MOROCCO

LUCAS PETERS

Contents

MOROCCO

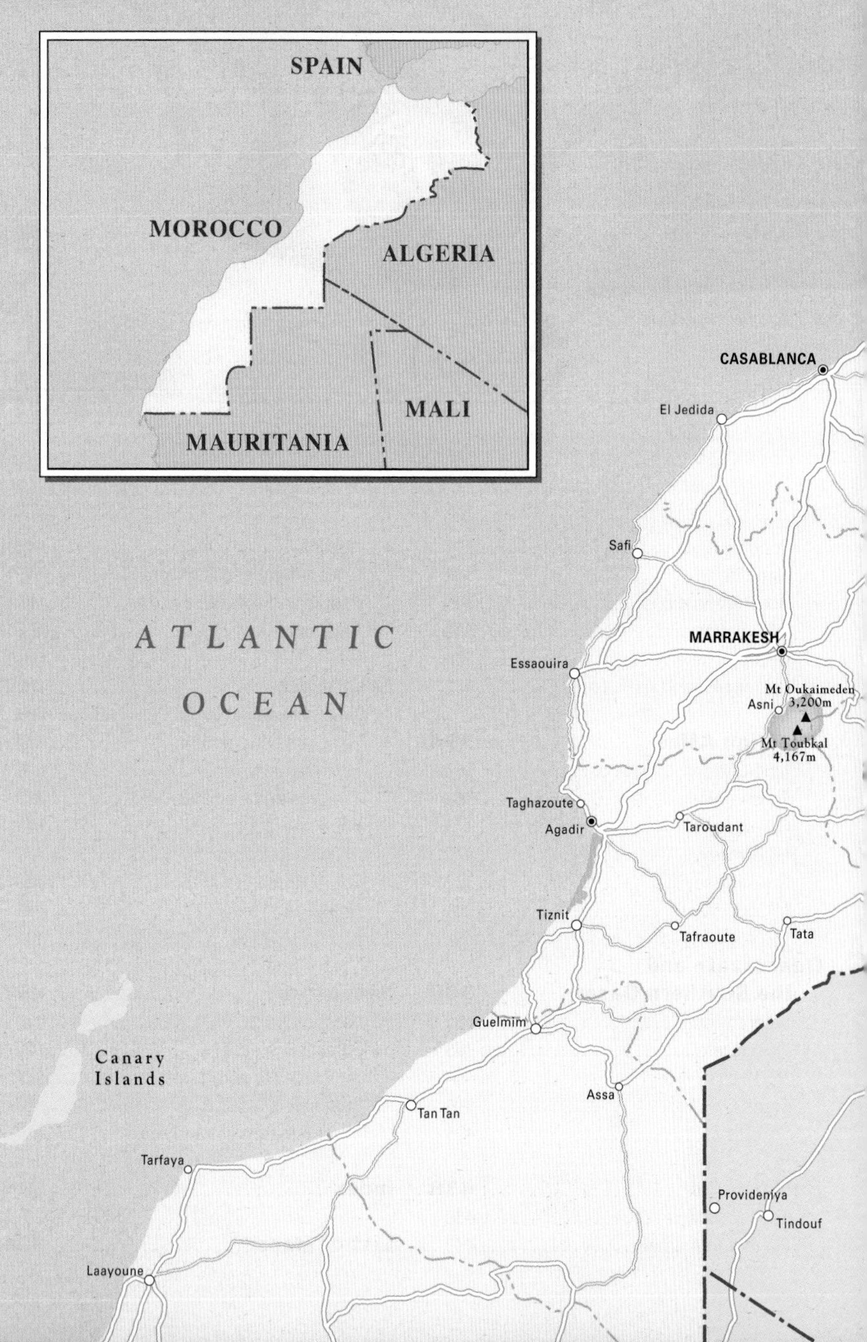

SPAIN
MOROCCO
ALGERIA
MALI
MAURITANIA
CASABLANCA
El Jedida
Safi
ATLANTIC
OCEAN
MARRAKESH
Essaouira
Mt Oukaimeden
3,200m
Asni
Mt Toubkal
4,167m
Taghazoute
Agadir
Taroudant
Tiznit
Tafraoute
Tata
Guelmim
Canary
Islands
Assa
Tan Tan
Tarfaya
Provideniya
Tindouf
Laayoune

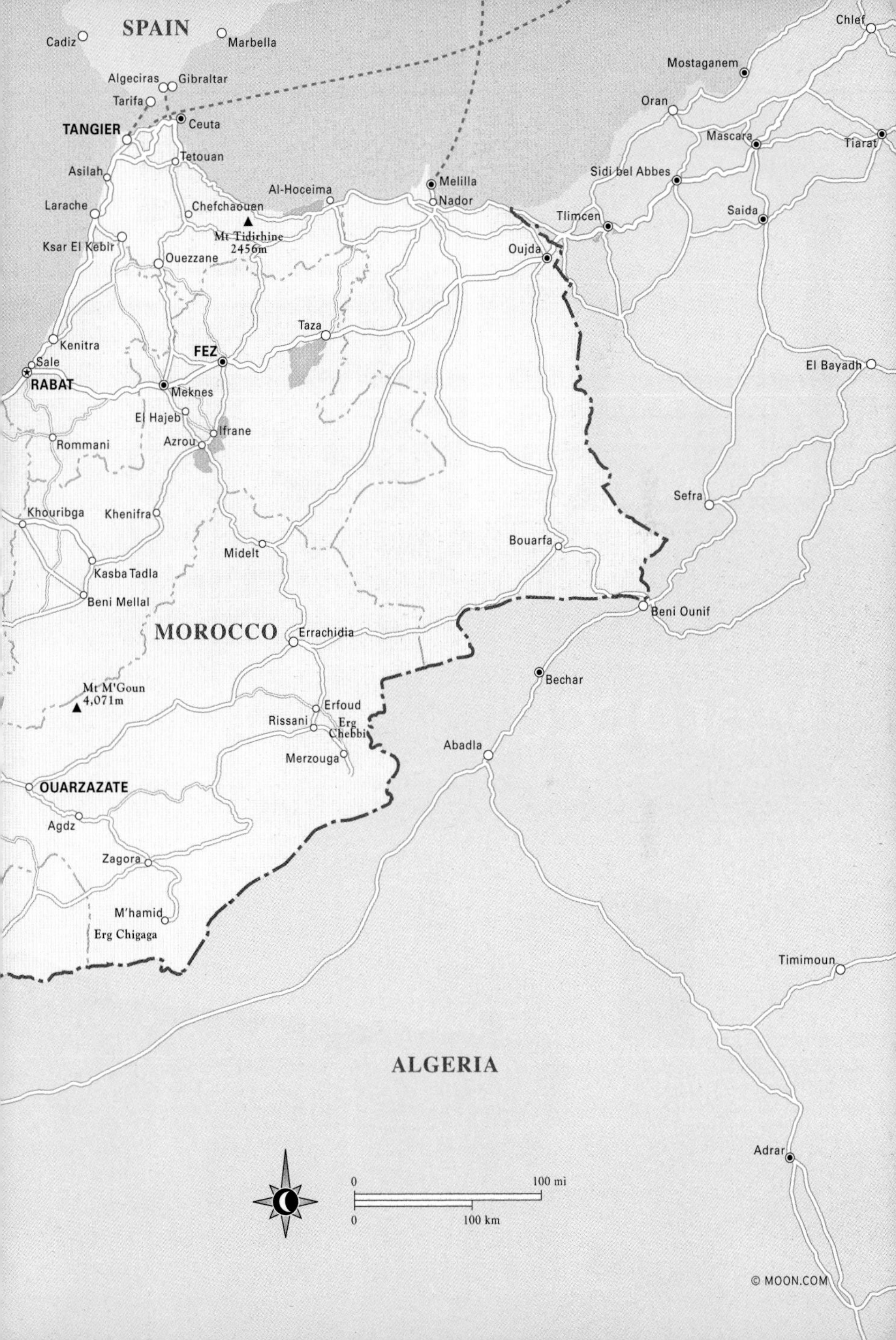

SPAIN
Cadiz
Marbella
Algeciras
Gibraltar
Tarifa
TANGIER
Ceuta
Tetouan
Asilah
Larache
Ksar El Kebir
Chefchaouen
Mt Tidirhine 2456m
Al-Hoceima
Melilla
Nador
Ouezzane
Oujda
Taza
Kenitra
Sale
RABAT
FEZ
Meknes
El Hajeb
Ifrane
Azrou
Rommani
Khouribga
Khenifra
Midelt
Kasba Tadla
Beni Mellal
MOROCCO
Errachidia
Mt M'Goun 4,071m
Erfoud
Rissani
Erg Chebbi
Merzouga
OUARZAZATE
Agdz
Zagora
M'hamid
Erg Chigaga
Bouarfa
Beni Ounif
Bechar
Abadla
Chlef
Mostaganem
Oran
Mascara
Tiarat
Sidi bel Abbes
Tlimcen
Saida
El Bayadh
Sefra
Timimoun
ALGERIA
Adrar
0
100 mi
0
100 km
© MOON.COM

DISCOVER

Morocco

Morocco is one of those destinations that has something for travelers of every stripe. Labyrinthine medieval cities, fast-paced urban centers, pristine stretches of beach, endless desert sand dunes, lush palm oases, snowcapped mountains, world-renowned cuisine, vast public markets, and the type of hospitality that will make you want to come back for more.

With its unique position in the northwest corner of Africa, just a few miles across the Strait of Gibraltar from Spain, Morocco is the true meeting of Europe and Africa, East and West, old and new. At each of these intersections is something unique, though understandably complex.

The more European cities of Casablanca, Rabat and Tangier, as well as the *villes nouvelles* of most major cities, provide modern comforts and maintain an air of their respective French and Spanish protectorate eras with wide boulevards, art deco architecture, sprawling urban gardens, and elegant French-style bistros.

Along the Atlantic Coast, you can also discover the idyllic, artsy towns of Essaouira and Asilah. These are more relaxing spaces where the Moroccan medina meets the ocean. Meanwhile, in the up-and-coming surf capital of Taghazoute, you're more likely to be greeted with a "what's up?" than *"salaam 'alaykoom."*

Clockwise from top left: Tangier's Kasbah gate looking to the Strait of Gibraltar; the Hassan II Mosque of Casablanca; a Barbary Macaque in the Ifrane National Park; tables and chairs on the beach; a hand-painted wood door; the fortress of Castelo Real of Mogador at Essaouira.

In the valleys and plains, you'll find the old, mud-walled Imperial cities of Marrakesh and Fez. Here you can experience Moroccan life as it has been lived for generations, with the muezzin's call to prayer wafting over the maze of pedestrian-only alleys and sprawling squares where artisans have been weaving, stitching, hammering, and welding hand-crafted goods for hundreds of years.

Morocco's four mountain ranges—the Rif, Middle Atlas, High Atlas, and Anti-Atlas—provide nature lovers with soaring peaks and winding mountain trails to explore by foot or by mule. Here is where you can most easily experience the culture of the Amazigh, the first people of Morocco who have lived here for thousands of years, and discover the picturesque town of Chefchaouen.

Out in the vast Sahara, blue-turbaned desert nomads lead camels through the sand dunes, past palm-lined oases to a series of Bedouin tents. Here, Morocco is most connected with the continent of Africa, and the Gnawa spirit rooted in the Sahara is alive and well.

In the last few years, Morocco has evolved from the sort of destination only your most adventurous friends might consider to a bucket-list destination for all of us looking for something a bit different. Whether you're planning your next romantic getaway, family vacation, solo travel adventure, or just a fun trip with your friends, this guidebook should help you tremendously.

Clockwise from top left: artisan chiseling stucco in Marrakesh; a local camel gets ready to head into the Sahara; the Andalusian Gardens of Rabat's Kasbah; old lamps in the Marrakesh medina.

11 TOP EXPERIENCES

1 Celebrating on the **Jemma el-Fnaa,** Marrakesh's largest plaza—a must if you want to truly feel the pulse of this magical land. Every night, it's a celebration (page 313).

2 Haggling in one of Morocco's famous **souks,** or markets, where navigating the hard-nosed bartering and opaque pricing structure is a rite of passage (page 329).

3 Getting lost in the **medinas** of Fez (page 252) and Marrakesh (page 313), infamous for their incomprehensibility. Embrace it. It's all part of the experience.

4 Sipping **mint tea,** the national beverage of Morocco, part of every greeting, every meal, and seemingly every business transaction, at a **café in Tangier** (page 195).

5 Wandering the "Blue City" of **Chefchaouen,** the most photogenic medina in Morocco (page 217).

>>>

6 Chilling on the **Atlantic beaches** of southern Morocco, where beaches like **Taghazoute** lead the way in year-round beach-going, sunsets, and surfing (page 99).

>>>

7 Spending the night in a ***riad,*** a traditional Moroccan house where hosting a guest, seeing to every need, and going above and beyond expectations is something of a national tradition (page 343).

8 Immersing yourself in Morocco's rich **Islamic history,** from waking to the sound of the muezzin calling the faithful to prayer before sunrise, to visiting the spectacular **Hassan II Mosque** in Casablanca (page 48).

9 Exploring spectacular **Roman ruins,** from the crumbling remnants of **Volubilis** near Meknes (page 286) to the less-visited ruin of **Lixus** outside Larache (page 162).

10 Relaxing in a Moroccan **hammam,** a full-body pampering experience, with steam rooms, exfoliation, and essential oils (page 265).

11 Sleeping out under the stars in the Sahara at the magnificent sand dunes of **Erg Chebbi** (page 432).

Planning Your Trip

Where to Go

Casablanca and the South Atlantic Coast

Casablanca is Morocco's largest city, with **art deco colonial-era buildings** and a vibe that is distinctly all business. This **cosmopolitan melting pot** gives way to traditional Morocco in smaller cities such as **Essaouira** and **Taghazoute** along the South Atlantic Coast, which also have some of the country's **warmest and most surf-friendly beaches.**

Rabat and the North Atlantic Coast

Along the North Atlantic Coast, the very European-feeling capital city of **Rabat** provides a gateway to a more relaxed stretch of **secluded beaches** and tranquil fishing ports along the coastline, the stunning Roman ruins of **Lixus** and **Banasa,** and the artsy coastal town of **Asilah.**

Tangier and the Mediterranean Coast

The days of the **Interzone,** a period when Tangier was ruled by no one government, giving host to legions of spies and artists, still ripple around the nooks of the Zoco Chico and along the cafés dotting the boulevards of the **edgy port city** of **Tangier.** The Mediterranean Coast hosts two **Spanish exclaves** in Morocco, **Ceuta** and **Melilla,** while the Moroccan coastline is a popular destination in August for vacationing Moroccan families. **The Rif** is home to the famous blue town of **Chefchaouen,** one of the most picturesque towns in all of Morocco, while

the bustling port of Essaouira

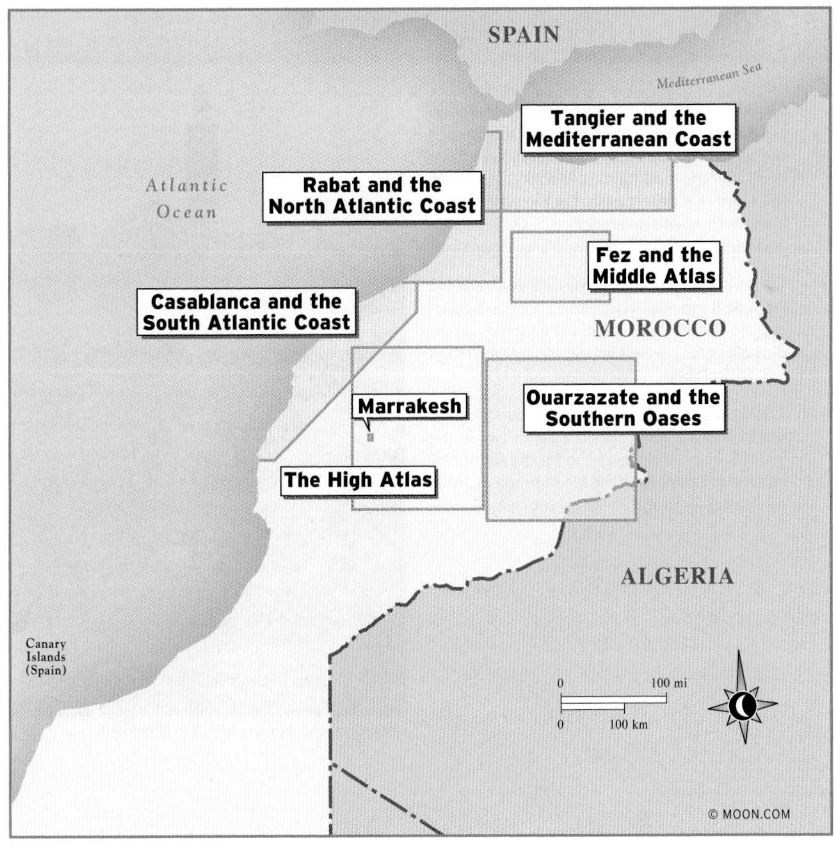

the surrounding mountains offer opportunities for **rock-climbing** and **trekking.**

Fez and the Middle Atlas

The old medina of **Fez** is considered the world's largest existing medieval city and a UNESCO World Heritage Site. Spending a few days getting lost in its twisting passageways is a rite of passage for any traveler to Morocco. The nearby city of **Meknes** provides a medina experience with less confusion, while **Volubilis** is one of the most well-preserved former Roman cities in all of Africa. The **Middle Atlas** mountains are stunning, particularly in spring, with opportunities for nature lovers to mingle with locals and visit some less touristed places, such as picturesque **Zaouia d'Ifrane,** a quaint village with a backdrop of cascading waterfalls.

Marrakesh

Europeans have long known the secret of **Marrakesh,** and now the secret is out for the rest of the world. With **world-class dining, shopping, and nightlife,** along with the more traditional experiences of the Moroccan **hammam** (bath), call to prayer, and confusing maze of **souks,** it is a true meeting of East and West, Africa and Europe, where the 24-hour carnival of the **Jemaa el-Fnaa,** the main square, reigns supreme. Marrakesh is a strategic location

If You Have...

- **One Week:** Head directly to Marrakesh. Spend 2-3 days wandering the souks and the famous Jemaa el-Fnaa, do a day trip to Essaouira, then head over the mountains to Merzouga to spend the night in a desert oasis. On the way back to Marrakesh, spend one night in the Dades Gorge and your last night in the High Atlas Mountains.
- **Two Weeks:** Continue from Merzouga to the Ziz Valley, and relax in a palm oasis before crossing the Middle Atlas to tour the medieval medina of Fez for 2-3 days with a stop by the Roman ruins of Volubilis.
- **Three Weeks:** Add a two-day excursion from Fez to Chefchaouen. Spend a day or two in the Rif Mountains and then head for the former Interzone of Tangier and the Mediterranean. Make sure to pass through Asilah on your way.

evening at the Jemaa el-Fnaa in Marrakesh

for travelers, with easy access to the nearby High Atlas, coastal cities of Agadir and Essaouira, and the vast Sahara. It's easy to see why Marrakesh is one of the top vacation destinations in the world.

The High Atlas

The snowcapped peaks of the **High Atlas** can be seen from nearby Marrakesh and in winter provide some of Africa's best slopes for **skiers. Toubkal National Park** is one of the prettiest national parks, full of alpine trees and frothy rivers. It's excellent for **trekkers** and **hikers** and a tranquil background for **nature lovers** looking for a getaway. **Adventurous travelers** should pack their skis, snowboards, ice picks, crampons, hiking boots, and binoculars to try to take in all that Morocco's tallest mountains have to offer.

Ouarzazate and the Southern Oases

Take in the movie studios of **Ouarzazate,** the **Hollywood of Africa,** before heading out to spend a night in the great sand sea of the **Sahara.** See the stars as you have never seen them before, seemingly in VR, then travel back in time through valleys of lush date palms lined with *ksour* (walled villages) and hike through the spectacular **Dades and Todra Gorges.**

When to Go

Morocco is a country with **four distinct seasons,** following other countries in the northern hemisphere, with summer lasting June-August, fall September-November, winter December-February, and spring March-May.

Fall

The **beginning of fall** is one of the better travel periods, after the kids have gone back to school and many European vacationers are back to work. Daytime temperatures are about perfect along the coast, averaging 16°C (60°F) to 27°C (80°F), and the **water is generally warm** throughout **September.** It's a real possibility that you'll have an entire beach to yourself. Toward the **end of fall** the Sahara becomes cooler, with **October** generally being an excellent month for **desert excursions. November** is a slower travel month, so deals can sometimes be had with hotels, restaurants, and tours around this period.

Winter

December is becoming a trendy time to visit Morocco, with many holiday-goers Christmas shopping in the medinas of Marrakesh and Fez, though temperatures can be surprisingly **chilly,** averaging 6°C (43°F) at night and 21°C (70°F) during the day. **January** typically kicks off the **short ski season** in Oukaïmeden, though the rest of the country is quieter, with some hotels and restaurants closing down for the month. In some destinations farther out, roads are sometimes washed out during the **heavy seasonal rains.**

Spring

Spring is probably the **best all-around time to visit,** with temperatures typically around 15°C (58°F) at night and around 26°C (78°F) throughout the day. The mountain snows have cleared, valleys are in bloom, and the entire country

Paradise Beach in Asilah in early September

Mohamed works his loom in Sefrou.

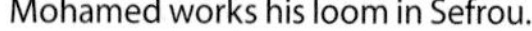

lounging outside a carpet bazaar in Essaouira

north of the High Atlas seems to erupt in shades of green, while just beyond the tall peaks of the High Atlas range the not-too-distant Sahara is warming up for the summer. Traveling around the country is typically easier, and the drives through the Ziz Valley and along the "Road of 1,000 Kasbahs" offer views of stunning snow-capped peaks against lively palm fronds and mudbrick *ksour* (walled villages).

Summer

During the **summer,** temperatures soar inland, in cities like Marrakesh and Fez averaging 38°C (98°F) with many days well above 40°C (102°F), making travel difficult and unbearably hot. Weather-wise, this is the **best time to be on the coasts. August** is crowded, as many Europeans and Moroccans have the month for vacation. Moroccan families crowd the Mediterranean beaches around Nador and Tetouan, as well as the North Atlantic Coast beaches of Essaouira and Larache, while Europeans flock to the packaged resort town of Agadir and other beaches along the South Atlantic Coast. The **Sahara should be avoided** during the summer, as travel is just too hot, with daytime highs well over 45°C (113°F).

Ramadan and Other Islamic Holidays

The busiest travel times for Moroccans, outside of the August vacation, revolve around the Islamic calendar, with the two largest holidays being the holy month of fasting, **Ramadan,** and the biggest holiday of the year, **Eid al-Adha.**

During the **month of Ramadan,** Moroccans are fasting throughout from sunrise to sunset. **Many businesses are closed,** including restaurants, or have shortened opening hours. Traveling by **public transport** can be difficult, with many **delays in service.** The exact dates of Ramadan and other Muslim holidays are not known in Morocco until there is a sighting of the moon by religious officials that matches with Islamic scripture. Roughly speaking, Ramadan should fall between April 23 and May 23 in 2020; between April 12 and May 11 in 2021; and April 2 and May 1 in 2022. The end of Ramadan is marked by Eid al-Fitr, often called Eid es-Seghir, or the "little holiday."

Eid al-Adha, often called plainly the "big holiday" or Eid al-Kabir, is easily the **biggest holiday** in Morocco. It is a **three-day festival** that occurs two moon cycles (or about two months) after the end of Ramadan and is the **biggest feast in the country,** marking when Ibrahim (Abraham) was willing to sacrifice his son for God. **Trains, public buses,** and ***grands taxis*** are **impossibly full** directly before and after this festival.

For Muslim and non-Muslim travelers curious about Islam, visiting Morocco during Ramadan or any of the other religious holidays, even with all the requisite traveling hiccups and delays, can be a rewarding experience. Many mosques have all-night *dikr,* a kind of spiritual chanting done in a group, while many families will open their doors to entertain guests. Some of the liveliest nights in Morocco happen during Ramadan.

Know Before You Go

Passports and Visas

UK, EU, Australian, New Zealand, Canadian and US nationals need to present a valid **passport** upon entry. Your passport should be valid for at least six months from your planned date of departure from Morocco, though you will not need to present proof of return. Customs officials will stamp a valid **90-day tourist visa** in your passport on arrival.

South African passport holders will need to obtain a visa before arriving, and will be required to provide proof of return travel and funds to support their stay in Morocco. Contact the Moroccan Embassy in South Africa for more information.

For all nationalities, for stays of longer than 90 days, you will need to request a visa from the nearest Moroccan embassy or consulate in your home country. Travelers to Morocco often cross back into Europe, sometimes via the Spanish exclaves of Ceuta or Melilla when they are close to their 90-day limit, and then reenter the country with another 90-day visa. Students and employees traveling to the country for studies or work should be assisted by the Moroccan-based university, school, or employer through the visa process, which generally happens after you have entered the country on a 90-day tourist visa.

Packing

Morocco is called a cold country with a hot sun. The cold is the most surprising element to travelers visiting Morocco for the first time. Pack **clothing for colder temperatures** in all seasons, except for during the summer months, especially during the winter and if going to the desert or mountains.

All travelers should pack **sun protection,** such as a wide-brimmed hat, sunglasses, and waterproof SPF 100 or higher sunscreen (though this you can find at most pharmacies), as well as light long-sleeved shirts and pants. Sun protection is particularly important if you are going to the desert or into the higher elevations in the mountain ranges.

Morocco runs on the **European 220-volt system,** with electronics having two round plugs. For those traveling from the United States, most electronics, such as laptops and battery chargers, require only a **plug adapter** and do not need a voltage regulator from 110 to 220, though check your device to be sure.

A pair of **earplugs, an eye mask, and a light scarf** to use as a shade for bus, train, and *grand taxi* trips will make traveling through the country much more pleasant.

It is a very good idea to bring your **toilet paper,** as many public restrooms in Morocco do not supply it.

Transportation

UK and EU travelers have a selection of **direct flights** with connections from most major European hubs to Agadir, Fez, Marrakesh, Rabat, and Tangier.

Most travelers from Australia, New Zealand, North America, and South Africa will arrive to the Mohammed V International Airport in Casablanca. Morocco's national airline carrier, Royal Air Maroc, has a monopoly on nonstop flights to and from North America, connecting Casablanca with Boston, New York, Miami, and Montreal. All other carriers in North America, as well as all flights from Australia, New Zealand, and South Africa, stop over in Europe or the Middle East.

There are a few nonstop in-country flights leaving Casablanca, including Agadir, Fez, Marrakesh, Ouarzazate, and Tangier, though most travelers use a combination of the easy-to-use intercity buses, trains, taxis, and car rentals to move around the country after their arrival.

From **Spain** and **France,** it is possible to enter the country by **ferry** to **Tangier** or the Spanish exclaves of **Ceuta** or **Melilla,** where you will then cross the land border into Morocco. Of these options, the quickest, easiest, and most practical is the 35-minute ferry that connects Tarifa, Spain, directly with Tangier.

Travel within the country is mostly accomplished by **train, bus,** and **car.** There are two primary **train lines.** The first line connects down the Atlantic Coast from Tangier to Casablanca and then turns inland to Marrakesh. The other follows a northeast trajectory from Casablanca through Fez to Oujda in the northeastern corner of the country. The new Al-Boraq high-speed train connects Tangier with Rabat (about 1 hour) and Casablanca (about 2 hours).

Between cities not connected by train there are **local and private buses,** as well as ***grands taxis*** that connect cities and towns.

Renting a car provides more mobility to travelers. The roads in Morocco are in generally good condition, though lighting is an issue for night driving.

plates and scarves in the Ait Ben Haddou kasbah

The Best of Morocco

See everything Morocco has to offer in two weeks, from the business capital of Casablanca to the great imperial cities of Marrakesh, Fez, Meknes, and Rabat. You'll travel deep into the calm oases of the desert, relax on the beaches along the Atlantic Coast, and literally walk through Roman history in Volubilis. This itinerary is best for those arriving directly to Casablanca. If you have less time, prioritize Marrakesh, Essaouira, and the desert excursion. If you have even less time, skip Casablanca completely by heading directly from the airport to Marrakesh. If you cut a day from your stays in Marrakesh and Essaouira and skip the night in the Dades Gorge, it is possible to do this itinerary in 10 days.

Casablanca and Marrakesh

DAY 1

Arrive in the afternoon at the Mohammed V International Airport and take the train into **Casablanca.** Get cozy in a beachfront or boutique hotel. Treat yourself to a night out at one of the myriad five-star dining options and sleep off any jet lag.

DAY 2

In the morning, take a tour of the **Hassan II Mosque** before catching an afternoon train for **Marrakesh.** Check into a three-night stay in a restored *riad* in the old medina. Spend this night walking around the giant plaza **Jemaa el-Fnaa,** taking in the circus-like atmosphere complete with monkey handlers and snake charmers, and eat dinner back at your *riad.*

DAY 3

After breakfast and a fresh orange juice, tour the sights, including the **Saadian Tombs, Bahia Palace,** and **Marrakesh Museum.** After some **street eats** for lunch, get lost in the **souks.** For dinner, experiment with Moroccan fusion cuisine in a restored *riad* like **Pepe Nero.**

the Hassan II Mosque in Casablanca

a cat lurks the streets of Essaouira

DAY 4

Tour some of the famed **gardens** of Marrakesh, such as the **Menara Gardens,** perhaps by horse-drawn carriage, and have lunch in the **Ville Nouvelle,** Marrakesh's French protectorate-era neighborhood, on the hipster strip of Rue de la Liberté. Spend the afternoon exploring some of the shops and cafés, but be sure to purchase your bus ticket for the following day to Essaouira. As darkness falls, head back to the **Koutoubia Mosque,** which comes alive when lit up at night, and have dinner at one of the food stalls on the Jemaa el-Fnaa.

Essaouira

DAY 5

In the morning, look out for goats eating argan nuts from the trees on the bus to **Essaouira.** Settle in for two nights in the old medina. Have lunch at one of the eclectic restaurants and explore the **medina** for souvenirs, getting to know a few of the artists, like the metal sculptor **Rachid Mourabit.** Catch the sunset from the ramparts, and for dinner treat yourself to the delicious fusion food of **Umia.**

DAY 6

Spend the morning preparing your own tajines, salads, and desserts in a **cooking class** at **La Table Madada,** where chef Mouna will have you slicing, dicing, and simmering your way to a delicious Moroccan meal. Then pack your swimsuits and towels for an afternoon at the **beach.** Lounge, take a **windsurfing lesson,** hike down the beach for more privacy, or consider a **beachside gallop** on a **horse** or a **camel.**

Imlil and the High Atlas

DAY 7

Catch the early morning bus for **Marrakesh** and meet your mountain guide at the bus station. You'll take the two-hour drive to **Imlil.** Have a hearty mountain lunch and spend the afternoon trekking through the villages and countryside before returning to **Domaine Malika, a rustic mountain lodge,** for a hearty dinner and a good night's sleep.

Ouarzazate and the Southern Oases

DAY 8

Be prepared for a long day of travel. Catch the morning bus to Marrakesh, and then catch the first bus to **Ouarzazate.** Have dinner out at French bistro **Accord Majeur** and tour the **Hotel Le Berbere Palace;** keep an eye out for visiting movie stars. Just remember to check in for the night somewhere more budget-friendly.

DAY 9

Catch the bus or drive through the oasis of **Skoura,** along the **"Road of 1,000 Kasbahs,"** taking in the date palm valleys and crumbling kasbahs set against the snowcapped peaks of the High Atlas. End your drive in the **Dades Gorge** at **Auberge Chez Pierre** for one of the best meals this side of the mountains.

DAY 10

Take a morning stroll through the mountain villages of the gorge, perhaps all the way to the **Monkey Fingers,** before heading back to the car for an afternoon drive (or bus ride) through **Tinghir** to **Merzouga.** Climb on a **camel** and make your way into the desert for a night under the stars at **Erg Chebbi.**

DAY 11

Wake up to watch the sunrise over the Saharan dunes. After breakfast, make the long drive through **Errachidia** and the **Ziz Valley** to the medieval city of **Fez.** (If traveling by bus, you'll have to wait for the Supratours night bus, which leaves Merzouga at 7pm.) In Fez, check in for a two-night stay in one of the restored *riads* that have been converted into boutique hotels.

Fez, Meknes, and Rabat

DAY 12

Spend the day getting lost in Fez's labyrinthine **medina** or take a guided tour of the breathtaking **Batha Museum** and the majestic **Medersa Bouanania,** a restored 14th-century Quranic school. Explore the **Chouwara tanneries** (after

a man in a traditional jellaba robe walks through the Bab Boujeloud gate in Fez

the extensive dunes of Erg Chebbi

a desert camp in the Sahara

plugging your nose with mint) and tuck in for a quick bowl of *bissara* at the **Elminchaoui soup stand.**

DAY 13

Drive or catch a *grand taxi* to the old Roman ruins of **Volubilis.** Spend the morning walking through history and then have a simple lunch in **Meknes,** on the **Place el-Hedim** looking at the impressive **Bab Mansour** gate. Consider shopping for souvenirs in the medieval medina, before taking the train to **Rabat.** Check into a luxury *riad* in the medina near the train station for your last night in Morocco. Rabat is just an hour northwest of Casablanca and your flight home the following day.

If You Have More Time...

Think about heading from Fez to **Chefchaouen** to start a four-day tour including **Tangier, Tetouan,** and **Asilah** before ending up at **Rabat.**

Spiritual Pilgrimage

Visit the holiest places in Morocco and discover why Fez is often called the "Mecca of the West." Despite pushback from orthodox Islamic scholars, who take a more hardline approach to idolatry, there is a strong presence of places of pilgrimage in North and West Africa. For Muslims, this is a particularly rewarding tour during Ramadan, though slower travel and delays mean you will likely need a few more days. Many of the sites, because they are places of worship, are intended only for Muslims, and non-Muslims will not be permitted entry. This itinerary is best for Muslims or those interested in different worship in all its forms.

Day 1

In **Casablanca,** take a tour of the **Hassan II Mosque,** a true feat of modern architecture featuring some of the best Moroccan craftsmanship. This is the largest mosque in Morocco; it holds 25,000 worshippers inside while another 80,000 can fit around the mosque grounds. Spend the night in one of the hotels along the corniche, listening to the surf pound against the shore below.

Day 2

Take the morning train to **Fez** and explore the medieval **medina,** home to many of the holiest sites in Morocco. Visiting Fez is a mini-pilgrimage for West Africans. The **Tijani Mosque and Mausoleum** houses the tomb of Sidi Ahmed al-Tijani, the man responsible for bringing Islam to countries such as Senegal and Mauritania. The nearby **Qaraouiyine Mosque,** founded in 859 by Fatima, a wealthy refugee from the city of Karaouin in Tunisia, is one of Morocco's oldest and largest mosques. Just a short walk from the mosque is the **Mausoleum of Moulay Idriss II,** the son of the founder of modern Morocco.

a door on the courtyard to the Mausoleum Moulay Ali Cherif in Rissani

Koutoubia Mosque

Best Beaches

Discover the tranquility of Mediterranean and Atlantic beaches, great for surfers, swimmers, and sunbathers alike. Windsurf in Essaouira, snag a wave in Agadir, and find yourself secluded in the aptly named Paradise Beach in Asilah. For calmer beaches, visit in September, just after the August crowds have subsided and the water is still at its warmest.

TAGHAZOUTE

This up-and-coming **yoga** and **surf** retreat maintains its surfer vibe and features one of the most relaxing beaches in Morocco. Many Europeans flock here throughout the year for the sun, the sand, and to disconnect (page 99). Just south is **Agadir,** with plenty of restaurants and bars for nights out.

ESSAOUIRA

Essaouira beaches are **welcoming to women travelers** and offer plenty of activities, including **bird-watching** over the **Îles Purpuraires.** The wind makes it popular with **kitesurfers** and **windsurfers** (page 77).

SIDI IFNI

This distant beach is a favorite with Europeans, with a distinct Spanish flavor and being a bit more out of the way. There are some **water sports** and **deep-sea fishing** possibilities, but most people come to **get away from the crowds** (page 112).

DAKHLA

The heavy winds that tear across the Sahara through the distant western city of Dakhla have made this beach a favorite with **kitesurfers** and **windsurfers,** as well as **paragliding** and **fishing enthusiasts** (page 435).

RABAT

Next to Kenitra, just north of Rabat, is the sunbathing-friendly **Plage des Nations.** Best avoided in late July and August, as it gets crowded, outside of these months it is a real delight (page 138).

a hidden beach outside of Mirleft along the South Atlantic Coast

ASILAH

The aptly named **Paradise Beach** is generally **deserted** outside of the busy summer months, making this a **romantic** daytime getaway (page 167).

TANGIER

Tangier has beaches on the Mediterranean and Atlantic. The popular **Mediterranean** beaches are good for **families** and small children, while the **trendy Atlantic** side allows you to catch some rays away from the crowds (page 193).

PLAGE DE TORRES

Hidden in the middle of **Al-Hoceima National Park,** the little-visited Plage de Torres is a gem along this stretch of the Mediterranean and one of the few **public beaches** not strewn with garbage (page 233).

Day 3

Catch a bus to **Moulay Idriss,** just an hour from Fez, above the ruins of Volubilis. The hilly town is the resting spot for the founder of the country, Moulay Idriss, who brought Islam to Morocco from the Middle East. His mausoleum and mosque are some of the most ornate in the country. In the afternoon, if the sun is not too hot, you might want to take the opportunity to visit **Volubilis,** the ruins of the former capital of Morocco.

Day 4

By bus or rented car, make your way from Fez through the **Ziz Valley** to **Rissani,** where you can visit the **Mausoleum Moulay Ali Cherif.** Moulay Ali was the founder of the current Alaouite dynasty that rules Morocco and is considered a direct descendant of the Prophet Mohammed. To contemplate spiritual matters, venture by camelback into the dunes of **Merzouga** to watch the sunset in the Sahara and spend the night in a Bedouin tent communing with nature. Consider taking a course with **Morocco Geo Travel** to understand how the people of the desert relate the stars and the local nature to their lives.

Day 5

In the morning, make your way back to civilization and catch the bus for **Ouarzazate.** You can spend the night in Ouarzazate or consider the nearby kasbah of **Ait Ben Haddou** to continue your contemplation. If time allows, you can stop on the bus at **Tinghir** or **Boumalne Dades** to explore the wonderful **Todra and Dades Gorges,** true works of natural art.

Day 6

Take a bus over the Tizi n'Tichka pass to **Marrakesh** and explore the medina, touring the glorious **Koutoubia Mosque,** which holds court over the vibrant plaza Jemaa el-Fnaa.

World Heritage Sites

Morocco is home to nine UNESCO World Heritage Sites, which make for a spectacular tour for archaeologists and Indiana Jones wannabes. Explore the maze of Fez's medina and discover the Roman ruins of Volubilis before heading north to the medina of Tetouan. Then it's back south, down the coast, to the Portuguese Cistern of El Jedida and medina of Essaouira, before tucking inland to the Red City of Marrakesh and over the High Atlas to the living Ait Ben Haddou kasbah on the edge of the Sahara. This tour is best divided in two parts: north and south; the order is interchangeable. It's best for those catching flights from Europe into either Fez or Marrakesh.

Northern Leg

DAY 1

Land in **Fez.** Prepare to spend 3-4 nights in the middle of the medieval, where donkeys and horses trod alongside pedestrians. Examine the traditional architecture of your *riad,* and settle in for a quiet night of sleep.

DAY 2

Spend the day exploring the nooks and crannies of Fez's **medina,** perhaps with a guide, paying special attention to sites such as the beautifully restored 14th-century **Medersa Bouanania** as well as the smelly but rewarding **Chouwara tanneries,** where leather is being cured as it has for centuries, with pigeon excrement and cow urine.

DAY 3

Take a *grand taxi* to the Roman ruins of **Volubilis** and spend the morning walking through Roman forums and examining the water irrigation system, the different stone and marble used for construction, and some of the mosaics still lying about. Couple this with an afternoon in the historic city of **Meknes** looking at the unrestored yet exquisite **Medersa Bouanania** there, the **Mausoleum of Moulay Ismail,** and the **granaries (Heri es Souani),** for an idea of the technological advancement of Moulay Ismail's empire.

DAY 4

Catch the 8am bus for the mountain town of **Chefchaouen,** tucked into the folds of the Rif, and have lunch and explore one of Morocco's more pleasant medinas. Before sunset, catch a cab onto **Tetouan** for two nights in one of the medina lodgings there.

DAY 5

Spend the day in Tetouan exploring the most lived-in **medina** in Morocco, and make sure to spend an hour or two at the **Archaeology Museum of Tetouan.** The collection of Roman-era mosaics is unmatched. If you have time, consider taking a walk out to **Tamuda**—the site is little more than rubble, but it is all that remains of one of the oldest cities in Morocco.

DAY 6

In the morning, catch a taxi for **Lixus** and spend the first half a day exploring this little-visited Roman ruin north of Larache. Have a picnic in the amphitheater overlooking the Loukkos River while contemplating life in this city 3,000 years ago. In the afternoon, make your way by bus for two nights in **Rabat** or Salé, just across the river.

DAY 7

Spend the day exploring the **Oudaïas Kasbah** in Rabat and duck into the souvenir shops along the Rue des Conseils before making your way to the **Chellah Necropolis,** where you will see the Roman-era city alongside the more recent ruins of the 12th- and 14th-century Almohad and Merenid dynasties. Consider adding a day to explore the other Roman ruins in this region, **Banasa** and **Thamusida.**

Southern Leg

DAY 8

From Rabat, take the train to **El Jedida,** south of Casablanca, to begin the southern half of the tour.

the living kasbah of Ait Ben Haddou

Essaouira ramparts

Spend the afternoon touring the **Portuguese Cistern** and city ramparts before calling it a day.

DAY 9

Take a bus along the beautiful coastal road to **Essaouira.** Walk on the ramparts at sunset and eat off some of the most diverse menus in all of Morocco. Plan on spending two nights in one of the friendly restored *riads* or hostels.

DAY 10

Spend the early morning hours exploring Essaouira's **medina,** keeping an eye out for the Jewish Star of David. You'll see plenty of these above the doors in the **mellah.** Spend the afternoon shopping in the friendly souks, book a cooking class to make your own Morocco tajines, or bum around on the long strip of beach just south of the medina.

DAY 11

Catch the morning bus for **Marrakesh,** where you'll spend two nights, ideally in the medina (the last World Heritage site on your tour). If you're feeling up to it, make your way to the **Jemaa el-Fnaa,** the carnivalesque main square, for a night you won't forget.

DAY 12

Spend the morning touring the medina sites, including the **Bahia Palace, Saadian Tombs,** and **Marrakesh Museum,** before plunging into the famed Marrakesh **souks,** where sights, sounds, and smells will be sure to dazzle you. Haggle with a shop owner or two to complete the experience.

DAY 13

Wake up bright and early to take a bus over the Tizi n'Tichka pass to **Ouarzazate,** where you will spend the afternoon at the wonderful **Ait Ben Haddou** kasbah, a real living kasbah with a few families still dwelling in mudbrick. This is one of the most striking examples of southern architecture. From here, if you have time, head out to explore the desert at **Erg Chigaga** or **Erg Chebbi.** Otherwise, stay the night in the kasbah and head back over the Tizi n'Tichka pass for your flight out of **Marrakesh.**

Adrenaline Rush

looking over the clouds atop Jbel Toubkal

Surf, ski, run, bike, climb, raft, and parachute your way around Morocco! Surf the southern coast, ski the slopes of Oukaïmeden, mountain bike through the High Atlas, climb the Todra Gorge, raft down the Ahansal River, and even run the most extreme footrace in the world—a six-day race through the scorching Sahara sun.

SURF

Whether you want to kitesurf, windsurf, or just plain catch a wave, there are companies that offer rental equipment, lessons for all levels, and guidance as to where the best waves are. Check in with **Surf Maroc** in the Moroccan surf capital of **Taghazoute** (page 100).

SKI

Oukaïmeden is one of the best ski resorts in Africa, though for most skiers, this is more of a novelty than a challenge. Check in with the folks at **Hotel Chez Juju** for rentals and lift tickets (page 371).

RUN

If running is your thing, there are picturesque jogs to be had along any beach and around any city. Some of the more popular runs are an early morning jog through the **Marrakesh medina** and the 10-kilometer run along the **beach of Tangier.** If you think you're tough, enlist in the grueling **Marathon des Sables,** a six-day, 250-kilometer race in the intense Sahara sun (page 397).

BIKE

Mountain biking is growing in Morocco. Today companies carry good equipment, including e-bikes, and lead tours through the winding passes of the **High Atlas** and into long stretches of Saharan desert road. Get your bikes with **Bike Adventures in Morocco** (page 360).

CLIMB

The High Atlas and the Rif offer good spots to climb, though the **Todra Gorge** is the dirt-bagging standard. You can find guides and hand-drawn maps of newer climbs there (page 411).

RAFT

Plunge downriver and into some whitewater in the **N'Fis and Ahansal Rivers.** In the spring the rivers are at their fullest, offering some breathtaking views that will get your heart pounding. Check for equipment and guides with **Morocco Rafting** (page 359).

Casablanca and the South Atlantic Coast

Casablanca is the beating heart of modern

Morocco. It's a Moroccan-style New York and the country's business capital, with all the hustle and bustle that entails.

Casablanca can be underwhelming for travelers to Morocco, who likely think of it in light of its romantic history.

Casa, as most of the locals call it, is a unique city in Morocco. Alongside Agadir, it's one of the few completely "new" cities in Morocco. Here, you won't find any of that ancient charm of Marrakesh or Fez, and if time is of the essence, you should consider skipping the city entirely. However, what Casa lacks in ancient charm it makes up for in ambition. As the economic capital of Morocco, Casa is on the cutting edge of industry and fashion. You can walk

Highlights

Look for ★ to find recommended sights, activities, dining, and lodging.

★ **Hassan II Mosque:** Tour the largest mosque in all of Morocco (the second largest in the world). Modern meets the traditional in this holy place, one of the few mosques non-Muslims may visit (page 48).

★ **Morocco Mall:** For a peek into Morocco's future, shop till you drop at this mall designed by Davide Padoa, featuring high-end brands from around Europe (page 51).

★ **El Jedida Portuguese Cistern:** Step into history at this eerily well-preserved landmark of late gothic design (page 64).

★ **Safi Pottery:** Stop by Potter's Hill in Safi to wander through the kilns and meet with the potters spinning, baking, and hand-painting their wares (page 69).

★ **Windsurfing, Kitesurfing, and Surfing:** The South Atlantic Coast offers up some world-class waves as well as the perfect wind to make windsurfing and kitesurfing a year-round adventure (pages 77 and 100).

★ **Cooking Classes:** Head to Essaouira and chop, dice, slice, and simmer your way through an afternoon, learning how to create your own delicious Moroccan cuisine (page 83).

★ **Taliouine Saffron:** Make your way into the Anti-Atlas and stop by the women's cooperative in the seldom-visited village of Taliouine to sample some of the best saffron in the world (page 104).

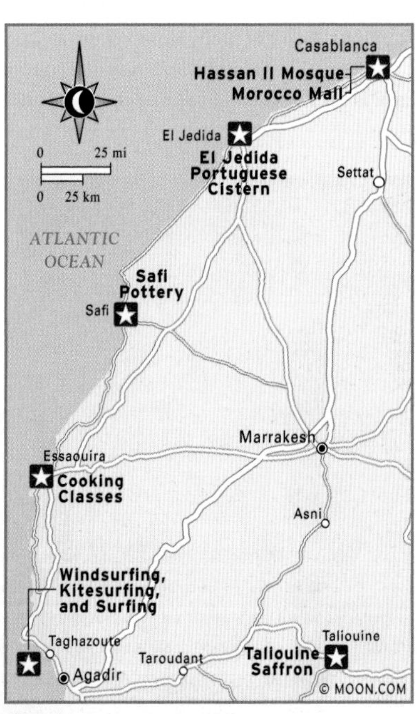

Casablanca and the South Atlantic Coast

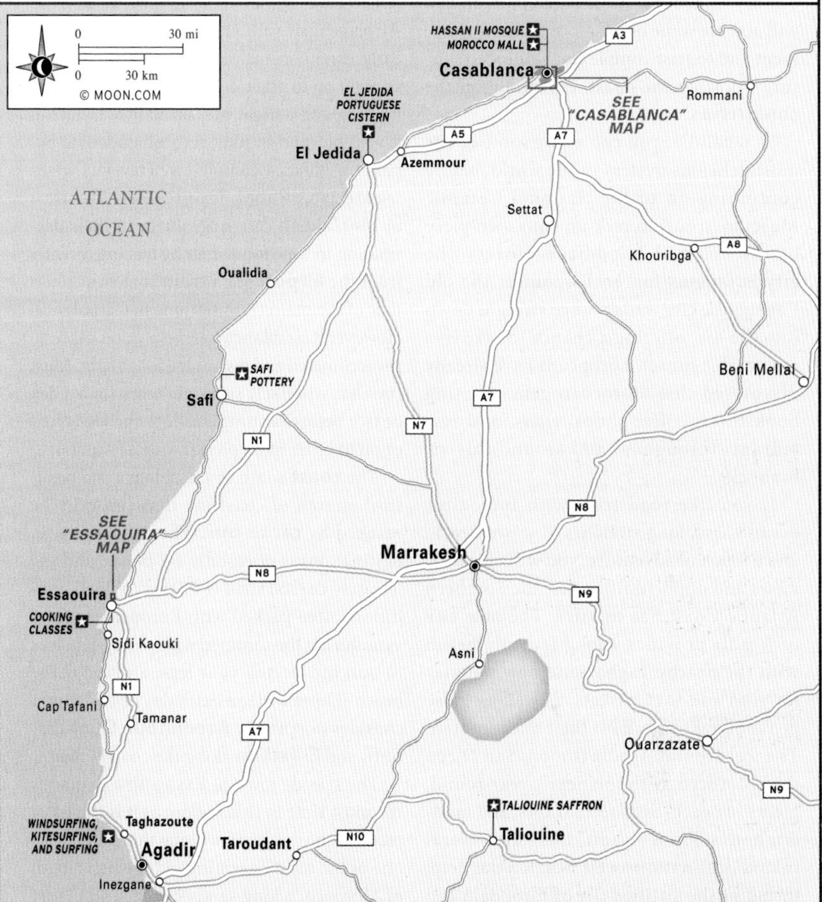

the art deco streets of Boulevard Mohammed V, shop for Gucci bags at the new Morocco Mall, visit the impressive Hassan II Mosque (one of the few mosques non-Muslims can enter in Morocco), and treat yourself to dinner at a five-star restaurant before heading out to a night at Rick's Café to hear some great jazz and the nightly staple, "As Time Goes By."

A few hours south of Casablanca, the southern Atlantic Coast is a beach lover's paradise. Here, you can find some of the most wonderful stretches of sand and surf in Africa. Quaint coastal towns dot this coast, some more touristed than others, and nearly all worth your while. The remnants of Morocco's varied past can be viewed along this coastline, from the restored

Previous: Moroccan T-shirt blowing in the wind; the 16th-century Portuguese cistern; couples at the Hassan II Mosque.

16th-century Portuguese ramparts of El Jedida and Essaouira to the crumbling 12th-century Almohad medina of Azemmour. You will also see some of the more modern apartment and tourist complexes—Morocco's future—dotting the coast, especially on the outskirts of Casablanca.

In Oualidia, you can enjoy some of the most delicious oysters in the world, before continuing on to the National Ceramic Museum in Safi to pick up your own piece of the colorful handmade pottery the city is famous for. In Essaouira, the old Portuguese city walls plunge straight down into the sea, offering a chance to take in a memorable sunset. Europeans have already discovered this Moroccan gem, opening bookstores, coffee shops, *riads,* and restaurants throughout and around this vibrant city.

If you like road trips with incredible ocean views, long stretches of warm beach, and a touch of adventure, you will enjoy the views and opportunities that the Southern Atlantic Coast has to offer. The new city of Agadir provides a long friendly beach with the nearby Taghazoute now popular for yoga and surf retreats, as well as those just looking to work on their vacation tan. The feel around Agadir is more San Diego than Morocco, with sun nearly year-round, plenty of beach-front restaurants, and modern hotels. From Agadir, there are several inland destinations well worth a day trip, including the fortified city of Taroudant and the capital of Moroccan saffron, Taliouine, a must-stop for foodies looking to stuff their bags with this precious spice. Further down the coast, travelers looking for smaller crowds would do well to check out Tiznit, a real up-and-coming destination, as well as the Spanish-flavored digs of Sidi Ifni.

PLANNING YOUR TIME

For many travelers coming from North America, Casablanca is the port of arrival. Airplanes generally arrive in the morning and early afternoon, making it possible to continue straight on to other destinations without having to spend a night in Casablanca. In fact, it is possible (and frankly, recommended) to bypass Casablanca completely. Travelers wishing to explore **Rabat, Tangier, Fez, Meknes,** or **Marrakesh** can generally be at their destination in time for dinner by leaving directly from the **airport** via a **train** that runs to either of the main train stations in Casablanca. However, Casablanca can be a good place to get acclimated and rest after a long flight. Most travelers will likely spend no more than a day or two before heading south to the **beaches** or on to other more picturesque destinations.

The **coast** south of Casablanca is a beautiful stretch of coastline that can only be reached by **car** or **bus**. The drive between destinations is often only 1-2 hours, and the leisurely coastal road (R301) is in good condition, often packed with European camper vans during the summer, with plenty of places to pull off, stretch your legs, and enjoy the beach. Those with an extra day or two might consider stopping by **Azemmour, Oualidia, Safi,** and **El Jedida** along the coastal road.

The seaside town of **Essaouira** demands the most time in this region, as it is the most picturesque destination along this route, with one of the most charming old medinas in all of Morocco, a long sandy beach, and plenty of nice restaurants for foodies. Essaouira is also a popular destination from Marrakesh. For many travelers, it will make a lot of travel sense to head straight to Marrakesh from Casablanca. Then, from Marrakesh head over to Essaouira and explore the rest of the Southern Atlantic Coast.

Itinerary Ideas

A DAY IN CASABLANCA

1 After arrival, hop on the train to Casa Port directly from the airport and then take the tram to **Ligue Arabe** to get settled in at the nearby **Hotel Point du Jour,** a simple, centrally located hotel right in the middle of Casablanca.

2 Once you've freshened up, hop in a taxi or enjoy the 40-minute walk past the Parc de la Ligue Arabe and the impressive art deco Sacred Heart Cathedral to the massive **Hassan II Mosque.** Join the first possible tour (Sat.-Thurs., nearly every hour 9am-4pm) to see inside this true modern wonder of architecture.

3 For lunch, stop by **Basmane** and enjoy a relaxing lunch in an ornate Moroccan salon.

4 After lunch, walk north along the waterfront **corniche** and take in the afternoon sun.

5 Hop on the tram or take a *petit taxi* back to your hotel to change into your nicest outfit. Then, consider diving into Casablanca's **medina.** Easy access into the medina from the main square is found near the old clock tower.

6 For dinner, you have to eat at **Rick's Cafe.** Just make sure to check the dress code and reserve in advance. Sip on a well-deserved cocktail in the **bar** after dinner. Of all the gin joints...

TWO DAYS ON THE ATLANTIC COAST

Day 1

1 After arriving in Essaouira on a combination of trains and buses from Casablanca via Marrakesh, check into the **Chill Art Hostel,** tucked away in the quiet corner of the medina, and tap into the town's hippie vibe.

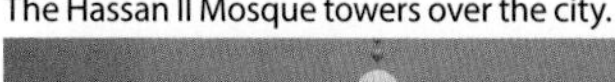

The Hassan II Mosque towers over the city.

A Day in Casablanca

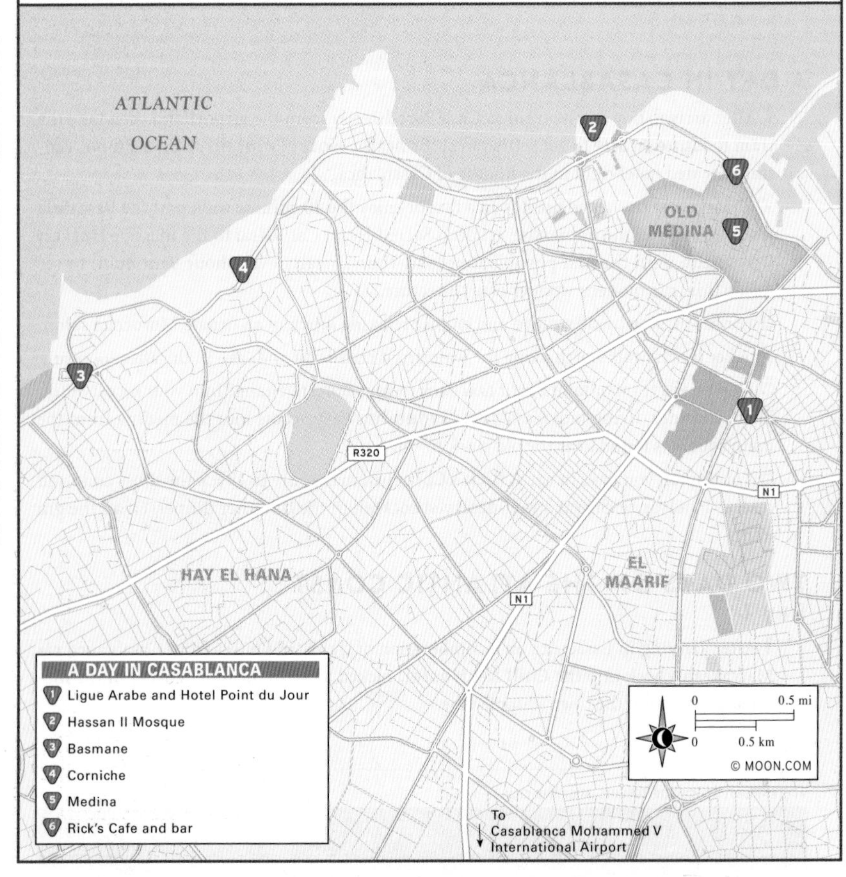

2 Cook your own lunch by taking a cooking class at **La Table Madada.** You'll tour through the local market before making your own Moroccan lunch.

3 Spend the afternoon and evening wandering the **medina,** ducking into the odd art gallery, touring the little streets, and checking out the artisans dotting the old town.

4 Have a light dinner at **Triskala.** Enjoy a fresh salad and some vegetarian-/vegan-friendly Moroccan fare.

5 That night, chill at the hostel and make a new friend on the **rooftop terrace.**

Two Days on the Atlantic Coast

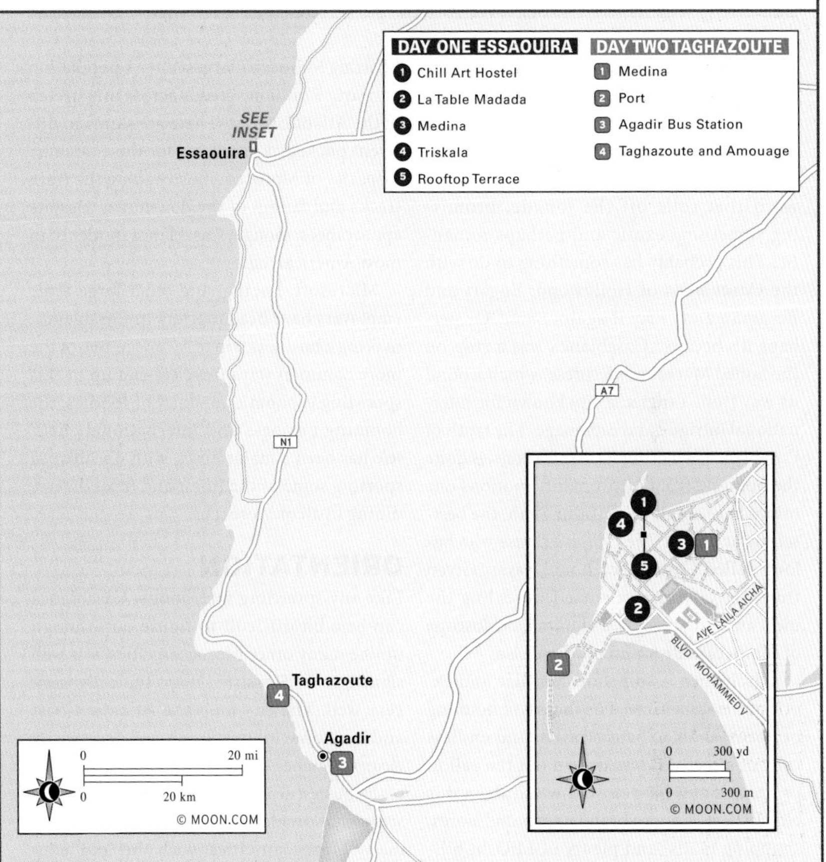

Day 2

1 Head out after breakfast and take one last stroll through the **medina.**

2 For lunch, barter with the fishmongers at the **port** and eat some of the freshest seafood you'll ever find.

3 Take the 2pm bus to **Agadir.** Though you could stay in Agadir, it's much more interesting to head to **Taghazoute,** just 20 minutes north. Catch a *grand taxi* from the **bus station** in Agadir to this up-and-coming destination.

4 Check into **Amouage** for the night and enjoy the seafood fusion menu for dinner. After dinner, head out into this little village to enjoy the surfer vibes of the locals and expats in this vibrant community.

Casablanca الدار البيضاء

I'm not going to mince words. The bustling city of Casablanca, Morocco's economic capital, typically ranks among the most disappointing travel destinations in the world. Maybe it's all in the name: Casablanca—a word that rolls off the tongue, promising something exotic and perhaps romantic. This probably has something to do with the *Casablanca* of Hollywood: Bogart and Bergman and "Play it again, Sam." Or perhaps it's because Casablanca was a stop on the famed Marrakesh Express, which wound its way from Tangier, a city known for international intrigue and espionage. The truth of Casablanca, whatever its associations, is quite the opposite from any romantic notions one might have about it. As Tahir Shah, the best-selling author of *The Caliph's House* who has long called Casablanca home, says: "Given time, the city unravels itself, revealing the most amazing corners, a vibrant kaleidoscope of Moroccan life found nowhere else."

Casablanca is somehow familiar and exotic at the same time. The incessant honking of horns, thick exhaust traffic, and endless calls of street vendors drown out the call to prayer and anything else old-world about this city. Expect Western brand names and stores, shopping malls, and plenty of LED-lit billboards advertising American name brands.

The dirty whitewashed facades of most of the buildings betray Casa's colonial past. The city has had many names as it passed from Carthaginian to Phoenician to Roman to Portuguese to Moroccan control, but it was the French—who took control of the city under the French Protectorate era in the first half of the 20th century—who built much of what Casablanca is today. Under French rule, the port grew in importance. The population boomed and Casablanca became the economic engine of Morocco. Intriguing art deco architecture of downtown is juxtaposed against new high-rises in glass and metal, befitting Morocco's largest city. A population of nearly 5 million spreads across this stretch of the Atlantic Coast. There are slums in different pockets, a showcase for the economic disparity of Morocco, mostly along the train tracks and far out of the downtown. Despite appearances, though, Casablanca is safer than most American cities.

Microsoft, Boeing, and other large-scale employers have headquarters in Casablanca, making a business trip to Morocco one of the more common ways travelers end up in this sprawling economic capital. For foodies, the booming business and international clientele has been a major boon, with Casablanca sporting some of the finest and most diverse dining in all of Morocco.

ORIENTATION

Like any sprawling metropolis, Casablanca can be a bit difficult to figure out, though unlike many other Moroccan cities, it is well signed, so GPS-assisted maps typically work very well. The city hugs the Atlantic Coast and has some long (though not necessarily clean) stretches of coastline, and it hosts one of the busiest seaports in Morocco. The city is somewhat divided into "old" and "new" like many Moroccan cities, with the "old" city being the Moroccan **medina** and the "new" being the rest of the urban sprawl of the **Ville Nouvelle.** The small, grubby medina forms a sort of focal point of the city, near the marina and the Hassan II Mosque along the coast, from where the rest of the city ripples out in a series of *rues* (streets), avenues, and boulevards.

The **Boulevard de la Corniche** follows the coast to the west. This wide, busy thoroughfare begins at the Hassan II Mosque and continues southwest past the lighthouse El Aank, a series of modern high-end hotels and resorts, the Anfa Place Shopping Center, and two beaches (Lalla Meryem and Aïn Diab) before ending at the Morocco Mall. Along the boulevard is the connection with the tram at Aïn Diab, which will take you back into the city. When the sun is out, as it often is in Casablanca, this can be a pleasant walk.

A rather less pleasant walk follows **Boulevard Sidi Mohamed Ben Abdellah,** which runs east from the Hassan II Mosque along the busy marina and industrial port to the seaside, where you can find well-priced seafood restaurants. Inland it passes by the neglected outer walls of the medina, where you will find Rick's Café, before arriving to the convenient Casa Port train station.

On the south side of the bustling Avenue des FAR from the medina is the vibrant **Place des Nations Unies,** the heart of Casablanca. Cafés and restaurants surround the square, with pedestrian-friendly streets to explore to the east in the Derb Omar neighborhood. The tram follows Boulevard Mohammed V, a car-free zone and a wonderful downtown art deco walk, to the **Marché Central.** This neighborhood is one of the better-preserved art deco neighborhoods in the world.

Farther south from the Place des Nations Unies and connected by the tram is the central **Park of the Arab League (Parc de la Ligue Arabe).** The park is usually busy with picnickers and families, as well as pockets of homeless, and isn't unlike New York's Central Park or London's Hyde Park. This is the middle of the colonial downtown of Casablanca. The streets around the expansive park are littered with art deco designs from the French protectorate era, as well as a few modern buildings. This is where the majority of museums, theaters, and restaurants can be found, as well as the more architecturally interesting buildings, such as the Palais de Justice and the Cathédrale Sacré Coeur. To the west of the park you'll find the U.S. Consulate. To the southwest is trendy **Quartier Habous,** a protectorate-era vision of a Moroccan medina with its slightly more upscale Moroccan markets and bazaars burgeoning beneath stone arches, popular with travelers seeking an alternative to the grungy markets of the medina.

SIGHTS

Medina

The old medina is relatively small, and an exit is never more than a few minutes away. This is a largely pedestrian-only zone, though plenty of scooters zoom about, adding to the chaos. **Bab Marrakesh,** across from the Place des Nations Unies near the clock tower, is the best entrance. Shuffle through lively fruit and vegetable sellers before plunging into the narrow,

the Hassan II Mosque

Casablanca

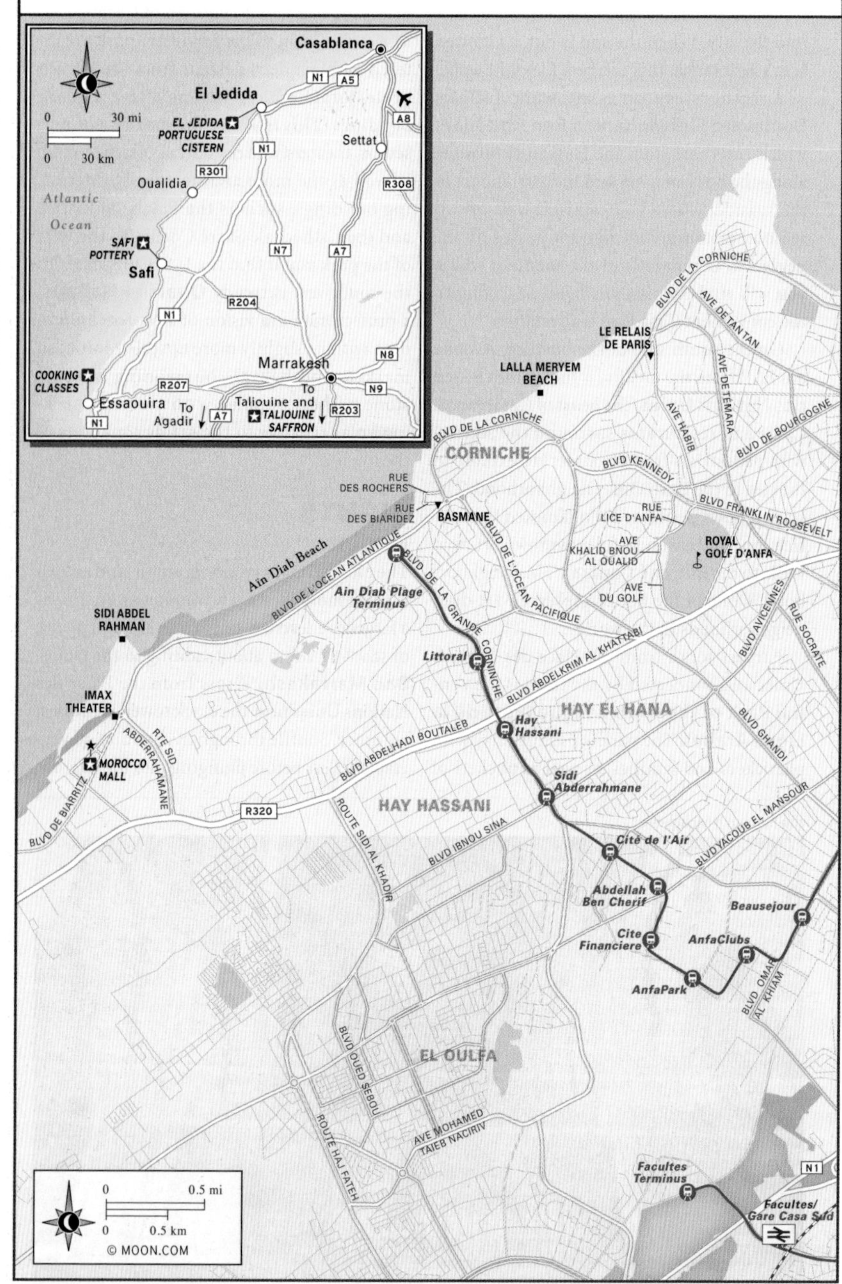
Casablanca
El Jedida
EL JEDIDA PORTUGUESE CISTERN
Settat
Oualidia
Atlantic Ocean
SAFI POTTERY
Safi
Marrakesh
COOKING CLASSES
Essaouira
To Agadir
To Talioune and TALIOUINE SAFFRON
N1
A5
A8
R301
R308
N7
A7
R204
N8
R207
N9
R203
0 30 mi
0 30 km
LE RELAIS DE PARIS
LALLA MERYEM BEACH
BLVD DE LA CORNICHE
AVE DE TAN TAN
AVE DE TÉMARA
AVE HABIB
BLVD DE BOURGOGNE
BLVD KENNEDY
BLVD FRANKLIN ROOSEVELT
CORNICHE
RUE DES ROCHERS
RUE DES BIARIDEZ
BASMANE
RUE LICE D'ANFA
AVE KHALID BNOU AL OUALID
AVE DU GOLF
ROYAL GOLF D'ANFA
Aïn Diab Beach
BLVD DE L'OCEAN ATLANTIQUE
BLVD DE LA GRANDE CORNICHE
BLVD DE L'OCEAN PACIFIQUE
Ain Diab Plage Terminus
SIDI ABDEL RAHMAN
Littoral
BLVD ABDELKRIM AL KHATTABI
BLVD AVICENNES
RUE SOCRATE
HAY EL HANA
IMAX THEATER
Hay Hassani
BLVD GHANDI
MOROCCO MALL
RTE SID ABDERRAHAMANE
BLVD ABDELHADI BOUTALEB
Sidi Abderrahmane
HAY HASSANI
BLVD YACOUB EL MANSOUR
R320
BLVD DE BIARRITZ
ROUTE SIDI AL KHADIR
BLVD IBNOU SINA
Cité de l'Air
Abdellah Ben Cherif
Beausejour
Cite Financiere
AnfaClubs
AnfaPark
BLVD OMAR AL KHIAM
BLVD OUED SEBOU
EL OULFA
ROUTE HAJ FATEH
AVE MOHAMED TAIEB NACIRIV
Facultes Terminus
Facultes/ Gare Casa Sud
0 0.5 mi
0 0.5 km
© MOON.COM

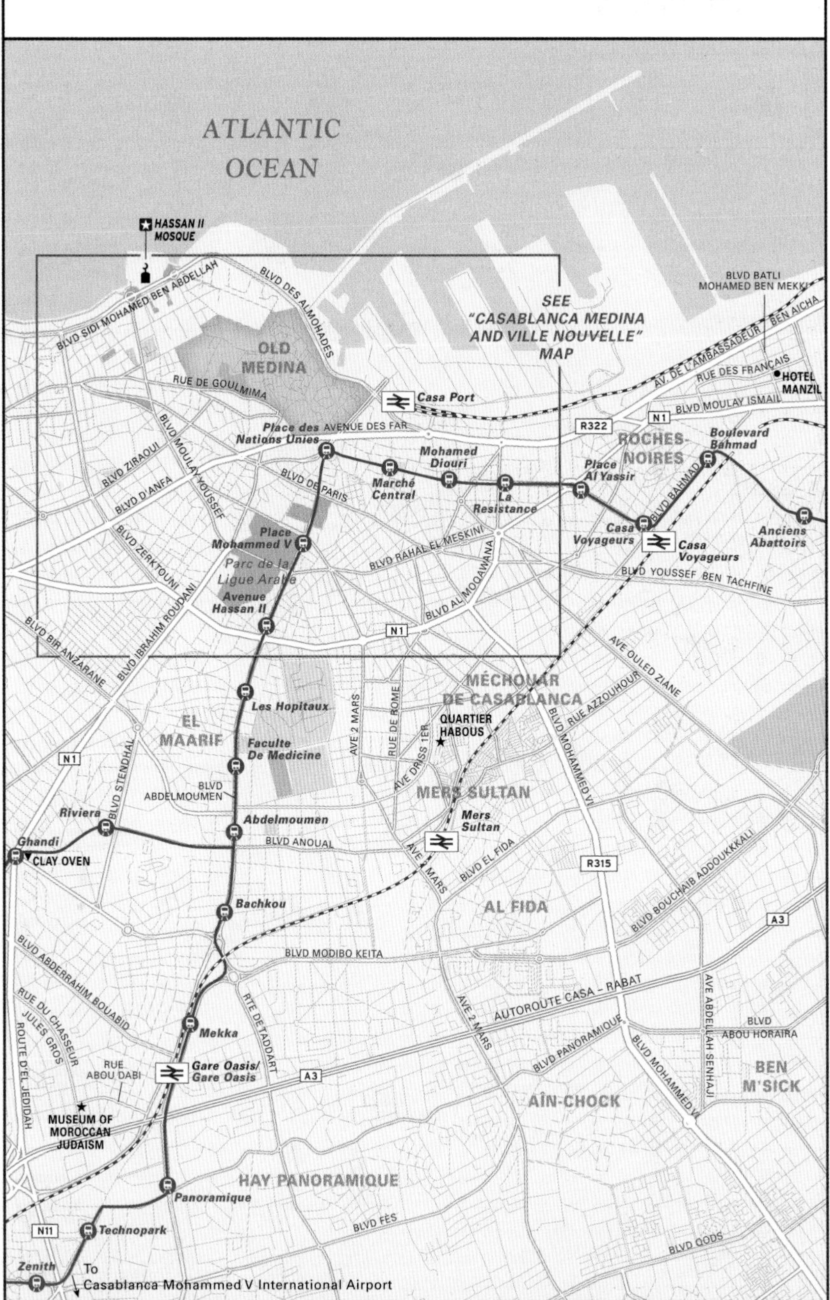
ATLANTIC OCEAN
HASSAN II MOSQUE
BLVD SIDI MOHAMED BEN ABDELLAH
BLVD DES ALMOHADES
SEE "CASABLANCA MEDINA AND VILLE NOUVELLE" MAP
OLD MEDINA
RUE DE GOULMIMA
Casa Port
Place des Nations Unies
AVENUE DES FAR
BLVD ZIRAOUI
BLVD MOULAY YOUSSEF
BLVD D'ANFA
BLVD DE PARIS
Marché Central
Mohamed Diouri
La Resistance
Place Al Yassir
ROCHES-NOIRES
Boulevard Bahmad
BLVD BAHMAD
Casa Voyageurs
Anciens Abattoirs
BLVD BATLI MOHAMED BEN MEKKI
BEN AICHA
AV. DE L'AMBASSADEUR
RUE DES FRANÇAIS
HOTEL MANZIL
BLVD MOULAY ISMAIL
N1
R322
Place Mohammed V
Parc de la Ligue Arabe
BLVD ZERKTOUNI
BLVD RAHAL EL MESKINI
BLVD AL MOQAWANA
BLVD YOUSSEF BEN TACHFINE
Avenue Hassan II
BLVD IBRAHIM ROUDANI
BLVD BIR ANZARANE
AVE OULED ZIANE
MÉCHOUAR DE CASABLANCA
RUE AZZOUHOUR
Les Hopitaux
EL MAARIF
Faculte De Medicine
AVE 2 MARS
RUE DE ROME
QUARTIER HABOUS
AVE DRISS 1ER
BLVD MOHAMMED VI
BLVD STENDHAL
BLVD ABDELMOUMEN
MERS SULTAN
Mers Sultan
Riviera
Abdelmoumen
BLVD ANOUAL
Ghandi
CLAY OVEN
BLVD EL FIDA
R315
Bachkou
AL FIDA
BLVD BOUCHAIB ADDOUKKALI
A3
BLVD MODIBO KEITA
BLVD ABDERRAHIM BOUABID
RUE DU CHASSEUR JULES GROS
ROUTE D'EL JEDIDAH
RTE DE TADDART
AUTOROUTE CASA - RABAT
AVE ABDELLAH SENHAJI
BLVD ABOU HORAIRA
Mekka
BLVD PANORAMIQUE
RUE ABOU DABI
Gare Oasis/ Gare Oasis
BEN M'SICK
MUSEUM OF MOROCCAN JUDAISM
AÎN-CHOCK
HAY PANORAMIQUE
Panoramique
N11
Technopark
BLVD FÈS
BLVD QODS
Zenith
To Casablanca Mohammed V International Airport

Casablanca Medina and Ville Nouvelle

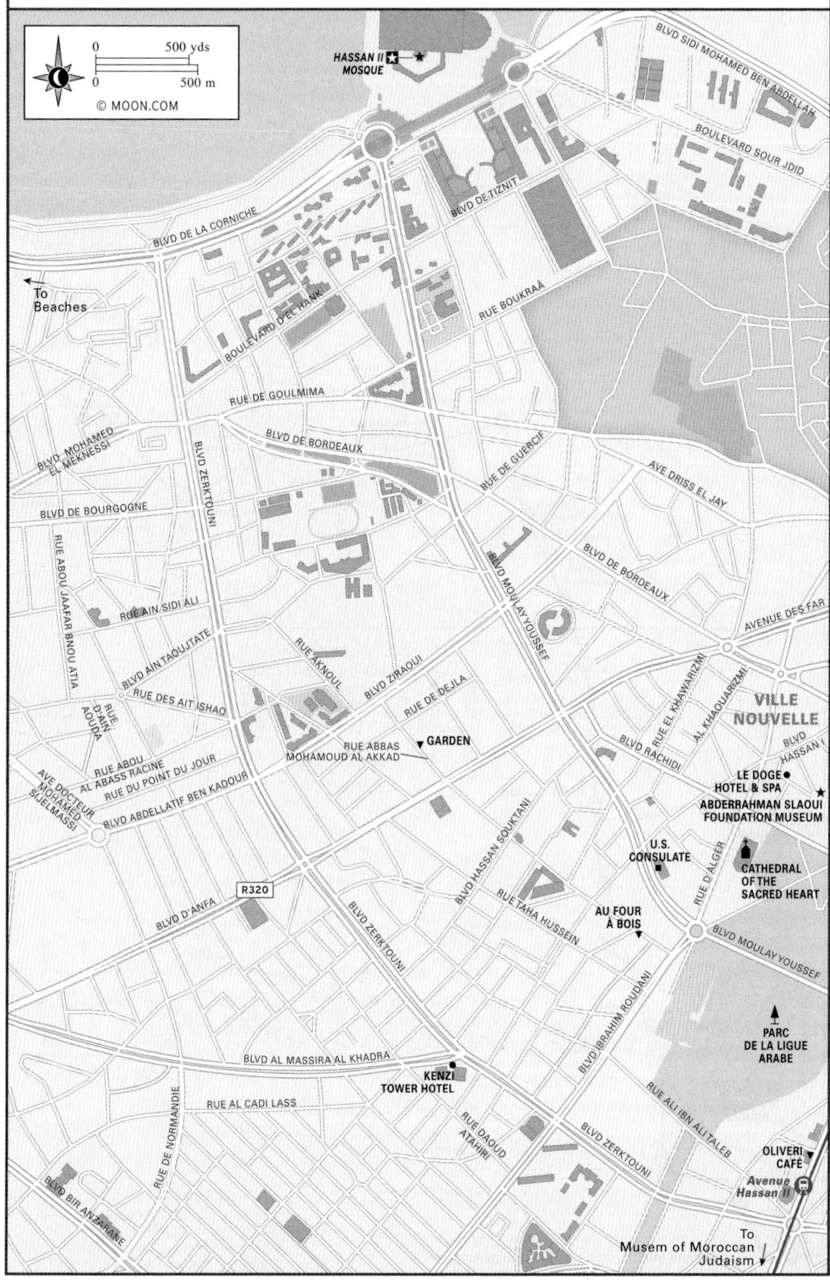

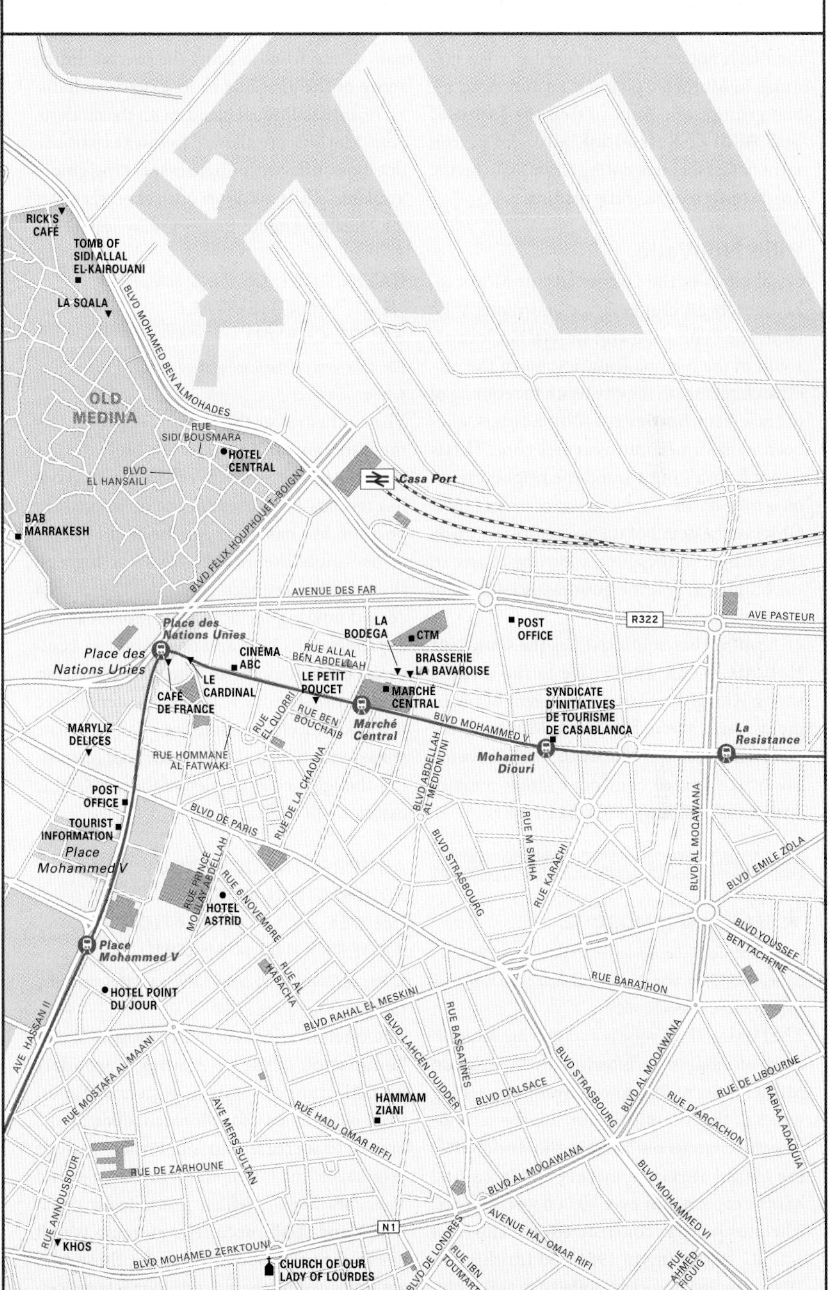
RICK'S CAFÉ
TOMB OF SIDI ALLAL EL-KAIROUANI
LA SQALA
BLVD MOHAMED BEN ALMOHADES
OLD MEDINA
RUE SIDI BOUSMARA
HOTEL CENTRAL
BLVD EL HANSAILI
BLVD FELIX HOUPHOUET-BOIGNY
BAB MARRAKESH
Casa Port
AVENUE DES FAR
R322
AVE PASTEUR
LA BODEGA
CTM
POST OFFICE
Place des Nations Unies
Place des Nations Unies
CINÉMA ABC
RUE ALLAL BEN ABDELLAH
BRASSERIE LA BAVAROISE
LE CARDINAL
LE PETIT POUCET
MARCHÉ CENTRAL
CAFÉ DE FRANCE
RUE EL QUORRI
RUE BEN BOUCHAIB
Marché Central
BLVD MOHAMMED V
SYNDICATE D'INITIATIVES DE TOURISME DE CASABLANCA
La Resistance
Mohamed Diouri
MARYLIZ DELICES
RUE HOMMANE AL FATWAKI
RUE DE LA CHAOUIA
BLVD ABDELLAH AL MEDIONUNI
POST OFFICE
TOURIST INFORMATION
BLVD DE PARIS
Place Mohammed V
BLVD STRASBOURG
RUE M SMIHA
RUE KARACHI
BLVD AL MOQAWANA
BLVD EMILE ZOLA
RUE PRINCE MOULAY ABDELLAH
RUE 6 NOVEMBRE
HOTEL ASTRID
BLVD YOUSSEF BEN TACHFINE
Place Mohammed V
RUE AL HABACHA
RUE BARATHON
HOTEL POINT DU JOUR
BLVD RAHAL EL MESKINI
AVE HASSAN II
RUE MOSTAFA AL MAANI
BLVD LAHCEN OUIDDER
RUE BASSATINES
BLVD STRASBOURG
BLVD AL MOQAWANA
RUE DE LIBOURNE
RUE D'ARCACHON
RABIAA ADAOUIA
BLVD D'ALSACE
HAMMAM ZIANI
RUE HADJ OMAR RIFFI
AVE MERS SULTAN
RUE DE ZARHOUNE
BLVD AL MOQAWANA
BLVD MOHAMMED VI
RUE ANNOUSSOUR
N1
AVENUE HAJ OMAR RIFI
KHOS
BLVD MOHAMED ZERKTOUNI
BLVD DE LONDRES
RUE IBN TOUMART
RUE AHMED FIGUIG
CHURCH OF OUR LADY OF LOURDES

maze-like streets of the medina. The outward-facing balconies are reminiscent of the medina of Tangier. Somewhat surprisingly, this medina is not nearly as touristed as other medinas in Morocco, giving it an authentic, albeit grungy, air. You can find the **Tomb of Sidi Allal El-Kairouani,** a sort of patron saint of Casablanca, dating from 1350, on the northwestern edge of the medina.

Ville Nouvelle

Casablanca is the largest city in Morocco, and nearly all of it is in the enormous Ville Nouvelle. The protectorate-era boulevards south of the medina feature some of the nicest architecture in the city. With the coming of the new tram, **Boulevard Mohammed V** has been transformed into a car-free zone. This is a spot for walking around the neighborhood on a tour of the art deco past of Casablanca. Observe the detail of the wrought-iron work, the strange arabesques adorning many of the buildings, and the quintessential funk of the signage.

A bit farther southeast lies the **Quartier Habous,** a chic alternative to the medina shops. Along the coast are different developments, such as the **Hassan II Mosque,** the **corniche,** and the **Morocco Mall.** Beyond, the urban sprawl continues into a mess of apartment buildings and office towers.

TOP EXPERIENCE

★ HASSAN II MOSQUE

Blvd. de la Corniche; guided tours Sat.-Thurs. 9am, 10am, 11am, 2pm, and 4pm, depending on prayer times; 120Dh, students 60Dh

The Hassan II Mosque is a staggering achievement of modern architecture by Frenchman Michel Pinseau that towers over the crashing waves of the Atlantic Ocean. It is the second-largest religious building in the world, after the Masjid al-Haram mosque in Mecca, and has the capacity for over 80,000 worshippers. The mosque was constructed in a flurry of activity beginning in 1986 and finishing in 1993, after local workers toiled day and night. Six thousand Moroccan master crafters were involved in the building, using their skills with *zellij* tile work, wood carving, and ornate stucco work to bring the overwhelming sense of the gracious to its expansive halls. Here, the traditional blends with the modern. Non-Muslims are allowed to enter as part of a one-hour tour with English-speaking guides available, while the doors open at prayer times for Muslims and for longer Friday services.

CATHEDRAL OF THE SACRED HEART (CATHÉDRALE SACRÉ COEUR)

Rue d'Algiers, on the edge of the Parc de la Ligue Arabe

The Cathedral of the Sacred Heart is a former Roman Catholic church built during the French protectorate era in the 1930s. It has recently been used for the occasional exposition but has otherwise been left for the birds—quite literally. Pigeons live high up the towering art deco columns. The church ceased holding services after Moroccan independence in 1956 and now serves as a cultural center. A guardian who usually watches over during the day will let you enter for free if you ask nicely. The interior, with its ornate stucco and stained glass, is somewhat interesting, though for most, a view of the neo-Gothic exterior will suffice.

ABDERRAHMAN SLAOUI FOUNDATION MUSEUM (MUSÉE DE LA FONDATION ABDERRAHMAN SLAOUI)

12 Rue de Parc; tel. 0522/206 217; www.musee-as.ma; Tues.-Sat. 10am-6pm; 30Dh

The often overlooked Abderrahman Slaoui Foundation Museum houses a wonderful collection of art deco posters (*affiches*) from old publicity for Morocco, done by the French to increase tourism. Posters include originals of the infamous *La Belle Fatma* and *Venez au Maroc,* which promoted a racial stereotype of Morocco. The museum is well worth the price of admission for those who are intrigued by these art deco masterpieces.

It also houses a collection of 19th- and 20th-century Moroccan jewelry, including some ornate headpieces, and paintings by Mohamed Ben Ali R'bati, known for his daily scenes of Tangier shortly after the turn of the 20th century. Information for the museum is only in French.

CHURCH OF OUR LADY OF LOURDES (ÉGLISE NOTRE-DAME DE LOURDES)

Rond-Point d'Europe; tel. 0522/263 537; free

The Church of Our Lady of Lourdes is a strange hulk of 1950s design, one of the last large-scale buildings under the French protectorate era, and not the prettiest. However, the stained glass inside is remarkable and captures the sunlight in arrays of colors, the immensity reminiscent of Paris's Sainte-Chapelle. The church still functions, serving the 20,000 Roman Catholics who call Casablanca home, making Sunday mass here a possibility.

QUARTIER HABOUS

Blvd. Sidi Mohamed Ben Abdellah

Sometimes called the "new medina," the Quartier Habous is something of an anomaly. The French constructed this medina to combat the overcrowding in the old medina and throughout the rest of the city in the 1930s. Though modeled on the design of Moroccan medinas, it incorporated modern plumbing and obeyed city planning ordinances and public health regulations in its construction. For a long time, Habous was neglected, though a revival effort recently took place and really cleaned up its streets. Now there are traditional crafts and bazaars, making this a less-authentic, though more-desirable, alternative to touring the old medina thanks to its relaxing atmosphere and general cleanliness.

MUSEUM OF MAROCCAN JUDAISM (MUSÉE DE JUDAÏSME MOROCAIN)

81 Rue Chasseur Jules Gros, Oasis; tel. 0522/994 940; www.jewishmuseumcasa.com; summer Mon.-Fri. 10am-6pm, Sun. 11am-3pm, winter Mon.-Fri. 10am-5pm, Sun. 11am-3pm; 40Dh

A bit east from the city center in the neighborhood of Oasis is the only known Jewish museum in an Islamic country, the Museum of Moroccan Judaism. The museum highlights the link of Morocco with its long, and proud, Jewish past. Religious texts, traditional garments, and sacramental artifacts make up much of the collection, with connections to the various mellahs (Jewish quarters) around Morocco. Much of the information is in French, though English versions are available—just ask. The museum is within walking distance from the Oasis train station.

Corniche

The corniche is host to two beaches, **Lalla Meryem** and **Aïn Diab,** as well as a couple of hotels and resort areas to the west of Boulevard de la Corniche. Set on a tiny island in the middle of this remote neighborhood, reachable only by a pedestrian bridge, is the mausoleum of **Sidi Abdel Rahman** (Plage Aïn Diab). Non-Muslims may not enter the mausoleum but may visit the merchants and healers around the mausoleum. For safety reasons, the island should be avoided at night. It provides a strange contrast to the relative opulence of the nearby **Morocco Mall.**

ENTERTAINMENT AND EVENTS

Performing Arts

Ground has finally broken on the **Casablanca Grand Theater** (slated to open in 2020) in the Park of the Arab League near Place Mohammed V. This theater, like its sister theater in Rabat, will house performances from around the world, including concerts, dances, and theater performances.

Events

Events, large and small, take place throughout the year. Check with the local tourist information center or your accommodation for the most up-to-date information.

1
2
3
4

CASABLANCA BOOK FAIR

www.salonlivrecase.ma; Feb.; free

Book nerds can salivate at the rows and rows of books at the annual Casablanca Book Fair, better known in Francophone-speaking circles as **Salon International de l'Edition et du Livre (SIEL).** It's held every February in La Foire International of Casablanca, an event space across from the Hassan II Mosque. This is one of the largest book events in Africa, with over 700 publishers attending and visiting authors from around the world. Titles are on hand, though they veer toward Arabic and French.

JAZZABLANCA

www.jazzablanca.com; late Mar./early Apr.; 200Dh

Of the festivals in Morocco, Jazzablanca has been one of the more successful. The Anfa Hippodrome plays host to most of the headliners, though there are plenty of sideshows throughout the city, at various hotels and restaurants. Sometimes jazz musicians gather at the Aïn Diab beach for a jam in the sand. This festival is at the end of March/beginning of April every year and features some of the biggest names in jazz from around the world. Tickets are reasonable at 200Dh.

AMAZIGH THEATER FESTIVAL

May; free

For about one week every May, the city of Casablanca hosts the **Amazigh Theater Festival.** These staged productions vary from horror to comedy and romance. The languages of the theater are different dialects of Amazigh, put on by those who claim their tribal Moroccan heritage. Even if you don't understand a word of Amazigh, it's still worth attending just to catch a glimpse into the culture and cultural pride of the people putting on the performances. Check with the tourist information center or your accommodations for more information, as the festival does not currently have a website and runs mostly by local advertising and word of mouth.

SHOPPING

Quartier Habous

Blvd. Sidi Mohamed Ben Abdellah

If Casablanca's medina proves to be a bit too much for the senses, head to Quartier Habous. This neighborhood, modeled on the design of Moroccan medinas, was constructed during the 1930s by the French to combat overcrowding in the city. The selection of traditional crafts and bazaars makes this a less-authentic experience than shopping in the dusty souks of Marrakesh or Fez, though it's a more desirable alternative to the grubby medina of Casablanca for those looking for traditional Moroccan goods.

★ Morocco Mall

Blvd. de la Corniche; tel. 0801/001 230; daily 10am-9pm

It might seem a little strange to come all the way to Casablanca only to head to the mall, but this is what the hip, trendy, and petit bourgeois of Morocco are doing. The Morocco Mall, at the end of the Aïn Diab beach, is a modern architectural treat. Opened in 2011, this is the largest indoor mall in Africa, with a curvy design by architect Davide Padoa that incorporates elements of the ocean that borders it. The outdoor musical fountain lights up at night, its classical score underscoring all the high-end retailers found here, such as Fendi and Gucci, as well as the more quotidian brand names, such as American Eagle and Starbucks. There is an Adventureland for kids, a three-story **aquarium** with an elevator plunging into its midst (Sun.-Thurs. 10am-9pm, Fri.-Sat. 10am-11pm, 50Dh), and a contemporary take on the Moroccan souk. The attached **IMAX movie theater** shows 3D movies and English-language films on Thursdays.

1: sunset soccer on Lalla Meryem Beach **2:** colonial art-deco architecture of downtown **3:** the art-deco Cathedral of the Sacred Heart **4:** kaftans for sale in the Quartier Habous

SPORTS AND RECREATION

Parks

PARK OF THE ARAB LEAGUE (PARC DE LA LIGUE ARABE)

Bordering Place Mohammed V is the Park of the Arab League. This is the widest green space in Casablanca, and after the crush of the city, it's the perfect place for a picnic. As in large public parks in other cities, there are some homeless people, though they keep largely to themselves. Around the park are some of the best examples of the colonial-era art deco French construction.

Golf

ROYAL GOLF D'ANFA

Lice d'Anfa; tel. 0522/365 344 or 0522/361 026; www.rgam.ma; 300Dh

With the economic affluence around Casablanca, it's no surprise that the local Royal Golf d'Anfa is one of the busier golf courses in Morocco. This is one of the few courses outside of Marrakesh where you will have to worry a bit about getting a tee time, so plan accordingly. Rental clubs, carts, and caddies are all available.

Hammams

Casablanca has high-end hammams and spas dotted throughout the city, each offering an experience not unlike what you might find back home. For a more authentic Moroccan hammam experience, you'll want to check out the offerings in the medieval medinas of Fez and Marrakesh.

HAMMAM ZIANI

59 Rue Abou Rakrak, Benjdia; tel. 0522/319 695; www.hammamziani.ma; 50Dh

Hammam Ziani offers a reasonable experience for a reasonable price, including a body scrub (20Dh) that will leave you feeling fresh and invigorated. This is about as authentic of a hammam experience as you can find in Casablanca. A vapor bath will relax you, while the humid heat activates your blood circulation and relaxes muscles.

LE DOGE HOTEL & SPA

9 Rue de Docteur Veyre; tel. 0522/467 800; http://hotelledoge.com; 500Dh

The on-site spa at Le Doge Hotel & Spa is one of the most luxurious spas in Casablanca and includes a refined traditional hammam as well as a hot tub, steam room, and rooms for manicures, pedicures, facials, and other treatments. Post- or pre-trip pampering here is highly recommended.

FOOD

Casablanca has one of the best food scenes in Morocco, which is to be expected given that it is the business hub of the country. Restaurants offer everything from traditional Moroccan dishes to French *haute cuisine*. Most restaurants still don't have a nonsmoking section, so this can be a problem for travelers sensitive to cigarette smoke.

Medina

LA SQALA

129 Rue Allah Ben Abdellah off Blvd. des Almohades; tel. 0522/260 960; daily 9am-11pm; 90Dh

If you're wandering the medina, ask around for La Sqala, a café and restaurant housed in the middle of the ruins of the old Portuguese fortress. For first-timers to Morocco, this is a great place to get familiar with different types of Moroccan cuisine, including the famous tajine, though the pumpkin soup and meat-filled pastries are not something to miss out on for those looking to dig into a tasty traditional Moroccan dish. Service can be a little bit slow, but this just gives you more time to take in the setting—eclectic traditional with a touch of modern. Take a look at the old black-and-white photos of Casablanca on display for a real sense of history. Breakfast is also served with an array of Moroccan crêpes, honey, confiture, and eggs, a spread fit for a king for less than 50Dh.

★ RICK'S CAFÉ

248 Rue Sour Jdid; tel. 0522/274 207; www.rickscafe.ma; daily noon-3pm and 6:30pm-1am; 300Dh

A stop in Casablanca is somehow incomplete without hearing Sam croon "As Time Goes

By" at Rick's Café—or rather, Issam, as the piano player is known in this Hollywood-come-to-life restaurant and bar. For those in love with the movie and wanting a dash of romance, Rick's Café does a wonderful job of re-creating the world of Bogie and Bergman. The menu features fresh vegetables and fish selected from the local markets and expertly thrown together. Goat cheese salads featuring perfectly ripe figs and seared swordfish steaks are menu staples. The rooftop terrace has views over the port, though likely you'll want to spend time in the gallant interior of this remarkable replica. Be sure to pack your fancy shoes, as the dress code is strictly enforced, and even with a reservation, you'll likely be turned away at the door if you're wearing sneakers and a baggy sweatshirt. Gentlemen will want to wear a button-down and slacks, and ladies should put on their fanciest threads! Of course, if dinner doesn't suit your palate, you could always just belly up to one of the finest gin joints in Morocco at the expansive bar.

Ville Nouvelle

CAFÉ DE FRANCE

Pl. des Nations Unies on Ave. Hassan II; tel. 0522/472 820; daily sunrise-11pm; 20Dh

Café de France is the best spot in town for people-watching, on the patio beneath the arcade, though you might have to fight off a few street vendors. This is a good haunt for literary types looking for a little inspiration as they watch the people from Casa breeze by across the busiest plaza in the city. For a thick hot chocolate worthy of its name, ask for a *chocolat fondant* (22Dh).

OLIVERI CAFÉ

Pl. Mohammed V on Ave. Hassan II; tel. 0522/982 898; www.oliveri.ma; daily 8am-10pm; 25Dh

If you're spending the day at the Park of the Arab League, the nearby Oliveri Café is a 1950s-styled ice cream parlor café, with a long wood bar and leather-backed chairs completing the look. This is a great stop for the kids, or the kid inside you, for an ice cream, sorbet, or milkshake. You might find a few of these cafés sprinkled around Casablanca. It's becoming a local tradition of sorts.

MARYLIZ DELICES

53 Ave. Hassan I; tel. 0522/471 282; daily 7am-9pm; 20Dh

Tucked off the Place des Nations Unies, Maryliz Delices features some of the most delicious pastries in town, including buttery croissants and spinach quiche, for a quick pick-me-up to take to the park or to the beach.

LA BODEGA

123 Rue Allal Ben Abdellah; tel. 0522/541 842 or 0522/312 203; www.restopro.ma/bodega; daily noon-4pm and 7pm-1am; 150Dh

La Bodega has a full bar, though at a price, including the most expensive bottle of Budweiser you'll likely ever have. Tapas start at 60Dh. The best deal is the "express midi" menu at 100Dh, which is large enough to serve two and includes a starter, main, and dessert. This is the place to go to throw a bit of an *olé* zest into your stay in Casablanca or if you have a hankering for some great Ibérico ham.

★ AU FOUR À BOIS

20 Jean Jaures; tel. 0522/221 718; daily noon-3pm and 7pm-11pm; 100Dh

The lovingly rustic Italian Au Four à Bois features pasta made in-house, and the meat is chargrilled *au four à bois* (French for "wood oven"). This is the house specialty, from where the restaurant takes its name. Decor is adopted from an Italian trattoria with tribal African touches. A mix of large round tables and smaller nooks make this place perfect for groups as well as more intimate dinners. Reservations are recommended for dinner. Pizzas are highly recommended. To avoid cigarette smoke and still get a delicious pizza, order from the **Au Four à Bois Express** (42 Omar Slaoui, tel. 0522/485 656, daily noon-11pm), which offers delivery to your hotel.

CLAY OVEN

245 Boulevard Ghandi; tel. 0522/992 133; daily noon-3pm and 7pm-11pm; 160Dh

Casablanca has seen a surge in Indian restaurants with an up-and-coming Indian population finding homes in and around Casa. Aptly placed right on Boulevard Ghandi, Clay Oven leads the way for those craving food with a bit more kick. Come for the butter chicken with naan bread and jeera rice with flavors that will take you straight back to Mumbai; stay for the good vibes and enclosed outdoor terrace.

LE CARDINAL

11 Blvd. Mohammed V; tel. 0522/221 560; daily noon-10pm; 95Dh

The popular Le Cardinal is a French-style brasserie, though with surprisingly great service, which somehow takes away from the Parisian-style dining (though perhaps in a good way). The restaurant is small and often full of smokers. *Entrecôte* (steak) with grilled mushrooms and a gratin of spinach and freshly caught fish highlight the menu, though to be clear, you're coming here for the ambiance more than anything.

BRASSERIE LA BAVAROISE

133 Ave. Allal Ben Abdellah; tel. 0522/311 760; Mon.-Sat. noon-3pm and 7:30pm-11:30pm; 250Dh

Just off the Boulevard Mohammed V, behind the Marché Central, the Brasserie la Bavaroise has a well-earned reputation for serving the best steaks in Morocco. The beef is sourced from locally grown, groomed, and herb-fed cattle indigenous to the Atlas Mountains. Entrecôte, New York, and T-bone steaks are all grilled to perfection in these rich confines. With oysters from Dakhla in the Western Sahara and fish caught right off the coast, this is the long-established classic steakhouse of Casablanca. Meat lovers should not miss out.

★ GARDEN

corner of Rue Mahmoud Akkad and Rue Commisaire Ladeuil; tel. 0522/200 333; www.garden.ma; daily 11am-11pm; 70Dh

If you're feeling a little heavy from the tajines and couscous, or if you're a vegetarian or vegan looking for a break, rejoice and head to Garden for a wide selection of salads, bagel sandwiches, and fresh juices. The few rope swing chairs will channel your inner child, while the good vibes will leave you feeling light, energetic, and ready to explore. The nonsmoking atmosphere is a welcomed retreat from the smoke-heavy restaurants in the city. Salads are always fresh, picked from local ingredients and the nearby markets, and you can customize your salad on the spot.

KHOS

44 Rue Announssour; tel. 0522/273 716; www.khos.ma; Mon.-Fri. 8:30am-5pm, Sun. 10am-3:30pm; 40Dh

Another wonderful stop for a quick soup and salad is Khos, close to the Park of the Arab League, near the hospital. The fresh salads and delicious soups on offer, all served in an incredibly hygienic atmosphere, are a good change-up from the heavier meals generally found around Casablanca. The Sunday brunch is worth a look if Saturday was a long night out.

Corniche

BASMANE

corner of Blvd. de l'Océan Atlantique and Blvd. de la Corniche; tel. 0522/797 532; www.basmane-restaurant.com; daily 7pm-midnight; 300Dh

If you're looking for a little belly dancing to go with your tajine, Basmane has just the spin for you. Set inside a traditional Moroccan house full of ornate stucco and complex *zellij* work, Moroccan tajines and heaps of couscous are served alongside the nightly entertainment, a parade of professional belly dancers who gyrate around the room, bringing the local male clientele to a near faint. Food is bland, but that's not the main draw anyway. It's popular with internationals and locals alike, both men and women, looking for something fantastical.

LE RELAIS DE PARIS

Blvd. de la Corniche, Hotel Villa Blanca; tel. 0522/391 510; daily 10:30am-midnight; 200Dh

Offering great dining just a short walk down the boulevard from the Hassan II Mosque, the classic French brasserie Le Relais de Paris should be visited on a warm day to enjoy a lunch of foie gras, seafood pasta, *magret de canard* (duck breast), or chateaubriand paired with one of the fantastic Moroccan wines on offer beneath a sunshade on the outdoor patio. The interior, though replete with white linens and fine woods, easily gets a bit crowded, and the tables are a bit too close for any real privacy.

BARS AND NIGHTLIFE

For most travelers, the local bars of Casablanca are places to be avoided. For the most part, the bars around here are of the "smoky dive bar" variety, feature seedy all-male clientele, and are home to rampant prostitution. That's not to say you can't have a nice drink, but just be aware. Here are a few of my favorite standby thirst-quenchers around town that are generally bereft of the less savory clientele lingering about other bars in Casa. There's always the bar at Rick's Café.

LE PETIT POUCET

86 Blvd. Mohammed V; tel. 0522/490 060; daily noon-11pm; 80Dh

Of the dive bars, perhaps the most interesting is Le Petit Poucet, famed for a number of French patrons, but most of all for Antoine de Saint-Exupéry, the author of *The Little Prince*, who stopped here often between flights as he was working for the French postal service as a pilot. Its long history of famous patrons also includes Albert Camus and Edith Piaf. The bar is typical of Moroccan bars, with generally male clientele and hard drinkers, though foreign females are welcomed—a completely authentic experience, if a bit edgy for most. It's the sort of place that might become your local hangout if you lived in Casa.

LA BODEGA

123 Rue Allal Ben Abdellah; tel. 0522/541 842; noon-1am; 150Dh

For a Spanish-themed evening, La Bodega has a full bar, though drinking is not cheap. Cocktails typically run north of 50Dh, with tapas starting at 60Dh. The clientele is a mix of locals, tourists, and hardened expats. The atmosphere is perfect for knocking back some suds with your amigos.

Nightclubs

Nightclubs in Casablanca should be avoided. Like most of the bars around the city, they are generally the provenience for the less savory characters of Casablanca, and they're incredibly expensive to boot. If nightlife is your thing, the more internationally friendly environs of Agadir, Marrakesh, Rabat, and Tangier are more genial to late-night fêtes.

Most large-scale hotels in Casablanca have their own nightclubs. If you absolutely have to get out, you could try the nightclub in your hotel; this way you can avoid being stranded somewhere late at night in the city or a host of other possible problems. The party never starts in Morocco until after midnight, with ladies and gentlemen often showing more skin than in most places in the United States or Europe. If you are traveling out, be sure to taxi back and forth, as these are the hours to avoid walking the streets. However, be aware that in some neighborhoods, taxis can be notoriously difficult to find late at night.

ACCOMMODATIONS

Accommodations can be had in Casablanca at virtually every price point imaginable, though decent accommodations at budget prices are difficult to find. Most of the budget options cater more toward illicit activities, such as prostitution, than they do toward travelers. Of all the cities in Morocco, Casablanca is perhaps the best choice for stretching your budget, not necessarily for what is offered so much as for the lack of availability of other types of accommodations. For the best deals, make sure to book online a few weeks ahead of time.

20
1
2
MAROC
3
4
GARE DE CASA VOYAGEURS

Under 400Dh

HOTEL ASTRID

12 Rue 6 Novembre; tel. 0522/277 803; 300Dh d

One of the better deals in the city is Hotel Astrid. The simple rooms have Wi-Fi, though it's often a bit slow, and en suite bathrooms. A generally clean hotel, though definitely in need of some renovation work, like all other budget hotels found throughout Morocco. This particular hotel suffers from problems with moisture during the winter. Those sensitive to molds should avoid the hotel in the cold months. The location near Place Mohammed V makes it centrally located and good for exploration. Breakfast will set you back an extra 35Dh.

HOTEL CENTRAL

20 Pl. Ahmed el-Bidaoui, old medina; tel. 0522/262 525; 350Dh d

The well-located Hotel Central is within walking distance of most of the major attractions, as well as the Casa Port train station. This hotel is easy enough to find, right on the edge of the old medina, though first-timers to Casablanca might consider taking a taxi, which can drop you close to the front door. A few of the rooms have balconies facing out toward the small square and Wi-Fi reception. The top-floor rooms open out with views over the medina and port, though Wi-Fi doesn't seem to reach all the way up. This is a good spot for single travelers to meet friendly faces also traveling Morocco.

400-800Dh

★ HOTEL POINT DU JOUR

10 Rue du Lieutenautberger; tel. 0522/279 207; www.hotelpointdujour.ma; 400Dh d

A centrally located two-star hotel with five-star service. Redouane, the manager, has done a great job hiring some of the most helpful, friendly staff in all of Casablanca. They can help you get around town and will even look after you if you've caught the traveler's flu. The hotel itself has been renovated, though the water pressure isn't the greatest and the Wi-Fi not the most robust. Breakfast is a good value, though you should look elsewhere for lunch or dinner. The elevator is a bonus if you have sore feet from walking around. Request a room opposite the road for a quieter night. Perhaps not the most romantic spot, though comfy and as welcoming for single travelers as it is for families.

HOTEL MANZIL

35 Rue des Français, Qu. Roches Noires; tel. 0522/242 020; www.manzilhotels.com; 500Dh d

Hotel Manzil is a bit out of the way from most of the major attractions, though taxis are available and can get you to the nearest train station, Casa Voyageurs, for about 10Dh. Rooms are clean, with Wi-Fi, air-conditioning, and television, and the beds are comfortable. The friendly staff can help you call taxis and navigate around the city, though taxis summoned to the hotel will cost more (typically a "pickup" charge of 30Dh or so). Breakfast is a reasonable value at 37Dh. A clean, cozy budget option, though the location leaves something to be desired.

Over 800Dh

KENZI TOWER HOTEL

Twin Center, Blvd. Zerktouni; tel. 0522/978 000; www.kenzi-hotels.com; 1,200Dh d

Even if you don't stay at the opulent Kenzi Tower Hotel, it's worth a visit to the top-floor Sky Bar 28 (daily 9am-1am) for panoramic views over Casablanca. Located in one tower of the Twin Center, the hotel has prompt, professional service. The ventilation system is good enough that, for the most part, cigarette smoke goes unnoticed. The beds are downy plush, and rooms have floor-to-ceiling windows that make the most of the view. There is a buffet breakfast and lunch, as well as the independent gastronomic restaurant Sens, though meals are not included with your stay. A full-service spa, business center, fitness room, and swimming pool make this a luxurious splurge.

1: Olives are a staple of Moroccan cuisine. **2:** a Moroccan wicker basket **3:** a Moroccan tajine **4:** the new Casa Voyageurs Train Station

★ LE DOGE HOTEL & SPA

9 Rue de Docteur Veyre; tel. 0522/467 800; http://hotelledoge.com; 1,700Dh d

If boutique hotels are your thing, Le Doge Hotel & Spa is wonderfully maintained with Jacuzzi-size tubs, rich wood furniture, plush beds, and art deco-period touches sprinkled throughout the hotel. The on-site spa is one of the most luxurious in the city. The salon is a private library with plenty of comfy seats to curl up with a book around the fireplace, while the fifth-floor garden terrace provides plenty of green space to catch some rays. The pampering available at Le Doge is well worth it.

INFORMATION AND SERVICES

The city code for Casablanca and the area is 22.

Visitor Information

TOURIST INFORMATION CENTER (DÉLÉGATION RÉGIONALE DU TOURISME DE CASABLANCA)

60 Ave. Hassan II; tel. 0522/206 266; www.visitcasablanca.ma; Mon.-Thurs. 9am-12:30pm and 2:30pm-6:30pm, Fri.-Sat. 9am-12:30pm and 3pm-6:30pm

The Tourist Information Center, right at Place Mohammed V, has some maps and updated information about city events, particularly about the numerous festivals and gallery showings.

SYNDICATE D'INITIATIVES DE TOURISME DE CASABLANCA

98 Blvd. Mohammed V; tel. 0522/221 524; Mon.-Fri. 8:30am-4:30pm

The Syndicate d'Initiatives de Tourisme de Casablanca also carries free information on events and happenings, though sometimes the brochures are a bit outdated. Malika is usually behind the desk. She speaks some English, is very friendly, and can help you find your way around Casa.

U.S. CONSULATE

8 Blvd. Moulay Youssef; tel. 0522/264 550; appointment only

U.S. citizens who need consular services or assistance, such as in the case of a lost or stolen passport, should contact the U.S. Consulate in Casablanca. The **U.S. Embassy** (tel. 0537/637 200) in Rabat is largely diplomatic. For emergencies, contact the **American Citizen Services hotline** (tel. 0522/642 099, Mon.-Fri. 8am-5pm, tel. 0661/131 939 after hours).

Safety

Casablanca is a relatively safe city, though with the booming population and shantytowns ringing the city, prostitution, drug use, and petty crimes remain high. Since a terrorist attack in 2003, the only one in recent memory, security has been beefed up to protect the economic interest of the country and the safety of its people. The new tram track provides safe, secure passage across different neighborhoods of the city, and police patrol the streets around the clock. Still, care should be taken with walking late at night because, as in most metropolitan cities, muggings are known to happen.

Post Offices and Courier Services

There are several post offices scattered around Casablanca, including Place Mohammed V, Boulevard Mohammed V, and Place Zallaqa. Post offices keep the same hours (Mon.-Fri. 9am-4:30pm, Sat. 9:30am-noon, with abbreviated hours during Ramadan).

Money

Cash machines are ubiquitous around Casablanca, though they only distribute 100- and 200-dirham notes.

At the Place des Nations Unies tram stop you'll find a handy **Attijarwafa Bank** (Mon.-Fri. 8:15am-3:45pm, Ramadan 9:15am-2:30pm) and **Wafacash Currency Exchange** with **Western Union** (Mon.-Fri. 8am-7pm and Sat. 9am-4pm) as well as the **Banque Populaire** (Mon.-Fri. 8:15am-4:30pm) and **BMCI** (Mon.-Fri. 8:15am-6:30pm, Sat.-Sun. 9am-6pm, Ramadan 9am-5pm). Right on Place Mohammed V there is a **Bank Al-Maghrib** (Mon.-Fri. 8:30am-3pm).

For travelers checks, foreign currency exchanges, and other services, it's best to use **BMCE.** The most convenient location for most travelers is across from the Cathédrale Sacré Coeur. Near the Hassan II Mosque you can find BMCE, Al Barid, and Banque Populaire (as well as a post office) on Rue Sanhaja.

Hospitals, Clinics, and Pharmacies

If necessary, head directly for **Hospital Dar Salaam** (728 Blvd. Modibo Keita, tel. 0522/851 414) for emergency services. There are pharmacies seemingly on every street in Casablanca. All keep posted hours for off-hour pharmacies. The **Grande Pharmacie Commerciale** (Pl. des Nations Unies, Mon.-Fri. 9am-12:30pm and 3:30pm-8pm, Sat. 9am-1pm) is one of the more conveniently located pharmacies, just off the Place des Nations Unies in the heart of the city.

GETTING THERE

By Plane

MOHAMMED V INTERNATIONAL AIRPORT

Nouasseur, about 30min south of Casablanca via the A7 or N9; tel. 0522/539 040; www.casablanca-airport.com

The airport train connects directly with Casa Voyageurs and Casa Port, the main train stations in Casablanca. Trains leave the airport every hour daily 3:55am-11:45pm (30min, 2nd/1st-class 43Dh/64Dh). You will find the station downstairs from the arrivals hall. This is the most convenient way in and out of the airport, especially after a long flight if you don't want to haggle for a taxi. If you're staying in Casablanca, consider debarking at the l'Oasis stop to connect with the tram.

Taxis are always available to shuttle travelers into the city (300Dh) and will be found just outside the arrivals gate, though you'll likely have to haggle your fair. At night, the prices are raised substantially (500Dh) and you should always try to bargain if you have the energy.

By Car

Casablanca is well-connected by the tolled autoroutes. Tolls vary according to type of automobile and where you'll enter/exit the tolled route. In principle, it's a good idea to travel with 400Dh just for tolls, though you'll likely not use it all.

From Rabat: Follow the A1 autoroute south for 90km/56mi, about 1 hour.

From Marrakesh: Follow the A1 autoroute north for 245km/153mi, about 3 hours.

From Meknes: Follow the A2 autoroute west to Rabat before taking the A1 south (232km/144mi, about 2.5 hours). There will be two tolls, one at Rabat (38Dh) and one on the Casablanca-Rabat autoroute (23Dh).

From Fez: Follow the A2 autoroute west to Rabat before taking the A1 south (292km/181mi, about 3.5 hours). There will be two tolls, one at Rabat (50Dh) and one on the Casablanca-Rabat autoroute (23Dh).

From Tangier: Follow the A1 autoroute south for 335km/208mi, about 4 hours. There will be two tolls, one at Kenitra (66Dh) and one on the Casablanca-Rabat autoroute (23Dh).

By Bus

CENTRAL STATION

23 Rue Léon l'Africain

Traveling by bus, the **CTM** (tel. 0800/0900 30, www.ctm.ma) shuttles to and from stops all over Morocco. The **central station** is well located in the middle of town, near several hotels and the tram and not far from the Casa Voyageurs train station. Check the scheduled information online or at the station for specific departure information and for "premium" buses that are a bit more comfortable and come with onboard Wi-Fi service. Premium buses tend to be about 30Dh more. Some of the more popular bus runs include: Agadir (7.5hr, 15 daily, 215Dh), El Jedida (2hr, 7 daily, 45Dh), Essaouira (7.5hr, 2 daily, 140Dh), Fez (5hr, 13 daily, 90Dh, premium available), Marrakesh (4hr, 16 daily, 80Dh, premium available), Meknes (3.5hr, 9 daily, 85Dh), Oualidia (3hr, 3 daily, 75Dh), Ouarzazate (9hr, 4 daily, 140Dh), Rabat (1.5hr, 30 daily, 40Dh), Safi (4.5hr, 9 daily, 100Dh), and Tangier (6hr, 3 daily, 100Dh, premium available).

By Train

Casablanca is a train hub. **ONCF** (tel. 0890/203 040, www.oncf.ma) operates two major train lines. The first follows the coast from Tangier to Marrakesh (this line gave rise to the popular Marrakesh Express) and the second crosses the country northeast through Meknes and Fez before ending at distant Oujda at the eastern border with Algeria.

CASA VOYAGEURS TRAIN STATION

at the eastern end of Blvd. Mohammed V

For those traveling to Tangier, the Al-Boraq **high-speed train** leaves from the newly remodeled **Casa Voyageurs train station** (at the eastern end of Blvd. Mohammed V) and whisks you to Tangier in just over two hours. It's a very good idea to purchase your ticket ahead of traveling. Online purchasing is possible, though fidgety. It might take a few tries to get the system to work. It's best to stop by the train station a day or two ahead of time if possible to purchase tickets. You can also keep an eye out for promotional fares that often cut the price by a third or more. The **Al-Boraq high-speed train** is just like the TGV in France. This train route was inaugurated in November 2018 and now whisks passengers along from Casablanca to Tangier in just over two hours. Prices vary according to demand. The first train leaves Casablanca at 6:00am with trains departing basically every two hours until 9pm. With the quick service, this makes a day trip to Tangier feasible (2hr, 9 daily, 149Dh-224Dh, with 1st class tickets typically costing about 70Dh more).

From the **Casa Voyageurs,** some of the more popular regular train lines run to and from Fez (4hr, 19 daily, 2nd/1st-class 110Dh/165Dh, sometimes with a train change at Sidi Kacem, check for the direct trains; regular train), Marrakesh (3.5hr, 9 daily, 87Dh/150Dh), Rabat (regular train 1.5hr, rapid train 1hr; trains leave every 30min daily 5:10am-12:30am, 37Dh/69Dh, rapid train 47Dh/96Dh), and Tangier (5hr, 10 daily, 125Dh/185Dh). Trains also connect directly with the Mohammed V International Airport every hour, just after the hour, 3am-10pm (30min, 19 daily, 43Dh/64Dh), making this a great option for getting to and from the airport.

CASA PORT TRAIN STATION

on the north end of Blvd. Felix Houphouët-Boigny, at the junction with Blvd. des Almohades

The centrally located Casa Port train station is within walking distance to downtown Casablanca.

GETTING AROUND

By Car

If you have a car, Casablanca is a place to park it and leave it for a few days. Navigating the city with its intense 24-hour traffic, aggressive drivers, and road signs that are not at all obvious to the uninitiated (or even to the initiated) is best avoided. Most hotels have guarded parking available, and street parking is generally safe, though likely you'll be asked to tip 5Dh or so to the guardian.

By Petit Taxi

The notorious red *petits taxis* of Casablanca are generally the quickest way around town, though taxi drivers are aggressive, both in driving and business. They often try to charge foreigners 3-4 times the going rate. Ask the taxi to use the counter. As with other taxis around Morocco, prices go up by 50 percent at night. If you're having trouble getting drivers to use the counter, even the "rip-off" rates are generally not exorbitant, with rides costing 50-100Dh.

By Tram

The clean, new, eco-friendly **tram line** (tel. 0522/998 383, www.casatramway.ma) is the cleanest way to get around town. The tram will take you near most major destinations. It runs daily 5:30am-10:30pm, with trains passing every 15 minutes or so. Purchase a ticket at any tram stop using the ATM-looking machines. Fares are 7Dh per trip (plus 1Dh for a rechargeable card that you can use for up to 10 trips), 60Dh for a weekly pass, and 230Dh for a month, plus 15Dh for the card itself. Change and credit cards are accepted (no paper bills), and instructions on the machine are available in English, though stops along the tram are only signed with their French and Arabic names. The tram connects with the main train stations near l'Oasis, Casa Port, and Casa Voyageurs, making train connections around the country, as well as to and from the airport, fairly easy.

South of Casablanca

AZEMMOUR

أزمور

The name Azemmour derives from the Tamazight *azemmur,* meaning "olives." Though olives are still found in the region and a main agricultural production, visitors to Azemmour tend to come here to escape the crowds. Azemmour was once a Portuguese-held fortress, as evidenced by the stone fortress walls surrounding the old medina, but these days is really a place to unplug and unwind.

Sights

Azemmour is a picturesque old town, not unlike the more popular towns of Essaouira to the south or Asilah to the north. What makes Azemmour a bit strange is that it really isn't that touristed ... yet. The very beginnings of something interesting are happening now in Azemmour. In a few years, this may just be Morocco's new hot spot, but as of now, it's all speculation and quiet along the riverfront. Unless you're really looking for an escape, Azemmour is perhaps best served as a short stop on your drive down the coast. You can tour the entire **medina** in less than an hour.

WALKING TOUR OF AZEMMOUR'S MEDINA

Starting from the north in the old medina, you begin at the old **mellah.** Notice the numerous Stars of David above the doors. Azemmour had a thriving Jewish community until the mass exodus after Moroccan independence in 1956 and the subsequent recruitment of Jewish citizens by the newly established country of Israel. An old **synagogue** is well kept and a sort of pilgrimage for Moroccan Jews from Israel. They also sometimes return to visit the small shrine of Rabbi Abrahim Moul Niss, a venerated, saintly figure in local Jewish lore. The **kasbah** is just south of the mellah. The gates are generally closed and it's slowly being left to ruin, though it is safe to walk around. The guardian in charge will let you in; he is usually around in the morning and for a couple of hours after lunch. After the kasbah, take a walk along the riverside, to the east, and take in the beautiful view over the river. If you're traveling along the coast, this is about as off-the-radar as it gets.

Food and Accommodations

All of the *riads* in the medina serve meals and there are a few cheap eateries across the street from the medina. The grill stations and cafés are unremarkable, on the whole, but can serve for a quick bite on the go if you're passing through town. Most travelers will likely want to dine at one of the local *riads.* Be sure to call ahead of time to make reservations. A day or two ahead of time is preferred, though the morning of is usually okay.

The few accommodations here cater mostly to French tourists. If you're planning on spending a night or two in this quiet backwater, it is a pensive alternative to Casablanca or nearby El Jedida. A couple of well-restored *riads* give an authentic medina experience for about half the cost of the equivalent in Marrakesh.

RIAD 7

2 Derb Choutka; tel. 0523/347 363; www.riad7.com; 350Dh d

One of the better options is the quaint Riad 7, lovingly restored and set in a traditional Moroccan house (*dar*). The small courtyard gives way to simple rooms that are cleaned regularly. It's not as elaborate as some of the other *riads* you might see around Morocco, but the modern decor provides an interesting contrast to the otherwise traditional setting. The rooftop terrace makes good use of the views over the river. Breakfast is included. Traditional Moroccan tajines are available for dinner on request.

L'OUM ERREBIA

25 Impasse Chtouka; tel. 0523/347 071; www.azemmour-hotel.com; 800Dh d

L'Oum Errebia is popular with the trendy French, with eclectic, vibrant paintings, sculptures, and books tastefully placed throughout the *riad* and spacious rooms in lots of beiges and creams, giving the impression that you're staying in something of an art gallery. The terrace views over the river, especially as the sun sets, are divine. It's a good getaway, if that's what you're looking for. Food is less Moroccan than French-Moroccan fusion. The rate includes breakfast. Dinners are possible.

Getting There and Around

By car, Azemmour is easily reachable from **Casablanca** (89km/55mi, 1hr) and **El Jedida** (16km/10mi, 15min). *Grands taxis* also shuttle back and forth between Casablanca (1hr, 89km, 40Dh) and El Jedida (15min, 16km, 15Dh).

The **ONCF** (tel. 0524/888 566 or 0524/885 632, www.oncf.ma) has services to the **Gare Ferroviaire Azemmour** station outside of town. From there, it is a 25-minute walk (2km/1mi) into town, or you can catch one of the *petits taxis* at the station for 10Dh.

EL JEDIDA
الجديدة

When I think about El Jedida, I think about a town with a lot of unrealized potential. The location is ideal, about 100 kilometers (60mi) southwest of Casablanca, and the views from the commanding Portuguese-era fortress atop the hill and over the Atlantic are stellar. The feel is truly unique in Morocco, but El Jedida is somehow always disappointing. Largely, this is because it caters to day and weekend tourists living in Casablanca, and the type of tourism that has taken hold has been swinging ahead at a rampant pace, with golf resorts and new beachfront hotels being quickly constructed along the coastline. Meanwhile, much of the old Portuguese city has been neglected, left to fall into ruin. With that said, El Jedida does host one of the more historically interesting sights to see in the area: the 16th century **Portuguese cistern.**

Just outside of the walled Portuguese fortress, a wide beach runs northeast just beyond the fishing port and the small Parc Abdelkarim el Khattabi. The beach is family-friendly, though trash can be an issue, and women traveling alone are likely to get hassled. From this northeast corner near the beach, the new city spreads south. The new city is where most restaurants, hotels, pharmacies, and cash machines can be found.

Sights

PORTUGUESE CITY

Better known in the 16th century by the Portuguese name **Mazagan,** the **fortress** is an "early example of the realization of the Renaissance ideals integrated with Portuguese construction technology," according to UNESCO, which certified the old Portuguese city (Cité Portugaise) as one of its World

1: the old Portuguese town of Azemmour **2:** the beachside of Oualidia

1
2

Heritage Sites in 2004. Stone walls with wide ramparts surround the city. These have all been restored and make for a nice walk, with an expansive terrace overlooking the ocean and usually some kids playing soccer nearby. The crumbling city houses one of the more important constructions from the Portuguese era in Morocco.

★ PORTUGUESE CISTERN (CITERNE PORTUGAISE)

Rue Hachmi Bahbah; daily 10am-noon and 3pm-sunset; 10Dh

Constructed to store water, the cavernous Portuguese Cistern is a bit eerie, and you can see why scenes from Orson Welles's *Othello* were filmed here. The design of the cistern building is attributed to João Castilho, the resident architect of old Mazagan. This Manueline-styled, late-Gothic cistern is a basic square plan. There are three halls, to the north, east, and south sides, as well as four towers. The partially underground central hall, built of thick stone and brick, once held thousands of gallons of water, which made their way to the cistern through a complex irrigation system throughout the fortress. This cistern's construction reflected a blend of Portuguese and Arab knowledge which ensured the water for the fortress, an incredibly important function for a fortress of this size and era.

CHURCH OF THE ASSUMPTION

Rue de Carreira

The Church of the Assumption dates from the beginning of the 16th century. Heavy rains and deterioration led to the roof collapsing many years ago—luckily nobody was injured. The church was restored sometime after the collapse, keeping the details and respecting the architecture of this period. After the Portuguese left in the 17th century, the church passed into secular use and was used as a town hall and meeting center. Decisions are still being made as to what to make of this wonderful representation of the architecture for this period.

Golf

MAZAGAN GOLF

Km7, Route de Casablanca; tel. 0523/388 076; greens fees 750Dh

El Jedida has a growing reputation as a golfer's vacation destination, with easy access to and from the airport at Casablanca as well as some of the most beautiful palm-lined courses north of Marrakesh, including Morocco's longest, the Gary Player-constructed, 7,484-yard Mazagan Golf.

Food

LA PORTUGAISE

Rue de Suez; tel. 0523/371 241 or 0660/401 398; daily noon-3pm and 7pm-10pm; 50Dh

The old standard in town, La Portugaise, in the old Portuguese city, serves savory, unpretentious Moroccan favorites, such as beef tajine with prunes and chicken with olives and candied lemon. Vegetarian options, including lentil soup and simple omelets, are also usually available. Red-and-white checkered tablecloths and the incredibly friendly staff will make you feel right at home.

LA CAPITAINERIE

Hotel l'Iglesia; tel. 0523/373 400; daily noon-3:30pm and 7pm-11pm; 100Dh

For a touch of fine dining in the heart of the old Portuguese city, head to La Capitainerie at the Hotel l'Iglesia. The hotel sits inside the 19th-century Spanish church of Saint Antoine of Padoue, while the dinner is served in the courtyard of the old U.S. Consulate, attached to the church. As interesting as the old consulate might be, it's the afternoon lunch on a sunny day, lounging on the terrace at the foot of the ramparts, that's the draw. Fresh fish straight from the port, French bistro specialties including *saumon aux poireaux* (salmon with leeks), and traditional Moroccan tajines are all rushed steaming to your table by the jovial waitstaff. Quality is something of an issue, as sometimes meals are wonderful and other times they leave a lot to be desired. Considering the price and location, it's worth it as long as you're going for lunch on the terrace. Reservations are required.

LE PRIVE

41 Ave. des FAR; tel. 0523/373 665; www.lepriverestaurant.com; Mon.-Sat. noon-3:30pm and 6:30pm-1am, Sun. 10:30am-3:30pm and 7pm-1am; 200Dh

Le Prive adds a touch of class to El Jedida. The shock of white and red adds a bit of Manhattan to the modern decor, while the tapas bring a little Spanish flavor, and the *duck à l'orange* is a classic French staple. The chef rotates the menu every three months according to the season (though it doesn't offer much for the vegetarian palate). This is an interesting option for those looking to break out of the mostly basic dining around town.

Accommodations

Consider staying in nearby Azemmour. The accommodations in El Jedida tend to veer toward the modern resort crowd, and there are few authentic-feeling *riads* or *dars*.

MAISON D'HOTES DE LA CITÉ PORTUGAISE D'EL JADIDA

9 Rue 8; tel. 0523/341 231; www.chambres-hotes-eljadida.com; 375Dh d

Check out the rather exuberantly named Maison d'Hotes de la Cité Portugaise d'El Jadida. As in other houses right on the water, the rooms can be a bit damp in winter, but during the warm months this guesthouse is a fine value, with many new furnishings adding an eclectic modern-decor touch to this otherwise traditional Moroccan house. Hassan, the manager, will make sure you have a happy stay. Breakfast (35Dh), lunch, and dinner are available—something to think about while lounging on the terrace, listening to the surf crash against the stone walls below.

RIAD SOLEIL D'ORIENT

131 Derb El Hajjar; tel. 0523/350 242; www.riadsoleildorient.net; 900Dh d

Tucked inside the popular neighborhood across the busy Avenue Moulay Abdelhafid from the old Portuguese city is the splendid Riad Soleil d'Orient. The rooms are spacious, with beds fit for a king or queen, and include private seating areas, TV, air-conditioning, and Internet access. Every room gives out over the interior courtyard with its giant banana trees. Olivier, the owner, will be happy to tell you all about growing banana trees and make sure that you are comfortable in your rooms. Dinner here is one of the best in town; make sure to reserve ahead of time, as seats are limited.

★ DAR AL MANAR

Route Haouzia; tel. 0523/351 645; www.dar-al-manar.com; 800Dh d

About 7 kilometers (4mi) northeast of El Jedida, just off the road leading to Azemmour, you'll find Dar Al Manar. This guesthouse is a true work of passion constructed from the ground up by Fatima, the resident owner and manager. This is one heck of a retreat, located off the coast on a rolling hill, much of it fenced in where cows, sheep, and goats graze, and overlooking the not-too-distant Atlantic Ocean. Rooms are airy and tastefully decorated, and feature plenty of coffee-table books to flip through while lounging in your private seating area, in the backyard, in the courtyard, or next to the fire in the living room on one of the cooler winter nights. The ripest fruits and vegetables are picked from the garden to be included with the meals, prepared in a kitchen that would be the envy of most house chefs. Breakfast is expansive and features fresh breads made in-house. Lunches and dinners (150-250DH) are on request and highly recommended, with wine available.

Information and Services

SYNDICATE D'INITIATIVE DE TOURISME

33 Pl. Mohammed V; Thurs.-Tues. 9am-12:30pm and 3pm-6:30pm

The Syndicate d'Initiative de Tourisme

keeps updated information on the city, surrounding events, and even restaurant recommendations.

MONEY

There are handy **BMCI** and **Banque Populaire** branches along the busy intersection of Avenues Mohammed V, Mohammed VI, and Hassan II, just one block inland from the fishing port.

Getting There and Around

BY CAR

By car, El Jedida is a short drive from **Casablanca** (105km/65mi, 1.5hr) and nearby **Azemmour** (16km/10mi, 15min). **Oualidia** (79km/49mi, 1.5hr) and **Safi** (147km/91mi, 2hr) are both relatively short drives, while **Essaouira** (268km/167mi, 4hr) and **Marrakesh** (199km/124mi, 3hr) are more distant. The coast can be a pretty drive, but drivers, especially around Casablanca, can be very aggressive, and driving at night should be handled with extreme caution.

BY GRAND TAXI

Grands taxis shuttle back and forth between **Casablanca** (1.5hr, 105km/65mi, 50Dh), **Azemmour** (15min, 16km/10mi, 15Dh), **Oualidia** (1.5hr, 79km/49mi, 45Dh), and **Safi** (2hr, 147km/91mi, 60Dh) regularly.

BY BUS

The **bus station** is on Avenue Mohammed V, about a 10-minute walk from the beach and a 15-minute walk from the old city. The **CTM** bus (tel. 0800/0900 30, www.ctm.ma) has connections with Casablanca (2hr, 9 daily, 45Dh), Oualidia (1.5hr, 3 daily, 30Dh), Safi (2hr, 8 daily, 60Dh), Essaouira (5.5hr, 3 daily, 110Dh), and Agadir (8hr, 2 daily, 170Dh).

BY TRAIN

Trains connect with the El-Jedida station from **Casablanca** (1.5hr, 9 daily, 35Dh/50Dh) via the **ONCF** (tel. 0524/888 566 or 0524/885 632, www.oncf.ma) railways, though there is no direct service on to other destinations. The station is a bit far from center of town at the end of Avenue de la Gare. Taxis are always around when trains arrive, though they charge a bit much (50Dh) for a ride into town.

OUALIDIA

الوليدية

From Azemmour and El Jedida, the drive to Oualidia is replete with leisurely beauty. Fields of wild vegetation and cultivation plunge straight into some wilder beaches. Fishing boats linger just off the coast, and on the beach fishermen cast out with long lines. After you pass a couple of big resort hotels, you arrive at the town of Oualidia itself, which hugs a small lagoon, while along the sea there is a solid rock shore that might look more in place on the moon. The effect is at once romantic and otherworldly. The Atlantic Ocean beats against the shore, forming pockets of water throughout the rocky landscape.

Over the last few years Oualidia has really grown. It's no longer the small resort town it once was. This is a very popular weekend and holiday destination for those living in and around Rabat and Casablanca. During the summer it fills with holiday-goers, and outside of the summer weekenders are increasingly flooding the town. Otherwise, in the middle of the week, Oualidia is usually still a pretty, tranquil spot on the coast, though with a few eyesores of new development along the beachfront.

Sights

COASTAL LAGOON

The coastal lagoon, one of the finest in Morocco, houses migratory birds, and the long stretch of beach is popular with jetsetters and those looking to ameliorate those tan lines. Popular activities focus on the lagoon, beach life, and enjoying the surf, with surfboards and lounge chairs available for rent, usually for 20Dh, though possibly more during peak tourist season. Probably the coolest thing to do here is to kayak through the lagoon.

Sports and Recreation

PLANCOËT CANOË-KAYAK

Ave. Hassan II; tel. 0622/514 934; http://canoekayakplancoet.free.fr; 9am-6pm; rentals from 100Dh/hr

Plancoët Canoë-Kayak offers canoe and kayak rentals, making a picnic in a boat on the lagoon a real possibility. Check that off your bucket list! You'll want to pack your own picnic—there is a local grocery right in the middle of town where you can get a few things to munch on. Feel free to haggle for boat prices, particularly if you happen to arrive midweek and there doesn't seem to be much demand.

If Oualidia is a little too crowded for your taste and you have your own transportation, take a short drive up to Cap Beddouza. This is a generally quieter little corner of the coast, with less-populated beaches and surf spots.

Food and Accommodations

Across from the coast, cheap eats include sandwiches, fries, and tajines. Generally, better food is in the upscale resorts and hotels, but even that can be hit-or-miss.

L'INITIALE

Oualidia beach; tel. 0523/366 246; restaurant daily noon-3pm and 7pm-11pm; 400Dh d

The hotel itself is a little dated, with tiny rooms and cramped bathrooms, and it's a bit of a walk to the town center. That said, for a cheap getaway with friendly service and fantastic sea views from a rooftop terrace, you can't do much better. Though the hotel may not be for everyone, the restaurant is one of the best deals in town. The *fruits de mer* (seafood) comes heaping, with a plate of clams, mussels, prawns, shrimp, oysters, and other seafood goodies available for 150Dh and big enough for two seafood lovers to split. Other options include pastas and pizzas, perfect for the kids, though understandably not the house forte at this seafood restaurant. Staff is friendly (though the service can be French-style slow), the decor unpretentious, and the terrace a lovely place to sip on a glass of *vin blanc*. When it's chilly out, dinners inside offer candlelit romance. Reservations are recommended.

ARAIGNEE GOURMANDE

Oualidia beach; tel. 0523/366 447; www.araignee-gourmande.com; 300Dh d

Araignee Gourmande is a hotel with wonderful terrace views right over the beach and surf, and a popular restaurant specializing in seafood. The hotel has basic rooms with en suite bathrooms, though the decor is tired and rooms can be a bit musty during lower travel times. For those looking for homey charm and wanting to stretch their travel funds, this is a good option. The on-site restaurant (150Dh) has improved over the years. Staff are friendly to a fault, the views are wonderful, and the seafood is as fresh as it gets.

OUALIDIA AUBERGE

121 Rte. Secondaire, near the entrance of Oualidia; tel. 0523/366 697; www.aubergeoualidia.com; 1,200Dh d

Right on the lagoon, the Oualidia Auberge is one of the more deluxe resorts. Rooms are draped with modern decor and textiles, adding a pop of color to the sweeping views over the lagoon and out to the water. Ask for a seaside view for this reason. Of the beach resorts, service is more personalized here and the experience notably more upscale. Breakfast, air-conditioning, and Wi-Fi are all included. The friendly staff can help to arrange activities in the area, and if you need an escape from the crowds on the beach, the terrace pool provides the perfect respite. The little whitewashed villa-hotel offers small, though charming, rooms complete with a pool. Best for couples looking for a more modern feel and who don't mind splurging a bit.

Getting There and Around

By car, Oualidia is a short drive from **El Jedida** (79km/49mi, 1.5hr) along the coastal route (R301) that runs south from **Casablanca** (184km/114mi, 3hr). From

Safi (59km/37mi, 1hr) or **Essaouira** (181km/113mi, 3hr), follow the R301 north.

For those traveling to Oualidia by public transport, the most convenient option is the *grands taxis* that leave regularly from El Jedida (1.5hr, 79km, 45Dh). It's possible to arrive via the **CTM** bus (www.ctm.ma) from Casablanca (2 daily, 3hr, 75Dh).

Safi

آسفي

Set along the banks of the Chaaba River, Safi (also: Asfi) is one of the busiest ports in Morocco. The city leads the sardine industry and exports the majority of the country's phosphates, textiles, ceramics, and other goods. All this lends a heavy sense of commercial growth to this vibrant little city, one of the oldest in Morocco. In many ways, Safi has a little sister vibe to Casablanca.

Just how old is Safi? Well, it is old enough that experts are not able to agree on approximately when it was founded, though some historians argue that it was founded by the Carthaginians, possibly on a previous tribal settlement. For generations, Safi has been one of the more sought-after ports along Morocco's Atlantic Coast, prized for its access to the river and for the towering cliffs along the coast, from where it was easy to stage a defensive position. The fortress standing proud atop the cliff is a leftover from the short Portuguese rule (1488-1541). The Portuguese abandoned the city because, though it was defensible to attacks from the sea, it proved difficult to fend off attacks from the land, which were numerous during the Saadian era.

Similar to El Jedida, there is a lot of unrealized potential in Safi. There are few interesting attractions, though the locally handcrafted and hand-spun pottery is one of the better-known examples of Moroccan pottery. However, perhaps because of the rapid expansion of the city, now with a population quickly approaching half a million, or because of a lack of interest in really building the tourist industry, the overall effect is underwhelming. Most of the sights can be seen in a day, and the local beach, often dirty, is one of the more unpleasant beaches in this part of Morocco particularly for women, who are constantly hassled. This is a place best visited in an afternoon, perhaps while following the stunning coastal road north toward Casablanca or south toward Essaouira.

SIGHTS

Sea Castle (Palais de la Mer)

Pl. de l'Indépendance

The Sea Castle makes for stunning photos and is the icon of Safi. The castle dates from the late 15th century when Safi was under Portuguese rule, similar to Azemmour, El Jedida, and Essaouira. This fortress was used to secure the Portuguese commercial interest in the region, which included gold and spices as well as slave ships. It includes quarters for the Portuguese governor and a dungeon for prisoners. The castle is now closed, with possible renovations to be completed over the coming years.

Medina

Across from the Sea Castle is the walled medina. You can enter the medina through Bab Lamassa just off the coastal road, Route du Port. From here, the main street, Rue du Souq, cuts northeast through the middle of the medina. Most of the bazaars, spice shops, and street cafés and grills are along this road.

PORTUGUESE CATHEDRAL

Safi Medina; daily 9am-noon and 3pm-6pm; 10Dh

Look carefully in the south part of the medina, shortly after the entrance at Bab Lamassa, to find the Portuguese Cathedral. It's a small ruin of a cathedral and easy to miss. Construction of the cathedral was begun by the Portuguese, though never finished. Lovers of architecture, ruins, and Catholic history of Morocco should make sure to visit while in Safi. For others, it's probably not worth the entrance fee.

National Ceramics Museum

Dar Sultan; tel. 0544/463 895; Wed.-Mon. 8:30am-6pm; 20Dh

If you're interested in learning more about the artisan pottery of Morocco, check out the National Ceramics Museum (Musée National de Ceramique). Housed in a citadel built by the Almohad dynasty in the 12th century, with commanding views over the medina, port, and sea, the building itself is well remodeled, and it alone is worth the price of admission. Under the Alaouite dynasty in the 18th century, the prince Moulay Hicham, the son of Sultan Mohamed Ben Abdellah, took over this fortress as his palace, likely the reason why the fortress is now better known as "Dar Sultan" rather than the original title, "Kechla."

The collection of pottery on display has been taken from different sites in Morocco and comprises different eras. There is pottery from the Neolithic and medieval eras, as well as rural pottery and wonderful examples of the rich traditional pottery found in Fez and Meknes. Unsurprisingly, a large part of the collection focuses on the pottery of Safi and its history and tradition, as well as contemporary examples from both Fez and Safi, the two indisputable pottery capitals of Morocco. Some information is available in English, though the majority is in Arabic and French. Still, this is worth stopping through before shopping for a piece of pottery of your own.

★ Safi Pottery

Safi pottery is recognized around Morocco as some of the best, generally vying with Fez. Whereas the pottery of Fez uses white clay and traditional design, the pottery of Safi uses a more brittle red clay, and the artisans here are more experimental. Often, local artisans in Safi will create a series of traditional designs and then experiment with some more commercial pieces featuring the likes of Spider-Man, Mickey Mouse, and other contemporary figures, as well as pieces that look heavily influenced by the works of the cubist work of Picasso. Most of the artisans are on **Potter's Hill** (Colline des Potiers), just outside of Bab Chaaba to the north of the medina on Rue du Souq.

The potters are generally nice, though touts

traditional pottery from Safi

tend to be more aggressive. Be prepared to be firm. The hill is small and you won't need a guide to wander up and down it. Pop into the different shops and watch the artisans spin, fire, or paint clay. If invited to watch or take photos, it is customary to give a small tip (5-10Dh), though it's better to buy something. Most items run 20-100Dh, with some of the larger clay bowls, plates, and vases going for 200-300Dh. Depending on the potter, sometimes the first price quoted is outrageous. A common tactic is to quote 800Dh for a medium-size plate or bowl, something which is almost never more than 100Dh, and even that assumes really good quality. Ashtrays are generally 30-70Dh, depending on size and style. Teacups, plates, and tableware can all be had generally for 20-40Dh apiece. Bargain accordingly.

FOOD AND ACCOMMODATIONS

Plenty of snack joints serve sandwiches and barbecued meats around town, though higher-end restaurants haven't yet made headway into Safi. Though Safi is not a huge tourist destination (most travelers stop for an afternoon), there are a few accommodations. Mostly these are for travelers who need a place to stay for one night as they make connections up and down the coast.

★ CHEZ HOSNI

7 Bis, Rue des Forgerons; tel. 0660/052 323; daily 11am-10pm; 80Dh

Near Potter's Hill, just a few minutes' walk outside the medina from Bab Chaaba, is Chez Hosni, generally regarded as one of the better tajine restaurants along the Atlantic Coast. Fish, chicken, and lamb tajines are all available, though save room for the dessert, a warm fruit tajine that will have your head swimming. This unassuming little restaurant, with an open kitchen and stacks of clay-fired tajine dishes piled around the chef, has seating outside on patio furniture. This is the place to go for warm hospitality, to tuck in to a mouthwatering tajine, and, if they're not too busy, to get a little lesson in how to cook a Moroccan tajine on the cheap.

RIAD LE CHEVAL BLANC

26 Derb el Kaouss; tel. 0524/464 527; www.riad-cheval-blanc.com; 420Dh d

Another good option in the medina is Riad le Cheval Blanc near the Bab Boudhab. The owners spent years restoring this *riad,* and the attention to detail shows. Intricate *zellij* tile work and rough stone arches are accented with local artists' work and traditional textiles. The rooms are airy, and the terrace views over the medina, ocean, and castle are splendid. Olivier, the owner/manager, will make sure you are comfortable in your stay. Breakfast is included. Dinners are available on request. In particular, the *boulette de sardine* tajine, a traditional tajine of sardine balls, seldom found in restaurants in Morocco (though popular in Safi), is generally available and always delicious.

INFORMATION AND SERVICES

The bustling Place de l'Indépendance, located between the medina and the Sea Castle, has a conveniently located **post office** and **banks,** including BMCI and Credit de Maroc. The **Mohammed V Hospital** is just across the street from the *gare routière* along Avenue John Kennedy, where you can find **pharmacies.**

GETTING THERE

BY CAR

Safi is easily reached along the coastal road (R301) from **Oualidia** (59km/37mi, 1hr) and **Essaouira** (122km/76mi, 2hr). From **Casablanca** (239km/149mi, 3hr) and **El Jedida** (145km/90mi, 2hr), you can follow National Road 1 (N1) before following signs along a secondary road (R202). The coastal drive along R301 is prettier, though the N1 to R202 is quicker. From **Marrakesh** (152km/94mi, 2.5hr), National Road 7 (N7) gives way quickly to the secondary road (R204), where you follow signs for Ras el Aïn and Chamaia before reaching Safi.

BY GRAND TAXI

Grands taxis shuttle regularly to and from Oualidia (1hr, 59km/37mi, 28Dh), El Jedida (2hr, 147km/91mi, 60Dh), and Essaouira (2hr, 125km/77mi, 60Dh).

BY BUS

CTM (tel. 0800/0900 30, www.ctm.ma) runs buses to and from Safi regularly from **Casablanca** (4hr, 6 daily, 100Dh), **El Jedida** (2hr, 7 daily, 60Dh), and **Essaouira** (2hr, 3 daily, 50Dh) and connects at the ***gare routière*** (Rue Ibn Khaldoun just off Ave. John Kennedy).

BY TRAIN

ONCF (tel. 0524/888 566 or 0524/885 632, www.oncf.ma) runs trains from **Casablanca** (5hr, 2 daily, 75Dh/120Dh) and Marrakesh (3hr, 2 daily, 65Dh/97Dh), though you'll have to transfer at Benguerir. The **train station** is along the waterfront south of the old medina and port along Avenue Sidi Ouassel.

GETTING AROUND

Most travelers will need only a decent pair of walking shoes to get around the old medina, Sea Castle, and Potter's Hill. These are all within **walking** distance of each other. Those spending a bit more time in Safi will likely be making much use of the *petits taxis*. As in other cities in Morocco, the taxis are regulated by meter, with most rides costing 10-20Dh.

Essaouira الصويرة

Once popular with artists and the hippie crowd, Essaouira has diversified in recent years, pulling in more travelers looking to escape from the crush of Marrakesh and searching for a more laid-back vibe in the south. Though no longer the sleepy village it once was, Essaouira has maintained its diversity, its love for art, and, yes, even its hippie crowd. There's a little something for everyone, and for most people traveling through this region, this city itself is a real highlight. The distinct cry of seagulls descending on the fishing boats entering the port, the chipped paint and weathered stone, the quiet mornings and lively evenings—these are just a few of the memories travelers come away with.

Within the old medina, you can feel history emanate from the walls that give shape to the city. These walls were first built under Portuguese rule in the 16th century, when Essaouira was known as **Mogador.** It wasn't until the 1960s and the more recent Arabization of Morocco that Mogador became commonly known by its Arabic name: Essaouira.

Essaouira has a long history with evidence of inhabitance from the 5th century BC, when the Carthaginians were spreading up and down the coastline of Morocco. At the beginning of the 16th century, when the region came under Portuguese rule, Mogador prospered as a major fishing port, as well as a strategic military post. For a time, like Salé to the north, Mogador was known for its trade in sugar and molasses, though it was the pirate trades and slavery that brought in the most wealth.

During the reign of Mohammed III in the 18th century, Mogador was transformed as the sultan oversaw a vast plan to reinforce the walls, add to the fortification of the city, and direct trade from Marrakesh through the port. The Jewish community was encouraged to relocate here for business. Nearly 40 percent of the population at this time was Jewish, as evidenced today by the large mellah, with stone carvings of the Star of David over many doors, the many synagogues, and the immense Jewish cemetery.

Today, Essaouira is better known as the Windy City for the near-constant wind that

Essaouira

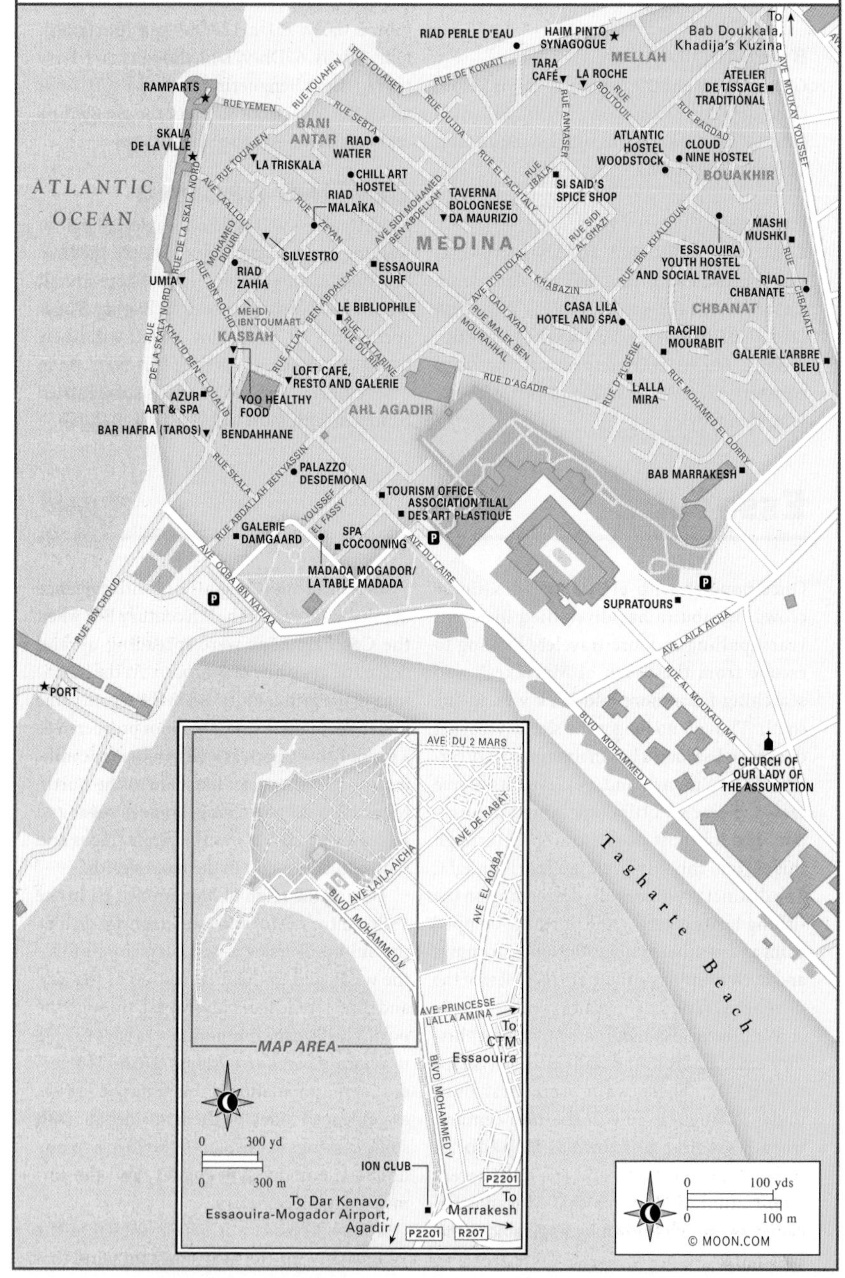
To Bab Doukkala, Khadija's Kuzina
RIAD PERLE D'EAU
HAIM PINTO SYNAGOGUE
MELLAH
TARA CAFÉ
LA ROCHE
ATELIER DE TISSAGE TRADITIONAL
RAMPARTS
RUE YEMEN
BANI ANTAR
RIAD WATIER
SKALA DE LA VILLE
LA TRISKALA
CHILL ART HOSTEL
ATLANTIC HOSTEL WOODSTOCK
CLOUD NINE HOSTEL
BOUAKHIR
ATLANTIC OCEAN
RIAD MALAÏKA
TAVERNA BOLOGNESE DA MAURIZIO
SI SAID'S SPICE SHOP
MASHI MUSHKI
MEDINA
SILVESTRO
ESSAOUIRA YOUTH HOSTEL AND SOCIAL TRAVEL
RIAD ZAHIA
ESSAOUIRA SURF
UMIA
RIAD CHBANATE
LE BIBLIOPHILE
CASA LILA HOTEL AND SPA
CHBANAT
KASBAH
RACHID MOURABIT
GALERIE L'ARBRE BLEU
LOFT CAFÉ, RESTO AND GALERIE
AZUR ART & SPA
YOO HEALTHY FOOD
AHL AGADIR
LALLA MIRA
BAR HAFRA (TAROS)
BENDAHHANE
PALAZZO DESDEMONA
BAB MARRAKESH
TOURISM OFFICE
ASSOCIATION TILAL DES ART PLASTIQUE
GALERIE DAMGAARD
SPA COCOONING
MADADA MOGADOR/ LA TABLE MADADA
SUPRATOURS
PORT
CHURCH OF OUR LADY OF THE ASSUMPTION
Taghart e Beach
RUE TOUAHEN
RUE DE KOWAIT
RUE SEBTA
RUE OUJDA
RUE ANNASER
RUE BOUTOUIL
RUE BAGDAD
AVE MOUKAY YOUSSEF
RUE DE LA SKALA NORD
AVE LAALLOUJ
MOHAMED DIOURI
RUE ZEYAN
AVE SIDI MOHAMED BEN ABDELLAH
RUE EL FACHTALY
RUE JBALA
RUE SIDI AL GHAZI
RUE IBN KHALDOUN
RUE IBN ROCHD
MEHDI IBN TOUMART
AVE ALLAL BEN ABDALLAH
RUE LATTARINE
RUE DU RIF
AVE D'ISTIQLAL
EL KHABAZIN
QADI AYAD
RUE MALEK BEN MOURAHHAL
RUE CHBANATE
KHALID BEN EL OUALID
RUE D'AGADIR
RUE D'ALGÉRIE
RUE MOHAMED EL QORRY
RUE SKALA
RUE ABDALLAH BEN YASSIN
YOUSSEF EL FASSY
AVE DU CAIRE
AVE OQBA IBN NAFIAA
RUE IBN CHOUD
AVE LAILA AICHA
RUE AL MOUKAOUMA
BLVD MOHAMMED V
AVE DU 2 MARS
AVE DE RABAT
AVE EL AQABA
MAP AREA
AVE PRINCESSE LALLA AMINA
To CTM Essaouira
ION CLUB
P2201
R207
To Dar Kenavo, Essaouira-Mogador Airport, Agadir
To Marrakesh
0 300 yd
0 300 m
0 100 yds
0 100 m
© MOON.COM

Essaouira in Pop Culture

Essaouira first memorably popped into the consciousness of Hollywood in 1952 with a selection of memorable scenes filmed by the renowned Orson Welles in his adaptation of Shakepeare's *Othello.* Since then, Essaouira has been featured in Terry Gilliam's cult classic *Time Bandits* as well as Ridley Scott's *Gladiator* and *The Kingdom of Heaven,* in which it was transformed into Jerusalem. More recently it has served as the background to the popular series *Game of Thrones,* in which it was thrust into the more imaginary realms of Astapor and King's Landing, as well as in the last installment of the *John Wick* action-movie trilogy.

By the 1960s, Essaouira's place on Morocco's hippie trail was firmly established, with local musicians joining with visiting musicians, such as Cat Stevens, to create fusion music that had never before been heard. Today, all around Morocco and throughout the world, you can now jam to Gnawa-Blues, a type of fusion arising from this era. Popular myth has it that Jimi Hendrix composed "Castles Made of Sand" while chillaxing on the beaches of Essaouira. The fact that Hendrix wrote "Castles Made of Sand" two years before he actually visited Essaouira hasn't stopped this myth from becoming something of a local legend, facts be damned!

cuts over the beach. It might be better called "Windsurfer City," as this pastime for locals and Europeans has come to define the beachfront south of the fortified walls.

There is a real international feel to the city, despite the medieval surroundings, and a touch of mass tourism. However, this isn't such a bad thing, particularly when looking for a nice place to go out and eat. If anything, Essaouira is replete with great restaurants catering to international tourism. But above all, it is the clean salt air, a crisp respite after a few days in Marrakesh, the heat of the desert, or the clutter of Casablanca, that is perhaps the most alluring.

ORIENTATION

Essaouira is easy to navigate. Its medina is less maze-like and quite a bit smaller than most of the others around Morocco. It's very safe (unless you count the occasional bellicose shopkeeper) and is a wonderful medina to explore with plenty of nooks and crannies as well as unique shops that provide delightful surprises.

The **medina** is surrounded by 18th-century walls and divided roughly into the following neighborhoods: the Kasbah, Bani Antar, the Mellah, Bouakhir, Chbanat, and Ahl Agadir. The **kasbah** is in the southwest of the city and is the area just around the tall citadel that watches over the harbor. Sometimes this is further divided into the "old" kasbah toward the north and the "new" kasbah on the southernmost corner of the medina. From the kasbah, you can easily walk along the ramparts or out of the medina to the port. Following the ramparts to the north, the neighborhood of **Bani Antar** to the northwest has many cafés and restaurants. The **mellah,** like the kasbah, is sometimes divided into "old" and "new." It runs adjacent to Bani Antar between the main thoroughfares of Avenue Sidi Mohamed Ben Abdellah and Avenue d'Istiqal—which turns into Avenue Mohamed Zerktouni before exiting through the north gate, **Bab Doukkala.** There are *riads* in the mellah as well as the heart of the medina, Souk Laghzal. The largely residential neighborhoods of **Bouakhir, Chbanat,** and **Ahl Agadir** lie to the east, farthest away from the ocean. There are a few larger *riads* here, and the streets of Rue Chbanate and Rue Mohammed el Qori host a number of shops. **Bab Marrakesh** is a popular exit to the east, along Rue Mohammed El Qori, and where most buses pick up and drop off.

SIGHTS

Though Essaouira is known more for its artists, activities like windsurfing, and events such as the Gnawa Music Festival, there are still several sights worth visiting during your stay.

Medina

RAMPARTS

The ramparts are thick, protective stone walls that surround the old city of Essaouira. They were first built by the Portuguese in the 16th century, though it was the work of Mohammed III—who had enlisted the service of a French engineer, Théodore Cornut, as well as a few other European architects and technicians—in the 18th century that gave Essaouira the medina and fortress for which it is known today. The ramparts include the harbor fortifications as well as the citadel watching over it, built by Ahmed el-Inglizi, or Ahmed the English, an Englishman of note who converted to Islam and spent much of his life in the pirate capitals of Salé and Essaouira. The most popular walk along the ramparts takes you up a flight of stairs to the **Skala de la Ville** (a walkway atop the ramparts) and a row of Dutch cannons that were purchased by Mohammed III and installed for defense of the city. *Game of Thrones* fans might remember Daenerys meeting her loyal army of Unsullied for the first time along these ramparts and at the Skala de la Ville. From atop these ramparts, the Îles Purpuraires and Mogador Island can easily be viewed to the south. A meditative sunset walk is something of a rite of passage here.

MELLAH

A walk through the mellah will put you in touch with several aspects of the history and culture of Essaouira. In the 18th century, the Jewish population made up nearly half of the city's populace. This is evidenced today by a large number of synagogues, the expansive Jewish cemetery, and the Stars of David engraved above many of the doors in this neighborhood.

HAIM PINTO SYNAGOGUE

Rue Mellah; tel. 0676/048 352; daily 10am-6pm; 20Dh (suggested donation)

Joseph Sebag, proudly the last Jew in Essaouira, has been the custodian of this Sephardic synagogue for years. He is usually around throughout the day to give a short tour, though he is not an official tour guide, and explain a bit about the Jewish history in Morocco and in Essaouira specifically. In the synagogue you'll find a photography exhibition that celebrates the Jewish history of Essaouira, while there are also all the necessary holy equipment for completing Jewish prayers, with separate salons for the men and women. On the ground floor you can also see the rabbi's quarters, left exactly as the last rabbi, Haim Pinto, for whom the synagogue has now taken its name, left it years ago.

Ville Nouvelle

CHURCH OF OUR LADY OF THE ASSUMPTION

Just outside **Bab Marrakesh** lies the Church of Our Lady of the Assumption (Église Notre Dame de l'Assomption). This is one of the very few churches in Morocco whose bells ring on Sunday for the call to service. You can hear them at 10am sharp every Sunday, marking the beginning of service. Construction began on the church in 1939. Weddings can be arranged at the church, and travelers on their way through Essaouira typically make up most of the congregation. This art deco church is seldom touristed. For those looking for a Christian service, it is a welcome respite and one of the few going strong in Morocco.

PORT

The famed port of Essaouira is a bustling place of activity, filled with fishers cleaning their nets and boats, getting ready to set sail, coming back with the day's catch, and calling back and forth about the good fishing spots of the day, the state of the ocean, and the coming weather. Flocks of seagulls cry overhead, plunge into the water, and scurry on the old wood docks. Cats lurk about, keeping to the shadows, sometimes lounging in the sun,

1: a door in Essaouira **2:** the synagogue of Essaouira **3:** the fishing port in Essaouira

1

2

3

Gnawa Music Festival

Since 1998, Essaouira has devoted a portion of its energies to transforming its little labyrinth of streets and wide beaches to rhythmic drumbeats of Gnawa musicians. Every May, over the course of four nights, a festival atmosphere envelops the city, featuring thousands of music lovers with the *kerketoo* rhythm of the *krakeb* (a large iron castanet-type rhythm instrument) and swaying with the lilting chords of the *hajouj* (a rustic base lute). This is Woodstock, Moroccanized.

Gnawa music can trace its roots to Sub-Saharan Africa, though Morocco and Algeria are the modern bastions of this ritual music that combines prayers, chants, and poetry with rhythm. Often, songs can continue for hours as the *mâalems* (primary singers) find themselves in the music, connecting and weaving their chants with the rhythm of the group. Though the more spiritual form of Gnawa music can still be heard privately and maintains its sacred energy, the Gnawa as it is practiced at the festival is more secular and more fusion-inspired. The artists performing open up Gnawa music to collaborations with jazz, reggae, and hip-hop, though the more natural collaborations happen with blues musicians, as both musical styles emphasize the third, fifth, and sometimes the seventh of the scale.

The free festival has concerts throughout the city on five stages: Place Moulay Hassan, Beach Stage, Dar Souiri, Borj Bab Marrakesh, and Issaoua Zaouia. Place Moulay Hassan and the Beach Stage typically host the biggest names in Gnawa and other headliners, free of admission charge, while Dar Souiri is the only paid entrance for more intimate performances. Borj Bab Marrakesh is a new stage, strictly for the Gnawa fusion, and features some of the most interesting musical performances throughout the festival, while Issaoua Zaouia keeps the Gnawa spirit alive with its all-night trance (*hadras*) performed by local musicians.

hoping for some fresh fish from a worker who will take pity on them. This is a good place for a morning stroll.

ARTISTS AND GALLERIES

Artists, both national and international, have long felt an affinity for Essaouira. Though the atmosphere of Essaouira is changing, there are still numerous painters, sculptors, and other artists who call Essaouira home. You'll find them in the bazaars lining Avenue Sidi Mohamed Ben Abdellah and tucked into the various little streets of the medina.

ASSOCIATION TILAL DES ART PLASTIQUE

4 Rue du Caire; tel. 0524/475 424; daily 8:30am-12:30pm and 2:30pm-7pm

Association Tilal des Art Plastique features work by female Moroccan artist Najia Kerairate, a Moroccan sculptor and painter specializing in the avant garde, as well as other artists. Art Plastique is sponsored by l'Association des Arts Plastiques d'Essaouira and is recognized by UNICEF for its contribution to disadvantaged youth. Perhaps a bit too on the cutting edge for some, though most should appreciate what this program does for the local youth community.

AZUR ART & SPA

15 Rue Khalid Ben Walid, Pl. Moulay Hassan; tel. 0524/785 794, www.azur-spa-essaouira.com/en; reservation recommended

With local artists on display, Azur Art & Spa is well worth a visit. A permanent collection rests downstairs, while upstairs you can sip on a tea and look at some of the new paintings, photos, and sculptures being exhibited. Contact for reservations. This is a great place to get to know a few of the local artists and their works.

BENDAHHANE

3 Rue El Hajjali; tel. 0661/347 262; www.bendahhane.com; Tues.-Sat. 10am-1pm and 3pm-6pm

Curated by Abdel Bendahhane, the gallery seeks to build bridges between artists and the public. Bendahhane tends toward pointillism, expressionism, and brutalist art. There is a wide spectrum of local talent on display. For those on a tight budget, but who still want some original art from Essaouira, check into the limited prints and art cards available.

GALERIE DAMGAARD

Ave. Oqba Ibn Nafiaa; tel. 0524/784 446; www.galeriedamgaard.com; Tues.-Sat. 10am-1pm and 3pm-6pm

Many local artists have spent some time being exhibited in the Galerie Damgaard, a gallery dedicated to showcasing the talent of artists from Essaouira since its inception in 1988. If you're in the market or curious about what the most contemporary artists in and around this corner of Morocco are putting on canvas, this is the place to stop.

RACHID MOURABIT

115 Rue Mohammed El Qori; daily, hours vary

Rachid Mourabit, an Essaouira native, creates sculptures from pieces of recycled metal, such as old cans, pieces from car engines, and greasy parts that you might find buried in your uncle's garage. He fuses these pieces together into whimsical forms, such as insect-looking musicians or comedic personas. The end product is clunky and robotic and maintains a sense of naive humor and ingenious charm. Rachid enjoys his work and enjoys every sale he makes. Prices will not hurt the pocketbook, starting at 100Dh or less for your very own small, twisted souvenir of Essaouira.

ENTERTAINMENT AND EVENTS

GNAWA MUSIC FESTIVAL

www.festival-gnaoua.net; May; free

Though its focus is on Gnawa music, the free annual Gnawa Music Festival includes rock, jazz, and reggae music. Dubbed the "Moroccan Woodstock," this four-day music festival held every May will leave even the most diehard music enthusiasts gasping for breath at the end. The festival now attracts nearly half a million visitors, making accommodations expensive and difficult to come by, not to mention the logistical problems with transportation in the region.

ANDALUSIAN MUSIC FESTIVAL

Oct.; free

Generally overshadowed by the Gnawa Music Festival, the less-popular Andalusian Music Festival is no less interesting, with days full of music performed by well-known groups from around Morocco and Spain. Oftentimes, musicians get together, improvising around town, creating new rhythms and melodies, fusing contemporary music composition with the more structured music of *al-Andalus*. Typically held at the end of October, this is a festival worth attending for those who love music, but are willing to skip the crowds.

SPORTS AND RECREATION

★ Windsurfing, Kitesurfing, and Surfing

If you're looking to learn how to **windsurf,** the long beach strip just south of Essaouira is the place to do it. Year-round, the geography of the land practically ensures a stiff breeze perfect for windsurfers. Beachside companies have updated, well-maintained equipment and offer lessons for beginners and long loops for advanced windsurfers. However, January and February can sometimes see lesser winds, great for beachgoers but a possible disappointment for those counting on a little wind to scoot around the surf. For slightly less expensive options, head a few kilometers south of Essaouira to the beachfront town of Sidi Kaouki.

ION CLUB

Blvd. Mohammed V; tel. 0524/783 934; www.oceanvagabond.com

Windsurfing, kitesurfing, and surfing instruction is available for all age groups and levels throughout the year at the internationally renowned Ion Club. Lessons start at 1,100Dh for a two-hour lesson, all equipment included. Instructors speak English, French, Spanish, and Arabic. The gear is the newest

1
2
Le
CURRY
MELANGE
POUR
COUSCOUS
3
4

available, including brands such as Triwave, Freewave, and Gecko. For those staying at Ion Club, free clinics are available.

ESSAOUIRA SURF

30 Avenue Sidi Mohamed Ben Abdellah; tel. 0645/742 030; www.essaouirasurf.com

If you're looking to expand your horizons, the team at Essaouira Surf has gear to really get you in the air. Instructors speak English and are well equipped for beginner windsurfers, kitesurfers, and surfers to explore what they can do on the waves and with the wind. Instruction is available starting at around 1,000Dh for gear and lesson. Those who are serious about learning might consider the week-long package deal that includes accommodations, breakfast, transportation in and out of Agadir or Marrakesh, and instruction and equipment throughout the week.

Camel Trekking and Horse Riding

If you just can't shake the dream of riding a camel on a secluded strip of beach, then there are several companies based in Essaoiura that can make this dream come true for you.

LIMA DROMADAIRE

tel. 0668/189 220; www.limadromadaire.com

Lima Dromadaire is the company of choice, with long treks along the beach and friendly professionals who will do their best to make you comfortable atop the relatively uncomfortable hump of a dromedary. Mostafa will happily show you the region of Essaouira, and overnight bivouac excursions are also available. Prices start at 150Dh for a short, one-hour ride. Children under five ride free with a paying adult.

EQUI EVASION

tel. 0666/780 561; www.equievasion.com

Finding yourself drawn to dromedaries but hooked on horses? Equi Evasion has both for you to ride. Rides can be arranged for as little as one hour (150Dh) and include safety helmets. Also available are half-day rides that include picnics and six-day treks that include stays in Bedouin tents along the Atlantic Coast. This is a great way to explore the region in harmony.

Hammams

As usual in Morocco, if visiting one of the local hammams in the old medina, just don't forget an orange to eat while you are relaxing in the cooling room. Ask your lodging where the nearest hammam is and, by all accounts, avoid Hammam Mounia.

AZUR ART & SPA

15 Rue Khalid Ben Walid, Pl. Moulay Hassan; tel. 0524/785 794, www.azur-essaouira.com; reservations only

The Azur Art & Spa offers the full Moroccan hammam experience, with a scrub of soap (*rhassoul*) and steam room starting at a reasonable 120Dh. Massages, facials, manicures, pedicures, waxing, and other options are available. For an upscale hammam experience, this is maybe the best option for value in Essaouira.

LALLA MIRA

14 Rue d'Algerie; tel. 0524/475 046; daily 9:30am-7pm

Lalla Mira, the oldest traditional hammam in Essaouira, though it has been remodeled, is still a bit dingy. You'll find it attached to the *riad* by the same name. The retrofitting of this hammam included solar thermal equipment, making it the first hammam in Morocco heated exclusively by solar power. From the natural *tadelahkt* walls and polished green clay tiles, you wouldn't know that this was once a hammam used historically by slaves. Today, the hammam is popular with tourists and locals alike, with a full exfoliation treatment with argan oil for 180Dh. Massages are also available, though given on plastic mats on the floor, so totally skippable. Reservations

---

1: windsurfing in Essaouira **2:** some of the funky bags and purses you can find in Essaouira **3:** spices for sale in the local market **4:** terrace at Riad Chbanate

are recommended for women and required for men. If you're looking for a local experience, it's expensive for what it is. Better locals can be found easily in Marrakesh and Fez.

SPA COCOONING

2 Rue Mohamed Ben Massoud; tel. 0524/783 035; http://spacocooning.com/contact; daily 9:30am-7pm

If money is no object or you don't mind splurging for a little self-care, make a beeline for Spa Cocooning. Aziza, Fatima, Sara, Souad, and the rest of the team will make sure you leave with your skin baby soft and your bones and muscles feeling like warm, fuzzy jelly. Go all out with the full hammam treatment with black soap scrubs and exfoliation, followed by a nice tea in the relaxing room before diving in for a full body massage. They use only the best Moroccan cosmetics, all 100 percent natural and great for your skin. Budget 400Dh or more for an unforgettable spa experience.

SHOPPING

A lot of the shopping is found along **Avenue d'Istiqlal** and **Avenue Sidi Mohamed Ben Abdellah,** though a detour down **Rue Chbanate** in the mellah and farther away from most of the touristed strips of the medina is well worthwhile, in terms of both price and interesting boutiques. On this strip, there are a number of shops of interest, each doing something a bit different than the standard tourist fare.

Just inside Bab Marrakesh, **Rue Mohammed El Qori** is another shopping strip, with plenty of popular *hanoots* (small stores) selling everything from laundry soap to bottled water, mixed in with a few specialized tourist shops and bazaars.

ATELIER DE TISSAGE TRADITIONAL

4 Bis Rue Ziane; tel. 0663/150 648; daily, hours vary

Atelier de Tissage Traditional, run by Abderrahim Hachetouf, has a selection of handmade blankets, towels, and scarves as well as some traditional carpets. Prices are honest and Abderrahim himself is friendly, charming, and willing to help you find just the right material or fit. He operates from two locations in Essaouira, this one on Rue Ziane and another at 31 Bis Rue Chbanate along the strip of boutique shops. To get to the second location, enter **Bab Doukkala** into the medina and take your first left. About 60 meters (200ft) down you'll find his other shop full of blankets, scarves, and cotton poufs.

MASHI MUSHKI

94 Rue Chbanate; daily 1pm-6pm, though hours vary

Mashi Mushki features funky designs alongside small paintings by local artists and replicas of vintage Moroccan record covers. Some of the proceeds benefit the Project 91 charity across the street. This is a good place to get a handmade silk scarf to keep your neck warm on those chilly Essaouira nights. The name is a play on the popular Moroccan phrase *mashi mushkil,* meaning "no problems."

GALERIE L'ARBRE BLEU

233 Rue Chbanate; Mon.-Sat. 10am-1pm and 3pm-7pm

Pop in for a little infusion tea and do some shopping at the Galerie l'Arbre Bleu, a boutique café featuring locally made and recycled jewelry as well as the paintings of local favorite **Monique Favière.** The jewelry makes for fun accent pieces.

LE BIBLIOPHILE

24 Rue de Rif; daily 10:30am-1pm and 3pm-7pm

Le Bibliophile has the best selection of English-language books around and focuses on classic titles, though a fair amount of genre and pulp fiction can be had. If you need a beach read, this is the place to go, though it's not only books on offer. Mohamed, the owner, has a thing for vintage vinyl and old postcards, which you'll also find in quantity.

SI SAID'S SHOP

199 Marché aux Épices; daily, hours vary

If spices are your thing, stop by Si Said's shop in the spice market. He has honest prices that are standard for the region and most of Morocco. You'll find that elusive Taliouine saffron and, if you're lucky, a "royal tea," a special Moroccan tea made of a combination of 15 spices. This is a great place to stock up on valuable spices before heading home. Look for Said's shop and the spice market hidden behind the fish market.

FOOD

More than perhaps any other city in Morocco, Essaouira is a foodie's paradise. With a number of traditional Moroccan restaurants, international restaurants, street eats, fusion foods, and fresh seafood, the one thing for certain is that your taste buds will come away from Essaouira absolutely delighted. Nearly all of the restaurants cater to the international crowd and international tastes. You'll find the dining in Essaouira overall more comfortable than just about any other corner of Morocco, with a number of options for nearly every budget and every palate.

A good selection of Moroccan street food is typically available outside of **Bab Doukkala,** including spicy chickpeas, snail soup, popcorn, grilled corn, and other seasonal treats. Most plates are 5-10Dh and make for a festive atmosphere, particularly at night before taking a stroll around the medina. For those looking for tasty street eats or to pinch pennies, this is a great option.

Seafood lovers can head to the port for huge plates of sardines, rouget (red mullet), shrimp, langoustine, and crab, though the callers working at the little fish shacks can be aggressive in trying to twist your arm into a meal. Plates start at around 100Dh (though you can always bargain) and are big enough for two to share. A large picnic area makes this a good spot for an afternoon lunch.

★ LA ROCHE

Place Taraa; tel. 0524/472 716; Sun.-Fri. noon-11pm; 80Dh

Located on a small square just out of the Jewish Quarter, La Roche entertains a surprisingly eclectic, international menu served up by Chef Amina. Though the staple couscous and tajines can be found (and are delicious), many travelers looking for a break from heavier Moroccan fare could look toward the selection of soups or even dive into Amina's club sandwich. The apple fritter (*beignet des pommes*) is a big hit with kids, while others might consider stopping in for a quick fresh-squeezed juice. For lunches, get here before 1pm to make sure you get your choice of everything from the menu, as stock is limited.

TARA CAFÉ

Place Taraa; tel. 0653/602 019; daily 9am-midnight; 30Dh

If La Roche is too full, pop across the street to Tara Café. This friendly out-of-the-way place is a great stop for a quick coffee, tea, or even a Moroccan salad or tajine for lunch. Though the menu isn't quite as varied as some of the other options, its location right on the Plaza Traa, in the mellah at the end of Avenue Sidi Mohamed Ben Abdellah, ensures a quieter lunch affair. A nice spot to meet friendly locals. Wi-Fi is available.

★ YOO HEALTHY FOOD

8A Rue Ibn Roch; tel. 0601/524 609; Mon.-Sat. 10am-10pm, Sun. 1pm-10pm; 70Dh

Vegans rejoice! This little shack tucked down an alley, cozy and clean, has a diverse menu that features all vegetarian and vegan food, including soy-based and lentil-based veggie burgers. For a quick pick-me-up, splurge on one of a number of slow-pressed fresh juices. Frozen yogurt is also an option, as well as the Shrek, a hearty milkshake loaded with bananas, chocolate, and cinnamon. Seating is limited, so it's best to eat a little early or late. If hummus, grilled veggies, salads, or a bunch of gluten-free options sound like they might hit the spot, you can't do any better.

★ LA TRISKALA

Rue Touahen; tel. 0524/476 371 or 0655/585 131; Tues.-Sat. 11am-7pm; 80Dh

Another great vegetarian option is La

Triskala, which has a quirky vibe with photos of Bob Dylan, Jimi Hendrix, and others decorating the walls. The owners strive to be eco-friendly and serve only all locally produced goods. The menu changes every day and depends on the freshest ingredients from the local souk—get the frothy cilantro gazpacho if it's available. If you're coming for dinner, it's best to show up early during the busy season, as they often run out of some of the more popular items. No wine or beer is available, but there is no corkage fee, so you can bring your own.

SILVESTRO

70, Rue Laalouj; tel. 0524/473 555; daily 7pm-11pm; 120Dh

Climb the grungy stairs to Silvestro, but don't let the stairs turn you off! Inside you'll find an explosion of flowered wallpaper and Moroccan stucco work set against a soft jazzy background. The menu offers up a fine choice of Italian classics like *penne arrabbiate* (spicy pasta), made with homemade pasta, and some killer gnocchi. Pizzas are all wood fired, and the seafood and mushrooms are fresh. There's a selection of wines and liquors, and it's nonsmoking.

TAVERNA BOLOGNESE DA MAURIZIO

7 Rue Youssef Ben Tachfine 7; tel. 0655/360 347; daily 7pm-11pm; 120Dh

If you're looking for a *tagliatelle alla bolognese* to fill that Italian craving, or maybe you just want a taste of something a bit more familiar than Moroccan fare, head to Maurizio's fine Italian diner. With a menu filled with some of his favorites from back home, including traditional recipes straight from Maurizio's hometown of Bologna, the only real disappointment is that the house wine isn't Italian (it's expensive to import), but it is Moroccan. Fortunately, Moroccan red wine shares a lot of the same body and properties as its Italian cousin.

LA TABLE MADADA

7 Rue Youssef el Fassi; tel. 0524/475 512; www.latablemadada.com; Wed.-Mon. 7:15pm-11pm; 250Dh

For an upscale, French-style dinner, pull up your chair under the stone arches of La Table Madada. The menu features some classic cuisine with a touch of local flavor, such as the spider crab and avocado tartare with a hint of argan oil and tiger prawns served with *charmoula* and Taliouine saffron rice. The bar has a full array of cocktails and a list of wines from France and Morocco. Tapas (35Dh) are also served, making the bar a wonderful place to stop in before heading out somewhere else for dinner. Cooking classes are available during the day.

LE LOFT CAFÉ, RESTO AND GALERIE

5 Rue Hajjali; tel. 0524/476 389 or 0638/949 793; Wed.-Mon. 9am-10:30pm; 120Dh

It's okay to hold lofty expectations when walking through the front doors of the Loft Café, Resto and Galerie. This is a particularly well-done concept café that blends vintage design and local art with one of the freshest menus around. Everything is seasonal, usually bought that day, with options for vegetarians. Some of the house favorites include spinach-cheese rolls and a mouthwatering saffron-vanilla crème brûlée.

★ UMIA

22 bis Skala St.; tel. 0524/783 395; Tues.-Sun. noon-3pm and 7pm-late; 250Dh

For delicate, delicious French-Moroccan fusion, this is perhaps the best address in the country. Candlelit and intimate, it is wonderful for couples looking for a special-occasion dinner or friends looking to sip on some full-bodied, cozy reds together. Fresh seafood is the highlight of the menu, as expected, and with the chef using local products, such as the locally sourced Taliouine saffron, with a deft French touch, it's easy to see why this is a foodie favorite. Go for the clam starter and consider the saffron cream monkfish as your main, but make sure to leave room for the oozy delicious chocolate soufflé.

DAR KENAVO

Douar Bouzama, Km13 Idaougard; tel. 0524/474 835; daily noon-3pm and 7pm-10pm; 120Dh

A few kilometers outside of Essaouira is the fantastic spread of Dar Kenavo. The organic, seasonal menu has possibilities to entertain anyone's dietary needs. With a wonderful garden and a heated pool, it's a bit more upscale, with three-course lunches and dinners, but for diners looking for something a bit different, a night at Dar Kenavo fits the bill in spades. Most ingredients are plucked straight from the on-site garden. If you're looking for a delicious break from the beach crowds, a break from the wind, or just want to spend an afternoon poolside, call them ASAP. Reservations are required.

★ Cooking Classes

In the last few years, cooking classes have increased in popularity, with many travelers interested in learning how to make their own tajine, couscous, and other Moroccan specialties. This is a great opportunity to really taste the culture and learn how to bring a piece of it home with you.

KHADIJA'S KUZINA

Avenue Allal Al Fassi, across the street from Pharmaice Bouhaira; tel. 0670/071 232; 300Dh

Khadija's Kuzina offers intimate Moroccan cooking classes inside the family home of Khadija. It's a cheerful environment to talk about and understand Moroccan culture and people better through its cuisine. The menu is completely customizable and can be catered to any dietary needs. Even better, Khadija and her husband, Lahoussaine, have been working with the Peace Corps since 2003. Not only do they host volunteers, but they have a passion for cross-cultural exchange that is evident throughout their work and life. Best for couples, friends, and families, and those looking for something a bit more than just learning how to cook a delicious meal.

LA TABLE MADADA

7 Rue Youssef el Fassil tel. 0524/472 106; www.lateliermadada.com; 500Dh

La Table Madada offers one of the most humorous, engaging cooking classes around, with Chef Mouna always telling you to "cut smaller" as you dice and slice the ingredients necessary for your own delicious tajine lunch. This cooking class includes a trip to the local souk to purchase vegetables, meat, spices, and

Chef Mouna guides the cooking class at La Table Madada.

other necessities. This is a great insider's look at Moroccan souks, and it provides a reference for how much things should cost. Those with a sweet tooth might want to consider the shorter Moroccan pastry workshop (220Dh) in the afternoon. Instruction is in English with French and Arabic also available.

BARS AND NIGHTLIFE

Notably more subdued than Marrakesh, the nightlife in Essaouira is more relaxed than it is vibrant. Many of the (overpriced) beach bars will close up by 8pm, while the others around town generally have last call well before midnight, unless there are festivals happening... in which case, Essaouira wakes up and never really seems to sleep.

BAR HAFRA (TAROS)

Ruette Layach; tel. 0524/476 407; daily noon-late

For a truly local experience, you couldn't ask for a better watering hole. Local fishermen and port workers sip suds and trade stories. Beers are the cheapest in town and internationals are welcomed, though some might be put off by the often raucous crowd, particularly if a football (soccer) match is on TV, while others will feel right at home. It's best to get here on a Friday or Saturday before 9pm when it's still possible to get a table. If there are no tables, feel free to squeeze up to the bar. Tapas are served (20Dh and up). Occasionally, buskers will stop by and play for tips, adding to the festive tableau.

DAR LOUBANA

24 Rue du Rif; tel. 0524/476 296; daily noon-11pm

The casual, beautiful patio of Dar Loubana features traditional live Gnawa music every Saturday night, which is worth seeing if you're not heading out to the Sahara. Outside of dinner hours, you can still make good use of the patio. Lunch is a relatively okay deal, with traditional Moroccan tajines starting at 80Dh, but **happy hour** is where it's at, with Moroccan-style tapas (10-40Dh) served daily 6:30pm-7:30pm and a selection of beer and Moroccan wine at standard prices.

LA TABLE MADADA

7 Rue Youssef el Fassi; tel. 0524/475 512; www.latablemadada.com; Wed.-Mon. 7:15pm-11pm

Tapas (35Dh) are served at the bar, making this spot a wonderful place to stop in before heading out for dinner or afterward for a nightcap. Good for wine lovers and those in need of a stiff cocktail, it's also a great place for couples or friends looking to have a chat.

ACCOMMODATIONS

There are plenty of great options in Essaouira for travelers of all budget types, making this a good time to scrimp and save on your journey or really splurge—however your wallet sees fit.

Under 400Dh

ATLANTIC HOSTEL WOODSTOCK

34 Rue Ellabanna; tel. 0629/652 268; 50Dh for a dorm bed, 240Dh d

For a clean, friendly hostel experience, Atlantic Hostel Woodstock caters to the many students and backpackers who come through Essaouira. Divided into two buildings (Atlantic and Woodstock) right next to each other, this hostel has slowly built a reputation for being one of the better ones in Morocco, with a quiet night of sleep the norm. For travelers on a tight budget, it's sometimes possible to sleep on the roof, weather allowing, for even less. This is a good place to meet fellow travelers and maybe make a new friend. Woodstock is typically quieter, while Atlantic has the kitchen and much of the socializing. Both buildings offer dorms and private rooms. Coffee, tea, breakfast, and kitchen access cost extra (usually 10Dh). Free Wi-Fi is available in the foyer.

CLOUD NINE HOSTEL

24 Rue Ellabanna; tel. 0615/931 061; http://hostelcloudnine.com; 60Dh for a dorm bed, 240Dh d

Another good bargain in Essaouira, the Cloud Nine Hostel doesn't have quite the same laid-back feeling of some of the other hostels. The staff is friendly and will gladly help guide you around the city, but the clientele is more of the young party crowd. You might not have the most restful night of sleep, but you could experience a really fun night that might just put you on cloud nine. ... Most of the furnishings, including the beds, are fairly new and comfortable. There's free Wi-Fi, and breakfast is an option.

ESSAOUIRA YOUTH HOSTEL AND SOCIAL TRAVEL

17 Rue Laghrissi; tel. 0652/014 569; 90Dh for a dorm bed, 220Dh d

Though not for everyone, the Essaouira Youth Hostel and Social Travel is another one of the well-priced hostels in Essaouira designed around a traditional *riad.* There is a bit more smoking at this hostel (shisha, hashish, and the occasional cigarette), which might put some guests off. It's not the cleanest of the hostels, but the location and price make it inviting for those who are smoke-friendly. Staff is welcoming and accommodating, though online booking is sometimes troublesome. It's best to call for a reservation. This is a place for the young and the young at heart.

★ CHILL ART HOSTEL

21, Rue Abderrahamane Eddakhil; tel. 0600/150 138; 95Dh for a dorm bed, 260Dh d

As chill as its name implies and easily the best hostel in Essaouira, if not in the whole country. Its location in the heart of the Essaouira medina, coupled with the vibrant, arty vibe make this a great place for musicians, students, artists, backpackers, and travelers looking to connect with like-minded people. Housed in a converted traditional *riad,* the hostel is run by Pierre and Elena, each married to Moroccan partners. A scrumptious breakfast is served every day at 10am (30Dh), and always includes a creative egg dish, such as spicy eggplant omelets, with a sweet finish (think caramel-drizzled croissants). Hearty dinners are served at 8pm (50Dh). The kitchen is open for everyone to use. You'll probably make a lot of nice friends out there, as Cat Stevens sings in the background. This is a nonsmoking property except for one corner on the rooftop terrace. The property sleeps around 35 people, which makes finding a bed at the last minute a definite possibility.

400-800Dh

PALAZZO DESDEMONA

Rue Youssef El Fassy; tel. 0524/472 227; www.palazzodesdemona.com; 500Dh d

The Palazzo Desdemona is an exceptional bargain in the medina. The rooms are wonderfully decorated with tribal rugs, canopy beds, and authentic Amazigh wood doors. The feeling is more upscale, but for half the price of more luxe hotels, and the rate includes breakfast. Rooms are spacious and clean and include working fireplaces for those cold winter nights. Panoramic views from the terrace overlook the ramparts, medina, port, beachfront, and nearby garden. It is basic, without air-conditioning or heating, but a good value nonetheless, and you'll be surprised at how you don't need all the mod-cons for a great night of sleep.

★ RIAD MALAÏKA

17 Derb Zayan; tel. 0524/784 908; www.riad-malaika.com; 750Dh d

For warm, friendly lodging, look no further than Riad Malaïka. Conveniently located in the heart of the medina, just off the main thoroughfare, this renovated *riad* has kept just enough historic detail to make it interesting, including the retro tile work leading to the rooftop terrace. The service and food are top-notch, and the staff have cleanliness on their minds, as a quick tour of the bottom-floor kitchen will attest. The rooms are cozy with plush beds, perfect for a quiet night of much-needed sleep. Wi-Fi, heating, and breakfast are all included. If you have any questions about Essaouira or the region, do not hesitate to ask. This is one of the few locally owned and run *riads* in Essaouira, and one of the best locally run *riads* in the entire country. All of the staff are proud of this and extremely knowledgeable about the area.

CASA LILA HOTEL AND SPA

Rue Mohammed el Qori; tel. 0524/475 545; 800Dh d

If you're looking for a great spa experience with your stay, the Casa Lila Hotel and Spa is a wonderful option. The spa treatments are available at the on-site Espace Bien-Être. The rooms all have themes of different spices, making a stay in paprika-, saffron-, or anise-accented bedding something of a novelty. The staff is friendly and helpful, though it's best to make use of your French or Arabic, as little English is spoken. As long as you're okay with this, there is nothing else you could ask for in this price range. Well located with all the amenities.

Over 800Dh

★ RIAD WATIER

16 Rue Ceuta; tel. 0524/476 204; www.ryad-watier-maroc.com; 900Dh d

One of the best-lit traditional *riads* in the medina is Riad Watier. This unique *riad* sports a couple of patios, which give a lot of natural light to the large, airy rooms, decorated with various painting and sculptures from local artists. Larger rooms are available for families, and babysitting is even available. The owner lives on-site and will see to your every need. If you want to feel a bit pampered, this is the place. Argan oil massages are available, along with a traditional, private hammam for your spa needs. Breakfast is delicious, and the traditional Moroccan tajines and other choices available for dinner are exquisite. The minimum stay is two nights, though most travelers leave wishing they had booked a longer stay.

RIAD ZAHIA

Rue Mohammed Diouri; tel. 0524/473 581 or 0524/473 581; www.riadzahia.com; 900Dh d

For a more eclectic experience, Riad Zahia features busy decor reminiscent of Ali Baba's famous cave, with red and yellow tribal designs competing with ornately carved wood and the work of featured local artists. The beds are comfortable and the showers hot. Service is friendly, and the breakfast spread will leave you ready for your day of trekking around town. Air-conditioning, heating, and speedy Wi-Fi are all included.

MADADA MOGADOR

7 Rue Youssef el Fassi; tel. 0524/475 512; www.latablemadada.com; 1,200Dh d

The team at Madada Mogador has put together a charming, traditional *riad* full of creamy beiges, rustic sands, and deep browns with torch lighting that instantly puts you at ease. This is a place for those looking to unwind. Large terraces give out to views over the ocean, and plenty of the rooms are big enough to really spread out. All rooms have air-conditioning, heating, and Wi-Fi and include a delicious breakfast of traditional Moroccan crepes (*miloui*) as well as homemade jams and jellies. Massages are available, which is just the thing when complemented by ocean views. The staff is friendly, and the attached restaurant, La Table Madada, is one of the best in town. Standard rooms, however, don't feature views. If you're already splurging, spend the extra 200Dh a night for views out over the Atlantic. You won't regret it.

★ RIAD CHBANATE

179 Rue Chbanate; tel. 0524/783 334 or 0668/034 757; www.riadchbanate.com; 1,600Dh d

One of the best high-end *riads* in the city is Riad Chbanate. Tucked into the back of the medina, just off the main shopping road leading from Bab Chbanate, this expansive *riad* has some fun designs, including a rope swing in one of the suites and wide bathtubs big enough for two. The ground-floor restaurant offers fine dining by candlelight. Breakfast, included with the room, is a veritable culinary experience with *viennoiseries* (pastries), fresh bread, Moroccan-style crêpes, and fresh orange juice. The terrace is private, with views out over Essaouira and the ocean, perfect for a little sun-tanning away from the crowds.

RIAD PERLE D'EAU

64 Rue du Kowaït; tel. 0661/601 955; www.riad-essaouira-perledeau.com; 1,800Dh d

With coffee and tea served in your room and a

real French-style breakfast, there is a lot to like about this hidden gem of a *riad*. The attention to detail is impeccable. For those looking for something with a bit more of a European flare, tuck in for your stay here. However, to really take advantage of the property, book one of the three rooftop suites to fully enjoy the sea views. This is becoming quite a popular getaway for the European jet-setting crowd, so be sure to reserve well in advance. Guests should also check out the on-site spa for some real pampering. Air-conditioning, heating, and speedy Wi-Fi are all included. Best for couples.

INFORMATION AND SERVICES

Cash machines are concentrated around Place Moulay Hassan in the south of the medina, near the port, including Banque Populaire, Attijarwafi Bank, and Crédit du Maroc. For emergencies, the **Sidi Mohamed Ben Abdellah Hospital** is outside of Bab Marrakesh, just across the parking lot. **Pharmacies** are sprinkled throughout the medina and the Ville Nouvelle.

TOURISM OFFICE

10 Rue du Caire; tel. 0524/783 532; daily 10am-6pm

The friendly Tourism Office (Delegation Provinciale du Tourisme) is directly attached to Morocco's ministry of tourism and handicrafts. It has updated maps of the city and hours for many of the museums and galleries.

GETTING THERE

BY CAR

The route to Essaouira is straightforward, just along the beachfront National Road 1 (N1), which connects with **Safi** (122km/76mi, 2hr), **El Jedida** (268km/167mi, 3.5hr), and **Casablanca** (359km/223mi, 5hr) to the north and **Agadir** (175km/108mi, 2.5hr) to the south, as well as newly widened National Road 8 (N8) from **Marrakesh** (178km/111mi, 2.5hr). For those coming from Casablanca and looking to bypass Marrakesh, it can sometimes be a slightly faster, easier ride to take the toll freeway (A7) from Casablanca to Marrakesh (240km/149mi, 2.5hr) and then follow the N8 to Essaouira from there.

Grands taxis commonly run to/from **Sidi Kaouki** (20min, 10km/6mi, 10Dh), Safi (2hr, 125km/77mi, 60Dh), **Agadir** (2.5hr, 175km/109mi, 90Dh), and **Marrakesh** (2.5hr, 177km/110mi, 90Dh).

BY BUS

CTM (tel. 0800/0900 30, www.ctm.ma) runs buses between Essaouira and **Marrakesh** (2.5hr, 2 daily, 75Dh) as well as **Casablanca** (5hr, 2 daily, 120Dh), **El Jedida** (5hr, 3 daily, 110Dh), and **Agadir** (3.5hr, 2 daily, 75Dh) from the **CTM Station** at Place 11 Janvier.

Supratours (tel. 0524/888 566 or 0524/885 632, www.oncf.ma) operates the buses affiliated with the national train line, ONCF. Buses depart directly from the Marrakesh train station to Essaouira (3hr, 6 daily, 120Dh) and are the most convenient way to get from Marrakesh to Essaouira for those traveling by train. Supratours also runs one bus to Agadir (3hr, 1 daily, 120Dh) that arrives in Agadir at 5:30pm and is a good way to connect with locations farther south without having to backtrack to Marrakesh. Supratours buses arrive/depart from right outside the medina walls off Place Bab Marrakesh, just off Avenue Lalla Aicha on the southeast corner of the medina.

BY PLANE

Essaouira has a small airport, the **Essaouira-Mogador Airport** (Route d'Agadir, Km 16, tel. 0524/476 704) that connects via Transavia (www.transavia.com) with **Paris.** For those bookending their trips with a stay in Paris or flying directly from Paris, this is a fantastic option for arriving directly in Essaouira (not to mention another possibility of bypassing Casablanca!) that should not be overlooked when planning your arrival.

GETTING AROUND

Most travelers seldom use a taxi around Essaouira, preferring to **walk** to and from the beach by foot. If you're pressed for time, *petits taxis* are a great way to get around the different entrance points of the medina, with most trips costing around 20Dh. Otherwise, Essaouira is a place for walkers. It is relatively flat without any discernible hills, though sometimes along the beach the wind will pick up and blow sand around. Be sure to bring something to cover your face, perhaps one of those blue Toureg wraps, as the sand can really sting.

AROUND ESSAOUIRA

Tamanar

تمنار

If the much sought-after **argan oil** is calling you, you can find many sellers and cooperatives featuring argan in the small town of **Tamanar,** an hour south of Essaouira along the N1 (67km/42mi, 1hr).

COOPERATIVE AMAL

Village de Arganier, off the main road; tel. 0524/788 141; daily 9am-6pm

Stop by the Cooperative Amal for good deals on argan to be used for cooking as well as argan for cosmetic purposes. This particular cooperative is also great for observing the entire process of making argan oil. It employs around 150 women on a part-time and full-time basis, and is one of the best cooperatives in all of Morocco for how it empowers the local women, giving them some financial autonomy, and also for working to preserve the argan tree, an endangered and precious resource, in Morocco.

In early November, there is a **Festival of Argan** with many sellers from around the countryside and all sorts of foods that use the distinctive flavor of argan, along with music and dancing.

GETTING THERE

The only real way to visit this region is by **car** via the coastal route (R301). There is no bus or train service to this region. Those more adventurous can hitchhike or bargain with *grands taxis* from **Safi** or **Essaouira** for pickup and drop off.

Sidi Kaouki

سيدي كوكي

If Essaouira proves a bit too hectic, consider heading just a few minutes south to Sidi Kaouki. It's a popular destination for those doing surf tours along this stretch of the Atlantic Coast, but otherwise is guaranteed to be calmer than Essaouira. The beach here can get blustery, much like the beach at Essaouira, which makes it sometimes not so

goats eating argan nuts from the trees around Tamanar

Daour of Regraga

Between Safi and Essaouira lies the beautiful region of **Chiadma.** Though it does sport a small natural park, this region is better known locally for its many *zawiyas* (mausoleums) and shrines. The best time to visit this region is in the spring, March-April, when the **Daour of Regraga** takes place. The *daour* (tour) totals 39 days, during which time the pilgrims are to visit all 22 *zawiyas* and all 44 shrines. The founding myth concerns seven local saints who went to Mecca to meet the Prophet Mohammed. These saints were Christians but converted shortly upon meeting the prophet, who understood their language. The prophet's daughter, Fatima, however, did not. The words they spoke to her sounded to her ears like *regraga,* from the Arabic meaning "empty handed." The prophet then told these seven saints to go back to their land and spread Islam, now that his daughter had given them a name. Before the coming of Islam to Morocco, it is said that these seven saints walked through the land on their *daour* to make sure that none in the tribe had strayed, and this was the beginning of the Daour of Regraga, or "tour of the empty handed." This is a sacred, festive time with fantasias featuring horseback riding as well as nightly storytelling, dancing, and music.

ideal for sunbathing, but it is great for windsurfing, and cheaper than up north. Other than catching a wave, there isn't much to do here, with a few local restaurants and newly built *riads* catering to those looking for a quiet getaway.

MOGA SURF

Beachfront; tel. 0618/910 431 or 0660/727 688; www.mogasurf.com

Moga Surf has a shop and a school for surfing, windsurfing, and kitesurfing, with friendly, knowledgeable instructors for beginners and intermediates, including lessons from world-class champion Ismail Adarzane. Advanced surfers can contact the shop to find out about conditions in the area and possibly get rides to other locations. Lessons start at 650Dh and include all the equipment you might need. On a calm day, also consider paddle boarding.

GETTING THERE

Grands taxis run between **Essaouira** and Sidi Kaouki (20min, 10km/6mi, 10Dh). Otherwise, it's a short, direct drive from Essaouira. There is no regular bus service or train to get to Sidi Kaouki.

Cap Tafani

تفني

Cap Tafani (also: **Tafelnay**) is a long stretch of beach that lies far off the main road between Essaouira and Agadir. There is little here except for a few fishing boats and a few farms, though the long stretch of beach is inviting and something that you could likely have to yourself, particularly during lower travel seasons. The town has no real restaurants to speak of, just a few snack shops serving grilled fish and fries for the fishers. For surfers, the waves are mostly calm and don't have the rise as in other parts of this coastline. This is a beach bum's paradise.

★ TASGUA-YAN HOTEL

Douar Ait Tamlal; tel. 0661/675 493; www.tasgua-yan.com; 900Dh d

For those looking to really disconnect, the Tasgua-Yan Hotel is wonderfully located, just off the beach, with a wide open terrace looking out over the ocean; simple, tasteful decor with plush beds; and the unbeatable ocean air that stirs the soul. The construction itself has been done in locally sourced wood and stone, grounding you in the experience of getting away from it all, and features a cozy salon with a circular fireplace to keep you warm if the night is chilly. Rooms include breakfast. Lunch and dinner are available, and all meals use products from the local farms. An on-site, recognized aesthetician uses local, traditional products.

GETTING THERE

Cap Tafani is reachable by car from Essaouira (63km/39mi, 1hr) and Agadir (137km/85mi, 2hr) along the R301. *Grands taxis* can be had, though you will have to negotiate the price. Expect to pay through the nose.

Agadir

اگادير

Agadir is the bustling capital of southern Morocco. It's the principal fishing port and well known for its expansive, clean 6-kilometer (4-mile) beach. There are typically over 340 days of sunshine a year, making the vibe almost Californian. This used to be one of the favorite cities of King Mohammed VI, who came here occasionally to jet ski. The extra attention from the king shows, with new construction and a neat waterfront boulevard. These days, Europeans come here in search of sun. Agadir has the most pleasant city beach in all of Morocco, and women travelers will be happy to sport their swimsuits without the extra attention given them in most other Moroccan cities. However, the tourism here has more of a packaged-holiday feel, akin to Cabo San Lucas in Mexico or Majorca in Spain.

The word *agadir* stems from the Tashelhit word for "slope" or "escarpment," a word more popularly known as a "granary" or a "bank." This makes more sense when you realize that the old city of Agadir was largely up on a big hill north of the modern city. The old city was fortified, much like the other old medinas of Morocco, but was destroyed by an 18th-century earthquake. Parts of this fortification can still be viewed atop the hill, now known as Oufella, which affords panoramic views over today's Agadir, the long stretch of beach, and the port below. There are generally snake charmers and street vendors here throughout the day. At night, the inscription "God, Country, King," which adorns many prominent hillsides in Morocco, is lit up in Arabic script along with the old kasbah walls.

Before World War I, under the pretext of protecting its interests in Morocco, Germany sent two ships to the Bay of Agadir. This action sparked the Agadir Crisis between France and Germany and led to the Franco-German treaty that established large swaths of Morocco as a French protectorate. After this, the French built large sections of Agadir, and by the 1950s, it boasted a booming population of nearly 50,000 and hosted events such as the Moroccan Grand Prix.

Another large earthquake struck on February 29, 1960. The earthquake, 5.7 on the Richter scale, hit 15 minutes before midnight and destroyed much of the city, killing one-third of its populace, about 15,000 people. Thus, unlike most other Moroccan cities, Agadir is now mostly a newer city, with buildings dating after 1960.

Today's Agadir is now a city of over 500,000 and one of the fastest-growing cities in Morocco. If you're looking for a traditional/authentic Moroccan experience, this is not the place. However, Agadir can be a great arrival destination while planning for a trip to the south of Morocco, as it also serves as the primary transportation hub in the south, with an airport that is well-connected with Europe.

That said, sun worshippers and beach bums may not want to leave due to the year-long temperate climate and relaxed lifestyle, particularly in nearby Taghazout.

ORIENTATION

Most of the restaurants, hotels, and nightlife hug the stretch of beach south of the port. This neighborhood is aptly named **Secteur Touristique** and sports the wide, wonderful Rue la Plage, a largely pedestrian-only boulevard that is lit up at night with restaurants and pleasant cafés. The **port** is a lively diversion around 10am and just before nightfall when fishermen bring in the fresh catch.

Those interested in purchasing the freshest seafood around can barter with the nearby fishmonger, though prices are generally very low. Snack shops and grills primarily serve fishers, and grill whatever is fresh simply and without much in the way of adornment. A typical plate costs 30-40Dh.

South of the Secteur Touristique, following either Boulevard de l'Oued Sous or Boulevard du 20 Août, is the **Founty** neighborhood, which has several large beachfront hotels and all-inclusive resorts as well as sectors of developed villas for wealthy locals.

Much of the rest of Agadir spreads inland and is largely referred to as **Nouveau Talborjt** (New Fortress or New City), though in reality it is several distinct neighborhoods. **Abattoir** is of some interest. It continues on the other side of the Avenue Hassan II from the beach, along Avenue Abderrahim Bouabid, and hosts the largest daily souk in the region, **Souk el Had,** as well as the *gare routière* for *grands taxis* and buses. **Boutchakat,** also on the east side of Avenue Hassan II, north of Abattoir, has several eateries as well as the Catholic church of Saint Anne. Around here you will also find the **Industrial Zone** and most of the budget accommodation.

South of Agadir is the suburb of **Inezgane,** a town in its own right but now seemingly swallowed by Agadir. Inezgane offers several golf courses and the primary bus and taxi station for traveling through the region.

SIGHTS

There are few buildings or sights of cultural or historic importance in Agadir. Most people come for the long, gorgeous stretch of beach, the sunny weather, and the nightlife.

Kasbah

on the tall north hill 7km outside of the city center; free

There isn't much left of Moulay Abdallah al-Ghalib's old kasbah, but there are some outstanding views over Agadir. The old fortified city is best reached by taxi (20-30Dh or more, depending on how well you can bargain and if the taxi will wait for you to descend), though it is possible to walk to the top of the steep hill. The fortress itself was constructed around 1570 and well situated to protect the harbor, keep watch over the territory, and keep the granary stores. A first earthquake destroyed the city in 1731. The Dutch helped to rebuild, and because of this the inscription that appears under the kasbah gate reads in Arabic and Dutch: "Fear and honor your king." Now, numerous street vendors and faux guides will try to direct your attention here, for a price. It might be worth paying 40-50Dh to discover a bit more about the history of this kasbah and see the fault line of the Great Leap Day Earthquake of 1960. Camels are available for a short ride and photo op (20-50Dh).

Municipal Amazigh Museum

Ave. Hassan II, Passage Aït Souss; tel. 0528/821 632; Mon.-Sat. 9:30am-1pm and 2pm-5:30pm; 20Dh

Dive into the history of the region at the Municipal Amazigh Museum (Musée Municipal du Patrimoine Amazighe), which has a small collection of Amazigh wood, pottery, and carpets from the Souss, Massa, and Draa regions that reveal the aspects of daily life in these environs just around Agadir. Myriad displays show the art of spinning pottery, weaving carpets, and carving the intricate wood designs seen all around. There are some English materials available, though the vast majority is in French and Arabic. Several eateries nearby make this an attractive stop to escape the heat, learn about the region, and then stop for lunch.

Medina of Agadir

Aéroport Militaire Bensergao; tel. 0528/280 253 or 0661/396 261; daily 9am-6pm; 40Dh

The Medina of Agadir hosts a variety of artisans. Many of them take Tuesday off, though the medina is still open. Here you can find quality Moroccan slippers, jewelry, textiles, mosaic tables, and carved wood as well as a café where you can rest your feet. While you're there, check out Chez Azzab Med's

1

2

shop (#Z1-57, tel. 0667/019 115). He has a great selection of silver jewelry for good prices, though you can always try to bargain down a bit. The shopping atmosphere is more laid-back than elsewhere in Morocco and, as far as replica outdoor medinas go, it is something of a novelty. Taxis will bring you from downtown Agadir (50Dh), though you might want to pay extra to have them wait for you, as finding a ride to leave can be a hassle.

Théâtre de Verdure

Blvd. Mohammed V, Centre Ville

Located right in the center of town, the Théâtre de Verdure is a charming outdoor theater, part of the Municipal Theater Complex. Throughout the year you can enjoy free concerts and plays that are both national and international, as well as modern, classic, and contemporary dance performances. Some of the more popular plays put on are reinterpretations of local folktales. Horsemen gallop in so close to the audience that you can literally smell the sweat of the horses and feel the earth shake beneath your feet. Plays typically feature characters dressed in traditional Moroccan garb, sporting authentic weapons, and often breaking into fantastic dances that boggle the mind. Check with your accommodation or the nearby Syndicate d'Initiative et du Tourisme for upcoming performances.

Bird Valley

off Blvd. du 20 Août near the Royal Atlas Hotel; daily 11am-6pm; free

Just off the beach, tucked in the folds of the hotels and shopping malls, lies Bird Valley (La Vallée des Oiseux), a local attraction with goats, peacocks, llamas, and other interesting animals that kids may enjoy, though animal lovers might be brokenhearted. There are numerous signs of distress from the animals. Most of the pens are dirty, if not filthy, and it seems that locals are accustomed to throwing any sort of food, including unsuitable items such as popcorn, for the animals to eat. It can be a good learning experience for children, as well as adults, about the fate of those less fortunate. I can't 100 percent recommend this, but without the support that these animals do receive, I wonder what else would happen.

1: the relaxing beach of Agadir 2: the artisan shopping center Medina of Agadir

BEACHES

The reason why Agadir is arguably the most touristed city in Morocco begins and ends pretty much at the **beachfront** and its long beachfront promenade. Moroccans and Europeans flock here for the long stretch of beach and the year-round sun. This long promenade, well-lit at night and full of people from around the world, is perhaps the best developed stretch of beach in Morocco. You can ride a camel along the beach, relax beneath a sunshade on a rented beach chair sipping on a cocktail, and then take in the sunset. Many of the younger local boys come out to play soccer on stretches of the beach, and women and men jog and power-walk at the edge of the surf. Farther out in the ocean, beginning and more experienced surfers try to catch waves, and children splash in the warm water, with trained lifeguards just a shout away throughout the daytime. Trade in your shoes for flip-flops for a day or, if it suits you, just go barefoot and sink your toes deep in the warm sand. This is as Hawaii as Morocco gets.

SPORTS AND RECREATION

Agadir is a sports enthusiast's dream. With nearly year-round sunny weather and a temperate breeze coming off the Atlantic, there are many activities to do, no matter the time of year.

Tree Climbing

ACCROBRANCHE

N1 at Ave. de l'Embouchure de l'Oued Souss; tel. 0546/153 579 or 0654/591 972; daily 9am-sunset; from 100Dh

If you fancy a climb in some trees, head to Accrobranche. Located in the Founty neighborhood near the golf courses, this challenging rope course will take you into the trees on five climbs over suspended rope bridges and up into the foliage. Each climb seems to be more daunting than the last. Staff are all well trained and the equipment is kept up-to-date. This is popular for a half-day excursion with children and wannabe children.

Golf

A few golf courses in Founty, the suburb just a few minutes south of the Secteur Touristique, are popular with Europeans and Moroccans. Golfing is still very much an upper-class pastime in Morocco, with the average greens fee, not to mention the cost of equipment, more than most locals can dream of managing.

GOLF DE L'OCEAN

Founty, tel. 0528/273 542, www.golfdelocean.com, 700Dh

Golf de l'Ocean features 27 wide holes with plenty of sand traps, water obstructions, a few long par 5s, and lots of ocean views. Caddies are mandatory (100Dh).

GOLF DU SOLEIL

Founty, tel. 0528/337 330, www.golfdusoleil.com, 500Dh)

Golf du Soleil is a slightly better deal and doesn't require caddies, though they're available. The course is well maintained, with beautiful water features and rolling fairways.

Camel Trekking

Those who can't resist the idea of taking a camel ride have a few options around town. Atop the hill at the north end of the town at the old kasbah are usually several camels you can take for a short jaunt and photo op (20-50Dh), though the more interesting option is to book a two-hour camel tour that will take you completely around Agadir, past the Royal Palace, through Bird Valley, and down to the beach just in time for sunset. Two hours on a camel will leave you sore, perhaps just in time for that hammam and massage you've been putting off. For a more bespoke, private experience, contact **Amodou Cheval** (tel. 0670/341 510, http://amodoucheval.com, 300Dh).

FOOD

There are many restaurant options in Agadir. After a long voyage through Morocco dominated by tajines and heaping plates of couscous, the variety is greatly appreciated. From snack stands to five-star meals, there is something for every price range. If you want to splurge on a meal, Agadir is the place to do it.

Seafood lovers should stop by the **fishing port** and its barbecues, open all day long. Sit and enjoy a freshly grilled seafood lunch with Moroccan round bread, olives, and mint tea for 40Dh. What's served is what has been caught that day. Be careful of the touts, though. They will try to steer you toward options where you might spend 3-4 times as much.

AYZAM AGADIR

Agadir port; tel. 0528/380 838; Sun.-Fri. 11:30am-10:30pm, Sat. 11:30am-11pm; 50Dh

A reliable option in the port is Ayzam Agadir for no-nonsense grilled fish and fried calamari. A fantastic place for families with young kids, as the large fish tanks and constant activity tend to keep the kids occupied. Before or after lunch, make your way down the slipway and check out the boats. The cacophony is half of the fun of eating at the port.

PATISSERIE L'ANICE

Rue de la Foire, at the bottom of the Hotel Studio; tel. 0528/848 164; daily 6:30am-10:30pm; 30Dh

For a solid continental breakfast, Patisserie l'Anice is perhaps the best around. Lunch and dinner are also available but a bit underwhelming given the other choices nearby. The patio can get a little warm, but it's well equipped with sun umbrellas, which make sipping on freshly squeezed orange juice or café au lait and people-watching a perfectly pleasant morning pastime.

TAFARNOUT

Immeuble Tigouarmine, Ave. Hassan II; tel. 0528/844 450; daily 6am-10pm; 25Dh

At the French-styled *patisserie* and *boulangerie* (pastry and bread bakery) Tafarnout, you can enjoy buttery croissants, *pain au chocolat* (chocolate croissants), *tartes aux pommes* (apple tarts), and breads of seemingly every shape, size, and grain. There is nonsmoking indoor service as well as service on the large outdoor patio, but you can take the pastries to go and enjoy at the beach, just a 10-minute walk away.

RIVIET

28 Residence Khalij Annakhil; tel. 0528/232 233, www.riviet.ma; daily 11am-11pm; 90Dh

There are a few Thai, Chinese, and Japanese restaurants around Agadir. Riviet is largely a sushi house, though some Thai-style noodles and soups are also available. The decor inside is self-styled Asian—clean lines with lots of red and black, and Shanghai fonts decorating the walls. If you're craving some sushi, dive in here for the *maki* rolls and sashimi. You won't be disappointed, except maybe by the service. It can be a little slow, even for Morocco. Free delivery is available anywhere in Agadir, making a night in or sushi on your beachside patio a definite possibility.

★ BUON GUSTO

42 Galerie Faiz, Pl. Cinema Rialto; tel. 0528/844 861; daily 11:30am-midnight; 70Dh

The super-popular Buon Gusto is known around town for its delicious wood-fired pizzas. The atmosphere is cozy (it's a pretty small restaurant), though bright and modern, while the little plants dotting the alleyway give it a homey touch, but you're really coming here for the Napoli pizza. Takeaway is available. When you need to get your Italian on or quiet the kids down, head here. The free garlic bread is a nice touch.

VIA VENETO

Blvd. Hassan II, in front of Pl. Al-Amal; tel. 0528/841 467; daily 11am-1:30am; 70Dh

Not far from Buon Gusto is another Italian favorite, Via Veneto, a friendly little joint on the main boulevard. The brick facade exudes a sort of rustic charm, echoed in the no-frills wood-fired pizzas, which have a bit more zest than some of the others in town (though not quite as good as Buon Gusto). Service is prompt and with a smile. The full bar is at your disposal, though the aperitif is an acquired taste.

★ PURE PASSION

Complexe Marina; tel. 0528/840 120; noon-3pm and 7pm-11pm; 300Dh

If upscale is your thing, make a beeline for Pure Passion, with fantastic views over the bay and marina, attentive staff, chefs that prepare your filet perfectly to instruction, and generous portions. From the amuse-bouche through courses of succulent crab croquettes, lamb with honey and thyme sauce, buttery monkfish, or perhaps the chateaubriand, your senses will be swimming, which seems appropriate given the location.

L'ATLANTIQUE

Sofitel Agadir Thalassa Hotel, Baie des Palmiers; tel. 0528/849 200 or 0528/388 000; Mon.-Fri. 11:30am-2pm and 7pm-11pm; 450Dh

L'Atlantique is perhaps the best seafood restaurant around. The tables are all lit by chandeliers with hanging glass bobbles reminiscent of Chihuly's work. Service is immaculate, as are the white linens, outdoor lounge, and open grill. Food is sourced daily from the local catch, and the menu includes many gluten-free dishes. Those not wanting cigarette smoke interfering with their meal are advised to dine outside.

LA SCALA

Rue de l'Oued Souss, Complexe Tamlelt; tel. 0528/846 773; Tues.-Sun. noon-3pm and 7pm-midnight; 250Dh

For a candlelit dinner, think about heading to

La Scala. The service is top-notch and the setting is charming, with an outdoor patio that makes the most of its location away from the beach, with warm lighting that sets the mood for a little romance under the stars. If it's too cold out for the patio, come early to avoid the possibility of a cigarette-smoking neighbor. The menu features some of the best steaks in the city as well as scallops in a rich Taliouine saffron sauce.

BARS AND NIGHTLIFE

Agadir is famed for its nightlife, and it's easy to see why. Europeans flock here for the summer sun, often dancing well into the morning hours. Most nightclubs are open year-round every night starting around 10pm or 11pm, though the party often doesn't get started until well after midnight. Hours change slightly according to season, as does the cover charge. Gentlemen can expect to pay 100-200Dh for a cover charge, while ladies often get in free. Dress codes are laid-back, as is the general atmosphere. Singles should be wary. The club scene is fertile ground for Agadir's prostitutes, both female and male. Sex tourism, unfortunately, is one of the dark draws for many Europeans and Middle Easterners to this part of Morocco. Many of the midrange hotels have their own nightclubs, an option for those not wanting to venture far from home or deal with late-night taxis. It's not unusual to walk from club to club looking for the right scene for the night. Most of them are within the **Secteur Touristique,** making this a fun, easy late-night parade with the possibility to unwind on the beach and catch a sunrise after dancing the night away.

If low-key is more your thing than a booming club scene, there are a few bars to choose from, but be warned: drinking in Morocco is not cheap. Most drinks run 40-80Dh. The bars tend to be fairly quiet in the off-season, though still busy during the weekends and holidays. Most large hotels have full bars with large terraces to lounge on and enjoy a tequila sunrise at sunset. And again, prostitution is rampant in Morocco. Forewarned is forearmed.

PAPAGAYO

Chemin des Dune; tel. 0528/845 400; 10pm-late; drinks about 100Dh

This long-standing favorite often has international DJs spinning the latest mixes from Europe, adding to the late-night crazy vibe of this 1,500-person club. You would be forgiven if you thought you were spending your night starring in a music video. Hired dancers populate the club most nights, gyrating and grinding to the newest beats while a veritable techno-laser show blazes across the dance floor. Like all nightclubs, a night out at Papagayo comes at a price. Drinks are typically 100Dh, so pace yourself.

THE FACTORY

Hotel Tafoukt, Blvd. du 20 Août, across from the English Pub; tel. 0528/221 314; www.lafactory.ma; 10pm-late; drinks about 100Dh

The Factory is a popular alternative to Papagayo, with specialized nights in techno, house, funk, and trance, with the occasional Moroccan Chaabi music thrown in just for local flavor. The atmosphere here is more of a nightclub feel than a music video, with fewer of the more undesirable elements and with more students studying abroad and young people on vacation having fun. Ladies' night is typically a great deal, with ladies getting free entry and free drinks starting at midnight.

ENGLISH PUB

Blvd. du 20 Août; tel. 0528/847 390; daily noon-1am

Of the local bars, the best of the bunch is the English Pub, which shows live sports, serves draft beer, and has karaoke every night. The pub food on offer, including English-style fish-and-chips (120Dh), hits the spot after a long night out. The variety of vegetarian-friendly options is attractive, and the large terrace is great for mingling and people-watching. Beers are a bit more expensive than at some other bars around town, though the atmosphere is a little less divey.

PIRATE PUB

4 Front de mer; tel. 0661/265 563; daily noon-1am

To sip on some suds and maybe snack while enjoying the beach, the Pirate Pub fits the bill nicely. With friendly service right along the beachfront and Moroccan and pub-style classics, this is one of the new favorites for those looking to chillax. The inside can get pretty smoky rather quickly and is mostly for drinking. Outside, just a few yards away from the beach, is where it's at.

THE PIANO BAR

Blvd. du 20 Août; tel. 0618/774 246; daily noon-2am; drinks about 100Dh

Women traveling alone looking to unwind and not be hassled should consider the Piano Bar in the Anezi Tower Hotel. The atmosphere includes lounge-style piano music (of course), friendly staff, and distance from the sport-fanatic crowd that seems to saturate other bars. Drinks are decently priced and competently cocktailed. Leather chairs and ornate cedarwood ceilings add to the Rick's Café vibe of this place. The outdoor pool makes for wonderful outdoor sitting if there are too many smokers inside.

ACCOMMODATIONS

Under 400Dh

Most of the real budget options in Agadir are well away from the beach and littered throughout the new city.

★ HOTEL TIZNINE

3 Rue Drarga; tel. 0528/843 925; 90Dh d

Hotel Tiznine in Nouveau Talborjt is refreshingly nonsmoking. Rooms are clean, though sterile, with drab tile work and no real charm to speak of. However, for the price, this is unbeatable. There are shared bathrooms (or you can ask for a room with an en suite bathroom for a bit more), and guests staying for longer periods are granted access to the upstairs kitchen. There's no breakfast served, though there are plenty of spots nearby to grab a good breakfast.

MOTEL AHL SOUSS

Ave. Arreda, Shell station; tel. 0528/835 091; 180Dh d

Along National Road 10 (N10), the Motel Ahl Souss, attached to the Shell gas station, runs a clean operation with quiet rooms toward the back. It's no frills, but it's easy to find, making it ideal for a late-night entry into Agadir. Otherwise, the other options are tucked around the Industrial Zone, with most having 24-hour reception for more illicit late nights, including a lot of prostitution.

TAGADIRT HOTEL

Blvd. du 20 Août; tel. 0528/645 228; 300Dh d

The Tagadirt Hotel is another no-frills option a bit closer to the beach, though best avoided in winter, as the rooms can get downright cold at night and there is no real heating to speak of. The common areas are charming and spacious and the staff friendly. The rooms, though clean, are outdated, with old TVs and threadbare towels. For two people splitting the cost, this is a good choice. The best rooms are away from the pub downstairs (with its loud music) and up a few floors. Terraces overlook the city.

400-800Dh

ATLANTIC PALM BEACH HOTEL

Sector A; tel. 0528/235 303; www.atlanticpalmbeach.com; 450Dh d

Just off National Road 1 (N1) in the Founty district you can find the Atlantic Palm Beach Hotel, a modern hotel with comfy beds and views out over the Atlantic, though ask for top-floor accommodations at booking to really take advantage of those views. The large pool is wonderful to cool off in, though the breakfast buffet, included with your stay, leaves a little something to be desired. Some rooms have kitchens so you can cook your own meals, as well as large terraces from which you can enjoy the stunning sunsets of this part of Africa. This is one of the best values going in Agadir.

Over 800Dh

Several large resort hotels in Agadir are along the beachfront and in the Founty district, each a true five-star experience with custom architecture, cozy beds, and service befitting the cost. For those in search of a "regular" high-end hotel, these are worth looking into, particularly online as you can find some good deals, though they're soulless and lacking any sort of local charm.

★ DAR MAKTOUB

Chemin l'Oued Souss, Founty; tel. 0528/337 500; www.darmaktoub.com; 900Dh d

If you're looking for a real retreat away from the resort crowds, head to Dar Maktoub, in the Founty neighborhood just a few minutes south of the Secteur Touristique of Agadir, nestled between golf courses. This sprawling guesthouse is tucked away into well-manicured grounds, replete with bougainvillea, aloe, daisies, and hundreds of other plants, and features a private pool, restaurant, Wi-Fi, and friendly staff that will see to your needs. The rooms all feature top-of-the-line beds and cozy linens with plenty of charm. Breakfast is included, and other meals are available on demand. Guests will likely want to have their own transportation to reach the nearby beaches, restaurants, and other sites and activities around the city, though taxis are always available and can be arranged by the guesthouse staff.

INFORMATION AND SERVICES

SYNDICATE D'INITIATIVE ET DU TOURISME

Blvd. Mohammed V; tel. 0528/840 307; www.visitagadir.com; daily 10am-5pm

For updated information on any local performing arts, including plays, concerts, and dance performances, check with the Syndicate d'Initiative et du Tourisme. There is information online and at the tourism office about local pharmacies, doctors, and bus schedules, plus a handy map of Agadir, though the office itself is often closed.

GETTING THERE

By Car

By car, Agadir is easily reached via National Road 1 (N1) from **Essaouira** (175km/108mi, 2.5hr) as well as the paid autoroute (A7) from **Marrakesh** (243km/151mi, 2.5hr). The roads are pleasant to drive, though extreme caution should be used when driving at night. **Taroudant** (82km/51mi, 1.5hr) makes for a good day trip inland along National Road 10 (N10). **Taliouine** (207km/129mi, 3hr) and **Ouarzazate** (378km/235mi, 5.5hr) are also reached via the N10.

By Bus

The **primary *gare routière*** is in Inezgane, just south of Agadir hugging the N1. Here, you can also find the **CTM station** (94 Ave. Mokhtar Soussi). There is another ***gare routière*** across the street from Souk el-Had in Agadir with a few *grands taxis* and local buses, though it is a bit far from the beach and run-down. From either station, take a *petit taxi* into town (around 20Dh).

CTM (tel. 0800/0900 30, www.ctm.ma) runs buses from here to **Marrakesh** (3hr, 16 daily, 120Dh), **Taroudant** (1.5hr, 2 daily, 35Dh), **Ouarzazate** (6.5hr, 2 daily, 150Dh), **Tiznit** (1.5hr, 9 daily, 40Dh), **Mirleft** (2.5hr, 1 daily, 60Dh), **Sidi Ifni** (3.5hr, 3 daily, 70Dh), **Guelmim** (4hr, 9 daily, 85Dh), **Tan Tan** (5.5hr, 9 daily, 130Dh), **Laayoune** (10hr, 9 daily, 240Dh), and **Dakhla** (19hr, 5 daily, 395Dh).

Supratours (tel. 0524/888 566 or 0524/885 632, www.oncf.ma) operates the buses affiliated with the national train line, ONCF. Buses run from the **Marrakesh** train station to Agadir (3hr, 12 daily, 120Dh) and are the most convenient way to get from Marrakesh to Agadir for those traveling by train. Supratours also runs buses to **Tiznit** (1.5hr, 3 daily, 50Dh), **Guelmim** (3.5hr, 6 daily, 70Dh), **Tan Tan** (5.5hr, 3 daily, 120Dh), and **Laayoune** (9.5hr, 4 daily, 220Dh).

By Grand Taxi

Grands taxis commonly run to/from the following locations: **Taghazoute** (20min,

20km/12mi, 10Dh), **Essaouira** (2.5hr, 175km/108mi, 70Dh), **Taroudant** (1hr, 85km/53mi, 32Dh), **Tiznit** (1.5hr, 92km/57mi, 32Dh), Mirleft (2hr, 140km/87mi, 45dh), **Sidi Ifni** (2.5hr, 165km/102mi, 65Dh), **Guelmim** (3hr, 200km/124mi, 70Dh), and **Laayoune** (8hr, 645km/400mi, 200Dh), as well as between Agadir and **Inezgane** (10min, 5km/3mi, 5Dh).

By Plane

AGADIR AL-MASSIRA INTERNATIONAL AIRPORT

20km/14mi east of Agadir, tel. 0528/839 112, www.agadir-airport.com

Many direct flights arrive from Europe to the Agadir Al-Massira International Airport. From the airport you can take a *grand taxi* directly to your hotel (30min, 220Dh, entire taxi only). Those wanting to skip Agadir could arrive at the airport and head directly for Taghazoute or perhaps Tiznit, each about 1 hour away by car.

GETTING AROUND

The ubiquitous *petits taxis* are the choice of travel for most getting around the city. Taxis are friendly and metered, and drivers know most of the major hotels and restaurants, but it is always good to have a map (either on your phone or paper) to show the driver. An average taxi ride will cost 7-20Dh, a relative steal. Otherwise, with wide sidewalks, pedestrian-friendly boulevards, and year-round sun, Agadir is one of the more pleasant cities to **walk** around.

Around Agadir

There are quite a few interesting towns and smaller cities around Agadir, all easily reachable by car or bus. Surfers will want to head north of Agadir to the laid-back surfing and fishing town of Taghazoute, where you can find waves nearly year-round. For those looking for something more traditional, the Anti-Atlas towns of Tiznit, Taroudant, Tafraoute, and Taliouine provide some great diversions and shopping opportunities. Taroudant and Taliouine can be visited either while en route for Ouarzazate and the southern oases or while doing a loop of the Anti-Atlas, starting with Tiznit. Taliouine is a must-visit for foodies looking for one of the best strands of saffron to be had in the world. Otherwise, south from Tiznit there are beach towns to explore on the way to Laayoune and the Western Sahara, including Mirleft and Sidi Ifni.

TOP EXPERIENCE

TAGHAZOUTE
تاغازوت

Just a short 20-minute drive north of Agadir lies Taghazoute (often: Taghazout), the surfer capital of Morocco. This growing little village hugs the coastline. Since 2015 or so, the stretch of beach just south of Taghatzoute has been under development. This once barren beach is now a haven of beach resorts, somewhat reminiscent of Hawaii. Taghazoute is already seeing a lot of growth from these developments, but its heart is still a beating fisher-surfer vibe, always in tune with the waves.

Surfers from around Europe, plus a few in-the-know Australians, Canadians, and Americans, make their way here to catch a wave, making Taghazoute a surprisingly international destination with a super-chill beachside vibe. This is a cheaper, more laid-back alternative to nearby Agadir, with a number of yoga and surf retreats becoming more popular. Taghazoute is a great place to unwind, catch a wave, and meet up with people from around the world. A word of warning for beachgoers: the beach right next to town with the fishing boats is not generally the cleanest. It's better to head out to the adjacent Banana Beach, just south of town near the resorts.

★ Windsurfing, Kitesurfing, and Surfing

SURF MAROC

Centre Ville; tel. 0528/200 230; www.surfmaroc.com; lessons from 250Dh, equipment rental from 200Dh

For English speakers, Surf Maroc is perhaps the best all-around option around Taghazoute. They have a great selection of well-kept boards and offer lessons for all levels. They can also arrange surf trips up and down the coastline and generally know the best surf spots on any given day. Solo female travelers or small groups of women should check out the girls-only surf program. The atmosphere is all surfer-friendly, with people helping each other out to give rides up and down the coastline and catch waves together, no matter the nationality. Two-hour coaching sessions start at 250Dh and include coach, board, and wetsuit. Additional (more expensive) options include transportation to other beaches as well as lunch. Board and wetsuit rental is 200Dh a day.

SURF CAMP TAGHAZOUT

Centre Ville; tel. 0665/611 288; www.surfcamptaghazout.com; lessons from 300Dh; retreats from 450Dh

If you are planning your surfing trip ahead of time, Surf Camp Taghazout offers a full range of services and can not only help with surfing equipment and lessons, but also has all-inclusive surfing retreats from the bargain-basement price of 450Dh, including accommodations, wetsuits, boards, meals, yoga classes, and surf instruction, as well as trips around the area and pickup from the Agadir *gare routière*.

Food and Accommodations

There are a number of *grillades* and snack shops lining the main street, alongside more surf shops than you can count. These can do in a pinch, but the real value is in the hotels. Each of them have an in-house café or restaurant, generally offering up some fantastic fare, much of it more sensitive than other places in Morocco to food allergies or preferences. Gluten-free, vegan, and vegetarian are par for the course. For breakfast, don't shy away from asking for that avocado toast you know you've been craving.

SURF MAROC

Centre Ville, on the main road overlooking the water; tel. 0528/200 230; http://surfmaroc.com; daily 9am-7pm; café 120Dh, 450Dh d

Travelers interested in a good beachfront café will want to check out Surf Maroc. This is a favorite spot for surfers to stay as well as other travelers looking for clean, friendly accommodations with waterfront views. On offer are surf classes and oceanfront yoga. Surf rentals are available on-site. In addition to the simple hotel rooms, private seaside villas are available for around 1,000Dh a night. For groups splitting costs, this is a good option. That said, the café is the real draw, with its wide oceanside windows, menu full of smoothies (try the vitamin booster with fresh-squeezed orange juice and carrots), and fresh catches coming in from the fishermen below. The free Wi-Fi is cool, but the fact they are fighting against plastic waste and have a clean on-site water tap is perhaps cooler.

SURF BERBERE

Centre Ville, on the main road overlooking the water; tel. 0528/200 290; 200Dh dorm-style bed

Similar but a bit rougher around the edges is Surf Berbere. The rooms are no-frills, though the views out over the water are breathtaking. It's a good option for students and backpackers, though there are cheaper options farther into town, off the water. The only option is sleeping in a room with eight bunk beds, which can be a way to cut down on costs. This might be attractive for some, though still not as inexpensive as one might imagine. The surf camp feel is intoxicating for those who have a love for the water. Rooms include breakfast.

★ MUNGA GUESTHOUSE

17 Rue Ilwite; tel. 0528/200 202 or 0698/680 680; www.mungaguesthouse.com; 1,000Dh d

Perfectly funky, Munga is something of a mix between a traditional B&B and cutting-edge art hotel. None of the 15 rooms or any of the common spaces are alike. Here, it's all salvaged wood and recycled materials. Multiple terraces offer up some of the best sunset viewing along the coast. The overall vibe is cozy, chic, arty, and chill. If you're looking to spend some time getting away from it all, this is the sort of getaway experience you imagine. Come for the surf and sun, but stay for the people. Not all rooms have views, so be sure to request a room with a view overlooking the water (preferably with a private balcony, of course). You'll find two dining options. Downstairs is a bit more simple and good for a quick catch of the day, though you'll want to make your way upstairs for rooftop dining and a glass of white to sip with your sunset. If you're really splurging, go for the magnum suite. It's a real treat for a real getaway.

Getting There and Around

From **Agadir** and **Inezgane**, *grands taxis* run back and forth to Taghazoute (20min, 20km/12mi, 15Dh). Those with their own cars will find plenty of street parking. A few local buses stop here as well. Once in town, all you'll need are flip-flops, a bathing suit, and a towel. Taghazoute is perhaps the most beach-friendly environ in all of Morocco, making it equally comfortable for men and women.

TAROUDANT

تارودانت

Along the road to the High Atlas and Ouarzazate is the city of **Taroudant,** nicknamed "Little Marrakesh" for its bustling markets and history of storytellers and street performers who entertain the crowds on Dsisa Square, just next to the Kasbah Gardens at the main entrance to the old city. Taroudant is a popular day trip for vacationers in Agadir. For a breath of something authentically Moroccan, check out the markets and maze-like medina streets, though much of it is less "traditional" than "contemporary Moroccan." For those interested in exploring the High Atlas, Taroudant has proven to be a popular alternative as a base camp to the more touristy Marrakesh, particularly for trekkers.

Around the main square, **Place Assarag** on Boulevard Mohammed V, you can find cash machines and cafés.

Sights

MEDINA

The centuries-old **ramparts** surrounding the medina are some of the best preserved in all of Morocco. Their pink shades take on deeper hues at sunset, particularly remarkable when the snowcapped High Atlas mountains are illuminated in the background, reminiscent of that other "Red City" over the Tizi n'Test pass to the north.

Shopping

The **souks** of Taroudant are locally famous for their diversity and for relatively low prices. However, most offerings veer toward the local and exclude many of the things of interest to most travelers in Morocco. For the ardent explorer of souks, this is as authentic as it gets. For shoppers, this is where you can count on prices that are a fraction of those generally found in Marrakesh.

LARBI EL HARE

Fendouk Elhare #28; tel. 0668/807 835; daily 9am-sunset, varying hours on Fri.

Purchasing a small carving by the local artist known as Larbi el Hare is something of a rite of passage in Taroudant. Larbi creates stone carvings, mostly of alabaster, using the same techniques that have been used in the region for generations, and drawing on the old Amazigh culture of Morocco, though with a modern twist. He's been featured in European

1

2

3

magazines, and you can read the news clippings he displays proudly on the wall in his small shop.

Food and Accommodations

If your accommodation doesn't include breakfast, consider heading to the **Café la Jeunesse** across from Hotel Indouzal. This is a clean place for breakfast, with simple omelets, baguettes served with jam, and freshly squeezed orange juice. Just inside Bab Targont you can find **Café Oulabas,** along Boulevard Mohammed V just down from Place Assarag. This is a fantastic spot for a quick morning *sfeng* (donut) and coffee. Just a few doors down, toward the center of the medina, is **Café Arena** for *msemen* (a type of flatbread) with cheese and/or honey.

DAR ZITOUNE

Boutarialt El Barrania; tel. 0528/551 141 or 0528/551 142; www.darzitoune.ma; noon-3pm and 7pm-11pm; 250Dh

If you're searching for a good dinner spot, Dar Zitoune serves one of the best meals in town and is a stellar *riad* to boot, though at a price (900Dh). The *riad* is about a 10-minute walk outside of the medina, and you will need reservations for dinner. A 20Dh taxi ride will take you right to the front door. The elaborate garden features orange trees around the inviting pool, providing some respite from the hot sun. There is outdoor/indoor dining, and the menu features traditional Moroccan dishes, made with vegetables and fruits plucked straight from the on-site garden. As well as the splendid gardens, the *riad* has a full-service spa and jacuzzi.

★ RIAD TAROUDANT DES PALMIERS

Blvd. Le Prince Heriter; tel. 0528/854 507; www.riadtaroudantpalmiers.com; 250Dh

There are few choices here for budget lodging that are not somewhat dingy around the edges. Several hotels in the medina dot the main square, though their charm is largely in their sort of scruffiness. However, the Riad Taroudant des Palmiers is one of the more distinctive choices. This was once a Spanish convent, built in the early 20th century, and it has been transformed into a budget hotel, with all of the proceeds going to help the orphanage next door. (It might not seem this way at first glance, but the tiles are really just that old!) Rooms are simple, though clean and comfortable, and the palm garden erupts with the soft chirp of birds in the morning. Note that the hotel fills quickly during the busy summer months; call 8am-6pm to book your stay. Meals are available on request and not included with your stay. Breakfast is around 20Dh in the attached café. For cheap eats, you can usually get a *bissara* or *harira* for less than 10Dh with a round of bread.

Getting There and Around

BY CAR

By car, Taroudant is a straightforward drive east from **Agadir** (82km/51mi, 1.5hr) on the N10. Those with their own cars will find plenty of street parking available for no cost. **Taliouine** (121km/75mi, 1.5hr) can easily be reached farther east on the N10 as part of the Anti-Atlas loop that turns south to **Tafraoute** (318km/198mi, 4.5hr) before joining the N1 at **Tiznit** (425km/264mi, 6hr). Taroudant is a half day of driving from **Ouarzazate** (292km/181mi, 4hr) on the N10.

BY GRAND TAXI AND BUS

Grands taxis run back and forth from **Agadir** (1hr, 85km/53mi, 32Dh) quite regularly. If it's hot out, make sure to get a seat on the shady side of the car. The ***gare routière*** is just outside the medina walls on Rocade Taroudant, to the south of the city. You can also find taxis to **Taliouine** (1.5hr, 121km/75mi, 45Dh). **CTM** (tel. 0800/0900 30, www.ctm.ma) runs buses to Taroudant from Agadir (1.5hr, 2 daily, 35Dh).

1: looking to catch a wave in Imsouane
2: Taghazoute, the colorful surf capital of Morocco
3: the finger rocks outside of Taliouine

★ Saffron: The Red Gold of Morocco

The harvesting of saffron happens in the early mornings, before sunrise, so that it has the most flavor. After sunrise, the saffron threads begin to lose their intensity. Saffron threads are taken from the purple saffron flower, with each flower typically giving three threads. During harvest season in Taliouine, usually October to early November, children as young as five years old are enlisted to assist with the harvest.

To pick one kilogram of undried saffron, it takes 400 hours and 160,000 flowers. This kilogram is dried, with the end result producing a final 200 grams, which can then be sold and used as spice. Because of the precious nature of this spice, and its golden red thread, it is no wonder why it is called the red gold of Morocco.

There are many ways to conserve saffron so that it keeps its intensity. It should always be stored in a cool, dark place and never exposed to sunlight. Once at home, it is possible to infuse warm water with a few threads of saffron, which may then be used in teas, soups, tajines, or other dishes.

A woman carefully plucks valuable saffron flowers.

TALIOUINE

تالوين

The seldom-touristed town of Taliouine is the capital of Moroccan saffron—making this a must-stop destination for foodies and chefs. The nearby mountain Jbel Siroua, part of the impressive Anti-Atlas range, provides some interesting opportunities for hikers and trekkers. There is a town 30 minutes from Taliouine by the name of Assaiss where there is a Wednesday souk for donkeys and mules, making this an interesting stop for trekkers in the region. Slightly further into the mountains from Assaiss you'll find a beautiful gorge in the Siroua Valley with large rock formations.

Saffron, the "red gold" of Morocco, is harvested in the fields around Taliouine, and it's generally recognized as one of the best varieties of saffron in the world. Every side-of-the-road café, auberge, and snack-food joint heaps a generous amount of this delicious spice in every tajine—not to mention couscous, sautéed vegetables, beef brochettes, and omelets—making the average tajine something infinitely more interesting. For a few days in early November, the annual **International Festival of Saffron** is held, featuring art, music, dance, and, of course, food from the region all decked out with saffron.

Shopping

COOPERATIVE SOUKTANA DU SAFRAN

Centre de Taliouine; tel. 0528/534 452; www.souktana.com; daily 8:30am-6:30pm with longer hours often in summer

The Cooperative Souktana du Safran is the oldest running cooperative in the area. Founded in 1979, it works with 154 families in the area to produce eco-friendly saffron of the highest quality. The average gram of saffron will run you about 35Dh. Lovers of this incredible spice will know exactly how inexpensive that is. Tours are available during harvest season. This is the most reputable place in town to buy saffron.

Food and Accommodations

AUBERGE RESTAURANT LE SAFFRON

Centre de Taliouine; tel. 0528/534 046 or 0667/297 142; www.auberge-safran.com; 260Dh

Just along the main road, the Auberge Restaurant le Saffron is a good stop for those passing through. The restaurant serves up the usual Moroccan goods, but with a saffron twist. The saffron omelet tajine is particularly well done. The auberge has rooms available (400Dh) as well as a pool and can arrange for treks into the surrounding Anti-Atlas and Jbel Siroua. The rooms have air-conditioning for the hot summers and panoramic views of the valley.

ESCALE RANDO TALIOUINE

Taliouine Kasbah; tel. 0528/534 600 or 0662/547 828; www.escalerando.com; 260Dh

For a home base in the region, this small, four-room open-patio guesthouse located in the ruins of the old Taliouine kasbah is comfortable enough. The mattresses could all use updating, but the service is friendly to a fault and the beds comfy enough. The real charm here, of course, is staying in the old kasbah. As there are not too many options for eating out in Taliouine, it is worth booking as a full pension (breakfast and lunch), unless you're packing your own food. If you have the time and nature beckons, strongly consider booking a trek here. Their guides are fantastic and will show you some real hidden gems in the region.

Getting There and Around

BY CAR

From **Agadir** (207km/129mi, 3hr) or **Taroudant** (121km/75mi, 1.5hr), you'll likely want to travel to Taliouine by car, as it is not well-serviced with buses and taxis. The N10 follows a valley between the High Atlas and Anti-Atlas mountain ranges and offers some nice views, particularly outside of Taroudant. It's also possible to come from **Ouarzazate** (171km/106mi, 2.5hr) via Tazenakht (84km/52mi, 1hr) along the same national road.

BY GRAND TAXI

Grands taxis run from **Taroudant** (1.5hr, 121km/71mi, 50Dh) and **Tazenakht** (1hr, 84km/52mi, 38Dh) fairly regularly. If it's hot out, consider purchasing two seats for comfort; if there is nobody else traveling, you might have to purchase the entire taxi.

TIZNIT

تزنيت

Tiznit doesn't sport the beaches of Mirleft, Sidi Ifni, or Tan Tan to the south; it's not quite far enough into the Anti-Atlas for some of the stunning rubble mountains that are ubiquitous farther away from the Atlantic; and it doesn't claim to have great souks like Taroudant. What makes Tiznit charming is something of a mystery, and perhaps this is why it might be the next "it" town in Morocco. Its location between the beaches and rocky Anti-Atlas mountains is fantastic, and a few wonderful accommodations make this an ideal location for a home base while you travel this less-explored region of Morocco through a series of day trips.

The old myth of the town revolves around Lalla Zanania. She was a poor but beautiful woman, and the Pasha fell in love with her, which made his wife jealous. The jealous wife arranged for men to come visit Lalla Zanania so it would look as though Lalla Zanania was a prostitute. Because of this, Lalla Zanania was exiled. In her exile, she befriended a dog who began digging into the earth. From the hole he dug, a well sprung up whose source came from an oasis in the desert hundreds of miles away. This is the famed "blue water" of Tiznit. You'll find this fountain, unlike any other in Morocco, right in the center of the old medina.

There are around 80,000 people living in Tiznit with just over 30,000 still calling the old medina home. The medina itself is pleasant to walk around and a touch cleaner than others in Morocco. The relative lack of automobiles and scooters means it lacks the frenetic pace of other medinas. The centuries-old wall of the old city was restored in 2015.

Within it, you'll discover a truly Moroccan medina that is a nice place to go for a stroll. Perhaps Tiznit's true charm lies in the medina and the mellah, these old pieces of Moroccan history where you are free to wander without the aggressive shop owners of some other cities like Marrakesh and Fez.

Sights

TIGMMI N' TAMAZIRT MUSEUM

center of town, next to the Grand Mosque; 70Dh

By the time this guide is published, the museum, located in the old Kasbah Aghenaj, should be open. This will be Morocco's largest museum dedicated to the indigenous peoples of Morocco, the Amazigh. The kasbah was restored by renowned architect Salima Naji, who has done a lot to restore many traditional Amazigh constructions, as well as raise awareness of the continued and historic importance of the Amazigh peoples of Morocco. Written information will likely be in French and Arabic. If you don't have either of these languages, to get the most out of your visit, it's highly recommended to book an English-speaking guide. The curation of the museum itself is wonderful (I got a sneak peek), but the restoration of the old kasbah has been equally incredible. Definitely worth a half-day visit, maybe just after breakfast or included as part of a tour of the medina.

Shopping

While wandering the medina, you'll likely be asked if you're interested in silver or jewelry. If you're not, then a firm "no" is enough (or rather, "*la*," if you're practicing your Darija). However, if you're in the market for some of that chunky tribal Moroccan jewelry, typically with the Hand of Fatima, to ward off the evil eye, or the *tazerzit* (Amazigh fibula) said to bring the *baraka* (blessing), then Tiznit is your place. Silver is sold by the gram (typically around 35Dh a gram) and will be stamped with the number 925. This means that the silver has been approved, checked, and passed through inspection.

BIJOUTERIE DE LA JOIE

35 Kissariat Louban; tel. 0548/862 277; daily, 9am-6pm

Si Mohamed is the honest man running this highly recommended silver shop. He doesn't speak English very well, but still you will quickly understand the difference between newer and older jewelry, as well as the different types of silver that can be had. As always, silver is sold by weight here. You can negotiate, particularly if you're purchasing a few different pieces, but his prices are already very friendly.

Food and Accommodations

The tranquil medina of Tiznit is a fantastic alternative to the medinas of some of the busier Moroccan cities. There are budget hotels to choose from just outside of the medina walls, though cleanliness can often be a problem. For those with a slightly higher budget, it's best to stick to the few *riads* in the medina. If you're staying for a few days in Tiznit and want to change scenery for dining, you can always call any of the *riads* to reserve for lunch or dinner.

L'OMBRE DE FIGUIER

22 Passage Akchouch Idzakri; tel. 0528/861 204; 200Dh

There are enough cafés and restaurants to get a quick bite to eat, though for a meal out the best option is l'Ombre de Figuirer with its outdoor dining options in the interior courtyard. It's best to reserve ahead of time as this is a place that is also, somewhat surprisingly, popular with local teens who come here to sip tea and study. Treat yourself to the succulent calamari, but just watch your head ducking into the door... it's a low one.

HOTEL IDOU

Ave Hassan II, just in front of Bab Ait Jerrar, tel. 0528/600 333, 350Dh d

Hotel Idou is the cleanest option of the budget hotels just outside the medina walls. It's a 1970s hotel that could stand to use some updating, but for the price, it's a good option for couples on a budget. The pool in the garden is refreshing and the staff are incredibly kind.

MAISON DU SOLEIL

470 Rue Tafoukt; tel. 0528/601 244; 500Dh d

At Maison du Soleil, the expansive sun terrace is alive with plants looked after by Hassan, the resident green thumb. This is really the place to be: the rooms are cozy (though lacking Wi-Fi, really only dependable in the common areas) and the staff, led by Slimane, super helpful. Breakfast is included and dinner is possible, though book ahead so they have time to shop at the souk for the freshest ingredients. It's well located right in the heart of the medina, just a few minutes by foot from the local markets.

★ RIAD JANOUB

193 Rue de la Grande Mosquée; tel. 0528/602 726; www.riadjanoub.com; 750Dh d

If you're looking to really make the most of your stay, Riad Janoub offers surprisingly opulent five-star treatment for about half the cost, complete with a swimming pool, hammam, and discreet massage room. *Tadelahkt* finishing, cement tiles, and locally crafted furniture all add to the charm of this veritable oasis. The boutique hotel, owned now by Pria (a British/Indian) and Aby (a Belgian/Moroccan), both anglophones, has really turned into something special. Aby will happily give you tips on getting around the medina and can arrange some incredible, one-of-a-kind day trips for you. He actually grew up in the region before moving to Belgium, so he knows a lot of undiscovered beautiful corners that most travelers don't get to visit. And if you're looking for some different dining option, the staff can whip you up a curry that will compete with the best in London, making for a great alternative to those ubiquitous Moroccan staples. Air-conditioning, heating, Wi-Fi, television, and breakfast are all included with your stay.

RIAD TIGMI KENZA

30 Rue Hay al-Mourabitine; tel. 0528/600 362 or 0666/203 054; www.tigmi-kenza.com; 800Dh d

For couples really wanting to spoil themselves, one could do worse than Riad Tigmi Kenza. The charm of this renovated, traditional Moroccan house is unmatched for sheer quaintness in the region. The staff will bend over backward for you, going so far as to purchase your bus tickets for you and even take you to the station. Quiet and intimate, with just four bedrooms and three suites, this is a place to spend a long weekend away from just about everything and be pampered for a bit. If the budget allows, go for one of the suites (1,100DH) for a super romantic getaway. Wi-Fi, air-conditioning, heating, television, and breakfast are all included.

Information and Services

There are banks, cafés, pharmacies, and restaurants outside the medina, alongside Avenue Hassan II and the R104 on the way to Mirleft and Sidi Ifni. You will find the post office next to the *grand taxi* stand, on Avenue Mohammed V and Avenue du 20 Août.

Getting There and Around

BY CAR

From **Agadir** (163km/101mi, 2.5hr), you can easily get to Tiznit by car following the N1 south. This is the beginning of two possible southern driving routes from Agadir. The coastal loop runs west from Tiznit to **Mirleft** (45km/28mi, 30min) and south down the coast to **Sidi Ifni** (73km/45mi, 1hr) before cutting back inland to **Guelmim** (110km/68mi, 1.5hr). It's possible to continue south to **Tan Tan** (237km/147mi, 3hr) and the Western Sahara. The inland loop through the Anti-Atlas branches east along the R104 to **Tafraoute** (107km/66mi, 1.5hr) and **Taliouine** (303km/188mi, 3.5hr) before turning back to Taroudant and returning to Agadir or forking east to **Ouarzazate** (440km/273mi, 7.5hr) along the N10.

BY BUS AND GRAND TAXI

CTM (tel. 0800/0900 30, www.ctm.ma) runs buses from **Agadir** (1.5hr, 9 daily, 40Dh), **Mirleft** (1hr, 1 daily, 20Dh), **Sidi Ifni** (1.5hr, 3 daily, 30Dh), **Guelmim** (2hr, 9 daily, 45Dh), **Tan Tan** (3hr, 9 daily, 95Dh), **Laayoune** (8.5hr, 9 daily, 200Dh), and **Dakhla** (17hr, 5 daily, 370Dh).

Supratours (tel. 0524/888 566 or 0524/885 632, www.oncf.ma) operates the buses affiliated with the national train line, ONCF. Buses run from **Agadir** to **Tiznit** (1.5hr, 6 daily, 50Dh), **Guelmim** (2hr, 6 daily, 50Dh), **Tan Tan** (3hr, 3 daily, 100Dh), and **Laayoune** (8.5hr, 5 daily, 220Dh).

Grands taxis regularly shuttle to **Agadir** (1.5hr, 92km/57mi, 32Dh), **Mirleft** (30min, 45km/28mi, 22Dh), **Guelmim** (1.5hr, 110km/68mi, 55Dh), and **Tafraoute** (1.5hr, 107km/66mi, 55Dh).

TAFRAOUTE

تافراوت

Tahir Shah, the famed writer of *The Caliph's House,* a story that chronicles his family's move to Casablanca, once said that in Tafraoute, he found the "secluded scrap of paradise" he'd been looking for. After arriving through a twisting, turning route through the Anti-Atlas mountains, it's easy to see why. Tafraoute is still very much a secluded oasis town, locked in granite cliffs in the middle of the Anti-Atlas, and popular with world-class rock climbers who come here for the challenging rock formations seemingly everywhere. Tafraoute can either be an interesting day trip from Agadir or, for those really wishing to travel back in time, a place where you could imagine staying for a few weeks, getting to know the friendly locals and maybe taking up rock climbing for good measure.

Along the two main roads connecting at the roundabout with the gas station and the pharmacy, there are several cafés and snack restaurants, as well as a more lively souk, which takes place every Wednesday. For real cultural immersion, there are few better places than Tafraoute, with its friendly community and honest shopkeepers.

Festivals and Events

ALMOND BLOSSOM FESTIVAL

Feb.

During the annual February Almond Blossom Festival, Tafraoute is transformed into a riot of pink-and-white almond blossoms. The Almond Blossom Festival sees villagers celebrate harvest time with Berber dancing, singing, and almond tasting. International musicians and actors mingle with local performers to produce live events. The festival generally occurs during the second week of February, but check on arrival to make sure of the dates.

Food and Accommodations

Cafés on the main road are suitable for a quick bite. During the Almond Blossom Festival, the few accommodations in town can fill up quickly, so it's best to call ahead for reservations. Accommodations are generally basic in the region, without any high-end options, though a few developments may be in the works. Currently, this makes for a really good stop for budget travelers and campers.

CHEZ SABIR

41 Rte. Ammeln; tel. 0666/419 968; 50Dh

Chez Sabir, tucked off the main streets, serves the tastiest tajine in town. You'll likely want to ask a local exactly how to get here. Abdellatif Bakrim, hailing from a long line of chefs, has turned his home into a restaurant where many Moroccan staples, such as *harira*, get a home-made touch. Come for the beef tajine, but don't skimp out on the Moroccan salads, including his wonderful *zallouk*, an eggplant and olive oil-based Moroccan specialty.

HOTEL SALAMA

Centre Ville, on the main road; tel. 0528/800 026; www.hotelsalama.com; 250Dh d

Hotel Salama has clean, comfortable rooms with private terraces that look out over the main road. The rooms toward the back are a bit quieter, though Tafraoute is generally a quiet town. The hotel is in a *riad* formation, with a shared central courtyard illuminated by stained-glass windows. The restaurant serves breakfast (20Dh) as well as lunch and dinner (50Dh). For those staying multiple nights, discounts are available, but you might have to bargain.

L'ARGANIER D'AMMELNE

Junction R105; tel. 0661/926 064 or 0528/800 069; www.arganierammelne.com; 500Dh d

Just 4 kilometers (2.5mi) north of Tafraoute is L'Arganier d'Ammelne, a budget hotel that caters to the European camper van crowd, though the rooms are perfectly adequate and have surprisingly nice bathrooms. A terrace has spectacular views over the Anti-Atlas, making this a great dining spot when the winds have died down. The *harira* is one of the better soups in the region and shouldn't be missed. The pool is nice for relaxing, especially after a long hike. Breakfast, Wi-Fi, and air-conditioning are included with your stay in this nonsmoking establishment.

★ EL MELARA

1 Route de Rochier Peints; tel. 0658/181 836 or 0695/909 292; www.elmalara.com; 500Dh d

Just a few kilometers out of Tafraoute, this is the kind of place you imagine when you think about getting away from it all. Something of a stone castle, taken from the region, this small guesthouse with eight large guest rooms hits all the right notes. Two generous suites are perfect for a couples' escape, while adventurous families will appreciate the easy access to some wonderful hiking, and kids will love the on-site pool. Friendly, festive, with a wonderful menu featuring Morocco classics taken from around the entire country, selected and adapted to a more international palate by Bernadette and Jean, the French owners, as well as Ahmed, their resident chef. Depending on the weather and time of year, meals might be served indoors, on one of three terraces, or poolside. Rooms are well heated and air-conditioned, making this a cozy, comfy place to rest your bones any time of year.

Getting There and Around

BY CAR

From **Agadir** (163km/101mi, 2.5hr), you'll likely want to travel to Tafraoute by car, as it is not well-serviced with buses and taxis. The quickest route from Agadir takes you south on the R105 through Ait Baha. It is possible to also drive via the R104 from **Tiznit** (107km/66mi, 1.5hr). However, one of the prettiest drives in the Anti-Atlas follows along the R106 from **Taliouine** (197km/122mi, 3hr), making driving a loop from **Agadir** and including **Tiznit, Tafraoute, Taliouine,** and **Taroudant** a stunning possibility.

BY GRAND TAXI AND BUS

Grands taxis run from **Agadir** (2.5hr, 163km/101mi, 70Dh) fairly regularly. If it's hot out, consider purchasing two seats for comfort, and if there is nobody else traveling, you might have to purchase the entire taxi. There are also taxis from **Tiznit** (1.5hr, 107km/66mi, 55Dh). **CTM** (tel. 0800/0900 30, www.ctm.ma) runs one daily bus from Agadir (6.5hr, 1 daily, 80Dh) and Tiznit (2.5hr, 1 daily, 40Dh).

MIRLEFT

ميرلفت

At first glance, Mirleft doesn't seem like much. It's little more than a rural Moroccan coastal town. Women are rarely seen on the streets, often working in the fields or at home with the children instead. Activity focuses on the main road cutting through town, with a few restaurants and dusty cafés. However, just a couple of minutes off the main street, toward the coast, there are other dining options as well as the reason why anyone escapes to a place like Mirleft—the beach.

Surfers have made their way to Mirleft, making use of the cove and regular swells. Most people traveling this section of highway pass Mirleft and make way for Sidi Ifni, but if you want to really get away, Mirleft is one of the hidden gems along this stretch. The big hotel chains have skipped this town, instead focusing their energies on Essaouira and Agadir, which means that the hotels are generally the work of individuals with a passion for the area, something any traveler can appreciate, with some wonderful deals to be had for accommodation. All of this makes Mirleft a great option for travelers looking to stretch their funds as far as possible.

Food and Accommodations

★ MIRLEFT SOUL HOSTEL

Derban, Mirleft Center; tel. 0659/299 778; http://mirleftsoulhostel.com; 60Dh for a dorm bed

One of the best hostels along this stretch of Morocco, the Mirleft Soul Hostel has quickly become a go-to spot for backpackers and surfers. Just steps away from one of the most popular beaches in the region and a short walk from the local markets and cafés, this is an awesome place to hole up for a few days and chill. Small groups of friends and families should check into the Berber-style tent to wake up with incredible ocean views. Breakfast, Wi-Fi, sheets, and towels are included, and Moroccan mint tea is free all day long.

SALLY'S BED & BREAKFAST

Mirleft les Amicales; tel. 0528/719 402; www.sallymirleft.com; 600Dh d

If awards were given for coziness, Sally's Bed & Breakfast would easily take it. Sally has a warm welcome for everyone, while her parrot, Bella, might have a few other choice words for you, and the dog, Moggy, will be happy with a scratch behind the ear. Located on a cliffside overlooking the Atlantic, the location is unbeatable with a good-size terrace for a little sunbathing, and it's a short walk to restaurants and cafés in town. The *tadelakt* bath can do wonders to restore your spirits, while the copious breakfast spread will make sure you start the day off on the right foot. All rooms (there are five) have en suite bathrooms and Wi-Fi connectivity (always a concern). For those coming for a longer stay or for small families, consider the Studio Room for some living space and a private terrace.

DAR NAJMAT

Plage Sidi Mohammed Ben Abdallah; tel. 0528,719 056; www.darnajmat.com; 1,400Dh d

Opened in 2016, this French-run boutique hotel has quickly garnered a reputation for hospitality and exquisite taste. Subdued creams and beiges blend with authentic Moroccan touches for an understated sort of elegance that seems to be a specialty of French decor. At Dar Najmat, all rooms have a safety deposit box, while some offer a terrace and private kitchens, perfect for longer stays or for families with kids. It's not usually a concern along the coast, but not all of the rooms are air-conditioned, so this is worth asking about. A continental breakfast is included and there is Wi-Fi in the public areas, which include an infinity pool, terrace, and garden. Local excursions, including via 4x4 to the "white beach," can also be arranged. Massages using local argan oil are also available upon request.

★ KASBAH TABELKOUKT

R104, 4km south of Mirleft; tel. 0524/387 567; www.kasbah-tabelkoukt.com; 1,600Dh d

Of the more upscale options, the Kasbah Tabelkoukt is the premier choice, particularly for couples looking for a little romantic getaway. In fact, shortly after opening, Kasbah Tabelkoukt was awarded the prestigious *Palme d'Or de l'Excellence et du Prestige*, an award carefully selected by the International Tourism Board. The rooms are all opulent, though for this category, the African room with the private terrace looking out to sunsets over the Atlantic is where it's at. The secluded beach ensures a good amount of privacy (particularly in comparison to the other local beaches). Of course, if the saltwater proves to be too much, the courtyard swimming pool with lounge chairs is a perfect alternative for a little sun-worshipping.

1: auberge Dar Najmat in Mirleft **2:** traditional silver jewelry in Tiznit

1
2

It's everything you would expect from a bespoke resort, though the feeling is more familial. Carved Marrakeshi doors and fireplaces in every room for those cool Atlantic evenings are just some of the touches that make this an outstanding retreat. Dinners are a touch expensive (250Dh), but you'll forget the price as soon as the chef puts down the bisque-style fish soup with aioli. The restaurant matches the hotel for tasteful grandeur.

Getting There and Around

BY CAR

From **Agadir** (142km/88mi, 2hr), you can easily get to **Mirleft** via **Tiznit** (45km/28mi, 30min) by car following the N1 south and then turning onto R104 at Tiznit. This is the beginning of a possible driving loop following the coastal road down to **Sidi Ifni** (28km/17mi, 30min) before cutting back inland into **Guelmim** (93km/58mi, 2hr).

BY GRAND TAXI

Grands taxis run regularly to and from **Sidi Ifni** (30min, 28km/17mi, 18Dh) and **Tiznit** (30min, 45km/28mi, 22Dh). **CTM** (tel. 0800/0900 30, www.ctm.ma) runs a daily bus from **Agadir** (1hr, 1 daily, 20Dh).

SIDI IFNI

سيدي إفني

The primary economic driver of the laid-back village of Sidi Ifni is fishing, easily observed by the relatively new fishing port and hassle-free atmosphere, though you'll likely see a fair bit of surfers throughout the season (roughly Nov.-Apr.).

The general vibe of Sidi Ifni stands in stark contrast to Mirleft, just a few minutes by car up the beach. Whereas Mirleft is decidedly more reserved, perhaps more influenced by the Amazigh who have settled here, Sidi Ifni is much more laid-back, a mix of influence from the Saharoui and its recent history hosting Spaniards. Today, a few expats have been lured to this quiet beach town, a bit farther from the more crowded cities of Marrakesh and Essaouira. You're more likely to hear Spanish from the locals here, due to intermittent Spanish rule until 1969. The cafés are vibrant and, notably, you'll see many more women around, often on the sidewalks taking their tea together, talking with friends and family, adding to the friendly, intercultural feeling.

The downtown has a distinct colonial air, with old blue-and-white-painted Spanish-era administrative buildings, including a former church (now courts of law), town hall, and Spanish consulate circled around the Plaza de España (now the Place Hassan II, though nobody calls it that). There is a short sloping terrace to the north overlooking the beach with a series of cafés that are good for a light breakfast or to take in the sunset.

Just outside of the Spanish old town lies the main market and a strip of cafés and places for a quick bite to eat. As in other Moroccan cities, there are new buildings popping up that spread out around the hillside and down the coastline. The beach, though sometimes not the cleanest, is one of the quieter stretches in the area and a great place to get away from it all.

Surfing

Sidi Ifni is growing in popularity with the surf crowd. For beginners looking to learn how to surf, this is generally a less-crowded alternative to Taghazoute.

IFNI SURF

47 Ave. Moualy Youssef; tel. 0662/533 717; www.ifnisurf.com; lessons from 200Dh, gear rental from 150Dh

Ifni Surf operates a fine surf camp, with lessons and packages for all skill levels starting at 200Dh and gear rental at 150Dh. You can also try **Camino Surf Camp** (www.camino-surf.com/en/surfcamp-morocco) at the Hotel Safa in the Spanish District by the hospital. They have great English-speaking guides with a variety of instructors from Europe and Morocco.

Food and Accommodations

HOTEL SUERTE LOCAL

7 rue Saffrou; tel. 0528/8745 350; sutereloca36@yahoo.com; 160Dh d

Replete with Spanish tile work and done up, like most of the town, in blues and whites, this hotel and restaurant has been a staple of Sidi Ifni since 1936, during the Spanish Protectorate era. Clean lodgings, with a rooftop terrace that's perfect for having breakfast or sipping on a cocktail. Wi-Fi is available, as are breakfast, lunch, and dinner. Demi-pension for two people (breakfast and dinner) is 370Dh. Though the lodgings are nice, the real treat is the restaurant featuring some Moroccan favorites, including *harira* (10Dh) and a deliciously spicy fish soup (15Dh), as well as Spanish staples, such as paella (55Dh) and seafood done *a la plancha* (55Dh).

IFNI SURF

47 Ave. Moulay Youssef; tel. 0662/533 717; www.ifnisurf.com; 320Dh d

For the basics, Ifni Surf offers comfy lodging with beachfront seats for surfing, beach bumming, watching crimson sunsets, and plunging your toes into the sand. Rooms are clean, if not bordering on sterile, but the terrace with the available kitchen makes for friendly encounters with other travelers. Breakfast and Wi-Fi are included. Dinner is available (70Dh), as is lunch (40Dh), served up by Asmaa, the friendly chef from Tangier.

★ HOTEL SAFA

Boulevard de Caire; tel. 0528/780 929; www.hotel-safa.com; 450Dh d

Located right in the heart of the old Spanish city of Sidi Ifni, Hotel Safa is the largest hotel in the region, though it still manages to have personal service. A known surfer hub for years, this hotel usually has rooms available even at the last minute. The bright yellow walls, exposed brick, and general layout of the hotel belay its Spanish origins. The rooms here are simple but clean, with comfy beds, hot showers, and private terraces. For the price, you won't find a better deal in the region. Singles will have a slight discount (300Dh). You can also try negotiating the price if you are staying for a few days. Often you can get a discount if they aren't full. The attached supermarket downstairs is handy for picking up picnic and road-trip essentials. Surfers can find the Camino Surf Camp across from the hotel reception. Wi-Fi and breakfast are included with your stay.

LOGIS LA MARINE

1 Ave. Prince Moulay Abdallah; tel. 0641/766 096; www.logislamarine.com; 600Dh d

Logis la Marine looks exactly like you'd want an art deco beachfront house to look like: spacious, lots of white with the occasional pop detail, plush leather couches, and a design that takes full advantage of the views out over the ocean. The rooftop terrace is perfect for catching a little sun. The rooms are immaculate, with lots of white linens and creamy beiges. Breakfast and free Wi-Fi are included with your stay. The guesthouse itself is quaint, with only a few rooms, and quickly building a local reputation for great service and quality, so be sure to book your stay ahead of time.

Getting There and Around

BY CAR

By car from **Agadir** (163km/101mi, 2.5hr), you'll pass through **Tiznit** (73km/45mi, 1hr) and **Mirleft** (28km/17mi, 30min) on your way, following the N1 south and then turning onto R104 at Tiznit. From **Sidi Ifni**, National Road 12 (N12) runs to **Guelmim** (65km/40mi, 1.5hr) and merges with the N1. This is a beautiful coastal drive, though of course be wary of night driving. Via **Guelmim,** the N1 dips farther south to **Tan Tan** (193km/119mi, 3hr) and **Laayoune** (504km/313mi, 6.5hr) or heads north toward **Tiznit** and **Agadir.**

BY BUS AND GRAND TAXI

Grands taxis run back and forth to **Mirleft** (30min, 28km/17mi, 18Dh), **Tiznit** (1hr, 73km/45mi, 40Dh), and **Guelmim** (1.5hr,

65km/40mi, 50Dh). **CTM** (tel. 0800/0900 30, www.ctm.ma) runs daily buses from **Agadir** (3.5hr, 3 daily, 70Dh) through **Tiznit** (1.5hr, 3 daily, 40Dh).

TAN TAN AND EL OUATIA (TAN TAN PLAGE)

طانطان and العربي

When people generally talk about going to Tan Tan, they mean Tan Tan Plage, not the fairly deserted town of Tan Tan just a short drive away on the N1, though this is where most of the buses and taxis will drop you off. There is little to do in Tan Tan outside of the Sunday souk. The place known as **Tan Tan Plage** is actually called **El Ouatia,** a small village with a charming fishing port just south of Tan Tan on the N1. You're coming here for the amazing beaches, though surfers can catch some waves while those interested in fishing can find some luck casting with the locals. Ask your hotel about tips for casting with local fishermen: corbine, sea bream, and bars are the daily catch.

Food and Accommodations

Most of the accommodations in this region are somewhat disappointing. Either you pay a lot and you don't get the services available in other parts of Morocco, or you don't pay much and receive little in return. Little has been done in the way of pensions, hostels, or boutique *riads* or internationally geared hotels. Most of the tourism seems aimed toward Moroccan families who rent apartments for their summer vacations, reminiscent of beach towns like Martil in the north of the country.

HOTEL HAGOUNIA

Hay Ettakadoum Ave. el Wahda, El Ouatia; tel. 0528/830 783; 300Dh d

The Hotel Hagounia is basic, and sometimes basic is just fine. The rooms are a bit cramped, though the beds are perfectly comfortable. Small, private terraces have views over the port, and breakfast is included with your stay. Lunch and dinner are also available on request. Wi-Fi is available, and the showers are wonderfully hot after a long day in the sand.

KSAR TAFNIDILT

N 28o32'775,W 010o59'569; tel. 0663/233 115; www.tafnidilt.com; 750Dh d

First things first: Ksar Tafnidilt is not an easy place to find on your own (refer to the GPS coordinates above). This is a more authentic *ksar* geared for those really looking to get away from it all. Though you're just about 20 kilometers (12mi) from Tan Tan, you'll feel like you're a world away. The location, for those craving a true taste of the desert, is a haven. However, because of its remoteness and reliance on its own generator for electricity, the power is cut at night (usually around 11pm) and doesn't come back on until morning. Make sure you charge your battery packs and phones before "lights out." But wow … when the lights are out, the sky glitters with a million stars. All around are different hikes for trekkers, advanced and beginner, which can be done by yourself or with a guide (around 400Dh for a day). The famed white sand beach is a short drive away and the pool is a real luxury, particularly in the midst of a hot day. Consider booking online for deals around half the listed price on their website. Breakfast and dinner (demi-pension) are included with your stay.

Getting There and Around

BY CAR

This is about as far south as most travelers drive. Those wishing to explore the long, dusty strip of the Western Sahara should continue along the N1, heading to out-of-the-way **Tarfaya** (212km/131mi, 3hr) before plunging into the Western Sahara city of **Laayoune** (311km/193mi, 4hr) and more farther afield **Dakhla** (840km/521mi, 10hr). Though you can make it directly from **Agadir** (333km/207mi, 4.5hr) in a day via the N1, consider a stopover along the coast at **Mirleft** (220km/137mi, 3.5hr) or **Sidi Ifni**

(193km/120mi, 3hr), or even the inland souk town of **Tiznit** (237km/147mi, 3hr) to break up the drive.

BY GRAND TAXI AND BUS

Grands taxis run back and forth from Tan Tan to El Ouatia/Tan Tan Plage (30min, 25km/15mi, 18Dh) quite regularly, as well as from Tan Tan to **Guelmim** (1.5hr, 128km/79mi, 45Dh).

CTM (tel. 0800/0900 30, www.ctm.ma) runs buses to Tan Tan from **Agadir** (5.5hr, 9 daily, 130Dh) through **Tiznit** (3hr, 9 daily, 95Dh) and **Guelmim** (1.5hr, 15 daily, 50Dh). **Laayoune** (5hr, 11 daily, 130Dh) and **Dakhla** (14hr, 5 daily, 300Dh) are possible destinations continuing south. **Supratours** (tel. 0524/888 566 or 0524/885 632, www.oncf.ma) also runs buses to Tan Tan from **Agadir** (5.5hr, 3 daily, 120Dh), **Tiznit** (3hr, 3 daily, 100Dh), **Guelmim** (1.5hr, 11 daily, 60Dh), and **Laayoune** (5.5hr, 5 daily, 140Dh).

Rabat and the North Atlantic Coast

If Casablanca is the New York of Morocco, Rabat is its Washington DC. Many travelers consider this city a real overlooked gem.

An hour north of Casablanca along the Atlantic Coast, Rabat is the political hub and home of the king of Morocco, Mohammed VI, as well as various ministries, dignitaries, and embassies. When the French invaded Morocco in 1912 to establish a protectorate, General Hubert Lyautey had the capital of Morocco moved from unruly Fez back to the old Almohad capital of Rabat, where it remains today. It was under French rule that the Ville Nouvelle was constructed, making it an administrative headquarters as it is now.

Rabat is the cleanest of all the major cities in Morocco with a

Highlights

Look for ★ to find recommended sights, activities, dining, and lodging.

★ **Oudaïas Kasbah:** Take an afternoon stroll through this ancient fortress. Enjoy the Andalusian Gardens, sip on mint tea at Café Maure, and take in the Atlantic from the expansive terrace that once protected the town from invaders (page 124).

★ **Hassan Tower:** If 12th-century caliph Moulay Yacoub had had his way, this tower would have been the tallest minaret in the world. Though it was never finished, it remains a landmark of Almohad-era architecture (page 130).

★ **MMVI Contemporary Art Museum:** This 2014 addition to Rabat cements the city's reputation as the new cultural center of Morocco. Check out what Moroccan artists have been doing for the last 100 years (page 132).

★ **Chellah Necropolis:** The oldest known settlement along the Bouregreg River is one of the best-preserved ruins in all of Morocco, with Roman, Almohad, and Merenid-era architecture all on display (page 132).

★ **Oulja Artisan Cooperative:** Spend a day at this cooperative, the largest and most pleasurable in Morocco, shopping for pottery, antique furniture, and *zellij* fountains (page 153).

★ **Merja Zerga National Park:** Head here during migrating season (Oct.-Mar.) and take a boat tour through the "blue lagoon" to see migrating pink flamingos (page 157).

★ **Lixus:** One of the few Roman amphitheaters in Africa is here, as well as one of the less-excavated ruins in Morocco, offering plenty of afternoon fun for history buffs and archaeology geeks (page 162).

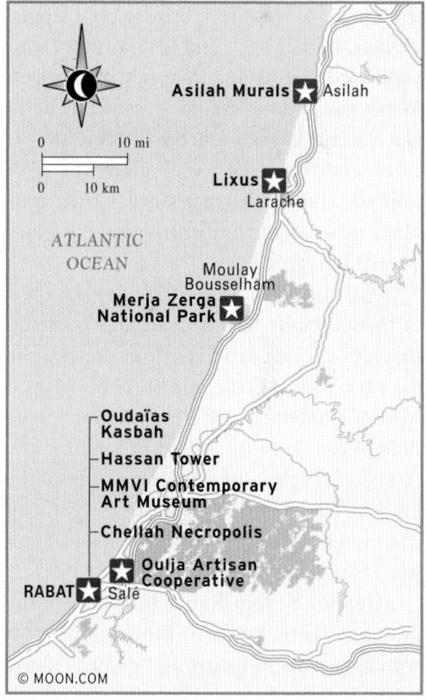

★ **Asilah Murals:** One of the cleanest, most vibrant medinas in Morocco is covered with murals that change every summer during the annual art festival (page 166).

vibe that leans more European, particularly around the downtown corridor. Cafés line the streets and there is a fine selection of international restaurants alongside a mix of languages—German, French, Arabic, and English—commonly overheard when out and about. With wide sidewalks and boulevards, friendly *petit taxi* drivers, and a tram to help commuters scoot around to the major destinations of Rabat and nearby Salé, it's also probably the easiest city in the kingdom to navigate.

Like most other Moroccan cities, Rabat has a medina. However, unlike most medinas in other cities around the country, it is situated on a grid, and prices here are all generally fixed, so you can stroll down the Rue des Consuls and enjoy the most hassle-free medina in all of Morocco. Browse the teapots, carpets, leather bags, and various other souvenirs without having to haggle over prices. When you're done shopping, continue up to the ancient kasbah, once a fortress for pirates, and then take a walk along the river and watch the fishermen display their glittery catches along the picture-perfect estuary of the Bouregreg River.

While in Rabat, make time to visit a few of the museums. The Archaeology Museum displays various artifacts from pre-Islamic dig sites, such as Lixus, and the newly opened MMVI Contemporary Art Museum, a true delight for those interested in modern art. And don't neglect the crumbling ruins of the Chellah Necropolis. If you plan it right, you can even listen to some world-renowned jazz musicians jam in these spectacular ruins.

Stretching from Rabat to Tangier, the North Atlantic Coast of Morocco offers a wonderful mix of nature and quaint fishing towns that dot the coast. During the month of August, Moroccans flock to the beaches to soak up the sun. Before and after August, some of these popular beaches are virtually abandoned. Don't be surprised if you find yourself all alone on a long stretch of beach or alongside casting fishermen in Moulay Bousselham. Outside of the summer months, this coastline transforms into the perfect place to get away from it all. Birders will want to make sure they catch a boat out on the lagoon in the Merja Zerga National Park to catch the migratory flocks stopping over here.

For those with an interest in ruins, this region is particularly rich. The history of this region is rife with myth and legend. Hercules is rumored to have completed his 11th labor here, fetching the "golden apples" from the Hesperides Garden at Lixus, and it was through the imposing Bab Mrisa that Robinson Crusoe sailed when he was taken captive by the Salé Rovers, the feared pirates of Salé. Amazigh tribes were likely the first inhabitants of the region. The Phoenicians, Carthaginians, Romans, early Moroccan dynasties, and Portuguese have all left evidence of their periods of power. You can visit the neglected ruins of Lixus with commanding views of the city of Larache and the Loukkos River, as well as the less-visited ruins of Banasa. However, for most, a stroll through the Portuguese walls of Asilah and into one of the smallest and most beautiful medinas in all of Morocco is among the most pleasurable experiences to be had along the North Atlantic Coast.

PLANNING YOUR TIME

Rabat is a city perhaps best visited toward the end of your stay. Only then will you truly be able to appreciate its stark contrast with the rest of the larger cities in Morocco. There are enough sights, museums, and activities to keep you busy for two or three days. Spend some time wandering the wide boulevards of the **Ville Nouvelle** and winding passages of the **Oudaïas Kasbah.** The neighboring city of **Salé** is just a few minutes by tram or ferry boat across the **Bouregreg River,** making it an easy day trip.

Previous: a girl running through the Rabat Oudaïas Kasbah; the Rabat Andalusian Gardens of the kasbah; the Chellah Necropolis of Rabat.

Rabat and the North Atlantic Coast

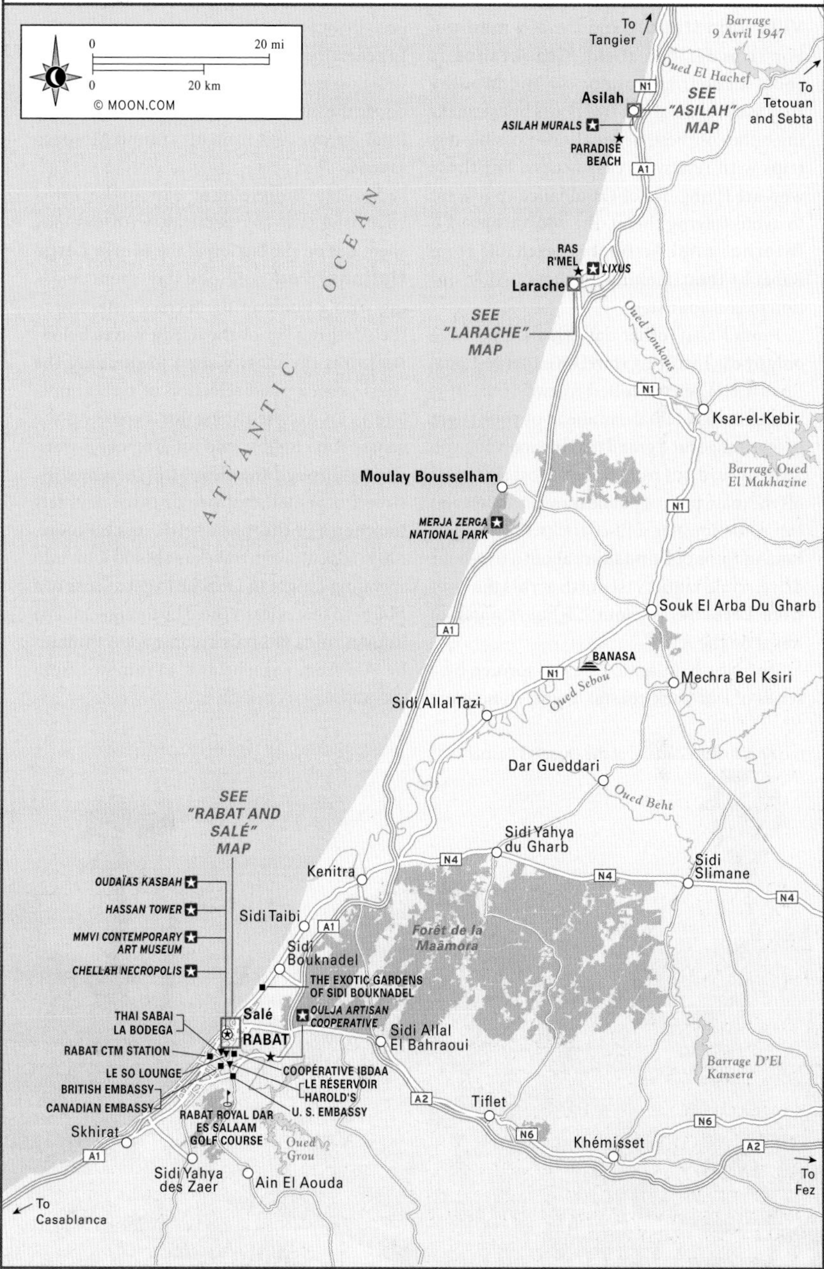

For getting around Rabat, the new **tram** services the nearby city of Salé, the generally calmer beaches of **Temara,** the **Rabat-Ville train station,** and the **old medina.** For trips farther afield, **Casablanca** is about an hour by train or car and **Moulay Bousselham** is about two hours by car, making either of these destinations possible day trips with relatively easy access. For those who are flying out of Casablanca (but want to avoid staying there), the **Mohammed V International Airport** is reachable from Rabat by train, making Rabat a possible option to end your stay.

From Rabat, other day trips are possible only by car, involving travel on either National Road 1 (N1) or the tolled freeway (A1). It is best to book a rental car ahead of your flight or to arrange for a *grand taxi* the morning you want to head out from Rabat. Most sights are off the main path of public transportation and can sometimes be a little tricky to find. The Roman ruins of **Banasa** are about a two-hour drive, while **Lixus,** just north across the river from **Larache,** is about 2.5 hours north of Rabat on the A1.

The North Atlantic Coast is formed by a series of laid-back coastal towns, some more developed than others. This is the region in which to relax with a good book, enjoy majestic sunsets, and mingle with the locals, especially outside of the busy summer months. In general, you'll want to avoid the traditional vacation month of August in this region to dodge the summer crowds who come not only from Europe, but from all around Morocco as well.

Moulay Bousselham can make for a charming two-day getaway, with one day spent out on the lagoon at the **Merja Zerga National Park** and one day spent relaxing with a book on the terrace listening to the soothing lap of the ocean waves below. **Asilah** is the most visited town along the coast, with a good selection of restaurants, and is an excellent base for exploring the coast. You could spend an afternoon wandering through the clean, frescoed medina streets of Asilah, but two or three days lets the charm of this place settle in a bit more. More adventurous travelers should look into spending a night in Larache to get a sense of a Morocco that is less-visited by foreigners. The Roman ruins of Lixus are just a few minutes by taxi from Larache and 45 minutes from Asilah.

the Andalusian Gardens of the Ouadïas Kasbah

Itinerary Ideas

RABAT AND SALÉ IN TWO DAYS

If you're flying in and out of Casablanca, it can make a lot of sense to spend your last couple of nights in Rabat. This is a great city for picking up last-minute souvenirs, and there are plenty of options for foodies.

Day 1

1 After a large, Moroccan-style breakfast at your *riad,* perhaps **Dar Shâan,** leave around 9:30am. You'll want to remember to wear a good pair of walking shoes and sunscreen.

2 Take a *petit taxi* to the **Chellah Necropolis** to beat the crowds (and the sun). Whether or not you take a guided tour, plan on spending 1.5-2 hours touring the ruins.

3 On your walk back from Chellah, escape the heat inside the **MMVI Contemporary Art Museum** and spend about an hour enjoying modern art.

4 Head over to **La Veranda** to relax on the terrace and enjoy a French bistro-inspired lunch and a cool glass of chardonnay.

5 Put on your sunscreen and make your way to the **Hassan Tower.** Remember to pay respects to the mausoleum of Mohammed V and Hassan II, the grandfather and father, respectively, of the reigning king of Morocco.

6 Stroll downhill to the riverside, pick up a gelato, and take a boat over to **Salé.** Spend the rest of the afternoon exploring the little-visited **medina** of Salé, including the incredible **Medersa Abu al-Hassan.**

7 For dinner, dine at **Le Repose** in Salé for one of the most creative Moroccan-vegetarian fusion menus in the country.

8 Take the tram over the river and back into Rabat. Consider a cocktail at the **Grand Comptoir** on your way back.

Day 2

1 For your last day in Rabat, keep it relaxed and start your day off with a Moroccan hammam. Consider doing it like a local at **Hammam Marassa.**

2 After your hammam, lunch at **Tajine Wa Tanjia** for an authentically delicious Moroccan meal. If it's a Friday, indulge in the couscous.

3 After lunch, wander through the **medina,** maybe get a little lost, and pick up any of those last-minute souvenirs.

4 Take a quiet stroll through the **Andalusian Gardens** in the kasbah and have a tea with a cookie or two at **Café Maure.**

5 Just before sunset, head up to the **kasbah terrace,** breathe in the ocean air, and take a photo to capture the setting sun.

6 For dinner, it's just a short walk to **Dar Naji,** where a veritable feast awaits. Walk off dinner through the medina and back to your *riad* for the night, but before turning in, enjoy the terrace views and the relative quiet of old Moroccan living.

Rabat and Salé in Two Days

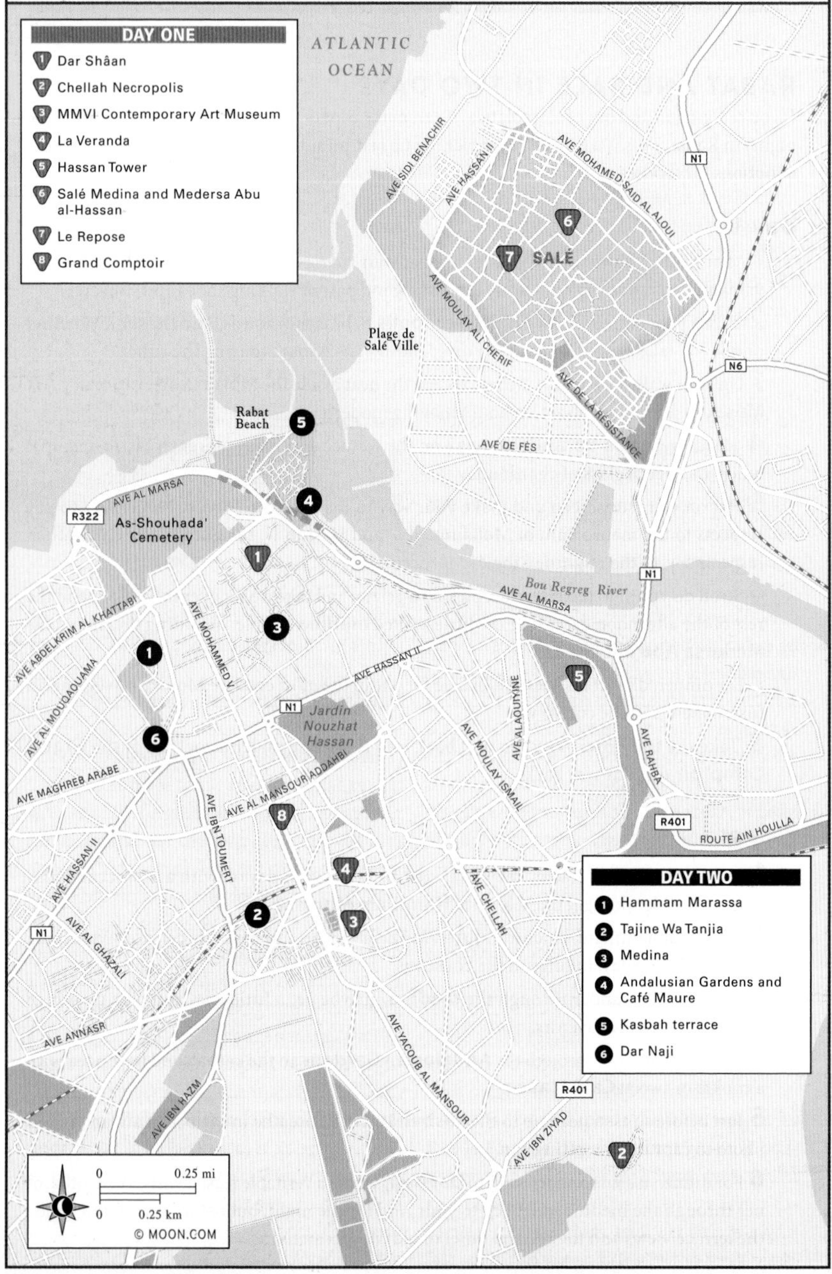

Day Trip to Moulay Bousselham

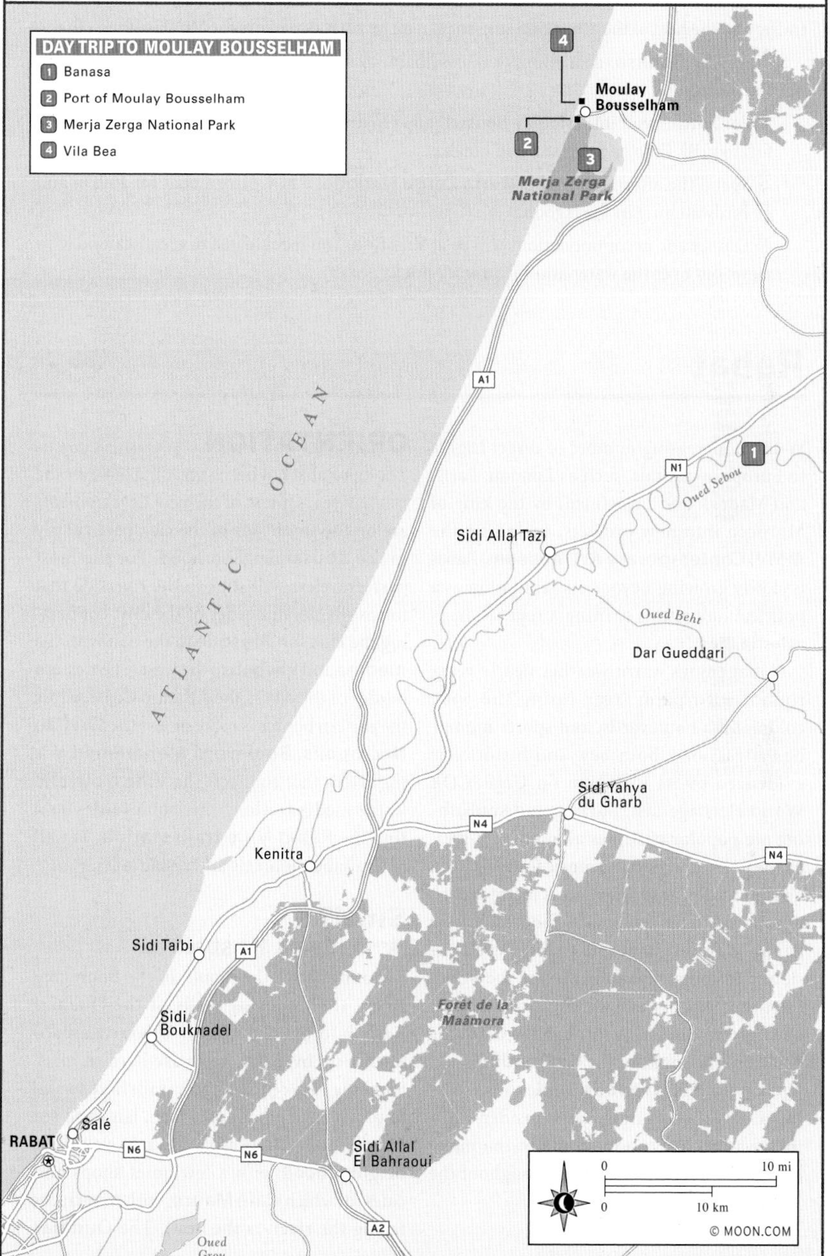

DAY TRIP TO MOULAY BOUSSELHAM

Moulay Bousselham is an easy drive north from Rabat, though you could also consider taking a combination of *grands taxis* and trains. You'll want to leave well before 9am to miss any possible traffic and the heat of the afternoon sun, so plan on an early departure for Moulay Bousselham.

1 Stop by **Banasa,** near Moulay Bousselham, to explore these unkept Roman ruins in the morning.

2 For lunch, head into Moulay Bousselham. Go directly down to the **port** to select your fish to grill. Enjoy a fresh seafood lunch.

3 Spend the afternoon in the **Merja Zerga National Park.** Hire a boat for 100Dh and go birdwatching in the lagoon.

4 Dinner and accommodations will be at **Vila Bea.** You'll be treated to great seafood with views out over the water and the infinity pool.

Rabat الرباط

With an increasing number of direct flights to European capitals, such as London, Paris, and Madrid, and investment by the king of Morocco into new projects, including the **MMVI Contemporary Art Museum,** Rabat is slowly growing beyond its reputation as a political hub and is earning a reputation as a destination.

Rabat enjoys warm weather nearly year-round, with palm trees lining the wide colonial-era boulevards, and sports numerous attractions, both new and historic, as evidenced by its inclusion on UNESCO's World Heritage List. Surfing and sunbathing are popular pastimes along the municipal beaches, and popular music festivals liven up the city. Because Rabat hosts many expats, dignitaries, and diplomats, foodies will be happy to find restaurants that feature classic and fusion menus from around the world. First-time visitors will want to spend at least one full day wandering through the **Oudaïas Kasbah,** the souks of the **old medina,** and **the Chellah Necropolis,** while those seeking a day of relaxation can consider whiling away an afternoon at one of the many European-style cafés dotted throughout the **Ville Nouvelle.**

ORIENTATION

Though Rabat has been spreading out over the last few years, most of the new developments are on the south side of the city, particularly in the **Soussi** neighborhood. For the most part, travelers will stick to the riverside that forms the north border of the city, connecting the **Hassan Mosque** to the east with the **medina** and **kasbah** to the west. The western border of the city is the Atlantic Coast, while the eastern border is more or less the **Chellah Necropolis. Boulevard Mohammed V** is the artery that connects the **Ville Nouvelle** to the medina. Along this boulevard, you'll find the **Rabat-Ville train station,** as well as a number of hotels and restaurants.

SIGHTS

★ Oudaïas Kasbah

Looming above the mouth of the Bouregreg River, the imposing walls of the Oudaïas Kasbah (often Oudayas or Udayas Kasbah) jutting up over the water are hard to miss. Since the 13th century, these walls have served to protect the inhabitants from land and sea attacks. Today, the kasbah is a relatively calm neighborhood with a few quiet shops and cafés (of which **Café Maure,** with its terraces facing the river, is the best). The **Oudaïas**

Rabat

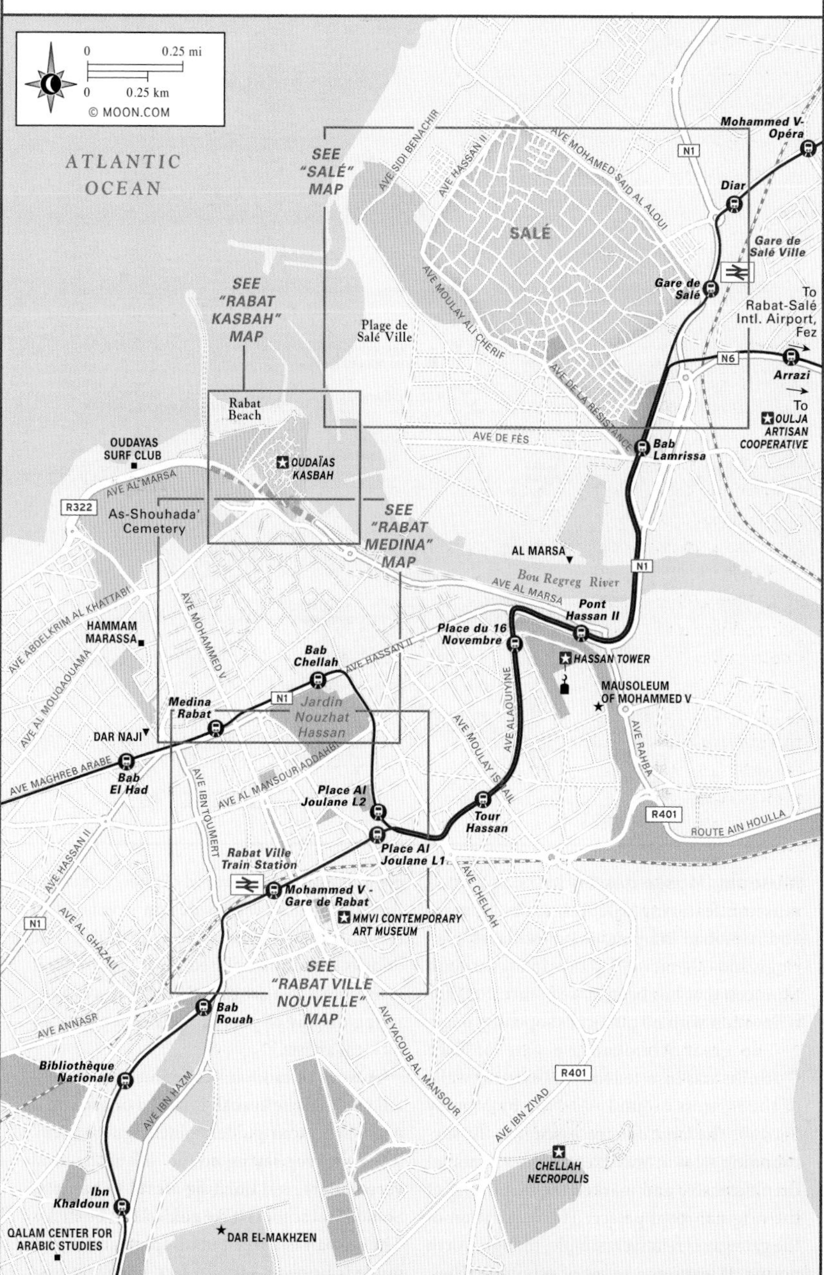
0
0.25 mi
0
0.25 km
© MOON.COM
ATLANTIC
OCEAN
SEE "SALÉ" MAP
SEE "RABAT KASBAH" MAP
SEE "RABAT MEDINA" MAP
SEE "RABAT VILLE NOUVELLE" MAP
SALÉ
Plage de Salé Ville
Rabat Beach
OUDAYAS SURF CLUB
OUDAÏAS KASBAH
As-Shouhada' Cemetery
HAMMAM MARASSA
DAR NAJI
AL MARSA
Bou Regreg River
Mohammed V-Opéra
Diar
Gare de Salé Ville
Gare de Salé
To Rabat-Salé Intl. Airport, Fez
Arrazi
To
OULJA ARTISAN COOPERATIVE
Bab Lamrissa
Pont Hassan II
Place du 16 Novembre
HASSAN TOWER
MAUSOLEUM OF MOHAMMED V
Bab Chellah
Jardin Nouzhat Hassan
Medina Rabat
Bab El Had
Place Al Joulane L2
Place Al Joulane L1
Tour Hassan
Rabat Ville Train Station
Mohammed V - Gare de Rabat
MMVI CONTEMPORARY ART MUSEUM
Bab Rouah
Bibliothèque Nationale
Ibn Khaldoun
QALAM CENTER FOR ARABIC STUDIES
DAR EL-MAKHZEN
CHELLAH NECROPOLIS
AVE SIDI BENACHIR
AVE HASSAN II
AVE MOHAMED SAID AL ALOUI
AVE MOULAY ALI CHERIF
AVE DE LA RESISTANCE
AVE DE FÈS
AVE AL MARSA
AVE ABDELKRIM AL KHATTABI
AVE AL MOUQAOUAMA
AVE MOHAMMED V
AVE MAGHREB ARABE
AVE IBN TOUMERT
AVE AL MANSOUR ADDAHBI
AVE ALAOUIYINE
AVE MOULAY ISMAIL
AVE RAHBA
ROUTE AIN HOULLA
AVE CHELLAH
AVE AL GHAZALI
AVE ANNASR
AVE IBN HAZM
AVE YACOUB AL MANSOUR
AVE IBN ZIYAD
N1
N6
R322
R401

Rabat Kasbah

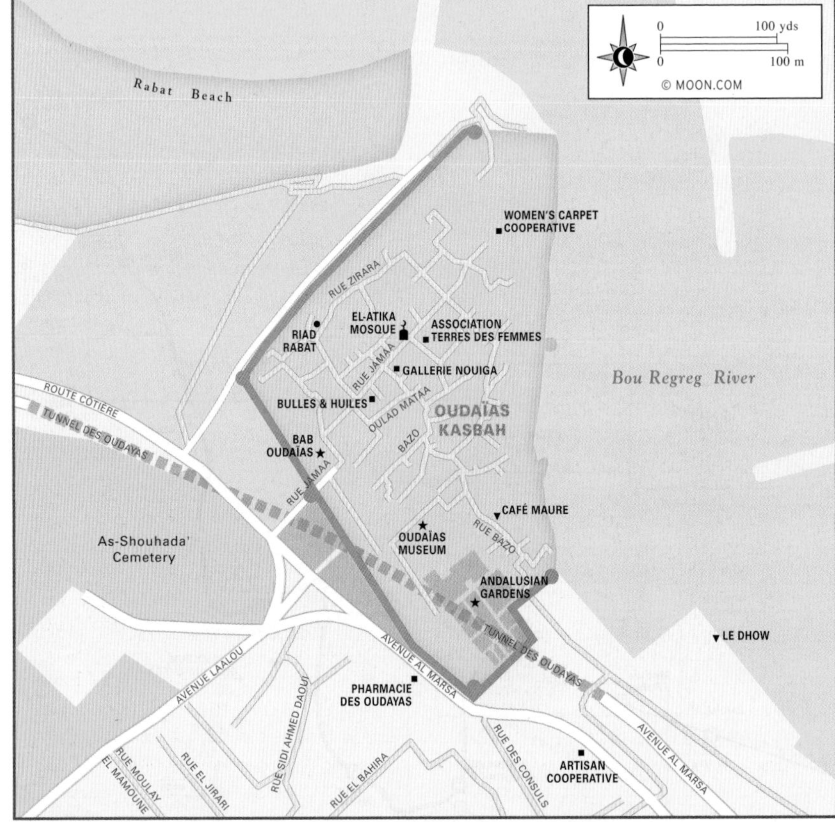

Museum (Musée des Oudaïas) is a small museum featuring paleolithic, pre-Roman, and Almohad-era pendants, necklaces, earrings, and other jewelry found in digs around Morocco that has been closed since 2017 for renovation with no publicized opening date.

The great Almohad-era gate of **Bab Oudaïas** was inserted into the existing walls of the fortress around AD 1195 by Moulay Yacoub. The large door recessed into the surrounding gateway was likely more ceremonial than defensive and marked the beginning of the original royal palace. The decoration of the gateway is relatively simple, though worth noting. It features a series of echoing arches, progressively elaborate in design, typical of the Almohad era. This design is echoed in the unfinished Hassan Tower nearby. The door is sometimes closed, though usually it is open to a free art gallery that features a rotating display of photography and paintings by local artists.

A word of caution: Sometimes people will tell you that the kasbah is closed or ask you if you want a tour guide. Politely ignore them, walk on, keep saying no (or "*la*" in the local vernacular), and don't be afraid to be firm. Some of these touts (fake guides) can be sticky. The kasbah is a free public space and a tour guide is unneces sary. In fact, once you pass the touts, these white and blue walls and general cleanliness of this area make it a great place to spend an afternoon.

ANDALUSIAN GARDENS

Both Rabatis and travelers come to this ancient corner of the city to take a pleasant stroll through the Andalusian Gardens and wind through the pedestrian-only cobblestone streets up to the expansive terrace overlooking the Atlantic Ocean, where a pensive moment is almost required while you take in the crashing waves, flirtatious couples, surfers in the cove, and a well-timed sunset. The gardens, ripe with banana trees, bougainvillea, and a variety of flowers and herbs, were planted by the French in the protectorate area and are a popular place to take a stroll or play with the friendly cats-in-residence. Near the terrace is a carpet workshop where you can peek in to see women working old looms and creating traditional Rabati-design carpets.

EL-ATIKA MOSQUE

Just off the main thoroughfare of the kasbah lies the El-Atika Mosque, originally built in 1050. It is the oldest functioning mosque in Rabat. Unfortunately, the mosque, like others in Morocco, is closed to non-Muslims. For Muslim travelers, it is well worth a stop to pray and admire the harmonious arches of the prayer hall. Others will have to content themselves with a view of the humble minaret that just peeks out over the tops of the neighboring houses.

Medina

Rabat's medina is often one of the more pleasant medinas in Morocco for tourists, even more so after the renovations that took place from 2016-2019. The culture of shop ownership here is much more reserved, with far fewer pestering bazaar owners. Rabat's medina is surprisingly easy to navigate. The primary street, **Avenue Mohammed V,** connects directly with the large boulevard in the Ville Nouvelle by the same name and runs parallel to **Rue des Consuls,** the main bazaar strip.

Most travelers will want to spend some time perusing the bazaars along the Rue des Consuls. Historically, this was the neighborhood where the consulates of Sweden, Denmark, Holland, and France all had offices prior to the period of the French protectorate. During the French protectorate, all administrative offices were moved to the Ville Nouvelle. The Rue des Consuls has since been transformed into a stretch of friendly, pressure-free bazaars featuring textiles, pottery, leather bags, and other Moroccan goods. This is a perfect place to grab that last-minute souvenir on your way home. Prices are fair and generally half (or sometimes less!) what you would find at similar bazaars in Marrakesh and Fez.

Connecting the Avenue Mohammed V and Rue des Consuls is the **Rue Souïka,** a shopping strip popular with the locals that sells newer goods. Here you can find herbs, spices, traditional soaps, pottery, and jewelry alongside goods made in China, from early in the day until late into the night. This is a great street to observe local life, and you can basically blend in with the crowd. The seldom-touristed **mellah** (Jewish quarter) in the far eastern corner of the medina could be interesting for those who wish to look at 19th-century synagogues, of which there are 17, though none are functioning.

BAB EL HAD

Though many of the medina walls and gates of entry date from the 12th century during the Almohad reign of Moulay Yacoub, Bab el Had remains the most impressive of these structures. Located at the southwest entrance of the medina on the Place Bab el Had, this gate opens to the central market. The gate has many of the features of Bab Oudaïas, including the three echoing arches and parallel designs on the top corners; however, Bab el Had is notably more minimalist in decor, with none of the decorative vines and flowers.

1
2
3
4

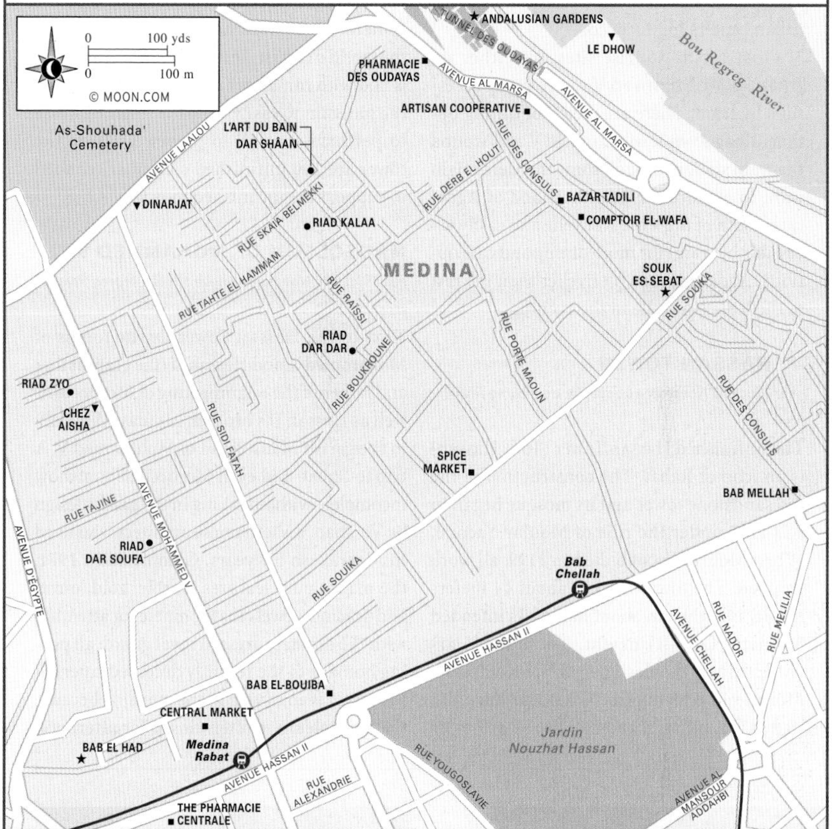

Nonetheless, it is an impressive site and an incredible relic of the Almohad era.

SOUK ES-SEBAT

The Souk es-Sebat, the "shoe souk," is basically a covered extension of Rue Souïka and is a wonderful place to shop for that pair of Moroccan *belghas* (slippers or *babouches*) to take home. You can reach Souk es-Sebat through **Bab Mellah** or follow Rue Souïka to its junction with Rue des Consuls. For music lovers, this is also a place to find ouds, *tarboukas*, and other traditional musical instruments.

1: the Andalusian Gardens in the Oudaïas Kasbah
2: a weathered painted door in Rabat's medina
3: the art deco Saint Peter's Cathedral **4:** a soldier on horseback at the Hassan Tower

Ville Nouvelle

Begun during the French protectorate in 1912 and expanded since Moroccan independence in 1956, Rabat's Ville Nouvelle has become a pleasant, if not quiet, urban center. Around the **Rabat-Ville train station** are many of the embassies and consulates, making it the diplomatic home of expatriates from around the world. The eclectic dining and luxury hotel options all reflect this influx of foreigners, as do the calm streets and

European-styled cafés. Rabat is the home of the king of Morocco, Mohammed VI, and as such, the streets are the safest in all of the urban centers in Morocco.

Most of the tourist sites are either on **Avenue Mohammed V** or are easily accessible by tram. There are plenty of dining options along Avenue Mohammed V and around the train station, though some travelers might want to explore the neighborhood of Agdal (just south of the Ville Nouvelle and easily accessible by tram) for more dining and café options. Agdal can be a bit livelier than the rest of the Ville Nouvelle in the evenings.

★ HASSAN TOWER

near Place 16 Novembre above the Bouregreg River; free

The unfinished Hassan Tower (Tour Hassan) is an icon of Rabat. The construction of the red sandstone tower and its mosque began in AD 1195 under the rule of Moulay Yacoub. When Moulay Yacoub died in 1199, all work stopped. The tower reaches about 44 meters (140ft) into the air, about half of its intended 86-meter (260-ft) height. The notable architect Jibar, the designer of the Koutoubia Mosque in Marrakesh, is said to have designed this minaret and mosque as well as its sister mosque, Giralda, in Seville, Spain. Jibar patterned these mosques after his design in Marrakesh. The Hassan Tower was to be the minaret of the mosque and would have been the world's largest. Instead of stairs, the tower is laid with ramps, which would have allowed the muezzin to easily scale the tower by horse to perform the call to prayer. Outside the tower are 200 unfinished columns, intended to support the unfinished mosque.

MAUSOLEUM OF MOHAMMED V

near Place 16 Novembre above the Bouregreg River; free

Next to the Hassan Tower lie the tombs of Mohammed V and Hassan II (the grandfather and father of the reigning king of Morocco) as well as Hassan II's brother, Moulay Abdellah, in the garish Mausoleum of Mohammed V. A trip to Rabat, and even Morocco, is somehow incomplete without taking in the gaudy design by Vo Toan, a Vietnamese architect who lived in Marrakesh for years. Completed in 1971, the mausoleum features marble, gold, onyx, and precious jewels that compete for attention with the ornately dressed royal guard, all paying homage to the recently deceased rulers of Morocco. Plan to visit in the morning because the mausoleum is often closed for afternoon

busy Rue Souïka in Rabat's medina

Rabat Ville Nouvelle

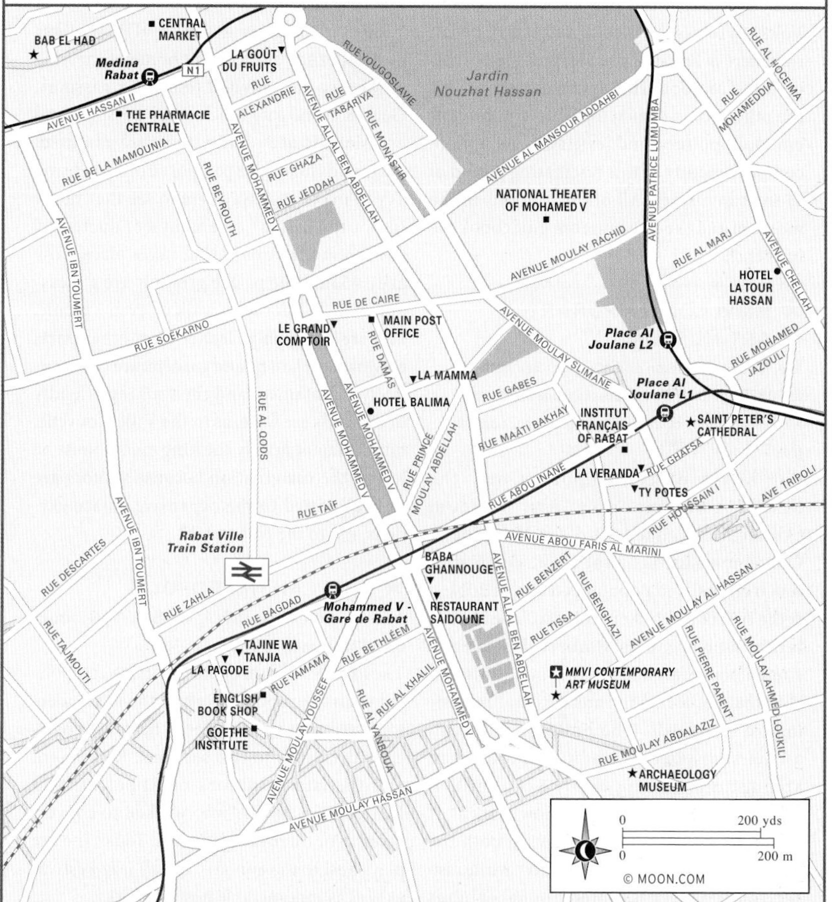

prayers. Visitors are allowed on the viewing platform with access to the rest of the mausoleum restricted.

SAINT PETER'S CATHEDRAL

Place al-Joulane; Mon. and Wed.-Fri. 10am-noon and 3pm-5pm, Tues. and Sat. 10am-noon; free

Saint Peter's (Cathédrale Saint-Pierre de Rabat) holds mass at 7pm every Saturday in French. Notable for its art deco construction, the cathedral was begun in 1919 and inaugurated by Hubert Lyautey, the French Resident-General of Morocco, in 1921. The iconic towers were added to the cathedral in the 1930s. This is the seat of the Archdiocese of Rabat.

ARCHAEOLOGY MUSEUM

23 Rue el Brihi; tel. 0537/701 919; Wed.-Mon. 9am-4:30pm; 70Dh

Rabat's Archaeology Museum (Musée Archéologique) is surprisingly small considering the wealth of material it houses. The most stunning pieces of this collection are the bronze Roman-period sculptures dating from the 1st and 2nd centuries that were collected from excavations throughout Morocco, from Volubilis to nearby Banasa and even Chellah right here in Rabat. If you are interested in this period of Moroccan history, make sure to visit the other floors displaying different Roman-era tools, pottery, and jewelry to get a more complete picture of this fascinating period of Moroccan history. All of the captions in the museum and the free museum guidebook are in French.

★ MMVI CONTEMPORARY ART MUSEUM

Ave. Moulay El Hassan and Ave. Allal Ben Abdella; tel. 0537/769 047; www.museemohammed6.ma; Wed.-Mon. 10am-6pm; 40Dh, bag and coat check free

For lovers of contemporary art, the MMVI Contemporary Art Museum (Musée Mohammed VI d'Art Moderne et Contemporain) is a real treat. Opened to much critical and popular acclaim in 2014, it is the first of its kind in Morocco. The MMVI is the first museum in Morocco dedicated to contemporary art and the first public institution that conforms to international museological standards. The building is bright, airy, and inspired by traditional Moroccan architecture, costing nearly $21.5 million USD. This museum is somehow typical of Morocco, dedicated to preserving both the past and the present of the country while also serving as a place for international exhibits of world-renowned artists such as Goya and Picasso. The permanent collection is divided into four sections (Early Pioneers, Artists of the 1950s, Masters of the 80s and 90s, and Developments Since 2000) that trace the last century of Moroccan art, although art lovers will want to keep a sharp eye on the museum's website to keep current on what has been an excellent run of exhibitions. Signage is in French and Arabic. Check-in for bags and coats is free.

ROYAL PALACE

Ave. Yacoub Al Mansour; tel. 0537/765 400; daily 9am-4pm; free

Visitors wishing to visit the Royal Palace (**Dar El-Makhzen**) and current home of the king of Morocco are advised to bring a passport. Guards at the gate check every passport and occasionally deny entry. If you are admitted, the guards hold your passport until you leave. Try to make your way here to see the "hoisting of the colors" ceremony conducted by the ceremonial guard that takes place daily at 10:45am. The palace grounds are a pleasant enough place for a walk or even a picnic, and are noticeably cleaner than other parts of Morocco. Lawns and gardens are immaculately maintained, and the walking-friendly boulevards are wide, as in the Ville Nouvelle, but the lap of luxury the king enjoys must be left to the imagination because visitors are only admitted to the expansive palace gardens, not to the palace itself.

★ CHELLAH NECROPOLIS

Ave. Yacoub al-Mansur and Blvd. Mouss Ibn Noussair; daily 9am-sunset; 70Dh

The impressive ruin of the Chellah Necropolis (Chellah Nécropole) is one of the few under-touristed sites in Morocco. The ruin is basically divided into two sections, Roman-era and the later additions of Almohad- and Merenid-era sultans who worked to convert the ruin into a royal necropolis. Today, the site plays host to the annual Chellah Jazz Festival as well as innumerable nesting storks.

Historically, Chellah, known as **Sala Colonia** in Roman times, is the oldest known human settlement along the Bouregreg River. Founded by the Phoenicians and then annexed successively by the Carthaginians and Romans, Sala Colonia was a powerful town. Its position here overlooking the river was strategic, and the springs that provided water in times of siege made it a forceful presence

1: the MMVI Contemporary Art Museum
2: a stork nest atop the mosque in Chellah
3: a street musician in the Rabat Kasbah

1
2
3

along the Atlantic Coast. As late as the Roman era, only a series of watchtowers and ditches provided any protection against enemy forces. The walls were a later addition by a 14th-century Merenid sultan, Abu el-Hassan.

The first area within the Chellah complex you visit is the **Roman-era section,** with ruins that date back to the 2nd century AD and perhaps earlier. This section is well signed and includes a triumphal arch, a forum, a temple of Jupiter, and Roman baths. Unfortunately, little remains of these once-great structures besides foundations. It is worth walking along the old Roman road and through the forum to get a feel for the expansiveness of this old city, which remained inhabited until AD 1154, when the city was completely abandoned and the inhabitants moved to nearby Salé.

The imposing main gate and fortress walls date from when the site was converted during the Almohad- and Merenid-era dynasties into a **royal necropolis** as early as the 12th century. Dating from 1339, the gate, an impressive structure featuring turreted bastions and honeycombed corbels (a staple feature of Merenid-era construction), towers overhead. Like many of the *medersas* and mosques, it features Kufic script, which reads "I take refuge in God against Satan." Through the gate, you continue down through a garden to a **viewing platform,** where you can take in the sprawling sight of the ruins against the impressive backdrop of the snaking Bouregreg River and the valley below.

Though the entire site was heavily damaged during the great Lisbon earthquake of 1755, the more recent necropolis is somehow better preserved. Here you can make out the impressive Merenid-era minaret, mosque, mausoleum, and royal tombs that form the area called **The Sanctuary.** Though the ceiling of the mosque has largely collapsed, you can walk among the archways and supporting columns and easily find the mihrab signaling the direction of Mecca. Various **tombs** are scattered about, including that of the "Black Sultan," Abu el-Hassan, and his wife, Shams al-Dawha, a well-known convert to Islam from Christianity. The nearby **spring** is venerated by locals, with women offering a boiled egg to the resident eels for fertility.

During most of the year, this area is replete with majestic storks, making it a prime stop for birders. English guides are generally available and charge 100Dh for a small group, sometimes more on busy days. For those without French or Arabic, this is a good value to really understand more of the history of this important archeological site.

ENTERTAINMENT AND EVENTS

Performing Arts

Rabat has an active schedule of international theater, orchestra, and ballet, and that is all about to get a giant boost with the help of the new **Rabat Grand Theater,** an indoor/outdoor theater by renowned architect Zaha Hadid that will sport three venues, including a main hall seating 2,050 people as well as an outdoor amphitheater seating 7,000 and a host of creative studios. The modern venue looks like something out of *Star Trek* and will be the showpiece of the king's new development along the Bouregreg River, but numerous delays have pushed back the opening indefinitely.

NATIONAL THEATER OF MOHAMMED V (THEATRE NATIONAL DE MOHAMMED V)

Ave. Al Mansour Addahbi; tel. 0537/707 300; www.tnm5.ma

The National Theater has a busy schedule of performances. Plays are mostly in Arabic and French. For avid francophones, this can be an interesting diversion for an afternoon. Consult the website for the latest show listings.

Events

In Morocco's capital city, there are numerous events held throughout the year, though many of these are in French or Arabic. For an updated list of entertainment on offer,

The Mawazine Festival

The annual Mawazine: Rhythms of the World Festival (www.festivalmawazine.ma) was created shortly after the attacks on the World Trade Center in 2001 as part of an approach to promote openness among all cultures throughout the world. The festival had modest beginnings, with musicians mostly from North and West Africa, though in the last few years it has grown and draws crowds well over 2.5 million, making it the second largest music festival in the world. The majority of the concerts are free, and the list of recent headliners reads like some kind of pop star hall of fame: Justin Timberlake, Mariah Carey, Rihanna, Lenny Kravitz, Scorpions, Jimmy Cliff, Gloria Gaynor, the Jacksons, Sting, Stevie Wonder, Shakira, Ricky Martin, Alicia Keys, Ne-Yo, Robert Plant, Jason Derulo, Elton John, Deep Purple, Enrique Iglesias, and Harry Connick Jr.

The festival has grown to include over 1,500 artists and 125 unique performances spread over seven locations. Recently, Mawazine has evolved to include other means of artistic expression. Senegalese sculptor Ousmane Sow has presented his works of art, as have Moroccan photographers such as Michel Nachef, Fouad Maazouz, and Touhami Ennadre. With the king's recent interest in building and supporting the arts in Rabat (evidenced by the recent additions of the MMVI Contemporary Art Museum and the construction of the Rabat Grand Theater), Mawazine promises to evolve into an even more diverse festival with music and art that seek to promote dialogue between cultures. For music lovers, Fez's **Sacred Music Festival** (www.fesfestival.com) is usually around the same time, making May and June a great, though crowded, time to schedule your trip to Morocco.

check in with the German-run **Goethe Institute** (7 Rue Sana'a, tel. 0537/706 544, www.goethe.de/ins/ma/fr/index.html) and the French-run **Institut Français** (1 Rue Abou Inane, tel. 0537/689 650, http://if-maroc.org/rabat). Francophones will enjoy the selection of free French films on offer. Most of the larger festivals are centered around music. Before going to Rabat, it is a good idea to check the event calendar to see if any events overlap with your stay. Accommodations can be difficult to find during events, and it is best to book in advance. Of these festivals, the largest is the **Mawazine Festival** (www.festivalmawazine.ma), which runs for a week or so over May/June every year and brings in headline acts from the United States and Europe.

CHELLAH JAZZ FESTIVAL

Chellah Necropolis; www.jazzauchellah.com; Sept.

The Chellah Jazz Festival has perhaps one of the most picturesque backdrops in the world, the Chellah Necropolis, and brings jazz musicians together for chill nights in the palms, under the stars, and in ruins.

INTERNATIONAL FESTIVAL DU CINEMA D'AUTEUR

Various locations throughout Rabat; www.festivalrabat.ma; Oct.-Nov., sometimes June

The annual International Festival du Cinema d'Auteur, which typically runs for about a week, is a lower-key festival, but it makes this an ideal time to visit Rabat for cinephiles. Most films tend to be in Arabic or French with subtitling generally in French.

SHOPPING

Shopping in Rabat is notably less stressful than shopping in any other large city in Morocco. Part of this is because, unlike Marrakesh and Fez, the city does not depend on tourist income; perhaps it's also because Rabatis see so many foreigners here on business with the government that any sort of novelty has worn off. Regardless, after trips in other parts of Morocco, the relaxed atmosphere as you peruse through stacks of Rabati carpets, Moroccan lamps, or Fassi leather bags is refreshing. Though you can bargain for slightly lower prices, most store owners are fair and do not gouge you . . . that much.

Kasbah

WOMEN'S CARPET COOPERATIVE

in the kasbah in the corner of the large terrace lookout; daily morning-sunset

Perhaps the most visited shop in the kasbah is the Women's Carpet Cooperative. The women weave carpets by hand on large looms. When the cooperative is open, you can take a look inside, though you will be expected to tip a small gratuity for this privilege (10Dh is good). Rabati carpets are often thought to be the best in Morocco, and the Persian influence is notable.

ASSOCIATION TERRES DES FEMMES

12 Rue Sidi M'Barik; tel. 0537/626 819; daily 10am-5pm

This small association has a selection of hand-spun pottery from smaller villages, such as Ain Kobb, Dhar, and Ifrane-Ali. Most of the pottery here is rustic and unpainted, standing in stark contrast to the pottery of Fez or Safi. Proceeds support women of these seldom-visited villages. Don't be put off by the cold reception. There are some really great finds here with proceeds going to a great cause.

BULLES & HUILES

23 Rue Jamaa; tel. 0658/807 208; k.ourich@yahoo.fr; daily 10am-2pm and 3pm-8pm

A fantastic little boutique next to the barber shop along the main road to the kasbah terrace, this shop has a wide selection of locally produced soaps and cosmetic oils, many of them made with argan, and all of them nicely packaged, which is great for the trip home or for gifts.

GALLERIE NOUIGA

42 Rue Jamaa; tel. 0610/624 419; daily 9am-6pm

This is another dependable shop along this strip with a variety of soaps, oils, body milks, and other eco-friendly, locally produced beauty products made with argan, aloe, camel milk, and other locally sourced materials.

Medina

RUE DES CONSULS

This is where you will find most of the bazaars in Rabat selling everything from carpets and spices to tea sets and ornate Berber-styled jewelry. Most shops are open every day, though many close on Friday. The best times for shopping are before lunch and later in the afternoon when all of the shops are open. If you're looking for a last-minute souvenir to take home, either for yourself or as a gift, this is the place to shop. Prices are generally fair and well-marked. Rabat is one of the few places where haggling isn't necessarily part of the purchasing process.

CARPET AUCTION

Rue des Consuls

On Monday and Thursday mornings, head to the medina for the carpet auction held just off Rue des Consuls. It's best to arrive shortly after breakfast in the morning. Generally, the earlier you are, the more likely you are to find a carpet of interest to you and at a bargain-basement price. Even if you're not in the market for a new handwoven piece, the often-chaotic melee is worth peaking in at just for the entertainment factor.

ARTISTAN COOPERATIVE

Avenue al-Marsa

Just around the corner from Rue des Consuls along Avenue al-Marsa is an Artisan Cooperative with a series of small shops. The shops where wood furniture is painted in traditional Moroccan fashions are of particular interest, as are the paintings done by local artists. You could easily stop in here and walk out with decorations for an entire room back home.

SPICE MARKET

Rue Souïka

Tucked away off Rue Souïka in the medina is a small spice market well worth the detour to get your *ras el hanoot* (a spice blend), saffron, *rhassoul* (clay soap), henna, and other herbs, spices, pigments, and oils. To get here, you'll have to keep your bearings about you as you walk down Rue Souïka. Look for a small passage about midway down the street on the westside that opens up to a small collection of spice sellers.

CENTRAL MARKET

Bab el Had

For fresh produce, head to the Central Market (Marché Centrale) just inside Bab el Had. The market itself is fantastic for photos and to experience how many locals purchase their basics. Budget travelers will want to head here with a shopping bag to fill up with fantastic produce. This is a must-stop for those planning their own meals and packing picnic lunches to enjoy on the beach.

COMPTOIR EL-WAFA

105 Rue des Consuls; tel. 0537/727 608; Sat.-Thurs. 9am-7pm

For leather goods, head to Comptoir el-Wafa. The leather is from Fez, though the work is mostly done in Rabat. Have a peek around the corner, off the Rue des Consuls behind the shop, for a look at leatherworkers plying their trade. Their wares are well crafted, with a few unique designs for small bags, purses, and even cases for your iPad or tablet.

BAZAR TADILI

39 Rue des Consuls; tel. 0661/149 806; Sat.-Thurs. 10am-7:30pm

This is a modest shop along this busy road with a selection of carpets from around Morocco and the Middle East. For those interested in *boucharouettes* (Moroccan rag rugs), the collection here is worth checking out.

Ville Nouvelle

ENGLISH BOOK SHOP

7 Rue al-Yamama; tel. 0537/706 593; Mon.-Fri. 10am-1:30pm and 4pm-7pm, Sat. 10am-1:30pm

The ramshackle English Book Shop is exactly what you would expect from a used bookstore in Morocco. Books in English are packed from floor to ceiling. Find classics and recent bestsellers for 20Dh on up. The owner, Muhammed Belhaj, opened the bookstore in 1985. There is no other bookstore like it in Morocco.

COOPÉRATIVE IBDAA

Rue El Gharb No 21 Aviation; tel. 0668/504 188; daily 9am-6pm

On the other side of the Chellah complex from the Ville Nouvelle is the Coopérative Ibdaa, a curious little cooperative of artisans working with blown glass to make pendants, bracelets, necklaces, and earrings, as well as sculptures

the English Book Shop near the Rabat-Ville train station

and vases. If you're looking to encourage local artisans, consider making the trip beyond Chellah to find this cooperative, though call ahead as hours sometimes vary.

SPORTS AND RECREATION

Hammams

If you're visiting a hammam, make sure to pack a fresh change of clothes. Many of the boutique hotels in the medina have their own, more expensive hammams available, which is ideal for couples and those looking for a more intimate experience.

HAMMAM MARASSA

Rue Qobros; tel. 0537/721 461; 5:30am-midnight; 20Dh

There are a few local hammams spread around the old medina, with Hammam Marassa easily the cleanest and most spacious of the bunch. Women have access throughout the middle of the day, while men can come in the early morning and after 8pm, though you should double-check the hours.

THAI SABAI

Avenue Fall Ould Oumeir; tel. 0537/675 158; open daily 9am-9pm; 200Dh

Sometimes after a long trip, you just need a really hard massage. Enter Thai Sabai, offering true Thai massages for those that really need to stretch out and work out some stress.

L'ART DU BAIN

24 Rue Jirari; tel. 0537/722 020; http://dar-shaan.com; daily 8am-9pm; 200Dh

Located in the supremely chic Dar Shâan boutique hotel, this traditional Moroccan hammam is a truly luxury plunge into the art of the Moroccan spa. Get slathered in essential oil-infused *savon bildi* (black soap) and enjoy an exfoliating experience like no other.

Beaches

Though Rabat is not generally thought of as a "beach" destination, some fun in the sand can be had. The Atlantic can be cold, undercurrents can be strong, and generally there are no lifeguards on duty. During the summer, these beaches swell with Moroccans and tourists all fighting for a patch of sand, but just outside of the summer months, they are much calmer. The mouth of the river has a couple of sandy inlets, particularly just across the river at Salé, and offers calmer waters.

RABAT BEACH

Oudaïas Kasbah

The western edge of Rabat is basically all beach. The Rabat Beach abutting the Oudaïas Kasbah is the busiest and most accessible beach in the region, and because of the port, it has the best protection from some of the strong Atlantic currents. You can get here by foot or take a *petit taxi* (10-15Dh).

TEMARA

A bit farther south of Rabat is neighboring Temara. The beach here is smaller than Rabat's, but it's also farther away from the crowds. Trains from Rabat to Temara (16Dh) leave every 30 minutes during rush hour and every hour or so during the day. The ride is short (about 15 minutes), and from the Temara train station you can take a taxi (10Dh) to the beach.

PLAGE DES NATIONS

Another option is to take the 9 bus (3.5Dh) north from Rabat and get off at Sidi Bouknadel. From the bus stop, it is a direct 2-kilometer (1mi) walk to the Plage des Nations beach. Just follow the smell of the sea due west. Of all the beaches, this is probably the cleanest and the nicest for women to sunbathe without the typical hassling that happens at other beaches, though it's also one of the more difficult beaches to access without a car.

OUDAYAS SURF CLUB

on Avenue Al Marsa, across from the Rabat Cemetery near the Oudaïas Kasbah and Rabat Beach; tel. 0537/260 683; http://oudayassurfclub.com; lessons start at 150Dh

There are a few surf clubs where you can rent

boards and gear for the day. The most well-known of these is the Oudayas Surf Club. In addition to the cost of the lesson, rental equipment requires a damage deposit of 500-1,000Dh plus the cost of the rental, from about 200Dh on up. The current king was one of the founding members. The club has a lounge and offers lessons for surfing and body-boarding.

Golf

RABAT ROYAL DAR ES SALAAM GOLF COURSE

Km9 Ave. Immam Malik; tel. 0537/755 864 or 0537/755 865; Tues.-Sun.; greens fees 330Dh, caddies required

Here you will find golfing fit for a king. There are three challenging courses denoted by color (Red, Blue, and Green). Nestled in a 400-hectare (988-acre) forest of cork trees, the 18-hole Red course, designed by Robert Trent Jones Sr., was intended to be one of the most challenging in Africa. There are plenty of sand traps and tough dog legs, though the signature par 3 ninth hole is entirely over water. For beginners and intermediates, the equally scenic 18-hole Blue or 9-hole Green courses are recommended, though these are still challenging courses.

FOOD

The selection of restaurants in Rabat is comparable to that of Marrakesh and Casablanca. There is a hub of political bodies from throughout the world who call Rabat home, making Rabat one of the more ethnically diverse locations in Morocco. This diversity is reflected in the numerous restaurants serving everything from American-style steak dinners to Chinese noodles and Lebanese falafels. The staple Moroccan couscous and tajine plates are also easy to find, though you would do well to check out some of the other dining options while you're in town.

Medina

The medina is the place to go for cheap eats. Several **grillades** inside the gate of **Bab el-Bouiba** have an assortment of barbecued meats. It's possible to get a large sandwich for about 10Dh, which might just be the quick thing to fill you up on your way through the medina. Some exotic meats are often available, including cow or sheep head. You can also find juice stands selling sugarcane juice with lemon zest. It's surprisingly refreshing and, at 5Dh, a great pick-me-up as you explore the medina.

CHEZ AISHA

80 Mohammed V at the corner of Rue Sidi Youssef; daily 9am-nightfall; 5Dh

Chez Aisha is a dependable *bissara* (soup/bean dip) stand along the main drag.

DINARJAT

6 Rue Belgnaoui; tel. 0537/704 239; daily noon-3pm and 7pm-11pm; 180Dh, reservations required

In the heart of the medina, Dinarjat has developed a reputation as one of the better restaurants in Rabat, though the decor and live music are kitschy. It's geared toward larger tour groups, and yet the Moroccan food is still mouthwateringly delicious. Try the *tajine de m'rouzia*, a tajine of honeyed lamb, sesame seeds, and raisins. Beer, wine, and alcohol are available.

LE DHOW

Quai des Oudaïas; tel. 0537/709 381; www.ledhow.com; Mon.-Fri. noon-2am, Sat.-Sun. 11am-2am; 220Dh

Hop aboard this restaurant, lounge, and coffee shop tucked aboard the pirate-looking sailboat docked on the Bouregreg River. The wooden planks and wrapped sails of Le Dhow truly channel the old patch-eyed, wooden-legged vibe of Rabat and Salé. Enjoy a selection of seasonal seafood and grilled steaks, but nonsmokers beware: the cabin seating fills with smoke fairly easily. If you're sensitive and the weather cooperates, ask to sit outside on the deck overlooking the river. Beer, wine, and alcohol are available and the cocktails are surprisingly competent. Yo ho ho, indeed.

Ville Nouvelle

LA GOÛT DU FRUITS

2 Avenue Allal Ben Abdellah; daily 8am-10pm; 15Dh

Located just on the other side of the tramway from **Bab el-Bouiba** (one of the gateways into the medina), La Goût du Fruits is a juice shop that is a popular stop with locals to get a freshly squeezed juice. Try the avocado and ginger or just order a *panaché* (blend) to get a mix of what's on offer. You can't get a better energy boost to keep you going on your way through the medina and up to the kasbah. For juicers, this is a must-stop.

RESTAURANT SAIDOUNE

467 Ave. Mohammed V; tel. 0537/709 226; Sat.-Tues. and Thurs. 11:45am-3pm, daily 6:30pm-2am; 20Dh

This grungy Lebanese gem is tucked in a small plaza off Mohammed V, across from the Terminus Hotel near the train station. Late at night, it gets a little seedy. You can find beer, wine, and alcohol on the menu here, though you must drink inside. This is the place to go for that falafel craving you've inexplicably had since landing in Morocco.

BABA GHANNOUGE

467 Ave. Mohammed V; tel. 0537/262 605; Tues.-Sun. 8am-2pm and 6pm-midnight; 25Dh

Come here for a good selection of shawarma sandwiches to go. Perfect for packing that lunch for a long train ride, as well as, of course, baba ghanoush and Syrian-style salads. The restaurant is non-smoking and family friendly.

★ DAR NAJI

Ave Jazirat Al Arab, facing Bab al-Had; tel. 0537/262 528; 50Dh

This is a very popular stop for locals and tourists just across from the unmissable Bab al-Had. There is a spectacular rotating menu of tajines, couscous, and seasonal Moroccan salads that feel right at home in the Saharan-like decor. Come for the *zaalouk, tajine min djej wa citron* (tajine with chicken and lemon), and the refreshing nonsmoking section.

TAJINE WA TANJIA

9 Rue Baghdad; tel. 0537/729 797; Mon.-Sat. noon-3pm and 7pm-midnight; 130Dh

This is an authentic, cozy Moroccan restaurant with a warm, traditional *tadelahkt* and *zellij* decor that serves to enhance the vibrant tajines and salads on offer. Friday is couscous day, and beer and wine are on the menu. The free Wi-Fi is especially handy to do a quick post of your lunch on Facebook to make your friends back home jealous.

LA MAMMA

6 Rue Tanta; tel. 0537/707 329; daily noon-3pm and 7:30pm-midnight; 100Dh

If pizzas and beer are what you're looking for, La Mamma does not disappoint. It is a Rabat institution that has been tucked away behind the **Hotel Balima** for over 50 years. An open kitchen greets you at this otherwise dimly lit establishment. There is a welcomed non-smoking room, but you have to brave a wall of smoke to get there.

LE GRAND COMPTOIR

279 Ave. Mohammed V; tel. 0537/201 514; daily 9am-midnight; 200Dh

This is the local favorite for treating yourself to a gourmet seafood or steak dinner. Grilled sirloin is served alongside dorado with oysters for appetizers, as long as they are in season. Nonsmokers should consider sitting near the door, away from the generally subpar live music on offer. Beer, wine, and alcohol are served.

LA VERANDA

1 Ave. Abou Inane; tel. 0674/841 244; Mon.-Sat. 10am-11pm, Sun. 10am-4pm; 100Dh

Located inside the French Institute, behind Saint Peter's Cathedral, La Veranda has a relaxed terrace on which to enjoy a French bistro-inspired lunch. It's a good place to meet Francophones. While you're there, why not take a look at the cultural offerings scheduled for the week? There's free Wi-Fi. Beer, wine, and alcohol are served.

TY POTES

11 Rue Ghafsa; tel. 0537/707 965; http://typotes.com; Tues.-Wed. noon-2:45pm, Thurs.-Sat. 7pm-11pm, Sun. 11am-3pm; 120Dh

If you're craving a good Sunday brunch, this is the spot. Located near Saint Peter's Cathedral and the French Institute, it has a true French-bistro feel and a wonderful garden patio. Pork lovers will be happy to find Spanish-cured ham and smoked ham making regular appearances on the menu. Beer, wine, and alcohol are served.

LA PAGODE

13 Rue Baghdad; tel. 0537/709 381; Tues.-Sun. 11:30am-3pm and 7:30pm-11:30pm; 60Dh

This is the Chinese-food staple of Rabat. It is one of the very few restaurants that will deliver. Delivery is free, though unfortunately not available for the medina or kasbah. It's close to the train station and open relatively late, but the faux-Chinese decor is a bit over the top.

BARS AND NIGHTLIFE

Drinking in most bars dotted around the Ville Nouvelle is not for the faint of heart. They are generally full with hard drinkers and prostitutes. Single women will likely be more comfortable at high-end restaurants and hotels.

The night scene in Rabat is shifting out toward the Soussi neighborhood, so you'll need to hop in a taxi and be ready for the mad Moroccan streets to have a great night out. If you do venture out, think about club-hopping, as all of these clubs offer something a bit different, though if you're looking for cheap drinks stop reading here. With cover charges and typically high drink prices, even by Moroccan standards, clubbing in Rabat is not for those on a shoestring budget. The weekends can be very busy with long entry lines. Like other club scenes in Morocco, this one doesn't really get going until well after midnight.

Bars

HOTEL LA TOUR HASSAN

26 Rue Chellah; tel. 0537/239 000; http://latourhassan.com; daily afternoons and evenings

The piano lounge at Hotel la Tour Hassan provides a classy backdrop for a drink in a hip, Moroccan-chic environ, though the real action here is on the outdoor terrace around sunset, cocktail in hand, admiring the stunning views over Rabat.

LE GRAND COMPTOIR

279 Ave. Mohammed V; tel. 0537/201 514; daily 9am-midnight

Along the main boulevard, Le Grand Comptoir is a local staple that channels the French protectorate era with heavy red curtains reminiscent of a Parisian bistro. Local musicians occasionally pop in to liven up the otherwise quiet scene.

LE DHOW

Quai des Oudaïas; tel. 0537/709 381; www.ledhow.com; Mon.-Fri. noon-2am, weekends 11am-2am

Along the river, head up to the chill deck aboard for cocktails dockside.

LA BODEGA

30 Ave. Michlifen; tel. 0537/673 300; daily noon-3pm and 6pm-2am

If you want to mix with the local expat crowd, consider heading to the neighborhood of Agdal to sip on a cerveza (beer) at La Bodega (also known as El Rancho), a Spanish-themed bar that serves tapas alongside beers, wines, and spirits. This is a lower-key place that picks up on the weekends.

Nightclubs

LE SO LOUNGE

Avenue Mohammed Hakam, Soussi; tel. 0614/134 303; Wed.-Sat. 9pm-3am; 100Dh

Le So Lounge in the Sofitel Hotel is the newest hot spot, with DJs spinning the latest in EDM fused with Moroccan and French hits as well as other international beats.

HAROLD'S

corner of Mohammed VI and Rue Ahmed Rifai, Soussi; tel. 0662/767 814; Wed.-Sat. 9pm-3am; 100Dh

Also in Soussi, you will find Harold's, which is typically more low-key and where the music changes nightly.

LE RESEVOIR

Centre Prestige, rue de Zairs; tel. 0537/750 909; Wed.-Sat. 9pm-3am; 100Dh

Resident DJ Slim spins a mix of disco and house, but what makes this worth a stop is the retractable roof, making this a sweet spot to hang with your friends.

ACCOMMODATIONS

Most of the accommodations here are in the form of hotels in the Ville Nouvelle, which range from seedy dives to opulent five-star hotels. Options for midrange budgets are few and generally disappointing. There are even fewer options for *riads* and guesthouses in the medina or kasbah. Rooms are typically booked well ahead of time. For most of Rabat, you would do well to make reservations before your trip, as various festivals, conferences, and political happenings can fill the city fairly quickly. For less expensive medina accommodations options, check out nearby Salé.

Medina

RIAD ZYO

5 Rue Moreno; tel. 0537/733 276 or 0661/110 896; 900Dh d

Traditional Morocco enters the 21st century in this stylish, recently refurbished modern *riad* in the heart of the medina. Easily accessible, just off Avenue Mohammed V. Comfortable beds are surrounded by all the mod-cons, such as air-conditioning, TV, and Wi-Fi. There is a small courtyard swimming pool to cool off in after a hot day. The neighborhood can get a bit noisy at night, so consider requesting a room off the street for a quieter night of sleep. Breakfast is included with your stay.

RIAD KALAA

5 Rue Zebdi; tel. 0537/202 028; www.riadkalaa.com; 950Dh d

A bit larger than most of the guesthouses in the medina, with a sprawling, maze-like floor plan and a bar/lounge space (though the drink menu is limited) just off the restaurant area. The service is top-notch, and on hot days, the terrace pool is refreshing. The rooms downstairs tend to be larger and more airy, while the terrace rooms are more cozy, though their large bathrooms make up for the smaller rooms. Accommodations include air-conditioning and Wi-Fi, as well as access to the spa and pool. Breakfast is included.

RIAD DAR DAR

13, rue Sidi Kadeem; tel. 0537/661 571 or 0661/480 558; http://rabatriads.com; 1,000Dh d

This homey, yet strange mix of Moroccan funk, oddities, and minimalist design opened in 2015. The service is friendly, as expected, and the rooms—all with TV, air-conditioning, Wi-Fi, and en suite bathrooms—make for a comfy night of sleep. Take advantage of the rooftop swimming pool, and to save a few dirhams, consider the cozy Wassila room on the 2nd floor. Dinner can be a real treat here with a deliciously fresh fish *pastilla* on the menu, as well as a number of tajines (200Dh). Just remember to reserve ahead of time.

★ DAR SHÂAN

24, rue Jirari; tel. 0537/722 020 or 0537/722 820; www.dar-shaan.com; 1,100Dh d

Welcome to the newest boutique accommodation in town. The attention to detail shows. From the clean lines to the select artwork from around Morocco adorning every room, including artists from Asilah, immaculate taste is combined with a friendly English-speaking staff, rooftop pool, quiet rooms, and nonsmoking dining room to make for an unforgettable stay. For the mobility-impaired,

---

1: Only Muslims are allowed in nearly all Moroccan mosques. **2:** the unfinished 12th-century Hassan Tower **3:** colorful leather saddle cushions **4:** Rabat's new tram is the best way to get around town.

INTERDIT AUX
NON MUSULMANS
FORBIDDEN
FOR NON MUSLIMS
1
2
3
4

there is even a small elevator, a real rarity in Morocco. Air-conditioning, Wi-Fi, and breakfast are all included with your stay. There is also a hammam/spa on-site (250Dh for a traditional Moroccan hammam and 250Dh for a massage). The restaurant is reservation only. Call by noon to make sure you have a table reserved. Directors Antoine Ansart and Nathalie Marmey have made it a point to include all the hotel amenities, but with the cozy, comfortable touch of a traditional Moroccan home.

RIAD DAR SOUFA

7 Impasse Souaf, Legza; tel. 0673/194 537; riaddarsoufa@hotmail.com; 1,200Dh d

Well located in a quieter part of the medina, this French-run hotel is a bright, airy establishment with clean, charming rooms. The owners, Benoit and Christine, provide friendly service and are helpful in getting you oriented in Rabat. The lounge and courtyard feature traditional Moroccan plaster and tile work.

Ville Nouvelle

Dotted around the Ville Nouvelle and in the medina are a number of budget hotel options.

HOTEL LE GAULOIS

corner of Mohamed V & Rue Hims, tel. 0537/730 573 or 0537/723 022, 220Dh

For students, backpackers, and budget travelers, the dated old colonial Hotel Le Gaulois is a well-located, generally clean choice, and prices are very reasonable. Rooms come with TV and Wi-Fi. It is often more expensive to book ahead of time, though if you don't, you run the risk of rooms possibly being sold out during events or festivals. Reception is often gruff, and you pay extra for en suite bathrooms. A shower will cost you an extra 20Dh, making the local hammam a tempting excursion.

HOTEL LA TOUR HASSAN

26 Rue Chellah; tel. 0537/239 000; http://latourhassan.com; 2,000Dh d

For opulence, you would be hard-pressed to find anything finer than Hotel La Tour Hassan. With a stylish blend of comfort and tradition, this is a hotel that seeks to please. Rooms are modern with the expected Moroccan touch. The unheated pool is pleasurable during the warm months, and the outdoor bar and lounge is a great place to unwind. In addition to the outdoor lounge, there are three excellent on-site restaurants and a piano bar, making this a wonderful nighttime stop for a cocktail and dinner even if you aren't staying in the hotel. The property also includes a spa and fitness room. Breakfast is included with your stay.

INFORMATION AND SERVICES

Embassies

BRITISH EMBASSY

28 Avenue S.A.R. Sidi Mohammed; tel. 0537/633 333; www.gov.uk/world/organisations/british-embassy-rabat

The British Embassy is in the Soussi neighborhood toward the south of Rabat. For emergency services while in Morocco, call the telephone number or visit the website. Some notarial, documentary, and legalization services are also available.

CANADIAN EMBASSY

66 Ave. Mehdi Ben Barka; tel. 0537/544 949

The Canadian Embassy also provides services to Australian citizens in Morocco. For emergencies, Canadian and Australian citizens can call collect to reach the **Emergency Watch and Response Centre** (Canada tel. 613/996-8885).

U.S. EMBASSY

2 Avenue Mohamed Al Fassi (formerly Ave. de Marrakesh); tel. 0537/637 200

The U.S. Embassy is largely diplomatic. For most services, U.S. citizens will want to visit the U.S. Consulate in Casablanca (8 Blvd. Moulay Youssef, tel. 0522/264 550). In the case of health, safety, or legal emergencies, U.S. citizens can contact the American Citizen Services hotline (tel. 0522/642 099 Mon.-Fri. 8am-5pm, tel. 0661/131 939 after hours).

Safety

With the king of Morocco calling Rabat home, it's no coincidence that this is the safest city in Morocco. Crime is very low and typically only seen in the far suburbs of the city. Of course, pickpocketing is always a concern, particularly on crowded buses and trams, so take precautions and don't leave all your money, valuables, and travel documents in your purse or wallet. Women generally feel more comfortable in Rabat than most other cities in Morocco. Harassment still occurs, but it is notably subdued. There are often protests outside of the Hotel de Ville with a police presence, so don't be alarmed if you run across a few police officers wearing riot gear or a small group of chanting protesters.

Internet Cafés and Telephones

In the medina, just off Rue Souïka are a couple of easy-to-spot Internet cafés; one is at the entrance of Rue Bouhlal on Rue Derbal Fasi and another is at 8 Bouchkaoi just off Rue Souïka. In the Ville Nouvelle, the cybercafé **Teleboutique** is right next to **La Mamma** by the **Hotel Balima.** Cybercafés are generally open by 10am and close around 10pm, with 20Dh buying an hour of Internet usage. Many cafés and restaurants around town now also have free Wi-Fi.

The city code for Rabat and the area is 37.

Post Offices and Courier Services

MAIN POST OFFICE

corner of Aves. Mohammed V and Jean Jaurès; Mon.-Fri. 8am-6pm, Sat. 8am-noon

To send packages and postcards, head to the main post office opposite the Bank Al Maghrib. Hours are shortened during Ramadan.

Bookstores, Newspapers, and Magazines

You can find several bookstores in the Ville Nouvelle. The **English Book Shop** (7 Rue al-Yamama) should suit most needs. Many newspaper stands dot **Avenue Mohammed V,** though most publications are in French or Arabic.

Foreign Language and Cultural Centers

QALAM CENTER FOR ARABIC STUDIES

2 Rue Ahmed Hiba; tel. 0537/755 790; www.qalamcenter.com

The Qalam Center for Arabic Studies offers classes in Modern Standard Arabic and Moroccan Arabic (Darija) for 1,500-3,000Dh a week. Classes also include cultural excursions and direction in the Arabic art of calligraphy.

INSTITUT FRANÇAIS OF RABAT

1 Rue Abou Inane; tel. 0537/689 650; http://if-maroc.org/rabat; Mon.-Sat. 8am-6:30pm

The Institut Français of Rabat, with its attached café, film-screening room, and library, is a great way to meet local Francophones and expats. The French Institute offers a series of free film screenings, lectures, and concerts. Check the website for details.

Money

For travelers checks, foreign currency exchanges, and other services, visit BMCE (Mon.-Fri. 8:15am-6:30pm, weekends 9am-6pm, Ramadan 9am-5pm). You can find the local branch along Avenue Mohammed V along with other options for ATMs.

Hospitals, Clinics, and Pharmacies

Rabat has plenty of hospitals and is probably the best place to be in Morocco if disaster strikes. For emergencies, call the Service Médical d'Urgence at tel. 0537/737 373 for admittance to their facilities.

PHARMACIE DES OUDAYAS

corner of the medina facing the Oudaïas Kasbah; tel. 0535/734 410; daily 9am-12:30pm and 3pm-7:30pm

A convenient, easy-to-find pharmacy. Handy to know if you need over-the-counter medicine or even need a replacement for your prescription.

THE PHARMACIE CENTRALE

Ave. Hassan II; tel. 0537/724 395; daily 9am-12:30pm and 3pm-7:30pm

The Pharmacie Centrale is right across the street from the Rabat-Ville train station. Every week the 24-hour pharmacy (*pharmacie de garde*) rotates, so check pharmacy postings for details or ask at your accommodation.

GETTING THERE

By Plane

RABAT-SALÉ AIRPORT

just off the N6 outside of Sal; tel. 0537/808 090; www.onda.ma

The Rabat-Salé Airport has a few carriers and a few flights direct to European capitals via low-cost carriers **Transavia** (www.transavia.com), **TUI Fly** (www.tuifly.be), and **Ryan Air** (www.ryanair.com), making Rabat an appealing option for those looking to fly into Morocco from Europe and wanting to avoid Casablanca. A shuttle will take you to the Rabat-Ville train station (20Dh) and leaves approximately 30 minutes after each landing. *Grands taxis* are also available and generally charge 200Dh for service direct to your accommodations, though this price is negotiable.

MOHAMMED V INTERNATIONAL AIRPORT

Nouasseur; tel. 0522/539 040; www.casablanca-airport.com

Getting to Mohammed V International Airport in **Casablanca** is straightforward, so you can spend the last night of your trip in Rabat and fly out of Casablanca. However, you will need to take two trains. From Rabat, purchase a train ticket to Casa Voyageurs, the main train station in Casablanca (regular train 1.5hr, rapid train 1hr; trains leave daily every 20 minutes or so 3am-11:55pm; regular train 2nd/1st-class 37Dh/69Dh, rapid train 47Dh/96Dh). At Casa Voyageurs, you'll purchase a second ticket for the airport (about 30min, trains leave every hour, 43Dh/64Dh). Alternatively, you could go through Casa Port, Casablanca's other major train station, which has nearly identical durations, frequency, and prices. Plan for two hours minimum to get to the airport, though three hours should leave you just enough time for the unexpected.

By Car

Rabat is well connected via the tolled autoroutes, N1, which travels north-south along the Atlantic coast, and N2, which travels west to east over the Middle Atlas mountains. Tolls vary according to type of automobile and where you enter/exit the tolled route. In principle, it's a good idea to travel with 400Dh just for tolls, though you'll likely not use all of it.

From Asilah: Follow the N1 south for 204km/126mi, about 2.5 hours.

From Casablanca: Follow the N1 north for 91km/57mi, about 1hour.

From Fez: Follow the N2 west for 201km/125mi, about 2.5 hours.

From Larache: Follow the N1 south for 168km/104mi, about 2 hours.

From Marrakesh: Follow the N1 north for 330km/205mi, about 4 hours.

From Meknes: Follow the N2 west for 141km/88mi, about 1.5 hours.

From Moulay Bousselham: Follow the N1 south for 137km/85mi, about 1.5 hours.

From Tangier: Follow the N1 south for 245km/152mi, about 3 hours.

By Grand Taxi

The *grands taxis* leave from **Bab Chellah** next to the medina, which is a convenient arrival and departure point. There are regular taxis to **Fez** (2.5hr, 201km/125mi, 80Dh), **Meknes** (1.5hr, 141km/88mi, 60Dh), **Salé** (15min, 4km/2.5mi, 10Dh), and **Kenitra** (30min, 47km/29mi, 35Dh). For taxis to **Casablanca** (1hr, 91km/57mi, 30Dh), you will have to make your way to either the CTM station or the local bus station near Place Zerktouni south of the city center. For most destinations, the train is preferable.

By Bus

Those arriving by bus, either CTM (tel. 0800/0900 30, www.ctm.ma) or another local service, will arrive to one of two bus stations about 5 kilometers (3mi) south of the city on National Road 1 (N1) to Casablanca. Most travelers will likely connect to other destinations by train.

The **CTM station** (Avenue Hassan II) is less crowded and offers buses with premium service, including Wi-Fi and larger seats. The CTM buses connect with **Casablanca** (1hr, 26 daily, 35Dh, premium available), **Fez** (3.5hr, 13 daily, 75Dh, premium available), **Larache** (2.5hr, 3 daily, 75Dh), **Marrakesh** (5hr, 9 daily, 140Dh), **Meknes** (2.5hr, 11 daily, 55Dh), **Tangier** (4hr, 6 daily, 110Dh, premium available), and other destinations.

The **local station** on Place Zerktouni has a left luggage service (10Dh a day), which may come in handy for travelers wishing to spend just a day in Rabat.

By Train

Rabat is served by two train stations, the brand new Rabat-Ville and smaller Rabat-Agdal, as well as two types of train lines, the regular (older, clunkier) national trains and new **high-speed Al-Boraq** trains, all run by the **ONCF** (tel. 0890/203 040, www.oncf.ma). From either train station, some of the more popular train lines connect with **Asilah** (3hr, 10 daily, 2nd/1st-class 88Dh/130Dh), **Casablanca** (regular train 1.5hr, rapid train 1hr, 40 daily, regular train 37Dh/69Dh, rapid train 47Dh/96Dh), **Fez** (2.5hr, 19 daily, 85Dh/127Dh), **Marrakesh** (4.5hr, 9 daily, 127Dh/195Dh), **Meknes** (2hr, 19 daily, 69Dh/95Dh), and **Tangier** (4hr, 10 daily, 101Dh/153Dh).

The **Rabat-Ville station** (Avenue Mohammed V) is conveniently located along Avenue Mohammed V and is most frequently used by travelers because of its central location in the Ville Nouvelle and proximity to the medina and kasbah. Most accommodations are located near Rabat-Ville with the medina being a 10-minute walk away. *Petits taxis* will take you from the stations to your accommodations, but they will only take three passengers. For larger groups, getting two or three taxis should be easy enough. The tram runs right next to the station, convenient for those heading to Salé or staying near the Hassan Tower.

If you're staying out in Agdal, meeting friends there, or riding the Al-Boraq, you will use the **Rabat-Agdal station** (Avenue El Hadj Ahmed Charkaoui). The **Al-Boraq** is just like the TGV in France and whisks passengers from Rabat north to **Tangier** very quickly. Prices vary according to demand. It's a very good idea to purchase your ticket ahead of traveling. Online purchasing is possible, though fidgety. It might take a few tries to get the system to work. You can also keep an eye out for promotional fares that often cut the price by a third or more. The first train heading north leaves Rabat-Agdal to Tangier at 6:50am, with trains departing every two hours or so until 9:50pm (1.5hr, 9 daily, 115Dh-172Dh). First-class tickets typically cost about 70Dh more.

GETTING AROUND

By Car

Driving in Rabat is noticeably more relaxing than in other cities, though still stressful. Parking is relatively easy to find along the streets of the Ville Nouvelle. Overnight **guarded parking** is available around the medina just off Avenue Misr, north of Bab el-Had, on Avenue al-Marsa on Place des Oudaïas outside the Oudaïas Kasbah (20-40Dh) as well as the underground car park Al Mamounia just off Boulevard Mohammed V near the medina (6Dh an hour day/3Dh an hour night).

By Taxi

The easiest way to get around Rabat is by ***petit taxi.*** Meters are regulated and taxi drivers are friendlier here than in most other cities. However, *petits taxis* are not allowed to cross into Salé. You will be able to get around most destinations in Rabat for 20Dh or less.

By Tram

The new **tram** (www.tram-way.ma, daily 6am-10pm, 7Dh) links Rabat to **Salé**. There are two main lines numbered 1 and 2. The **1 line** cuts through town, stopping by the Rabat-Ville train station, while the **2 line** passes by the medina. Both lines meet in the middle of town and cross to Salé while the 1 line continues out to **Agdal**, making this an attractive transportation option for getting around town.

By Boat

For crossing into Salé, the most fun way is by boat. Head down to **Quai des Oudaïas** and catch a ride on a rowboat across the river to the new development in **Salé** for just a few dirhams. Though it's not the most practical way to get across the river, and it is a bit of a walk to the Salé medina from the riverside, this is by far the most adventurous public transport in town.

The North Atlantic Coast

With its verdant forests, tucked-away beaches, and quaint coastal towns, the North Atlantic Coast is the quintessential escape from the bustling medinas and big cities of Morocco. This region stretches 250 kilometers (155mi) north from Rabat to Tangier. There are plenty of all-day excursions, particularly among the unkempt ruins of Roman-era cities, and a number of cozy beaches to catch a romantic sunset. As you head north, you will notice more of a Spanish influence in the language and culture where the evening *paseo* (stroll) and tapas become the norm. By far the best time to visit this stretch of coast is in early September after most of the summer crowds have gone and while the ocean is still warm enough for a good swim.

ORIENTATION

Spanning roughly from **Rabat** to **Tangier,** the North Atlantic Coast forms the northwesternmost tip of the continent of Africa, ending where the waters of the **Mediterranean** meet the **Atlantic.** There are two main roads running north-south, the **national road (N1)** and the tolled **autoroute (A1).** The national road is the slower, though immensely more scenic, of the two.

SALÉ

سلا

Located just a short bus, tram, or boat ride across the river from Rabat, Salé is an overlooked little sister to that city, perfect for those looking for something less touristy. A walk through the medina is much calmer than in some of the busier cities, with people going about their daily lives without much thought to foreigners. If anything, you might be asked what you are doing in Salé. Don't worry, they aren't being rude—tourism just hasn't quite caught on yet in this little commuting city, a boon for those looking for something a little off the beaten track but not too far afield.

Salé's strategic position makes it an ideal location, both for military and trade, along one of the major rivers of Morocco and a commanding presence along the Atlantic Coast. It is no surprise that it abutted the oldest known city along the North Atlantic Coast, Sala Colonia, founded by the Phoenicians and then taken over by the Carthaginians, Romans, and then the Benu Ifran tribe. The city is most famous for the Salé Rovers, a group of Barbary Pirates who formed the Republic of Salé in the 17th century and ruled the seas, from the Americas to Africa. Robinson Crusoe spent time in the captivity of these pirates before escaping from the mouth of the Bouregreg River.

The **Candle Festival** is a religious *moussem* held every year in Salé to commemorate Sidi Ben Hassoun on the eve of Mawlid, the Prophet Mohammed's birthday, on the 12th day of the Muslim month, Rabi' al-Awwal.

Salé

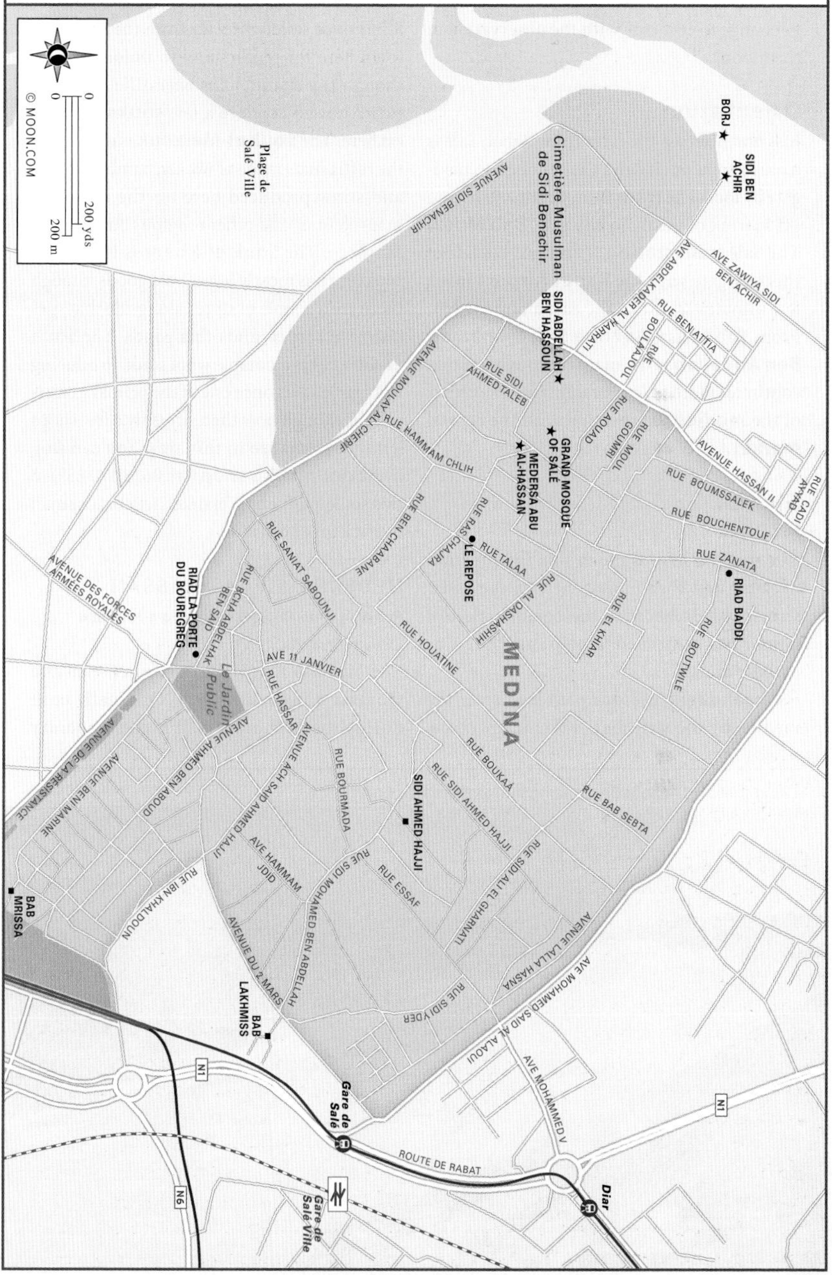

BORJ
SIDI BEN ACHIR
Plage de Salé Ville
Cimetière Musulman de Sidi Benachir
AVENUE SIDI BENACHIR
AVE ZAWIYA SIDI BEN ACHIR
AVE ABDELKADER AL HARRATI
RUE BEN ATTIA
RUE BOULAAJOUL
SIDI ABDELLAH BEN HASSOUN
RUE SIDI AHMED TALEB
AVENUE MOULAY ALI CHERIF
RUE MOUL GOUMRI
RUE AOUAD
GRAND MOSQUE OF SALÉ
MEDERSA ABU AL-HASSAN
RUE HAMMAM CHLIH
AVENUE HASSAN II
RUE CADI AYYAD
RUE BOUMSSALEK
RUE BOUCHENTOUF
RUE ZANATA
RIAD BADDI
RUE BEN CHABANE
RUE RAS CHAJRA
LE REPOSE
RUE TALAA
RUE AL QASHASHIH
RUE EL KHIAR
RUE BOUTWILE
RUE SANIAT SABOUNJI
RUE BCHA ABDELHAK BEN SAID
RIAD LA PORTE DU BOUREGREG
AVENUE DES FORCES ARMEES ROYALES
MEDINA
RUE HOUATINE
AVE 11 JANVIER
Le Jardin Public
RUE HASSAR
AVENUE AHMED BEN ABOUD
AVENUE DE LA RÉSISTANCE
AVENUE BENI MARINE
AVENUE ACH SAID AHMED HAJJI
RUE BOURMADA
SIDI AHMED HAJJI
RUE SIDI AHMED HAJJI
RUE BOUKAA
RUE BAB SEBTA
RUE SIDI ALI EL GHARNATI
AVENUE LALLA HASNA
AVE HAMMAM JDID
RUE IBN KHALDOUN
BAB MRISSA
RUE SIDI MOHAMED BEN ABDELLAH
RUE ESSAF
AVENUE DU 2 MARS
BAB LAKHMISS
RUE SIDI YDER
AVE MOHAMMED SAID AL ALAOUI
AVE MOHAMMED V
N1
Gare de Salé
ROUTE DE RABAT
Diar
Gare de Salé Ville
N6
0 200 yds
0 200 m
© MOON.COM

In 2019, the Prophet's birthday will fall on November 9, and in 2020 it will fall on October 28 (the dates in Morocco are subject to change to coincide with the observation of the moon).

Orientation

Just north across the river from Rabat, Salé is a much smaller city and easy enough to navigate by foot. The **tram** from Rabat will let you off in front of the main city gate, **Bab Mrisa.** The Salé **train station** is also just outside of this city gate with the **Rabat Airport** just a few minutes by car to the east along the **N6.** From Bab Mrisa, **Avenue Sidi Mohamed Ben Abdellah** is the main thoroughfare that continues more or less straight into the center of the **medina,** connecting with the central **market.**

Sights

MEDINA

The medina here is much like the medinas of Rabat and Taza in that they feature wider streets, likely because the construction of houses has continued largely atop the ruins of older houses.

The most picturesque path is to enter the medina by the well-marked main entrance, **Bab Mrisa,** a large gate dating from the 13th century, across from the train station named for it (Bab Lamrissa) along the southeast wall. Ships once sailed directly from the river into town here for repairs and to unload goods, though the channel has been filled for centuries now. There are a few **souks** of interest here. The **Souk el-Merzouk** is devoted to the raffia mats made of wicker, bamboo, palm, and straw produced here for the mosques, mausoleums, and other religious buildings of Morocco. The **Souk el-Kbeer** is the largest souk and has mostly household goods, though there are a couple of stores alongside that specialize in carpets and other goods. The **Souk el-Ghezel** is a notable wool souk. Producing wool goods was once one of the primary crafts of Salé, though now there are only a few shops left that specialize in this area. You can stop by **Abdoumalik's shop** (tel. 0675/170 257) in this souk to pick up a blanket, jellaba, or small bag at a great price.

MEDERSA ABU AL-HASSAN

Rue de la Grand Mosquée; daily 9am-noon and 2:30pm-6pm; 70Dh

The Medersa Abu al-Hassan functioned as a Quranic school until 1927. Originally built during the 14th century, it is contemporary

a long stretch of Atlantic Beach along the North Atlantic Coast

with the Bouanania *medersas* of Fez, Meknes, and Marrakesh. It was commissioned by the Sultan Abu al-Hassan. Though one of the smallest *medersas,* it is one of the most beautiful and least visited, with exquisitely formed stucco, elaborate carved wood, and unique *zellij* work that was renovated from 2000 to 2005. Make your way up the narrow flights of stairs to examine the dormitories of the boys who once studied here, and take in the view from the terrace, where you can overlook Rabat to get a sense of the scale of the Hassan Tower and the looming presence of the Oudaïas Kasbah across the river.

GRAND MOSQUE AND THE MAUSOLEUMS

Near the *medersa* is the Grand Mosque of Salé, and as you follow the Rue de la Grand Mosquée toward the Atlantic, you will also pass three important mausoleums dedicated to the three patron saints of Salé: **Sidi Abdellah Ben Hassoun, Sidi Ben Achir,** and **Sidi Ahmed Hajji.** Non-Muslims will only be able to look at the exterior of these buildings, but of course Muslims are encouraged to enter, pray, and discover the ornate interiors of these mausoleums.

The Grand Mosque dates from the 12th-century Almohad era and is one of the largest in Morocco. There are seven gates to the mosque, though they are all opened only for Friday prayer. The north gate is the one most generally opened throughout the day for prayer. Of particular note are the mihrab and prayer hall, which are original.

Of the three mausoleums, or *zawiyas*, the **Zawiya Sidi Abdellah Ben Hassoun** is arguably the most important. For Moroccans, Ben Hassoun is something like the patron saint of travelers—something you might want to keep in mind as you visit this mausoleum. Ben Hassoun lived in Salé in the 16th century, and the mausoleum dates from the same era. On the eve of the Muslim holiday of Mouloud a giant procession of candlebearers winds its way through Salé in respect for this venerated figure, with various groups contributing music, dance, and general conviviality through the early evening.

Sidi Ben Achir, noted for his ability to cure madness, blindness, and paralysis, was nicknamed "The Doctor" by the people of Salé. His mausoleum marks the western edge of the city. Ben Achir was born in Spain near Jerez de la Frontera and died in Salé in 1364. He is the oldest of the three patron saints of Salé.

The mausoleum of **Sidi Ahmed Hajji** is dedicated to the memory of this venerated marabout and general who famously led a group of 300 men in battle to drive the Spanish out of Mehdia, a small town held captive north of Salé. It was this act that accorded him the status of a saint after his death in 1691. He is the last of the great saints of Salé, and it is said that in his family, the *baraka,* or blessing, was passed from him to subsequent generations.

BORJ

Following Rue de la Grande Mosquée past the cemetery and the three mausoleums, you will find yourself at the Borj, a fortress dating from the 16th century. Though it's generally closed, you can often find the guard there (daily around 10am-6pm), and if you're nice, he might let you in. It's okay to give a small tip (10-20Dh) if you're moved to do so. The views over the beach and crashing waves are spectacular. However, the real treat is the prison where Robinson Crusoe was said to have been a captive. Follow the stairs down into this stone dungeon; a few chains still fastened to the wall send the spine tingling.

THE EXOTIC GARDENS OF SIDI BOUKNADEL

Km13 on N1; tel. 0537/822 756 or 0537/822 758; www.jardinsexotiques.com; daily 9am-sunset; free

Built in 1951 by French horticulture engineer Marcel François, the Exotic Gardens of Sidi Bouknadel (Les Jardins Exotiques de Bouknadel), just a few minutes north of Salé, offer an interesting diversion for families and couples looking for a quiet respite from

1
2
3
4

city life or to cool down during the summer. Much wilder than the Majorelle Gardens of Marrakesh, these gardens feature plants from around the world. François spent 10 years accumulating exotic plants, including diverse species from Southeast Asia and Central Africa. Today, the gardens are dotted with secret passageways, waterfalls, bridges, walkways, and fountains, and they sport an active aviary. Tour guides are available in English for 100Dh. The gardens are easily accessible by the 9 bus leaving from Bab el Had in Rabat or Bab Mrisa in Salé (3.5Dh).

Shopping

★ OULJA ARTISAN COOPERATIVE

Just off Route Ain Houalla a few kilometers east of the Salé medina; daily 9am-6pm

The largest, most expansive artisan complex in Morocco is the Oulja Artisan Cooperative (Complexe Artisanal Oulja). Originally built to host a small group of artisan potters from nearby Salé, the complex has expanded over the years to include nearly every type of traditional Moroccan craft, with many artisans practicing traditional methods as well as working to incorporate more modern designs. For shoppers, this is the place to spend an afternoon. The complex is something like an indoor-outdoor shopping mall with a couple of cafés and restaurants to take a lunch break. Make sure to stroll down the small streets outside the main complex, marked by ornate *zellij* fountains and wicker furniture, to have a look at Moroccan-made furniture using wrought iron, cedarwood, and wicker. Oulja is perhaps best visited at the end of your trip so you don't have to lug souvenirs around the country.

Food and Accommodations

There are not too many options for accommodations in Salé. Several *riads* have either remained incomplete or have gone out of business.

1: looking out to Salé from the Rabat Kasbah **2:** the Medersa Abu al-Hassan **3:** the traditional *shishiya* hat from the north **4:** a boy getting water from the public fountain in Salé

BARAKA

Bab Chaafa, on the waterfront; daily 11am-4pm; 30Dh

For a quick bite to eat, check out Baraka. The ladies here serve up whatever is fresh that day—typically calamari, shrimp, marlin, and sole can be had. It's popular with the local crowd. On busy afternoons, you might have to wait for a seat.

AL MARSA

Quai des Oudayas; tel. 0537/702 302; daily 10am-2am; 200Dh

Along the new marina, part of the Bouregreg development along the riverfront, there are a few cafés, though the real treat is this riverfront restaurant overlooking the Hassan Tower, the kasbah, and the rest of Rabat. The Spanish-style menu features a fine selection of wine, beer, spirits, and cigars, and fish such as salmon and redfin tuna *a la plancha,* as well as grilled steaks, lobster, and other fine dining classics. A less-expensive bistro menu is available noon-7pm. This is a good spot for those looking for a glass of wine and a big European-style splurge. Reservations are recommended.

RIAD BADDI

Derb Zanata; tel. 0537/885 875; 400Dh d

Riad Baddi is a clean establishment and can be a budget option for single travelers with single rooms for as little as 200Dh a night. The rooms are themed on local names. Though the Bouregreg room is probably the most comfortable, the Zenata room is farther away from the street and is a lot quieter. Wi-Fi, air-conditioning, TV, and breakfast are all included with your stay.

RIAD LA PORTE DU BOUREGREG

6 rue Ab Delilah Bensaid; tel 0611/343 550; 800Dh d

This up-and-coming project by Frenchman Jean-Luc and his Moroccan partner Fatima promises a charming mix of modern and ancient Morocco, with touches of their love for music everywhere. There is an on-site hammam perfect for a couples' spa and massage (hammam is included with the room; a massage will cost 100Dh). When Jean-Luc and Fatima aren't around, Zineb, the chef, takes over. Saveurs de la Medina is the gastronomic-quality restaurant. Television, air-conditioning, Wi-Fi, and breakfast are included.

★ LE REPOSE

Talâa Zankat; tel. 0537/882 958; www.therepose.com; 600Dh d

This vegetarian, Muslim-friendly *riad* is a treat for those seeking to get away from it all for a weekend. For vegetarians and non-vegetarians alike, dinner here is a must. The menu—perhaps one of the most creative in all of Morocco—features organic, locally sourced produce spun together in unique combinations (such as a pomegranate, grated carrot, and beet salad) that are simply delightful. Call at least a few hours before to book dinner (150Dh and up) or a vegetarian-friendly Moroccan cooking class. Air-conditioning, Wi-Fi, and breakfast are all included with your room.

Information and Services

Several pharmacies dot the medina. **Pharmacie Fennich** (Bab Cherffa, tel. 0537/883 932, daily 9:30am-9pm) is easy to find next to the large cemetery. Along Rue Boutouil you can find an **Internet café** (daily 10am-2:30pm and 4pm-9pm), usually full of kids playing video games. And near Bab Mrisa, there is a **Currency Exchange-Bouregreg** (Pl. de Marche, tel. 0537/845 839, daily 8am-12:30pm and 2:30pm-7pm).

Getting There and Around

The train, bus, and *grand taxi* stations are all on the eastern side of the medina.

BY BOAT

The most fun way to get to Salé is by **rowboat** from across the banks of the Bouregreg River from Rabat. This short ride will cost you about 5-10Dh and take all of 10 minutes. Though perhaps impractical for those arriving with luggage, it's still a must-do for most visitors and is a convenient way to go back and forth between the two cities. You can find the ports along the riverfront walk, just down from Le Dhow in Rabat.

BY TRAM

The **tram** (www.tram-way.ma) is another easy way to get back and forth between cities. It will take you from in front of the Bab Mrisa to the Hassan Mosque and the Rabat-Ville and Salé train stations for 7Dh.

BY TRAIN

The **ONCF train** (Route de Rabat, tel. 0890/203 040, www.oncf.ma) connects with **Asilah** (3hr, 10 daily, 2nd/1st-class 86Dh/127Dh), **Casablanca** (regular train 1.5hr, rapid train 1hr, 40 daily, regular train 41Dh/74Dh, rapid train 51Dh/101Dh), **Fez** (3hr, 12 daily, 85Dh/126Dh), **Marrakesh** (5hr, 9 daily, 128Dh/195Dh), **Meknes** (2hr, 12 daily, 63Dh/94Dh), **Rabat** (15min, 40 daily, 15Dh/27Dh), **Tangier** (3.5hr, 10 daily, 101Dh/149Dh), and other destinations.

BY BUS

The **CTM** (tel. 0800/0900 30, www.ctm.ma) does not call on Salé (only Rabat), though most other local bus companies will stop in front of the Bab Mrisa.

BY TAXI

Grands taxis can take you to **Moulay Bousselham** (1.5hr, 135km/84mi, 55Dh), **Rabat** (10min, 2km/1mi, 5Dh), and other destinations, though you may have to haggle for a good price. The most convenient spot to find grand taxis in Salé is at the Salé train station.

Petits taxis are available for travel within Salé, though they are not allowed to cross the bridge into Rabat. Most trips around Salé won't cost more than 15-20Dh.

BANASA

There are many semi-abandoned archaeological digs of some importance in this region, with Colonia Iulia Valentia Banasa being one of the better-excavated sites. For those interested in archaeology or the pre-Islamic history of Morocco, this can be a fascinating daytime excursion, and you will likely have the entire site to yourself. The only people that generally visit these sites are archaeologists, historians, and the occasional school group. Entrance is free, as the sites are not fenced in, and there is usually a friendly security guard on-site who will be happy to let you have the run of the ruins.

Banasa was a former outpost of the Roman era, though its history, like the history of the more popular sites of Lixus and Volubilis, stretches back before the Roman era. The layout of the cities and the architecture left of these ruins is largely Roman in origin. Over a period of 300 years, the city flourished: There was a thermal bath, a temple dedicated to Venus, and numerous merchant houses. Though the Romans had retreated north by the end of the 2nd century, the city continued to thrive as a largely Christian community until its eventual abandonment around the 3rd century. The 15-hectare (37-acre) site has plenty still to uncover, with the more recent finds, including several bronze statues, on display at the Archaeology Museum of Rabat.

Near the forum you can see some wonderful Latin inscriptions detailing trade laws with the local Amazigh tribes. Its commanding position along the Sebou River is breathtaking. Much of the decorative mosaic work and the few bronze statues found here are now housed at the Archaeology Museum of Rabat. The various houses and shops left to ruin are still waiting for archaeologists to unearth clues as to the daily life of the people here; however, exploration of the site has been paused until more funding has been found.

Rachid Arghabi (tel. 0672/288 061) is the curator and custodian of the sites and can arrange for group tours or provide more historical information for visitors interested in Banasa and the other digs around this region of Morocco.

Getting There

Because of Banasa's location in the interior of the region, where road signage is rarely used, it is best to either **hire a guide** or to use **GPS,** though even with GPS, you will likely be a little lost or turned around as you're trying to find the site. Roads are unnamed, though the road numbers below should help if you're using GPS.

The best direction is to take the tolled N1 autoroute **north** from Rabat. Take the Sidi Allal Tazi exit (about 40 minutes from Rabat). From the tollbooth, follow the signs straight down the P4234 to Sidi Allal Tazi. In Sidi Allal Tazi, the P4234 breaks. You have to take a right at the T-intersection and cross the Sebou River, then take your first left to get back onto the P4234. Look for a small white sign for Banasa on the left side of the road. Take the left and continue along the road for about 2 kilometers (1mi) until you reach the site.

MOULAY BOUSSELHAM

مولاي بوسلهام

During the off-season, Moulay Bousselham is a haven for those seeking a bit of relaxation and something a bit more idyllic. Along the hillside beach, sunbathers mingle with fishers and swimmers with shellfish collectors. Its location off the autoroute and the noticeable absence of a CTM or railway connection mean that Moulay Bousselham isn't touristed by many internationals, though its popularity with those seeking sun and something off the beaten track has grown in recent years. Largely, this is a weekend destination for many Rabatis and other local tourists, though in the summer months, the village population swells with vacationing Moroccans renting houses along the beach for their families. The summer crowds make this a place to avoid in late July and August.

The town derives its name from a 10th-century Egyptian saint. His tomb and the tomb of his friend, Sidi Abd el-Galil, lie across the mouth of the river. They provide a sort of protection or blessing to the charming

1

2

lagoon of the Merja Zerga National Park, an extremely popular stopover for bird-watchers.

Locally, Moulay Bousselham is known for its strawberries. A strange, battered strawberry sculpture stands testament to this at the roundabout at the end of the *marché* (market), overlooking the Atlantic. The best season for the berries, most believe, is January.

★ Merja Zerga National Park

For nature lovers and bird-watchers, a boat trip into the Merja Zerga, or Blue Lagoon, is a real treat. This 4,500-hectare (11,000-acre) park is a popular winter layover for migratory birds making their way from Europe to Africa. During the migrating season (Oct.-Mar.), you can expect to see coots, Eurasian wigeons, gadwalls, gray plovers, marbled teals, northern shovelers, pied avocets, ruddy shelducks, and slender-billed curlews, though it's the greater flamingos, more commonly known as pink flamingos, that really steal the show here.

This saltwater lagoon stretches south from Moulay Bousselham into a reed-lined cove. During the day, locals harvest worms for fishing bait along the muddy shores. Over 100 bird varieties dine in the lagoon, whose humidity makes it a perfect breeding ground for various types of insects, most notably the mosquito, which the birds feast on throughout the year. For this reason, water-resistant bug spray is recommended for any foray into the lagoon. If the tide is out, parts of the lagoon are not passable by boat, and you'll likely have to hop into the shallow lagoon and march through the wetlands. It's all part of the birding adventure!

There are numerous boats for hire (100Dh per hour) to take you on a tour of the lagoon. **Hassan Dahlil** (tel. 0668/434 110) is the only officially recognized bird guide, though most other guides here are reasonably trained. In recent years, many of them have become avid birders, and most carry with them a birding book to help identify species. Nearly all of them know the lagoon well, what flocks have recently arrived, and the general migratory patterns and species. However, because Hassan has been featured on numerous television shows and in other travel guides, many guides will claim to be Hassan. It is best to call Hassan directly (he speaks English) to arrange a tour with him or arrange one through your accommodation. In practice, you can show up to the lagoon and hire a guide straight away for minimum fuss.

The entrance for the Merja Zerga National Park is on the south end of Moulay Bousselham at Chez Nassim. Watch out for the turnoff from R406 across the street from the Attijariwafa Bank and follow the road down to the fishing boats and campground on the banks of the lagoon.

Food

AL MOUSTAIN

Accueil du Centre d'Estivage; sunrise-early afternoon; 7Dh

Across from the Accueil du Centre d'Estivage, one of the few good landmarks around the central market, is a reliable *bissara* stand, Al Moustain. You'll see fishers packing this small stand in the morning before heading out.

CAFÉ IZAGUIRRE

Merja Zerga, at the port; tel. 0537/432 445; 8am-10pm; 80Dh

This clean, chill place down by the port sports slightly obstructed views over the lagoon, insanely photographic blue dinghy boats, and the fish market. Come here for the seafood. Fish are brought in straight from the port, just a handful of steps away, and put directly to the grill. You can even go shopping for your own fish on the port, buy direct from the fisherman, and take it here to grill (20Dh) or to fry (15Dh per kilogram). It doesn't get much fresher than this.

1: Greater flamingos take flight in the Merja Zerga National Park. **2:** the Roman forum in Banasa

VILLA NORA

20 Front de Mer; tel. 0537/537 432 071; 400Dh per night; 170Dh dinner

I can't recommend Villa Nora for sleeping; however, the location next to the beach with terrace views and the delicious seafood tajines on offer make for a great sunset dinner on the terrace. Make sure you reserve ahead of time for either lunch or dinner. If you really needed a roof for the night, this should be your last resort—when I was there in 2015 and again in 2018, the bed was a literal box spring (no mattress) and the guest rooms were all very musty.

Accommodations

Nearly all of the lodging options in Moulay Bousselham are geared toward local tourism (unadvertised rented houses), so hotels and guesthouses are sparse. If you're traveling during the busy summer months or on weekends, you will want to reserve in advance. Luckily, there are usually options available in the off-season for last-minute arrivals during the week.

HOTEL LE LAGOON

R406, at the beginning of town; tel. 0537/537 432 650 or 0537/432 649; 300Dh d

The Hotel Le Lagoon, with views of the lagoon and sea, is okay in a pinch. The rooms are clean-ish; there always seems to be some flies and mosquitoes about, and the linens are a bit rough. For the price point in this part of Morocco, it's a decent value.

★ VILA BEA

41 Front De Mer; tel. 0537/537 432 087; www.vilabea.com; 900-1200Dh d

This is the chic option: retro art deco Miami Beach meets Japanese minimalism and genuine Moroccan hospitality. Amenities include en suite bathrooms, rooftop hammam, workout room, cinema, terrace bar, and a heated infinity pool that opens out over the ocean. There are numerous lounging spots perfect for curling up with a book and listening to the crashing surf, or just getting a little sun. Dinner is available (reservations required, 270Dh) and includes a variety of seasonal salads, fresh fish, and vegetarian options. Wi-Fi, television, air-conditioning, and breakfast are all included with your stay. Though all rooms sport a sea view, the property only has three rooms that directly face the sea. Consider paying more to enjoy unforgettable sunsets from the comfort of your bed.

CAMPING

tel. 0537/432 477; 80Dh (camping car, two-person summer, electricity, shower, toilet all included)

Camping is another option at the Merja Zerga National Park. The campground is right next to the lagoon. Because of this, you'll want to make sure you have plenty of mosquito repellent. There are services onsite for showers and hookup facilities for camper vans. This is one of the nicer camping parks in Morocco, particularly outside of the summer season.

Information and Services

At the entrance of town you will find the post office and several banks, each with Western Union. **Banque Populaire** and **Credit Agricule** have the same hours (Mon.-Fri. 8:15am-3:45pm, Ramadan 9:30am-2pm). The many pharmacies around town keep the same hours (daily 9am-1pm and 3pm-7pm). **Pharmacie Moulay Bousselham** is in the *marché,* and **Pharmacie Al Moustain** is at the start of Front de Mer, just one block past the *marché.* There are a couple of **Internet cafés** near the entrance and one on the north end of town that is open in the summer and well-signed. **Villa Nora** along the Front de Mer hosts a cultural center with free Wi-Fi.

Getting There and Around

BY CAR

The easiest way to get to Moulay Bousselham is by car. There are well-posted signs along National Road 1 (N1) and the tolled freeway (A1). From **Rabat,** it is about a 1.5-hour drive on the tolled freeway. The N1 is a bit more scenic as it hugs the Atlantic Coast and detours through farmlands, but slower speeds and occasionally slow-going farming equipment generally make this a 2.5-hour drive.

BY GRAND TAXI AND BUS

If you haven't rented a car, you will probably have to hire a ***grand taxi.*** The *grand taxi* stand is right at the beginning of town and has taxis leaving 5-10 times a day for Kenitra (1hr, 89km/55mi, 15Dh) and Ksar el-Kbir (1hr, 70km/43mi, 15Dh). To book a taxi for another location, you will likely have to pay both fares, to-and-from, with **Asilah** and **Tangier** each costing around 700Dh, and **Rabat** and **Larache** 600Dh. Local buses also stop here, though there is no CTM service.

Larache العرايش

With the nearby Roman Ruins of Lixus, as well as a number of fantastic constructions left from the Spanish Protectorate era, an old Kasbah, and its picturesque position directly above the Atlantic Ocean, Larache is something of a hidden gem that lacks polish. It's a laid-back port town nesting high above the Atlantic Coast and the mouth of the Loukkos River. This is a destination best left to more adventurous travelers.

Historically, Larache was a stronghold of the Spanish empire and a strategic port. Some of the ruins here date from the various periods of Spanish rule in the 15th, 16th, and 17th centuries. Everywhere you look, Spanish heritage is very much in evidence. Along the Place de la Liberation (still known by the locals as Plaza de España), you can find various colonial-era hotels, cafés, and even a church that still gives Sunday mass. The nightly *paseo* (stroll) on the newly built Patio Atlantico and the pedestrian-only Avenue Hassan II is a daily event; café menus typically include the Spanish dishes *gambas a la plancha* (pan-grilled shrimp), paella, and *pollo de asado* (grilled chicken); and flamenco music can often be heard just above the crash of the surf below.

There is a sense of faded, if not dying, European decadence throughout this old Spanish port town, perhaps best symbolized by Fort Kebibat crumbling into a magnificent ruin threatening to plummet into the ocean at any moment, and immortalized by the French writer Jean Genet. He spent the last decade of his life here when Larache was more cosmopolitan in nature, similar to nearby Tangier.

ORIENTATION

Located about midway between **Tangier** and **Rabat,** Larache borders the Atlantic Ocean to the west, with the **Loukkos River** to the north. Across the river you'll find the Roman ruin of **Lixus** as well as the popular beach of **Larache.**

SIGHTS

Spanish Cemetery

The Spanish Cemetery (Cementerio Español) overlooks the crashing waves thundering against the cliffside and is a breathtaking spot to take a photo or wander among the dead. Ring the buzzer to the right of the gate to call the guardian. Tip them 5Dh to open the gate. Many tombs remain nameless. Those with names are largely military, though of course the French bad-boy writer **Jean Genet** (1910-1986) is the resident celebrity. He is easy to find. Walk along the only paved path from the gate until the path's end to his burial spot. Don't forget the flowers.

The cemetery is located along the southwest corner of Larache hugging a bluff overlooking the ocean along Avenue Moulay Ismail.

Church of Our Lady of the Pillar

Ave. Mohammed V

Church of Our Lady of the Pillar (Iglesia de Nuestra Señora del Pilar) is a Spanish-built

Larache

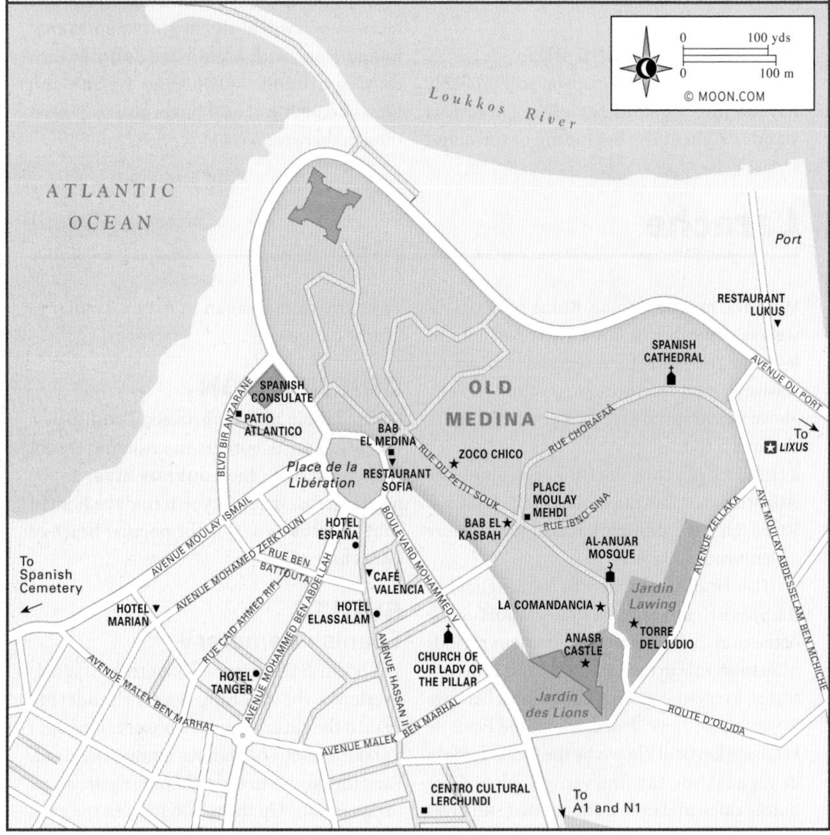

20th-century church. The facade recalls Andalusian mosques, echoing the al-Anuar Mosque in the medina, though the interior is more typical of Spanish cathedrals. Mass is held here, in Spanish, on Sunday at 11am.

Medina

The standout **Bab el Medina** gate at the Place de la Liberation leads directly into the **Zoco Chico,** a Moroccan market where everything from fruits, vegetables, and meat is on sale next to secondhand goods and Chinese-made pots and pans. From here, take a right through the ancient **Bab el Kasbah** and into one of the more pleasant medinas in Morocco. The blue-and-white-washed medina is relatively small, though a bit hilly, and hasn't been gentrified. It's a great medina in which to get a feel for the quickly fading traditional Moroccan city living, complete with neighborhood *farrans* (traditional public wood ovens) and children kicking soccer balls up and down the surprisingly tidy streets.

As you walk through the Bab el Kasbah, look to the left to see a map of the medina

1: the Spanish colonial architecture of Larache **2:** a woman walking through the streets of the Larache medina **3:** final resting place of Jean Genet at the Spanish Cemetery

1
2
3
Jean Genet
19 Dec 1910
13-14 Avril 86

that highlights several places of importance, including a couple of 15th-century walls as well as the **Anasr Castle.** Cross Place Moulay Ismail and continue down Rue Moulay el-Mehdi to **Plaza Dar El Majzen,** perhaps the most picturesque square in the medina. From here, you can view the octagonal **al-Anuar Mosque,** the remodeled **La Comandancia,** and the **Jewish Tower (Torre del Judio).** Head back into the medina, take your first right down Sidi Abdelkarim, past the mausoleum, and turn left onto Calle Jebiil. Follow the road down to the main to the T-intersection with Calle Real 2 Mars (road is unmarked), and turn right. A few steps down, at the corner of Calle Del Jartzi, is a 15th-century **Spanish Cathedral** falling into ruin, one of the only known cathedrals in a Moroccan medina. Stop for a mint tea and a much-needed bottle of water at one of the smoke-free outdoor patio cafés dotting the edge of the medina on the corner of the decrepit **Fort Kebibat,** built in AD 1491 by Moulay en Nasser and later used as a pirate stronghold. Relax with views over the Atlantic, the beach, and the mouth of the river before continuing around the fort and back up to the Place de Liberation.

Ras R'mel

Across the river to the north is Ras R'mel, a small strip of beach largely empty outside of the busy summer months. This is a great spot for beachgoers, though swimmers beware! The undertow along this strip of coast is very strong and there are no lifeguards. The easiest way to get there is to hire a boat at the port (5Dh) to take you across, though during the summer the 4 bus (3.5Dh) can get you there. It runs every 20 minutes or so.

TOP EXPERIENCE

★ Lixus

On a hillside across the Loukkos River from Larache lies the ancient city of Lixus, with commanding views over the valley and the mouth of the river, making it easy to imagine why this was such a strategic city. It is a city rich with lore, as well. Ancient Greeks believed this to be the location of the legendary Hesperides, the keepers of the golden apples, and the site of the penultimate labor of Hercules, where he was charged by King Eurystheus to steal the golden apples. It is not hard to imagine that the locally grown tangerines were indeed the golden apples of myth.

the ruins of the Roman forum in Lixus

Lixus was founded in the 7th century BC by the Phoenicians and later conquered by the Carthaginians, much like the Chellah Necropolis (Sala Colonia) in Rabat and Mogador in Essaouira. When the Romans conquered Carthage, they annexed these cities, which became outposts in their province Mauretania Tingitana.

The ruins consist of a series of vats where *garum* (a local fish sauce) was produced, as well as a fantastic amphitheater (the only one of its kind in Morocco), baths, Roman walls, a paleo-Christian church, temples, and a confusing network of crumbled houses and walls that once made up the trade center of the forum. Some work was done to recreate columns, and though the patchwork of cement and plaster somehow takes away from the authenticity of the site, it helps to imagine what the networks of roads and buildings must have looked like at one time.

Once, murals decorated many of the floors of the houses and buildings, though nearly all of these have been dug up and taken away. Most are on display at the Archaeology Museum of Rabat or in Tetouan. The one remaining mural, featuring Neptune, is in the main square of the baths, though it is currently covered by a protective layer of plastic and earth until future excavation is possible.

Only about 20 percent of the 75-hectare (185-acre) site has been excavated, which means that a lot of the site is still buried under dirt and rubble, though it can awaken the nascent archaeologist inside you and provides hours of fun for kids. It's hard not to look over the mounds of earth and grass and wonder at what lay beneath. What has been excavated, including the amphitheater and baths, makes for a picturesque half-day excursion. There is a visitors center under construction, though it is likely that there will not be funding for this for some time and construction has halted. The site is guarded by locals, though entrance is free. There are no hours or official guided tours, though Jalil or Noureddine, the custodians, are usually around during daylight and will give tours of the ruins. You'll be expected to tip 20-50Dh. It is best to agree on this ahead of time.

Lixus is easy enough to find. From the N1, take the turn onto the Ras R'mel road, just a couple of kilometers north of Larache. The site entrance is directly on the hillside corner. Taxis are easily had from Larache (20-30Dh) and will let you off at the entrance, though you'll want to agree on a time for the driver to meet you at the gate for the return trip, as there are no taxis from Lixus. It is possible to walk back to Larache (4km/2.5mi).

FOOD AND ACCOMMODATIONS

Several cafés and small restaurants sit tucked beneath the arches along the Place de la Liberation. Clean, inexpensive former Spanish hotels surround the Place de la Liberation, though breakfast is not included, there are few nonsmoking options, and the decor is dated. **Hotel El Assalam** (9 Ave. Hassan II, tel. 0537/916 822, 100Dh) is a favorite budget option, though none of the rooms are truly nonsmoking. **Hotel Tanger** (on the corner of Ave. Moulay Mohamed Ben Abdellah and Rue Tanger, tel. 0537/916 814, 140Dh) is another option, a bit newer, though much the same.

RESTAURANT SOFIA

Pl. de la Liberation; daily noon-midnight; 50Dh

Head to Restaurant Sofia for *pescado a la crema* (fish in cream sauce) and *pollo asado* (grilled chicken). The free Wi-Fi is a bonus, as is the flamenco music that kicks up most nights around 8:30pm.

CAFÉ VALENCIA

Avenue Hassan II; daily 8am-10pm; 30Dh

Along the main pedestrian road, Avenue Hassan II, Café Valencia just outside the Hotel España serves up a solid breakfast. Get eggs sunny-side up, toast, Moroccan *bildi* cheese, coffee, and a freshly squeezed orange juice for 30Dh.

RESTAURANT LUKUS

Zone Portuaire; tel. 0537/539 914 640; daily noon-11pm, closed Ramadan; 100Dh

This venture, by a German-Moroccan couple, is a walk down the hill from the **Spanish Consulate,** right next to the port. Walk past the immaculate kitchen on your way upstairs to a dining room that overlooks the colorful fishing boats anchored in the harbor. Ask for the freshest catch of the day. Start with *zaalouk* (a traditional Moroccan eggplant salad) and dive into a grilled dorado served with potato croquettes and vegetable béchamel gratin.

HOTEL MARIAN

Ave. Mohamed Zerktoun; daily noon-midnight; 100Dh

This protectorate-era hotel is conveniently located just a block off of the **Patio Atlantico** and features a menu of standard Spanish classics, including *gambas a la plancha* and *tortilla española* (a Spanish omelet), though the real draw here is the wine and beer menu, as the hotel is one of the few places in town with a liquor license.

★ HOTEL ESPAÑA

6 Ave. Hassan II; tel. 0537/913 195; www.hotelespanalarache.com; 260Dh d

One of the better-kept colonial-era Spanish hotels with real nonsmoking rooms on offer. The rooms are basic, and if you are facing the street, it can get a bit noisy. It's one of the better values in the region. The staff is accommodating and, most importantly, the beds are dependably comfortable and clean. There is even Wi-Fi, as well as air-conditioning and TVs in every room.

INFORMATION AND SERVICES

Banks, ATMs, and the local post office are all found on **Avenue Mohammed V,** just up from Place de la Liberation, including: **Banque Populaire** (Mon.-Fri. 8:15am-3:45pm, Ramadan 9:30am-2pm), **Credit Agricule** (Mon.-Fri. 8:15am-3:45pm), and the **post office** (Mon.-Fri. 8am-4:15pm, Ramadan 9am-3pm).

CENTRO CULTURAL LERCHUNDI

13 Ave. Hassan II; tel. 0537/098 673

On Avenue Hassan II, you can find the Centro Cultural Lerchundi, which offers language classes in French, Spanish, and English.

PHARMACIE GHATNATA

Ave. Moulay Ben Abdullah; tel. 0537/912 929; Mon.-Fri. 10am-1pm and 3pm-7:30pm

The conveniently located Pharmacie Ghatnata is also here on Avenue Hassan II.

MARNET CYBER

corner of Ave. Moulay Mohamed Ben Abdellah and Rue Mouatamid Ben Abad; Mon.-Sat. 10am-11pm

There are a few Internet cafés, with Marnet Cyber being one of the more convenient options.

GETTING THERE AND AROUND

Larache is small enough to **walk** around, but ***petits taxis*** are an inexpensive way to get down to the port and back.

By Car

Larache is connected via the tolled autoroute (A1) with **Rabat** (168km/104mi, 2hr).

By Grand Taxi and Bus

Other *grands taxis,* CTMs, and buses use the ***gare routière*** (sometimes referred to in Spanish as *estaciastillo Anasr*) just off Avenue Moulay Mohamed Ben Abdellah. Regular ***grands taxis*** leave for **Asilah** (30min, 42km/26mi, 15Dh) and **Ksar el Kbir** (30min, 36km/22mi, 15Dh). The **CTM** (tel. 0800/0900 30, www.ctm.ma) connects with **Casablanca** (4hr, 1 daily, 105Dh), **Fez** (4hr, 4 daily, 80Dh), **Meknes** (3hr, 4 daily, 60Dh), **Rabat** (2.5hr, 2 daily, 75Dh), **Tangier** (1.5hr, 4 daily, 35Dh), and other destinations. Other bus companies are available for additional locations. At the *gare routière,* there is a well-signed **baggage**

consignment (*consigne des bagages*), 7Dh per day, 10Dh for overnight.

For **Lixus** (10min, 3km/1.8mi, 5Dh) or **Ras R'mel** (15min, 4km/2.4mi, 7Dh), you can book a *grand taxi* from Castillo Anasr near Plaza Dar El Majzen.

Asilah أصيلة

This up-and-coming destination is just off the beaten track enough to still be charming despite the tour groups (mostly day-trippers from Spain) that have found their way here. For many years, Asilah (formerly Zili, a small town of Phoenician origins) was mostly known as a picturesque fishing village, where the waves from the Atlantic pounded at the 500-year-old stone walls of this former Portuguese outpost. Paul Bowles and a few other expat writers and artists have found their way here, but it wasn't until former Foreign Ambassador Mohamed Benaïssa and the Asilah-born artist Mohammed Melehi decided to revamp the town through their passion for painting, sculpture, and the arts that this little fishing village began to transform. In 1978 the first ever Cultural Moussem of Asilah took place, and the town was forever altered.

Today, the self-proclaimed "City of Art" hosts the yearly Cultural Moussem of Asilah, which draws artists, art dealers, musicians, poets, and performers from around the world. To commemorate the summertime festival, many of the medina walls are used as murals, making the entire medina one of the major tourist attractions. The Zilachis take pride and help to clean their city, which unfortunately can't be said of the city beaches. However, Paradise Beach, about 4 kilometers (2.5mi) south of the city, is a gem. Outside of summer months, it's possible to have the entire beach to yourself.

Many apartments, residences, and other projects are in the works in Asilah, including a complete rebuild of the main mosque in the medina, adding to the overall feeling of growth in this otherwise small town.

ORIENTATION

A few hours north of **Rabat** and just an hour south of **Tangier,** located directly on the Atlantic Ocean with an old **medina** nestled inside of a 500-year-old **Portuguese fortress,** there is a lot to like about Asilah. Though the medina is where most travelers spend their time, the area just north of the medina is where you'll find the **municipal beach,** the **port,** and a number of surprisingly fantastic **restaurants.**

SIGHTS

Medina

The Asilah medina is one of the cleanest and most welcoming in Morocco. Tucked inside protective walls dating from a period of Portuguese rule, this small medina has become gentrified over the last decade, with many Spanish buying vacation and rental homes, though it has retained much of its charm.

Surrounding the medina are the **ramparts,** one of the more notable features of Asilah. The impressive stone structure dates from 1471, when the Portuguese took over the town from El Hakim II, the caliph of Córdoba, and fortified the city. The ramparts are dotted with many towers (*borj*). Many locals and tourists take in the sunset at the ***krakiya,*** a line of stone that juts out into the ocean, where Gnawa musicians strum and chant. When the tide is high, teenage boys jump from the *krakiya* and plunge 15 meters (50ft) down into the ocean. Next to the *krakiya* you can look down on the picturesque mausoleum of Lalla Mennana, the daughter of a famous Sufi leader. She was said to have died on her wedding night, taking the form of a white dove to fly into the afterlife.

Asilah

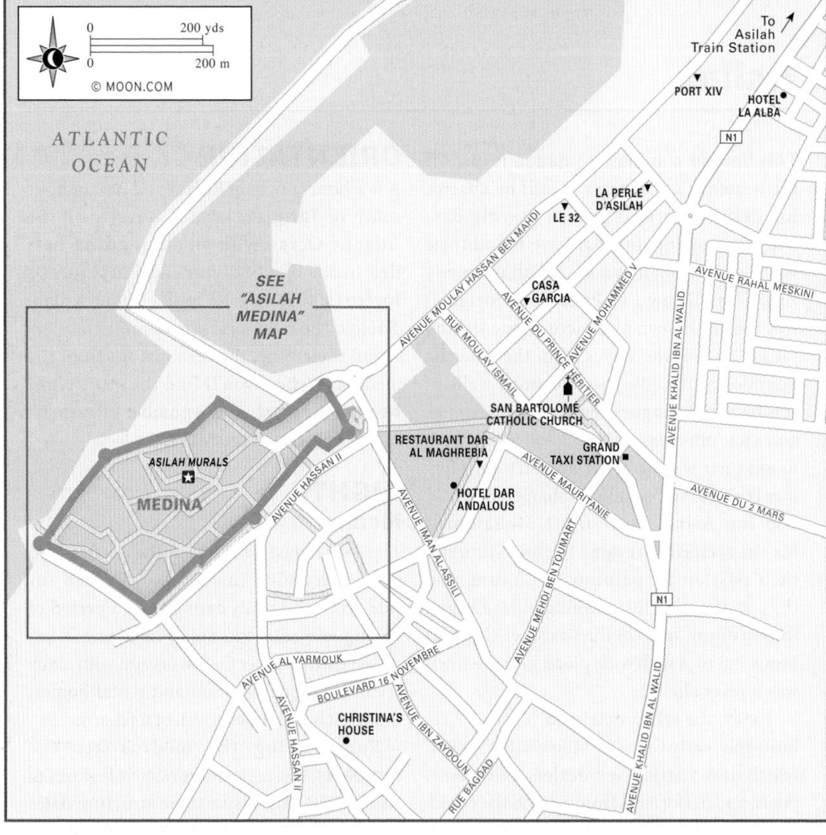

★ ASILAH MURALS

At the beginning of every summer, the town gets together and paints the entire medina in whites and blues, covering up any of the murals that were painted the previous year to create a fresh canvas. Then, in preparation for the yearly art festival held in August, artists are enlisted from around the world; each is given a wall, and new murals are painted. Around every corner, it seems, a new mural lurks, waiting to be appreciated.

HASSAN II CENTER

Rue al-Kasabah, across from the Grand Mosque of Asilah; hours vary; free

The Hassan II Center (Centre Hassan II) is a cultural center that has a revolving exhibit of contemporary art selected from artists throughout Morocco. Admission is free. The hours are often unpredictable and limited due to various special events, though it is generally open in the early mornings before lunch and right after lunch.

TCHIKAYA U'TAMSI GARDEN

Directly outside Bab Kasaba

The Congolese poet Tchikaya U'Tamsi wrote,

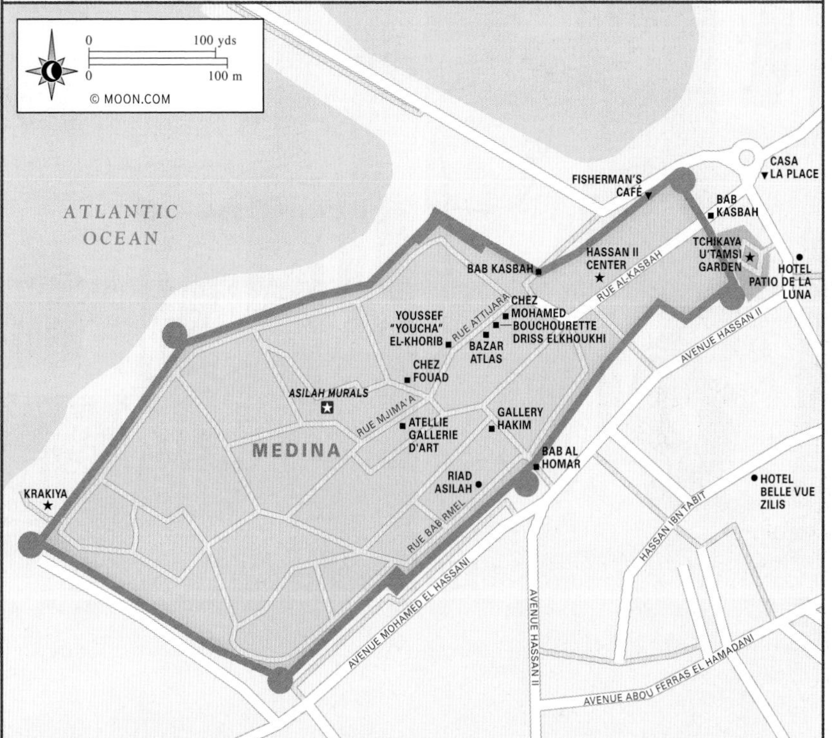

"The Walls of Asilah are the showered songs of the hands that built them." He participated in Asilah's first Afro-Arab Cultural Forum in 1981 and every subsequent year until his unexpected death in 1988. There is a biennial poetry prize awarded in his honor. The Tchikaya U'Tamsi Garden (Jardin Tchikaya U'Tamsi) is nestled below the ramparts, where U'Tamsi liked to sit and watch the sunset. One of his poems is engraved here.

Outside the Medina

SAN BARTOLOMÉ CATHOLIC CHURCH

Corner of Ave. du Prince Héretier and Ave. Mohammed V; mass Sat. 7pm

The San Bartolomé Catholic Church (Iglesia San Bartolomé) was built by Franciscan monks in 1927 while Spain was functioning as the protectorate for the north of Morocco. The church holds mass in Spanish or French (though many in the congregation speak English) every Saturday evening at 7pm. San Bartolomé is one of the few churches in Morocco that are allowed to ring the bell for mass—something a bit strange to hear in the midst of this otherwise Muslim country.

PARADISE BEACH (PLAGE DE R'MILAT)

One of the real pleasures of spending a few days in Asilah is found on Paradise Beach just a few kilometers south. This crescent-shaped stretch of sand is packed in the summer with tourists from Morocco, Spain, and other parts of Europe, but outside the summer it is largely

1
2
3

empty. Swimming along this stretch can be dangerous and there are no lifeguards, so exercise caution. It's best visited after the summer, when crowds are gone, the weather is still warm, and the Atlantic is relatively mild. You can hike there, but for most it will be better to get there by *petit taxi* (50Dh). You can usually find horse-drawn carts along Avenue Mohamed el Hassani or near the roundabout next to the Tchikaya U'Tamsi Garden. Bargain for cost or have your accommodation arrange transportation.

ENTERTAINMENT AND EVENTS

ASILAH ART FESTIVAL

www.asilahinfo.com; Aug.

The Cultural Moussem of Asilah is an arts and cultural festival started by two friends, Mohammed Benaïssa, now the mayor of Asilah, and Mohammed Melehi, a celebrated Moroccan artist. Benaïssa and Melehi had traveled throughout Europe and saw how art could change a community. In 1978 they came together and began the festival as a platform for cultural dialogue and exchange between different countries, with a different guest nation every year. In 2014, the guest nation was Qatar. Previous guest nations include Mexico, Portugal, and Kuwait. Each year, this guest nation takes center stage and showcases its culture through art exhibitions, folk dances, concerts, conferences, and much more. Unfortunately, many of the events are by invitation only.

SHOPPING

Shopping in Asilah is low-key, relaxed, and honest. Very few people engage in high-pressured sales tactics, making this a destination for shoppers to not only take in some sun, but also to pick up souvenirs for everyone back home. Along Rue Tijara in the medina there are several shops worth noting, all conveniently near one another. Throughout the medina, artist galleries and studios sell reasonably priced works, which can make it easy to support the local arts while finding that must-have painting, photo, or sculpture to pack home.

BAZAR ATLAS

25 Rue Tijara; tel. 0539/417 864

This small shop has a wonderful selection of handwoven carpets at fair prices and offers hassle-free shopping. The owners are pleased to show you what they have on offer, and can ship back to your home country so you don't have to worry about packing a large carpet with your luggage. If you're looking to pick up a traditional, handwoven Moroccan carpet, this is one of the best places for selection, service, and price in the region.

CHEZ MOHAMED

9 Rue Tijara; tel. 0661/924 782

Mohamed has a wonderful rotating selection of lightweight blankets and carpets, Fassi pottery, and small tiles for sale. Like most other sellers in Asilah, he is low-pressure and incredibly honest. He'll also be happy to advise you if you need a little help getting around town or finding a specific souvenir or gift to take home.

BOUCHOURETTE DRISS ELKHOUKHI

27 Rue Tijara; tel. 0661/924 782

This is one of the few shops in all of Morocco that deals exclusively with *boucharouettes* (Moroccan rag rugs). These popular handwoven carpets are made from recycled fabrics, machine-washable, and small enough to pack in your suitcase. Prices range from 200-500Dh, making these carpets not only eco-friendly but extremely affordable. Driss, the owner, will be happy to show you his selection and tell you about where the carpets are from and their importance in today's Morocco.

1: Kids go to school within the muraled walls of the medina. **2:** carpets for sale in Asilah **3:** the Portuguese Ramparts and Municipal Beach

CHEZ FOUAD

8 Zagori; tel. 0638/058 303

Offers various handmade goods, including lightweight throws, blankets, rugs, and Fassi pottery. Fouad sources his material from around Morocco and often has some interesting pieces, such as blankets from the Rif and Middle Atlas, that you probably won't see elsewhere and for fair prices.

Local Artists

HAKIM GHAÏLAN

14 Pl. Sidi Benaïssa; tel. 0661/799 535; hakimghailan@yahoo.fr

Hakim Ghaïlan runs the **Gallery Hakim,** where he mostly exhibits younger artists, many of them fresh graduates from the Université des Beaux Arts in Tetouan. He usually has a few engraved postcards for sale, as well as other engravings and printings, which can make for a perfect gift.

RABIE EL-MESNANI

Rue Attijara; tel. 0672/492 087

Rabie el-Mesnani can usually be found at his **Atellie Gallerie d'art,** where much of his abstract work, as well as the work of a couple of other local artists, including his brother, is on display. Rabie is one of the more popular young artists of Morocco, and many of his large, abstract canvases can be found in several hotels around Morocco as well as Spain. He has also been featured in several magazines in Europe and is one of the faces of the new generation of contemporary Moroccan art. Stop by his gallery for a look. Pieces range from 200Dh and up.

YOUSSEF "YOUCHA" EL-KHORIB

Rue Tijara; tel. 0534/226 018

Youcha has a colorful gallery right on Rue Attijara. He has been featured in numerous French, Spanish, and Swiss magazines, and is often written about as a "master of the naïve." Youcha once owned a café but sold it to pursue his dream of making art. His dreamlike paintings depict a world struggling with religion, war, immigration, lust, and other monsters that haunt him. His paintings are some of the most affordable larger-scale canvases you'll find and are ideal for packing home. Poster-size originals start around 400Dh.

FOOD

Asilah has a surprising number of good restaurant options for a small town, mostly geared toward weekenders from Spain and day-trippers from Tangier. A convenient

Asilah is home to many artists.

Art in Asilah

The nearby Université des Beaux Arts in Tetouan, one of the few fine art schools in Morocco, as well as the proximity of Tangier and Europe, helps to make this region a hotbed for contemporary art in Morocco. Several artists from France and Spain have found this charming seaside town, and with the advent of the annual art festival, the face of Asilah has been transformed by the arts. Throughout the year, you can find artists from Morocco, Europe, and sometimes other places in residence working on their craft, painting, sculpting, engraving, and often engaging in cross-culture dialogue and attempting to make sense of life on the edge—the edge of Africa and Europe, Atlantic and Mediterranean, North and South, East and West.

liquor store is near the park along the pedestrian route, Avenue Abdel Moumen Ali Bnou, on the way to Place Mohammed V in the Ville Nouvelle. Along Avenue Mohammed V, across from the police station is a great **bissara stand** (7Dh) as well as a good selection of local cafés for a light breakfast or snack.

FISHERMAN'S CAFÉ

The Fisherman's Café along the medina wall outside of Bab al-Baher, tucked behind a bamboo fence, serves mint tea and is a local tradition. Fishers have long gathered here to while away the hours playing Parcheesi ("par-cheese" in the local dialect), sipping tea, smoking kif, and waiting for the tides.

CASA LA PLACE

7 Ave. Moulay al-Hassan Ben Medhi; tel. 0539/417 326; daily noon-11pm; 100Dh

Casa la Place is conveniently located just outside Bab Kasaba, making it the perfect stop for a grilled-fish lunch followed by a stroll past the boats and up the boulevard to the beach. Reserve ahead of time for the seafood *pastilla* (savory pie). Wine and beer are served.

CASA GARCIA

Angle Ave. Prince Héritier et Melilal; tel. 0539/417 465; daily noon-3pm and 7:30pm-11pm; 120Dh

Once a small restaurant on the beach, this Asilah standard needed a bigger location to deal with all the traffic, and rightly so. Its modest roots are reflected in the decor, fitting of a captain's lounge. It's popular with locals and tourists. The succulent, buttery John Dory is filleted and grilled to perfection. Other tasty, simple, fresh seafood dishes are available, including *gambas a la plancha* and grilled sole, as well as pastas and sandwiches. Beer and wine are served. Reservations are recommended during high season.

LE 32

32 Ave Moulay Hassan Ben Mahdi; tel. 0539/416 452; www.asilah32.com; daily 8:30-11:30pm; 200Dh

This new kid on the block is an upscale restaurant with clean lines reflecting its minimalist French flavor imparted by owners Laurent and Marie Claes and chef Johan Couland. However, the menu is eclectic, catering to travelers around the world. Come here for Thai-style spring rolls, Spanish-inspired *sopa de pescado,* seasonal tajine, and crispy teriyaki monkfish, and stay for the homemade ice cream. Smoking is allowed throughout the restaurant and patio.

★ PORT XIV

14 Ave. Moulay Hassan Ben Mehdi; tel. 0539/416 677 daily noon-4pm and 7pm-midnight, closed mid-Jan.-Feb.; 200Dh

A short stroll north of the medina, past the moored fishing boats and to the municipal beach, lands you at Port XIV, a regional leader in fine dining. Karim, the Scottish-Moroccan owner, studied in restaurants around Europe and the details show, from the spot-on service to the spot-free crystal glasses and meticulously clean open kitchen. Go for the oysters, sourced locally from Morocco, but remember to save room for the rest of the menu, including swordfish steaks that are seasoned to perfection, and lightly battered English-style fish and chips served with hand-cut french fries. Full bar is on offer here, as well as a surprisingly robust wine menu. With the combination of quality, service, and price (and nonsmoking interior), this might be the best restaurant north of Marrakesh.

RESTAURANT DAR AL MAGHREBIA

7 Rue Al Banafsafe; tel. 0633/662 377; daily noon-3pm and 7:30pm-11pm; 100Dh

If couscous is your craving, then head here for your fill of lamb, chicken, beef, or fish couscous as well as Moroccan salads and tajines. The interior here is more Moroccan-kitsch and tends toward the stuffy and staid, but it is perhaps the best Moroccan restaurant in town, with a killer seafood tajine that will make you momentarily forget the decor.

LA PERLE D'ASILAH

Rue Allal Ben Abdallah and Ave. Melilla; tel. 0539/418 758; daily noon-3pm and 7:30pm-11pm; 150Dh

An upscale restaurant just a short walk from Place Mohammed V, buried a little bit in the Ville Nouvelle. The varied menu features seafood, steaks, and creative vegetarian dishes done with seasonal fruits and legumes. For vegetarians exhausted of veggie pizzas, tajines, and couscous, this is perhaps the best stop in northern Morocco.

ACCOMMODATIONS

HOTEL BELLE VUE ZILIS

19 Rue Hassan Ben Tabit; tel. 0539/417 747; 70Dh dorm, 200Dh private room

The least-expensive budget option for students and backpackers, with a large dorm-style room with a dozen bunkbeds. Throughout most of the year, college-age Europeans stop here for a couple of nights. The original murals and tile work are somehow reflective of Asilah, just a touch on the tacky side. Rooms are clean and nonsmoking, though the beds are a bit dated. There is Wi-Fi, though it barely reaches past the ground floor, so much of your web surfing will likely be done in the downstairs Moroccan salon.

HOTEL DAR ANDALOUS

30 Rue al-Banafsaje; tel. 0539/417 840 or 0539/417 840; 210Dh d

Another solid budget option, though not recommended for nonsmokers. Its location just off the Place Mohammed V makes it easy to find. In the off-season, it's possible to bargain for price, and rooms can be had for 200Dh or less. Wi-Fi and TV are available.

★ CHRISTINA'S HOUSE

26 Rue Ibn Khatib; tel. 0677/276 463; 250Dh d

A popular favorite, particularly with students and backpackers. This cozy *riad* features a large terrace to relax on, a shelf full of English-language books to choose from, delicious breakfast, and clean rooms. This is one of the better options around Asilah for the price, and the company you'll find is unbeatable. Wi-Fi is available.

HOTEL PATIO DE LA LUNA

12 Pl. de Zelaka; tel. 0539/416 074; www.patiodelaluna.com; 450Dh d

With rustic Andalusian-Arab decor and a location right outside of Bab Kasara, Hotel Patio de la Luna is a charming, convenient place to stay for a couple of nights. Service is simple, if not friendly, and the rooms are clean. The hotel is usually closed from mid-January until the beginning of April. The rooms here are all en suite, and the back terrace, though small, can be a nice place to relax on a windy day.

HOTEL LA ALBA

35 Lot. Nahil; tel. 0613/429 190; 600Dh d

A quaint, Spanish-run guesthouse, this is a bit of a walk from the medina, but the friendly service and views of the beach from the terrace are worth it. The clean architectural lines of the house and quiet rooms make for the perfect getaway. The hotel has a spa and restaurant on-site, though reservations are needed for an afternoon in the traditional hammam for massages, facials, and a good Moroccan-style scrubbing. Wi-Fi and air-conditioning are in all the rooms. Breakfast is included with your stay.

★ RIAD ASILAH

64 Rue Bab r'Mel; tel. 0539/417 979; 650Dh d

If you're looking to stay in the old medina, this is the only true guesthouse. It is easy enough to find, near Bab el Souk toward the east side of the medina. The terrace is closed off from the sea, though it is a tranquil spot to kick back, read a book, or just disconnect for a bit. If you're looking for a quiet getaway, this is just the spot. The beds are comfy, the towels are fluffy, and the water is hot. Wi-Fi, air-conditioning, and breakfast are all included with your stay.

INFORMATION AND SERVICES

Outside of the medina, almost everything you might need is off Place Mohammed V. **Banque Populaire** (Mon.-Fri. 8:15am-3:45pm, Ramadan 9:30am-2pm), **BMCE** (Mon.-Fri. 9:15am-5pm, Ramadan 9:15am-2:30pm), and **Credit Agricule** (Mon.-Fri. 8:15am-3:45pm) are found here. You will also find a couple of pharmacies: **Pharmacie l'Ocean** (10 Pl. de Zelaka, daily 9am-9pm) and **Pharmacie Avicenne** (Ave. Khadir Ghailan, daily 8:45am-11:45pm). Just off this main plaza is the **post office** (Ave. de Prince Héritier, Mon.-Fri. 8am-4:15pm, Ramadan 9am-3pm), along with an Internet café, **Al Ahram** (Rue Al Banafsaje, daily 10am-11pm).

Inside the medina you can find a few currency exchanges, including **Currency Exchange Asilah Change** (Rue Barcesat, Mon.-Thurs. 9:30am-8:30pm, Fri.-Sun. 9:30am-12:30pm and 2:30pm-6:30pm), as well as an Internet café, **Association National pour le Development Humain** (4 Barcesat, daily 11am-midnight).

GETTING THERE AND AROUND

By Car

Asilah is connected via the tolled autoroute (A1) with **Rabat** (204km/126mi, 2.5hr).

By Train

The easiest way to arrive to Asilah is the **ONCF** (tel. 0890/203 040, www.oncf.ma) train. Any regular train (not the Al-Boraq high-speed train) going to or from Tangier stops at the **Asilah station** (along the national road to Tangier, north of the medina), making it an easy stop along this part of the coast. Direct trains are available to **Tangier** (45min, 12 daily, 2nd/1st-class 16Dh/25Dh), **Rabat** (3hr, 11 daily, 88Dh/130Dh), **Casablanca** (4.5hr, 11 daily, 115Dh/173Dh), **Fez** (4hr, 5 daily, 92Dh/136Dh), **Marrakesh** (9hr, 9 daily, 196Dh/301Dh), and **Meknes** (3.5hr, 5 daily, 74Dh/108Dh). The overnight train to Marrakesh leaves at 11pm; you will want to book ahead to reserve a sleeping car (*couchette*) for the trip. For any destination south (such as Casablanca, Rabat, Fez, or Marrakesh), you might have to transfer at Sidi Kacem or Casa Voyageurs. Consult the ONCF website or the ticket operator and inquire about direct trains.

From the Asilah train station there are usually *petits taxis* that will take you into town for 20-30Dh. If no taxis are available, it's an easy, short 15- to 20-minute walk into town.

By Bus and Grand Taxi

There are local **bus** services from the ***gare routière*** (Avenue Imam Assili, across the national road from the medina) to **Tangier** (1hr, 10 daily, 15Dh), though *grands taxis* are generally more convenient.

The ***grand taxi*** station in Asilah is on Place Mohammed V by the mosque. Regular taxis leave for **Tangier** (1hr, 47km/29mi), 20Dh) and **Larache** (1hr, 82km/51mi, 28Dh) with other routes possible, though you'll likely have to negotiate a price and hire the entire taxi.

Tangier and the Mediterranean Coast

William Burroughs once called it the "Interzone." Though Tangier has long given up its status as an international zone, a definite spirit of internationality exists in Tangier as in no other city in Morocco.

After the Portuguese Conquest in 1471, control of the city passed from Portugal to Spain and then back to Portugal before finally, in 1662, Tangier was given as part of a dowry for Catherine of Braganza's marriage to Charles II, the king of England. A scant 22 years later, the British would give up on Tangier because it was too expensive to maintain. Tangier has remained part of Morocco ever since.

As a result, in Tangier, you are as likely to go out for tapas as for a tajine. Travelers who make the stop here are rewarded with some

Highlights

Look for ★ to find recommended sights, activities, dining, and lodging.

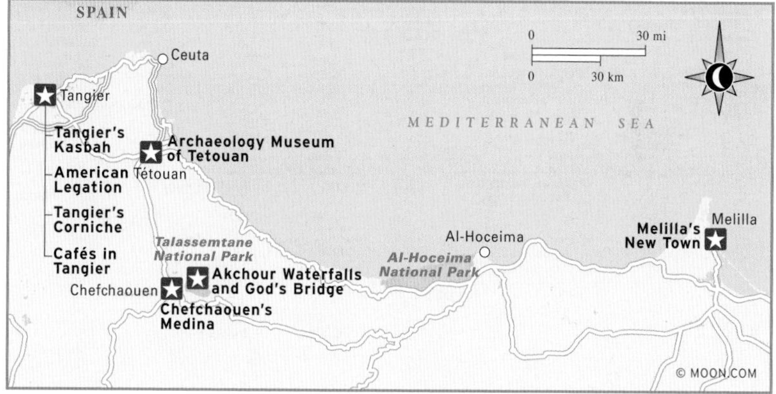

★ **Tangier's Kasbah:** Explore the maze-like streets of the towering fortress that rises over Tangier and keeps watch over the Strait of Gibraltar (page 183).

★ **American Legation:** Visit the United States' only National Historic Landmark located outside the country and learn a bit more about the history of Tangier, U.S.-Morocco relations, and Tangier's most famous expat, the American writer Paul Bowles (page 185).

★ **Tangier's Corniche:** Walk like the locals along the new corniche, enjoying the fresh breeze blowing off the strait, the bright Mediterranean sun, and the view of ships rocking in the distant waves (page 190).

★ **Cafés in Tangier:** The city's lively cafés have a rich literary history. The most storied hangout is Café Hafa, with past famous visitors such as William Burroughs and Tennessee Williams. It still has one of the best mint teas in town and unbeatable views across the strait (page 195).

★ **Archaeology Museum of Tetouan:** There is no better place to view the Roman mosaics once adorning the ancient cities of Lixus, Banasa, and far-flung Volubilis, which are featured in this underrated collection (page 213).

★ **Chefchaouen's Medina:** This medina, with its mellow shopkeepers and clean, wonderfully blue and white walls, is a true pleasure to explore (page 220).

★ **Akchour Waterfalls and God's Bridge:** Not to be missed in the spring months is a hike through Talassemtane National Park to the waterfalls and natural bridge of Akchour (page 229).

★ **Melilla's New Town:** Make your way to the seldom-touristed Spanish exclave of Melilla and walk through its gorgeous New Town (Ensanche), featuring a mix of art deco, Catalan modernist, and baroque architecture, and nibble your way through an Andalusian-style tapas tour (page 237).

Tangier and the Mediterranean Coast

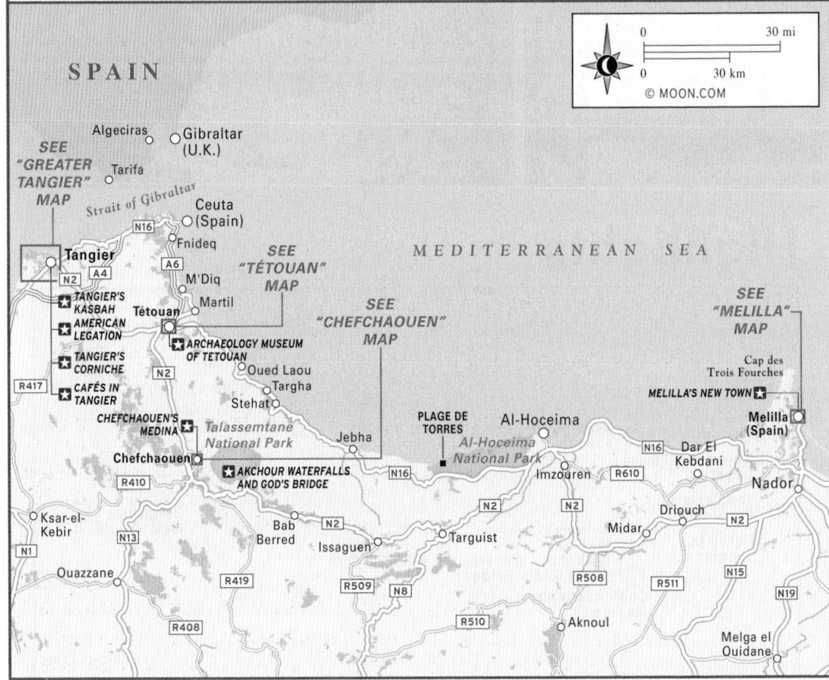

breathtaking views and a good laugh—Tanjaouis, as the natives of Tangier are called, are well known throughout Morocco for their wit and joie de vivre.

Though Tangier was neglected (and sometimes even ridiculed) by the previous king, Hassan II, his son and successor, Mohammed VI, has rediscovered this area. He stays at his palace in Tangier for one month or so out of the year, usually in the summer. The entire region has benefitted greatly from his renewed interest. Perhaps the most notable developments are along the old fishing port, where a new port is being built to house yachts and high-end apartments, and in the old medina and kasbah, whose facades have been beautifully restored. There are also new roads all along the entire Mediterranean Coast, from Tangier to Al-Hoceima, making this one of the best, and most breathtaking, road trips you can take in all of Morocco.

In Tangier, you can visit the only U.S. National Historic Landmark not located within the U.S. at the Tangier American Legation: under George Washington's administration, Tangier became the site of the first U.S. consulate. Take in a sunset at the Cave of Hercules, where the mythical hero is rumored to have rested after completing his 11th labor. Travelers will also want to tour Tangier's historic kasbah and lively medina and take a *paseo* (stroll) in the evening with the locals along the Avenue Pasteur and along the newly paved corniche.

Previous: backstreet of Tangier; the distinctive mosque of Tangier's Grand Socco; a man walking through the Chefchaouen medina.

Beyond Tangier are three cities to the west of the Rif Mountains that should be of interest to most travelers. The closest, Tetouan, is the least touristed of the group, though it offers perhaps the most authentic experience in the region. Tetouan sports a thriving medina, well-preserved remnants of Spanish-era construction, and a few museums to entice visitors, including an archaeology museum with the best collection of Roman mosaics in the country.

A bit farther into the mountains, at the foot of Jbel el-Kaala, lies the Instagram-friendly environs of Chefchaouen, known as the "Blue City" for its stunning blue medina. This long-established stop for backpackers has experienced a real boom in tourism since 2015. Near Chefchaouen is Talassemtane National Park, a spectacular destination for hikers and rock-climbers, particularly in the spring and early fall.

The third city, Ceuta, is the closest of the Spanish exclaves, though maybe not the most interesting. That designation belongs to Melilla, the other Spanish exclave farther east. Many travelers looking for a cold beer and tapas head over the Spanish border to one of these cities, particularly during Islamic holidays, to enjoy a touch of Andalusia.

Adventurous travelers, especially those that have already traveled quite a bit of Morocco, might consider exploring the Mediterranean Coast and the Rif Mountains. Though this area is well known to Moroccans, with many flooding the beaches of Martil, Cabo Negro, and Al-Hoceima during the summer months, it is an area of the country much less traveled by internationals. This region is known to be more conservative than the rest of Morocco. With the opening of the Oujda airport in 2012 and the latest investments by the king, this area will likely see more growth in the coming years.

PLANNING YOUR TIME

With the new **Al-Boraq high-speed train** connecting Tangier with **Rabat** and **Casablanca,** exploring Tangier as a day trip is possible, as do many travelers taking the **ferry** over from **Spain.** Tangier is easy to explore by **foot.** However, 2-3 days here really let the charm of this old seaside port town settle in. Beyond Tangier, you will need to travel by **bus** or **car.** Some of the mountain roads are impassable in winter and temperatures can dip well below freezing. The ideal time to visit is the **late spring** or **early autumn** when the roads are clear, the driving is easy, and the summer crowds haven't crammed the **beaches.** The roads throughout this region are well maintained, though in spring, potholes often dot the higher mountain roads.

From Tangier, several easy day trips are possible. **Tetouan** is the less explored option, though it is an up-and-coming destination with great access to the Mediterranean beaches. **Chefchaouen** is farther in the **mountains,** about two hours away, and can be done as a day trip, though most people spend at least two days there. The Spanish exclave of **Ceuta** is another option, especially for those looking to day trip into Europe. Along the North Atlantic Coast—stretching from Tangier south to Rabat—**Asilah, Larache,** and the nearby Roman ruins of **Lixus** (covered in the Rabat chapter) are also worth considering. And with the new high-speed train, Rabat itself, or even Casablanca, could be considered for a day trip.

Itinerary Ideas

TANGIER, TETOUAN, AND CHEFCHAOUEN

Day 1: Tangier

1 Whether you arrive in Tangier by ferry or train, drop off your bags at your hotel or *riad*. Consider staying at **Dar Chams.** Its location is unbeatable and the service is the best in the north. They'll watch your bags until it's time to check in.

2 Head to **Café Baba** for a mint tea or a coffee, and take in the Beat-era vibes to get your Tangier experience off to the right start.

3 Make your way downhill, into the **medina.** Meander, take photos, check out any shops that are of interest, but don't forget to stop by the **American Legation Museum** before lunch.

4 For lunch, make your way to the Petit Socco and get a quick sandwich at **Ray Charly,** a Tangier staple for over 50 years. Feel free to eat at the counter, or maybe tuck into one of the cafés on the square for a bit of people watching.

5 Head back to your hotel or *riad* to check in, freshen up if needed, and then head up to the **kasbah.**

6 Stop into the **Museum of Moroccan Art and Antiquities.** Note the Roman mosaic taken from Volubilis and stroll the gardens.

7 A little before sunset, head to **Café Hafa** and enjoy a mint tea while the sun sets over the Atlantic, casting nearby Spain into shadow.

8 For dinner, dive into the **El Morocco Club.** An after-dinner drink in the piano bar would be a fitting tribute to your first night in the former Interzone.

Day 2: Tetouan

You'll want to leave Tangier before 10am to dodge most of the city traffic.

1 Head directly into Tetouan's old medina, drop off your bags at **Dar Rehia,** your accommodation for the night, and relax with a mint tea.

2 For lunch, head to **Casa España** for tapas and, if the mood strikes you, a much-deserved cerveza.

3 Spend the first part of the afternoon at the **Archaeology Museum of Tetouan** and take in the incredible Roman mosaics that once adorned the Roman cities of Morocco.

4 Next, head to the **Museum of Modern Art** to get a look at some contemporary Moroccan artists and new-age Moroccan architecture.

5 Dinner is at **Riad Blanco,** but make sure to make reservations at least a day or two in advance.

6 Enjoy a quiet walk through the **medina** before bed.

Itinerary Ideas

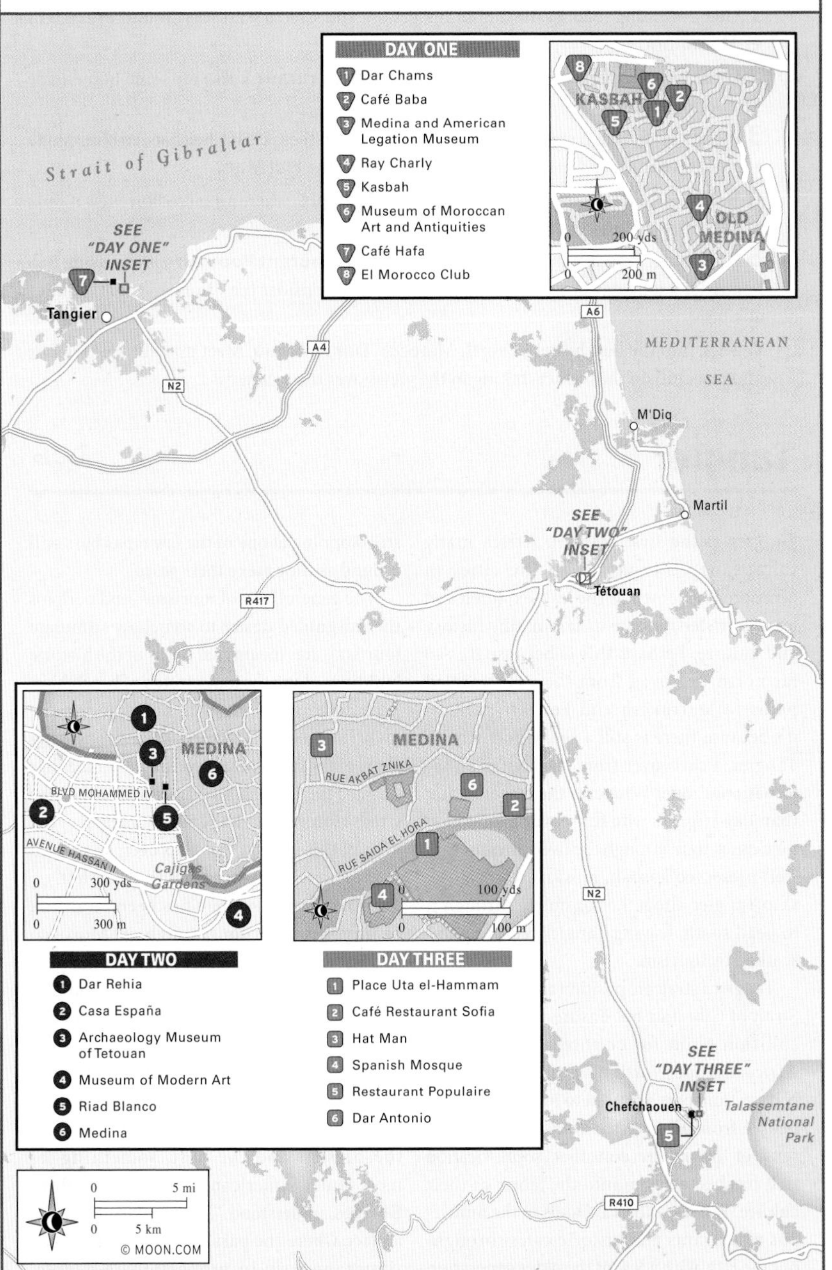

Day 3: Chefchaouen

Get ready to hit the road for the "Blue City" as soon as you finish breakfast.

1 After a winding road up the mountain, get out and stretch your legs around **Place Uta el-Hammam.**

2 If the weather permits, dine outside at **Café Restaurant Sofia** for some homemade Moroccan cuisine.

3 Spend the afternoon exploring the medina, taking in the special Chefchaouen blue. Make a few new friends, and pick up some new threads at the **Hat Man.**

4 Before sunset, take the trail to the **Spanish Mosque,** where an incredible view awaits of the entire city and valley below.

5 For dinner, keep it simple with a quick bite at **Restaurant Populaire** just outside Bab Sor. After a long day of walking, a quick sandwich (consider the "Tangier") is all you really need.

6 Tuck into the best hostel in north Morocco, **Dar Antonio.** Meet up with new friends and just chill on the terrace, taking in the views over the valley.

Tangier طنجة

Tangier is the first place in Africa many Europeans visit—yet of all the cities in Morocco it is somehow the least explored and least touristed, despite its fascinating history and culture. Perhaps this is because it is so far north, removed from the well-traveled paths to Marrakesh and Fez? Or perhaps it's because there is still a seedy-port vibe to Tangier, a carryover from its days as an international zone? Whatever the reason, other than day-trippers who ferry over from Spain for a quick tour through the lively medina and well-preserved kasbah, most travelers either skip Tangier altogether or hustle through it to head south, leaving Tangier relatively unscathed by tourism.

Tangier's strategic position along the famed Strait of Gibraltar has ensured that this be a collision point for cultures from all over Africa, Europe, North America, and beyond. Native Tanjaouis are used to interacting with people from all over the world, imparting a sense of "been there, done that" sophistication that has been woven into the fabric of their culture. You'll see the Tanjaouis in the numerous restaurants and historic cafés throughout the city, with a few of the older generation still stopping at one of the few tapas bars still around as they make their *paseo.*

The general lack of tourism—and perhaps the misguided desire to somehow stimulate tourism—has meant that many of the historic buildings along the long stretch of beach have been destroyed, with giant hotels and apartment buildings replacing them, repeating some of the unfortunate construction that has plagued the Spanish Mediterranean across the strait. However, with the recent interest of the king in this region, there has been a renewed interest in what historic buildings are left.

In recent years, there has been an influx of immigrants from throughout Morocco and sub-Saharan Africa, with some looking for passage into Europe and others looking for jobs at the factories that now dot the suburbs around the old city. This has changed the character of Tangier somewhat, though it has always been in flux, between cultures, histories, governments, and even between the present and the past, something its most famed American expat resident, **Paul Bowles,** understood. "Tangier," he wrote, "is a place where the past and the present exist simultaneously in proportionate degree,

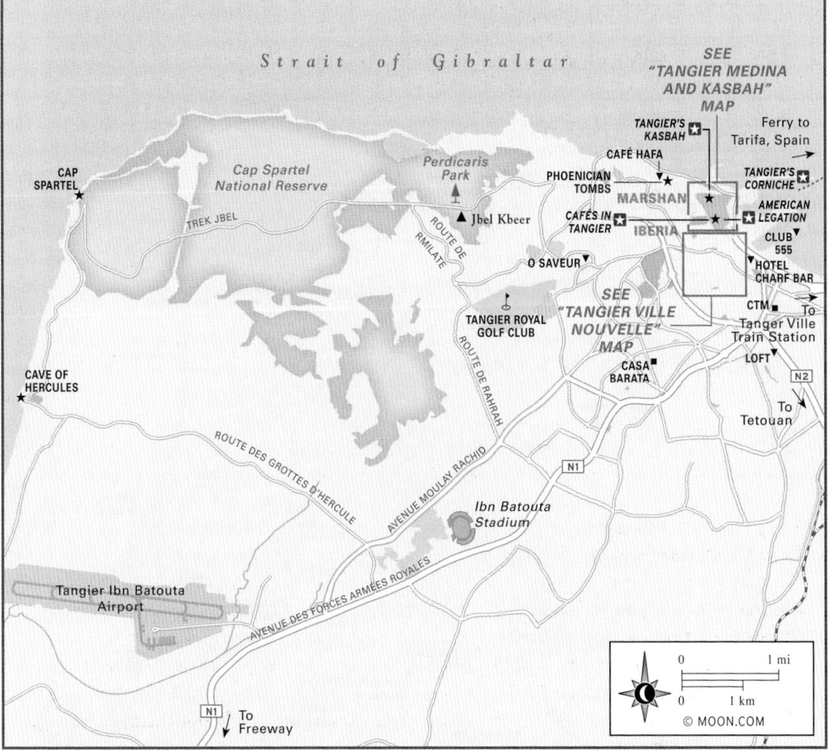

where a very much alive today is given added depth of reality by the presence of an equally alive yesterday."

This flux between cultures and eras, as well as its location between Europe and Africa, means that it maintains a degree of mystery. All of these elements have contrived to lend Tangier an artistic air, unique among Moroccan cities. Many expat writers and artists have found inspiration in crooks of the medina, traipsing through the Jbel Kbeer, or sipping on a mint tea at Café Hafa while peering over the strait to Spain. From the aforementioned Bowles, to William Burroughs, Jack Kerouac, and Allen Ginsberg, to artists such as Eugene Delacroix and Henri Matisse and musicians like the Rolling Stones and Jimi Hendrix, Tangier has long been a siren calling out across the water, inviting passersby to enjoy the conflux of space, time and culture.

ORIENTATION

Tangier rests on the northwestern tip of Africa, along the Strait of Gibraltar, at the strait's narrowest passage. Just 14 kilometers (8mi) separate Morocco from Spain. **Cap Spartel,** the cape on the westernmost edge of Tangier, marks the meeting point of the Atlantic Ocean and Mediterranean Sea. The city of Tangier is divided into three main sections: the old medina, the kasbah, and the Ville Nouvelle.

The **old medina** is one of the more lived-in medinas in Morocco. A few main entrances, or *babs,* lead into it through the ancient wall that surrounds the old city. From the famed

Tangier Medina and Kasbah

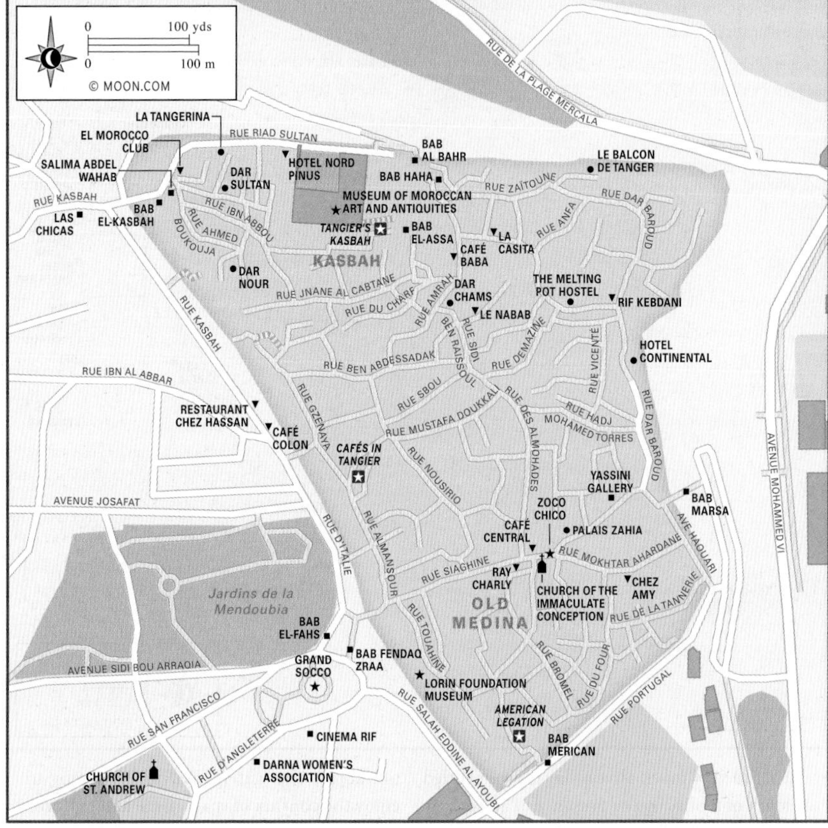

Grand Socco (now marked "Place du 9 Avril 1947" on most maps, though this plaza is still called "Grand Socco" by all the locals), duck beneath the **Bab el-Fahs** or **Bab Fendaq Zraa** to plunge directly onto the bazaar-lined **Rue as-Siaghin** and onward to the historic square known as the Zoco Chico. This is the center of the old medina. From here, you can explore the different quarters of the medina.

The **Ville Nouvelle** (New City) of Tangier is home to many of the city's things to see and do, which makes it unlike many of the other *villes nouvelles* of Morocco. There is now a long pedestrian path along the beach, the corniche, that curves around the kasbah and back into the city. Everything in the city seems to orient toward the beach, with many hotels, houses, and apartment buildings taking advantage of the view north across the strait to Spain. There are a few neighborhoods worth visiting in the new city. **Centre Ville** lies just outside the medina, with **Place de France,** the famed **Gran Café de Paris,** and **Soor el-Ma'agazine** (Wall of the Lazy People) forming the heart of the new city. To the west of the kasbah, even farther into the hills, lies **Marshan.** This is where several elaborate villas are located, as well as **Café Hafa** and the **Phoenician tombs.** South of Marshan is **Iberia,** where you will find the soaring Grand Mosque of Tangier, the mosque of Mohammed V, and the Spanish-run Cervantes Institute, which are handy navigational landmarks.

Jbel Kbeer (Big Mountain) lies to the west, just outside the main city, and is less of a mountain than a large, sloping hill full of forested natural parks, such as the splendid **Perdicaris Park,** as well as elaborate palaces and mansions. Beyond Jbel Kbeer is Cap Spartel and the Cave of Hercules along the Atlantic Coast.

Safety

With the king of Morocco spending more time in Tangier, it's no coincidence that the city is slowly shaking its sleazy past. The medina is a lot safer, especially at night, though visitors should take general precautions. Other than the occasional pesky tout and typical sorts of enthusiastic vendors, the city is relatively subdued, though there is a vibrant, up-and-coming feeling to it. The harassment of single women or women walking in groups still occurs, though this is mostly verbal, and if you don't understand Darija, it's easy to ignore. The one place to exercise extreme caution is along the beach, where muggings are known to occur in the early morning hours.

SIGHTS

★ Kasbah

Towering above the rest of Tangier and watching guard over the Strait of Gibraltar is the splendid kasbah of Tangier. The ancient fortifications that were once in charge of the city's defenses are still largely intact hundreds of years after their erection and, happily, were wonderfully restored from 2016-2019. These days, quite a few of the historic buildings and palaces of the kasbah are owned by Europeans and have been turned into private homes or converted into boutique hotels and restaurants.

The two most common entrances to the kasbah are the **Bab el-Kasbah** to the west, off Place du Tabor, and **Bab Haha** (Don't laugh! This gate is actually named for a region around Essaouira) to the east, coming from the medina. **Place du Mechouar** (often referred to as Place de la Kasbah) is next to Bab Haha. There is paid, guarded parking. Touts gather here and will offer to give you a guided tour, though this is unnecessary. The kasbah is small, and to the left of Bab Haha there is a small map highlighting the walk you can do around it.

MUSEUM OF MOROCCAN ART AND ANTIQUITIES

Pl. du Mechouar; tel. 0539/932 097; Wed.-Mon. 9am-4pm; 10Dh

Just off Place du Mechouar, the Museum of Moroccan Art and Antiquities (Musée des Art Marocains et des Antiquités) houses various relics from the Stone Age through the turn of the 20th century, displaying the rich history of Tangier. You can see evidence of the many, many peoples that have inhabited or ruled this region. Not to be missed is a beautiful mosaic taken from the Roman city of Volubilis. Be sure to take a nice stroll through the gardens.

Medina

Tangier's famed medina is something of an anomaly in Morocco. Parts of it are touristed and fairly tidy, though much of the medina remains residential with only a few boutique *riads,* unlike the hundreds that dot the medinas of Marrakesh and Fez. You can feel this "lived in" vibe all around the medina. Perhaps this is the reason why Tangier has provided the backdrop for movies such as *Inception* and *The Bourne Identity.* Though the Tangier medina has shed much of its seedy reputation of years past, it still stands in stark contrast to the adjacent, mellow, well-touristed kasbah.

Pass through the **Bab el-Fahs** or **Bab Fendaq Zraa** off the Grand Socco and stroll down **Rue as-Siaghin,** the former Jewish gold market of the medina, and you will end up in a small square called the **Zoco Chico.** If Tangier had a heart, this would be it. The famed Zoco Chico is also known as the Petit Socco (Little Market) and dubbed the Souk Dakhel (Interior Market) by locals. Once a

1
2
KASBAH
3
4

hotbed of nightclubs and seedy bars and home to Tangier's red-light district, the Zoco Chico is much more chill these days. The nightclubs and bars have all been replaced by cafés, while the brothels have transformed into bazaars. That said, this is still the place to be to spy Tanjaouis sipping on a coffee or tea and to take in the hustle of the medina. Just off the Zoco Chico, a few steps further down Rue as-Siaghin, you can also find the 19th-century **Church of the Immaculate Conception,** now a functioning nunnery.

The medina is divided into five separate quarters (though it might be difficult to tell) all around the Zoco Chico, most of them residential. From the Zoco Chico, many merchants can be found along **Rue des Almohades** (most Tanjaouis still call it "Rue des Chretiens"), selling Berber carpets, mosaic tables, ceramics, and various antiques. You won't want to miss walking through the faded splendor of the 19th-century **Hotel Continental** and enjoying a beverage on the patio, which has a panoramic view over the bay.

Tangier was one of the first cities in Morocco to fall under the influence of Europeans. One of the real treats of the medina is noticing the differences between the Andalusian, Moorish, Colonial, and Moroccan architecture packed together. Unlike in the medinas of Fez or Marrakesh, typically you'll be hassled a lot less by touts and store owners.

★ AMERICAN LEGATION

8 Rue d'Amerique; tel. 0539/935 317; http://legation.org; Mon.-Fri. 10am-5pm, Sat. 10am-3pm, closed Sun. and holidays; 20Dh

Close to the aptly named Bab Merican, the Tangier American Legation Institute for Moroccan Studies is the only U.S. National Historic Landmark outside of the United States. The museum itself is a wonderfully restored three-story house dating from the 17th century, featuring tall wood-beamed ceilings, ornate stucco and *zellij* (mosaic tile) work, and a sprawling outdoor patio. The museum holds a letter from George Washington; many paintings from American, European, and Moroccan artists; and a collection of models recreating historic battles in the region, including the famed Battle of the Three Kings. A large library specializing in North Africa holds a collection of the first 100 years of the *Tangier Gazette* (a multilingual newspaper that began printing in the 19th century), many antiquarian maps, and travel accounts from the 17th to 19th centuries. Visitors will not want to miss the **Paul Bowles Wing,** a section off the patio dedicated to the life, writing, and music curation of Tangier's most famous expat resident, Paul Bowles, from when he first moved to Tangier in 1947 up until his death in 1999. Guided tours are available (50Dh per person) and are highly recommended to get the most from your visit to one of the most unique landmarks in all of Morocco.

1: medina of Tangier **2:** Bab el-Fahs off the Grand Socco **3:** signs in the medina point the way to the kasbah **4:** the gardens of the Museum of Moroccan Art and Antiquities

LORIN FOUNDATION MUSEUM

44 Rue Touahine; tel. 0539/334 696; Sun.-Fri. 11am-1pm and 3:30pm-7:30pm; free

Easy to find right off the Rue as-Siaghin, the Lorin Foundation Museum (Musée de la Fondation Lorin) is housed in an old synagogue. On display are old newspapers, photographs, posters, and other items related to the history of Tangier since the 1930s, as well as contemporary paintings. Exhibitions are regularly held. Admission is free, but donations are appreciated and go to help the disadvantaged children in the area.

GRAND SOCCO

Just outside of the medina, the main plaza, dubbed Grand Socco by the locals, used to be the largest market in town, where sellers from all over the region came to offer fresh fruits, vegetables, and livestock. Though not quite the large market it was historically, the Grand Socco still has quite a few sellers along

On the Beat Path: Tangier's Famous Writers and Artists

the Paul Bowles Wing of the American Legation

Tangier has long had a pull for writers. Perhaps this is because of its geography? There is something about Tangier that instigates and challenges. Or perhaps this is because, like its namesake Tinjis, a beautiful goddess, there is something irresistible about it. The list of writers who have experienced something of Tangier that made them take pen to paper is astonishing: Alexandre Dumas, Hans Christian Andersen, Mark Twain, Edith Wharton, Paul and Jane Bowles, Jean Genet, William Burroughs, Jack Kerouac, Allen Ginsberg, Truman Capote, Tennessee Williams, and George Orwell, to name just a few.

Henri Matisse famously stayed at the Villa de France in the Ville Nouvelle, painting scenes from his walks through the medina and kasbah. Another painter, the French master Eugène Delacroix, also spent time in Tangier, amazed by the colors, the vibrancy, the life.

The Rolling Stones and the Beatles found inspiration (among a few other things) while exploring musical possibilities.

However, it is Paul Bowles and the Beats who are most associated with Tangier. Paul Bowles first visited Tangier in 1931 with composer Aaron Copland at the advice of Gertrude Stein. He finally settled permanently in 1947 with his wife, Jane Bowles, where he wrote his most famous novels, including *The Sheltering Sky, Let It Come Down,* and *The Spider's House.* Despite their rather unconventional marriage, the Bowleses were fixtures in Tangier. The Beats quickly followed. William Burroughs, the man whom the locals called "The Invisible Man," was running from the law and from a long history of drug abuse. Burroughs wrote *Naked Lunch* while living in Tangier and battling drug addiction. Ginsberg and Kerouac would visit, both of them struck by the city as they tried to help their friend put together his masterpiece.

Rue d'Italie at the foot of the **Mendoubia Gardens.**

The southernmost edge of the Grand Socco is now a roundabout, **Place du 9 Avril 1947,** at the primary entrance of the medina, making it a good meeting point for groups. The nearby, newly remodeled **Cinema Rif** is a relaxing place to sit back and sip on a coffee while you're waiting for friends to show up. Nearby, the **Grand Hotel Villa de France,** a storied five-star hotel reopened in 2014 after a seven-year renovation, once housed the cream

Tangier Ville Nouvelle

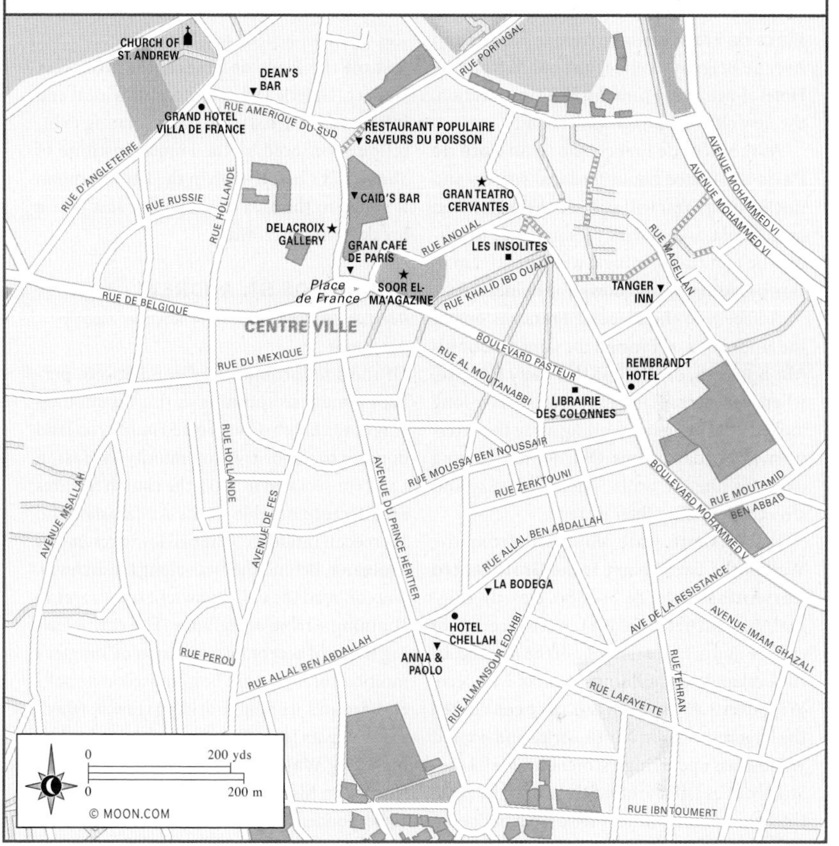

of Tangier's society and their friends. Henri Matisse stayed here in 1912-1913, in room 35, painting various scenes and people from around Tangier. His room is now a mini-museum with a print of his famous painting, *Paysage vu d'une fenêtre (View from a Window),* that he painted while staying here. Room 35 can be accessed for free if you ask nicely at reception during the day, though it's polite to tip the staff 10Dh for their time.

Ville Nouvelle

Unlike many of Morocco's other cities, much of Tangier's charm lies in the Ville Nouvelle just outside the confines of the kasbah and medina, where the city begins its great spread out over the hilly landscape, plunging westward over Jbel Kbeer into the Atlantic and embracing on its north face a long stretch of beach and numerous hilly inlets, giving it an unmatched topography that is home to many of the things to see and do in Tangier. There are many neighborhoods here; most of the places of interest are in Centre Ville, the Grand Socco, Marshan, and Iberia, with a couple of nightclubs, restaurants, and hotels along the beach.

SELF-GUIDED WALKING TOUR OF CENTRE VILLE

Centre Ville, or "downtown," centers on the **Place de France,** where Avenue Pasteur and Avenue Belgique collide, just uphill from the Hotel el-Minzah. From this little intersection, the new city of Tangier spiders out.

At the Place de France, the **Gran Café de Paris** is a famed haunt for local writers and intellectuals. You will still see them gathered here, books and newspapers in hand, watching the foot traffic mingle with the stream of cars parading up and down the boulevard.

Adjacent to the Place de France is one of the landmarks of Tangier, the famed **Soor el-Ma'agazine,** or **Wall of the Lazy People,** where Moroccans and expats alike have long looked over at Spain, whiling away the afternoon lost in daydreams. Old, nonfunctioning cannons line the walls, where kids play and street sellers sling their wares.

Just a short walk downhill from the Wall of the Lazy People is the **Gran Teatro Cervantes** (Calle de Murillo, closed), originally constructed in 1911, once a center of culture and art, and now one of the most beautiful dilapidated buildings in all of Morocco. With over 1,400 seats, it was once considered the largest theater in North Africa and housed world-class opera singers, orchestras, and theater troupes from around the world. In 2007, the Spanish government released a budget of €94,000 to help with the restoration of the theater, but thus far nothing has been determined and the building continues to fall into ruin.

From the Place de France and the Wall of the Lazy People, you can continue down Avenue Pasteur, where most Tanjaouis take their evening *paseo*. This strip is vibrant throughout the day and well into the night with cafés, shops, electronics stores, and a historic bookstore, the Librairie des Colonnes. From the boulevard, you can continue down to the beach or walk uphill and explore the Grand Socco and Marshan.

DELACROIX GALLERY (GALERIE DELACROIX)

86 Rue de la Liberté; tel. 0539/941 054; Tues.-Sun. 11am-1pm and 4pm-8pm; free

Just off the Place de France, the Delacroix Gallery (Galerie Delacroix) features local and international artists and has a rotating exhibition sponsored by the French Institute of Tangier. It's best to stop in the late afternoon if you're in the area to cool off or just take a break from the crowds.

CHURCH OF ST. ANDREW

Rue d'Angleterre; tel. 0539/314 469; open roughly 9am-sunset

Of the sites around the Grand Socco, perhaps none is so stunning as this functioning Anglican church. Constructed in 1894 on land donated to the British community by Hassan I and consecrated in 1905, the church features architecture notable for its Andalusian and Moroccan influence. The bell tower resembles a minaret. Behind the altar, along the archway, you can read the well-known Lord's Prayer in stunning Arabic calligraphy. The entire feeling is one of acceptance. A vision of Tangier's multicultural past can be glimpsed in its halls and around its neighboring gardens, where many expats from Tangier have been buried, including **Walter Burton Harris,** a Tangier legend. In his lifetime, Harris was the local correspondent for *The Times* and was involved in much of the political intrigue that gripped Tangier while it served as an International Zone. Nowadays, Harris is most known for his travel work, *Morocco That Was*. The British humanitarian Emily Keene, a.k.a. the Sherifa of Ouazzane, responsible for introducing the cholera vaccine to Morocco, also has her final resting place here. The grounds are free to access, though 50Dh is the going rate for entry to the church and a guided English-language tour with Yassine, the caretaker, and highly recommended. Attending service, of course,

1: the American Legation in Tangier **2:** women selling their produce in the Grand Socco **3:** the Gran Teatro Cervantes falling into ruin **4:** the interior of the arabesque Church of St. Andrew

1
2
GRAN
TEATRO CERVANTES
1913
3
4

is free and perhaps the best way to get a feel for the vast diversity of Tangier's resident Christian community.

★ Corniche

A stay in Tangier isn't complete without a sunset stroll along the new corniche. The corniche runs along the north edge of town, following Avenue Mohammed VI.

To the **west,** this route passes between the fortified walls of the medina and the kasbah uphill and the port along the sea before opening up into the **Route de la Plage Mercala.** This particular strip of the corniche is great for walkers and runners. It's possible to follow the route around the western corner, at the small **Mercala Beach,** and continue back up through town, through the backside of Marshan, though most will want to stick with the beachfront.

To the **east,** the wide pedestrian-only walkway is full, day and night, with kids playing on the beach and on the new playgrounds, kicking around soccer balls. At night, there are often family-friendly festivals along the new walkway with lots of live music.

Marshan

In the wealthy neighborhood of Marshan are the former Forbes Mansion and the Marshan Palace, which housed deposed sultans of Morocco, as well as the first football (soccer) stadium in Tangier. The king keeps an office here, and there are green spaces and wonderful views over Tangier and across the strait. Make sure to visit the **Phoenician tombs** (just off Ave. Hadj Mohamed Tazi; follow the signs). There are several scattered around Marshan, though the most famous overlook the strait. The tombs themselves are little more than rectangular holes in the hard rock. This is now a meeting point for many young local couples and a spot for quiet contemplation. Couples often sit at these empty tombs, catching a quiet moment in the afternoon and staying until sunset.

A short walk away from the tombs is Morocco's most storied hangout, **Café Hafa.** Located on the cliff overlooking the meeting of the Mediterranean and Atlantic, Café Hafa tumbles down in a series of steppes, each with a few cheap chairs and tables. Paul Bowles, William Burroughs, the Beatles, and the Rolling Stones have all sipped on the mint tea here and (more than likely) partook in the hash or kif that is invariably around.

EVENTS

For the most up-to-date information on the festivals happening throughout the year, check out the monthly ***Tanger Pocket*** (www.tangerpocket.com), a predominantly French-language publication, available online and at most restaurants and hotels.

SPRING BOOK AND ART FESTIVAL

https://printempsdulivretanger.org; Apr/May; free

For a week in April/May, Francophone book nerds and art lovers can delight in the Printemps du Livre et des Arts (Spring Book and Art Festival), a joint collaboration between Morocco and France run by the French Institute near Place de France. Talks generally concern the history of Morocco and France; the relation between the two countries and cultures; recent economic, social, and political developments in Morocco; and art and literature around Africa. The **French Institute** (www.if-maroc.org/tanger) also runs several events throughout the year, usually one a month, to promote French language and culture. Check the website for more information about events and the Spring Book and Art Festival.

TANJAZZ

www.tanjazz.org; Sep; 200Dh

Since 2000, Tangier has celebrated its musicality annually with the biggest music festival in north Morocco, Tanjazz: Festival de Jazz de Tanger. Helped with support from the local Lorin Foundation, the festival brings acts from around the world for a five-day celebration of music in September, with everything from big band to swing, Delta blues to Moroccan fusion. With tame crowds and a sophisticated air, Tanjazz evokes the city's long history of cultural, and musical, fusion. Passes are 200Dh a day or 1000Dh for the length of the festival.

MEDITERRANEAN SHORT FILM FESTIVAL

http://www.ccm.ma; Oct; free

Movie buffs and cineasts should check out the Mediterranean Short Film Festival of Tangier run by the Centre Cinématographique Morocain, which runs for a week in early October. Films range far and wide, with a selection of 46 films from 18 different countries. Films are linguistically diverse, with offerings usually in English, Arabic, French, Spanish, and other languages.

SHOPPING

Curious shoppers may want to head to **Casa Barata,** the sprawling flea market that is well known among those searching for antiques, black-market goods, and discount items, along Avenue Moulay Abdelhafid near Place du Maroc in the Ville Nouvelle. Otherwise, most of the shopping happens in the medina (for more traditional, handmade crafts) and just outside, along Avenue Mexique and Avenue Pasteur (for electronics, clothes, and everything else).

Medina

The medina can be difficult to navigate, and there are many bazaars selling lamps, carpets, *zellij*-tiled furniture, ceramic tajines, teacups and plates, antique-looking doors, sculptures purportedly from sub-Saharan Africa, traditional jellabas, and decorative kaftans, among many other typically Moroccan goods on offer. Sellers can be aggressive, but much less so than sellers from other medinas around Morocco. From the Zoco Chico, head up **Rue des Almohades** (most Tanjaouis still call it "Rue des Chretiens"), where most of the bazaars can be found. In general, you will need to bargain. The negotiation, typically over a mint tea, is a sort of game for the shop owners and can be exhausting, so be prepared. There are several shops with posted prices, though even these are often a bit on the expensive side. If you want less expensive goods and an even more laid-back shopping experience, it's worth thinking about a day trip to nearby **Asilah** to shop in the pleasant medina with a near-nonexistent hard sell.

YASSINI GALLERY

Rue de lar Marine, Petit Socco; tel. 0539/948 023

Over the years, this gallery has developed a fine reputation for quality carpets and low hassle. You will find an excellent variety of rare and precious carpets, though the best deals are found with the newer carpets with many modern, cubist designs. Those interested in interior design and who want to see a large variety of Moroccan carpets would do well to spend an hour or two perusing the selection here.

DARNA WOMEN'S ASSOCIATION

Rue Jules Cot; tel. 0539/947 065; Mon.-Sat. 9am-noon and 3pm-5pm

Founded in 2002, Darna is a little complex that includes a boutique shop and small restaurant, just a short walk from Cinema Rif. Its mission is to help women of the area, particularly those suffering from difficult divorces and who have been abused. On offer are numerous textiles and handmade goods that the women involved have created. A great place to spend your money and place it directly in the hands of people who could really use it.

Ville Nouvelle

LIBRAIRIE DES COLONNES

54 Ave. Pasteur; tel. 0539/936 955; www.librairie-des-colonnes.com; Mon.-Sat. 9:30am-1pm and 4pm-7pm

Tangier's most famous bookstore, founded in 1949 by the Gerofi family, is still running after all these years, stewarded by Simon-Pierre Hamlin, who also edits the local multilingual literary journal, *Nejma.* Samuel Beckett, Tennessee Williams, Paul Bowles, and nearly every other writer who has come through Tangier has spent time in

1
2
3

this historic bookstore. The works of many of the Beat Generation writers who spent time in Morocco are usually available, and the shop will most likely have a copy of William Burroughs's *Naked Lunch* on hand. English books are on offer, though the majority of the wonderful selection is in French. A great place to pick up a read for a train ride or a coffee table book for home. Check out the website for a list of author readings.

LES INSOLITES

28 Rue Khalid Ibn Oualid; tel. 0539/371 367; http://lesinsolitestanger.com; Mon.-Sat. 9:30am-12:30pm and 3pm-8pm, Sun. 12:30pm-4pm

Les Insolites is the newest, hippest bookstore of the bunch. Conveniently located just off the Wall of the Lazy People, it holds many contemporary art showings and readings. The owners are usually around and are happy to talk to people traveling through. They will gladly recommend a nearby café or restaurant.

Kasbah

LAS CHICAS

52 Rue Kacem Guennon near the Bab el-Kasbah; tel. 0539/374 510; Mon.-Sat. 10:30am-7:30pm

Perched just outside the kasbah is this chic boutique where you can find all sorts of items carefully curated and all made in Morocco, including jewelry, linens, furniture, mirrors, paintings, ceramics, and candles, all signed by their young creators and designers.

SALIMA ABDEL WAHAB

Bab Kasbah; tel. 0539/930 793

A Tangier native, Salima Abdel Wahab is one of Morocco's most successful fashion designers. For fashionistas, this is a must-stop boutique in Tangier, though you can now find Salima's other boutiques in Marrakesh and Fez. Though her roots are in Tangier, Salima has a mixed Moroccan, Spanish, and German heritage she fulfills in her designs, which embody her eye for detail and love for comfort. These are timeless pieces in historically noble fabrics in touch with today's men and women.

1: colorful Moroccan slippers in the medina 2: a little boy reads a book in the Librarie des Colonnes bookstore 3: a regular evening on Tangier's busy beachfront boulevard

SPORTS AND RECREATION

Parks

PERDICARIS PARK

Rmilat on Avenue Mokhtar Gazoulit; daily sunrise-sunset; free

Perdicaris Park (Parc Perdicaris) lies just 15 minutes outside of the city on the road to the **Cave of Hercules.** The parks and its paths were renovated in 2016-2017 and boast stellar views out over the Atlantic, across the Strait and through lush Mediterranean flora. This is a perfect spot for a picnic and to take a break from the city. There is a juice stand at the entrance of the park, but otherwise food is scarce, so plan accordingly. You can hire a *grand taxi* or take the #5 bus (3.5Dh per ticket, every 30min) from Sidi Bouabid by the Grand Mosque (across from the Cervantes Institute in the Iberia neighborhood). If you're driving, take Avenue Sidi Mohamed Ben Abdellah northwest from the big roundabout at the Mohammed V Mosque and follow the road signs for **Rmilat.**

Beaches

As Tangier is a beach town, there is plenty of free swimming to be had along the Mediterranean and Atlantic Coasts. The currents along the Atlantic make it a somewhat more dangerous swimming place, and those with children should exercise extreme caution. The Mediterranean beaches, particularly the city ones, are family-friendly and safe places for swimmers, though swimmers must keep well clear of the port. Women, whether alone or in groups, will inevitably be hassled. For a harassment-free beach day, strongly consider spending a few dirhams to enter in one of the cabanas run out on the Atlantic Coast. There are a series of private beach areas just south of the Hercules Caves and Cap Spartal.

Horse and Camel Riding

Along the municipal beach, horse and camel rides are generally available for 10-20Dh, though you will likely be quoted much more. Bargain, gallop along the beach, and remember to take a picture.

Golf

TANGIER ROYAL GOLF CLUB

Route de Boubana; tel. 0539/938 925; www.royalcountryclubtanger.com; 400Dh

This golf club offers a challenging 18-hole course over 65 hectares (160 acres) just 3 kilometers (1.8mi) away from the middle of Tangier. This was one of the first golf courses in the Mediterranean basin and is one of the oldest in Africa.

Hammams

Traditional hammams in the medina are great places to meet locals. You can wash for 10Dh or so, though all hammams cater to either men or women or have separate hours for the genders. Check with your lodging to find the closest local hammam in the medina. Otherwise, the higher-end hammams are the answer for couples and travelers who are uncomfortable with braving the local hammams with their unfamiliar social etiquette.

LA TANGERINA

19 Riad Sultan; tel. 0539/947 731; http://latangerina.com; 250Dh

La Tangerina is a fantastic traditional hammam in the style that was once common in the homes of the wealthy, who wouldn't use the public hammam. It supports up to four people, and couples are welcome. The 45-minute traditional hammam includes a body scrub using *rhassoul* (clay soap). Massages are also available. Afterward, be sure to lounge on the terrace for spectacular views over the strait.

LE BALCON DE TANGER

28 Rue Bouhachem; tel. 0539/948 213; http://lebalcondetanger.com; 250Dh

This boutique hotel right in the middle of the old medina offers an in-house hammam and an opportunity to indulge in an hour-long massage, which is a perfect antidote to a long stretch of medina haggling and shopping.

FOOD

Though Tangier hasn't developed the culinary reputation of Marrakesh, Casablanca, and Rabat, the fare on offer is thankfully down-to-earth. Restaurants offer fresh, delicious dishes in a variety of cuisines, catering to both locals and travelers.

A woman wearing a traditional hat looks out over Parc Perdicaris.

TOP EXPERIENCE

☆ Cafés

Tangier has a famed café history, with many of the literati having spent time sipping on a *café con leche* while composing their latest masterpieces. Today, the many cafés peppering Tangier draw a lively mix of locals, expats, and travelers while offering up some of the best people-watching this side of the Strait of Gibraltar. What follows is a list of some of the best cafés in Tangier.

inside Tangier's famed Café Baba

- **Café Hafa:** William Burroughs, Paul Bowles, Tennessee Williams, the Beatles, and countless others have stopped by Café Hafa to sip on a mint tea and look out over the Mediterranean to Spain (page 198).
- **Gran Café de Paris:** The centrally located Gran Café de Paris has a rich literary history and, even now, is considered somewhat of a hot spot for local writers (page 197).
- **Café Colon:** Maybe best known for its 15 minutes of fame in Bernardo Bertolucci's adaptation of *The Sheltering Sky,* this quintessentially Tanjaoui café has remained largely unchanged in the last 40 years (page 196).
- **Café Central:** A trip to Tangier wouldn't be complete without a stop here, where Tangier's expat crowd used to meet up for a cocktail (page 197).
- **Café Baba:** Founded in 1941 and famously patroned by the Rolling Stones, this café serves up some mean mint tea and heavy Turkish-style coffee alongside views over the medina and the Mediterranean from the indoor balcony (page 197).

Kasbah

HOTEL NORD PINUS

11 Riad Sultan; tel. 0661/228 140; daily 1pm-3pm and 7:30pm-9:30pm; 300Dh

This hotel restaurant offers traditional Moroccan fare, including tajines on a wood fire, grilled fish and vegetables, candied lemons, and Moroccan soups. Spirits, beer, and wine are available, making an afternoon cocktail on the terrace overlooking Tangier and the Strait of Gibraltar an enticing idea. Skip the food and come for a cocktail and the view.

★ EL MOROCCO CLUB

1 Rue Kachla; tel. 0539/948 139; http://elmoroccoclub.ma; Tues.-Sun. noon-3pm and 7pm-midnight; 200Dh

Just outside the medina is this reincarnation of the iconic residence designed by famous American architect Stuart Church and frequented by the Beats and Mick Jagger during their sojourns in Tangier. Dishes are French-Moroccan fusion and include chicken with *bakoula* (a sort of cooked spinach-like vegetable) and grilled sardines lathered in *charmoula* (a Moroccan olive oil sauce with coriander, cumin, garlic, and paprika). The downstairs **Piano Bar,** though a bit small, can be a real treat with live music, competent cocktails, and fresh oysters served starting at 8pm.

LA CASITA

91 Rue Mohamed Ben Seddik; tel. 0539/334 592 or 0675/035 145; lacasita-amrah@gmail.com; Tues.-Sun. noon-3pm and 7pm-midnight; 90Dh

One of the most colorful entrepreneurs in Tangier, Bilal, has worked with his family to bring their version of Tangier cuisine to life. Serving a delicious mix of soups and salads, as well as the staple tajines and heaping mounds of couscous, this is regional cuisine done right. Ingredients are seasonal and fresh from that morning's souk while Bilal's mother oversees the kitchen, ensuring that each plate is something she would happily serve her own family. A light lunch with a traditional Moroccan soup, such as *harira* or *bissara,* is possible for 25Dh, making this a really excellent budget option.

RESTAURANT CHEZ HASSAN

Rue Kasbah, at the bottom of the hill; tel. 0613/769 293; daily noon-midnight; 100Dh

This is a fantastic hole-in-the-wall restaurant located just down the hill from the Bab Kasbah and easily found just outside the medina, a short walk up from the Grand Socco. The charismatic proprietor, Hassan, serves up fresh seafood and traditional seasonal regional dishes. Tajines are made to order, so be prepared to wait for a few extra minutes. You can pick from a selection of fresh fish, chicken, beef, and vegetarian options, but you really should consider the shark tajine—it's one of a kind. Snag a seat on the patio for some unbeatable people-watching.

Medina

CHEZ AMY

16 Rue Mokhtar Ahardan; tel. 0607/409 543; daily noon-10pm; 30Dh

One of the better hole-in-the-wall restaurants in Morocco, Chez Amy offers up some of the most authentic Senegalese dishes this side of Dakar. Go there for the *maffé,* a fried rice dish with chicken, pepper, ginger, and a blend of hot Senegalese spices bathed in a fresh peanut sauce. If you're feeling big-hearted, you can also buy meals here to help feed the numerous sub-Saharan refugees struggling in and around Tangier.

RIF KEBDANI

14 Rue Dar el-Baroud, downhill from the Hotel Continental; tel. 0539/939 497; daily noon-11pm; 50Dh

Known locally as "Dar Baroud," this is a good break from the street food and quick snack vendors in the medina. The usual mix of lamb, chicken, and meatball tajines, as well as Moroccan salads and *pastilla,* are on offer, though you really want to stop in here for the rather theatrical service set in the beautifully tiled courtyard and open kitchen.

LE NABAB

4 Rue al-Kadiria; tel. 0661/442 220; daily noon-3pm and 7pm-11pm; 125Dh

Though a bit difficult to find, this local spot is a good introduction to Moroccan cuisine, serving a variety of tajines, including chicken with candied lemon and lamb with prunes, and Moroccan salads, including *zaalouk*, a roasted and chilled eggplant salad. Service can be slow, but it's honest, and the tajines are well worth the wait.

RAY CHARLY

Zoco Chico; daily 10am-10pm; 50Dh

A Tangier staple for 50 years, this burger and kebab joint right on the Zoco Chico is fantastic for a quick snack or easy afternoon lunch. Sit on one of the few barstools and look out over the travelers and touts hustling back and forth through the medina while you munch on some chips. If you're generally adverse to liver, you might change your mind after tasting the incredibly seasoned Moroccan version. Order the *kedba* sandwich—trust me on this one.

CAFÉ COLON

rue d'Italie; daily 7am-11pm; 10Dh

Café Colon, just outside of the medina, adjacent to the Grand Socco on Rue de la Kasbah, across from the falling-into-ruin Cinema Alcazar movie theater, may best be known for its 15 minutes of fame in Bernardo Bertolucci's adaptation of *The Sheltering Sky.* This café has remained largely unchanged in the last 40 years. As at most cafés in Morocco, the clientele is largely male, but it's a nice place to recharge after a few hours in the medina and is perhaps the most quintessentially Moroccan café in Tangier.

CAFÉ CENTRAL

Zoco Chico (Petit Socco); 7am-11pm; 10Dh

A trip to Tangier wouldn't be complete without a stop at Café Central, right on the Zoco Chico, in the heart of the old medina of Tangier. It's hard to believe this was a hot spot in the Tangier International Zone days, with brothels around the corner, opium dens across the street, and Tangier's expat crowd meeting up here for a cocktail. The cocktails are no longer (selling alcohol is forbidden in the medina), but you can sip on a coffee and watch the characters of Tangier and the day-trippers from Spain mingle as they pass through.

CAFÉ BABA

Rue Zaitouni; 7am-11pm; 10Dh

Farther up the medina toward the kasbah is the historic Café Baba. Founded in 1941, this café serves up some mean mint tea and heavy Turkish-style coffee, with views over the medina and the water from the indoor balcony. Most clients, including kings of Spain and Sweden as well as the Rolling Stones and filmmaker Jim Jarmusch, come here not for what's served, but for the "smoke what you like" policy. Of all the cafés, this might be the most difficult to find. Ask for directions around Bab Haha if you're having trouble.

Ville Nouvelle

★ RESTAURANT POPULAIRE SAVEURS DU POISSON

2 Excalier Waller; tel. 0539/336 326; Sat.-Thurs. 12:30pm-4pm and 7pm-10pm; 200Dh

After a few short years, this restaurant has become a favorite for locals and travelers alike. The charming, though rough-around-the-edges, restaurant does brisk business, with everything on offer seemingly made in-house, even the wooden cutlery and clay plates. This is a fixed menu, boasting some of the best traditional Mediterranean-Moroccan food in the region, which means that you won't order so much as sit down and be served whatever the chef has on hand. All dishes use fresh seafood selected by the owner (a former fisherman who goes by "Popeye"), and lots of local herbs and spices. No reservations are taken, so come early to avoid a long wait. It's refreshingly nonsmoking and a can't-miss experience.

O SAVEUR

15 Rue Boubana in the California neighborhood; tel. 0539/949 660; Mon.-Sat. 8pm-11pm; 400Dh

Of the few French restaurants in Tangier, O Saveur is *le top.* Dishes vary seasonally and according to the chef's whims. You might find bluefin tuna prepared three different ways: carpaccio with rocket (arugula) and parmesan, cooked with sesame, or kissed at the grill with crushed tomatoes, crystallized garlic, and basil. The tuna may be followed by a bread brioche with pineapples roasted with vanilla for dessert . . . or you might find something else. Trust the chef. Don't forget to order dessert. And, when the weather permits, which it usually does in Tangier, consider dining in the outdoor garden beneath the stars.

ANNA & PAOLO

77 Rue Prince Héritier; tel. 0539/944 617; Mon.-Sat. noon-3pm and 7:30pm-11pm; 125Dh

Located in the newer part of Tangier across from the Hotel Chellah, this is a cozy, family-owned Italian bistro with largely Mediterranean-Italian fusion options, including particularly well-done delicate house-made pasta and real Italian pizzas. The seafood selection abounds with fresh catches of the day. Food, service, and atmosphere are generally pleasant, though one smoker can ruin the entire restaurant as it is small.

GRAN CAFÉ DE PARIS

Pl. de France; daily 7am-11pm; 15Dh

The centrally located Gran Café de Paris has a

rich literary history and, even now, is considered somewhat of a hot spot for local writers. The colonial decor inside is mostly maintained with plush leather seats. Grab a spot on the terrace, order a fresh-squeezed orange juice, recharge, and people-watch.

Marshan

★ CAFÉ HAFA

rue Hafa; Mon.-Fri. 8:30am-11pm, Sat.-Sun. 8:30am-2am; 20Dh

In Marshan, close to the Phoenician tombs, Café Hafa is a must-do experience. William Burroughs, Paul Bowles, Tennessee Williams, the Beatles, and countless others have stopped by Café Hafa to sip on a mint tea and look out over the Mediterranean to Spain. Kids from the local schools come here to do homework, and young men get together to play Parcheesi ("par-cheese" in the local vernacular). The tapping of their dice clinking across the glass top of the game board blends into the background with the wind, the surf, and the inevitable one or two bees that find your mint tea as delicious as you do. At night, there is often music. If anyone smokes anything other than a cigarette, a strict "don't ask, don't tell" policy should be adhered to.

BARS AND NIGHTLIFE

Tangier is famous for its nightlife, and rightfully so. During the summer, the young and hip (and wannabe young and hip) used to flock to the numerous nightclubs that lined the beach along Avenue Mohammed VI. These have all been torn down, and now with the new port development, the party has changed drastically, with the best nightclubs having relocated there. Bars and nightclubs aren't cheap, though women generally get in free. Nightclubs all boast loads of security and can help you get taxis back to your accommodations at the end of the night. Prostitution is a concern, and some nights it can feel as though the club is packed solely with them and their escorts. The clubs are best enjoyed in groups, and usually open Thursday-Saturday nights, though hours and days are generally expanded in the busy summer months. It might be worth contacting the club to make a reservation for the night. This can make things smoother at the door.

Most of the bars of Tangier are not for the faint of heart. With few exceptions, they are male-dominated, very smoky, and rough around the edges with rampant prostitution. That said, there are a few bars of historic note and a couple of tapas bars well worth a visit.

Locals enjoy mint tea with a view at Café Hafa.

HOTEL CHARF BAR

25 Rue al Farabi; daily noon-midnight; 25Dh

Perhaps the best remaining tapas bar in Tangier. You won't find a nonsmoking section, but you will find plenty to eat as long as you sit and drink. If you ask to go upstairs, you'll be treated to panoramic views of the Mediterranean Sea and Spain. Best of all, in true tapa-style, whatever is put in front of you to eat is free. Grilled sardines, Moroccan salads, fried calamari, and whatever else is fresh in from the port that day will find its way onto a plate for you. Kick back, sip on a bottle of suds, and imagine you're buddying up to the bar with Jack Kerouac. The downstairs corner bar is about as authentic of an experience of Tangier bar-hopping as it gets.

DEAN'S BAR

2 Amerique du Sud; daily noon-1am; 20Dh

One of the more storied bars of the 20th century, though you wouldn't know it by looking at it. The small plaque reading "Dean's Bar - 1937" has been torn off. Now the only thing to distinguish it is the "33" beer sign above the door. Dean was a man of unknown origin who opened his own bar here and supplied the residents and visitors of Tangier with just about everything. He was known to arrange travel visas and pawn jewelry, and he was even thought to be a spy employed by the British, French, or Germans, depending on who you believe. During his reign, Dean served cocktails to Ian Fleming (vodka martini, shaken, not stirred, one would imagine), who stayed at the Minzah dictating his book *Diamonds Are Forever*, as well as Truman Capote, William Burroughs, Barbara Hutton, T.S. Eliot, and countless others. Now, there is a load of Spanish soccer memorabilia and a clientele of Moroccan men defining hard drinking, which makes the history of this bar somewhat hard to believe.

TANGER INN

1 Rue Magellan; daily 11am-11pm; 20Dh

A great stop to soak in the literary history of Morocco. Knowing your barstool once supported the likes of Frederico Garcia Lorca, Tennessee Williams, and Jean Genet can add a bit of erudition to your beverage of choice. Located just uphill from Avenue Mohammed VI and the beach, this area can be a little sketchy at night, so it's best to travel in groups or have a taxi drop you off and pick you up.

LA BODEGA

Rue Allal Ben Abdellah, near the Hotel Chellah; daily 11am-2am; 25Dh

This tapas bar doesn't disappoint, with Ibérico ham, *queso manchego* (cheese), *boquerones* (anchovies), and numerous other Andalusian specialties on offer. Quieter on weekdays and during happy hour, the bar picks up toward the end of the week. It's one of the cleanest bars in Tangier, catering more to the business and tourist crowd than locals, and is also a comfortable spot for women looking for a beer, cocktail, or glass of wine. With the decor of deep reds and sharp black, as well as the occasional live music, including flamenco, performed here on the weekends, there is a real Andalusian vibe to be had.

CLUB 555

Marina Bay, Ave. Mohammed VI; tel. 0654/085 321; www.beachclub555.com; 200Dh

The gold standard for clubs in Tangier. The music varies nightly with guest DJs spinning lots of upbeat R&B, international hip-hop, and house to keep you dancing. Tables are available, though you'll have to buy an overpriced bottle of alcohol. Women don't pay cover, and they get free whiskey, vodka, and mixers on Ladies' Night (night varies). A dress code applies—no flip-flops or tennis shoes.

LOFT

Rue de Boubana; tel. 0651/636 044; www.loftclub-tanger.com; 200Dh

Loft is the largest nightclub in northern Morocco, with up to 2,000 visitors per night, located in a complex that also features a lounge and a pool. The club itself has multiple stories, with inward-facing balconies and billowing muslin drapes that give the sensation of truly dancing the night away. Entry is free before midnight; women always get in free.

ACCOMMODATIONS

Kasbah

DAR NOUR

20 Rue Gourna; tel. 0662/112 724; www.darnour.com; 700Dh d

The owners of Dar Nour combined three separate houses to form this complex, a charming maze reminiscent of the sprawling labyrinth of the Tangier kasbah and medina. The furniture and decor reflect the energy and cosmopolitan history of Tangier, a city open to European, Moorish, African, and Jewish influence while being marked by the artists who passed through. Breakfast and Wi-Fi are included with your stay. Dinner is available as well, on request.

★ LA TANGERINA

19 Riad Sultan; tel. 0539/947 731; http://latangerina.com; 800Dh d

This is what you imagine when you picture a *riad* in the kasbah of Tangier. The location couldn't be more stellar, with a wide terrace holding a few chaise lounges for you to relax in as you soak up the views over the kasbah and the Strait of Gibraltar. The rooms are spacious without being palatial; some have private patios. The simple, Mediterranean-Moroccan decor is a breath of fresh air after a stressful day in the medina. The service is outstanding and friendly without being intrusive, and the daily freshly cut flowers add to the sense of being at home. Breakfast and Wi-Fi are included, as is afternoon tea. There is an on-site hammam for couples, and dinner is available upon request.

DAR SULTAN

49 Rue Touila; tel. 0539/336 061; www.darsultan.com; 1,000Dh d

Walking into this guesthouse can feel a little like walking into one of the medina bazaars, with shiny lamps, ornate carpets, and other bric-a-brac lying about. The rooms are clean and comfortable, though the real treat is to pay extra for the Chambre Charf—this way you'll have your own private terrace looking out over the Mediterranean and sprawling medina below. Wi-Fi and breakfast are included. The cigar cave/smoking room might be of interest to some, while the private massages are great for couples.

Medina

★ THE MELTING POT HOSTEL

3 Rue de Tsouli; tel. 0539/947 731; www.meltingpothostels.com; 110Dh dorm-style bed, 250Dh d

Of the cheaper options in the medina, this is the cleanest and most reliable. Beds are comfortable, sheets are clean, and towels are provided. Popular with backpackers and weekenders, especially from Spain, the hostel serves up a free, though lean, breakfast. The friendly staff provides pointers for the medina and around Tangier. A wonderful rooftop terrace offers views over the port. Wi-Fi is included.

HOTEL CONTINENTAL

36 Rue Dar El Baroud; tel. 0539/931 024; 400Dh d

One of the most storied hotels may likely disappoint, but it will leave you with a story, which shouldn't be all that disappointing. Winston Churchill and many other notables stayed here, and it doesn't seem as though much has changed since then in this 19th-century National Heritage site. Beds are often uncomfortable, breakfast can be a hit-or-miss affair, and the electricity cuts on and off sporadically. Otherwise, the service is friendly, rooms are clean, and the long terrace (overlooking the port and strait) and outer dining room (with its sculpted ceiling and stained-glass windows) are stellar, though the dinner doesn't quite live up to the surroundings. How could it?

★ DAR CHAMS

2 rue Jean Kabtan; tel. 0529/332 323; www.darchamstanja.com; 900Dh d

A stone's throw from the kasbah, and just down the hill from Bab el-Essa linking the kasbah with the medina, Dar Chams has been a traveler favorite for over a decade. Situated next to the storied Cafe Baba and Sidi Hosni (Barbara Hutton's mythic Tangier mansion), the location is perfect for exploring Tangier. From the moment you step out the door, you'll be exploring one of Tangier's most colorful, chic neighborhoods. The only problem with this boutique hotel is that the service is so top-notch that you might find yourself reluctant to head out the door. This welcoming, Moroccan-chic *riad* has enough nooks and crannies, including a reading room, lounge, and outdoor terrace, that you could easily spend a day exploring the property. Luckily, the manager, Khadija, is knowledgeable not only about the latest hot spots around Tangier, but all around the country, so she'll make sure you get out. The traditional on-site hammam with available full-body massages can relax the vacation right into you. A scrumptious breakfast spread is included with your stay. Rooms have TVs, Wi-Fi, air-conditioning, minibars, and lockboxes.

PALAIS ZAHIA

76 rue de la Marine; tel. 0539/934 000; www.palais-zahia.com; 1,200Dh d

A little expensive but with a great location, right next to the Zoco Chico. Formerly the first branch of the National Bank of Morocco, the entire building has been renovated by a caring Moroccan family, with beautiful stucco work, painted wood, and carved cedar everywhere. Rooms overlooking the street can be pretty noisy, with the traffic and the morning call to prayer—ask for rooms farther away from the front door for a quieter night. With a rare elevator, the *riad* is wheelchair accessible, and breakfast is included. Dinner with Chef Louba should not be missed! Try the *kebab maghdour* ("fooled meat"), a tender, stewed, well-spiced meat dish. Veggie lovers would do well to ask about a seasonal favorite: *bakoula*, a hearty green, much like collard greens or kale, slow cooked with plenty of garlic and olive oil. No alcohol is served. Wi-Fi, televisions, air-conditioning, minibars, and lockboxes are included.

Ville Nouvelle

HOTEL CHELLAH

47-49 Rue Allal Ben Abdellah; tel. 0539/321 002; 400Dh d

This long-time staple with business travelers and visitors to Tangier is beginning to show its age. The mix of Moroccan *zellij* and art deco has a noticeable, worn veneer. The beds are comfortable, though the rooms feel as though they still belong to the 1970s. The back courtyard and pool area is a great spot to relax, and the breakfast buffet is one of the best in Tangier. Air-conditioning, Wi-Fi, and breakfast are all included.

REMBRANDT HOTEL

Ave. Pasteur; tel. 0539/937 870; www.rembrandthotel.ma; 400Dh d

Located right on Avenue Pasteur, just a few minutes from Place de France, the Rembrandt Hotel's rooms are a bit noisier than some of the other options around the city. It's best to request rooms higher up and facing the strait, though you will be at the whim of the small elevator that shuttles slowly up and down. The vibe is all 1950s, with many period pieces throughout the hallways and in the rooms of this colonial hotel. One of the better values in town, particularly for the use of the pool. Air-conditioning, Wi-Fi, and breakfast are included.

GRAND HOTEL VILLA DE FRANCE

Rue d'Angleterre; tel. 0539/333 111; http://grandhotelvilla.hotelspages.com; 1,500Dh d

There is now a bit of class restored to Tangier; after a seven-year renovation, this stunning hotel that once housed the cream of Tangier's society reopened in 2014. Henri Matisse stayed here in 1912-1913, painting scenes of the medina and Tangier's people in room 35, now a mini-museum. Rooms are all modern, though styled from the 1930s; the beds are luxurious and the linen divine. The hotel abuts the Grand Socco, making it one of the best locations for exploring Tangier. Air-conditioning, Wi-Fi, and a great breakfast are all included. The only downside is the occasional large party or wedding hosted on-site that may be noisier than you'd want.

INFORMATION AND SERVICES

The city code for Tangier and the area is 39.

Post Offices and Courier Services

The main **post office** (33 Blvd. Mohammed V, Mon.-Fri. 8am-4:15pm, Sat. 8am-11:45am) has Western Union services.

Money

There are a couple of banks in the Grand Socco: **SGMB** and **BMCE** (Mon.-Fri. 8:15am-3:45pm). Otherwise, head down Avenue Pasteur and Boulevard Mohammed V to find a string of banks. **Banque Populaire** (corner of Blvd. Mohammed V and Rue Allal ben Abdellah, Mon.-Fri. 8:15am-3:45pm) exchanges travelers checks and has a handy 24-hour exchange ATM. **WafaChange** (across from Banque Populaire on Blvd. Mohammed V, Mon.-Fri. 8am-6pm, Sat. 9am-1pm) is the only bank with weekend hours. The state-run **Bank al Maghrib** (Blvd. Mohammed V, Mon.-Fri. 8am-3pm) will generally cash travelers checks.

Hospitals, Clinics, and Pharmacies

Pharmacies are found easily throughout Tangier and are generally open Monday-Friday 9am-1pm and 4pm-8pm. All pharmacies have a list of after-hours and weekend pharmacies posted on their front door. In the Ville Nouvelle, **Pharmacie du Paris** and **Grande Pharmacie Pasteur** are both on Place de France, and a bit farther down Avenue Pasteur is **Pharmacie Centrale.** On Rue as-Siaghin in the medina you will find **Pharmacie Anegax.** If you have a more serious health issue, a **private ambulance service** (tel. 0539/954 040 or 0539/946 976) is available. One of the better private clinics is **Clinique Assalam** (10 Ave. de la Paix, tel. 0539/322 558).

GETTING THERE

By Bus and Grand Taxi

Grands taxis and buses arrive and leave from the ***gare routière,*** which is at the Place de la Ligue Arabe (though everyone still calls this "Ronds-Points Dial Tetouan"). Popular runs for *grands taxis* are **Asilah** (40min, 46km/28mi, 30Dh, though you'll likely have to hire the entire cab), **Tetouan** (1hr, 60km/37mi, 45Dh), and **Cap Spartel** (15min, 15km/9mi, 15Dh).

The **CTM** (tel. 0800/0900 30, www.ctm.ma) is the most reliable bus service and runs buses to **Tetouan** (1hr, 3 daily, 45Dh), **Chefchaouen** (2.5hr, 2 daily, 65Dh), **Fez** (4.5hr, 4 daily, 110Dh), and **Rabat** (4hr, 6 daily, 110Dh).

By Car

Tangier is connected via the tolled autoroute N1, which runs along the Atlantic coast. Tolls vary according to type of automobile and where you enter/exit the tolled route. In principle, it's a good idea to travel with 400Dh just for tolls, though you'll likely not use all of it.

From Rabat: Follow the N1 north for 250km/155mi, about 3 hours.

From Casablanca: Follow the N1 north for 335km/208mi, about 4 hours.

From Fez: Follow the N2 west toward Rabat before joining with the N1 going north toward Tangier, for a total of 305km/190mi, about 4.5 hours.

From Marrakesh: Follow the N1 north for 572km/355mi, about 6.5 hours.

By Ferry

Tangier is just a short 35-minute ferry ride from **Tarifa, Spain**. There are two ferry companies that operate directly from **Tangier-Ville,** a small port at the foot of the Tangier medina: **FRS** (www.frs.es/en) and **Intershipping** (www.intershipping.es/fr). The companies alternate departures every hour on the hour throughout the day. Tickets are available online and right at the ferry terminal for single passengers (420Dh), cars (1,920Dh), and caravans (2,050Dh). You will want to make sure to arrive at the ferry 30 minutes prior to departure if you are walking. If you are taking an automobile, you'll want to get there at least an hour early. Take special care if purchasing tickets online to select Tangier-Ville (not Tangier-Med). They are two different ports serving two different cities in Spain.

There is a free bus that departs a few minutes after each ferry arrival on the Spanish side that connects the Tarifa ferry terminal with the Algeciras ferry terminal. The Algeciras ferry terminal is a short walk to the bus station, making this a great connection for those traveling on foot by public transport and continuing their adventure to (or from) Andalusia.

If there are high winds, the ferries from Tangier-Ville will stop running. This is the only time I would advise trying the larger ferries departing from the **Tanger-Med port**, about a 30-minute drive east of Tangier. Even then, I would only do this if you are really in need of crossing immediately. Ferries from Tangier-Med connect with Algeciras. Though tickets are generally less expensive than the Tangier-Tarifa ferry, the travel time is usually doubled, if not tripled, with longer lines and longer travel times on bigger, older, slower ferries.

By Train

There are two types of trains that serve Tangier, both operated by the **ONCF** (tel. 0890/203 040, www.oncf.ma). The older, dilapidated trains serve nearly all destinations, while the sleek new **Al-Boraq high-speed trains** make only a few connections. There are direct trains for most destinations, though for some destinations your trip will perhaps include a transfer at Sidi Kacem. Check your ticket for details. Popular connections include **Asilah** (30min, 12 daily, 2nd/1st-class 16Dh/25Dh), **Casablanca** (5hr, 11 daily, 125Dh/185Dh), **Fez** (4.5hr, 5 daily, 105Dh/155Dh), **Meknes** (4hr, 5 daily, 85Dh/130Dh), and **Rabat** (4hr, 11 daily, 95Dh/145Dh).

Trains leave from **the Tangier-Ville station** (Gare Ferroviare) to **Marrakesh** (9.5hr, 10 daily, 2nd/1st-class 205Dh/310Dh), though most trains change at Casa Voyageurs or Sidi Kacem. The only direct train to Marrakesh is the **overnight train** that leaves Tangier at 10pm and arrives in Marrakesh at 8am without a transfer. It's best to book the *voiture-lit* single/double or couchette (sleeping cars) at the train station a day or two before departure. These cannot be purchased online but must be purchased at the train station. Prices per bed start at 350Dh and they can sell out quickly during peak travel seasons.

The **Al-Boraq** is just like the TGV in France. This train route was inaugurated in November 2018 and now whisks passengers along from Tangier to **Casablanca** in just over two hours. Prices vary according to demand. It's a very good idea to purchase your ticket ahead of traveling. Online purchasing is possible, though fidgety. It might take a few tries to get the system to work. You can also keep an eye out for promotional fares that often cut the price by a third or more. The first train leaves Tangier at 5:55am, with trains departing around every two hours until 9:55pm. With the quick service, this makes a day trip from Tangier to **Rabat** or Casablanca feasible. From Tangier, connections on Al-Boraq include Kenitra (1hr, 9 daily, 93Dh-139Dh), Rabat (1.5hr, 9 daily, 115Dh-172Dh), and Casablanca (2hr, 9 daily, 149Dh-224Dh), with first-class tickets typically costing about 70Dh more.

By Plane

TANGIER IBN BATTUTA AIRPORT

Boukhalef, 8km/5mi southwest of the town center, tel. 0539/393 649, www.onda.ma

The airport is easy enough to navigate, located a short 30min drive south of downtown Tangier. For those flying in from Europe, alongside Fez and Marrakesh, this is one of the best airports to use in Morocco. The airport does provide service to cities throughout Europe via mostly budget providers such as **Air Arabia** (www.airarabia.com), **Ryan Air** (www.ryanair.com), and **Transavia** (www.transavia.com). From the airport, *grands taxis* can shuttle you to the *gare routière* in the city for 200Dh.

GETTING AROUND

As in other cities in Morocco, driving around Tangier can be stressful thanks to many drivers ignoring the rules of the road. Most hotels have **parking** included with your stay, and there is street parking around the Grand Socco. It's possible to drive into the kasbah through the Bab Kasbah and park at the main square there if you're staying in or visiting the kasbah.

Red ***petits taxis*** can shuttle you around the city, though outside the train station the drivers will often try to get you to agree on an exorbitant price rather than use the counter, as they legally should. Feel free to demand the counter be used, and if a driver ever disagrees, simply refuse to take the taxi. Most taxi rides should cost 15-20Dh.

City buses (3.5Dh) owned by Alsa (http://alsa.ma) run dependably daily 7am-9pm around Tangier. The handiest for travelers looking to explore the western edges of Tangier is bus 5, which runs every 30 minutes from Sidi Bouabid by the Grand Mosque (across from the Cervantes Institute in the Iberia neighborhood) past Perdicaris Park and all the way to Cap Spartel.

Segways have also been taking Tangier by storm with MobilBoard (tel. 0606/000 311, www.mobilboard.com/tanger, 170Dh for 30min). The most enjoyable Segway ride is perhaps the circuit on the new waterfront pedestrian-only boulevard (1h, 300Dh). Helmets are available (and recommended). It's best to reserve a few days in advance.

Otherwise, you will be walking through the kasbah and medina, and along Avenue Pasteur and the long corniche bordering the beach, so bring a good pair of shoes.

AROUND TANGIER

Cap Spartel

About 15 minutes west of Tangier on the Atlantic Coast is Cap Spartel, an extraordinary cape that wraps around the northwestern edge of Africa. From here, it's possible to see the different waters of the Mediterranean Sea and Atlantic Ocean mingle.

CAVE OF HERCULES

Route des grottes de Hercule, just south of Cap Spartel

The stunning Cave of Hercules (Grottes d'Hercule) is rumored to be the resting place of Hercules after he completed his 11th labor, the Apples of Hesperides (or "The Golden Apple"). After Hercules obtained the golden apple, it is thought he rested in this cave near Cap Spartel.

However, as interesting and surprisingly beautiful as the newly restored Cave of Hercules is, it is also a bit of a tourist trap. Avoid any guides, as this cave is simple to navigate. There are some unremarkable shops catering to tourists on the terrace, but once you enter the cave, remember to look up to see where locals have carved out round stones from the cave walls, used for milling grain, for generations. The cave's opening, in the shape of the continent of Africa, looks out toward the Atlantic. If you can, try to get there at sunset.

GETTING THERE

Driving to Cap Spartel and its environs is easy, though getting out of the city can prove to be a little tricky, and the drive is quite pretty. You meander through a palatial neighborhood and through **Perdicaris Park.** Often, women and children will be selling pine nuts or other seasonal fruits alongside the road. These are generally delicious and always inexpensive. To find your way west out of the city of Tangier, toward the

---

1: beach lovers at the municipal beach of Ceuta
2: a boat makes its way through the rampart passage

1
RIBERA
2

Atlantic, follow the signs for "Cap Spartel" and "Grottes d'Hercule" and "Rmilate" that dot the main thoroughfares.

To get to Cap Spartel without a car, it's best to go to the Grand Socco. You can hire a **taxi** there for 20Dh per person round trip. You could also take **bus 5** from the Grand Mosque (3.5Dh), which will let you off at Cap Spartel, where it's a short walk down the coast to the Cave of Hercules.

The Northern Mediterranean

CEUTA (SPAIN)

سبتة

After a long wait at the grimy land border between Morocco and Spain, the enclave of Ceuta (often called **Sebta** in Morocco, its Arabic name) comes as a tranquil surprise. At night, the city is lit up in gold, twinkling over the Mediterranean. The cerveza flows and *gambas a la plancha* (grilled shrimp) seem to be everywhere. Many expats living in Morocco, as well as Moroccans from the region, regularly cross into Ceuta for the low-tax shopping and ease of getting goods common in Europe. Ceuta's reputation as a shopping hub is thanks to its status as an autonomous city within Spain. Today's Ceuta has the feel of an outdoor shopping mall, with plenty of chic designer labels, high-end cars, and jewelry on sale. For beach lovers, the stretch of sand alongside **Calle Independencia** makes a nice beach, and women should enjoy much less harassment here than across the border. However, Ceuta does hold a special place in history, and thus, there's quite a bit to see and do for cultural vultures.

The history of Ceuta is quite long, beginning in the 5th century BC with the Carthaginians, who called the city Abyla and saw its military value as a post along the strait. The Romans then took control, calling the city Septem, from which it derives its Arabic name, Sebta. The Vandals, Visigoths, and Byzantines all had their turns controlling this strategic outpost. The city fell into ruin during the 8th century, though not before the famed military commander Tariq Ibn Zaid used this as a staging ground for his invasion of Spain. Interestingly, the Rock of Gibraltar carries the commander's name. The original name of Gibraltar was "Jbel Tariq" or "Tariq's Mountain." Andalusian and Moroccan dynasties controlled Ceuta until the Battle of Ceuta in 1415, when the Portuguese took control. After the Treaty of Lisbon in 1668, Portugal recognized the city's allegiance to Spain, to whom it has belonged since, despite a 33-year siege by the notorious tyrant sultan Moulay Ismail in the 17th and 18th centuries as well as ongoing disputes with Morocco.

Of course, mythology also plays a large part in this part of the world. According to the Greeks, Africa and Europe were once connected by a mountain range. The two continents were divided when Hercules threw down his mace while fighting with Antaeus and opened what we know of now as the Strait of Gibraltar. There were two pillars the Greeks identified that marked this event: Calpe (Gibraltar) in Europe and Abyla (Hacho Mountain) in Africa. There are a surprising number of sculptures dotted throughout Ceuta, including a statue commemorating Hercules's mythological separation of the two continents front and center in the main Plaza de la Constitutión.

Orientation

Though Ceuta lacks some of the historic and architectural interest and importance of its sister enclave city, Melilla, it is the more popular of the two because of its relative ease of access, just two hours west of Tangier and 45 minutes from Tetouan to the south. Nearly all of the **museums** and cultural points of interest are closed on Sundays, many also closed Mondays, as are a number of **shops** and **restaurants**, so these two days are best avoided. However, beachgoers might make it a point to go on a Monday as many of the weekenders have cleared out of town. Many of the town's shops and restaurants are also shuttered during Spanish holidays, so it's best to consult a list of Spanish National Holidays before crossing the border.

Sights

There are quite a few small military museums throughout Ceuta that are all free entry, though nearly all information is in Spanish and often carries a not-so-subtle colonial air. If you can read Spanish and are interested, then these are perhaps worth stopping in. Otherwise, this collection of museums is perfectly skippable.

WALKING TOURS

For those interested in local culture and wanting to check out some of the sights, consider the very affordable walking tours (€2), which cover sights from the Royal Walls to the Tardorramana Basilica. In fact, there are two sights that are only possible to visit while on a tour: the **Arab Baths (Baño Árabe)** and the **Caliphal Gate (Puerta Califal).** Unfortunately, you can't see these both on the same tour or even on the same day. The tours are guided by professionals from the Tourist Office, and you can get tickets and view schedules online (www.ceuta.es) or by visiting the ticket booth at the local Theater Revellín (Plaza Nelsón Mandela, tel. 0956/500 303).

ROYAL CITY WALLS

Ave. González Tablas; Mon.-Fri. 10am-2pm and 5pm-8pm; free

The walk along the Royal City Walls (El Conjunto Monumental de las Murallas Reales) offers beautiful views over the city and across the Strait of Gibraltar to mainland Spain. Signage in English explains the historic significance of the fort and the various parapets, jetties, walls, and moats along the walk. This is a declared Spanish Heritage Site. The walk is free, but the photographic possibilities are priceless.

MUSEO DE LAS MURALLAS REALES

Conjunto Monumental de las Murallas Reales; tel. 0956/511 770; Tues.-Sat. 10am-2pm and 5pm-8pm; free

Take a moment in the air-conditioned confines of the lovely Museo de las Murallas Reales, located within the Royal City Walls. Not only will you glimpse the history of the region, but the museum has a rotating exhibition that usually features artists from Spanish-Morocco, such as Mariano Bertuchi, a Spanish painter who was largely responsible for the Spanish visualization of "Spanish Morocco" in the first half of the 20th century. Many Moroccan and Spanish painters have found homes for their work in this museum.

CALIFAL GATE

Conjunto Monumental de las Murallas Reales

Located within the monumental complex of the Royal City Walls, the Caliphal Gate (Puerta Califal) was discovered by chance in 2002. This gateway once allowed access to the old medina of the city while it was under Moroccan rule. Its construction dates from the 10th century. In 1415, the Portuguese expanded the wall, leaving the door buried for centuries, which has allowed for its good state of preservation. From the ramparts of the Royal City Walls, you descend to the Califal Gate, though you will need to be on a tour to access the stairway down. Be sure to join the walking tour on Mondays or Thursdays to gain access (€2).

CATHEDRAL OF SAINT MARY OF THE ASSUMPTION

Plaza de Africa

The 15th-century Cathedral of Saint Mary of the Assumption (Catedral de la Asunción de Ceuta), originally constructed by the Portuguese under their rule of the city, combines baroque and neoclassical elements that

Tapas Time!

Undoubtedly, the majority of the meals you'll have in Ceuta, Melilla, or anywhere else in Spain will comprise a series of tapas. Tapas are varied snacks that may be served **cold** (such as slices of aged cheese or Ibérico ham) or **hot** (like fried chorizo in garlic or baked mussels). The concept behind tapas is that, instead of focusing on a large meal, you have a little snack that you nibble while focusing on the conversations with the friends around you.

The word *tapa* comes from the Spanish *tapar,* meaning "to cover." Historically, drinkers in Andalusia would cover their sweet wines or sherries with a piece of bread or slice of meat to keep fruit flies from landing in their beverage. Today, the tapa has evolved into a staple of Spanish culture and cuisine. Because Spanish dinners are served late, generally after 9pm, one of the more popular times to enjoy tapas is just after work. This is when most of the bars are usually at their most boisterous.

For the tapa tourist, it is important to know a few words in Spanish:

- Draft beer generally comes in three sizes: ***caña, tubo,*** and ***jarra*** (small, medium, and large).
- A bottle is a ***botella.***
- Wine comes by the ***chato*** (glass) with your choice of ***vino tinto*** or ***vino blanco*** (red or white).

Tapas are sometimes free, though generally €1-2. Some of the more common tapas dishes are:

- ***queso:*** usually a cured, semi-hard cheese
- ***jamón ibérico:*** Ibérico ham
- ***aceitunas:*** olives, usually stuffed with anchovies or red pepper
- ***bacalao:*** salted cod
- ***boquerones:*** cured white anchovies
- ***ensaladilla rusa:*** potato salad, often with tuna and vegetables
- ***patatas bravas:*** fried potato cubes, usually served with a spicy tomato sauce
- ***tortilla española:*** a type of frittata with fried potatoes and onions

Enjoy your tapas. *Una caña y una tapa de queso por favor! Gracias!* (One small beer and one tapa of cheese, please!)

have been added throughout its construction. The cathedral was built on the site of a 6th-century Christian church and hosts a collection of art dating back to the 17th century. The cathedral is currently part of the Roman Catholic Diocese of Cadiz and Ceuta.

ARAB BATHS

Plaza de la Paz

This is an interesting diversion for those interested in ancient waterways and old cleansing rituals, but make sure to join the "Medieval Ceuta" walking tour (€2) on Wednesday or Sunday to view these Arab Baths (Baño Árabe). You'll be taken inside to see the well-preserved traditional Moroccan-style hammams. For those who have experienced a Moroccan hammam treatment (or will be in the near future), this short tour can provide lots of historical insight and appreciation for a bathing ritual that is as old as the Sahara.

TARDORRAMANA BASILICA

Calle Queipo de Llano; free

The ruins of the Tardorramana Basilica were discovered in the 1980s during some construction. The site was then excavated and the museum was erected atop it. The construction of an indoor bridge over the old basilica is well executed. While visiting, you will be able to see the remains of several buildings, various items from the epoch, and even a few skeletons reposed in their coffins. The entrance can be a little difficult to find and all signage is in Spanish, making this a good chance to practice your Spanish, or join an English-speaking Sunday walking tour. A great stop to get an insight into ancient Ceuta.

Food

★ DE BUENA CEPA

40 Calle Real; tel. 34-956/201 056; Mon.-Fri. 8:30am-midnight, Sat. 1pm-midnight; €16-20

An authentically unique tapas experience. The tapas veer far away from the staple ham and cheese. Seared foie gras with orange zest and shaved chocolate, venison carpaccio, and seared ahi tuna coupled with apple marmalade are just a few of the tapas on offer, each with a carefully selected wine pairing. The menu changes every day and is written on a chalkboard at the bar. This small, cozy bar with its delicious tapas and friendly service will have you coming back.

EL PESCAITO FRITO

5 Calle Pedro de Menesses; tel. 34-956/516 935; Mon.-Fri. 8:30am-midnight, Sat. 1pm-midnight; €15

This joint keeps a selection of fresh catches on hand, including their well-done staple: *gambas a la plancha* (grilled shrimp). This small, nondescript bar is generally full of locals who come here to tell stories, catch up, and enjoy the inexpensive food.

EL LUCAS

Avenida Martinez Catena; tel. 34-956/509 487; Mon.-Thurs. 9am-10pm, Fri.-Sun. 9am-midnight; €10

For sheer quantity, this tapas bar can't be beat. The plates are piled high with grilled mussels, clams, scallops, crab, lobster, and other fresh catches of the day. The location right next to the Cepsa gas station isn't exactly ideal, but the entrance, with seafood displayed on an ice shelf, should quickly turn the palate.

Accommodations

Most of the accommodations in Ceuta are streamlined, basic hotels without much in the way of variation, with most rooms costing €80-100 per night. For budget travelers, there aren't too many options.

HOSTEL CENTRAL

15 Paseo del Revellin; tel. 34-956/516 716; www.hostalcentralceuta.com; €50 d

This hostel is the best option for most travelers. It's well located, just steps from the Plaza de la Constitución, and within walking distance to the attractions in the city. The rooms are spartan but clean, and the beds comfortable. Wi-Fi, air-conditioning, and TV are also included. Reserve directly on their website to get the best rates.

ULISES HOTEL

5 Calle Camoens; tel. 34-956/514 540; www.hotelulises.com; €80 d

For more of a boutique hotel with some basic business hotel functions, handy for digital nomads, this hotel has all the amenities one would expect. The decor is contemporary Spanish with a touch of the Moroccan thrown in. The rooms feature lots of rich browns and beiges, are large and clean, and have balconies that look over the hotel pool and across the city to the boats making their way in and out of the harbor. Wi-Fi, air-conditioning, TV, and a friendly staff are the order of the day.

Information and Services

TOURIST OFFICE (OFICINA DE INFORMACIÓN TURÍSTICA)

Edificio Baluarte de los Mallorquines; tel. 34-856/200 560; Mon.-Sat. 10am-2pm and 4:30pm-8:30pm, Sun. and holidays 10am-2pm

The Tourist Office is right between the beach and the port, with plenty of maps and pamphlets in English to help you get around.

Getting There

Ceuta is roughly two hours away from Tangier by car and just 45 minutes from Tetouan, but keep in mind that you do have to cross a land border into Spain. Lines here can often be long, by car or on foot, often taking more than an hour. Touts will try to sell you passport forms and offer to fill them out for you at the border, often taking your passport as collateral until you give them cash; just roll up your window and avoid them. The forms are free at the Moroccan customs office; however, you will be expected to provide your own pen, as customs officials almost never have pens on hand.

BY CAR

By car, Ceuta is about 1.5 hours east of **Tangier** (76km/47mi), 40 minutes north of **Tetouan** (42km/26mi), and 1.5 hours north of **Chefchaouen** (103km/64mi). The roads in this area have all been upgraded and are safe, though night driving is still a bit dangerous. If you have rented a car, you will not be able to bring it across the border into Ceuta. There is **overnight guarded parking** in Fnideq on the Moroccan side (30Dh), from which you can take the bus to Ceuta, or you could chance parking your car on the road on the Moroccan side of the border. Either way, you'll have to park your car and walk across the border.

BY BUS AND GRAND TAXI

By bus, getting to Ceuta is a little trickier. First you take a bus to Fnideq, and then you take a taxi from there to the Ceuta border (60Dh for entire taxi, 10Dh for a place, though this is always negotiable and sometimes taxi drivers will try to charge more). The **CTM** bus (tel. 0800/0900 30, www.ctm.ma) runs directly to Fnideq from **Tetouan** (30min, 1 daily, 15Dh), though it leaves at 5:30am. Another CTM bus stops in Fnideq at 2pm and will take you to Tetouan (45min, 1 daily, 15Dh).

BY FERRY

Three companies run ferries to mainland **Spain** via Algeciras and leave from the port every day: **Transmediterranea** (Spain tel. 34-902/454 645, www.transmediterranea.es), **Baleària** (Spain tel. 34-966/428 700, www.balearia.com), and **FRS** (Spain tel. 34-956/681 830, www.frs.es). Check their websites or the local newspaper for the latest departure and arrival times. A typical one-way ticket for two passengers with a car ranges from €120-150. If you are heading to Málaga, there is a bus that connects with the arriving ferries in Algeciras, making the rest of Spain easily accessible by train or plane.

Getting Around

Ceuta is small enough that you will get around just fine on your feet. If you have a car, **parking** is free on the streets, and there are a few scattered parking garages. **Taxis** are metered, inexpensive, and available throughout the city if you need to quickly get from your hotel to a restaurant.

TETOUAN
تطوان

Just an hour east of Tangier lies a real gem for those looking for something a bit less traveled—Tetouan. This city, the former capital of Spanish Morocco, is still rough around the edges, but it is an up-and-coming destination with plenty of historic value and fine museums. There is a notable Arab-Andalusian influence throughout the city. The only similar city one might find in Morocco is Melilla, which you'll have to cross the Rif Mountains and the Spanish border to see.

Orientation

Like most other Moroccan cities, Tetouan is divided into two parts—the new, protectorate-era city (Ville Nouvelle) and older Moroccan city (medina).

Tetouan's **Ville Nouvelle** (often called by its Spanish name, **Ensanche,** by the locals) spreads out from grand **Place Moulay El-Mehdi,** still known to the locals as **Plaza Primo,** a large, Spanish-era plaza with a selection of cafés as well as the Andalusian-influenced Spanish Church, **Iglesia de Nuestra Señora de la Victoria.** Recently renovated, the church boasts some stunning mosaic work and still holds mass (in Spanish)

Tetouan

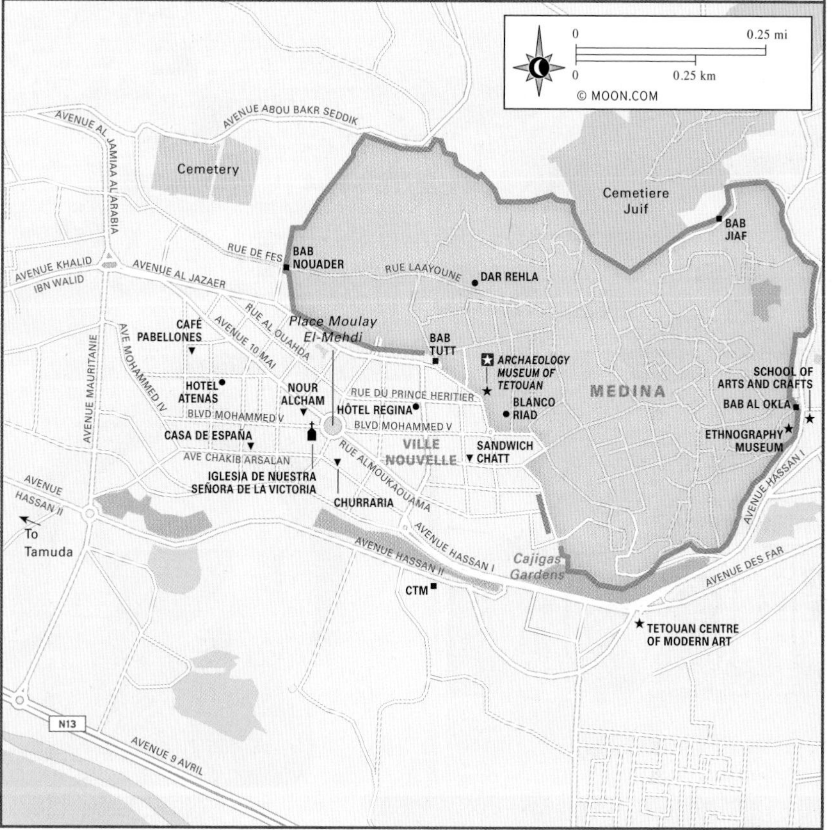

every day at 7pm and Sundays at 11am. The main pedestrian drag, **Mohammed V** (often called the *paseo*), runs from this plaza. Keep an eye out for the nondescript bookstore across from Passage Aidir, which sometimes carries English books, and the many private club cafés dotting this pleasant walking strip—leftovers from the Spanish protectorate. **Boulevard Ouadha** has a selection of banks, cafés, shops, and snack food places, as well as a few travel companies. Meanwhile, the new Feddan Park located on the south edge of the city has guarded **underground parking** and is a great space for kids, picnics, and views out over Tetouan.

The **medina** is one of the better preserved and most lived-in medinas in all of Morocco. Recently, plaques in Arabic, English, and Spanish that explain the historical importance of many of the medina houses, fountains, and public ovens have been posted throughout the medina to give travelers a better idea of the cultural and historic value of these otherwise crumbling structures. Some work has been done recently to renovate the medina, and there are none of the bazaars typical of the medinas in nearby Chefchaouen or Tangier, to say nothing of Fez or Marrakesh. The medina of Tetouan is a place for living more than souvenir shopping.

1
2
GARE ROUTIERE
3
4

Sights

KASBAH AND MEDINA

The Kasbah de Al-Mandri, a 15th-century fortress falling into ruin at the top of the medina, is largely inaccessible. Funds have been dedicated for renovation, but it will likely be years before it is opened to the public. It's worth taking a walk through the medina's working-class neighborhoods to the kasbah to take in the views along its walls atop the medina.

Otherwise, the medina is pleasant to stroll around. There are very few bazaars, and the traditional goods that are for sale are used by the locals. Most goods on offer are of the secondhand or made-in-China variety popular with many Moroccans for their inexpensiveness and availability. Of particular interest for many Muslim tourists are several of the signed ***zawiyas*** (mausoleums). Two of the more picturesque squares are **Souk el-Hoot,** where they no longer sell fish, but where you can pick up a *mendil* (the white-and-red-striped wraps traditionally worn by the women of the area) for around 35Dh. From here, head uphill to snap photos at the bustling **Souk Swika** at the top of the medina.

★ ARCHAEOLOGY MUSEUM OF TETOUAN

Rue Al-Jazaer at Bab Tut; tel. 0530/676 081; Mon.-Sat. 10am-6pm; 20Dh

The Archaeology Museum of Tetouan (Musée Archéologique de Tétouan) primarily showcases the wealth of Roman history in Morocco. There is an incredible selection of **Roman murals** from the 2nd century sourced from Lixus. Of particular note is the Venus with Adonis mural. In addition, there is a small collection of bronze statues, coins, pottery, vases, and jewelry from Roman sites such as Tamuda, Banasa, and Volubilis. Beyond the Romans, there is also a reconstruction of the 4th century BC megalithic monument of M'zora (outside of Asilah), as well as prehistoric stone tools from the Acheuleans who lived in the area 500,000 years ago. Most signage is in Arabic, French, and Spanish, though that shouldn't stop you from visiting.

1: looking across the medina of Tetouan 2: the ornate *gare routière* (transportation hub) of Tetouan 3: entering the Tetouan medina through the arched Bab Rouah 4: churros with hot chocolate

TETOUAN CENTRE OF MODERN ART

Ave. Al Massira; tel. 0539/718 946; Tues.-Sat. 9am-4pm; admission free until the ministry decides on admission prices—likely 20Dh

Opened in 2012, the Tetouan Centre of Modern Art (El Centro del Arte Moderne de Tétouan) is reminiscent of the Musée d'Orsay in Paris in that it is housed in a remodeled train station. The collection of paintings and sculptures follows the progression of art in Morocco starting just after Moroccan independence in 1956 and the establishment of the Tetouan School of Fine Arts the following year, following a progression from this period until the present day. Special attention is paid to artists from the area as well as their influences from Europe. A pamphlet in English is available, though all signage is in Arabic and Spanish.

ETHNOGRAPHY MUSEUM

Bab El-Okla; tel. 0539/970 505; Mon.-Sat. 9am-4pm; 20Dh

The Ethnography Museum (Musée d'Ethnographie), founded in 1928, contains a collection of 20th-century pottery made in Fez and Safi, as well as a few elaborately painted arabesque doors and tools used for working leather from the 19th century. On the second floor you can follow a typical Tetouan life and learn about hosting guests and marriage rites. Signs are in Arabic, French, and Spanish.

SCHOOL OF ARTS AND CRAFTS

Bab El-Okla; tel. 0599/972 721; Mon.-Thurs. 8am-6pm; 20Dh

Across the street from the Ethnography Museum and Bab El-Okla is the School of Arts and Crafts (École des Arts et Métiers)

The Spanish in Tetouan

the *Phoenix of Tetouan,* a statue dating from the Spanish protectorate era

Tetouan has a long history of Spanish influence, beginning with the Moors who fled Spain in the 15th and 16th centuries. Many of the Moors expelled by King Felipe III in the 17th century found refuge in Tetouan. The descendants of these fleeing families are still nostalgic about their homes in Andalusia. In fact, there is a 400-year-old Tetouan tradition in which the keys of homes left behind in Spain are passed on from generation to generation, with some inhabitants still owning the keys to their family homes in old Andalusia.

During the protectorate era of 1912-1956, Tetouan served as the Spanish capital of North Morocco, overseeing other cities in the area, including the Spanish enclaves of Ceuta and Melilla. During this period, Spain embarked on building the Ensanche—a widening of the city that spread out from the ancient medina. You'll find balconies and windows framed by iron grilles, shaded squares, and patios with refreshing Moorish-Andalusian fountains, white plasterwork, and the occasional strum of flamenco.

where you can see students following the instruction of local masters as they learn how to do embroidery and how to work with wood, leather, iron, and other traditional materials. The best time to visit is 9am-3pm, when students are generally in attendance. On the ground floor, you can see some current student work and take a stroll through the pleasant, even inspiring, gardens.

Food

In the north, a typical quick lunch consists of a ***bocadillo*** (sandwich) stuffed with fries. **Café Pabellones** (corner of Rue Abdullah Ibn Yassine and Blvd. Zarktouni) has free Wi-Fi. In the medina, there is a reliable ***bissara* stand** through Bab Tut, just up Ben Azuz.

SANDWICH CHATT

Corner of Boulevard Mohamed Torres and Boulevard Sidi Mohamed Abderrahim; daily 11am-4pm; 10Dh

One of the more popular snack joints is Sandwich Chatt, where you can get a little sandwich from 7Dh.

NOUR ALCHAM

5 Blvd. 10 Mai; daily 10am-10pm; 20Dh

For a quick shawarma, head to Nour Alcham. The menu features burgers and pizza, but the

7Dh falafel and other Syrian-style treats are where it's at.

CHURRARIA

Boulevard Yacoub Mansour, just off the Moulay et Mehdi; daily 7am-5pm; 10Dh

For those seeking Spanish-style *churros* for breakfast, head to the authentically shabby Churraria. Be sure to order hot chocolate to dip your churros in, just like they do in north Morocco and all around Spain.

CASA DE ESPAÑA

4 Ave. Chakib Arsalane; tel. 0539/967 083; daily noon-3:30pm and 7pm-10:30pm; 80Dh

Housed in a still-functioning playhouse, this Spanish restaurant sports a fresh selection of seafood, tajines, and tapas. The theatrical decor is undercut by the TVs blasting Spanish channels. The real draw is the bar; the fresh tapas are comparable to those of Granada. It's good for change-of-pace dining and a fresh cerveza (beer).

Accommodations

There is an interesting mix of more traditional *riads* and *dars* in the medina as well as a good selection of hotels in the former Spanish town (Ville Nouvelle). In the medina, the mellah neighborhood across the plaza from the king's palace has a wide selection of pensiones and budget hotels. Everything here is basic.

HOTEL REGINA

8 rue Sidi Mandril; tel. 0539/962 113; 180Dh d

Hotel Regina is almost double the price of the local pensions, but it's infinitely more comfortable, clean, and centrally located. If you need all your modern conveniences and are okay with a more spartan hotel, this is a good choice. Wi-Fi works in the main lobby but can be hit-or-miss in the rooms. Mostly importantly, beds are comfortable and the water is hot.

★ DAR REHLA

3 Rue Habibi; tel. 0539/711 768; 350Dh d

This charming house is well located just off the Rue de Fes in the old medina. Brahim, the owner and manager, is from Tetouan and will happily arrange to show you around and even meet you at your arrival point. The service is friendly, beds are comfy, and the remodeled home is done up in tasteful traditional decor with the requisite bright Moroccan touch. Wi-Fi, air-conditioning, and breakfast are all included. Massages, manicures, pedicures, waxing, and facials are available on request. For those looking to stay in the medina, this is one of the better-situated *riads,* just along a main thoroughfare that has many vegetable and fruit sellers and is a short walk from the Bab Nouader.

HOTEL ATENAS

Blvd. Allal Ben Abdellah; tel. 0539/700 065; www.hotelatenas.ma; 450Dh s, 650Dh d

Outside the medina, conveniently located near the Place Al-Aadala, is the Hotel Atenas, with clean, comfortable beds. The restaurant and café of this Tetouan staple are both refreshingly nonsmoking, which can be a real treat in the colder winter months when sitting outside isn't really an option. Typical tajines, salads, and pastas are available, but with a Spanish twist. The fresh, seasonal seafood options are more extensive than at most other restaurants in the area and include a sizable swordfish steak and a plate of mixed grilled seafood big enough for two for just 60Dh. Rooms are fairly standard, but are an option if the few medina *riads* are all booked or if you're looking for a break from the medina. Rooms are equipped with TV, and Wi-Fi and breakfast are included with your stay.

BLANCO RIAD

25 Rue Zawiya Kadiria; tel. 0539/704 202; http://blancoriad.com; 800Dh d

This is the poshest spot to catch some much-needed rest or dig in a for a gourmet meal in Tetouan. This bright, airy *riad* is tucked just inside the souk near the royal palace. The seasonally diverse menu is sourced from the nearby souks. Staples include the cannelloni stuffed with eggplant and the seafood *pastilla*. Reserve at least a few hours in advance of your meal (160Dh); the day before is better. The *riad* once served as the home for the Spanish consulate as well as the local pasha. The rooms feature traditional mosaics mixed with the more contemporary mosaic work in the courtyard. The overall vibe is a little more cool than cozy, but after a hot day out, this can be just the ticket. Wi-Fi, air-conditioning, and breakfast are all included. Guests and non-guests may want to stop in for lunch or dinner.

Information and Services

The main **post office** is right on Place Moulay Mehdi, alongside numerous cash machines. The **Grande Pharmacie du Nord** (11 Blvd. Mohammed V, Sun.-Fri. 9am-1pm and 3:30pm-8pm, Sat. 9am-1pm) is along the *paseo*. The **Medical Center (Centro Medico)** is just outside Bab Tut on the corner of Boulevard Sidi El-Mandi and Avenue Al-Jazaer. A couple of currency exchanges are on Mohammed V, at Place Moulay Mehdi: **Al-Adaresa Change** (Sat.-Thurs. 10am-2pm and 4pm-8:30pm, Fri. 10am-noon and 4pm-8:30pm) and **Change Tetouan** (Mon.-Sat. 8:30am-2pm and 3:30pm-8:30pm).

Getting There and Around

BY CAR

Tetouan is about an hour southeast of **Tangier** (61km/38mi, 1hr) and roughly six hours north of **Fez** (256km/160mi, 6hr). The roads in the mountains of this area can be a little narrow, and drivers should be wary of farm equipment, particularly on the sharper turns, as well as drivers trying to pass on blind turns. Night driving should be avoided. From Tangier, the drive avoids most of the mountain roads and is relatively straightforward.

BY GRAND TAXI AND BUS

There is a convenient ***grand taxi* station** on the corner of Boulevard Sidi Mohamed Abderrahmen and Avenue Al Majlis Al Baladi with service to **Martil** (15min, 12km/7mi, 10Dh), **Tangier** (1hr, 61km/38mi, 50Dh), and **Chefchaouen** (1hr, 61km/38mi, 50Dh).

The new ***gare routière*** is on the southern outskirts of the city off of Avenue 9 Avril (N13). Buses and *grands taxis* leave from here to most destinations around Morocco. **CTM** (tel. 0800/0900 30, www.ctm.ma) runs buses to **Tangier** (1hr, 5 daily, 45Dh), **Asilah** (2hr, 6 daily, 40Dh), **Chefchaouen** (1hr, 6 daily, 45Dh), **Fez** (6hr, 8 daily, 100Dh), and **Rabat** (4hr, 6 daily, 140Dh). If you are continuing east along the Mediterranean, you will have to first go to Oued Laou (1hr, 1 daily, 40Dh) and transfer to another CTM from there; the only CTM bus that leaves from Tetouan for Oued Laou rather inconveniently departs at 11pm.

BY PETIT TAXI

To get around town, ***petits taxis*** are easy enough to find and are particularly useful coming in and out of the medina as well as to and from the ***gare routière.*** Taxis are metered, and 10Dh will get you to practically any destination in the city. For destinations in the medina, it is best to tell the taxi driver what gate (*bab*) is the closest (e.g., Bab Nouader or Bab Rhuh).

Chefchaouen and the Rif

TOP EXPERIENCE

CHEFCHAOUEN

شفشاون

Often regarded as one of the prettiest towns in Morocco, Chefchaouen doesn't disappoint. Sometimes shortened to "Chaouen" or "Xaouen," the name derives from the Rifi word for "antlers" or "horns," an allusion to the peaks that crown the region, often snowcapped in winter. The narrow blue passages give way to wide squares where the historic Andalusian influence on the town is easily notable in ornate archways, doorways (the most famous of which is a ruin at the entrance of town), windows, and the sprawl of red-tiled rooftops. This is the place to head for that photo op to make all the friends back home envious.

Chefchaouen has long been a strategic mountain town. The location was originally

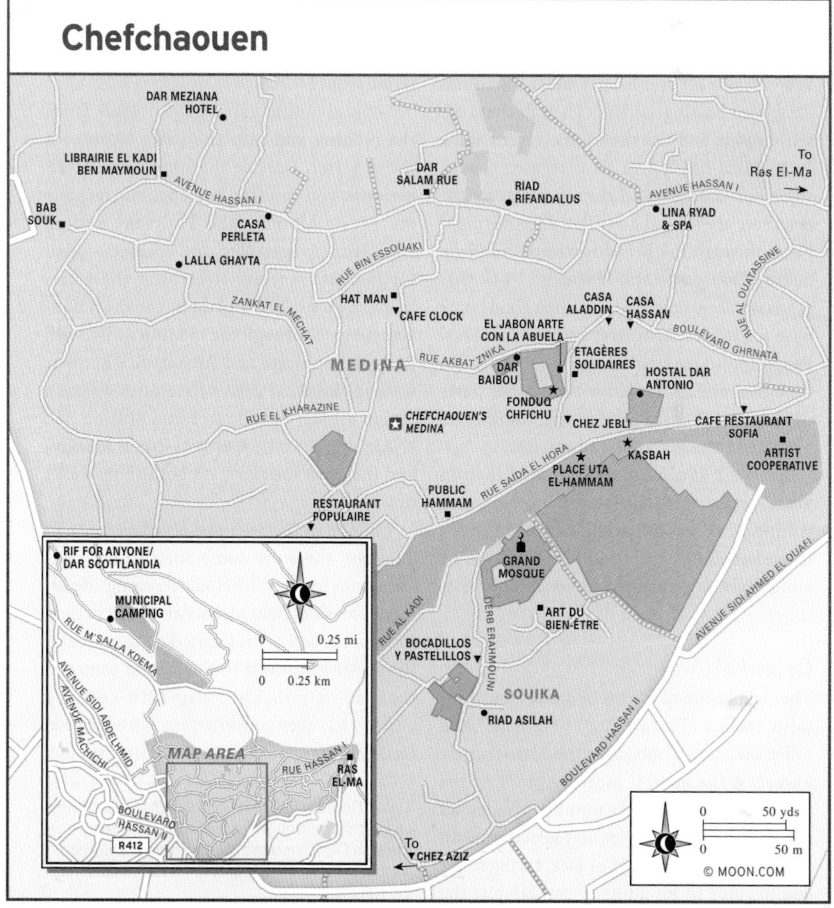

discovered as a secret city from which to launch attacks against the Portuguese in Asilah, Tangier, Ceuta, and Ksar Seghir during the Portuguese conquest of 1471, as attested to by the fortified kasbah.

In the 16th century, Andalusian immigrants descended on the city seeking refuge from the Spanish Inquisition, resulting in a rapid expansion of the city and the settlement of the districts. In 1760, the sultan ordered the local Jewish population to relocate into the medina for their protection. They formed a mellah and built outward-facing balconies while painting the exterior of their homes a light blue, introducing the color that is now so associated with Chaouen.

Firmly entrenched on the backpacker circuit, presumably for the easily obtainable (and very illegal) kif and hash, Chefchaouen has long been hosting visitors. Though there are still hostels and pensiones, the recent spike in tourism has led to an increase in boutique hotels, *riads*, and *dars*. For nature lovers, there are several day hikes and overnight hikes through the **Rif Mountains** and into nearby **Talassemtane National Park** that are easily accessible, making this a good home base for hikers, campers, and backpackers. People in this region are usually very friendly, though more conservative than other parts of Morocco in terms of dress and traditional, gendered roles in public and private.

Even if it is a bit more touristed than in years past, with its pleasant medina and stunning hikes at its back door, Chefchaouen has retained its charms and continues to be a highlight for seasoned travelers and first-timers alike.

Orientation

The cobblestoned **Place Uta el-Hammam** (also spelled "Plaza Outa el-Hamam" and other variations) outside of the 15th-century kasbah is the central meeting point in the **medina.** You will find a number of cafés, all generally equal in service and selection, with men waving menus in your face, trying to get you to come in for a bite to eat. Despite the hard sell, sitting and people-watching in this square is one of the wonderful afternoon pastimes. From the square, the medina is roughly divided into seven different districts. **Souika,** downhill to the southwest, is the main shopping district and is where some of the pensiones and hotels are. Uphill, to the north, is the district of **Al-Andaluz,** where there is more shopping and accommodations. To the east of Al-Andaluz are **Bab Souk** and **Jarrazen,** where many of the other accommodations are tucked into quaint side streets and the occasional bazaar can be found. To the west of Al-Andaluz is **Onsar,** a largely residential district. Lastly, the old **Jewish mellah,** a bit poorer, quieter, and ragged around the edges, is downhill, southeast of the main square, next to **Sebanin,** where you can find the waterfalls **Ras el-Ma.**

Several main gates (*babs*) lead from the medina and into the **Ville Nouvelle (Ensanche).** Outside the aptly named **Bab el-Souk** you can find the open-air farmers market on Monday and Thursday, selling fresh fruits, vegetables, and seafood—great for budget travelers stretching their dirhams. **Bab el-Ain** is perhaps the most convenient gate through the medina walls, with Banque Populaire and Attijarwafa Bank as well as the local post office and Western Union all just outside it. From outside Bab el-Ain, the **Marché Central** (Main Market) and the ***gare routière*** are both short walks downhill.

Though not as well preserved as those in Tetouan, there are some Spanish-era constructions in the Ville Nouvelle alongside cement blocks of new Moroccan construction. Most of the activity is focused on the circular **Place Mohammed V,** the former center of the Spanish town. The **early-20th-century church** has been converted into an education facility to give youth further training, though

1: the "Door to Chefchaouen," which is reproduced on keychains throughout the town **2:** twisting through Chefchaouen's blue medina **3:** a woman washing oranges in a fountain **4:** knitted hats from the Hat Man

the facade is largely intact. It's among the few examples of early-20th-century Spanish colonial architecture remaining in Chefchaouen. For most people from Chefchaouen, this is where the evening *paseo* begins.

Sights

★ MEDINA

The ancient medina is nestled in a sharp valley between mountain peaks and is one of the more pleasurable medinas to visit in all of Morocco. It's often painted by the locals in shades of blue that have been combined to make the stunning "Chefchaouen blue."

It's one of the cleanest medinas in the country, with comparatively little trash lying openly on the footpaths. Plaques in Arabic, Spanish, and English explain the historical importance of some of the medina buildings. However, as is often the case, some things are lost in translation: Many of these translations contradict each other, or leave out information altogether.

The oldest buildings in the Jewish mellah date from the 16th century, though most of the Jewish population didn't move into the medina until the sultan's command in the 18th century. Despite its advanced age, it is still known as **Mellah el-Jedid** (New Mellah), because the old mellah was outside of the medina walls and even older still, though nobody knows exactly how old. Today, there is just the one mellah in Chefchaouen.

The medina is more hassle-free than most others in Morocco. There are still a few touts and nagging store owners, but a firm "no, thank you" is generally sufficient to deter them. No doubt you will be asked many, many times to buy kif, a local specialty, often by young men passing by. Be wary. Kif is a derivative of the marijuana plant and is still very illegal in Morocco, though in Chefchaouen you will likely see people openly smoking in cafés, hostels, storefronts, and even in the streets.

The main square, the cobblestoned Place Uta el-Hammam, and the kasbah that towers over it, date from the 15th century, when Moulay Rachid first constructed the kasbah as part of his war against the Portuguese.

KASBAH

Pl. Uta el-Hammam; Wed.-Mon. 9am-1pm and 3pm-6:30pm, Fri. 9am-12pm, closed Tues.; 10Dh

The red-walled kasbah, built in 1471, has been renovated and houses a small **Ethnography Museum.** Moulay Ali Ben Rachid continued his cousin's declared war against the Portuguese, who had seized control of Tangier, Asilah, and other port towns. Moulay Rachid was concerned with the defensive nature of his war, which was the chief reason he built his fort in Chefchaouen. The graffiti-strewn walls of the small prison still have the chains that once held the inmates. Most information is in Arabic, French, and Spanish.

GRAND MOSQUE

Pl. Uta el-Hammam

Just next to the looming kasbah, the delicate Grand Mosque (Jamaa Kbeer) (Pl. Uta el-Hammam) rises, calling the faithful to prayer five times a day. Though non-Muslims are not permitted entrance, its architectural uniqueness can be observed from the outside. The mosque was built by Moulay Mohamed, the son of Moulay Rachid, in 1560, but its minaret, inspired by the Torre de Oro in Sevilla, was built much later, in the 18th century. The octagonal minaret features three tiers of blind arches that wrap around the tower, with each tier of arches being distinctive.

FONDUQ CHFICHU

Zanka Targhi, 20ft from the main square

At one time, there were four or five major *fonduqs*—open courtyards surrounded by stables and shops—that served as hubs for traders, artisans, and shopkeepers in the medina. Today, the only one remaining is Fonduq Chfichu. This 16th-century *fonduq* just off Place Uta el-Hammam is a reminder of this era of Andalusian-influenced architecture. Currently, wood and iron workers are making use of the *fonduq*, and usually a distinct odor of kif will accompany your visit.

Hiking

There is plenty of hiking to be had on the outskirts of the Chefchaouen medina. Just behind the city rises the mountain **Jbel el-Kelaa.** Several valleys are accessible from well-marked walking paths alongside Ras el-Ma and provide wonderful day hikes into the fields, through the fields, and up the peaks of the Rif Mountains.

RAS EL-MA WATERFALLS

outside Bab Ras el-Ma

The Ras el-Ma waterfalls are just beyond Place Sebanin through Bab Ras el-Ma. There are usually ladies who will dress you like a local (*jeblia* for girls, *jebli* for boys) for 5-10Dh. This is a fantastic photo op and should be taken advantage of given the colorful nature of the traditional clothing in this region. This area makes for a nice morning or afternoon stroll with plenty to see and do. The municipality has built wood shacks where the local women often take their laundry to scrub, and just a short hike along the hillside will bring you to the recently renovated, though unused, **Spanish Mosque** overlooking the city.

THE SPANISH MOSQUE

from Ras el-Ma; 2km/1.2mi; 1hr roundtrip; easy

This hike offers an easy path to the best view over Chefchaouen. Start at Ras el-Ma and follow the main path. You will likely pass some villagers bringing sheep or goats into the city. This is also their main route into Chefchaouen. At the end of the path is the Spanish-built mosque at the top of the hill overlooking the city. The mosque is closed, though it underwent a renovation in 2010 funded by Spain. You can peek inside the windows, but most people hike here for the view. A large terrace overlooks the valley. This is best visited in the morning when the sun is at your back, illuminating the white and blue city below.

INTO THE MOUNTAINS

from the giant Hotel Atlantis overlooking Chefchaouen; 10km/6mi; 4hr roundtrip; medium

Just above the medina, an often-used trail runs through a steep valley into the mountains. This is a cannabis-growing region and is sometimes patrolled by the police, but the people are friendly and the hike offers some spectacular views over the valley of Chefchaouen. If you continue for about 2.5 hours for a longer full-day hike, the trail opens up into a beautiful valley, the beginning of the Ketama region of the Rif.

CIRCLING THE RIF

from Ras el-Ma, past the Spanish Mosque; 30km/18.6mi; 12hr loop; difficult

A long circuit hike takes you around the Rif, through valleys, and around mountains. The trail is well marked in places, though you'll likely want to have either a guide (Fatima Habté, tel. 0672/743 347) or, if possible, GPS. Leave from Chefchaouen by Ras el-Ma and follow the trail into the mountains toward Mechkralla. This hike takes you through winding forests and many cannabis farms. The small, isolated towns of Tissouka, Plaza España, and Bab Taza are all visited on your way back to Chefchaouen.

Hammams

Just off the main square, Place Uta el-Hammam, are two hammams of interest for those looking for a true Moroccan experience in cleanliness.

PUBLIC HAMMAM

Place Uta el-Hammam

The public hammam, used by many of the local men and women, is just across the square from the large mosque, next to the Pension Castellana. The times allowed for men and women change regularly. (Historically, Chefchaouen, like many other Moroccan cities, had separate hammams for men and women. Today, many hammams share a space and have separate times for the two genders to bathe.) Expect to pay about 25Dh, and bring plastic sandals, soap, a shower scrub, and a towel.

ART DU BIEN-ÊTRE

one street west off the Place Uta el-Hammam, behind the mosque; tel. 0539/989 908; daily 10am-1pm and 3:30pm-8pm

For a more luxurious experience, head to the Art du Bien-Être (Art of Good Living). Though not exactly traditional, this is a more upscale spa with massages, foot soaks, facials, and exfoliations. This business operates with a local women's cooperative to create all of their all-natural products. Many of the products are for sale in the entryway. Reservations are required for the hammam, though often they are able to accommodate same-day requests. Expect to pay 100Dh or so for a facial, 150Dh for a hammam, and 250Dh or more on a fuller spa experience.

Shopping

Artisan shops around Chefchaouen specialize in local crafts. For the most part, sellers are low-key and pressure sales are minimal. As always, you can try to bargain for the best price, though typically in Chefchaouen, bargaining is minimal and prices are clearly labeled. Most shops keep hours throughout the day, generally 10am-8pm, though hours are flexible, depending on business and the season.

EL JABON ARTE CON LA ABUELA

Zanka Targhi, just up from the Place Uta el-Hammam; daily 10am-10pm

For a wide selection of handmade, all-natural, artisanal soaps, scrubs, and other bath products, the easy-to-find El Jabon Arte Con La Abuela (The Art of Soap with Grandma) is an incredibly eclectic shop. Where else can you find soaps made with chocolate, thyme and lemon, or cinnamon? Spices, herbs, teas, and incense are all available in convenient gift packs for just 80Dh.

ETAGÈRES SOLIDAIRES

corner of Djebki on Zanka Targhi; daily 10am-10pm

Etagères Solidaires is a women's cooperative that sells a wide selection of argan oils, olive oils, locally farmed honey, and soaps. Socially conscious shopping is just a short walk up from the Uta el-Hammam.

DAR SALAM RUE

Taylia; tel. 0539/993 230

For jewelry, carpets, and furniture, make your way to Dar Salam Rue, where you can find a wide selection of well-priced chunky tribal silver jewelry and carpets from around Morocco. Hassan, the co-owner, speaks great English and will be happy to tell you about where his stunning jewelry and furniture is designed and made as well as where all of his carpets are sourced from. No hard sells here—just a friendly chat, a tea if you want it, and some shop talk about Moroccan goods.

HAT MAN

Rue Targui, not far from Casa Aladdin; daily, hours vary

No trip to Chefchaouen is complete without a hand-knitted hat from the Hat Man. Atman, dubbed locally as the "Hat Man," is usually in attendance for a few hours in the mornings and then again in the afternoon, knitting some of the most outrageous hats this side of the Atlantic. Look for hats in an assortment of bright colors, with the occasional set of antennae, ears, or poufs. Scarves, mittens, and legwarmers, equally inventive and colorful, can also generally be found.

LIBRAIRIE EL KADI BEN MAYMOUN

corner of Hassan I and Derb El Kadi Maymoun; daily, hours vary

If you finished your vacation read on the long bus ride in, check out Librairie El Kadi Ben Maymoun, with books in English, Arabic, French, German, and Spanish. The selection is small, but there is usually a good find. Right next to it is a handy cybercafe.

ARTIST COOPERATIVE

Plaza el-Majzen

Artist Cooperative has a series of shops featuring work by local artisans. This is a good place to start shopping for that new, brightly colored blanket or carpet. Sometimes the artisans will be here crafting, which is a good time for a photo-op, though of course ask before snapping away, and leave a tip (10Dh is the norm). At the very least, this is a good place to get an idea of the basic prices of rugs and blankets before making your way into the bazaars, as the artisans are dictated prices by the government.

Cooking Classes

CAFE CLOCK

3 derb Tijani, Hay Souk; tel. 0539/988 788; www.cafeclock.com; daily 10am-3pm; 150Dh

Though some *riads* can accommodate for cooking classes, the tried-and-true formula of Cafe Clock makes for the fun-loving sort of courses ending with some delicious meals you're looking for while in the country. Classes usually run about five hours, beginning in the morning and ending with a late lunch. It's a good idea to book a few days ahead of time, if not a few weeks, particularly in the busy spring and fall months. For those who have already done a cooking class, consider taking the shorter (3hr) Moroccan pastry class (100Dh).

DAR MEZIANA HOTEL

Bab Souk, 7 Derb Zagdoud; tel. 0539/987 806; www.darmezianahotel.com; daily 10am-2pm; 150Dh

For a cozier atmosphere, the cooking classes hosted by Dar Meziana are where it's at. Here, you'll experience all the wonderful hospitality of a real Moroccan house while chopping, slicing, boiling, and baking up your Moroccan feast. Classes typically start in the morning and can include a quick stop by the souk for fresh ingredients.

Food

CHEZ JEBLI

Place Uta el-Hammam; daily 7am-late; 35Dh

The Chez Jebli, across from the entrance to the kasbah, serves one of the better breakfasts, with *harsha* (a semolina pancake), *miloui* (a Moroccan-style crepe), *amlou* (a paste of nuts, including argan, that is somewhat like peanut butter), *jbin arabi* (locally made goat cheese), and freshly squeezed orange juice.

BOCADILLOS Y PASTELILLOS

Zanka al-Kaida; daily 11am-10pm; 20Dh

For a quick sandwich, Bocadillos y Pastelillos, tucked into the corner just off the Place Uta el-Hammam on Zanka al-Kaida, around the corner from the Grand Mosque, is conveniently located. Also look at the homemade date cookie (*halwa dial tmar*) that crumbles wonderfully in your mouth.

CHEZ AZIZ

Bab el-Ain; daily 11am-late; 20Dh

Chez Aziz, just outside Bab el-Ain, is the local favorite for *bocadillos* (Spanish sandwiches) and pizza. It's a clean restaurant and great place for a quick pick-me-up or to pack up sandwiches for a picnic lunch, for instance, if you're looking to do the afternoon hike out to the Spanish Mosque.

CAFE RESTAURANT SOFIA

Place Uta el-Hammam, Khadraine Escalier Roumani; tel. 0671/286 649; daily 10am-10pm; 35Dh

Travelers of all stripes hopping through the blue environs of Chefchaouen settle down in this curbside treat. The chefs here do amazing food at a very, very fair price point. Traditional Moroccan tajines come with some wonderful options, including couscous and soups, for vegetarians. The perfect sort of thing to stave off some of that mountain chill. Save some room for crepes for dessert. There are no restrooms, so plan accordingly.

CAFE CLOCK

3 derb Tijani, Hay Souk; tel. 0539/988 788; www.cafeclock.com; 10am-10pm; 110Dh

Those who have already traveled through Fez and/or Marrakesh might be familiar with Cafe Clock. Like its sister branches in Fez and Kesh, you'll be able to find camel burgers, cooking classes, and even calligraphy classes at this version of a local favorite. The new property has a friendly, helpful staff and a great rooftop to enjoy sunsets. Make sure to stop in for at least one meal or class while you're in Chaouen.

CASA HASSAN

22 Rue Targui; tel. 0539/986 153; www.casahassan.com; daily 10am-10pm; 80Dh

Traditional tajines, couscous, and kebabs are particularly well done at Casa Hassan. For vegetarians, the veggie *pastilla* is a real treat, with finely chopped zucchini, carrots, bell peppers, green beans, onion, and garlic stuffed with vermicelli inside a delicate phyllo dough, folded and baked golden. The restaurant is set in an eclectic, traditional Moroccan *riad* with hand-painted details, including the elaborate wood ceiling. Downstairs, the open kitchen becomes a veritable show when the chefs are busy with the crackle of grilled vegetables and tajines seemingly thrown one after the other onto the fire. The friendly staff members speak English and will be happy to help you with information about their restaurant or Chefchaouen, as long as they aren't too busy. Indoor seating is nonsmoking.

CASA ALADDIN

Rue Tangier; tel. 0539/989 071; daily 10am-10pm; 85Dh fixed menu

Popular, but a little tricky to find. Walk uphill from the Uta el-Hammam, taking the path to the left. Look out for signs that read "Lampe Magique" and "Casa Aladdin." The decor is what you would expect in Chefchaouen, with lots of blues and oranges, but the views over Place Uta el-Hammam and the old kasbah are unbeatable. The vegetable *pastilla* is a nice change of pace from the standard vegetarian fare, though it can be a bit bland, so ask for extra spices. The anchovy tajine, a seafood affair slathered in spicy tomato sauce, is a northern specialty and shouldn't be missed.

★ RESTAURANT POPULAIRE

Rue Elkharrazin; tel. 0660/261 128; hours vary, usually daily 9am-11pm; 80Dh

A backpacking trip through Chefchaouen wouldn't be complete without a stop at this joint next to Bab Sour. The menu is varied and seasonal, but you can usually find the "Tangier" on offer, a mouthwatering slow-cooked strip of tender beef seasoned with garlic, onion, and cumin and layered with a sharp yogurt sauce. Vegetarians will be happy to find sautéed mushroom caps. Decor is humble in the popular (if not somewhat tacky) style of the region, but the food is can't-miss.

Accommodations

★ HOSTAL DAR ANTONIO

36 Calle Garmata; tel. 0539/989 997; www.darantonio.com; 150Dh s, 250Dh d

Just off Place Uta el-Hammam is this funky hostel. Popular with college students and Spanish backpackers, this colorful hostel is one of the best budget options in the region; reserve ahead during the busy season. The rooms are bright and clean, the Wi-Fi connection is solid, and the kitchen is available for everyone to use; just remember to clean up after yourself!

RIAD RIFANDALUS

151 Ave Hassan I (Lmdaaka); tel. 0539/986 612; 300Dh d

Combining a love for the Rif and an acknowledgment of the Andalusian heritage of the region, this *riad*, with comfy beds and panoramic rooftop views, can be great for backpacking couples and close friends. There's plenty of Moroccan charm to spare—with traditional *zellij* works and carved headboards, friendly hosts, and a close location to the center of the medina, there is a lot to like. The rooms are not too large, though, and sometimes it can be a little noisy, depending on the clientele. Air-conditioning, Wi-Fi, and breakfast are included. Most rooms have security boxes for your valuables.

RIF FOR ANYONE/ DAR SCOTTLANDIA

H'Naine; tel. 0539/988 116; http://home2.btconnect.com/rif-for-anyone; 300Dh s, 400Dh d

For those wishing to stay out of the bustle of the medina, this guesthouse, run by a Scottish family, is one of the best options out of town. The family has really made Chefchaouen their home. They can easily arrange tours for you in Chefchaouen, as well as hikes to many of the more remote villages. The accommodations are spartan, though clean, and most rooms have en-suite showers. Like most other places in Chaouen, the outdoor patios and terraces are all smoking friendly, but the rooms are nonsmoking. The Wi-Fi is strong, which means uploading your latest Instagram masterpiece from the rooftop terrace overlooking the sun setting over the Rif Mountains is a snap.

RIAD ASILAH

19 Rue Imam Chadil; tel. 0539/883 000; 450Dh d

For location this can't be beat, being right off the main plaza, Place Uta el-Hammam. The decor echoes the medina in arches painted blue and white with touches of mosaic and comfy furniture. Rooms are bright and clean, though the beds can be a bit too firm for some. The bathrooms are all custom, with some interesting *zellij* tile work. The breakfast (included with room) includes freshly made Moroccan-style donuts (*sfinge* in Darija) on demand. Wi-Fi is good, and the staff is friendly.

★ CASA PERLETA

Bab el-Souk; tel. 0539/988 979; www.casaperleta.com; 600Dh d

A newly remodeled home that has truly kept alive the Andalusian vibe of Chefchaouen can be found here. The helpful staff speaks English, and all are locals from Chefchaouen. They are quick to help you with recommendations and can even double as your guide on hikes through the Rif if they have the time. The rooms are cozy, well heated, and equipped with Wi-Fi as well as air-conditioning. Breakfast is included with your stay, and if you happen to visit in winter, the downstairs living room with the fireplace is a great spot to relax with your vacation read.

DAR BAIBOU

22 Rue Targui; tel. 0539/986 153; www.casahassan.com; 700Dh s, 800Dh d

This is one of the larger options to stay in the medina. The unmarked door just off the main plaza opens to an elaborate *riad*. The owners combined three houses to create this arabesque dream with lots of natural stone work, traditional mosaics, tasteful fountains, carved wood, and bricked arches. A private hammam is on-site (150Dh) and offers traditional body scrubs. Price includes Wi-Fi, air-conditioning, heating, breakfast, and dinner.

DAR MEZIANA HOTEL

Bab Souk, 7 Derb Zagdoud; tel. 0539/987 806; www.darmezianahotel.com; 700Dh s, 800Dh d

A superbly charming *dar* with a large open patio and central kitchen that adds to the warmness of the welcome, particularly in the colder months and chilly evenings. This sprawling, maze-like *dar* is wonderful for kids to explore and for those that are little kids at heart. The upstairs terrace looks out over the mountains for some incredible sunsets and makes for a perfect background for a late breakfast. An on-site hammam and cooking classes are great options to round out your stay. Air-conditioning/heating, Wi-Fi, and breakfast are included.

LINA RYAD & SPA

Rue Moualy Hassan I; tel. 0645/069 903 or 0660/239 906; www.linariad.com; 1,700Dh d

For a true getaway, head to this little oasis within Chefchaouen. The rooms on the upper floors have better views, and some have private balconies. It's the only true high-end

Rif-er Madness

kif pipes for sale in Chefchaouen

Marijuana, hash, and kif are derivatives of the cannabis plant, which grows throughout the Rif Mountains and has a long history of being cultivated and harvested. Likely, people will offer you some form of cannabis while you're in the Rif and in a few other spots in Morocco that are popular with backpackers and the hippie crowd. Sometimes this is a friendly offer, though usually it is more of a business proposition. Regardless, keep in mind that cannabis, despite its relative availability, is strictly illegal in Morocco. If caught with any amount of cannabis product, you will likely face a steep fine, possible jail time, and possible deportation.

Farmers in the Rif have soil that generally gives poor crop yields except for the cannabis plant, which has become a staple source of income in the region, albeit on the black market. The industry here is controlled by a loose kind of mafia who work at exporting hash globally, particularly into the European market. It is estimated that the Rif produces 70-80 percent of the hash for Europe and 30-40 percent for the world. Morocco as a whole is the largest exporter of hash in the world. There is a lot of money in this industry, and where there is money, there is corruption, greed, and people willing to cut deals. One of the more common practices is for a dealer to sell a tourist hash, only to turn that tourist in to the local police.

Exactly how much money is in the hash industry is anyone's guess. The best estimates put the value at nearly US$2 billion per year. Ahmed Ben Chemsi, the editor for *Tel Quel,* a more liberal French-language weekly magazine published in Casablanca, is calling for legalization. According to his estimates, gleaned from sales of rolling papers and loose tobacco, Moroccans smoke 1.1 billion joints a year. With prices of hash typically hovering around 6-15Dh per gram, it's easy to see the inexpensive draw of this illegal substance.

accommodation option for most travelers coming through Chefchaouen, and the on-site spa service is second to none, with a couples bath as well as in-house massages (the massages are only for women as of this writing). The traditional hammam is wonderful, and so is the staff. Wi-Fi is available in the reception area, and breakfast is included.

LALLA GHAYTA

10 Lalla Ghayta, near Bab el-Souk; tel. 0674/839 216 or Spain +34 696 43 20 65; 2,200Dh d

This historic property, dubbed "The House of Nations," has provided refuge for many important political players in Morocco over the past few hundred years. The granddaughter of Lalla Ghayta has lovingly restored the *riad,* keeping it as the traditional Moroccan *riad* it has always been, with lounge spaces, an interior courtyard, two bedrooms (one with an en-suite bath), and a rooftop terrace. If you've ever fancied what it might be like to live in a house in a Moroccan medina, this is your chance. Families, couples, or a few good friends should take advantage of this fantastic villa tucked inside the medina, the only one of its kind in Chefchaouen. Lunches and dinners (300Dh) are available on request, as is breakfast (70Dh), though the house is impeccably furnished and has everything you need to make your own meals. Maid service is in the mornings.

CAMPING

There is a well-marked municipal campground on the eastern hillside of town in the H'nain district. Depending on your setup, a night will run around 80Dh. Like most municipal campsites, it's equipped with hot-water showers (10Dh) and is vehicle friendly. Free overnight camping is also possible along the waterfall trail in nearby Akchour.

Information and Services

Just outside **Bab el-Ain** you can find **Banque Populaire** (Mon.-Fri. 8:15am-3:45pm) and **Attijarwafa Bank** (Mon.-Fri. 9am-4:30pm), as well as the local **post office** (Mon.-Fri. 8am-4:15pm, Sat. 8am-11:45am) and a **Western Union** (Mon.-Fri. 8:30am-4:30pm).

Getting There and Around

Getting around town is easy enough. For the most part, you will be **walking** up and down the hills of the medina. For trips to and from the ***gare routière*** or other locations out of the medina, ***petits taxis*** are reliable, though they don't have meters like taxis in the big cities. Most rides around town cost 7-10Dh. A taxi from Bab El-Ain to the *gare routière* is 8Dh.

BY CAR

By car, Chefchaouen is about two hours southeast of **Tangier** (115km/68mi), one hour south of **Tetouan** (64km/40mi), and four hours north of **Fez** (204km/127mi). The roads in this area can be a little narrow, and drivers should be wary of farm equipment, particularly on the sharper turns, as well as drivers trying to pass on blind turns. Night driving should be avoided.

There is a convenient parking lot on **Place Makhzen** for 20Dh a night, and there is a 24-hour guard on duty. **Chaouen Car** (Ave. Hassan II, 0539/986 204, daily 10am-1pm and 3:30pm-6pm) has car rentals and various excursions into the Rif available, including on 4x4s and quad bikes.

BY BUS AND GRAND TAXI

Just off Place Mohammed V is a ***grand taxi*** stand. *Grands taxis* go regularly to **Tetouan** (1hr, 61km/38mi, 35Dh).

By bus, getting to Chefchaouen is fairly straightforward, though leaving can be somewhat stressful. There is a **CTM office** in the *gare routière*, but it is preferable to book tickets in advance from another CTM office because the CTM buses generally arrive full to Chefchaouen on their way to other destinations, and it can be difficult to find a seat otherwise. The **CTM** (tel. 0800/090 030, www.ctm.ma) bus connects with **Fez** (4.5hr, 6 daily, 100Dh), **Tetouan** (1.5hr, 6 daily, 45Dh), **Tangier** (2.5hr, 2 daily, 65Dh), **Al-Hoceima** (7hr, 1 daily, 110Dh), **Nador** (11.5hr, 1 daily, 160Dh), and **Rabat** (4.5hr, 1 daily, 110Dh).

THE RIF MOUNTAINS

جبال ريف

The Rif Mountains have a notorious past, and people from this region are wary of visitors—and rightly so. Around the smaller cities like Chefchaouen and Tetouan, locals are used to seeing foreigners and tourists of all stripes and are seldom bothered, but venture a little farther into the mountains and the cultural landscape changes. The locals are more suspicious and generally more reserved. This is one of the more conservative regions of Morocco and one of the more insular. The Rifis have a long history of warring with the various ruling monarchies of Morocco as well as European powers. Rifis generally marry among each other, even those who have moved overseas, and, notoriously, marijuana and drug trafficking have become this region's primary economic source of income.

However, the natural beauty of the region is irresistible to many, especially in the spring when the wildflowers are in bloom. Rock-climbers have been making routes over the rockier regions to the northwest, around Akchour, and mountain bikers are often found in the mountains in the late spring and early summer months. Most of these activities

1

2

3

are confined to **Talassemtane National Park,** although a few other venturous souls traverse less-traveled paths farther east.

Crossing the mountains via the N2 from Chefchaouen, this particular strip is considered one of the more dangerous drug-trafficking corridors in Morocco. In particular, be wary of invitations to farms. More than likely, if you have luggage or a vehicle, it will get searched as you finish the pass through the mountains.

Talassemtane National Park
المنتزه الوطني تلاسمطان

Along the north side of the Rif Mountains spreads Talassemtane National Park, a 59,000-hectare (145,000-acre) park boasting a unique Mediterranean ecosystem with over 200 plant species, many of which are endangered, including the Atlas cedar and black pine. Talassemtane National Park offers plenty of hiking. For longer excursions in the park, consider a guide. **Fatima Habté** (tel. 0672/743 347) arranges trekking in the park and is the most reliable guide in the area, with a master's degree in ecotourism. Her hikes include both one-day hikes and multi-day backpacking excursions through the park.

There are numerous caves and caverns, as well as seemingly hidden valleys, to uncover in this region. A good guide can be indispensable in finding these and leading you around to the fantastic views afforded by Jbel Khizana, one of the taller mountain peaks.

For those spending a few days in the park, the small town of Bab Taza just off the N2 is a good place to shop for goods.

★ AKCHOUR WATERFALLS AND GOD'S BRIDGE

The Akchour Waterfalls and God's Bridge are popular day hikes with Moroccans and internationals alike, branching from the same trailhead located a short 30 minutes from Chefchaouen just off the road to Tetouan. You can get to the Akchour trailhead by *grand taxi* (400Dh); just make sure to arrange a pickup time. From Chefchaouen, the road to the trailhead is well-signed—just follow the signs for Akchour along the road to Tetouan. If you have your own car, it will be easy enough to find.

There are two basic hikes. At the trailhead (the stone bridge with the cascading water), you can go left or right. The **left path** follows the river. There are several **waterfalls** here. It's a two-hour easy-medium hike to get to the largest waterfall. Along the way there are cafés and barbecues for a quick tajine, brochette, tea, or coffee.

The **right path** goes up the mountain. At the fork, marked by a little café, you can continue downhill, across the river, and then up over **God's Bridge,** a natural rock formation a bit like those in Utah, where erosion has caused the rock to form a natural bridge over the river, which is about 45 meters (150ft) below. You will likely have to wade into the river to get there; this can be dangerous when the water is high. The easier (and less wet) trek follows the mountains up the ridge from the fork at the little café, and it offers a fantastic view of the bridge as well as some breathtaking views of the limestone cliff faces. From here, you can continue across the ridge to the bridge. This steep hike to reach God's Bridge will take 30-45 minutes.

The trails can be busy during summer months and major holidays. During and just after these times the hikes can be dirty with the garbage of other hikers who are evidently unaware of the environmental damages that occur from littering. If you can, hike with a bag and a pair of gloves to do your part to help clean up these otherwise stunning hikes.

ROCK-CLIMBING

Over the last five years or so, various semiprofessional climbers from Germany, the Czech Republic, and Slovakia have been opening up climbing routes throughout Talassemtane National Park. Climbers can look forward to

1: Women ride back home after a long day in the fields. **2:** hiking through Talassemtane National Park **3:** the Akchour Waterfalls

single-pitch and multi-pitch climbs with various levels of difficulty. To date, about 300 or so routes have been opened, though there are a couple thousand unexplored possibilities. **Café Refuge Rueda** just outside of Akchour has been the climbing hub in these parts. There you can find an updated log of climbs in the area. For climbers, this is currently the best region in Morocco.

Accommodations

Free overnight **camping** can be had along the route to Akchour along the riverbanks and throughout the national park. Outside of the park, things can be a little more dicey with drug lords and cannabis farmers about. In this region, campers should exercise extreme caution.

GITE TALASSEMTANE

Just outside the national park; tel. 0672/743 347; www.gitetalassemtane.com; 400Dh d

This is maybe the best *gîte* (guest house) in the Rif Mountains. Fatima, the owner, will be happy to arrange day hikes and visits to local women's co-ops as well as tasty meals at her *gîte*. The accommodations are some of the coziest around, with plush beds and a cozy lounge. Fatima works hard with the local women, and it is clear that she is invested in her community. She arranges not only guides, if needed, but also homestays throughout the region, so that you can hike from place to place with a warm bed waiting for you after a long day of trekking.

Mediterranean Coast Road Trip

If you love a good road trip, consider a drive along the newly paved National Road 16 (N16), which runs along the north Mediterranean Coast, and take the six-hour drive (350km/218mi) from Tetouan to the Spanish city of Melilla. This drive features majestic cliffs plunging into the blue-green sea below, long stretches of seldom-visited beaches, the occasional national park, and a few protected lagoons that dot the way. Every 20 or 30 kilometers there is a small village, though unfortunately most of these are being developed with the square brick and cement structures common in the *villes nouvelles* in all Moroccan cities. This strip is popular with Moroccan tourists in the summer, and the more popular beaches are often strewn with trash, though if you keep an eye out, you might run across one of the more secluded beaches between Martil and Al-Hoceima.

STARTING THE DRIVE

From Tetouan, you can follow the N16 directly from town, following signs to Oued Laou (48km/30mi, 1hr). From Chefchaouen, you can either backtrack to Tetouan or take the newly repaved P4105, which twists through the Rif past the dam at Barrage Oued Laou and a couple of picturesque Moroccan villages, before joining up with the N16 in **Oued Laou** (56km/35mi, 1.5hr), a laid-back fishing town that fills up with Moroccans enjoying the beach in the summer.

Leaving Oued Laou, the road immediately begins to climb the steep cliffs of the northern point of the Rif Mountains, where they plunge into the sea below. Amazingly, these are part of the same mountain system that gave rise to the Sierra Nevada of Spain just across the strait. The road climbs back and forth through green pine-studded hills and red cliffs.

TARGHA
تارغة

Targha (17km/11mi, 20min) is the first of many small towns you will reach after Oued Laou. Note the small fort atop a huge rock along the coastline. Built during the Spanish protectorate, this crumbling fort was once a base for Spanish dominance in the region. Because of its strategic location, this rock also has a long history of pirates using it as a hidden outpost. Today it is rarely visited, except by shepherds with their goat flocks, which graze along the steep rock.

STEHAT

سطحت

Farther along, after another climb up the Rif, is another, more ruined fort in the valley at Stehat (12km/7mi, 20min from Targha). This is a good place to stop if you need a break after the winding mountain road or want to relax for a few days.

Accommodations

NAZL STEHAT

Rue Principale; tel. 0539/884 061; http://hotel-stehat.com; 200Dh d

The Nazl Stehat has simple, clean rooms, Wi-Fi, and a restaurant. The rooms are a bit spartan, though they will do in a pinch. The hotel can arrange cycling, fishing, and personal watercraft rentals.

JEBHA

الجبهة

East from Stehat, the drive is less green, though not less interesting. The rock formations of this part of the Rif are picturesque and provide a stunning contrast to the Mediterranean. From here, the transformation from the mountainous region to a more arid, high-desert Mediterranean region is apparent. Rocky mountains give way to oasis-like valleys.

Jebha (55km/35mi, 1hr from Stehat) is a small village with an exceptional stretch of beach over a small mountain to the east of town, though it is accessible only by foot, which makes it a real joy to get to. The town offers a few beachfront grills with nearby parking. Sardines, *bissara,* and fish tajines are the order of the day. Tuesday is the weekly souk in Jebha, one of the biggest and liveliest around.

AL-HOCEIMA

الحسيمة

Al-Hoceima (109km/68mi, 1.5 hr from Jebha) was found by the Spanish in 1925 and called Villa Sanjuro after a Spanish general. However, not much remains of this Spanish protectorate-era town. Like most Spanish-styled cities, everything seems to radiate out from a main plaza, today's **Place Mohammed VI.** Most visitors head down from Place Mohammed VI to the Mediterranean, where a couple of new hotel complexes are looking to capitalize on the exclusivity of the small **Quemado Beach,** resting in the natural cove the bay provides. If you want to break up your road trip with a good night's sleep, Al-Hoceima is a decent place to do it.

Besides the nearby national park, the city has no other major attractions and is mostly a series of new Moroccan construction of the cement/brick variety. For Moroccan tourists, the draw is the beaches. They are swarmed in the summer months, particularly August. Unfortunately, the trash left behind from these visitors can be a real problem. As in the rest of this region, the best time to visit the beaches is just outside the summer months, in May and June as well as September.

Sights

AL-HOCEIMA NATIONAL PARK (PARC NATIONAL D'AL-HOCEIMA)

www.eauxetforets.gov.ma

Just before the city of Al-Hoceima is Al-Hoceima National Park (Parc National d'Al-Hoceima). This is likely the least-visited national park in all of Morocco and, because of that, a bit of an undiscovered gem that stretches for 485 square kilometers (187 square miles). You won't find the hordes of backpackers along well-trod paths that you'll find during the high travel season in other parks. Instead, the many dirt paths that crisscross through the park, from the coastline into the mountains, serve as main thoroughfares for the people of the local Rifi tribes who still live in small villages scattered throughout

1
2
APPART HOTEL
3
4

the park. This is an idyllic spot for hikers and mountain bikers. The park serves as a refuge for many species of flora and fauna, including the endangered thuya wood.

PLAGE DE TORRES

Be on the lookout for signs to Plage de Torres, a beautiful beach a few kilometers off the N16. This is a much more secluded beach than others in the area and less touristed, which makes it a generally cleaner beach. A fantastic stop for adventurous travelers wanting to take a little dip and sunbathe.

Accommodations

CALA IRIS

Campers might consider moving on to Cala Iris, farther down the beach, where there is **Camping Amis de Cala Iris** (80Dh), which has hot showers for 10Dh and beautiful views over the rest of the national park. From Cala Iris, you can take the 1.5-hour coastal hike to Peñón de Velez de la Gomera, one of the small territories still controlled by Spain in this region.

HOTEL VILLA FLORIDO

40 Pl. del Rif; tel. 0539/840 847; http://florido.alhoceima.com; 250Dh s, 350Dh d

Conveniently located in one of the more picturesque areas of town, Plaza del Rif, and only a 15-minute walk from Quemado Beach. This colonial-era hotel dates from 1929 and offers spacious lodgings and a comfortable, though noisy, night of sleep. The rooms on the corners can comfortably sleep three. This is a backpacker favorite, especially during the off-season, when prices plunge to 150Dh a night, including breakfast and taxes.

1: the spectacular, wild coast of the Mediterranean **2:** The drive along the Mediterranean Coast is breathtaking. **3:** Al-Hoceima's Quemado Beach outside of high season **4:** Melilla's 15th-century Old Town, called El Pueblo by locals

HOTEL LA PERLA

Ave. Tarik Ibn Zayid; tel. 0539/984 513; www.hotelperlamorocco.com; 700Dh d

Perhaps the best night of sleep in town, with updated beds that feel heavenly after a few nights of camping. Wi-Fi and air-conditioning are found in each room, and there are nonsmoking rooms. Each room features modern decor that wouldn't be out of place in New York. The restaurant is refreshingly nonsmoking as well and serves traditional Moroccan cuisine. The location just up from Place Mohammed VI, near the stadium, is well situated for exploring Al-Hoceima and the beaches.

CAP DES TROIS FOURCHES

رأس المذرات الثلاث

After Al-Hoceima, the drive becomes more arid. The landscape features rust-colored cliffs that seemingly drop into the turquoise abyss below. There are several viewpoints along this part of the drive, as well as snack restaurants on the side of the road every few miles, though restrooms can be hard to find. For several stretches the road follows alongside the Mediterranean, in particular at **Plage Sidi Driss,** where a straightaway across a shallow plain offers a few turnoffs for relaxing.

Along this stretch, one of the more interesting diversions is the Cap des Trois Fourches (Cape of Three Forks). To get there, take the Bni Chiker/Iazzanen exit about 100 kilometers (62mi) east of Al-Hoceima, on the left. From here, the road is a bit more rocky, though you won't need a four-wheel drive. The road winds through a few villages. There are two turnoffs, but signs for Cap des Trois Fourches point the way (always, it seems, to the left). The last part of the drive continues up, over a mountainous road that drops straight down into the water, before ending at the Cap des Trois Fourches lighthouse. This is the easternmost tine of the three-pronged fork. The middle prong is the stunning Wali Sidi Amar, a mausoleum for the local saint, and the westernmost prong is an uninhabited crop of rocks. This is a wonderful area to hike to seldom-visited beaches, though the winds are often strong.

MELILLA (SPAIN)

مليلية

After the long coastal road and the seemingly longer wait at the border, stepping into Melilla is something of a welcomed surprise. After spending time in Morocco, life in Melilla can be a bit of a shock. Just over the border, suddenly cars are stopping for pedestrians in crosswalks, people are walking dogs, and there is a tapas bar with cold beer on tap at virtually every street corner. Make no mistake—this is Spain. Melilla is the often-forgotten sister city to Ceuta, the other "Spanish" city in Morocco.

In some ways, the remoteness of Melilla has made the city somehow more Spanish than many places on mainland Spain. There is a relative lack of international tourism, but with the daily flights and ferries to Spain, Melilla is where the Spanish come for vacation when they don't want to fight the crowds on continental European beaches. However, all this is set to change in the near future. With the new freeway built from Fez to Oujda, Melilla is now only a four-hour drive or so from Fez.

Melilla has long been a strategic point along the Mediterranean Coast. As in many other cities in this corner of Africa, the Phoenicians were the first known settlers, followed by Carthaginians, Romans, and the Moroccan dynasties. Various tribes from the Rif Mountains settled here along the coast sometime in the 7th century. It wasn't until the arrival of the Spanish in the 15th century that the city began to take shape. The Spanish began building the medieval fortress over two centuries after taking the city in the Conquest of Melilla. Tunnels through the rock, in use since Phoenician times, are still accessible through various gates in the fortress. The fortress, dubbed Melilla La Vieja, or "Old Melilla," has been restored and now is home to many important historical sites, including the Church of the Conception, Hospital del Rey, and the ethnography and military museums.

Melilla underwent another growth spurt in the late 19th and early 20th centuries, expanding out in grand baroque, Catalan modernism, and art deco style with the famed architects Enrique Nieto and Lorenzo Ros Costa, credited for many of the more outstanding examples of this period. After Barcelona, Melilla boasts the most important modernist heritage in all of Spain. Like his mentor, Gaudí, in Barcelona, Nieto is largely seen as the "Architect of Melilla" and is responsible for many of the buildings forming the "Golden Triangle," a largely commercial area just off the Plaza de España with many shops and tapas bars.

Today, Melilla is a bright, relatively unexplored city with lots of possibilities. During the warm summer months the municipal beach offers a fairly clean alternative to many of the other beaches in northern Morocco. And for shoppers, the autonomous nature of Melilla holds a certain monetary allure, as all purchases made in the city are tax free, much as in airport duty-free shops. The sheer beauty of the city's architecture, authentic European vibe, and the feeling that not too many tourists make it out to this distant corner of Spanish Morocco make it a true pleasure to visit.

Orientation

Because of its relative compactness, it is possible to visit all of the major sites in Melilla in a single day, though two days at a more relaxed pace with a few stops for tapas and maybe an afternoon siesta on the beach fit more into the local culture. Like other smaller towns in Spain, in Melilla nearly everything is closed on Sunday, and many of the **museums** are closed on Monday as well as for a few hours in the afternoon. For the best feel of the city, try to visit during midweek to see Melilla in full swing.

Melilla

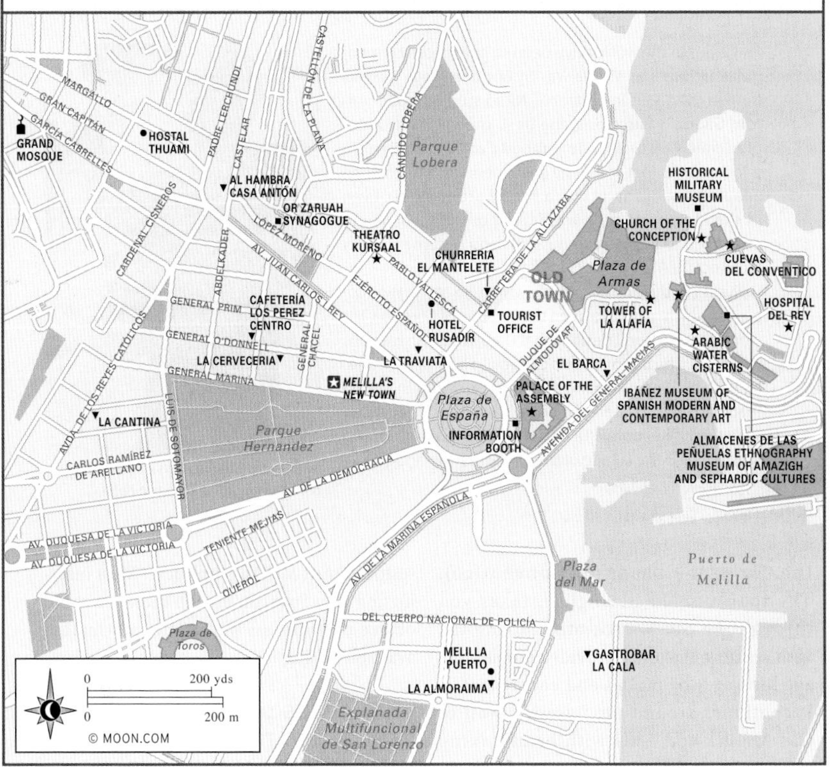

Sights

OLD TOWN

The Old Town (Melilla La Vieja), affectionately called El Pueblo by the locals, is a hilltop fortress divided into four precincts. The first precinct was begun in the 15th century. It consists of the imposing defensive structures towering above the pounding shore. They encompass the museums and most historical buildings in the Old Town. A bridge over the **Foso de Santiago,** a moat, leads into the open-air second precinct at the **Plaza de Armas.** Below the plaza were the underground dungeons, and above you can still see the remains of the **Shrine of Victory,** which used to house the patron saint of Melilla. The third precinct is accessed from below the Old Town in the Plaza de las Culturas through the **San Fernando Tunnel.** Here you can find the only remaining medieval tower, the **Tower of La Alafía.** The fourth precinct was built much later, in the 18th and 19th centuries. Cannons were fired from the forts of **El Rosario** and **Las Victorias** to decide the current boundaries of Melilla.

Most sights are concentrated in the first precinct, including several museums of interest as well as the 15th-century **Arabic Water Cisterns (Aljibes)** and **Church of the Conception (Iglesia de la Concepción),** the oldest structures in the city.

Before climbing up the hill to the Old Town, be sure to stop in at the Tourist Office to arrange a free guided tour of the **Caves of**

Enrique Nieto y Nieto: Architect of Melilla

Few cities in the world have been so influenced by a singular architect as Melilla was by Enrique Nieto y Nieto. Born in the 1880s in Catalonia, Nieto studied under Antoni Gaudí in Barcelona, the best-known practitioner of the architectural style dubbed Catalan modernism (*modernisme*) that would be so influential to Nieto as he adapted Gaudí's style into a sort of art nouveau. Even as the modernist style was falling out of favor, Nieto continued to receive commissions and became the city architect for Melilla in 1939.

Nieto cited many influences within his style, the biggest of which may have been the Mosque of Córdoba. His works feature floral designs that drape over curvaceous balconies. The bright turrets command a sort of symmetry with his works. Among the many buildings in Melilla that Nieto designed are the newly remodeled Teatro Kursaal, the La Reconquista department store, the Grand Mosque, and the facade of the Or Zaruah Synagogue.

a statue in Melilla's Ensanche commemorating Enrique Nieto

the Convent (Cuevas del Conventico). The tour, offered in English, takes you through the caves, excavated during the 18th century, that once provided ample storage for sieges by pirates and enemy forces. It continues around the towering wall of Old Melilla and ends with breathtaking views out across the water from the Cala de Trápana, with its crystal-clear water and private beach access. Take in the looming 19th-century lighthouse and the parabolic arch. On the tour, you can get a real feel for the protection the city's walls provided during the Renaissance era, and you'll learn other juicy tidbits of Melilla's history.

HOSPITAL DEL REY

1 Pl. de Parada; tel. 34-952/680 144; Mon.-Fri. 9am-2pm, Sat.-Sun. 10am-2pm, closed holidays; free

Tucked inside the old "King's Hospital," from which it takes its name, this museum houses a collection of photographs, lithographs, maps, and manuscripts that follow the progression and restoration of Melilla. Of particular interest are the comparative photographs taken nearly 100 years apart that make the restoration of Melilla prominent. Most information is in Spanish, though there is a stand of free publications with some information available in English.

ALMACENES DE LAS PEÑUELAS ETHNOGRAPHY MUSEUM OF AMAZIGH AND SEPHARDIC CULTURES

2 Calle de la Maestranza; tel. 34-952/976 216; www.museomelilla.es; Tues.-Sat. 10am-2pm and 4pm-9pm, to 8pm in winter, Sun. 10am-2pm; free

The Almacenes de las Peñuelas Ethnography Museum of Amazigh and Sephardic Cultures (Almacenes de las Peñuelas Museo Etnográfico de las Culturas Amazigh y Sefardí) is an archaeology, ethnography, and history museum that houses a rich collection of Amazigh and Jewish cultural artifacts, tracing the history of the region from the Neolithic period through contemporary times. Of particular interest are the Sephardic Hebrew amulets and stone mosaics on display. One of the real highlights of the visit is the building itself, constructed in 1781 as a store for perishable goods. In 2007, the building underwent a vast renovation to make it suitable to use as a museum.

HISTORICAL MILITARY MUSEUM

Baluarte de la Concepción; tel. 34-952/976 216; www.museomelilla.es; Tues.-Sun. 10am-2pm; free

The Historical Military Museum (El Museo Histórico Militar) provides an engaging perspective on the importance of Melilla as a military stronghold, from the first Phoenician settlement on this rocky outcrop to the present day. As one might imagine, most of the focus is on the might of the Spanish military the use of Melilla as a strategic military post on a high bluff overlooking a narrow passage along the Strait of Gibraltar.

IBÁÑEZ MUSEUM OF SPANISH MODERN AND CONTEMPORARY ART

Pl. Pedro de Estopiañán; tel. 34-952/699 232; Tues.-Sat. 10am-2pm and 4pm-9pm, to 8pm in winter, Sun. 10am-2pm; free

Across the plaza from the Ethnography Museum is the Ibáñez Museum of Spanish Modern and Contemporary Art (Museo Ibáñez de Arte Español Moderno y Contemporaneo), which is teamed with the Casa Ibáñez in Almeria, one of the most important museums in eastern Spain. It follows 200 years of Spanish art, with special attention given to 19th-century realism, new figuration, and photographic documentarism. On the ground floor, you will find paintings by Salvador Dalí and Pablo Picasso as well as engravings by Francisco Goya. In the museum you also have access to the Torre de la Vela, a 16th-century tower with the remains of a small chapel for Christian worship dating from this time.

★ NEW TOWN

The charming, palm-tree lined **Plaza de España** is the nerve center of Melilla. From Old Town, you arrive here and are able to branch out to any one of the stylish neighborhoods. There is work currently underway to make Melilla a World Heritage City and it is largely thanks to this area, with its nearly perfect urban design and monumental architecture that has been fused from various schools of architecture and design. Like the Spanish town of Tetouan, this part of Melilla is dubbed **Ensanche,** Spanish for "widening." Many cities in Spain undertook an *ensanche* plan in the later part of the 19th century, and beside Barcelona, Melilla holds claim to having one of the most intact *ensanches* in Spain.

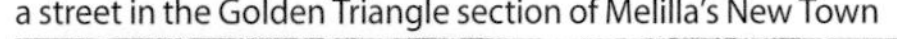

a street in the Golden Triangle section of Melilla's New Town

The most beautiful section to walk has been dubbed the **Golden Triangle (Triángulo de Oro).** This area extends from the Plaza de España between **Calle General Marina** and **Avenue Juan Carlos I, Rey** and is the commercial center of the city, with plenty of shops, cafés, and tapas bars.

Pay special attention to the towering **Palace of the Assembly (Palacio de la Asamblea),** an art deco Nieto design from 1932 that curves along the Plaza de España. The Palace of the Assembly still features the personal coat of arms of General Francisco Franco, who used the city as a staging ground to begin the Spanish Civil War in 1936. A statue of him can still be found on the street, the only one of its kind in Spain. In this area, you can also find the **Or Zaruah Synagogue,** designed by Nieto in the 1920s, along Calle López Moreno (named for the sculptor of the *Heroes of Battle* monument along Avenue Juan Carlos I, Rey). If you pay attention to the decorative elements of the windows, the doors, the railing and balconies, the molded parapets, and the grand arches, you can glean a feeling of the unity and the fragility of the architectural development of this Ensanche district, which combines many different elements, from the arabesque to the baroque, Catalan modernism, and art deco.

One of the surprising elements of Melilla is the harmony in which Christians, Hindus, Jews, and Muslims share the city. Though Melilla is primarily Catholic-Christian, there has been a sharp rise in the Muslim population (primarily from the Rif) and a steady, though small, population of Hindus and Jews. Each of these populations has a house of worship, and it is possible to visit them on a guided tour called the **Route of the Temples (Ruta de los Templos)** with the Office of Tourism or the Information Booth at the Plaza de España for €4. Tours are offered in English. The standout of this tour is the **Grand Mosque** of Melilla, a Nieto construction from 1945, along Calle García Cabrelles.

TEATRO KURSAAL

8 Calle Cándido Lobera; tel. 34-952/699 296

Check out the Teatro Kursaal for local happenings. There are often inexpensive, sometimes free, concerts showcasing local and international musicians and troupes. The theater was designed in 1930 by Enrique Nieto, one of his art deco and Catalan modernism-inspired buildings. It was remodeled in 2011 to recover the original facade of the building, though the interior has been updated with state-of-the-art equipment.

Food

There are plenty of dining options for a small town, though most food steers toward traditional Spanish, including tapas bars. Many dishes include ham (*jamón*), which may be just the thing after a week or two in a Muslim country where pork options are extremely limited. Keep an eye out for hanging legs of **Serrano** and **Ibérico ham,** deliciously cured ham that is one of the specialties of Andalusia in southern Spain.

★ CHURRERIA EL MANTELETE

9 Calle Teniente Aguilar de Mera; tel. 34-679/016 547; €3

For a traditional Spanish breakfast or snack, drop what you're doing and head here. Immediately. This nondescript, industrial-looking restaurant serves only one kind of food: churros. Churros are a type of deep-fried Spanish treat akin to a donut. These are considered by locals to be the best churros in town. Order churros by the plate (for one, two, three, or more!) and dip them into one of the thickest hot chocolates you've ever had.

CAFETERÍA LOS PEREZ CENTRO

5 Calle General Paraje; tel. 34-952/670 666; Mon.-Fri. 6:30am-12:30pm and 3pm-8pm, Sat.-Sun. 6am-12:30pm; €3

Right in the middle of the Golden Triangle, Los Perez offers up a more diverse breakfast, with a few Moroccan specialties as well as churros, croissants, donuts, and fresh fruit juices. The café is more New York than traditional Spain, though this is truly contemporary Spain, where tradition has given way to anything modern. Staff is friendly and the location is perfect for a quick breakfast or a snack while you're shopping in the area.

★ LA CANTINA

19 Calle Alonso Martín; tel. 34-952/681/704; Tues.-Sun. 1pm-5pm and 8pm-midnight; €3

Founded in 1981, this family-friendly tapas bar channels a cozy flamenco vibe with exposed wood-beam ceilings and walls cluttered with mounted bull heads, framed bullfighting posters, hanging legs of Serrano and Ibérico ham, and crates of wines stacked to the roof. The street-side bar is great for a drink and a bite on the go. Besides the cured Spanish ham, the artichoke hearts preserved in olive oil and spices are delicious. La Cantina is what you think of when you think of a Spanish tapas bar.

EL BARCA

11 Gral. Macías, across from the port; Mon.-Fri. 6:30am-12:30pm and 3pm-8pm, Sat.-Sun. 6am-12:30pm; €5

For toasted sandwiches, crepes, and croissants for breakfast. A quick lunch can be had for €3. The decor is nondescript, but for those moving from the Old Town into the New Town (or vice versa), it is a well-located place for a quick sandwich, a cold beer, and a breather.

AL HAMBRA CASA ANTÓN

3 Calle Castellar; hours vary; €5

A Spanish tapas bar with anchovies preserved in vinegar and olive oil, *gambas a la plancha* (grilled shrimp), *queso manchego,* and other tapas favorites. With a cozy, friendly vibe and nice staff, this is a good stopover if you are doing a tapas tour of Melilla.

★ LA CERVECERIA

23 Calle General O'Donnell; tel. 34-952/683 427; www.cerveceriamelilla.com; Tues.-Sun. 1pm-5pm and 8pm-midnight; €5

Popular with the young, hip, and social, this is one of the better-decorated tapas joints in town, with a Gaudí-inspired bench that wouldn't look out of place in Park Güell in Barcelona. A traditional tapas menu features Spanish tortillas, Ibérico and Serrano ham, olive oil-cured cheese, and *gambas al pilpil* (garlic shrimp). Come early for a seat.

LA ALMORAIMA

Explanada de San Lorenzo; tel. 34-952/695 525; daily 1pm-4pm and 8pm-midnight; €20-30

For more of a sit-down dinner (or more tapas if you want), head here for a varied Mediterranean-based menu, including Spanish and Moroccan favorites, as well as vegetarian and vegan options. Sushi can be had on Friday and Saturday. The menu includes favorites such as tenderloin with foie gras, Atlantic cod dressed with orange *pilpil,* and wild mushroom parmesan risotto. The decor is sleek with modern pink and black lines, a contemporary take on the Spanish tendency toward the garish and bright.

LA TRAVIATA

Calle Ejercito; tel. 34-952/268 925; daily 1pm-4pm and 8pm-midnight; €25

Don't let the rather humdrum decor fool you: this local favorite sizzles with Spanish zest. From the goat cheese salad to the lamb shoulder, the incredibly spiced menu, served by a friendly, fun-loving staff, sends your taste buds spinning, while the lengthy wine menu might leave your head a little lighter. Make sure to leave room for the boozy sorbets.

GASTROBAR LA CALA

6 Puerto Noray Local; tel. 34-952/678 107; Mon.-Sat. noon-4:30pm and 8pm-12:30am; €20-30

For something a little different than Spanish staples, head to the port, where you can find Gastrobar, serving up one of the more innovative menus in Melilla, complete with chicken curry, *enchiladas verdes* (enchiladas in green tomatillo sauce), and chicken pops. The wine menu is top-notch, and most wines can be had by the glass. The music can be a bit loud.

Accommodations

Hostels and hotels are fairly limited in Melilla. There are few real values to be had. Most accommodations are sufficient, if a bit on the expensive side. Most visitors will want to stay in the New Town, around the Golden Triangle. Be wary of accommodations outside of the main Ensanche district. Many of the hotels on the outskirts of Melilla have had problems with drug trafficking and prostitution.

HOSTAL THUAMI

13 Calle General García Margallo; tel. 34-952/686 045; €45 d

The best deal for travelers on a budget, this hostel is a short five-minute walk to the Golden Triangle neighborhood. The rooms are spacious, offer air-conditioning, and comfortably sleep two or three. Whatever this hostel lacks in charm, it makes up for in cleanliness.

HOTEL RUSADIR

5 Calle Pablo Vallescá; tel. 34-952/681 240; www.hotelrusadir.com; €55-82 d

Named after the old Phoenician name of Melilla, this hotel is perhaps the best mid- to high-range option around town. Rooms are clean and come equipped with air-conditioning, TV, and Wi-Fi. The location is ideal, just a block from the Plaza de España and on the edge of the Golden Triangle. Staff is friendly, patient, and helpful. Nonsmoking rooms are available.

MELILLA PUERTO

Explanada de San Lorenzo; tel. 34-952/695 525; €75-89 d

A bit of a splurge, especially considering some of the other hotels run by TRYP. However, if you are craving stunning seaside views over the port and the Mediterranean, this is the clear winner. It's just a short walk to the Golden Triangle and the Old Town and has some of the most comfortable beds in town, though the rooms lack any sort of personality, which might be just the ticket for some travelers tired of quaint, full-of-charm boutique hotels.

Information and Services

An **Information Booth (Punto de Información)** (Mon.-Fri. 9am-1pm) right on the Plaza de España, outside the Palacio de la Asamblea, has information on events and cultural activities. It is possible to arrange tours as well.

TOURIST OFFICE (OFICINA DE INFORMACIÓN TURÍSTICA

Pl. de las Culturas; tel. 34-952/976 190; info@melillaturismo.com; Mon.-Sat. 10am-2pm and 4:30pm-8:30pm, Sun. and holidays 10am-2pm

Just a short jaunt from the Plaza de España, the tourist office is staffed with friendly, helpful people.

Newspapers

The newspaper is alive and well in Melilla with three daily papers—*El Faro, Melilla Hoy*, and *El Telegrama*. All are in Spanish, though they print handy updated schedules for ferries and planes to Spain as well as addresses for 24-hour pharmacies and gas stations. You can find newspapers at the reception of most hotels as well as cafés, bars, and newspaper stands.

Health and Safety

For emergencies dial 112 for medical assistance or 092 to reach the local police, though you will likely want to have someone who speaks Spanish help you. There is a convenient pharmacy, **Farmacia Puga** (Pl. de las Culturas, Spain tel. 34-952/682 054), in the main plaza by the Tourist Office.

Getting There

Please note that touts will try to sell you passport forms and offer to fill them out for you at the border. They ask for money to do this. It is unnecessary, as the forms are free at the Moroccan customs office. However, you will be expected to provide your own pen, as customs officials will not have pens on hand to give you.

BY BUS

By bus, getting to Melilla is a little more tricky and involves taking a taxi from nearby **Nador** (220Dh for entire taxi, 35Dh for a place, though this is always negotiable and sometimes taxi drivers try to charge less or more). **CTM** (47 Rue General Ameziane, Nador, tel. 0536/600 136 or 0800/0900 30, www.ctm.ma) runs lines from **Fez** (5hr, 3 daily, 210Dh), **Tetouan** (10.5hr, 2 daily, 160Dh), **Chefchaouen** (11.5hr, 1 daily, 160Dh), and **Al-Hoceima** (4hr, 2 daily, 80Dh) to Nador.

BY CAR

By car, Melilla is about four hours northeast of **Fez** (330km/200mi), two hours east of **Al-Hoceima** (130km/81mi), and 5.5 hours east of **Chefchaouen** (335km/202mi). The roads in this area have all been upgraded and are safe, though night driving is still dangerous. If you have rented a car, you will not be able to bring it across the border into Melilla. There is **parking** in Nador, and on the Moroccan side of the border is free street parking, which should be fine for overnight, though take precautions and don't leave your valuables behind.

BY FERRY

Two companies run ferries to mainland **Spain** (Almeria, Málaga, and Motril) and leave from the port every day: **Transmediterranea** (Spain tel. 34-902/454 645, www.transmediterranea.es) and **Naviera Armas** (Spain tel. 34-902/456 500, www.navieraarmas.com). Check their websites or the local newspaper for the latest departure and arrival times.

BY PLANE

The **Melilla Airport** (Ctra. de Yasinen, Spain tel. 34-902/404 704) lies in the southwest corner of Melilla, about 4 kilometers (2.5mi) from the city center. Several airlines run daily flights to mainland **Spain** (45min-1hr). Melilla Airlines, AirEuropa, and Africa Travel have daily flights to Málaga. Air Nostrum also offers flights to Almeria, Granada, and Madrid. Airfares fluctuate wildly depending on the season, ranging from €50-300 each way.

Getting Around

Melilla is small enough that you will get around just fine on your feet. **Parking** is free on the streets and in the scattered parking garages. Several local **buses** (http://coamelilla.com, €1) can take you around town. You can also call for a **taxi** (Spain tel. 34-952/683 623) in the city, with an average fare running around €5. A convenient taxi stand is located on the corner of Avenida de Candido Lobera and Avenida Juan Carlos I, Rey, right in the middle of the Golden Triangle.

Fez and the Middle Atlas

When you pass under the great blue gate of Bab Boujeloud into the old city of Fez, known as Fès el-Bali, you are walking into the largest car-free urban area and one of the largest UNESCO World Heritage Sites on our planet.

Founded in AD 789 by Moulay Idriss I and home to roughly 150,000 people, the Fès el-Bali is a fully functioning medieval city. The streets are narrow, some not even shoulder-width, and occasionally steep as they descend toward the Fez River, the heart of the city. The only traffic here is pedestrian, donkey, and horse, with the occasional motor scooter slowly making its way through the crowds, up the main road of Talâa Kbira.

Highlights

Look for ★ to find recommended sights, activities, dining, and lodging.

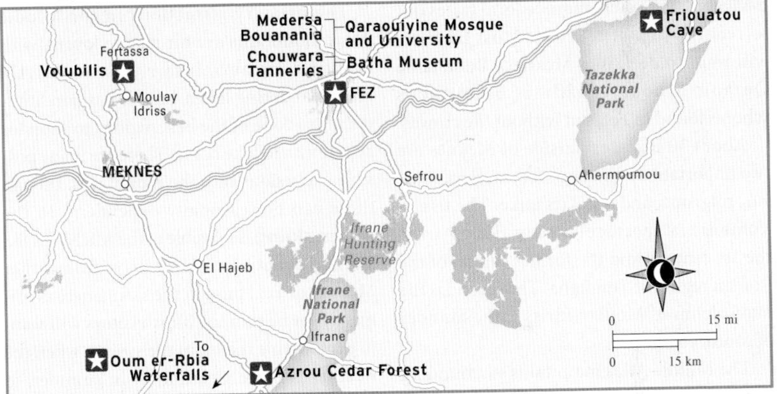

★ **Medersa Bouanania:** Lace-like stucco work combines with intricate woodcarving and fine *zellij* in this newly restored 14th-century Quranic school in Fez (page 254).

★ **Qaraouiyine Mosque and University:** Venture into the heart of the old Fez medina and to the oldest university in the world, and then stop for a quick bowl of *bissara* to keep you going (page 254).

★ **Chouwara Tanneries:** Check out a medieval trade that hasn't really changed in the last few hundred years, but be sure to plug your nose (pages 256)!

★ **Batha Museum:** Take a stroll through the artisan history of Morocco while enjoying the palatial surroundings of this restored 19th-century palace (page 259).

★ **Volubilis:** Take a walk through Roman history, strolling down the Decumanus Maximus, under the Arch of Caracalla, and into the House of Venus (page 286).

★ **Azrou Cedar Forest:** Get off the beaten track with Barbary macaques, experience the tranquility of the Middle Atlas, and rough it for a couple of nights (page 291).

★ **Oum er-Rbia Waterfalls:** Take a plunge and cool off at the bottom of this locally famous waterfall. After you dry off, grab lunch at one of the numerous family-run tajine tents (page 294).

★ **Friouatou Cave:** Go spelunking in one of Morocco's largest caves in the heart of Tazekka National Park. Examine majestic underground formations that look like a thousand giant jewels (page 301).

Admire Fez's 500-year-old Chouwara tanneries, where tanners cure and dye leather as they have for nearly a thousand years. Sift through the local hand-thrown, -painted, and -fired pottery in the Henna Souk. Listen to the metalworkers hammer brass and copper into shape at Seffarine Square, and inhale the scent of freshly cut cedarwood from the nearby Nejjarine Square, where carpenters ply their trade. Listen to the call to prayer softly croon over this ancient city, a calm reminder of Fez's status as the spiritual capital of Morocco.

Perhaps because of its proximity to the more-touristed Fez, the old imperial city of Meknes is often overlooked by travelers. The medina in Meknes is relatively small and navigable, and caters more to local tastes due to relative lack of tourism. Most travelers will want to peek into Meknes's Bouanania Quranic School, equally as beautiful as schools found in Fez, but without the crowds.

About 30 minutes outside of Meknes are two important destinations for travelers, tourists, pilgrims, and scholars alike. The first is Volubilis, a spectacular ruin dating from the 1st century and the former capital of the Roman region of Tingitana. The second is the mausoleum of Moulay Idriss I, the founder of Morocco.

The Middle Atlas mountains surrounding Fez and Meknes are a nature lover's dream. This relatively unexplored region rewards travelers with some of the most beautiful landscapes Morocco has to offer. Take in the waterfalls at Oum er-Rbia, watch eagles and crimson-winged finches soar below from the snowy peaks of Michlifen, or trek alongside Barbary macaques and sheep in the lush rolling valleys—especially during the vibrant spring this mountain range is known for.

PLANNING YOUR TIME

You will need three days, at least, to explore Fez, but four or five days is ideal to include day trips to nearby **Meknes** and **Volubilis**. If you have more time, are a nature lover, or want to explore some smaller towns, consider another two or three days to visit the **picturesque towns** and **national parks** in the region.

Meknes, Volubilis, and **Azrou** are each about one hour from Fez by hired car and can all be done in separate day trips, making Fez an ideal base from which to explore the region. Meknes makes another excellent base for those seeking a calmer, less touristed experience; the laid-back atmosphere of this former imperial city makes up for the lack of options. Most visitors tour both Volubilis and **Moulay Idriss** in the same day, often on tours arranged by their accommodations.

The primary attractions in the Middle Atlas mountains are for nature lovers, with beautiful streams, lush rivers, waterfalls, and meandering hikes, but for bargain hunters, this is one of the best regions to shop for **souvenirs** to take home. There are many possible excursions into the mountains, though these can be seasonally dependent. In the winter, **skiing** is possible at the Michlifen Ski Station, about a two-hour drive from either Meknes or Fez, though the skiing here is primarily for beginners. Most visitors will want to explore this region in the spring, when the weather is more pleasant, or in summer, to break away from the heat of the nearby cities.

Buses and ***grands taxis*** travel between all points in this region, though you will likely have to first take a ***petit taxi*** to get to either the taxi or bus station. Once at the station, you may have to wait for a bus to depart or for a taxi to get enough clients to set off for your destination. All of this adds time to your trip. For those pressed for time, hiring a taxi or renting a car is the best solution for making the most of your stay in this region.

For backpackers, Azrou makes a great base for exploring the Middle Atlas. It has plenty of low-cost accommodations, and its location

---

Previous: a lantern hanging in the Fez medina; Medersa Bouanania; ornate tile detail in Fez.

Fez and the Middle Atlas

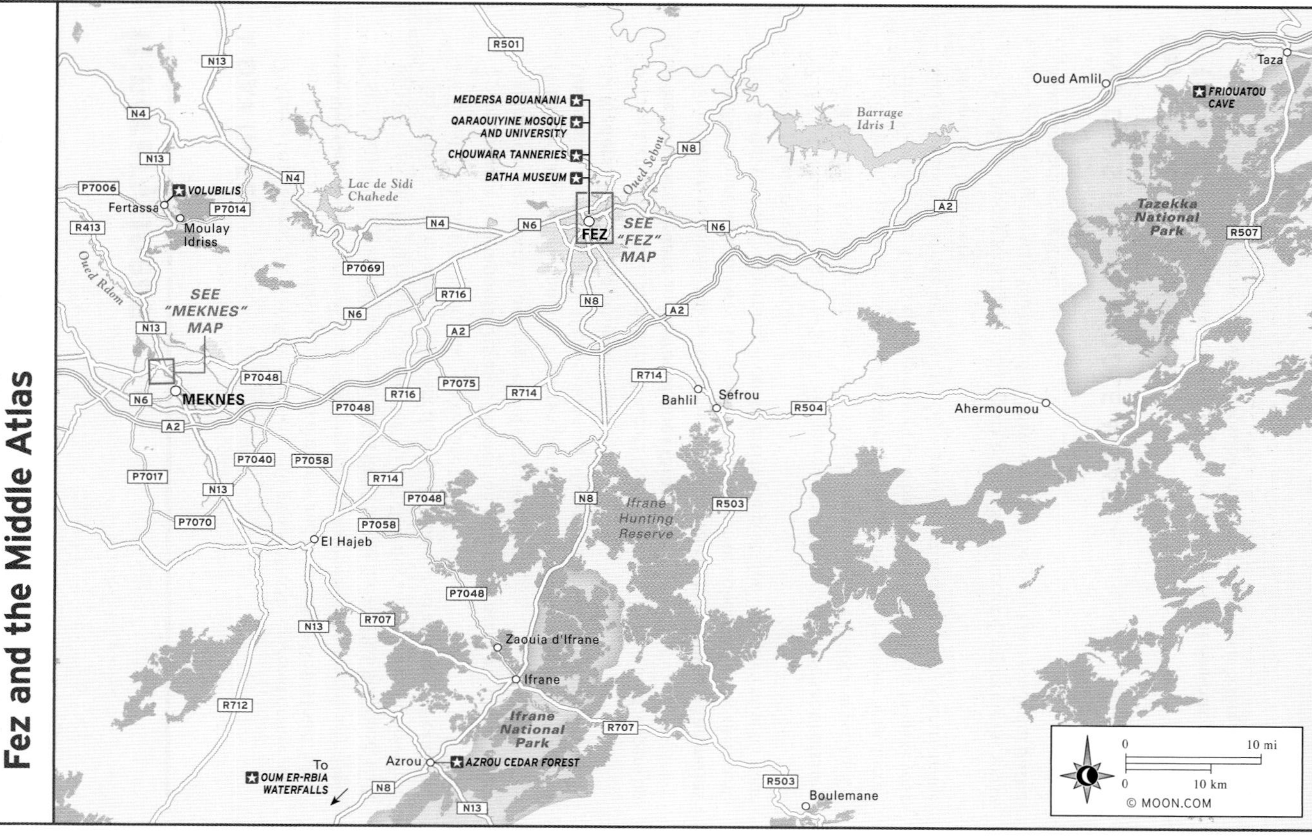

in the middle of **Ifrane National Park** is ideal. You can spend a few days backpacking through the park and then continue north into **Tazekka National Park**, dotted with villages and small rock homes whose families happily welcome visitors for a night.

Itinerary Ideas

A DAY IN FEZ

1 After a large Moroccan breakfast, complete with plenty of fresh-squeezed orange juice and coffee, wear your comfiest pair of walking shoes and head to **Bab Boujeloud,** a.k.a. the Blue Gate.

2 Start your morning walking tour down **Talâa Kebira.** Pass through Bab Boujeloud, walk past the cafes on the plaza, and look for a left turn. Follow this and take a right, downhill. Talaa Kebira is well-marked. If you walk through Bab Boujeloud and past the cafés and are forced to take a right, backtrack; you've gone too far.

3 Stop in at the **Bounanania Quranic School** (on your right, near Café Clock) before making your way downhill into the belly of the souks.

4 Follow Talâa Kebira until the T intersection. This is the **Qaraouyine Mosque and University** directly in front. If time allows and it's not too crowded, you could also visit the **Medersa El-Attarine** at this location.

5 Take a left at the T intersection (rue Rhabat l'Qais), following the path until it opens up at the **Seffarine Square** and **Qaraouiyine Library.**

6 From Seffarine Square, follow rue Chouara (to the right). The **Chouwara Tanneries** are a five-minute walk this way. The smell of tanneries can be unbearable in the afternoon. Even at this time in the morning, it can be pretty pungent. You'll be given mint for your nostrils to help block the smell.

7 For lunch, backtrack near the Seffarine Square and tuck into the **Elminchaoui *bissara* stand** on Place Aachabine for some hearty fava bean soup and a truly local experience.

8 After lunch, make your way to the **Nejjarine Museum** and spend an hour or so discovering the woodcrafts. This is also a good spot for a bathroom break. Be sure to make your way to the rooftop terrace for an incredible view over Fez and the nearby Qararouiyine Mosque and University.

9 Finish up the day walking up Talla Sghira back to Bab Boujeloud, exploring the souks and shops along the way. You should still have enough time to visit the wonderful **Batha Museum** before nightfall.

TWO DAYS IN THE MIDDLE ATLAS

Day 1: Volubilis and Meknes

1 The Roman ruin of **Volubilis,** your first stop today, is exposed to the elements, including the sun. You'll want to arrive as early as possible in the morning to tour before the harsh

A Day in Fez

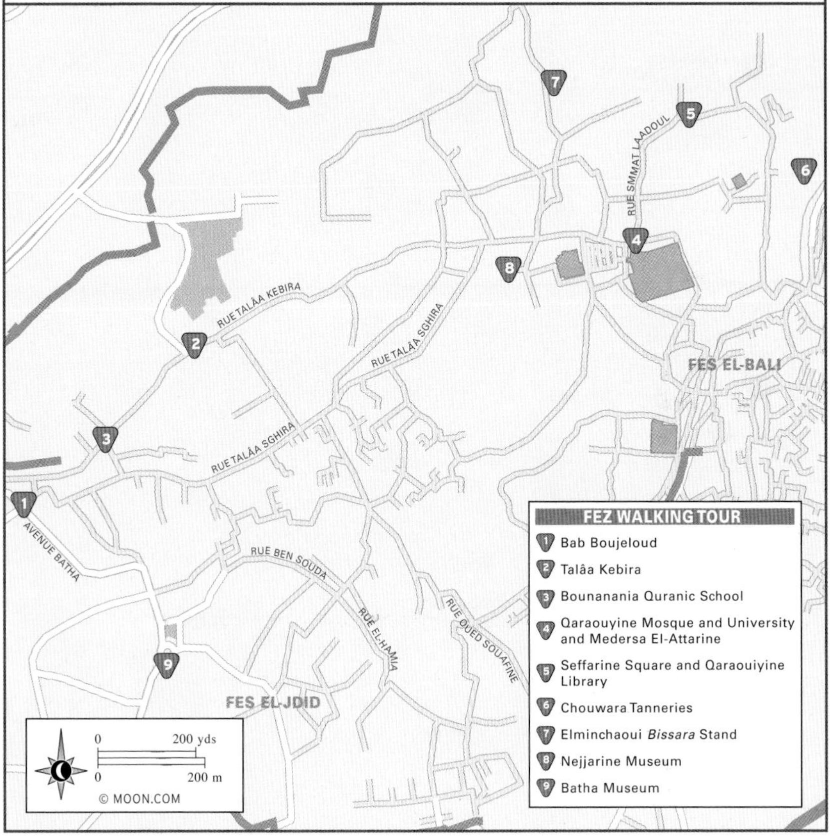

RUE TALÂA KEBIRA
RUE TALÂA SGHIRA
RUE TALÂA SGHIRA
RUE SMMAT LAADOUL
FES EL-BALI
AVENUE BATHA
RUE BEN SOUDA
RUE EL-HAMIA
RUE OUED SOUAFINE
FES EL-JDID
0 200 yds
0 200 m
© MOON.COM
FEZ WALKING TOUR
1 Bab Boujeloud
2 Talâa Kebira
3 Bounanania Quranic School
4 Qaraouyine Mosque and University and Medersa El-Attarine
5 Seffarine Square and Qaraouiyine Library
6 Chouwara Tanneries
7 Elminchaoui *Bissara* Stand
8 Nejjarine Museum
9 Batha Museum

afternoon sun hits the hilltop. Plan on spending a minimum of one hour here, though 2-3 hours is more likely. The ruins of this once great city leave plenty to explore, from weather-worn mosaics to sculpted ornamental stonework.

2 Head to **Meknes,** about an hour away. Have a porter from your accommodation meet you at the square and check into your lodging in Meknes for the night.

3 Eat lunch out on the main square before diving into the less-toursited **medina** of Meknes. The markets here are typically less expensive than nearby Fez, making for relative bargains, while the medina itself is calmer and a truly local experience. Be sure to visit the **Medrasa Bouanania Quranic School** in the medina. Head to the rooftop terrace for stunning views over Meknes.

Two Days in the Middle Atlas

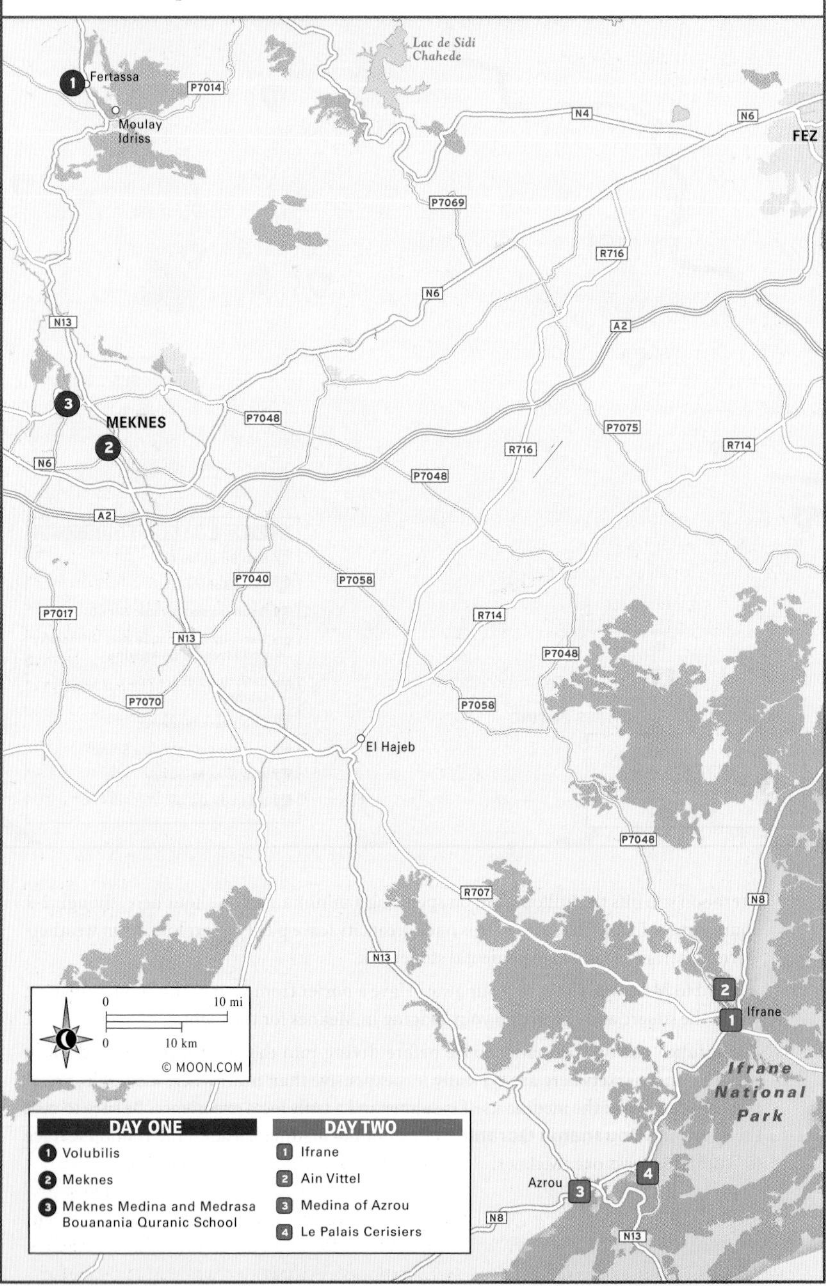

Day 2: Ifrane and Azrou

1 Head to **Ifrane,** about an hour drive, where you'll park in "centre ville" and have lunch at one of the restaurants off the main square.

2 After lunch, walk around the local parks or drive down to **Ain Vittel** for some hiking through the cedar forests and small waterfalls.

3 In the late afternoon, head down the mountain to **Azrou,** about a 30-minute drive, and check into your lodging. The **medina** of Azrou is one of the best places for bargain shopping. Peruse the local bazaars and consider getting a souvenir.

4 For dinner, drive up to **Le Palais Cerisiers,** just outside of Azrou alongside the road to Ifrane, for one of the finest mountain meals you'll ever find.

Fez

فاس

There is nowhere else in the world quite like Fez. There is something mystical about entering into the labyrinthine old city, walking its shadowy pedestrian paths, wandering in the cool early mornings through the souks surrounding the Qaraouiyine Mosque, ducking into a quiet café for a break from the crowd, and catching your breath as the muezzin's call to the faithful seems to break the heat of the sudden afternoon. Most travelers will lose themselves at least a couple of times in this city. Don't panic. It's all part of the experience.

The history of Fez (often spelled Fès or Fes) is full of war and art. For nearly a thousand years, it was the primary cultural, religious, and political hub of Morocco. Fez was founded by Moulay Idriss I as Medinat Fas in AD 789. One of the great stories of the founding of Fez is that Moulay Idriss I threw his *fez* (the Arabic word for "axe") into the river, and where the axe struck, he declared the city founded. The city was then aptly named for this *fez*. Though this story is entertaining, it's likely more myth than anything else.

Until 1070, Madinat Fas and sister settlement Al-'Aliya across the river were rivals, fighting until both settlements were conquered by the Almoravids and united under the name Fez, though the capital was moved to Marrakesh. Under the Almohad empire at the beginning of the 13th century, the old city walls of Medinat Fas and Al-'Aliya were destroyed, bridges were built over the river, and new walls were constructed joining the cities. These walls form the outline of today's Fès el-Bali, the old medina. During this time, Fez became a cultural hub under the leadership of the second Almohad ruler, Ibn Tashfin, and Andalusians sought refuge in the city, thus endowing it with certain architectural and cultural traits often associated with Moorish Spain. By 1170, Fez was the largest city in the world, with an estimated 200,000 inhabitants. An important trading hub serving Europe and Africa, it was on the gold route from Timbuktu, and its famous tanneries were known for producing fine *al-Daraqeen* (leather shields).

In 1250, the Merenid dynasty had displaced the Almohads and taken firm control of Morocco. They reinstated Fez as the capital. In 1276, they founded Fès el-Jdid, the new medina, and made it an important military and administrative center. During this era, Fez's reputation as an intellectual center continued to grow. Seven schools (*medersas*) were built, and, architecturally, the "Fassi" style, a mix of Andalusian and Almohad traditions, was born, of which the Bouanania and el-Attarine *medersas* are excellent examples.

Through the next few centuries, Fez was largely a contested city throughout the Wattasid, Ottoman, and Saïdian dynasties, though it remained an important hub for trade and cultural and intellectual pursuits. Fez was also the home of a special sort of nationalism and violently rebelled against the emir in the 19th and 20th centuries. It was the capital until 1925 when, under the French protectorate, the capital was moved to Rabat, where it remains today.

The Ville Nouvelle outside the old Almohad walls of the old city was built during the French protectorate from 1912 to 1956. Originally, it housed French administration and military. Today, this is where most of the one million or so people in Fez live, in more modern apartments and housing developments.

Because of the medieval medina's uniqueness among world destinations and the palace's connections with the city (the king's wife is from Fez), today's Fez has been affected by tourism, with people speaking more English and signs advertising Coca-Cola dotted throughout the medina. But it retains much of its storied past within its mudbrick walls.

ORIENTATION

Fez lies at the foot of the Middle Atlas mountain range, about 300 kilometers (186mi) from Casablanca and 200 kilometers (125mi) from the Atlantic Coast of Rabat. The city is divided into three main sections: the **old medina (Fès el-Bali),** the **new medina (Fès el-Jdid),** and the **Ville Nouvelle.** You will want to spend most of your time in the old medina, as this is where most of the sights and sounds are, though there are a few things of interest in other parts of Fez.

The entirety of the old medina of **Fès el-Bali** is surrounded by a giant wall that has largely existed since the Almohad empire in the 13th century. The streets here are winding and you will likely get lost. There are few real street signs, and not many people use the names of streets. You are best off navigating the medina by the newly placed colored signs that lead to different points of interest, though even these will likely confuse you. The two main thoroughfares, Talâa Kbira and Talâa Sghira, begin at the Bab Boujeloud, the western gate of the medina, dividing into two roads that meet again near the Henna Souk and the Qaraouiyine Mosque and University in the middle of the medina.

Outside of the old medina is another medina by the name of **Fès el-Jdid** (which translates as "New Fez"). Built during the Merenid empire in the 13th century, this extension of Fez was the political and administrative hub. The streets here are longer and more straightforward. It holds the first Jewish ghetto (mellah) in Morocco, constructed in the 15th century, as well as the Jewish Cemetery, a few synagogues, and the **royal palace.**

As in most Moroccan cities, under the French protectorate period a *ville nouvelle,* or "new city," appeared alongside the older Moroccan city. Fez's **Ville Nouvelle** lies a few kilometers to the southwest of the old medina, beyond Fès el-Jdid and the Louaririyine Forest. Here is where most Fassis live today, in modern apartment complexes and villas built of brick and cement. Visitors will likely not spend a lot of time in the Ville Nouvelle, though there are several restaurants and cultural events that may be of interest, and of course the transportation hubs are all located in and around this area. Avenue Hassan II is a main thoroughfare that provides plenty of people-watching in nicer weather, especially just after sunset, with lots of small cafés and restaurants. The N6 and N8 lead directly out to the tolled autoroute (A2), marked by large blue billboards with directions leading toward Oujda (northeast) and Rabat (southwest).

About an hour by car or train (70km/43mi) to the west of Fez lies the great imperial city of Meknes, making a day trip a possibility. Direct train runs every hour or so to Meknes. The ruins of Volubilis and Moulay Idriss, also west of Fez (64km/40mi), are best visited in a combined day trip by hired taxi or car.

The primary road leading south from Fez is the N8, which takes you into Ifrane, Azrou, and the heart of the Middle Atlas mountain range before continuing onto Marrakesh. At Azrou, most travelers will want to change

Fez

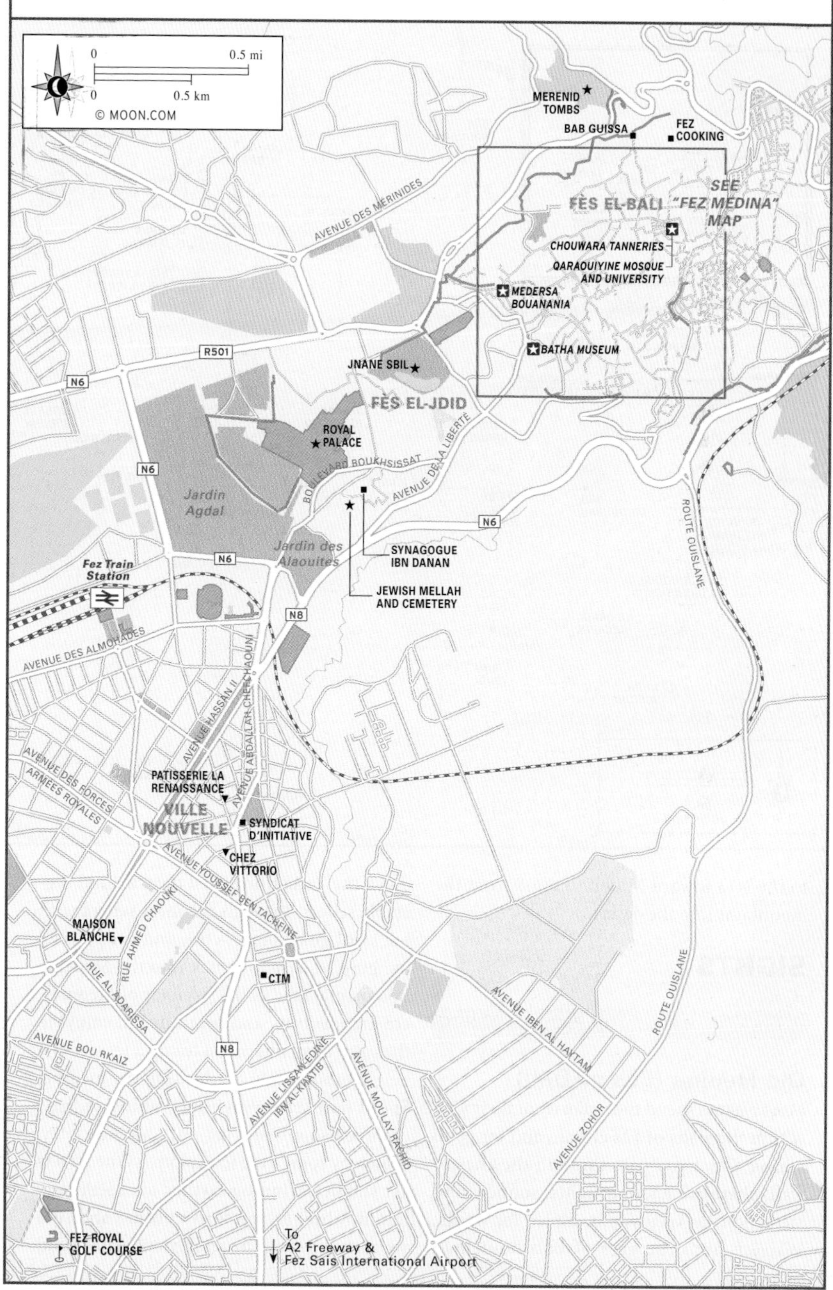
0
0.5 mi
0
0.5 km
© MOON.COM
MERENID
TOMBS
BAB GUISSA
FEZ
COOKING
SEE
"FEZ MEDINA"
MAP
FÈS EL-BALI
CHOUWARA TANNERIES
QARAOUIYINE MOSQUE
AND UNIVERSITY
MEDERSA
BOUANANIA
BATHA MUSEUM
AVENUE DES MERINIDES
R501
N6
JNANE SBIL
FÈS EL-JDID
ROYAL
PALACE
BOULEVARD BOUKHSISSAT
AVENUE DE LA LIBERTÉ
Jardin
Agdal
Jardin des
Alaouites
SYNAGOGUE
IBN DANAN
JEWISH MELLAH
AND CEMETERY
ROUTE OUISLANE
Fez Train
Station
N8
AVENUE DES ALMOHADES
AVENUE HASSAN II
AVENUE ABDALLAH CHEFCHAOUNI
AVENUE DES FORCES
ARMEES ROYALES
PATISSERIE LA
RENAISSANCE
VILLE
NOUVELLE
SYNDICAT
D'INITIATIVE
AVENUE YOUSSEF BEN TACHFINE
CHEZ
VITTORIO
MAISON
BLANCHE
RUE AHMED CHAOUKI
RUE AL ADARISSA
CTM
AVENUE BOU RKAIZ
AVENUE IBEN AL HAYTAM
AVENUE LISSAN EDINE
IBN AL KHATIB
AVENUE MOULAY RACHID
AVENUE ZOHOR
FEZ ROYAL
GOLF COURSE
To
A2 Freeway &
Fez Sais International Airport

Fez Medina

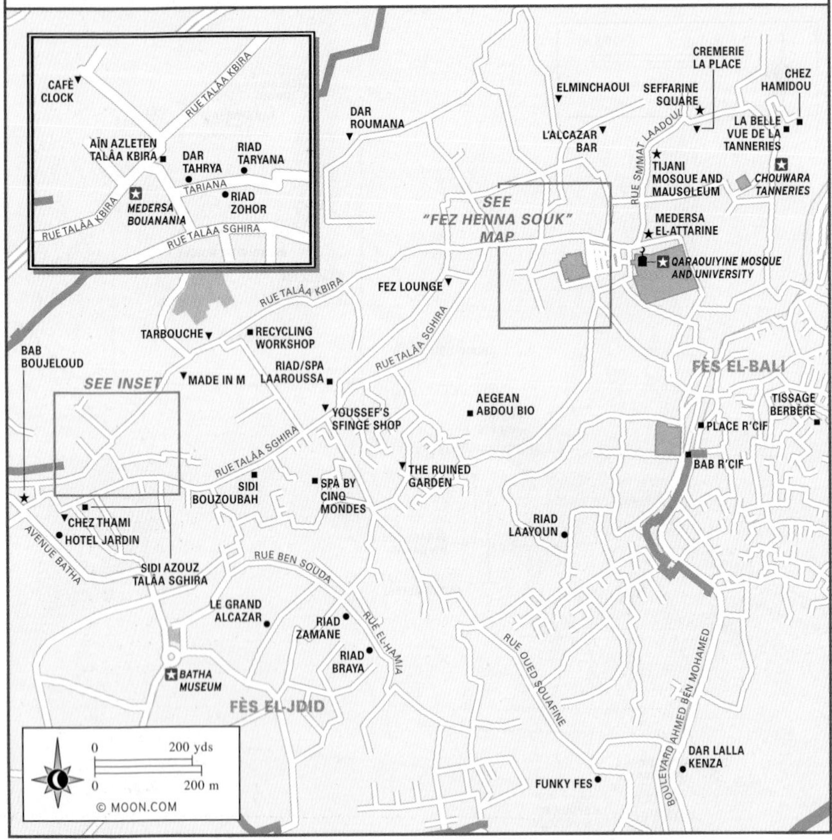

to the N13 toward Midelt to cross from the mountains into the desert.

SIGHTS

TOP EXPERIENCE

Old Medina (Fès el-Bali)

Most visitors spend the majority of their visit within the walls of Fès el-Bali, and for good reason. Once you pass through the ancient walls there are enough sights, sounds, and attractions to keep you occupied for weeks. Wander from the gate of Bab Boujeloud down the Talâa Kbira, past the fruit and vegetable sellers, through the meat sellers with hocks of goat, sheep, cow, and even camel hanging on display. Duck into the Medersa Bouanania, take in the splendor of Merenid-era architecture, and continue on, enjoying the calm of an afternoon tea on a terrace at a neighborhood café overlooking the medina. Speed past sellers inviting you inside their cramped shops, and get lost on a side alley, drawn by some urge to explore, as the streets get smaller, winding farther on, seemingly into nowhere as you turn a corner and find yourself inhaling the freshly cut cedarwood

Mosque Basics

Arabic script of praise and allegiance runs around the Medersa Bouanania.

The early morning call to prayer, *fajr*, is the first of **five calls to prayer** sung daily, the others being *dhohr, a'sr, maghreb,* and *a'sha*. The **muezzin** is the man responsible for calling the faithful to prayer, and it is his voice you hear. In Fez, there are more than 100 functioning mosques spread throughout Fès el-Bali, so the call to prayer becomes a chorus you will hear five times a day.

The most well-known mosques are the Qaraouiyine Mosque and the Tijani Mosque, though you will see several more impressive mosques along your walk through the medina. Often, there will be young men at the door to stop non-Muslims from entering. This rule was actually established by the French, though today Moroccans hold fast to this regulation.

The basic mosque construction contains a **fountain** in a courtyard near the entry to perform ablutions. Next to this is a series of **covered arches** that orient the faithful toward the **qiblah,** the direction of Mecca. The **mihrab,** a small notch from which the imam delivers the **khutbah,** his speech, is always located on the qiblah end of the covered arches. The **minaret,** usually square in form in Morocco, towers above it all, and it's from here that the muezzin traditionally delivers his call to the faithful five times a day.

Non-Muslims should be sure to stop in at the beautifully restored Medersa Bouanania while in Fez. This is the only *medersa* with a minaret in Morocco, and you can get a very good idea of the basic mosque construction from a religious building that is currently in use. Non-Muslims will not be able to visit any other mosques in Fez, though the Hassan II Mosque in Casablanca and the Tin Mal Mosque in the High Atlas remain open to visitors.

of the Nejjarine Souk, where carpenters are putting together gaudy wedding chairs and banquettes. Remember that in the old medina of Fez, getting lost is half the fun.

For most visitors, the **Bab Boujeloud,** on the western edge of the old medina, is their first entrance into Fès el-Bali. Nicknamed the "Blue Gate," this is one of the newest gates of the medina (only the Bab Jdid is newer). The gate was built in 1913 at the beginning of the French protectorate and features blue *zellij* tile work on the outside and mirrored green *zellij* on the inside—blue is the color of the city of Fez, and green is the color of Islam. This is a very handy meeting place, a must-shoot for photos, and a great landmark for directions.

★ MEDERSA BOUANANIA

Meknes Medina; daily 5:30am-10pm, depending on prayer time; 10Dh, free entry to Muslims for Friday prayer

Enter the medina through Bab Boujeloud and follow the road to the left, past a group of cafés, onto the Talâa Kbira. Just a short walk through the food stalls and across from the Dar al-Magana, a water-run hydraulic clock, lies the Medersa Bouanania, the most impressive *medersa* in all of Morocco. Ornate 14th-century Merenid-era architecture appears in every facet of the construction, from the intricately carved cedar work (an exquisite example of the Moroccan *laceria,* or knot carpentry) to the marble floors of the courtyard. Note also the play of air and light reflected in the *zellij* work, which itself is separated from the stucco by elaborate Kufic script (a Moroccan style of calligraphy). Somewhat surprisingly, this script is a list of endowments given for the building of the *medersa* and not Quranic script.

The *medersa* was first constructed under the leadership of the Sultan Bou Inan and finished in 1357. More recently, the *medersa* underwent a nine-year restoration project from 1995 to 2004 with the help of local artisans following the original design of the *medersa.* The result is something truly spectacular. With its minaret clearly visible through the arches of Bab Boujeloud, this is one of the very few actively used religious buildings non-Muslims are able to visit in Morocco, and well worth the stop for any visitor to Fez.

★ QARAOUIYINE MOSQUE AND UNIVERSITY

The Qaraouiyine Mosque and University (pronounced "kare-a-ween") complex is something to behold and, for non-Muslims, will likely remain a mystery. One of the main doors is at the end of the Talâa Kbira, where visitors can glimpse at the vast courtyard inside, something that somehow doesn't quite reflect the huge size of this complex. Muslims are welcomed inside for prayer and to visit the university grounds, though sometimes classes are in session. More often than not, one of the worshippers will be happy to lead Muslim visitors around to show them the wonders of this truly marvelous structure.

The mosque and university were founded in 857 by Fatima al-Fihri, the daughter of a wealthy refugee from Kairouan, Tunisia. The mosque has undergone several renovations and expansions. The largest expansion came in the 12th century under the Almoravids, who expanded the prayer halls and footprint of the mosque to hold 22,000 worshippers. The adjacent University of al-Qaraouiyine is sometimes referred to as the oldest university in the world, though it was not officially granted university status until joining Morocco's educational state system in 1963. Originally, the University of al-Qaraouiyine was a *medersa,* founded with the adjacent mosque, and is recognized as the world's oldest continually operating educational facility by UNESCO.

MEDERSA EL-ATTARINE

rue Rhabt l'Qais; daily 5:30am-10pm, depending on prayer times; 10Dh

If you are arriving to the Qaraouiyine Mosque from the Talâa Kbira, take a left directly in front of the Qaraouiyine complex and walk for a few yards until you come to the Medersa el-Attarine. Though slightly less impressive in stature than the Bouanania, the el-Attarine is well worth a visit. The ornate stucco work mingles with carved cedarwood and elaborate *zellij* work every bit as wonderful as at the Bouanania. This *medersa* was home to many visiting scholars and students of the Qaraouiyine University next door. You can still visit their tiny rooms surrounding the courtyard, which may make you appreciate the size of your college dorm room a bit more. If the door to the terrace is open, glimpses of the courtyard in the Qaraouiyine complex are well worth peeking in. Like nearly all

1: the restored Medersa Bouanania **2:** the Qaraouiyine Mosque and University

1
2

mosques in Morocco, this remains closed to non-Muslims.

TIJANI MOSQUE AND MAUSOLEUM

Continue from the Medersa el-Attarine down toward Seffarine Square to arrive at the Tijani Mosque and Mausoleum, which houses the tomb of Sidi Ahmed al-Tijani (1735-1815), a venerated saint and founder of the Tijaniyya Sufi order. Sidi Tijani was born in Algeria and welcomed to Morocco by the Sultan Moulay Sliman in 1796. Sidi Tijani was responsible for spreading the message of Islam throughout West Africa and Sub-Saharan Africa, particularly modern-day Mali, Nigeria, and Senegal. Many pilgrims from these countries make the journey, often on their way to Mecca, to give thanks, to pray, to read the Quran, and to take part in *dikr,* the night-long chanting of suras from the Quran and other religious songs. Like the Mausoleum of Moulay Idriss II, this is closed to non-Muslims, though the 18th-century entrance is something to be admired on your way to Seffarine Square.

SEFFARINE SQUARE

You'll hear the pounding of dozens of hammers on metal before you arrive to Seffarine Square. Though the nearby school of coppersmiths is under repair with no end date in sight, coppersmiths still hammer metals in the square, and a few shops are worth checking out. Most visitors will want to continue on their tour after taking a photo or two.

★ CHOUWARA TANNERIES

Rue Chouwara; 10-20Dh

The Chouwara tanneries are one of the most spectacular sights of the medina and are difficult to miss. Between the faux guides continually trying to show you the way and the smell, trust that you will get there.

A few leather-good shops just outside the tanneries will allow you onto their balcony and give you mint to plug into your nose, though you will almost assuredly be pressured to buy something in exchange for the view. It is a fair tradeoff for the bird's-eye view to witness a process that hasn't changed much since the 16th century. The leather is first cured in vats of pigeon dung, and then the hides are laid out in the sun to dry and cure. Water pours through the tanneries and men shuffle from one colorful vat to another. The system here is family run, with families inheriting and passing on skills and materials from one generation to another.

There has been one change visitors should

the famous Chouwara Tanneries

know: The dyes used for the leather were once vegetable-based, using antimony (black), indigo (blue), mint (green), poppy (red), and turmeric (yellow). However, in recent years these have all been replaced with chemical dyes. The workers' health has suffered with this change.

If a guide, typically a young boy, takes you, it is appropriate to give them 5-10Dh in exchange for their service, though they will inevitably ask for more. Be wary of guides trying to take you to the smaller Guéliz tanneries and not the larger Chouwara tanneries.

It is possible to go into the tanneries. If you stand by the door, someone will offer to take you in for 10-20Dh, though you must wear good shoes and take some mint to plug into your nostrils to guard against the powerful smell.

MERENID TOMBS

off Ave. des Merenides, just outside the medina walls to the north; free

Watching over the city in glorious ruin are the Merenid Tombs, on the northern hillside overlooking the old medina. These are best visited at dusk, when the sun sets behind you, lighting Fez in golds and greens. From here, you can make out the many monuments of Fez, the minarets of the mosques, the green pyramid roofs of the Qaraouiyine complex and the Mausoleum of Moulay Idriss II. On either side of the old medina you can see the cemeteries crawl up the slopes of the hills, and on a clear night you can make out the distant outline of the Middle Atlas mountains.

The massive, crumbling tombs date from the 13th-century Merenid era, and it is thought that royalty or some other persons of importance are buried here, though nobody knows for certain. What is certain is that the views are stellar.

The tombs are best reached by *petit taxi.* The closest is through **Bab Guissa** near Seffarine Square. The taxi should cost around 5Dh, but you should pay extra to have the taxi wait so you can enjoy the view and not worry about walking back to the medina after dark. The walk between the tombs and the medina, though relatively short, is dangerous and muggings have occurred here, during both day and night.

Around Henna Souk

MAUSOLEUM OF MOULAY IDRISS II

Nearby the Qaraouiyine Mosque and University lies the Mausoleum of Moulay Idriss II, a *zawiya* dedicated to the son of Moulay Idriss I. Many Fassis consider the Idriss II to be the founder of today's Fez. The gaudy Alawi-style mausoleum was finished in 1824, though it has been newly renovated with local artisans contributing to the vast majority of restoration. Elaborate traditional wood, tile, and stucco work colorfully adorns the walls, inside and out. Many pilgrims stop here to pray for good fortune, and many women pray for fertility, making this a popular visit for Muslims. Though non-Muslims are not permitted inside, the facade and environs make this a must-see stop on your way through the old medina. Past the stalls of candy, fruit, nut, and candle sellers is a small slit in the wall where you can place a donation to help the mausoleum with its expensive upkeep.

NEJJARINE MUSEUM OF WOOD ARTS AND CRAFTS

Pl. Nejjarine; tel. 0535/740 580; daily 10am-7pm except holidays; 20Dh admission, 10Dh for drink on terrace

In Nejjarine Square (the carpenters' square near the Nejjarine Souk, famous for its woodcrafts and ornate wedding chairs) you will find a renovated caravanserai, once a stopping place for horses and traders, transformed into the well-kept Nejjarine Museum (Musée Nejjarine). On display here are 14th- to 18th-century ornately carved cedar doors, chairs, tables, and other furniture, as well as some jewelry, chests, and daggers. Half of the charm is the building itself. The renovated caravanserai, with its indoor courtyard and period-specific tile work, makes for an interesting diversion, particularly to break a hot afternoon. Also of note: The bathrooms here

1
2
3
4

are nicer than usual and free to use with admission. Make sure you head up to the terrace and take in the panoramic view of Fez!

New Medina (Fès el-Jdid)

The "new" medina of Fez, Fès el-Jdid, founded in the 13th century, is surprisingly easy to walk around, with sidewalks and wider streets. Notably, this area housed the first Jewish Quarter (mellah) in Morocco, though today the area is predominantly Muslim with nearly all the Jewish inhabitants having moved to the Ville Nouvelle, Casablanca, or farther afield (France, Israel, or the United States). The Fez mellah is one of the best preserved and most atmospheric in Morocco, with balconies that look out onto the street, jewelry shops, a wonderful cemetery, and a fine synagogue.

From Fès el-Bali, the easiest access point for Fès el-Jdid is to exit from Bab Boujeloud. Then continue on foot to the Batha Museum or head straight across the parking lot to the Jnane Sbil Gardens. From **Bab R'cif** or **Bab Ftouh,** take a short taxi ride to Bab Boujeloud or directly to the Batha Museum and continue from there.

★ BATHA MUSEUM

Pl. de l'Istiqlal; tel. 0535/634 116; Wed.-Mon. 9am-5pm, closed holidays; 10Dh

Just a short walk from the Bab Boujeloud, the Batha Museum (Musée Dar el-Batha) is one of the more impressive buildings in Fez. This former 19th-century palace has been fully restored and houses some wonderful period pieces of Moroccan arts and crafts dating back over eight centuries. The artisan work on display includes ornate wood furniture, wrought-iron tables, embroidery, jewelry, a surprisingly holistic collection of astrolabes, and, of course, elaborate carpets. There are also stucco sculptures and a large collection of pre-20th-century coins.

Pay special attention to the collection of Fassi pottery dating from the 14th century. Note the traditional "Fez blue" cobalt color that is unique to the pottery from this region. The process to obtain the glaze for this color was discovered here in the 10th century, and the color has become emblematic of Fez, as evidenced by the iconic blue gate of Bab Boujeloud. The patterns on the displayed pottery are largely intricate floral patterns of various blue shades overlaid on a white enamel background.

The true highlight of the Batha Museum is the museum itself, with its inspired tile work, ornate courtyards, and lush central garden enveloped by a giant holm oak that helps to cool down visitors after a long stroll through the medina. Because of its popularity, the museum is best visited shortly after opening or an hour or so before closing. Public bathrooms are available, though you should pack your own toilet paper just to be on the safe side.

JNANE SBIL GARDENS

Ave. de l'UNESCO; daily sunrise-sunset; free

Just beyond the Bab Boujeloud, across the parking lot and through the gate straight ahead (the left-most gate), you will pass through another gate, typically busy with crossing traffic. There, across the street on your left, lie the pleasant, well-shaded Jnane Sbil Gardens (Jardin Jnane Sbil), formerly known as the Boujeloud Gardens, a name locals still sometimes use. Renovated in 2010 with extreme detail paid to its original 19th-century planning, the 7.5-hectare (18-acre) garden has recently been replanted with a wide range of vegetation, bamboo, papyrus, eucalyptus, palms, weeping willows, roses, cacti, and ferns. With a large pond and many fountains, the garden offers a relaxing stroll through a veritable paradise. An old, non-functioning waterwheel stands testament to how the medina was once powered by the water from the local rivers. A well-maintained public toilet is near the center of the park (2Dh or more for gratuity).

1: Two women walk beneath wood beams that support many walls. **2:** a woman taking bread to the public oven **3:** the Attarine Quranic School (Medersa El Attarine) **4:** the Nejjarine Square

The Fez Sacred Music Festival

The city of Fez rings in the summer with the annual **Sacred Music Festival** (www.fesfestival.com), launched back in 1994. It was the first of its kind. Today, musicians descend on Fez from nearly every corner of the globe, as do the spectators, making this one of the most crowded, though joyous, times of the year to visit Fez. Though many of the city's landmarks are turned into stages for music, the Batha Museum is one of the more impressive venues, providing a backdrop that has complemented such performers as Ben Harper, Paco de Lucia, and Björk, as well as groups from Mali, Syria, France, Indonesia, India, and Cuba.

Begun as a means to highlight the more beautiful aspects of religions, the festival celebrates music and spirituality from around the world. It is thought by the organizers that music is a central part of our faiths, and as we share our music, we share our different faiths. Now, there are sacred music festivals found throughout the world based on the inclusive program developed in Fez.

JEWISH MELLAH AND CEMETERY

After a few days in Fès el-Bali, it is nice to wander through the Jewish mellah, where the streets are still winding but are wider, and balconies of curved wood and wrought iron face out over the street. Historically, the Jews were in charge of salting the heads of the beheaded prisoners of the sultans, and it is thought by some that this is where the term "mellah" (which is related to the Arabic word for salt) originated. The Jewish population was also protected by the sultans for their trade in precious metals. In the 14th century, when the Jews were forced to live in the mellah, they were told that it was for their protection from the larger Muslim population (purges were known to occur). However, their travel was strictly regulated. From the 14th to the 20th century, Jews were not allowed to leave the mellah without papers and, outside the mellah, were not allowed to wear shoes.

Within the mellah is the Jewish Cemetery (free, though faux guides will often ask for a token payment of 10Dh). There are nearly 13,000 Jews buried here, making for a small sea of tombs. The candles and pebbles found in the nooks of the tombs, and often on top of them, are evidence of them having been visited. The beautifully restored Slat Alfassiyine synagogue can be found at the cemetery. It has recently been converted into a museum (admission by donation). The nearby **Ibn Danan Synagogue** is also worth checking out. Both synagogues date back to the 17th century.

ENTERTAINMENT AND EVENTS

NATIONAL FESTIVAL OF ANDALUSIAN MUSIC

Feb./Mar.; free

The National Festival of Andalusian Music kicks off the festival calendar in February/March with a week-long focus on the history of Andalusian classical music, featuring performances by orchestras and other musical groups from throughout Morocco. Festival organizers also promote history and poetry of the Islamic period of Andalusia in a series of lectures (generally in French and Arabic). Check with your accommodations for details.

FESTIVAL OF SUFI MUSIC AND CULTURE

www.festivalculturesoufie.com; Apr.; free

In April, the Festival of Sufi Music and Culture focuses on the more cultural, spiritual, and mystic aspects of various forms of Sufi music for a few days. This successful festival was started in 2007. The popularity of this festival has grown, as have the entry fees to some of the shows and spectacles associated with it.

SACRED MUSIC FESTIVAL

www.fesfestival.com; May/June; free-250Dh

The largest of all these festivals in Fez is the world-renowned Sacred Music Festival, held every May/June. For a week, this festival brings together music from different religions around the world. Concert venues are spread throughout the city, with the more popular musicians entertaining crowds in the lush surroundings of the Batha Museum, though tickets are becoming pricy, with festival passes selling for more than 3,000Dh.

FESTIVAL OF AMAZIGH CULTURE

July/Aug.; free

The festival calendar ends with the Festival of Amazigh Culture in late July/early August. There are numerous free concerts, and the festival is well worth a stop to learn more about the history, culture, and traditions of the Amazigh tribes spread throughout Morocco. Check with your accommodation for details.

SHOPPING

The Fez medina offers countless shops, vendors, and so-called cooperatives. The two main streets, **Talâa Kbira** and **Talâa Sghira**, offer shops with leather goods, pottery, carpets, jewelry, spices, and essential oils. A popular saying goes "not everything that sparkles in Fez is made of gold"—something to keep in mind as you shop for souvenirs and gifts. Often, you will have to be patient to arrive at an agreeable price. The Fassi storekeepers are expert hagglers. If you don't want to bargain, it's best to stick to the few stores with posted prices.

Besides the two main streets, there are several popular **souks.** Historically, these were divided by trade, though today many of the souks have a variety of sellers. Local trades include woodwork, *babouches* (slippers), silver jewelry, tailored clothing, leatherwork, pottery, mosaic tiling, brass and copperware, cotton and silk weaving, and drums.

Try the **sweet sellers** lining the streets outside the Mausoleum of Moulay Idriss II, where 10Dh buys a delicious mix of Spanish-style *torreon* (a type of nougat) as well as roasted sesame seeds, peanuts, and almonds to take home or as a quick pick-me-up on the go.

For an idea of prices for traditional goods, such as carpets and pottery, you can visit the government-run **Centre Artisanal** (Ave. Allal Ben Abdallah, tel. 0535/621 007, daily 9am-12:30pm and 2:30pm-6:30pm), where prices are fixed. Though often the fixed prices are a touch more expensive than the "local" price, it will still give you an idea of the going rate for certain items.

RECYCLING WORKSHOP

Talâa Kbira, near Made in M; Sat.-Thurs. 10am-8pm

Along the Talâa Kbira you can find the Recycling Workshop on the right, a few minutes walking downhill from the Medersa Bouanania, where Hasna creates bags, clutches, and jewelry from recycled rubber from tires and innertubes. This is a unique project in Morocco, and the prices are posted and reasonable. A must-shop for the fashion-forward and eco-conscious.

SIDI BOUZOUBAH

Talâa Sghira, near the tombstone chiselers; Sat.-Thurs. 10am-8pm

On the Talâa Sghira near the tombstone chiselers, Sidi Bouzoubah offers hand-woven baskets from 10Dh on up. These baskets make wonderful containers for gift selections of spices, herbs, soaps, and essential oils you can pick up farther down in the medina.

Tanneries and Leather

The tanneries are big business for the medina. Cow, goat, sheep, and camel are all used to make leather, with camel being the most expensive. Quality is sometimes an issue, but the bags and cushions are mostly well made. Jackets are rarely treated for water and will not usually "bead" like similar jackets in the United States, Canada, or Europe.

It is difficult to get a fair price at most of the tanneries and shops in the medina for leather goods, particularly around the Chouwara tanneries, because, as at any sight known for

1
2
3

tourism, prices tend to be steeper than usual. For those traveling to Rabat or a smaller local town, like Azrou, it might actually make more sense to do leather shopping there.

To give you an idea of decent prices in Fez, a large bag should cost around 500Dh, briefcases around 250Dh, handbags 150Dh or so, and embroidered ottomans 60Dh. You might pay a little more or less, depending on your haggling abilities and the type and quality of the leather.

LA BELLE VUE DE LA TANNERIES

64 Derb Sidi Bouaza Blidi Chouara; tel. 0535/637 950; Sat.-Thurs. 10am-9pm

One of the best selections in the medina, though for good prices you will have to bargain hard. There are several floors of leather bags, purses, clutches, and jackets. If you're in the market for leather goods, you could easily spend a couple of hours here just looking through their selection, which includes many different styles, cuts, colors, and treatments. If you have the time, you can even get custom-fitted for a new coat.

Spices and Essential Oils

Though it is being slowly transformed by numerous pottery sellers, the **Henna Souk,** with its large central plane tree, is still a pleasant shopping experience for henna, herbs, and spices. Most shops are open daily 9am-7pm but have shorter hours or are closed on Friday. Head to **Mohamed's Herb Shop** (tel. 0675/595 891 or 0649/653 623, Sat.-Thurs. 9am-7pm), the stall nearest to the old hospital Maristane Sidi Frej, to pick up your *rhassoul* (soap), dried herbs, traditional makeup, and natural products to help you create your own Moroccan hammam kit.

RACHID'S SPICE SHOP

Henna Souk; Sat.-Thurs. 9am-7pm

Also in the Henna Souk is Rachid's Spice Shop, where you can pick up quality spices, including saffron, cumin, and *ras el hanoot* (a spice blend), for great prices.

AEGEAN ABDOU BIO

148 Guerniz Sidi Moussa; tel. 0669/964 056; Sat.-Thurs. 9am-7pm

Aegean Abdou Bio features organic, eco-friendly, Moroccan-made cosmetics, spices, and essential oils, including products made from argan, and provides friendly, honest service. The shop can be difficult to find, though it's not a long walk from the Henna Souk. If you call ahead of time, someone can meet you and take you to the shop. Ask for Malika.

Pottery

In the Henna Souk you will also find pottery sellers, each with a small display in front and another, larger storage space.

CHEZ MOHAMED

Henna Souk; tel. 0674/012 700; Sat.-Thurs. 9am-7pm

The best option here is Chez Mohamed. Here you can learn about the different sorts of pottery from around Morocco, but you will likely want to stick with the gray clay pottery of Fez,

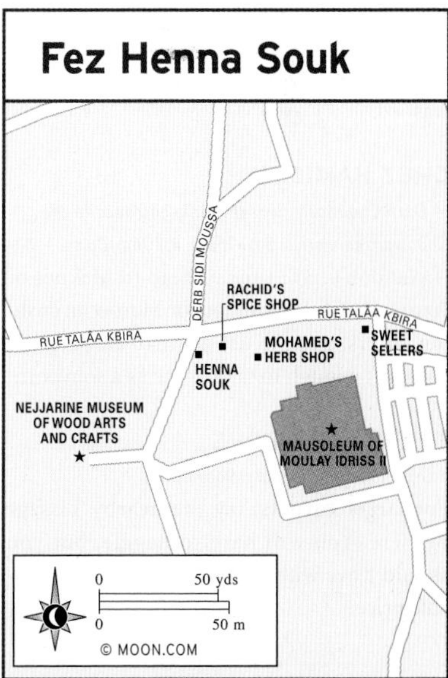

1: an artisans sews 2: along the Talâa Sghira in Fez
3: the peaceful Jnane Sbil Gardens

as it is quite a bit stronger and stands a better chance of arriving back home intact. Even better, you can order specialized pottery and have it shipped back directly to your home.

CHEZ HICHAM AND MEHDI

2 Henna Souk; Hicham tel. 0661/503 895, Mehdi tel. 0660/654 012; Sat.-Thurs. 9am-7pm

Just off the Talâa Kbira near the Souk el-Attarine, you'll often find two brothers who run Chez Hicham and Mehdi tending to their small shop. Stop in, say hi, and don't be alarmed when they take you through the maze of souk streets to their larger storage, where you can find well-priced souk goods in their bazaar.

Carpets and Rugs

Those serious about carpet shopping should stay away from buying carpets, rugs, and tapestries in Fez. Better prices with less hassle can be had in Rabat, Azrou, and Meknes. Carpet dealers will often tell you that carpets in these other cities are not the same quality, but unless you know your carpets, do not believe them. If a carpet seller tells you that the shiny fabric you're staring at is from "cactus silk," it is probably time to run for the door. "Cactus silk" is the local slang for "rayon" and the color will fade quickly and will bleed if washed.

CHEZ HAMIDOU

14 Derb Chouwara, near the main entrance to the Chouwara tanneries; Sat.-Thurs. 8:30am-6pm

If you don't have time to head to Meknes or Azrou, try Chez Hamidou for Moroccan cushion covers, great to use as small carpets and compact enough to take home as a souvenir.

TISSAGE BERBÈRE

4 Derb Taouil; Sat.-Thurs. 9am-6pm

For larger carpets, try the nearby Tissage Berbère. You will have to haggle, but you should leave with a good piece for a reasonable price.

Antiques

ALI'S ART GALLERY

Riad Jouha; tel. 0535/633 022; aliartgallery@yahoo.com; Sat.-Thurs. 9:30am-6pm

There are countless antiques and faux-antiques stores in the medina. For one of the more reputable ones, head to Ali's Art Gallery. It is best to call ahead to make sure they are open.

SPORTS AND RECREATION

Golf

FEZ ROYAL GOLF COURSE

Km17, Route d'Imouzzer; tel. 0535/665 006; fesgolf@menara.ma

The 18-hole Fez Royal Golf Course is an open, though challenging, par 72 course designed by renowned architect Cabel Robinson. Tee times and prices are best reserved through your accommodation. Expect to pay 400Dh or more for greens fees.

Hammams and Spas

There are basically two options for hammams and spas in the medina: traditional hammams and more upscale options. Although getting freshened up at one of the local hammams is a great experience, some visitors, particularly traveling couples, might feel more comfortable in the more upscale options, as all of the traditional hammams in the medina keep separate hours for men and women, and most of the upscale hammams offer couples' sessions.

AÏN AZLETEN TALÂA KEBIRA

Medersa Bouanania; men daily 6am-12:30pm, women daily noon-8pm; 15Dh

One of the more popular local hammams is near the Medersa Bouanania. Because of its proximity to many of the boutique hotels and *riads* dotting the Talla Kebira, this is a good choice for most travelers to stick close to their home base while experience this local bathing ritual. Scrubs (20Dh) and massages (50Dh) are available. Just ask the attendant greeting you as you arrive or the person supervising the bathing areas.

TOP EXPERIENCE

How to Hammam Like a Local

To bathe like the locals, head to one of the many inexpensive hammams (Moroccan baths, generally 10Dh) spread throughout the old medina. For just a few dirhams, you can take part in the bathing ritual and be part of a real cultural experience. You will want to come prepared with the following:

- flip-flops or sandals
- a plastic bucket
- a cup (traditionally this would be brass, but any cup will do)
- a towel
- a *kis* (the scrubbing glove)
- *savon bildi* (black soap)
- *rhassoul* (clay soap)
- shampoo
- conditioner
- shower gel or soap bar
- something to cover your lower half (bathing suit or underwear, though keep in mind they might get stained if you're going to have henna applied or might get stretched out because of the steam)
- a clean change of clothes
- an orange to eat while you are relaxing in the cooling room before you change into fresh clothes

The typical hammam consists of four rooms: changing room, cool room, warm room, and hot room. When you first enter the steamy confines of the hammam, you will strip down to your bathing suit or underwear and put your belongings in a cubicle in the changing room. Next, you can apply the *savon bildi* in the cool room and then head into the warm room, or go straight to the warm room, where you can rinse and scrub. Some people just head straight for the hot room and do everything there while they breathe in the steam. The basic idea is to gradually increase the temperature of the air and water as you go from room to room, while washing using your bucket and cup. Usually, there will be someone on hand in the changing room to lead you through the hammam ritual: soaping, rinsing, and exfoliating. They will also vigorously (if not violently) rub you down for a small charge of 40-50Dh. Most locals opt to do everything themselves, usually going with a friend or family member to have a chat while they are scrubbing down.

SIDI AZOUZ TALÂA SGHIRA

Talâa Sghira; men daily 6am-1pm and 10pm-2am, women daily 1pm-10pm; 13Dh

Near the Hotel Lamrani, this is another local favorite that is close to many of the popular *riads*. Though perhaps a touch dingy around the edges, that's part of the charm and, to be frank, part of the local experience. As all local hammams, you will want to come equipped with your own bathing goods. For a really hard massage that will get all the knots out, ask for Khadija (50Dh).

SPA LAAROUSSA

Derb Bechara, Talâa Sghira; tel. 0674/187 639; www.spalaaroussafez.com; daily noon-8pm; 330Dh spa or massage

In Riad Laaroussa, the Spa Laaroussa, a more upscale yet remarkably traditional hammam and spa, is guaranteed to make you feel like royalty. Choose from either a hammam featuring a body scrub with eucalyptus-infused black soap or a relaxing massage with essential oils. Reservations are recommended.

SPA BY CINQ MONDES

5 Derb Ben Slimane Zerbtana; tel. 0535/947 610 or 0535/741 206; www.riadfes.com; daily 8am-10pm by appointment; 400Dh

The Spa by Cinq Mondes in Riad Fez offers a thoroughly relaxing, high-end experience with specialized 50-minute massages for your back, face, or feet. Epilation is also available, though most will want to splurge on the traditional hammam, which includes black soap and olive oil.

Cooking Classes

The Fassis have a reputation throughout Morocco as being some of the best chefs in the country, and after a cooking course, it's easy to see why! Many *riads* now offer cooking classes for a reasonable price, and some offer this free for guests. Make sure to inquire with your reservation.

CAFÉ CLOCK

7 Derb El Magana; tel. 0535/637 855, fez@cafeclock.com; http://fez.cafeclock.com; 600Dh

Café Clock runs one of the more popular cooking courses, offering a range of traditional tajines, couscous, *pastillas* (meat pies), and salads to prepare. Classes begin with a tour of the souk, where the chef explains to you the different vegetables, meats, herbs, and spices you will purchase with seasonal recommendations.

FEZ COOKING

Riad Tafilalet, 17 Derb Miter Zenifor; tel. 0615/866 144; www.fescooking.com; 400-500Dh

A slightly less expensive alternative is Fez Cooking, where you begin with a trip to the local souk to pick your ingredients. Chef Lahcen Beqqi speaks English, French, Spanish, Tamazight, and Arabic, and explains why you soak your knife in orange blossom water before chopping dates and what is the freshest produce in the market. Vegetarians can make a vegetarian *pastilla*! For those wanting more of a culinary tour of Morocco, Lahcen can also arrange 7- to 10-day tours, from Fez to Marrakesh, where you prepare and sample cuisine from around the country.

FOOD

Fez is one of the better Moroccan cities for a sampling of street food. Most food in the medina is of the traditional variety, and outside of a few *riads*, there is no alcohol available. In the Ville Nouvelle there is a wider variety of dining options. Most accommodations in the medina include breakfast, and many have dinner available upon request.

Though the cafés around Bab Boujeloud are always ripe with entertainment of the people-watching variety, head down to the Place R'cif around sunset to take in a truly local experience. Children chase each other and women look on from the stadium-style seating.

In the Ville Nouvelle, stick to the Avenue Hassan II, where couples, young and old, stroll up and down this bustling center full of street vendors. There are numerous cafés facing the boulevard to choose from when you've had your fill of walking and want to sit and watch the spectacle unfold. If the local Fez soccer team has just won a big match, be prepared for a more raucous night than usual.

Medina

YOUSSEF'S SFINGE SHOP

corner of Talâa Sghira and Zkak Rouah; daily 7am-10am and 3pm-7pm

For **Moroccan donuts,** the perfect breakfast

food or afternoon high-calorie pick-me-up, head to Youssef's Sfinge Shop along Talâa Sghira on the corner with Zkak Rouah. It's a simple shop with two choices of Moroccan donuts: sugarered or unsugared. Donuts come with a simple paper cover and are meant to be eaten immediately. Be warned: If you come once, you'll likely come again, and again, and again. These donuts are addictive.

SNAIL STAND

Derb el Hora, daily, hours vary

If escargot is more your speed, check out the snail soup on offer daily at the Snail Stand on Derb el Hora. Snail soup is the Moroccan way to enjoy these squirmy delicacies. The soup is flavored with licorice, bay leaves, and the local spice blend, *ras al hanoot*, giving it a rich texture. On those surprisingly chilly days in Fez, this hits the spot.

CREMERIE LA PLACE

Pl. Seffarine; daily 8am-8pm; 25Dh

Take in the hammering of the copper workers of Seffarine Square with a freshly squeezed orange juice at Cremerie La Place. Food is available, but stick with the pastries.

CHEZ THAMI

near Bab Boujeloud at the head of the Talâa Sghira; daily 9am-10pm; 20-50Dh

This local favorite features the usual mix of salads and tajines, though the quality here is a notch better than the surrounding options. Behind Chez Thami is an old cinema, Cinema Boujeloud, that is no longer in use but worth peeking into.

CAFÉ CLOCK

7 Derb El Magana; tel. 0535/637 855; http://fez.cafeclock.com; daily 9am-10pm; 40-80Dh

This is a staple of the college and backpacker crowd. It features a laid-back atmosphere offering free Wi-Fi and the locally famous "Camel Burger." On Sunday nights, check out the calendar for live traditional Issawa, Gnawa, or Nomad Fusion music. Check the calendar online for details. This is a good place to meet fellow travelers, hang with a few liberal locals, and enjoy a meal on the terrace.

★ ELMINCHAOUI

69 Pl. Aachabine; tel. 0677/768 658; Sat.-Thurs. 8am-4pm; 8Dh

One of the more popular options for a quick lunch in the medina is to eat like many of the local workers at one of the *bissara* stands

fresh Moroccan salad

scattered throughout the medina. There are stalls around the Qaraouiyine complex in the center of the medina. Head for Place Aachabine and look for Elminchaoui's soup stand, a clean, nonsmoking, veritable hole-in-the-wall. You'll probably have to wait a few minutes for a seat, but it will be well worth it for a thick bowl of *bissara* topped with a generous splash of olive oil, cumin, and red chili pepper and served with half a round of bread.

TARBOUCHE

43 Rue Talaa Kebira; tel. 0535/638 466; daily 11am-10pm; 80Dh

This relatively new concept restaurant has quickly become a favorite for travelers looking for a quick lunch or light dinner in the medina. The menu is Moroccan-Mexican fusion, something that you'll be hard-pressed to find anywhere else in Morocco. There is not a lot of seating, so you might have to wait for a seat. Definitely go for the Moroccan-style chimichanga. Consider saving room for dessert: The gooey chocolate brownie is just the thing you didn't know you were craving.

★ MADE IN M

246 rue Talaa Kebira; tel. 0535/634 116; daily 10am-10pm; 10Dh

You might come here for a spot of people-watching and a caffeine boost, but that would be a mistake. It's really the wonderful ladies who staff this café that make it the cozy spot that it has quickly become. You can have a full lunch or dinner here. The tajines are flavorful, as to be expected, but don't be afraid to have a go at the veggie rolls. Perhaps the most welcomed surprise is the coffee to go. Feel free to pop in right when they open and grab a quick pastry and a flat white to energize yourself for a day of medina exploration.

RIAD BRAYA

7 Derb El Hamia, near the Batha Museum; tel. 0535/638 725; www.riadbraya.com; daily noon-3pm and 7pm-10pm; 250Dh

You would be forgiven for thinking dinner out at Riad Braya is a black-tie affair. It's not, but this restaurant and *riad* was once a palace of local nobility. The restaurant features a menu of mixed French and Moroccan cuisine. Take in the view from the terrace. A limited (but more-than adequate) bar serves up mixed cocktails and a varied wine list. This is the place to go to if you're craving a steak. Reservations are required.

★ DAR ROUMANA

30 Derb el-Amer, Zqaq Roumane; tel. 0535/741 637; www.darroumana.com; daily 7:30pm-11pm; 150Dh

A can't-miss for foodies. Enjoy a pre-dinner aperitif complete with an amuse-bouche on the terrace, and take in the sunset before heading downstairs to a fine-dining experience in the sumptuously decorated courtyard. The cold roasted tomato with crab, coriander, and pesto is a must-have starter, and the pan-seared salmon is exquisite. Reservations are required. The French-style menu can be tailored to fit dietary needs, including gluten-free options—just be sure to tell them when you make your reservation.

THE RUINED GARDEN

Siaj, Sidi Ahmed Chaoui; tel. 0535/633 066; http://ruinedgarden.com; daily 1pm-9:30pm; 40-120Dh

This is a unique concept. Unlike most addresses in Fez, there has been no real restoration work done here. Instead, you dine in the ruin of an old merchant house. The kitchen is a small shack off to one side that prepares seasonally fresh food grown in the on-site garden. There are plenty of options for vegetarians, including a scrumptious artichoke, chickpea, and saffron tajine, though sometimes the food is hit or miss. Don't miss the freshly squeezed juice concoctions!

Ville Nouvelle

PATISSERIE LA RENAISSANCE

at the intersection with Rue El Mohktar Soussi; daily 10am-9pm; 15Dh

This local favorite is best for their fresh juices and is worth a small detour if you're wandering the Ville Nouvelle. The sidewalk terrace is a little quieter than the main drag and can be a pleasant place to sip on a juice and reenergize.

CHEZ VITTORIO

21 Rue Brahim Roudani; tel. 0535/624 730; daily noon-3pm and 6pm-midnight; 70Dh

A popular stop for travelers, though one gets the impression this is largely because of the availability of wine and beer. Skip the pastas and stick to the pizzas and steaks. Decor is spot-on Italian. The nonexistent ventilation can be problematic for nonsmokers because a single smoker will make your pizza taste like an ashtray. It's best visited for an early dinner.

★ MAISON BLANCHE

12 Rue Ahmed Chaouki; tel. 0535/622 727; www.mbrestaurantlounge.com; daily noon-3pm and 7pm-11pm; 300Dh

This has been a foodie favorite for a few years, and for good reason. Italian-inspired French designer Christophe Pillet teamed with the chef responsible for the Café Faubourg in Paris to create this Moroccan-French fusion restaurant set in stone and glass. Have the carpaccio for starters, then the pan-seared Saint Pierre fish served with risotto mixed with preserved lemon for your entrée, but save room for the *sphère tout chocolat* with Amaretto. The menu features one of the better wine and alcohol selections in Fez. Reservations are recommended.

BARS AND LOUNGES

FEZ LOUNGE

95 Zkak Rouah; tel. 0633/284 874; www.fezlounge.com; 1:30pm-10pm

Fez Lounge draws some of the younger, hipper crowd in the midst of the old medina with loud house music, live DJs, and a shisha (or "hookah") lounge. For shisha smokers, this is the place to be. The decor is somewhat lacking, though this is standard for Fez nightlife.

L'ALCAZAR BAR

5 Derb Ben Slimane Zerbtana; tel. 0535/947 610 or 0535/741 206; www.riadfes.com; noon-late

Looking for a drink poolside? Head to l'Alcazar Bar at the sumptuous Riad Fez in the medina for an upscale cocktail or glass of champagne.

ACCOMMODATIONS

Fez is a top tourist destination in Morocco and is predicted to challenge Marrakesh soon for number of visitors per year. Most visitors want to stay in the old medina, where all the accommodations listed here are situated. Many foreigners have fallen in love with Fez, purchased old medina houses, restored them, and opened them up to guests as *riads*. There are many midrange to high-end options, even within the same *riad*. For the most part, the *riads* are quiet and comfortable. Generally, the bottom floors house larger rooms, though they can be a little noisier in the mornings and evenings with traffic outside of your room in the courtyard from other travelers coming and going. For travelers with tighter purse strings, there are a number of hostels dotted around the medina. Some are more relaxed than others and many have a curfew and lockout period. Ask ahead about any rules and regulations before booking your hostel.

The October-April season is typically busier than the hotter summer months, when temperatures can climb well past 100°F. November-March can be very rainy and surprisingly cold, particularly at night. Though snow is rare, it is possible in the winter months. Travelers should check with their lodging for heating and cooling options.

During the Sacred Music Festival, usually in June, rooms should be reserved well in advance.

Under 400Dh

FUNKY FES

60 Arset Lamdelssi near Bab Jdid; tel. 0535/633 196; www.funkyfes.com; 85-175Dh depending on demand

Funky Fes is the local branch of the Spanish-run Funky Hostels. There are mixed dorms, though no private rooms, with free Wi-Fi access and, thankfully, air-conditioning for the hot summer months. It fills up quickly, so you'll want to make sure to book ahead of time.

★ DAR LALLA KENZA

5 Derb Sidi Hssayne Klaklieyener; tel. 0613/504 732; 130-150Dh mixed dorms, 160-300Dh private rooms

Buried deep in the labyrinthine Fez medina, this is the hostel of choice for those who really want to stay somewhere with a ton of local flavor. The friendly owner, Ben, is a Fez native who will gladly help you get oriented in the medina and help you with most questions you might have. The rooms are simple but comfy. Free Wi-Fi will help you keep connected while a delicious breakfast is available (20Dh) and can get you going for your morning.

HOTEL JARDIN

153 Kasbat Boujloud; tel. 0644/302 151; 150-600Dh d

Located just outside the Bab Boujeloud gate, this is one of the larger hotels around the medina, with 32 rooms, and is a popular stop for larger groups and families looking to explore the Fez medina. Elaborate *zellij,* wood, and tile work decorates this comfortable, if uninspired, hotel. The showers are awkward for people over six feet tall. Take your breakfast on the large terrace and enjoy the commanding views of the medina and the surrounding hills. Wi-Fi, TV, and breakfast are included with your stay.

400-800Dh

DAR TAHRYA

9 Rue Taryana, Talâa Kbira; tel. 0535/638 756 or 0667/823 576; www.dartahrya.com; 350-800Dh d

Popular with budget travelers and adventurous couples looking to experience something outside of the standard fare, this cluttered *dar* features six rooms, all with en suite toilets. Prices for single rooms go as low as 350Dh. For privacy, request the second floor. It can be a little noisy, though usually the guests will quiet down at night, and the suites are spacious. Just a short walk from Bab Boujeloud and close to both of the main thoroughfares of the medina. Cooking classes are available for 300-350Dh; call 24 hours in advance to arrange. Wi-Fi and breakfast are included with your stay.

RIAD TARYANA

8 Rue Taryana, Talâa Kbira; tel. 0535/638 540; www.riadtaryana.com; 400-700Dh d

One of the more modern midrange options in the medina. The *zellij,* stucco, and cedarwood throughout this surprisingly sleek *riad* were all done by the workers responsible for remodeling the nearby Medersa Bouanania, and the high level of craftsmanship shows. For those tired of the ramshackle quaintness many of the other *riads* offer in this price range, this might be just the ticket. Staff are friendly to a fault and will gladly help you get around Fez and can arrange for transportation for a day trip to nearby Volubilis and Moulay Idriss. Breakfast, air-conditioning, and Wi-Fi all included.

RIAD ZOHOR

19 Rue Triara, Talâa Sghira; tel. 0535/638 598 or 0679/674 570; darzohourguesthouse@gmail.com; 550Dh d

This is affiliated with nearby Riad Rahba, Riad Yasmine, and Dar Tahrya. All rooms feature en suite toilets. The draw here for budget travelers is the large terrace. In low season, it's possible to book the single room on the terrace for 150Dh. Sleeping on the terrace is possible in warm seasons with a light blanket or sleeping bag. The local staff, headed by Youssef and Noureddine, is extremely helpful. Air-conditioning, heating, Wi-Fi, and breakfast are included with any room reservation.

★ RIAD LAAYOUN

47 Derb Thakharbicht, near Bab R'cif; tel. 0535/637 245 or 0670/200 196; 550-800Dh d

A clean, calm respite from the hustle of the medina, with a beautiful courtyard fountain, rooms with private terraces, and plenty of nooks and crannies for you to explore. It's one of the better midrange options for the medina. The terrace opens up over the Place R'cif and the hillside, where you can see the smoke from the pottery kilns. The owner, Jean-Claude, and his manager, Simo, are very welcoming and make you feel at home. The breakfast is not as elaborate as at some other *riads,* but the service makes up for this. Book one of the suites or the rooms off the ground floor. Air-conditioning, heating, Wi-Fi, and breakfast are all included.

Over 800Dh

RIAD BRAYA

7 Derb El Hamia, Douh, near the Batha Museum; tel. 0535/638 725; www.riadbraya.com; 900Dh d

This *riad* gets its name from the particular color of blue used throughout the building. It's beautifully restored, if a bit monochrome, with lots of modern glass, marble floors, and faux-tique claw-foot bathtubs that offset the traditional *zellij* and courtyard setting. Best for those looking for a modern twist. A stay in their suite includes transportation to and from the train station or airport. Heating, air-conditioning, TV, and Wi-Fi are all included.

LA GRAND ALCAZAR

15 Derb Guebas, Batha; tel. 0684/232 373; www.legrandalcazar.com; 900Dh d

One of my new favorite boutique hotels in Fez, the property and the service are impeccable: from tasty meals to spotless, traditional *riad* rooms with exquisite ornamentation, from the carved plasterwork to the hand-painted wood. The location, right next to Batha on the edge of the medina, is fantastic, particularly for those traveling by car. The deluxe king suites are well worth the additional price for the royal splurge if the budget allows. Heating, air-conditioning, TV, and Wi-Fi are all present, as well as wonderful views over the Fez medina from the rooftop terrace.

RIAD ZAMANE

12 Derb Skallia, Douh; tel. 0535/740 440; www.riadzamane-fes.com; 900Dh d

This is a great option, conveniently located near the Batha Museum in a quieter part of the medina with easy access to parking and to the driving routes, which is helpful for those road-tripping. Sakina, the proprietor, is a gracious hostess and will accommodate all your needs. If your budget allows, try to reserve the Green Suite with the private terrace. Heating, air-conditioning, Wi-Fi, and breakfast are all included.

★ RIAD LAAROUSSA

3 Derb Bechara; tel. 0674/187 639; www.riad-laaroussa.com; 1,200Dh d

A real highlight of any trip to Morocco. It took a few years to remodel this former palace to its glory, but it was well worth it. The refinished woodwork, intricate *zellij* tiles, palatial suites with roaring fireplaces for the winter, and fine attention to detail all help to make this *riad* one of the best in Fez. With a helpful staff, wonderful terrace views, delicious breakfast, great location, and an on-site traditional hammam, Riad Laaroussa has it all. The owners, Fred and Cathy, are invested in the local community, and it shows with their staff and the respect the Fez community has for them. Rooms are themed by color. If you can't splurge for a suite, try the Blue Room, with a wonderful reading nook overlooking the courtyard. The Blue, Yellow, and Brown rooms open on a shared salon with sofas and fireplace, perfect for larger families or groups. If you're staying for a few days, make sure you take advantage of the free cooking course offered in their wonderful kitchen for guests. Fireplace heating, air-conditioning, Wi-Fi, and breakfast are all included.

INFORMATION AND SERVICES

The city code for Fez and the area is 35.

Visitor Information

SYNDICAT D'INITIATIVE

Pl. Mohammed V; tel. 0535/624 769; Mon.-Fri. 8:30am-noon and 2:30pm-6:30pm

Head to the Syndicat d'Initiative, in the Ville Nouvelle near Cinema Rex and Jardin Lalla Amina, to buy festival tickets or a city map, though the maps are also available in the medina and elsewhere. Occasionally information regarding festivals and events can be found here, though often you are better off checking with your accommodations.

Internet Cafés

You will find Internet cafés throughout the medina. The most reliable is the **Cyber Café Bab Boujeloud** (daily 9am-10pm, 5Dh per hour), near Boujeloud mosque just outside Bab Boujeloud.

Post Offices and Courier Services

In the medina, head to the Place de l'Istiqlal or the Medersa el-Attarine to send packages and postcards. If you're in the Ville Nouvelle, head to the corner of Avenue Hassan II and Boulevard Mohammed V for the main post office. All post offices keep the same hours (Mon.-Fri. 8am-4:30pm, Sat. 8:30am-noon, shortened hours during Ramadan).

Bookstores, Newspapers, and Magazines

A couple of bookstores in the medina on Talâa Sghira, toward Bab Boujeloud after the cafés as you are walking into the medina, sell books in English, French, Spanish, and Arabic. Another option is the bookstore at the **American Language Center** (2 Rue Ahmed Hiba, tel. 0535/624 850, Mon.-Fri. 9am-noon and 3pm-6:30pm) in the Ville Nouvelle.

Arabic Language Courses

The **Arabic Language Institute in Fez** (2 Rue Ahmed Hiba, tel. 0535/624 850, www.alif-fes.com) in the Ville Nouvelle offers classes in Modern Standard Arabic and Moroccan Arabic (Darija) in either three-week (6,300Dh) or six-week (10,900Dh) intensive course options or by the hour. Instructors speak English and French.

American Language Center

Coupled with the Arabic Language Institute, the **American Language Center** (2 Rue Ahmed Hiba, tel. 0535/624 850, http://alcfezbook.com, Mon.-Fri. 10am-1pm and 2pm-4:30pm) in the Ville Nouvelle offers a free series of film screenings, lectures, and concerts. Check the website for details.

Money

There are two handy ATMs by the Medersa el-Attarine in the middle of the medina—a Poste Maroc and another by Banque Populaire. The Banque Populaire, however, keeps regular bank hours and their ATM is closed on weekends. There is another ATM on the Talâa Sghira near where it merges with Talaâ Kbira, as well as one outside Bab Boujeloud and many scattered throughout the Ville Nouvelle. Please note: The ATM in the airport is often out of service. For travelers checks, foreigner currency exchanges, and other services, it's best to use BMCE. You can find branches in the Ville Nouvelle at Place de Florence, Place d'Atlas, and Place Mohammed V.

Safety

Fez is a relatively safe city. Muggings are a rarity in the old medina, though the first time walking after dark through the quiet, dimly lighted pedestrian pathways will likely send shivers through the most seasoned traveler's spine. General precautions apply.

The most likely annoyance will be nagging children and faux guides. Be firm but fair with them, telling them no thank you, no matter how much they follow you. If you do ask for directions and are led to a destination, a small tip of 5-10Dh is plenty, though you will always be asked for more.

Also keep watch out for hustlers. Common hustles include someone asking you to go to their "cousin's shop" or "brother's shop" to pressure you into buying something or telling you upon arrival that your accommodation is closed and suggesting another place.

In the medina, watch out for people calling "*Belek! Belek!*" or "*Smah Belek*" so you don't get run over by an overburdened donkey or man pushing an impossibly full wheelbarrow.

Harassment toward women occurs throughout Morocco, and Fez is no exception. Women are encouraged to travel in groups, though during the day and on the more traveled paths through the medina it is as safe as anywhere else in the world.

Hospitals, Clinics, and Pharmacies

If you have a medical emergency, it is best to head for the hospital in Rabat. Fez has several hospitals, but none of them seem well equipped. For non-emergencies, it is better to use private clinics in the Ville Nouvelle. **Dr. Jamal Wakkach** (2 Rue Benzakkour, tel. 0535/656 565 or 0555/960 000) speaks English and should be able to assist you for any nonemergency. **Dr. Benyahia Tabib Ali** (21 Blvd. Chefchaouni, tel. 0535/624 295), another general practitioner, speaks French and Spanish. There are several pharmacies just outside the Bab Boujeloud. The 24-hour **Pharmacie du Municipalité** is on Avenue Moulay Youssef near the Place de la Résistance.

Laundry

Most *riads* offer an inexpensive laundry service. They do not charge much, generally around 50Dh, and will wash, dry, and fold your laundry. Hotels usually cost quite a bit more for the same service. You won't find launderettes here, but numerous dry-cleaners will wash and press your laundry. You pay by item. The closest dry cleaners to the medina is just outside Bab Boujeloud in Place de l'Istiqlal next to the post office. In the Ville Nouvelle, there are numerous options in every neighborhood.

GETTING THERE

BY CAR

Fez is connected with the tolled A2 autoroute, making getting to the city from other major cities easy.

From Casablanca: Follow the A1 autoroute north to Rabat before taking the A2 east (292km/181mi, about 3.5 hours). There will be two tolls, one on the Casablanca-Rabat autoroute (23Dh) and one at Fez (50Dh).

From Marrakesh: Follow the Follow the A1 autoroute north to Rabat before taking the A2 east (529km/329mi, about 6 hours). There will be three tolls, one at Casablanca (80Dh), one on the Casablanca-Rabat autoroute (23Dh), and one at Fez (50Dh).

From Meknes: Follow the A2 north for 70km/43mi, about 1 hour. The toll is 15Dh.

From Rabat: Follow the A2 east for 201km/125mi, about 2.5 hours. The toll is 50Dh.

From Tangier: Follow the A1 south and take the Kenitra Centre/Khemmisset exit (the third Kenitra exit from the autoroute). Take a left off the exit followed by another quick left to take the road to Khemmisset. At Khemmisset, continue straight through the roundabout to connect with the A2 autoroute heading east. The whole journey covers 400km/249mi, about 4.5 hours. There are two tolls, one at Kenitra (66Dh) and one at Fez (50Dh).

For locations along the Atlantic Coast and Tangier, the national road may look shorter than the tolled freeway on a map, but often traveling by the national road takes longer because of slow-moving traffic and road conditions. Other locations, such as **Chefchaouen** (204km/127mi, 4.5hr) and **Merzouga** (467km/290mi, 8hr), are connected only by the national road system, which can make the driving painfully slow.

BY TRAIN

The **Fez Train Station,** just off the Avenue des Almohades in the Ville Nouvelle, serves the national lines run by **ONCF** (tel. 0890/203 040, www.oncf.ma). There are direct trains to and from **Casablanca** (4.5hr, 19 daily, 2nd/1st-class 110Dh/165Dh), **Marrakesh** (8hr, 8 daily, 195Dh/295Dh), **Meknes** (1hr, 23 daily, 20Dh/30Dh), **Oujda** (5hr, 3 daily, 110Dh/160Dh), **Rabat** (3.5hr, 19 daily, 80Dh/120Dh), and **Tangier** (5hr, 6 daily, 105Dh/155Dh, early morning train transfer at Sidi Kacem), with stops in between.

Most travelers will likely continue from here straight to the old medina. Red *petits taxis* are available from the main road. The fare from the station to most of the gates (*babs*) should be 10-20Dh; you will pay a bit more at night. *Petits taxis* take only three passengers. For larger groups, it might be better to pay slightly more for the *grands taxis.*

BY BUS

Those traveling by bus will most likely arrive near the **CTM station** in the Al-Atlas neighborhood near the large Youssef Ibn Tachfine mosque just off the N8. Local buses arrive at the *gare routière* near the train station. From either, it is possible to take the red *petits taxis* on to your destination for around 15Dh.

The **CTM** bus (tel. 0800/0900 30, www.ctm.ma) connects with many cities around Morocco with a few premium buses that offer onboard Wi-Fi and larger seats. Popular connections include **Casablanca** (4hr, 12 daily, 90Dh, premium available), **Chefchaouen** (4hr, 3 daily, 75Dh), **Ifrane** (1hr, 2 daily, 25Dh), **Marrakesh** (5.5hr, 6 daily, 170Dh, premium available), **Meknes** (1hr, 10 daily, 25Dh), **Rabat** (3hr, 13 daily, 75Dh, premium available), and **Rissani** (10hr, 1 daily, 160Dh). The overnight Rissani bus leaves Fez at 9:30pm and is one of the best ways to travel by public transportation to Merzouga and the desert.

BY PLANE

The **Fés-Saiss Airport** (5km/3mi south of the city, tel. 0535/620 663, www.onda.ma) serves mostly budget airlines from Europe, such as **RyanAir** (www.ryanair.com) and **Transavia** (www.transavia.com), as well as the national carrier, **Royal Air Maroc** (www.royalairmaroc.com). A new terminal was recently built to cater to the predicted growth in tourism.

To get into the city, you have a few options. You can arrange for pickup through most hotels and *riads* (make sure to verify this with your booking). Most travelers rely on *grands taxis,* which can take up to six passengers; they run for 120Dh from the airport to the train station and 150Dh to the medina, though night prices can run up to 200Dh. A newer option is the **Fez-Airport bus**, which also runs approximately every half hour and takes you directly to/from the train station for 20Dh.

GETTING AROUND

Cars are not allowed into the medina, so once you enter the gates of Fès el-Bali, the only mode of transport is your own two feet. Make sure to pack a comfortable pair of walking shoes.

There is guarded, overnight **parking** near Bab R'cif just after the Bab Jdid and another lot near Hotel Batha. Both are 20Dh a day with overnight parking sometimes a bit more. Pay when you leave, not in advance, unless you receive a ticket.

If you're traveling outside the old medina, make your way to one of the main gates (Bab Boujeloud, Bab R'cif, Bab Guissa, or Bab Ftouh) and catch a red ***petit taxi.*** These metered taxis are a great value. Destinations in the Ville Nouvelle and the Merenid Tombs can be reached for 10-15Dh during the day; prices go up 50 percent after 8pm. Though all taxi drivers are familiar with the different gates into the medina, the train station, and the Merenid Tombs, they are not familiar with different restaurants, hotels, and street names, so if you're taking a taxi to one of these locations, it is best to have a map either loaded on your electronic device or printed out to show the driver.

City buses run 6am-10pm from Bab R'cif to the train station (**bus 19**), Bab Boujeloud to Bab Ftouh (**bus 12**), Bab Ftouh to the train station (**bus 10**), and from the airport to the train station (**bus 16**). Other routes are used more by locals than tourists as schedules are not dependable. Look at the sides or fronts of the buses (not the back) to find the bus numbers.

Meknes مكناس

The old medina of Meknes (also spelled Meknès) is more relaxed than that of nearby Fez. Visitors can stroll with very little hassle from shopkeepers through its winding streets, narrow alleys, and countless mausoleums. Keep a lookout for elaborately decorated doors throughout the medina for some fantastic photo ops.

The souks are a pleasure to browse, and sales tactics here are much lower pressure. Prices will be significantly less expensive than in nearby Fez, though you are still expected to negotiate. The entire medina is fairly compact, just big enough to feel a little lost. For carpets, decorated wood chests or tables, *zellij*

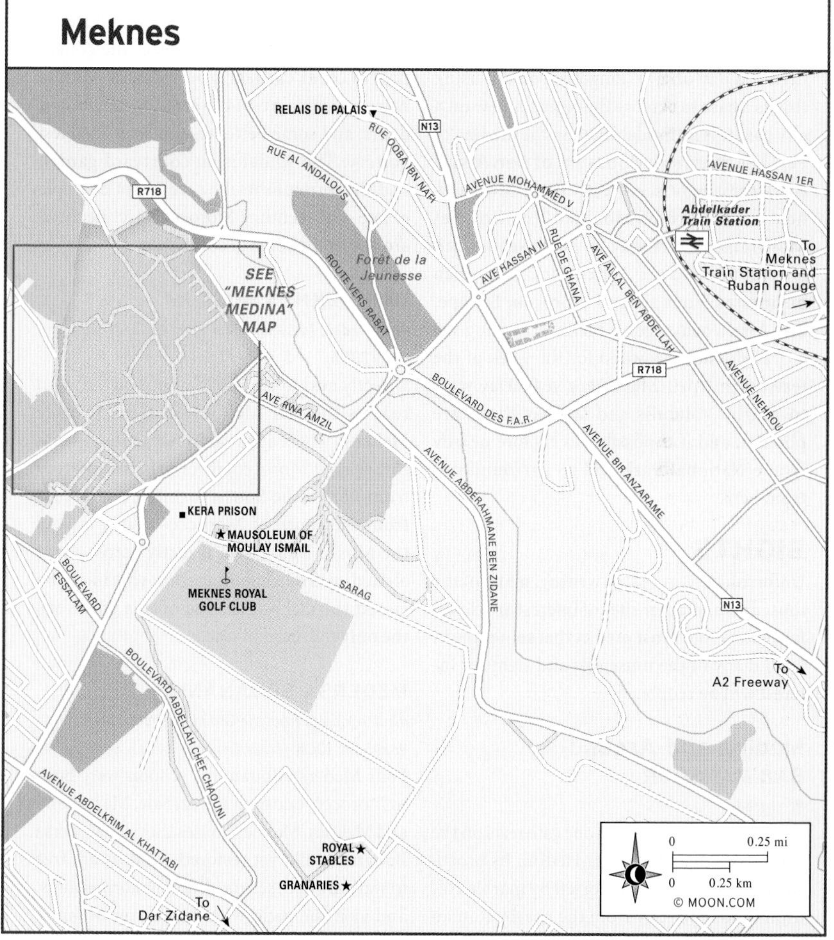

fountains or tables, spices, herbs, or pottery, Meknes is well worth the stop.

The tyrant sultan Moulay Ismail, who reigned in the 17th and 18th centuries, formed Meknes into a great imperial city through the use of slave labor and his desire to have the greatest palace in the world. Unfortunately, the materials used for the construction of his vast fortress and elaborate palaces were not strong enough to avoid near complete destruction with the great Lisbon earthquake of 1755, just a few years after Moulay Ismail's death. The imposing gate of Bab Mansour and its sister gate, Bab Bardaine, stand as testament to his heavy-handed rule.

Meknes has enough sights to warrant staying for a day or two, longer if you are using this as a base to explore the region and want a city base less intimidating than the medina of Fez. The theatrical **Moussem of Ben Aïssa,** the largest *moussem* (festival) in Morocco, held on the eve of Mouloud, the Prophet Mohammed's birthday, is worth seeing, but it's best to avoid the Agricultural Fair, when businesses from around Morocco, Europe, and Africa converge on Meknes, making the city impossibly crowded for the week of the festival in April/May every year. Day trips to nearby Volubilis and Moulay Idriss are popular, and it is possible to explore nearby Ifrane National Park and its surroundings from here.

SIGHTS

Unfortunately, as of this writing, many of the museums and other sites of interest are closed for renovation. Most predict that sometime in 2020 many of the museums and sights of interest will be reopened.

Medina and Around

BAB MANSOUR

Pl. el-Hedim

The impressive Bab Mansour gate rests on the southeast edge of Place el-Hedim. Its broad, square bastions are supported by marble columns taken directly from the nearby Roman ruin of Volubilis. Nearly the entirety of the gate is decorated with ornate scripture and complex green and black *zellij* work. The scripture extols the virtuosity of Moulay Ismail and his successor, Moulay Abdellah, and exclaims that it is a gate without equal. This is a great meeting point for travelers. The plaza here is the most lively in Meknes, particularly at night, when it transforms into a smaller version of Marrakesh's Jemaa el-Fnaa.

DAR JAMAÏ MUSEUM

Pl. el-Hedim; closed for renovations until 2020/21

Across the Place el-Hedim from the Bab Mansour is perhaps the most interesting museum in Meknes, the Dar Jamaï Museum (Musée Dar Jamaï). It houses a fine collection of local carpets from various Middle Atlas tribes, carved 14th-century cedarwood doors, and some better examples of Meknesi pottery. The Andalusian courtyard garden and the museum itself, a well-kept example of late-19th-century Moroccan architecture, are worth the price of admission.

DAR MEKNES MUSEUM

Pl. el-Hedim; Tues.-Sun. 9am-6pm; 10Dh, official tours 20Dh

Directly next to the Bab Mansour on the main road is the Dar Meknes Museum (Musée Meknes). There are a variety of artifacts from throughout Morocco, from old Fassi pottery from Fez to the Soussi farming equipment from the south of Morocco on display. As the Musée Dar Jamaï, directly across Place el-Hedim from Bab Mansour, will likely be closed throughout the life of this guide, it's the only museum in town.

MEDERSA BOUANANIA

medina, across from the Grand Mosque; daily 9am-5pm; 10Dh

Four Medersa Bouanania schools were built in Morocco, one each in Fez, Salé, Marrakesh, and Meknes. Meknes houses the only Medersa Bouanania not yet restored. Visitors are free to walk around, see the different dorm rooms, and visit the patio with views over Meknes. Though some of the undecorated walls are

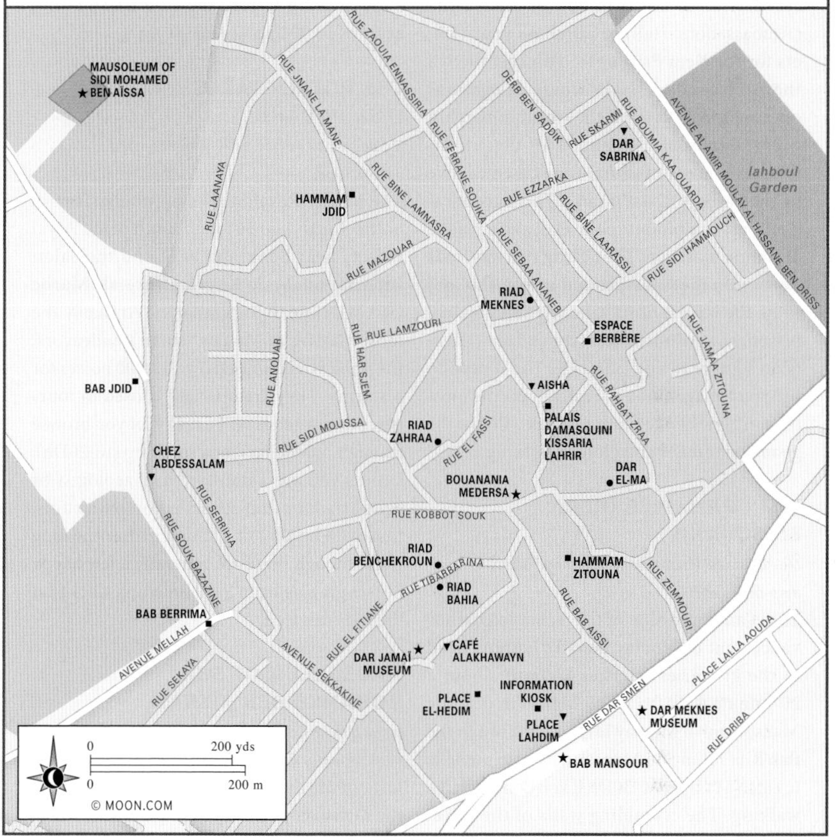

showing age, much of the original stucco, wood, and *zellij* work, dating from about 1358, is in fantastic condition. The light, lace-like stucco work gives a particularly balanced look that is somehow lost on its restored sister *medersas*.

MAUSOLEUM OF MOULAY ISMAIL

across from Place el-Hedim, through Bab Mansour; closed for renovations until 2020/21

The Mausoleum of Moulay Ismail is one of the few active religious buildings in use where non-Muslims are allowed entry, though they are barred from passing through the annex to the sultan's tomb. There is a window just outside the annex, on the right side as you approach the tomb, through which you can spy the tomb and the famed grandfather clocks standing on either side that came as a gift from Louis XIV of France. Women from all over Morocco come to visit to receive the *baraka* (blessing) from the remains of the sultan. It is common to see them praying and chanting around his tomb. The mausoleum is best visited in the early morning on your way to the granaries, when the air is still cool and you can take your time to examine the ornate *zellij* work and carved stucco.

KERA PRISON

Bab el-Khemis; 10am-6pm; 70Dh

Head first to the Koubba el Khayatine (Ambassadors' Hall) to purchase your tickets for the Kera Prison. Don't forget to visit the Ambassadors' Hall, where delegations once met from around the world to bargain over the ransoms demanded for the prisoners below, many of whom were taken captive by the Barbary Coast pirates. There are occasional art exhibitions in the Hall and a plaque of commemoration. The nearby stairway leads down into the underground prison thought to be the largest of its kind. Around 50,000 prisoners were once incarcerated here. There is no signage in any language. You'll need to use your imagination to really make the most of your time here. Photographers will like the geometric arches and gloomy lighting.

THE GRANARIES (HERI ES-SOUANI)

Moulay Ismail Palace; daily 9am-noon and 3pm-6:30pm; 70Dh

To get an impression of the technological advancement of Moulay Ismail's empire, head to the granaries (Heri es Souani), about a 20-minute walk from Bab Mansour, past the Mausoleum of Moulay Idriss and through the Bab Rih. From Bab Mansour, it's also possible to catch a taxi for 20-30Dh if you don't feel like walking. The crumbling walls of the Royal Palace line either side of this walk, with no real shade to speak of during midday, so make sure you've applied plenty of sunscreen before you head out. The Meknes Royal Golf Club is to your right as you follow the road until it slopes down to the right and leads directly to the Heri es-Souani, the granary stores of Moulay Ismail for times of drought or siege. The granaries are a surprisingly intact series of archways, though the roof has long since decayed, making them unusable today. Perhaps the most impressive sight is the system of buckets chained together in each of the vaulted storerooms, which gives you an idea of how 17th-century plumbing functioned. Moulay Ismail's palaces all had underground plumbing nearly a century before it would be used in Europe. These granaries once held enough grain to feed the sultan's standing army of 12,000 horses for 20 years.

THE ROYAL STABLES (THE ROUAH)

Moulay Ismail Palace; daily 9am-noon and 3pm-6:30pm

The former Royal Stables of Moulay Ismail, or the Rouah, can be found south of the Royal Palace, near Benhlima Park and the Salon Internationale de l'Agriculture au Maroc (SIAM), close to the granaries. Arguably the most massive of Moulay Ismail's endeavors, the stables once housed over 12,000 horses for his army. They are officially closed to tourists, but the guard will usually let you browse (though not too far) for a small tip (10-20Dh). Unless you are a die-hard archaeologist or equestrian, or find a fascination with ruins, these can be a bit of a letdown after the long walk, though there are generally a few happy horses grazing from local breeding stock that the kids can feed.

MAUSOLEUM OF SIDI MOHAMED BEN AÏSSA

in the Muslim Cemetery off Trek Bab Jdid; free for Muslims, entry not permitted for non-Muslims

Just outside the west end of the old medina lies the Mausoleum of Sidi Mohamed Ben Aïssa. Ben Aïssa founded the Aissaoua sufi brotherhood in the 15th century and bestowed upon his followers the power to ingest anything without any harm coming to them. Though the mausoleum is closed to non-Muslims, all visitors will be able to witness the largest *moussem* (festival) in Morocco held here on the eve of the Muslim holiday of Mouloud. For Muslims stopping into the mausoleum, there are prayers and often *dikr* happening throughout the day and night.

1: the Mederasa Bouanania of Meknes
2: *bissara* soup, a vegetarian staple of Morocco
3: underground in the Kera Prison **4:** the Bab Mansour gate of Meknes

1
2
3
4

ENTERTAINMENT AND EVENTS

Moussem of Ben Aïssa

Eve of Mouloud (Islamic Calendar), around Oct. 29, 2020, Oct. 19, 2021, and Oct. 8, 2022

The Moussem of Ben Aïssa, the largest *moussem* (festival) in Morocco, is held at the saint's mausoleum on the eve of Mouloud, the Prophet Mohammed's birthday. Historically, followers of Ben Aïssa would go into trances during the *moussem* and eat poisonous snakes, broken glass, and live sheep (among other things) to prove their devotion. Today's *moussem* is much less violent. Most visitors will want to see the corresponding fantasia, a kind of celebration of the history of Berber knights and their bravery that occurs near Bab Mansour, and enjoy the dancing and music. The galloping horses, gunfire, and the theatricality of this event are worth seeing.

SHOPPING

Shopping in the Meknes medina is noticeably more tranquil than nearby in Fez and a lot more hassle-free. You will still be expected to bargain, though sellers here generally begin with a fair price, so negotiations here are typically over a few dirhams, not a few thousand dirhams, as can be the case in Fez.

ESPACE BERBÈRE

32 Rue Tiberbarine; daily 9am-6pm

If you are shopping for a carpet, pillowcases, or arabesque light fixtures, head to Espace Berbère, where Abdelrahim will happily guide you through one of the best selections of carpets in the area while explaining the region, type, and history of each piece. Prices are generally firm, though there is always room for a little negotiation. This is one of the most honest carpet sellers in the country, and his selection usually has some real gems.

PALAIS DAMASQUINI KISSARIA LAHRIR

Pl. Kissaria; Sat.-Thurs. 7am-7pm

One of the more interesting shops in the medina, tucked into the corner of the Kissaria Souk. This is one of the oldest establishments in Meknes that works with silver damascene, a particular type of inlay often used in fine jewelry, sculptures, and vases. There are pictures of his majesty Mohammed VI shopping here. The sculptures, cups, and jugs make for interesting souvenirs and are not something you might typically think of when shopping in Morocco.

SPORTS AND RECREATION

Horseback Riding

Meknes is famous for its horses. You can hire a guide and head out on a mare or a stallion for a morning, afternoon, or a few days of horseback riding through the nearby valleys, rivers, and plains, past nearby Volubilis and up into the mountains surrounding Moulay Idriss. This is a wonderful (and more environmentally friendly) way to tour Morocco. Contact your accommodations for a reservation, or the local horse riding club, **Club Farah** (www.clubfarah.com), to book a guided excursion. Club Farah keeps a calendar of their trips on their website; for groups of four or more, other excursions are possible. For beginners, horse-riding courses are available. Prices start from a few hundred dirhams for a day trip to a few thousand dirhams for an all-inclusive one-week trek through the mountains.

Hammams

HAMMAM ZITOUNA

Grand Mosque; men daily 6am-noon and 9pm-midnight, women daily 1pm-9pm; 10Dh, massage 30Dh

Across from the Grand Mosque is one of the better local hammams, Hammam Zitouna. Like many hammams near the mosques, this hammam is a bit cleaner than some of its other counterparts, though not quite as charming as Hammam Jdid (listed below). Pay attention to the hours for men and women. You will want to pack a swimsuit (going fully naked may be inappropriate), flip-flops, and your soaps and shampoos. For a real local experience, be sure to pick up some of the *savon bildi* and a scrub before arriving.

HAMMAM JDID

22 Derb Hammam Jdid; men daily 6am-noon and 9pm-midnight, women daily 1pm-9pm; 10Dh, massage 30Dh

Hammam Jdid, a few streets farther into the medina, is another, perhaps a touch more picturesque, option to bathe like the locals. What sets this hammam apart is some of the traditional *zellij* (tile) work that is still in evidence around the hammam, as well as the *tadalakt*, a sort of traditional coating used on the walls as humidity protection.

Golf

MEKNES ROYAL GOLF CLUB

J'nane Bahraouia, Bab Belkari; tel. 0535/530 753; www.royalgolfmeknes.com; 200Dh green fee

Right in the middle of the old imperial city of Meknes lies this little nine-hole. Tee off among the minarets protruding from the surrounding medina and take in the ornate *zellij* fountains and, especially at sunset, the soft smell of orange blossom and jasmine floating on the air.

FOOD

Mekness is not known for its variety of restaurants. If you are staying in one of the *riads*, you will likely want to have breakfast and possibly dinner there, too. This is often the best choice and you'll have the chance to taste some really hearty, delicious home cooking.

Every afternoon and into the early evening, Place el-Hedim serves as a smaller, less chaotic version of the Jemaa el-Fnaa in Marrakesh, with vendors and fortune tellers, snake charmers and soothsayers crowding the plaza. Early evening is the best time to sit down at one of the many cafés lining the square and take in the festivities.

Medina

CAFÉ ALAKHAWAYN

Pl. el-Hedim; daily 10am-11pm; 20Dh

The real draw to this café in front of the Dar Jamaï Museum is the unrestricted view across the square to Bab Mansour. On a day with a strong sun, the sun shades are worth their weight in mint tea. Tuck in for a drink and take in the carnival ambiance.

PLACE LAHDIM

Pl. el-Hedim across from Bab Mansour; daily 9am-11pm; 15Dh

For more of a bird's-eye view, head to Place Lahdim. The drinks will set you back about 10Dh more than at other cafés on the plaza for the terrace view, but what a view!

★ CHEZ ABDESSALAM

near Bab Jdid; Sat.-Thurs. 9am-4pm; 7Dh

If you're craving *bissara,* make your way here for one of the best *bissaras* around, a delicious thick bowl doused with local olive oil and sprinkled with cumin. It's a perfect lunch to keep you going, or even a breakfast! For those looking to rub elbows with locals, the cozy confines of Abdessalam's *bissara* stand is the place to be. The atmosphere is 100 percent working-class Moroccan, with the local workers stopping in for a quick bowl (or three) for breakfast and lunch.

★ AISHA

14 Rue Kababine; tel. 0660/876 545; daily 10:30am-11:30pm; 80Dh

Everyone's favorite hole-in-the-wall restaurant in the old medina does not disappoint. Three small tables form the entirety of the dining room, just off the walking street, with a tiny kitchen where mouthwatering veggie couscous and *rfissa* (a local specialty, particularly great during the colder months) are lovingly prepared. Service is friendly, though if they offer to take you shopping for spices or anything afterward, politely decline.

DAR SABRINA

145 Blvd. de Lahboul; tel. 0664/019 914; daily noon-3pm and 7pm-11pm; 130Dh

At this new favorite, you have your choice of Moroccan salads (try the roasted pepper salad) and chicken, beef, lamb, or camel tajines. The museum-like decor features pieces from around Morocco that add to the intimate, romantic atmosphere. The *dar* can be difficult to find; call and someone can meet you to take you to this lovely gem. Reservations are required.

DAR EL-MA

4 Derb Sidi Besri; tel. 0661/514 824; daily noon-3pm and 7pm-11pm; 200Dh

Enjoy some of the most delicious Moroccan cuisine with a hint of a French twist served up by Amina, a local who enjoys making staples from the region, such as *charmoula* (a traditional paprika and olive oil-based sauce) and *zaalouk* (roasted eggplant salad). In the winter, don't miss out on the roast chicken tajine with green olives, with a locally produced glass of Bordeaux-styled red. Reservations are required. Let them know of any dietary restrictions when you make your reservation.

Ville Nouvelle

In the Ville Nouvelle, numerous French-styled boulangeries (bakeries) are great if you're looking to pack for a picnic in Volubilis or find a delicious pastry for the road.

RUBAN ROUGE

Ave. des Forces Armées Royales; tel. 0535/510 010; daily 7am-9:30pm; 5Dh

The Ruban Rouge, near the Meknes train station, is the best bakery in town, with a larger selection of sweet and savory pastries. A round of bread will set you back 2.5Dh, like most other bakeries around Morocco, while croissants, baguettes, and other French-styled treats abound here.

RELAIS DE PALAIS

46 Rue Okba Ben Nafia; tel. 0665/186 818; daily noon-3pm and 8pm-midnight, lounge open 5pm-2am; 250Dh

A standard, if slightly overpriced, French restaurant a few blocks off Avenue Hassan II, northwest of the Institut Français. The menu serves up some classics, including foie gras. The lounge is nice, but the terrace with a commanding view over the medina is the place to be. The ample wine menu is a welcome treat for those needing to wet their whistle. Reservations are recommended.

★ DAR ZIDANE

15 Rue Arrazi; tel. 0535/538 406; daily noon-3pm and 7pm-11pm; 250Dh

Khadija, the French-trained chef at this guesthouse, had a restaurant near Lyon not long ago but now serves up some of the finest French-Moroccan fusion in Meknes. Seasonal dishes with fresh fruits, vegetables, and perfectly cooked chicken, lamb, or beef are finished with a special Lyonnaise twist. The environs will make you feel right at home, with friendly service and cushy chairs surrounding shaded tables in the grassy backyard. If you're looking for a place to stay, you could consider this boutique hotel, just a five-minute taxi ride from Bab Mansour, ensuring a bit more quiet for those looking for something outside the maze-like medina, but close enough to the major sights. The rooms are cozy, keeping nice and warm in the cooler winter months.

ACCOMMODATIONS

The numerous remodeled *riads* in the old medina offer the best value. The hotels in the Ville Nouvelle seem to cater to more local, rather unsavory clientele.

Under 400Dh

RIAD ZAHRAA

5 Rue Sidi Abdallah Elkasri Touta; tel. 0667/768 302; 150Dh d

Best for single travelers, with dated, comfortable rooms that are good for those traveling light. The included breakfast is an incredible value, particularly before heading out for a big day. During the peak travel seasons (spring and fall) the *riad* fills up with the younger European backpacker crowd, so it's best to reserve ahead of time.

RIAD BENCHEKROUN

8 Derb Mekka Tiberbarine; tel. 0535/535 406; 350Dh d

A good option for single travelers, the backpacking crowd, or those looking to save a few dirhams. The beds here are generally stiff, though you'll sleep well after a big day of walking around. The overall vibe is a little like staying at grandma's with some odd trinkets scattered about, but it's charming nonetheless. The terrace is a great place to catch the sunrise and listen to the muezzin call for the first prayer of the day.

400-800Dh

★ DAR EL-MA

4 Derb Sidi Besri; tel. 0661/514 824; 550Dh d

Centrally located on a quiet street near the Grand Mosque just off the Kissaria Souk, this is perhaps the best value-price deal in town. The suites are roomy, but the best options are the Red and Gray rooms upstairs. When the weather is nice, head to the terrace to take a dip in the small pool. For colder months, the salon has a nice fireplace to cozy up around. Two ladies, both named Amina, are friendly and will help you with finding your way around the medina and with anything else you need. Dinner should not be missed. Air-conditioning, TV, heating, Wi-Fi, and breakfast are all included with your stay.

★ RYAD BAHIA

Derb Tiberbarine; tel. 0535/554 541; www.ryad-bahia.com/en; 600Dh d

This maze-like, sprawling *riad* has lots of nooks and crannies in which to cozy up with a book and is an ideal spot for families. You'll find great access to the medina and friendly, hospitable service. Bouchra, the owner and manager, speaks fantastic English and will be happy to help you arrange activities around Meknes or even day trips to Volubilis and Moulay Idriss. The Maharaja Suite on the terrace can sleep a family of four or a small group of friends, while couples might consider the Rim Room, which has a private terrace and views over the main square. Heating, Wi-Fi, and breakfast are included. Lunch and dinners are available on command. For the best prices, contact Ryad Bahia to book directly. If you're looking for a little getaway, consider their second property outside of Meknes, Les Jardins de Ryad Bahia.

RIAD MEKNES

79 Ksar Chaacha; tel. 0535/530 542; 650Dh d

Housed in the only remaining palace of the sultan Moulay Ismail. One of the multiple courtyards features a small swimming pool, one of the few in Meknes, which can be just the thing for a refreshing dip in the hot summer months. The pool is unheated and often drained for colder months. Just a short walk from the Bab Mansour, this well-located guesthouse is a fine choice in the medina. The rooms have an understated, chic quality, and are light and airy, emanating a distant sense of royalty. Air-conditioning, heating, Wi-Fi, and breakfast are all included.

INFORMATION AND SERVICES

The city code for Meknes and the area is 35.

Visitor Information

There is an **information kiosk** (Pl. el-Hedim, Fri. 9am-1pm, Sat.-Mon. 9am-4:30pm) across from Bab Mansour that can direct you around the medina and help you get oriented. The **tourist office** (27 Pl. l'Administrative, Mon.-Fri. 9am–4:30pm) in the Ville Nouvelle is a good place to get up-to-date information for events and concerts. The staff is eager to help and can speak English.

Post Offices and Courier Services

In the medina, head to the post office on Rue Smen down from Bab Mansour to send packages and postcards. If you're in the Ville Nouvelle, the post office (Pl. Administrative) is near the Hotel de Ville. Offices keep the same hours (Mon.-Fri. 9am-4:30pm, Sat. 9:30am-noon, shortened during Ramadan).

Arabic Language Courses

The Swedish-run **Ambergh Education** (www.ambergh.com, arabic@ambergh.com) offers Arabic courses starting at US$840 for two weeks; accommodations can be added to your tuition for US$700 or more a week, including the option of staying with a guest family. Classes focus primarily on Modern Standard Arabic, though classes in Darija are available.

Money

There are two handy ATMs northeast of Bab Mansour along Rue Dar Smen (the Banque Populaire will be on your right and the BMCE on your left) and a convenient BMCI ATM on the Pl. el-Hedim near the Dar Jamaï Museum. The Abdelkader train station has an ATM, and many others are scattered throughout the Ville Nouvelle. For travelers checks, foreign currency exchanges, and other services, it's best to use BMCE. The most convenient location for most travelers is at 66 Rue Rouamzine in the medina, near Bab Mansour.

Safety

Meknes is a lot more relaxed than other major Moroccan cities. The normal caution should be exercised, as there are the occasional pickpockets, especially around Place el-Hedim after sunset. Otherwise, the medina is quite safe and mostly full of families.

Hospitals, Clinics, and Pharmacies

If you have a medical emergency, it is best to head for the hospital in Rabat. There are several hospitals in Meknes, but none seemed to be well equipped. For non-emergencies, it is better to use private clinics in the Ville Nouvelle, such as **Polyclinique Ibn Rochd** (Blvd. Bir Anzarane, Route d'el Hajeb, tel. 0535/515 577). For a pharmacy, try the **Grande Pharmacie** (21 Bouderbala, Imm de la Mosquée, tel. 0535/546 355, daily 9am-8pm) in the Ville Nouvelle, and watch for the posting that lists the weekend and 24-hour pharmacies (these change every week).

GETTING THERE

BY CAR

Meknes is connected with the tolled A2 autoroute by two exits, Meknes East and Meknes West. Cities connected with Meknes along the tolled freeways include **Casablanca** (232km/144mi, 2.5hr), **Fez** (70km/43mi, 1hr), **Marrakesh** (469km/291mi, 5hr), **Oujda** (383km/237mi, 4hr), **Rabat** (141km/88mi, 1.5hr), and **Tangier** (341km/212mi, 4hr). **Azrou** (69km/43mi, 1hr) is just over an hour away along National Road 13 (N13).

BY BUS

The **CTM** (tel. 0800/0900 30, www.ctm.ma) buses arrive and depart from the CTM station along Avenue de Fez. Popular connections include: **Casablanca** (4hr, 7 daily, 85Dh), **Fez** (1hr, 10 daily, 25Dh), **Marrakesh** (7hr, 3 daily, 160Dh), **Rabat** (2hr, 9 daily, 55Dh), **Rissani** (9hr, 1 daily, 150Dh), and **Tangier** (5hr, 4 daily, 100Dh). The overnight bus to Rissani leaves at 10:30pm and is perhaps the best way to get to the **Merzouga** and the desert.

From the CTM station it is easily possible to flag down *petits taxis* to take you to the medina, train station, or other places around the Ville Nouvelle and the Avenue de Fez. For the medina, it's best to ask for Bab Mansour (20Dh).

Those arriving by *grand taxi* or local bus will usually arrive near either Bab Bardain or the Souk Atriya. Those arriving at the Souk Atriya will only have a short uphill walk to Bab Mansour and Place el-Hedim. Those arriving at Bab Bardain will be in the north end of the medina and will have to either navigate their way through the medina or take a *petit taxi* around to the main entrance at Bab Mansour (20Dh).

BY TRAIN

Travelers can arrive and depart from two stations in the Ville Nouvelle, either the **Meknes**

train station (often called Gare de Meknes or Grand Gare) a few kilometers west of the medina off the R718, not far from the CTM station, or the **Abdelkader train station** (Gare el Amir Abdelkader), also west, though closer into the main walking routes in the Ville Nouvelle along Rue Amir Abdelkader.

There are direct trains run by **ONCF** (tel. 0890/203 040, www.oncf.ma) from **Casablanca** (4hr, 19 daily, 2nd/1st-class 90Dh/135Dh), **Marrakesh** (7hr, 8 daily, 174Dh/265Dh), **Oujda** (6.5hr, 3 daily, 130Dh/190Dh), **Rabat** (3hr, 19 daily, 65Dh/90Dh), and **Tangier** (5hr, 6 daily, 85Dh/130Dh), with stops in between. Early morning trains to Tangier have a transfer at Sidi Kacem. Not all trains stop in Meknes at Abdelkader, though it is a little closer to the medina and there are a few hotel options nearby. If you're traveling to/from Tangier, consider transferring at Kenitra to save a bit of a time on the high-speed Al-Boraq train, making the trip about 3 hours.

Blue *petits taxis* are available at either train station. From either train station, you can walk one block directly from the train station to a main street where you can find a taxi relatively easily most of the time. The fare from either train station to Bab Mansour should be 15-20Dh, though you will pay a bit more at night. *Petits taxis* take only three passengers. For larger groups, it might be better to pay slightly more for the *grands taxis* that are usually hanging out along the main road in front of both train stations.

GETTING AROUND

Like the other medinas in Morocco, the Meknes medina is accessible only by foot.

There is **guarded overnight parking** inside Bab Bardain and down from Place el-Hedim near the Meknes Royal Golf Club for 20Dh a day. Pay when you leave, not before.

Petits taxis are the most convenient way to shuttle between the Ville Nouvelle and the medina. Taxis are metered and generally cost 10-20Dh to go just about anywhere in Meknes.

Local buses run 6am-9pm (5Dh). The 2, 3, 5, 6, and 7 lines run between Place el-Hedim and the Ville Nouvelle, with the 5 and 6 continuing to either of the train stations and the primary bus station.

The Middle Atlas

The Middle Atlas is still primarily a series of Amazigh villages, some more interesting than others, set between limestone plateaus, stony fields, and forests of scrub oak, pine, and cedar. The history of these seminomadic people is relatively unknown, existing more in story and myth than anything else. Recent discoveries have indicated that nomadic civilizations have used the mountains for thousands of years, usually during the more welcoming summer months, sometimes dwelling in caves and other times living in tents and loose stone buildings throughout the mountain range, while herding livestock.

The people mostly speak Tashelhit (one of the Tamazight languages indigenous to Morocco), with Moroccan Arabic (Darija) as a second language and often some French, Spanish, or English as a third language. Tribal meetings take place seasonally throughout the region, and often you will see tents or loose stone houses along the roadways, much like they have existed since time immemorial.

The Middle Atlas is a relatively unexplored gem for nature lovers. Here, evergreens are a constant, along with the Azrou Cedar Forest and the rolling hills of the Ifrane and Tazekka National Parks. There are several good hiking trails throughout the region, plenty of spots for bird-watching, and the opportunity to visit with the local Barbary macaques. Hiking and fishing throughout the region are excellent, particularly in the spring and fall months, with May and June perhaps being the best two months to explore the region by foot, when the winter snow has melted and the flowers are all in bloom. Trails here are predominantly well established and often used by locals as much as tourists. Hikers should be warned that a run-in with wild dogs or shepherd dogs is common, though actual attacks are very uncommon. Still, it can be a startling sight for the unprepared.

Tourism is only beginning in the Middle Atlas. There are few options for upscale lodging. Most accommodations here are geared toward travelers comfortable with camping and cold water, wanting a real "Berber" experience. The people here are generally friendly, though poorer and less educated than in many other parts of Morocco. Many Peace Corps volunteers are spread throughout the smaller villages of this region, working on education and local infrastructure and sometimes helping with tourism projects.

A couple of well-kept national roads cross through this region (the N8 and N13). However, much of the driving takes place on small, unmaintained roads. Many are difficult, if not impossible, to traverse through the snowy winter months.

TOP EXPERIENCE

★ VOLUBILIS

daily 8am-6:30pm, 10Dh; guides available for 150Dh an hour but unnecessary

Volubilis—known better to many of the locals by its Arabic name, **Walili**—makes for a breathtaking day trip from either Fez or Meknes. You will likely make out the impressive ruin of Volubilis long before you arrive. It is a phenomenal scene that unfolds along a series of winding roads and, in the spring, seems to rise from the lush green hills and limestone cliffs on a plateau, a sort of echo of the nearby white-washed town of Moulay Idriss, tucked in the folds of the Zerhoun Mountains.

Though the ruins of Volubilis are primarily Roman, the town itself existed long before the arrival of the Roman empire. There is evidence of a settlement existing here as long ago as 3,000 BC due to its fertile valley and commanding position. Neolithic pottery has been found in the area, and there is ample evidence of a Phoenician and subsequent Carthaginian outpost that existed a few centuries before the Romans arrived.

For many years, Volubilis was a prosperous town of about 12 hectares (30 acres) in size,

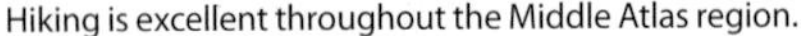

Hiking is excellent throughout the Middle Atlas region.

A Little Roman History of Morocco

a roman mosaic left to the elements

After the fall of Carthage in AD 40, Rome annexed most of what is now Morocco into its territories, though rule was done through subservient Amazigh tribal kings. The region was named Mauritania Tingitana. Gradually, Rome expanded its administrative and military occupation. Under Emperor Augustus, Roman rule expanded from locations in the north, such as Cotta in Tangier and Lixus near Larache, to Thamusida and Banasa until it reached the literal end of the Roman Road in Volubilis. Augustus established three colonies with Roman citizens, introduced Christianity, and (it is thought) dispatched outposts of Roman legionnaires as far south as modern-day Casablanca in a town named Anfa.

The few centuries of Roman rule saw great economic prosperity, with the newly established roads making the travel, sale, import, and export of goods easier. Olive oil, silver and bronze work, and a type of rancid fish oil were among the primary sources of wealth. However, it was under Roman rule that much of the region's wildlife, including the Atlas bear and Barbary lion, became endangered. They were prized for their size and ferocity and sent back to Rome for gladiatorial matches.

Around AD 278, the capital of Mauritania Tingitana was moved from Volubilis to Tangier, signaling the beginning of the Roman exodus from the region. The brief Roman rule of Morocco gradually declined with the waning power of the Roman empire. In AD 429, the Vandals put a definitive end to Roman control in the region, though by this time, most of Morocco was back in the control of the more powerful Amazigh tribes.

developed on a pattern typical of Phoenician and Carthaginian settlements, enclosed by a long protective wall with the small city gate near today's parking lot being one of the entrances. An aqueduct, likely constructed in the 1st century AD, fed the city with water into its public baths, houses, and fountains through a complex network of channels. The Romans expanded the city to about 40 hectares (100 acres). During this time, olive oil was the primary source of wealth. Some 58 oil presses have been discovered on the site.

The ruins you see today are primarily from the 2nd and 3rd centuries AD, when the Romans annexed the region into their empire and made Volubilis the literal end of the road that stretched across France and Spain, into Tangier and south until

Volubilis. The Romans retreated from the area late in the 3rd century. Volubilis continued to prosper under local rule, functioning as an Amazigh capital of the region, housing Christian and Jewish settlers after the Romans were driven out.

It was here that Moulay Idriss first came when he sought refuge in the 8th century, establishing the first Moroccan empire, the Idrisid dynasty, in 788. Over the years, the inhabitants moved elsewhere, many to the neighboring town of Moulay Idriss, and Volubilis slowly fell into ruin. Its demise came when Moulay Ismail pillaged the city for its marble and precious stone and had them carried by his slaves to his lavish palaces in Meknes. Whatever was left was likely decimated by the 1755 Lisbon earthquake.

Volubilis has been listed as a UNESCO World Heritage Site since 1997. Excavation is a slow but ongoing process. Only about half of the site has been excavated, and discoveries are still being made. It is best to visit in the early mornings before the sun is too strong. The ruins are on an exposed hill with no real shaded areas to be found, and heatstroke can be a real concern, especially during the summer. Unlike the Roman ruins of Rome and elsewhere in Europe, these ruins are not particularly well guarded, and it is possible to wander unmolested, but respect the ruins to preserve them as well as possible.

Diana and the Bathing Nymphs

As you meander the ruin, keep an eye out for some of the most wonderful mosaic work to still be found *in situ* in a Roman ruin. Along the main thoroughfare, the **Decumanus Maximus,** you will find several mosaics in the surrounding houses. These are all starting to show signs of wear, and their bright colors have faded from years of exposure and neglect. Of these mosaics, the most impressive is *Diana and the Bathing Nymphs,* located in the **House of Venus** on the eastern side of the city. The mosaic depicting Venus has been moved to the Museum of Moroccan Art and Antiquities in Tangier, but *Diana and her Bathing Nymphs* has been left behind. The mosaic shows the goddess Diana with one of her companion nymphs being surprised by Actaeon. Notice the horns growing from his head, indicating his transformation into a stag, a punishment meted out by the displeased goddess.

Triumphal Arch

The stone **Arch of Caracalla** is one of the more distinctive sights of Volubilis, constructed in 217 by the city's governor to honor the Roman emperor Caracalla and his influential mother, Julia Domna. Before construction had finished on the arch, the emperor was murdered while relieving himself on the road between Edessa and Carrhae. The arch was reconstructed during the French protectorate between 1930 and 1934, with the inscription being based on the journal entries of the English antiquarian John Windus, who visited in 1722. The Latin inscription reads:

> For the emperor Caesar, Marcus Aurelius Antoninus [Caracalla], the pious, fortunate Augustus, greatest victor in Parthia, greatest victor in Britain, greatest victor in Germany, *Pontifex Maximus,* holding tribunician power for the twentieth time, Emperor for the fourth time, Consul for the fourth time, Father of the Country, Proconsul, and for Julia Augusta [Julia Domna], the pious, fortunate mother of the camp and the Senate and the country, because of his exceptional and new kindness toward all, which is greater than that of the principes that came before, the Republic of the Volubilitans took care to have this arch made from the ground up, including a chariot drawn by six horses and all the ornaments, with Marcus Aurelius Sebastenus, *procurator,* who is most deeply devoted to the divinity of Augustus, initiating and dedicating it.

House of the Columns

Turning from the arch, there is a series of ruins of houses easily found by looking for the one remaining house with several columns protruding. This is the House of the Columns. Adjacent to this house is the House of Ephèbe, built around a courtyard and pool, named after a bronze statue that was found in the ruins here. The Knight's House next door features a mosaic of Bacchus, the god of wine and a good time, while the House of the Labors of Hercules has a series of mosaics featuring the great acts of Hercules.

Basilica

Just a few short steps south from the Arch of Caracalla is the impressive basilica, measuring 42.2 meters (138ft) long by 22.3 meters (73ft) wide. The original building was two stories tall, though you wouldn't know it by looking at it today. The interior is lined on either side by two rows of columns framing the apses at either end of the building. The outside looks over the forum, where local markets were held. Small temples, public offices, and perhaps other businesses lined the forum. The pedestals you see now once held statues of emperors and local dignitaries. Little else is known about the buildings because many were torn down and 3rd-century constructions were built on their foundations.

Getting There

The Roman ruins of **Volubilis** are perhaps the most popular day trip from either Fez or Meknes. Whether by car, hired taxi, or bus, you will travel either west from **Fez** (84km/52mi, 1.5hr) or east from **Meknes** (64km/40mi, 45min) following the signs for **Moulay Idriss** along the N13, a winding, sparsely forested road that connects Fez to Meknes and makes for a scenic drive, taking you through several hills and valleys before Volubilis and Moulay Idriss suddenly appear from the surrounding hills like magic. These two ancient cities lie along the same road, just a few kilometers apart, offering a glimpse into Morocco's storied past.

You can get to Volubilis from Meknes by bus. The **15 bus** (5Dh) departs near the Place Ferhat Hachid in the Ville Nouvelle and serves Moulay Idriss. The bus runs every hour, though unreliably, and the ride is about an hour long. *Grands taxis* can be hired from the bus stations and train stations in Meknes. It's best to negotiate the price for a half day (250-400Dh) so the taxi will wait for you while you tour Volubilis and Moulay Idriss.

Prices for renting a taxi from Fez typically range from 400-800Dh and are the most reliable transport available.

the hillside town of Moulay Idriss

MOULAY IDRISS

Sitting on a hill within the short Zerhoun Mountains, the small town of **Moulay Idriss** is home to one of the holiest destinations in Morocco, the Mausoleum of Moulay Idriss I. The town was closed to non-Muslims for many years. It has only been in the last few decades that non-Muslims have been allowed within the city (and, even then, it's only since 2004 that they have been allowed to spend the night in the city), though access to sights such as the Mausoleum of Moulay Idriss I are still off-limits to non-Muslims. As such, there is a small, but growing, tourist industry. Lodgings are relatively inexpensive, though they are without exception more of a home-stay than sleeping in a hotel. For most travelers, this is an opportune time to see a side of Morocco that is relatively untouched by tourism and, in many ways, still very traditional.

As in most of the region, springtime is the best time to visit, when the surroundings are green and in bloom and the temperatures more agreeable. The town itself is full of stairs and hills, some of which provide great vantage points. It is best to locate the main square—Place Khiber—and then the Mausoleum of Moulay Idriss I. Nearly all directions in Moulay Idriss are in reference to these two main points. From the main square, facing the main mausoleum entrance, you can take a passage to the left and follow the signs for Sidi Abdallah el Hajjam (another mausoleum at the top of the hill) for a bird's-eye view of the entire town. From here, you can get a good idea of the size of the mausoleum, though you'll likely be a little short of breath, and not just from the view.

Unofficial guides can lead you around the city for about 50Dh, which is a good idea if you wish to save yourself some walking time. Many of the streets abruptly end, and though the medina is not particularly large, it is very hilly and confusing. It is possible to walk from Moulay Idriss to Volubilis. There is a good trail that takes about an hour (about 4km/2.5mi) and is downhill for the most part.

Mausoleum of Moulay Idriss I

Without a doubt, the Mausoleum of Moulay Idriss I, the founder of modern-day Morocco and the town's namesake, is the primary reason for most travelers to visit the town of Moulay Idriss. Moulay Idriss I fled the Abbasid caliphs of Baghdad in the 8th century and took refuge in nearby Volubilis. He is a known descendant of the Prophet Mohammed and founded the first Arab-Muslim dynasty. Many pilgrims make their way here to show their respect. As at many of the other mausoleums around Morocco, you can expect to find many women here to receive the powerful *baraka* (blessing) from Moulay Idriss. For Moroccans, a visit to this mausoleum is worth one-fifth of a full hajj to Mecca. Located directly in the heart of town off Place Moulay Idriss I, the mausoleum has been recently cleaned and can be well admired from outside from the streets above. Inside, the elaborate arches, *zellij* work, and carved wood dating from the reconstruction under Moulay Ismail in the 18th century make this architecturally stunning mausoleum a real treat. The mausoleum is closed to non-Muslims.

Medersa Idriss I

Uphill from the main square you might come across a circular minaret covered in green tile. This is the Medersa Idriss I (closed to visitors), and the minaret is the only one of its kind in Morocco. After completing the hajj, a pious man came back and built this *medersa* in the 1939 using materials taken from nearby Volubilis. The design was purportedly inspired by the minarets he had seen in Mecca. The ornate Arabic script circling this unique minaret is a chapter from the Quran.

Accommodations

MAISON D'HÔTES HANNOUI

5 Rue Ben Yazgha; tel. 0535/544 106; www.riadhannoui.eu.ma; 200Dh s, 300Dh d

One of the better choices in the medina, with musical entertainment available most nights. Zakia, the proprietor, offers cooking courses (50Dh an hour, not per person, so a great value for small groups; reservations required), traditional hammams (100-300Dh with massage), and even picnic trips to Volubilis by foot, donkey, or horse (150Dh). Try to get one of the rooms upstairs, as the rooms on the bottom floors smell a bit musty. Breakfast is included.

CAMPING

Tagourart Ain Karma

Just a couple of kilometers toward Meknes off the main road is a free campsite with wonderful views, a popular stop for travelers, caravaners from Europe, and pilgrims making their way to Moulay Idriss. Though the camping is free, showers will set you back 10Dh, and there is very little infrastructure here.

AZROU

ازرو

Though plenty of tourists make their way to Azrou, the city has maintained its sense of authenticity and literally circles around the town namesake: the central, crowned *azrou* (the Tashelhit word for "rock"), an imposing outcropping of rock that sits astride the old medina and the Ville Nouvelle just below the Grand Mosque. The small medina is easily navigable and the town boasts a large Tuesday souk, one of the more popular in the region. Most travelers will likely spend most of their time around Place Mohammed V. Shops and cafés line the square, making it a pleasant place to spend a couple of hours writing postcards, talking with friends, or reading a book. On the plaza you can also find ATMs (Banque Populaire and BMCE).

Azrou is the place to buy souvenirs. The prices are much lower than you will find elsewhere, and the shopkeepers are generally more honest, though haggling is still sometimes necessary.

For most hikers and nature lovers, Azrou is where they make their home base. From here, many trails wind through the surrounding cedar forest. You can check in with the famous Barbary macaques, shuffle down limestone cliffs and across pastures of calendula, poppies, and flax, and find the occasional orchid.

Sports and Recreation

★ AZROU CEDAR FOREST

www.eauxetforets.gov.ma

The Azrou Cedar Forest is part of the larger Ifrane National Park and well known throughout Morocco. It boasts cedars that are over 400 years old, some growing to over 60 meters (200ft) high. Though logging has taken a toll on the population, locally there is a sense of preservation with several initiatives that have been encouraged, including the expansion of the Ifrane National Park, which houses most of the cedar trees in the Middle Atlas region. Most Moroccans take pride in the cedar forest, and the local community is beginning to understand its importance to their survival. Logging is now better regulated and replanting frequently occurs. Hiking, bird-watching, fishing, and visiting with the Barbary macaques are all popular activities.

Birders will want to come prepared with a good pair of binoculars. In the cedar forests of the national park, along the banks of many of the small lakes, while driving along and even while walking around the small towns of the region, numerous species are readily spotted. Storks, herons, lesser kestrels, and the hooting scops owl are some of the larger birds to spot, while the Moussier's redstart, Atlas flycatcher, North African tit, and Levaillant's woodpecker should make any ornithologist's list.

Hiking in this region is encouraged. Several trails snake through the cedar forest, with the most popular a 14-kilometer (8.5mi) hike that takes you to the top of the rock jutting out above Azrou. This hike slopes uphill through the cedar forest and some rocky outcrops. It's taxing but not difficult. Pack plenty of water. You'll find the trailhead behind the Azrou medina, at the foot of the hill south of the large mosque. Most locals are very familiar with this hike and the path is obvious the entire way. This is perhaps the

Barbary Macaques

Often and incorrectly referred to as the "Barbary ape," the Barbary macaque is a unique species found in Morocco, Algeria, Libya, and across the Mediterranean on Gibraltar. It is marked by a vestigial tail and is one of the best known Old World species of monkey. Like many other Old World species, the tribes are matrilineal, with daughters staying with their mothers for life. Most tribes either have one male to drive off the other males, or the males in the group establish a hierarchy. A full-grown female is about 56 centimeters (22in) in height and weighs approximately 10 kilograms (22lb), while a male is 66 centimeters (25in) and weighs about 15 kilograms (32lb). They take their name from the Barbary Coast region of North Africa. The macaques around the region are generally accustomed to people. There is a popular stop on the road to Midelt (N13, just a kilometer or so south from Azrou) where people feed and take pictures with the monkeys, though feeding is discouraged. There are problems now with overweight monkeys being unable to climb trees to avoid predators. This has taken a toll on the numbers of the local population in recent years.

easiest access point for the forest. You'll want to give yourself a full day, if time allows, so pack a picnic and plenty of water.

Shopping

Azrou has long been a stopover for traders and merchants due to its strategic location. Because of this, a wide variety of shops and bazaars line the main square and are sprinkled throughout the medina. Most of these shops do not engage in the high-pressure tactics common in many of the other cities, which makes shopping a lot more enjoyable. You will easily be able to find cedarwood boxes, locally woven Amazigh carpets, Fassi leather bags, Moroccan slippers, silver jewelry, argan oil, locally produced honey, and pottery.

DAR NEGHRASSI

22 Rue des Tapis; tel. 0670/360 998 or 0673/578 393; darneghrassi@gmail.com; daily 9am-10pm

Si Moha and his son Abdou run a homey bazaar at Dar Neghrassi. They will happily tell you about the history of the region, good hiking trails, and, of course, the history of their unique carpet collection. There is no pressure to buy, though it might be difficult to leave without at least a small rag rug, known as a *boucharouette,* rolled up and stuffed in the bottom of your bag.

CHARIFI ABDELLAH ET SES FILS

Pl. Mohammed V; tel. 0535/560 799; bazarhcarifi@hotmail.com; daily 9am-8pm, closed Fri. morning

The fixed-price Charifi Abdellah et Ses Fils is a great place for Moroccan slippers, leather bags, cedarwood boxes, silver jewelry, and other goods you have probably seen in most bazaars in Fez or Marrakesh.

ENSEMBLE ARTISANAL

Blvd. Hassan II; daily 8am-6pm

The government-run Ensemble Artisanal, on the other side of the medina from Place Mohammed V, down the street from the Grande Mosquée, houses small shops, each with fixed prices, displaying their specialized craft. Head here for pottery, newer carpets, cedarwood bowls, and occasionally wood and stone sculptures. You'll help support the artisans in continuing their craft.

MOUNIR'S SHOP

Zankat Moulay Achrif; tel. 0670/620 066; open daily, but hours vary widely

If you are in the market for a *wahtar* or *gimbri* (types of Amazigh guitar-like instruments), head to Mounir's Shop. Mounir is well known throughout Morocco, and his instruments made of goat skin, sheep intestines, walnut, poplar, and cedar are sold throughout the world. Sometimes you can see Mounir working at his shop in the Ensemble Artisanal and playing some of the great songs of the Middle Atlas to pass the time.

Food and Accommodations

In Azrou, there are a few good options for cheap eats outside of the hotels, of which there are many budget options, with the best being located closer to the forests and hiking trails. There are a couple of hotels in town.

CHEZ AZIZ

Zankat Ait Ghriss next to the mosque in the medina; daily 8am-10pm; 5Dh

Check out Chez Aziz for a great bowl of *bissara*. Not only is the soup top-notch, but it's a real local experience with workers in the neighborhood all gathering here for a quick bowl. Top off your bowl with as much olive oil and *sudani* (crushed red peppers) as you can manage.

BOULANGERIE PÂTISSERIE L'ESCALADE

5 Pl. Hassan II; tel. 0535/563 419; lescaladeboulangerie@hotmail.com; daily 6am-9pm; 10Dh

Just off Place Mohammed V on the corner facing the big mosque is Boulangerie Pâtisserie l'Escalade, which has savory pizzas, *pastillas*, a good selection of breads, and French-style sweets.

HOTEL RESTAURANT LES CEDRES

Pl. Mohammed V; tel. 0535/562 326; daily 11:30am-3pm and 7pm-10pm; 90Dh

Hotel Restaurant Les Cedres is a simple option for a quick bite overlooking the plaza. Stick with the trout—they get it fresh every day. Indoors it's a bit gloomy, but on a nice day, the terrace is a wonderful place to people-watch in the bustling afternoon and early evening.

AUBERGE LA FORESTIERE

Km33, Route d'Errachidia, Timahdite; tel. 0635/560 403 or 0662/096 899; elgraimy46@yahoo.fr; 250Dh d

For hikers, a great option is Auberge la Forestiere, near the village of Timahdite 33 kilometers (20mi) south of Azrou. The rooms are all rustic and can be quite cold during the winter months, so ask for extra blankets. Breakfast runs 60Dh.

PANORAMA HOTEL

Parc Tarsemt; tel. 0535/562 010 or 0535/562 242; panorama_hot@menara.ma; 500Dh d

The Panorama Hotel was built in the 1930s in a wooded chalet style. It's dated but comfortable, if overpriced. However, a well-equipped bar generally has a roaring fire in the winter.

★ LE PALAIS DE CERISIERS

just off the N8 on Route du Cèdre Gorou; tel. 0535/563 830 or 0649/321 321; restaurant 150Dh, hotel 900Dh d

This is the high-end option around Azrou, complete with full-service hammam, bar, restaurant, and swimming pool. It's decorated in a chalet style with lots of wood and marble. Though perhaps the lodgings are a touch overpriced, the restaurant is top notch and a nice change of pace from the run-of-the-mill tajines on offer in the region. With new French-Moroccan owners arrived to settle in the mountains after their last few years in the hustle and smog of Casablanca, the weekends here can be extremely busy. Reserve ahead of time and go for the salmon burger or another French bistro staple. Local trout are featured, and if the duck is on the menu, it's another winner.

EUROCAMPING

Ougmès; tel. 0513/143 030; www.camping-morocco.com/euro_camping.html; 20Dh for 1 camper van

Along the road to Ifrane (R17), just a couple of kilometers after you leave Azrou, is Eurocamping, also known as the Emirati Tourist Center. Though tent camping is possible, the facilities cater to the Europeans driving through Morocco with camping cars. A swimming pool (10Dh), laundry (10Dh), hot showers (10Dh), bathrooms, and a small market can all be found on-site.

Getting There and Around

Historically, Azrou was a major stop on the route from **Fez** (83km/52mi, 1.5hr) to **Errachidia** (261km/162mi, 4.5hr) and the desert. It served as a transportation hub, as it does today. The conveniently located ***gare routière*** on the N13 across from the large mosque has local bus and **grand taxi service** to most nearby destinations, such as **Ifrane** (30min, 19km/12mi, 9Dh), **Meknes** (1hr, 69km/43mi, 38Dh), and **Fez** (1.5hr, 83km/51mi, 45Dh); for *grands taxis* to **Ain Leuh** (30min, 28km/17mi, 12Dh), **M'Rirt** (1hr, 58km/36mi, 35Dh), or **Khenifra** (1.5hr, 81km/50mi, 45Dh), head to the secondary taxi station across from the Ensemble Artisanal.

The Azrou Cedar Forest surrounds Azrou. It's easily possible to begin a **hike** from the center of town. Those with cars might want to take the road south toward Midelt, where there are several places to park just a kilometer or so out of Azrou that offer easy access to the forest.

★ OUM ER-RBIA WATERFALLS

أم الربيع

The impressive waterfalls of Oum er-Rbia (sometimes "Oum Rabie") are about a two-hour drive from Azrou and make for a fine day trip. Local cafés line the pathway along the river to the waterfalls, each serving a family-style tajine for about 35-50Dh. The cafés are little more than a series of rickety structures that are often washed away with the winter rains and rebuilt every spring. Travelers often stop here for lunch on the fun walk to and from the waterfalls.

The waterfalls themselves are an impressive sight, cascading over a sheer, though climbable, rock face. Forty-three different springs meet to form the river just before the waterfall. During the warmer months, the pool at the base of the waterfall becomes a popular spot with local youths and hikers to take a swim and cool off.

Getting There and Around

You'll have to get to Oum er-Rbia by **car.** From **Azrou** (60km/37mi, 1.5hr) you can take the route to **Ain Leuh** (turn off the N13 onto the P7215) and continue from there, though often this road is backed up and it can be quicker to take the N8; just look for a turn-off near M'rirt for the Source d'Oum er-Rbia. ***Grands taxis*** from Azrou (45Dh) are sometimes available, though it is likely you'll have to pay for the entire taxi.

The town is small enough that you'll be **walking** around, though streets can get muddy here during storms.

IFRANE

إفران

Dubbed by the locals as the "Little Switzerland" of Morocco, this small mountain village is one of the most popular in-country tourist destinations for Moroccans during holidays and weekends. In winter there is often snow at the nearby Michlifen Ski Station for those learning to ski or sled. In the summer it provides a cooling respite from the hotter cities in the region. Ifrane is home to one of the king's palaces and a growing number of resorts and hotels.

Many Americans and other international students find themselves in Ifrane studying at **Al Akhawayn University** (www.aui.ma), a small university based on an American-style liberal arts curriculum. Classes here are primarily taught in English. Though the school is still thought of by most Moroccans as an elite university only for the rich, scholarships and increased activity in the local community are beginning to change this perception.

Ifrane is somehow less "Moroccan" than other towns. It's generally clean, and its lush green spaces are a nice change of pace from the rest of the country, making it an adequate base to explore the region throughout the Ifrane National Park, from nearby Azrou to farther afield Taza, Oum er-Rbia, and Zaouia d'Ifrane. However, because of its popularity among locals, accommodations are generally more expensive and have less value. For alternatives, check out nearby Azrou.

If you're passing through Ifrane for a day or spending more time here, be sure to take your picture in front of the stone lion near Centre Ville. The lion commemorates the last of the Atlas lions, who have now gone extinct in the wild. The story is that the lion was carved by a prisoner—either Italian or German, depending on whom you believe—but more recent scholarship points to a high school art teacher completing the sculpture in the early 1930s, modeling it on the famous Court of Lions at the Alhambra in Granada, Spain.

For those looking to stay in the city limits, the **Ain Vittel waterfalls and park** on the northern edge are wonderful for a picnic and an easy stroll. Signs for Ain Vittel are posted all over the city, and during the summer months and busy weekends there are a lot of local tourists. It's possible to walk to Ain Vittel from the city center, but most people take a *petit taxi* (15Dh). A short horseback ride is available for about 20Dh. Those looking for guides can check **Tourisme Vert** (http://tourisme-vert-ifrane.com/page1.html) or nearby **Moroccan Unexplored** (11 Street des Abatiers, Azrou, tel. 0535/561 876).

Hiking, Biking, and Bird-Watching

Hiking and biking are fairly common weekend activities throughout the region. There are plenty of well-traversed trails, especially toward Ras el-Ma and Michlifen. A popular trail leads through the different **lakes (*dayats*)** of the region: Aaoua, Ifrah, Afourgah, and Iffer (Dayat Aaoua and Ifrah are the largest). The beginning of the hiking trail at Lake Aaoua is about 12 kilometers (7mi) north of Ifrane. An easy-to-spot road sign leads the way to Lake Aaoua off the route to Fez (N8). The hike itself is easy, though occasionally the footing gets a bit loose. Lake Aaoua is a popular picnic stop with the locals and is a fantastic spot for birding. Keep an eye out for coots, herons, egrets, black-winged stilts, and reed warblers.

Along the trails and into the cedar and oak forest, there are tits, chaffinches, short-toed treecreepers, jays, greater spotted woodpeckers, and raptors, including black and red kites, Egyptian vultures, and booted eagles. Foxes and jackals have been spotted in the region.

Another popular, considerably easier hike, is a pretty 8-kilometer (5-mi) trek that circles the **king's castle** and property, taking you through pine trees and down to the Zarouka Pond, another great stop for bird-watchers, though a little less tranquil with the noise of the passing traffic on the nearby road to Fez.

Winter Sports

MICHLIFEN

After a good snow, Moroccan skiers and sledders lose no time making their way to **Michlifen.** Equipment is available for rent, but it's extremely outdated and you will have to bargain. The vintage ski-tows are rarely, if ever, turned on, and you will have to climb one of two runs to make your way down. This is best for beginners and those who don't mind the crowds. More advanced skiers should check out nearby Jbel Hebri. You can take a green *petit taxi* from Ifrane for about 200Dh. Michlifen is about a two-hour drive from either Meknes or Fez.

JBEL HEBRI

Nearby Jbel Hebri is a few meters lower than Michlifen and less popular with the locals, which makes for less-crowded slopes, though the bottoms will still be packed with children and adults on sleds or just enjoying the snow. The ski-tows here are seldom functional, though with the surrounding cedar forest, the off-piste potential is greater for advanced skiers.

Food and Accommodations

There are a surprising number of restaurants around Ifrane. In the market (*marché*) there are several options, all serving the same pizzas and sandwiches, more or less.

1

2

3

DAIFA

Marché municipale #1, tel. 0624350956; daily 11am-10pm; 25Dh

One of the more popular options is Daifa, better known to the locals as "Wad la Hajj," near the parking lot of the market toward Boulevard Mohammed V. Look for the gaudy bright red signs. The food is fast and service is good, with takeout available. It's an especially good option for sandwiches and panini to pack on a picnic.

LA PAIX

Ave. de la Marche Verte; tel. 0535/566 262; 100Dh

In town center (*centre ville*), the ever popular La Paix (Ave. de la Marche Verte, tel. 0535/566 262; 100Dh) features a gaudy though spacious interior and serves up a varied menu, including staples such as pastas, pizzas, tajines, steaks, salads, and couscous. It's a safe, if uninspired, choice for lunch or dinner. The terrace is a prime people-watching spot in the center of town overlooking the small gardens.

★ BONSAI SUSHI

Quartier Hay Riad, near the Beethoven Café down the street from the Grand Hotel; tel. 0673/348 265; daily noon-3pm and 5pm-11pm; 70Dh

Hakim, a former Al Akhawayn University student, is the man responsible for this nonsmoking establishment that features genuine spring rolls, sashimi, sushi rolls, and various Thai-style noodle bowls. The decor is spot-on. This is a popular spot for local university students and faculty, who quickly crowd the small dining space. Luckily, takeout is available. Sushi picnic? It's possible!

PERCE NEIGE

Rue des Asphodelleshay; tel. 0535/566 350; 800Dh d

This is one of the better standard hotels in town, with generally clean rooms and friendly staff. The street can be noisy out front, so it's best to ask for one of the rooms away from the front of the building for a quieter night of sleep. The restaurant downstairs is adequate and has a small selection of local beers and wines. There is smoking in the downstairs bar, which can waft up to the rooms on the first floor (second American floor). Those sensitive should request rooms far away from the bar and main staircase. Air-conditioning, TV, heating, and Wi-Fi are all included.

HOTEL MICHLIFEN SUITES & SPA

north edge of town; tel. 0535/864 000; www.michlifenifrane.com; 3,000Dh d

This palatial property boasts a full-service spa, three restaurants, an indoor/outdoor swimming pool, basketball courts, workout rooms, conference rooms, a 200-person theater, and a lodge-style bar serving up some of the best cocktails in the region. The prices are steep, but the service is what you expect from a five-star hotel. The commanding views over the surrounding mountain peaks and steeple-roofed town make this worth a stop, if only for a coffee. Wi-Fi, air-conditioning, TV, fireplace heating, and breakfast are all included for those wanting to indulge.

CAMPING

The **municipal campground** is near the central market on Boulevard Mohammed V. If you are arriving into town, you can also follow the signs for the **Farah Inn by Best Western** (tel. 0535/567 130, www.bestwestern.com), which has a campground available, though this is farther on the outskirts of town. Basic equipment is available at either campground, with hot showers for 10Dh and tent camping for 15Dh per person.

Getting There and Around

Ifrane is serviced by the N8 from the north, which cuts through town as it connects **Fez** (71km/44mi, 1hr) with **Azrou** (19km/12mi, 20min). A secondary road (R707) connects with **Meknes** (65km/40mi, 1hr) to the east.

Grands taxis to Ifrane are found in **Fez** (1hr, 71km/44mi, 30Dh) near the CTM station, in **Meknes** (1hr, 65km/40mi, 30Dh)

1: a boy riding his donkey through the Tazekka National Park **2:** people sledding in the snow in Ifrane **3:** the picturesque mountain town of Zaouia d'Ifrane downhill from Bab Mansour, and in **Azrou** (30min, 19km/12mi, 9Dh). The **CTM** (tel. 0800/0900 30, www.ctm.ma) bus connects with **Meknes** (1hr, 1 daily, 25Dh) and **Fez** (1hr, 2 daily, 25Dh), as well as **Casablanca** (5hr, 1 daily, 120Dh).

Green *petits taxis* run around town; most fares cost 7-15Dh. Meters are not used here.

ZAOUIA D'IFRANE

زاوية إفران

Well off the established travel route of most tourists, this is one of the most picturesque villages in the entire Middle Atlas. After exiting the national road, you take a 20-minute drive down a zigzagging farm road that leads you through a dry valley before twisting into a small village of mud and rock homes, nestled in the shadow of looming moss-covered cliffs with cascading waterfalls. The accommodations are all rustic, though serviceable. It's a fantastic stop for one or two nights to experience how locals live. For those less adventurous, a day trip is recommended from Ifrane or Azrou.

Shopping

ZAOUIA D'IFRANE WOMEN'S COOPERATIVE

daily 2pm-7pm, except holidays

The **Zaouia d'Ifrane Women's Cooperative** was founded in 2007. You can find the cooperative near the parking lot at the beginning of town following the main road. The cooperative will be on your left, though the sign is written only in Arabic. Textiles, couscous, *sfoof* (a type of ground nut mix), and sometimes other goods are sold. Proceeds help stop deforestation of the region.

Hiking

There are beautiful, relatively easy hikes around Zaouia d'Ifrane where you can walk through farmlands and beneath cascading waterfalls, then take a refreshing drink at the local spring. Follow the signs through town to "Gite Challal" to find the **main trailhead** at the edge of town. Follow the trail either up to the plateau or down to the river. Both hikes can be done in just a couple of hours with well-traveled paths also used by locals with their donkeys and mules shuttling goods back and forth.

Up the plateau there are usually grazing horses, mules, donkeys, and cattle, and stunning views of the valley and the cedar- and oak-forested mountains. Following the route along the plateau and then down the other side, where you follow the dried out riverbed, will bring you to the other side of town and past the large waterfall. A hike to the top of the plateau can easily be done in an hour, which is perfect for those packing a picnic.

Along the river is a relatively flat trail where you can expect to find a few tents selling tajines and, in the warm months, kids diving into swimming holes. Keep a lookout for Barbary macaques swooping in to eat the local figs. This is a short, easy hike, about 45 minutes, though you have to cross the shallow river on slippery rocks. Be sure to pack a good pair of waterproof shoes.

Food and Accommodations

All of the local accommodations have food options. If you don't reserve your lunch or dinner ahead of time, you'll likely have to wait one hour or more as your *tajine* is being cooked. All accommodations will ask you if you want breakfast, lunch, and/or dinner included. It's usually a good idea to have all meals included unless you've packed food ahead of time.

CHEZ HACHIMI

town center; tel. 0535/560 578; 500Dh d, no meals

Chez Hachimi features an exposed outdoor courtyard with a bubbling fountain. Decor is simple, with standard Berber carpets from the region covering the floors. There are five rooms—three downstairs with beds, two upstairs without mattresses where you will sleep on a pile of carpets. As in most buildings in Zaouia d'Ifrane, there are patches on the walls from humidity, though a stay here includes the ability to use the rustic hammam. This is best for a family or group, as rentals are only available for the entire house.

GITE RAHA

town center; tel. 678/416 827; 50Dh without meals, 200Dh with all meals

Locals know Gite Raha as "Chez Hyatt" or "Gite dial Hyatt." Hyatt, the manager, is the smiling face that greets you here. The well-run, clean *gîte* is decorated with small rock wall sculptures, starting with the entrance. It offers four rooms—three rooms with beds, one with Berber-style sleeping on a pile of lush wool carpets on the second floor across from the café. Hot water is available. There are two separate kitchens, and you are welcome to make your own food.

GITE AMNAY

tel. 0659/546 586 or 0535/563 857; fatihi1@hotmail.com; 100Dh wihtout meals, 250Dh with all meals

Right next to the mosque, the Gite Amnay is the most modernized *gîte* in town, with hot water and regular toilets (not the holes in the ground that are common in these rural areas), and offers friendly service. Downstairs all rooms have fairly comfortable single beds. One room has an en suite toilet. This is the best lodging for those who want to spend a comfortable night or two. The terrace offers a café with wonderful views of the cliffs, waterfalls, and valley.

Getting There and Around

Zaouia d'Ifrane is about an hour drive from **Azrou** (45km/30mi, 1hr) and difficult to reach without a car. Take the N8 from Azrou toward Beni Mellal. The turnoff from the N8 is well marked, but afterward, the drive is long and winding with many blind turns and should not be driven at night. ***Grands taxis*** from Azrou (35Dh) are sometimes available, though it is likely you'll have to pay for the entire taxi.

BAHLIL

البهاليل

For a look at troglodyte living, spend an afternoon in Bahlil examining the cave houses of this quaint town clinging to the hillside. This charming town is a series of winding stone paths leading up and down the hill, over bridges and through narrow passageways. Many homes are open for visitors and are painted in yellows, pinks, blues, and other loud colors. Locals will often offer you tea and whatever they are having for lunch as you tour their small cave homes. Several unlicensed guides are perfectly kind and will give you a tour of the medina for 50-100Dh, depending on the time and the number of people in your group.

As you tour the medina, you might see women with mounds of thread at their feet, gabbing away as they make the elaborate buttons (or *'aqaad* in Darija, meaning "knots") for jellabas and kaftans. This time-intensive work is not well paid, with each button fetching about a dirham.

If you are looking to escape from the hustle of the larger cities, Bahlil is a good place to do it.

Accommodations

DAR KAMAL CHAOUI

60 Kaf Rhounie; tel. 0535/969 174; www.kamalchaoui.com; 550Dh d

Dar Kamal Chaoui is an unexpected treat in the middle of the village. The owner, Kamal, is passionate about this town and Morocco in general. The *dar* itself is charming, with a clean, rustic decor full of traditional wood furnishings, smooth *tadelahkt* (a traditional type of anti-humidity wall coating) bathrooms, and a wonderful bamboo-covered terrace that overlooks the valley. Ask to stay near the terrace. Kamal will likely give you a free tour of the medina. Naima cooks up a delicious dinner (180Dh)—just save room for her dessert!

Getting There and Around

From **Fez** (30km/19mi, 45min) you take the route to Sefrou (R503)—just look for a turnoff before Sefrou for Bahlil. ***Grands taxis*** from Fez (20Dh) are sometimes available at the taxi stand near the McDonald's on the roundabout at the north end of Avenue Hassan II, though it is likely you'll have to pay for the entire taxi.

TAZA

تازة

From Fez, Taza is about a two-hour drive. The local Tazekka National Park and its location off the A2 autoroute make Taza a possibility for those looking to get a little off the beaten track and explore a city relatively untouched by tourism. Historically, Taza was an extremely important post controlling the route connecting Oujda and the rest of North Africa with Fez. It is thought to have been inhabited as long ago as the Paleolithic period. The modern-day city of Taza was founded in the late 7th century by the Miknasa Amazigh tribe, who quickly pledged allegiance to the Idrisids in 790.

Today, Taza is divided into two parts (medina and Ville Nouvelle), like most cities in Morocco. Because of the medina's location atop the hill, the locals refer to it as Taza Haut (High Taza) and to the French-built Ville Nouvelle as Taza Bas (Low Taza). There are few hotels in Taza Bas and fewer options in the medina.

Sights

MEDINA

In the quiet, easily navigable medina, perhaps the most interesting attraction is the **Provincial Museum of the Resistance and the Liberation Army** (Musée Provincial de la Résistance et de l'Armée de Liberation) (Ave. Allal El Fassi Immeuble, tel. 0535/673 832, 10Dh) across from the Medersa Ibn Bar, a functioning Quranic school. However, the hours are sporadic. It's best to call ahead to make sure someone is there to open the museum so you can see the extensive military library, including the magazine *Adhakira Al Wataniya (National Memory)* and scientific studies on the military movements of the resistance of Moroccans while under French rule in the early part of the 20th century. Uniforms and weapons used by the resistance fighters are on display.

The 14th-century **al-Andalous Mosque** is known for its unique minaret, which is wider at its top than its base. The newly restored **Mosque and Mausoleum of Sidi Azzouz** (a venerated local saint) has elaborate, fine stucco work. **Hammam Cleopatra** (daily, women 8am-9pm, men 9pm-8am) is open 24 hours and is a good place to wash off the dust and sweat from an arduous hike through the Tazekka National Park.

On the other side of the main square from the medina lies the Grain Souk, where you can sneak a glimpse at the former prison of Moulay Ismail (closed) that is falling into ruin. Here is where the tyrant sultan, who reigned in the 17th and 18th centuries, kept many of his prisoners. The prison is thought to be an extension of an older Merenid Palace, though this seems more rumor than fact.

Tazekka National Park

منتزه الوطني تازكة

The Tazekka National Park (Parc National de Tazekka) (www.tazekka.com) is a 14,000-hectare (35,000-acre) park full of goats, sheep, and reintroduced Barbary deer. The park sports 365 caves, one for every day of the year, and a lush cedar forest. If you enter from the east at Bab Azhar, you will see a sign in Arabic that translates to "Forests are for our generation and for the generations after us," which summarizes how the people of the region view this national treasure. There is sometimes snow here during the winter, though it doesn't often stick around. You will need a guide and authorization to see certain spots in the park where **hunting** is available. These sections are closed off to hikers for obvious safety reasons. For hunters, boar and pheasant are the most popular game. To obtain hunting authorization, it's easiest to check with your accommodation or contact

Lanato Chasse (tel. 0661/193 129, www.lanatochasse.com).

One main road (R507) crosses the park; several rest stops have picnic tables and trailheads. If you're lucky, you'll spot a Barbary deer. The 9-kilometer (5.5-mi) road to the summit of **Jbel Tazekka** is only navigable by four-wheel drive, making this a possible hike, and the information center is still under construction. The turnoff is well marked with shoulder parking for your car. From the summit, you'll command views of the entire park.

There are several **hikes** posted, though the trails are not all well kept, and on a few of them it is easy to lose your way. It's best to make sure you have a working GPS in this park. All trails are marked by difficulty (easy, medium, and hard). The shortest hike is a circular, easy hike of about 20 minutes, and the longest is a 4.5-hour hike through the cedar forest. Both hikes have a few sloping uphills. Along the way, keep an eye out for eagles, squirrels, otters, foxes, hedgehogs, and lesser horseshoe bats.

Additionally, you will likely want to explore a few of the **caves** of this region. Friouatou Cave is the most developed cave in the park, perhaps in all of Morocco, and is popular with local tourists.

★ FRIOUATOU CAVE

مغارة فريواطو

daily 7am-9pm; 5Dh for entrance, 200Dh guide, 50Dh spelunking equipment

Undeniably, the biggest attraction in Tazekka National Park is Friouatou Cave (Gouffre Friouatou). Friouatou translates from the Amazigh language as "The Wind Cave," but local legend tells us another possible meaning of the name—this one a touch more romantic and involving star-crossed lovers. A man pledged himself to a woman he loved named Itto, but he was forced by his family to marry another woman against his wishes. Because of the decision, the man decided to commit suicide in the nearby Assoukh cave. Itto could not bear the pain and she spent ages crying in the *fri,* the local word meaning "cave," and the cave forever after became known as Fri wa Itto or "The Cave of Itto." Over time, the name was shortened to what it is known as today, Friouatou.

The cave system is thought to be about 6 kilometers (3.7mi) long, though you will only be able to visit the first 2.5 kilometers (1.5mi) or so. The entrance is impressive. The sun shines down directly through the crater opening in the summer months in the early afternoon. There are over 500 steps to the bottom. From there, a small crevasse leads into the longer body of the cave. The path is generally slick with moisture and unlit, so you will have to rely on lights fastened to helmets, cameras, or flashlights. Though most of the cave is relatively large, exploring the longer cave is not for the faint of heart. Those who do make their way will be treated to some wonderful formations (speleothems), including drip stones, flow stones, pour deposits, and pool deposits. Impressive columns have formed throughout, as well as a natural "table" you can climb up and sit on, seemingly floating in the dark of one of the larger caverns.

Accommodations

HOTEL D'ETOILE

39 Ave. Moulay Hassan, Taza Haut; tel. 0535/270 179 or 0663/582 889; 50Dh per person

Perhaps the best option in Taza, in terms of location, price, and cleanliness. The pink and blue retro decor is nice, though it feels as though not much has changed since its opening in 1927. Rooms here can hold up to four people comfortably.

★ AUBERGE AIN SAHLA

59 Oued Amlil near Bouchfaa; tel. 0661/893 587 or 0670/196 094; www.ainsahla.com; 550Dh s, 700Dh d

The most interesting accommodation in the area is on the northeastern side of Tazekka National Park, about a 30-minute drive from Taza. Omar, a Moroccan who spent most of his life in Algeria and Switzerland, came back to Morocco to construct this sprawling, eco-friendly guesthouse using local stones. The guesthouse is now at 80 percent independence from the infrastructure, uses recycled water for the bio garden, and is nearly reliant on solar power. The rooms are simple and clean, and the service is fantastic. The meals served up by Azziza are well worth paying for, with plenty of creativity for vegetarians and the ability to accommodate other dietary needs. For those interested in exploring the area, this is perhaps the best place to stay in the region.

Information and Services

Place de l'Armée is the main plaza at the entrance to the medina. Here, you can find most everything you might need. There are two banks, **BMCE** (Mon.-Fri. 8:15am-4pm, Ramadan 9:15am-2:30pm) and **Attjariwafa** (Mon.-Fri. 8:15am-3:45pm, Ramadan 9:15am-2:30pm, no ATM), as well as a **post office** (Mon.-Fri. 8am-7pm, Ramadan 9am-3pm), **Western Union, Pharmacy Aharrach** (look for the phone numbers posted there for the nearby 24-hour weekend pharmacies—the sign is in Arabic), and **Maroc Telecom.**

Getting There and Around

If you are traveling by taxi, train, or bus, you will most likely arrive at the **Taza train station** (Gare de Taza) run by **ONCF** (tel. 0890/203 040, www.oncf.ma) on the north edge of town off the N6. Connections are available to and from **Fez** (2hr, 6 daily, 2nd/1st-class 40Dh/56Dh) and **Oujda** (3hr, 3 daily, 74Dh/111Dh). Other connections such as **Casablanca** (6hr, 6 daily, 136Dh/204Dh), **Marrakesh** (10hr, 4 daily, 210Dh/322Dh), **Meknes** (3hr, 7 daily, 56Dh/82Dh), and **Tangier** (7.5hr, 4 daily, 140Dh/212Dh) typically have transfers in Fez, Sidi Kacem, or Casa Voyageurs.

The **grand taxi** station is about one block east of the train station, on the other side of the large grocery and home goods store, Marjane. *Grands taxis* arrive from and leave to **Fez** (1.5hr, 117km/73mi, 45Dh) and other local destinations.

From either of these stations, you can walk out to the main boulevard (Blvd. Bir Anzaran, N6) and easily flag down a ***petit taxi*** that will take you up to the medina for about 6Dh.

To get to **Tazekka National Park,** there is a secondary *grand taxi* station on the road to the Tazekka National Park from which taxis can take you to the Friouatou Cave and back for about 220Dh. Ask for Sidi Salaam or give him a call (tel. 0665/033 418) to arrange for transportation into the national park.

The local bus, the **Foughal Bus,** will take you to different parts of Taza for 3Dh. It's a good way to explore different parts of this sprawling town.

Marrakesh

Ancient bamboo-covered souks, an endless

array of bazaars, five-star restaurants, lush palm groves, snake charmers, fortune tellers, and characters of all sizes and shapes make up modern-day Marrakesh.

Any visitor to Marrakesh would be forgiven for believing this city sprang directly from the pages of *One Thousand and One Arabian Nights.* The snowcapped peaks of the High Atlas Mountains provide a picturesque backdrop to this living dream that is in a near-constant state of transformation. From the bustling souks, circus-like atmosphere, and frenetic nightlife of the Jemaa el-Fnaa, to the contemplative hush of the Menara Gardens, to candlelit dinners and spiritual tranquility tucked in the quieter corners of the medina, this is a city

Highlights

Look for ★ to find recommended sights, activities, dining, and lodging.

★ **Jemaa el-Fnaa:** Spend a night reveling in the carnival charm of Morocco's most famous public square (page 313).

★ **Koutoubia Mosque:** Take in the most well-preserved Almohad-era minaret in all of Morocco (page 314).

★ **Marrakesh Museum:** Discover the history, culture, and people of the region in this converted palace (page 319).

★ **Bahia Palace:** The most splendidly decorated of Marrakesh's many palaces was formerly the residence of the sultan's most cherished concubine (page 322).

★ **Majorelle Gardens:** Take a stroll through this art deco masterpiece curated by famed fashion designer Yves Saint Laurent (page 325).

★ **Storytelling at Café Clock:** Experience the ancient art of oral storytelling as it has been practiced for generations (page 327).

★ **The Souks of Marrakesh:** It's more than a shopping experience—wandering through the labyrinthine souks is a real cultural pastime (page 328).

★ **Moroccan Cooking Classes:** Take a piece of Morocco home with you to share with your friends and family by learning how to make your own tajine, *pastilla,* or couscous (page 334).

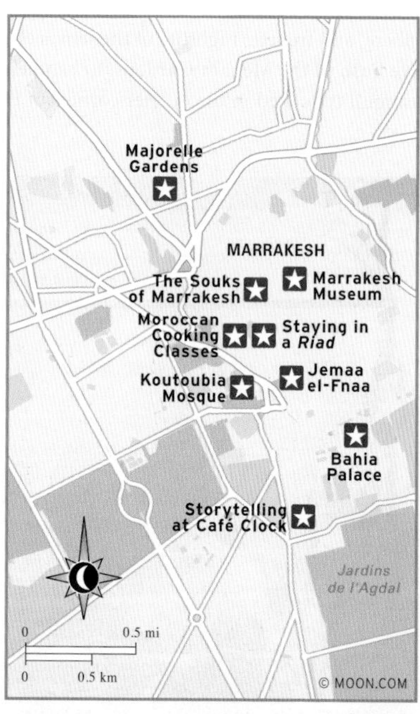

★ **Staying in a *Riad*:** Spend a night, or more, in one of the hundreds of traditional refurbished Moroccan *riad* guesthouses, each offering its own unique touch (page 343).

that opens like a ripe pomegranate, inviting travelers of all stripes.

Since the Almoravids first crowned it their capital in the 11th century, Marrakesh has played a historically important role in Moroccan and world history. Marrakesh was so identified with Morocco that many travelers referred to it as "Morocco City," while in countries such as Pakistan, the entire country of Morocco is still known as "Marrakesh." Today people like to joke that "Marrakesh" actually derives from an old way of saying "get out of here," or that it even stems from the English: "more cash." As you probably already know, Marrakesh is popularly also called the "Red City," "Pink City," or "Ochre City" because of the red earth used in the construction of the medina and medina walls.

To experience Marrakesh, you no longer have to take the "Marrakesh Express" train from Tangier after a long ferry ride from Spain. Its airport is well-connected with daily flights from over 20 European cities, three per day from Paris alone. The fact is that "Kesh"—as the locals call it—is a "must-see" destination, now firmly established beside London, Paris, Tokyo, or New York. However, Kesh is not a city to "see." Rather, it is a place to experience.

Take a stroll through the gardens, learn how to make your own tajine in a cooking class, work on your bartering skills in the souks, inhale the night musk along the medina walls, and then dance your tail off until late into the night. There are countless activities to do, restaurants to try, and accommodations to fit nearly every budget and every interest. So maybe it shouldn't come as a surprise that Marrakesh is one of the most popular destinations in the world.

Tourism is nothing new in Marrakesh. Moroccans, foreigners, and traders from around the world have long been coming here for business, pleasure, and a taste of the exotic, making it a great crossroads of language, culture, and civilization. Coupled with a healthy supply of water from the mountains, Marrakesh's strategic location—at the end of the famed Salt Road that crossed the Sahara, near the ports of Agadir and Essaouira, as well as on the major routes north to modern-day Casablanca and Rabat—ensured its importance. Some travelers make their way over the Sahara and to the Atlantic, while others stay in Marrakesh to experience life at the crossroads. The wealth of diversity that has marked this city through its long history continues to thrive in its medina and Ville Nouvelle.

As a longtime trade station, the old medina of Marrakesh has evolved over the centuries into a honeycomb of souks, representing a variety of different neighborhoods. Each of the souks was originally the home of an individual group of shops with certain specializations. Metal workers, wood workers, leather workers, spice merchants, and others each had their own distinct district in the medina, recognizable from the sights, sounds, and smells associated with each trade. Today, tourist bazaars are crowding out some of the more specialized businesses, though vestiges of the original souks are still identifiable. Because of the interest from travelers coming to Marrakesh, there has been a small revival of traditional crafts, which is helping to keep these artisan industries alive.

Of course, a stay in Marrakesh would not be complete without a night out on the Jemaa el-Fnaa, the giant plaza that is the carnival heart of the city. Fortune tellers, jugglers, medicine men, musicians, henna artists, storytellers, and snake charmers all gather to entertain the crowds as they have for a millennium. Sip on freshly squeezed orange juice (4Dh) and peer through the veil of smoke from the grilling lamb, chicken, and beef brochettes on offer at the numerous food stands while the Gnawa drumbeat rhythmically draws you further into the festivities. This is a quintessential Marrakeshi scene and something to behold.

Previous: eating out on the Jemma el-Fnaa; dried fruits and nuts for sale; narrow passage in the Souk Haddadine.

Marrakesh

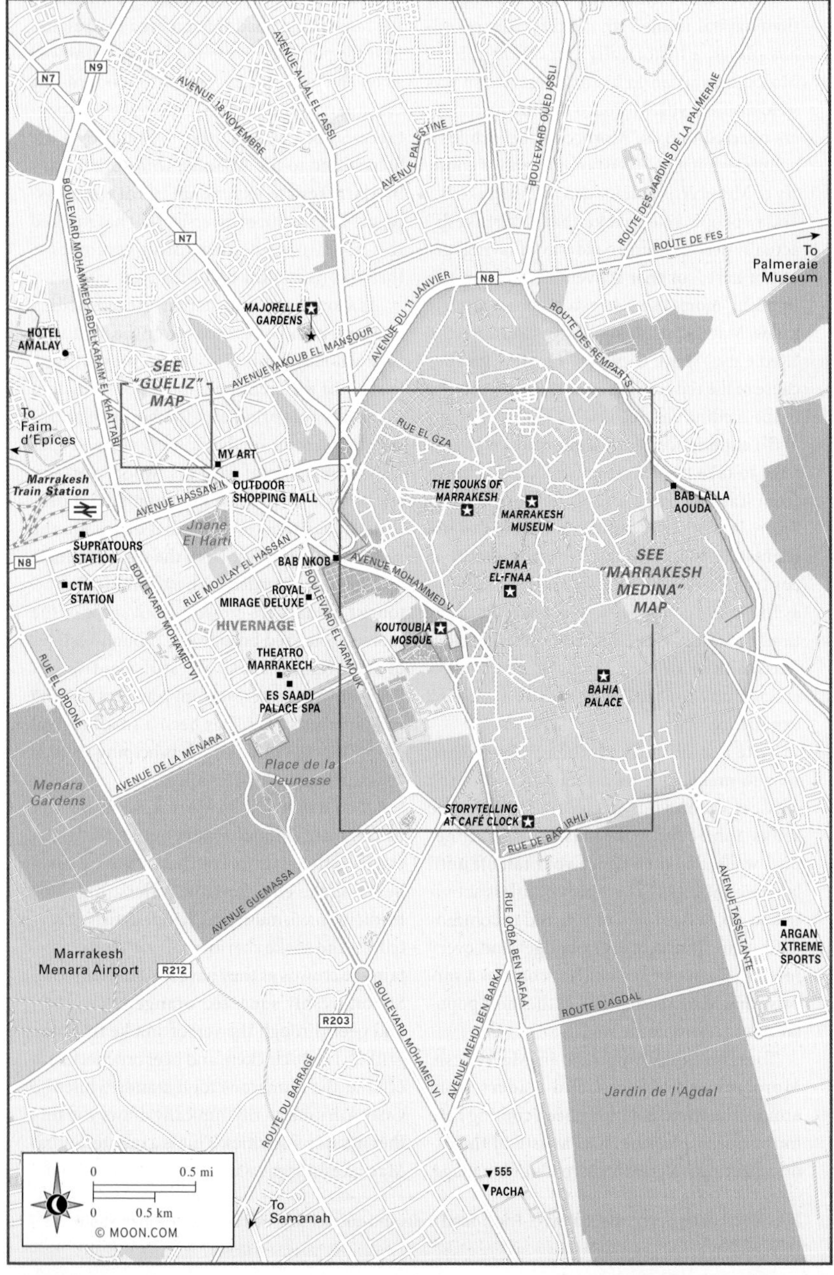
N7
N9
AVENUE 18 NOVEMBRE
AVENUE ALLAL EL FASSI
AVENUE PALESTINE
BOULEVARD OUED ISSLI
ROUTE DES JARDINS DE LA PALMERAIE
ROUTE DE FES
To Palmeraie Museum
N8
AVENUE DU 11 JANVIER
MAJORELLE GARDENS
HOTEL AMALAY
AVENUE YAKOUB EL MANSOUR
ROUTE DES REMPARTS
BOULEVARD MOHAMMED ABDELKARAIM EL KHATTABI
SEE "GUELIZ" MAP
To Faim d'Epices
RUE EL GZA
MY ART
OUTDOOR SHOPPING MALL
Marrakesh Train Station
AVENUE HASSAN II
THE SOUKS OF MARRAKESH
MARRAKESH MUSEUM
BAB LALLA AOUDA
Jnane El Harti
SUPRATOURS STATION
BAB NKOB
AVENUE MOHAMMED V
JEMAA EL-FNAA
SEE "MARRAKESH MEDINA" MAP
CTM STATION
RUE MOULAY EL HASSAN
ROYAL MIRAGE DELUXE
BOULEVARD EL YARMOUK
BOULEVARD MOHAMED VI
HIVERNAGE
KOUTOUBIA MOSQUE
THEATRO MARRAKECH
ES SAADI PALACE SPA
BAHIA PALACE
RUE EL ORDONE
AVENUE DE LA MENARA
Place de la Jeunesse
Menara Gardens
STORYTELLING AT CAFÉ CLOCK
RUE DE BAB IRHLI
AVENUE GUEMASSA
RUE OQBA BEN NAFAA
AVENUE TASSILTANTE
ARGAN XTREME SPORTS
Marrakesh Menara Airport
R212
AVENUE MEHDI BEN BARKA
ROUTE D'AGDAL
R203
BOULEVARD MOHAMED VI
ROUTE DU BARRAGE
Jardin de l'Agdal
0
0.5 mi
0
0.5 km
© MOON.COM
555
PACHA
To Samanah

Touring Marrakesh by Bus

The red double-decker buses run by **Alsa** (tel. 0524/335 270, www.alsa.ma, daily, 9am-sunset), seen throughout the city, provide a relaxing way to see many of the sights from the comfort of a cushy bus seat, though they also double as a handy way to get to distant parts of the Ville Nouvelle. Tickets are available to purchase (145Dh for a day pass, 165Dh for a two-day pass) when you board the bus, which leaves every 20-30 minutes every day from the station in Gueliz across from the Tourist Information Center on Avenue Mohammed V.

There are two bus circuits. The **Historic Tour** makes stops at the Jemaa el-Fnaa, the tourist office, Menara Gardens, and the train station, and the **Oasis Tour** makes a circuit through the Palmeraie. Each bus takes approximately one hour to make a full circuit. Your ticket is valid for 24 hours, and for those who want to see more of the city but don't want to deal with unreliable taxis or figuring out the local bus schedule, this can be a huge timesaver. For people wishing to tour the Palmeraie, the views from the top of the bus can't be beat. They allow you to peer over some of the walls that otherwise obscure many of the elaborate villas spread throughout this giant palm grove.

The Ville Nouvelle offers some of the best restaurants in town as well as some of the best parks in Morocco, not to mention some of the best nightclubs in Africa. Though there is not a lot of sightseeing to do in the Ville Nouvelle, a trip through the palm groves could easily make it on your itinerary, perhaps coupled with an early morning at the Majorelle Gardens. Shopaholics and foodies should plan on spending some time browsing in the shops and nibbling in the restaurants.

PLANNING YOUR TIME

Most people spend at least two to three days in Marrakesh. This is just enough time to see the sights, absorb the life in the **medina,** and make a trip into the **Ville Nouvelle** to see the **Majorelle Gardens,** the **Palmeraie** (Palm Groves), and a few of the other attractions, while also giving yourself enough time to lounge for an afternoon in the luxurious spread of your *riad.* The wide variety of restaurants and the abundant entertainment make longer stays feasible and often (happily) unavoidable.

For those looking to spend more time in the area, Marrakesh can serve as a base for a number of other activities, including treks into the **High Atlas** and longer seaside adventures in **Agadir** and **Essaouira.** The more popular day trips are to High Atlas hiking destinations such as the **Ourika Valley** and **Imlil.** Though guides are not necessary, they can be helpful, providing insights into the local culture and taking you to some sights and local villages off the trodden tour circuit. Using a guide can also be a time saver for those who want to see more of the country but don't want to spend the time learning the often-confusing network of roads. However, after a few days in Marrakesh, most travelers opt to continue their journey, either heading west to the Atlantic or southeast, up and over the mountains and into the Sahara. Whatever your direction, continuing on from Marrakesh is easy enough, though you may find yourself wishing you had spent a little more time here. Travelers planning on spending a week in Marrakesh only to find themselves passing a lifetime in the Red City are not unheard of.

Guided City Tours

MARRAKESH BY LOCALS

tel. 0659/165 696; www.marrakechbylocals.com; 200Dh

For guided tours of Marrakesh, this new walking tour outfit is incredible. They run two different types of tours, both of which are for those interested in the culture and history from a local perspective. One is a walking tour for families and friends who want to be

Photography Etiquette

Among photographers, Morocco is known for being both extremely beautiful and extremely hard to photograph. This is particularly the case when attempting to photograph people. Over the last 20 years, tourism in Morocco has grown exponentially. In some ways, this has been positive, with better public transportation and better citywide infrastructure, as well as the fostering of cross-cultural understanding and exchange. However, over-aggressive tourists with their cameras pointed in the faces of people going about their daily lives have taken a toll on some of the population. There can sometimes be a real aggression toward photographers. In no place in Morocco is this more apparent than in Marrakesh. Here are a few tips to help you grab the most Instagrammable photos.

photo sensitivity in Marrakesh

- It is respectful to ask to photograph a person or a person's shop before taking a photo. Most shop owners will agree, particularly if you've just spent some money in the shop. Strangers on the street will usually decline, but they will be much happier you asked, and you may be surprised: Every once in a while someone will say yes!
- Occasionally you will be asked to pay, generally a token of 5-10Dh. In the Jemaa el-Fnaa, it is customary to pay for photos featuring the various monkey handlers and snake charmers. The going rate is 20Dh-100Dh; this is how they make their living. However, if you spend some time here, you probably won't like how they treat the animals.
- Photographers who are polite, ask permission, and tip occasionally when asked generally make new friends and have a pleasant experience, though this isn't to say there won't be some aggression, particularly with street photography.
- Use Darija. This is a great time to practice. Know your please (*afek*) and thank you (*shokran*) in Moroccan Arabic. It can do wonders, particularly in smaller towns.
- Shoot landscapes. If you're obviously shooting a landscape, you likely won't be bothered at all.
- For those interested in street photography, it's a good strategy to tuck away in a quiet corner, carefully compose your shot, and wait for the right person to walk by.
- Be discreet. If your camera has a silent shutter option, this can be a good way to be more discreet with your photography. Also consider the gear you're using. The bigger and more intimidating, the more likely it is you'll provoke undesirable reactions. A good smartphone camera can work wonders.
- Most people love selfies. If you have an experience with someone and would like to mark it with that person by taking a selfie, this has become the standard. Moroccans are no exception to the selfie craze.
- Just remember—even though you're shooting, it's not a war. Smile and be friendly, and if someone gives you a hard time, be humble and apologetic.

Hiring a Guide

Hiring a guide anywhere in Morocco, particularly in Marrakesh, can be a little tricky. The market is crowded with self-proclaimed experts and locals trying to make a quick buck and who are not afraid to overcharge for their services. When in doubt, you can ask to see the certification given by the Moroccan Ministry of Tourism or play it safe and stick with one of the guides listed here.

One of the common local cons is to pose as a guide, particularly in and around the Jemaa el-Fnaa. Though policing has gotten better in recent years, many travelers to Marrakesh often fall prey to one of these local conmen. Though occasionally the prices will be higher than licensed guides, the real issue is that many of these faux guides have not been certified or schooled and thus often spew lots of misinformation. To get the real scoop on Marrakesh, or any other Moroccan city, make sure to contact a certified local guide or company.

One of the best travel strategies is to reserve a guided tour for your first full day in Marrakesh. This way, as you're learning more of the culture and history, you'll also be able to have a friendly face to help orient you in the confusing medina.

Because of the rising popularity of Marrakesh, there can be a scarcity of guides during busy seasons (spring, fall, and winter holidays) and during festivals. It is best to arrange for a guided tour ahead of your arrival. The guides listed throughout this guidebook have all been vetted, speak English unless otherwise noted, and are certified whenever certification is available.

in privacy and do not want to "share" their guide with someone else; the other tour is for travelers who prefer to share the experience with like-minded souls.

★ MARRAKESH FOOD TOUR

tel. 0666/261 545; https://marrakechfoodtours.com; 600Dh

If you're anything like me, you probably like to travel through your stomach. Lucky for us, resident Marrakesh expat and influential blogger Amanda Mouttaki has put together a tour just for us. Tours are limited to around eight people and usually meet in the Jemaa el-Fnaa. From this busy plaza, you'll quickly dive into the local souks to sample Marrakesh's slow-cooked specialty *tangia* and the ever-popular Moroccan donuts, *sfeng*, to a number of other dishes scattered throughout the medina that will leave your belly happy and your taste buds glowing.

Itinerary Ideas

TWO DAYS IN MARRAKESH

Day 1

1 After an expansive Moroccan breakfast at **Riad Boussa,** strap on a comfy pair of walking shoes.

2 Meet Saeed, your English-speaking guide from Marrakesh by Locals, at the **Koutoubia Mosque** and get ready for an exploratory outing to some of the Red City's most iconic landmarks. Stop for lunch at a local eatery with Saeed and dig into a Marrakeshi classic: ***tangia.***

3 Dive back into the **medina** and learn some tricks from Saeed to help you navigate the

Itinerary Ideas

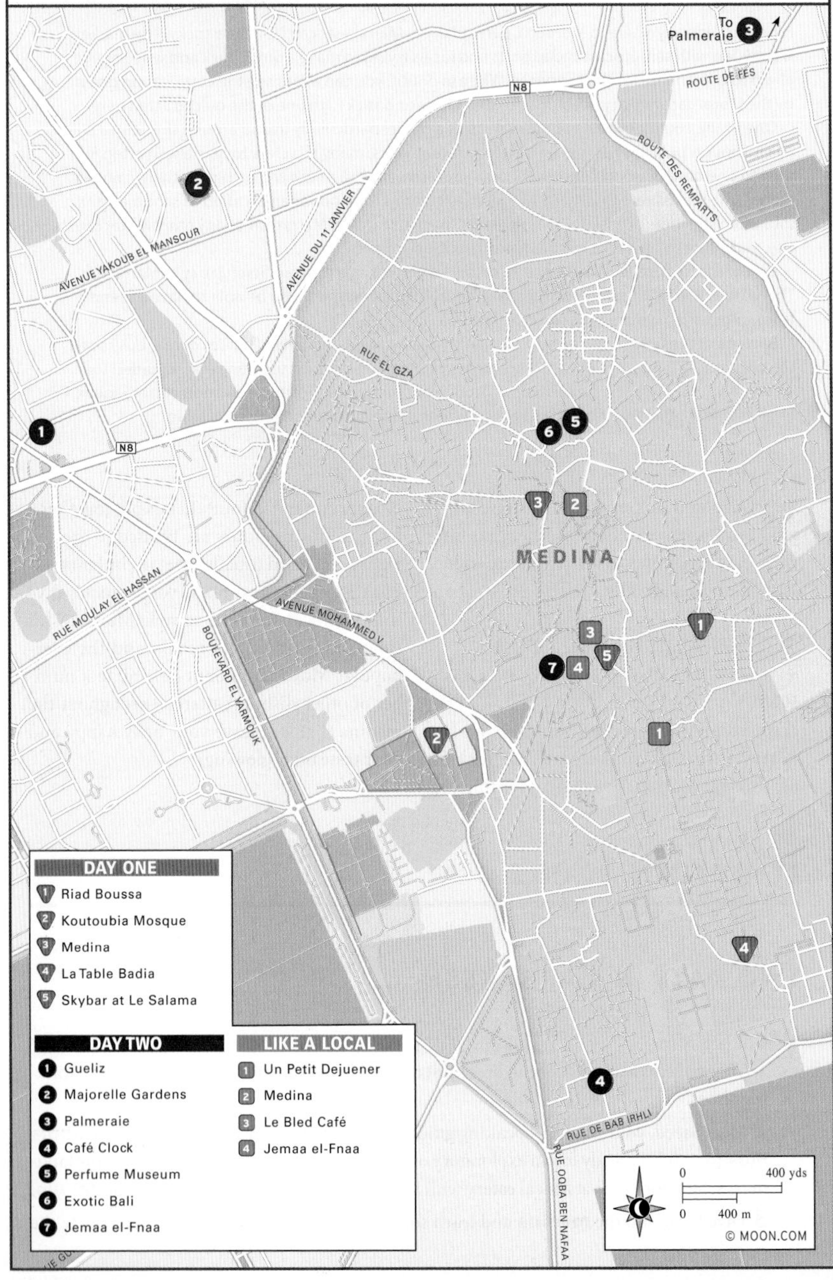

confusing twists and turns of the souks on your own. After a lot of walking, unwind on the terrace of your ***riad*** enjoying the late afternoon.

4 Cozy into **La Table Badia** and enjoy an exquisite Moroccan dinner, replete with dishes that will defy your taste buds to identify which is the sweet and which is the savory.

5 Stop by the **Skybar** at Le Salama for a nightcap before testing your medina knowledge to find your way back to your *riad.*

Day 2

This more relaxed day is full of photo ops. Be sure to pack your camera.

1 Head into **Gueliz** and hop on the red bus run by Alsa for a quick tour of the medina.

2 Hop off the red bus at the **Majorelle Gardens.** Get there early for a little quiet. This will be a great spot for a photo op in the gardens with the stunning cobalt blue backdrop.

3 Take the bus out to the **Palmeraie.** Be sure to grab a seat on the top to see into some of the more palatial spreads. Dab on a bit of extra sunscreen if needed.

4 For lunch, it would be hard to pass up diving back into the medina for a camel burger at **Café Clock.**

5 After lunch, take in a few museums that capture your fancy, like the offbeat **Perfume Museum.**

6 Relax into dinner at **Exotic Bali** for a taste of the Far East and experience a delicious array of Indonesian food prepared in a beautiful Moroccan *riad.*

7 Head out onto the **Jemaa el-Fnaa** to take in the very best of Marrakesh's nightlife.

MARRAKESH LIKE A LOCAL

1 After waking up at Kammy Hostel, head toward the Jemaa el-Fnaa, but stop for a quick breakfast first at **Un Petit Dejuener.**

2 After a nice breakfast, do what any good Moroccan does when they first visit Marrakesh: get lost. Spend your first hours wandering through the souks, dodging scooters, and puzzling your way out of the **medina.** For lunch, ask for the nearest ***bissara*** **stand** and get elbow-to-elbow with the local workmen eating lunch. Don't be afraid to ask for seconds.

3 Make your way back to the Jemaa el-Fnaa (follow the signs) and sit out on a terrace sipping a coffee or mint tea. **Le Bled Café** is a good spot to delve into the Moroccan art of people-watching.

4 As the sun sets, head out on the **Jemaa el-Fnaa** and enjoy the festive atmosphere, musicians, storytellers, soothsayers, snake charmers, monkey handlers, and the rest of the madness. When hunger calls, head to one of the food stands on the Jemaa el-Fnaa and order up dinner. Just be sure to bargain.

ORIENTATION

Like other Moroccan cities, Marrakesh is divided into two parts: the old medina and the Ville Nouvelle. The old **medina** of Marrakesh is one of the largest in Morocco. The main square, **Jemaa el-Fnaa,** a UNESCO World Heritage site since 1985, can easily be found—it's hard to miss the towering mass of the Koutoubia Mosque, the central meeting point of the medina. Easily found signs peppered throughout the medina also point the way to the Jemaa el-Fnaa. Streets are usually unnamed; there are many confusing, often frustrating, dead ends; and though the rest of the medina is divided into neighborhoods, these are generally indistinguishable to most visitors and are not well signed. Many locals, however, do know the neighborhoods, so if you're staying in the medina or looking for a restaurant, it's a good idea to know the name, if only to ask someone to point you in the right direction.

It is incredibly easy to become disoriented in these old medieval cities. Though Google and Apple maps of the Marrakesh medina are quite good, you'll still likely get turned around a time or two. Not putting pressure on yourself to see a bunch of sights makes it easier to stop in at a café or dawdle a bit longer over lunch, or perhaps reserve that much-needed massage, all in the name of relaxation, particularly after an adventure in getting lost, which is bound to happen and is part of the experience.

In the medina is where you'll find the majority of sights that are of touristic interest. From the Jemaa el-Fnaa, the popular **souks** of Marrakesh, the traditional **artisans,** and residential neighborhoods lie to the north. To the east are streets lined with cafés, shops, and ***riads.*** There are residential neighborhoods to be found here as well as the **tanneries.** To the south you'll find the **mellah, kasbah,** and current **royal palace** of the king of Morocco, while to the west sprawls the **Koutoubia complex** and the most elaborate of the **city gardens.**

Several gates enter into the old medina. **Bab Jdid** leads from the west, past the splendid Koutoubia Gardens down Avenue Houman el Fetouaki. **Bab Nkob** is perhaps the most used gate, separating the old medina from Gueliz near the Place de la Liberté along Avenue Mohammed V. To the north, near the *gare routière,* are **Bab Doukkala** and **Bab Moussoufa,** used often by those arriving via *grand taxi.* There is a handy guarded parking lot near Bab Doukkala for drivers, while

There are 19 kilometers (about 12 miles) of walls around the old medina.

the entrance by Bab Moussoufa provides a straight path along Rue el Gaz (which turns into Rue Riad el Arous) to the back of the souks. To the east is **Bab Lalla Aouda,** near the tanneries, and it's one of the better signed gates in the medina.

Avenue Mohammed V cuts through the medina, right between the Jemaa el-Fnaa and the Koutoubia Mosque. This is the main artery leading from the medina into **Gueliz,** the most popular section of the **Ville Nouvelle,** with lots of shopping and popular cafés and restaurants. Gueliz extends north and west from the city beyond the large **Place de la Liberté.** Here you will find the **train station** as well as the major **bus stations.** The train station is along Avenue Hassan II, turning west from Avenue Mohammed V at Place du 18 Novembre. The Supratours station is behind the train station, and just a block south of the Supratours station is the CTM station. Most *grands taxis* and other bus companies use the *gare routière,* outside of the medina near Bab Doukkala.

Hivernage is the other neighborhood in the Ville Nouvelle most travelers should know. It's west of the medina, southwest of the Place de la Liberté. The five-star **resorts** are located here, along with some of the more upscale dining options, bars and nightclubs, and big boulevards. You'll also find the Menara Gardens here.

Sights

TOP EXPERIENCE

MEDINA

Though not the largest medina in Morocco—that distinction belongs to Fez—the Marrakesh medina is one of the liveliest. Most of the sights in Marrakesh are within the walls of the medina, as are numerous cafés, restaurants, and renovated *riads.*

Most of the sights in the medina can all be seen in a day, most efficiently with a guide. You can usually book a reliable guide through your lodging. It's more relaxing to spread sightseeing out over a few days, clustering sights with their neighborhoods, while the rest of the time is spent dining, shopping, or just wandering the labyrinthine streets, taking in the Marrakeshi way of life.

The famed Marrakesh souks are gathered north of the Jemaa el-Fnaa. Though many of the original artisans have moved to separate quarters, displaced by the numerous bazaars, vestiges of this artisan history remain. See the Shopping section (page 328) for detailed information about the souks.

TOP EXPERIENCE

★ Jemaa el-Fnaa

The giant plaza comprising the center of the medina is the Jemaa el-Fnaa (also Djemma el-F'nâ and other variations), one of the most storied public squares in history. By day, it looks like little more than a dusty crossways of traffic with *grands taxis* and donkey-pulled carts plodding through the pedestrian traffic. There are usually a few monkey handlers and snake charmers about. The best action doesn't start until late afternoon, after the hottest part of the day, and continues well into the night. This is when most of the performers and musicians really come alive. Food stands grill all sorts of meat, fish, and vegetables, and there are also stands for *harira* soup and freshly squeezed orange juice. Beware of pickpockets in more crowded areas. The LGBT community should be aware that this is also prime cruising ground, particularly for gay men. However, any advances by any Moroccan should be taken with extreme caution, as prostitution is a serious issue in Marrakesh. The feel of this is something like a large county fair, but mingled with the

Behind the Scenes of the Jemaa el-Fnaa

a water seller on the Jemaa el-Fnaa

Morocco is a country replete with characters, and in no place is this more evident than a night out on the Jemaa el-Fnaa. The large square comes alive at night with storytellers and snake charmers, monkey handlers and fortune tellers, musicians and henna artists, as well as more modern carnival entertainments such as putt-putt golf. It seems hard to believe that people can make a living these days as a snake charmer, but in Marrakesh, anything is possible. However, there are a few things to consider while making your way around the square.

Though the snakes and monkeys are a staple of the Jemaa el-Fnaa, those considering animal welfare might want to keep in mind that the hooded cobra snakes used by the snake charmers have their venom pockets removed, essentially killing the snake over the course of a few days. These snakes are bred specifically for the purpose of entertainment, and while they are generally well taken care of because they are the source of income for these performers, the end of the snake's life is thought to be painful. The monkey handlers spend years working with their animals so that they might perform certain tricks, again as entertainment. Some handlers are kinder than others.

Otherwise, entertainment is to be had for people of all ages. Children love the dancers, animals, and musicians, while adults enjoy looking into their future with fortune tellers and discussing their latest henna tattoo with the artist. Tipping is the norm. Before taking photos or engaging with a performer individually, it's best to agree on a price ahead of time, 20-100Dh depending on what the performer is being asked to do, while tipping 5-10Dh to musicians or storytellers is acceptable.

essentials of Moroccan culture in all of its carnivalesque glory.

★ Koutoubia Mosque

Ave. Mohammed V

The Koutoubia is the mosque and minaret that established the Moroccan style that is seen throughout the country, from the new Hassan II Mosque in Casablanca to the cherished Qaraouiyine Mosque in Fez. This is also one of the best-preserved examples of Almohad architecture. The minaret dates from the mid-12th century. Work was likely begun shortly after the Almohads conquered the Almoravid empire in 1150, and continued under the rule of Sultan Moulay Yacoub al-Mansour. One of the more striking features of the mosque is that the stones used in its construction are of visibly varying size. They would have been covered with a coat of plaster and painted—something local authorities were considering when the tower was renovated in 2000—but fortunately they settled for just cleaning the mosque and didn't cover the stones with plaster and paint. Today, the Koutoubia is lit up at night and comes alive.

The tower is an outstanding example of the Almohad style, with other key examples being the unfinished Hassan Tower in Rabat and the Giralda in Sevilla. One of the first things you'll notice are the varying decorative arches centered on the tower. These arches are layered upon each other around the mosque, framing the windows and varying from floor to floor. Note how the arches change from one side to the other, with each face of the mosque. Those arches found on the third floor of the tower on the southeast window have become synonymous with Almohad gates found throughout Morocco and Spain. There are some fascinating stories about the origin of the four gold balls that are stacked atop the minaret, many of which find themselves woven into tall tales spun by the storytellers every night on the Jemaa el-Fnaa. As legend has it, there were originally only three gold balls; however, when al-Mansour's wife accidentally ate during Ramadan, she had her gold jewelry melted down to add a fourth ball to the minaret. When the gold balls were replaced with brass balls nobody seems to know.

The foundations of the mosque next to the minaret were excavated during the renovation and restoration of 2000. The excavation proved one of the architectural theories of the mosque: Evidence was found of the mosque having to have been rebuilt because it was not oriented correctly toward Mecca. This mistake in orientation is possibly the same reason why the Tin Mal Mosque found in the High Atlas is no longer in use. Though non-Muslims are free to wander the abandoned Tin Mal Mosque, they are forbidden entrance to the Koutoubia Mosque.

TOMB OF FATIMA ZOHRA

Koutoubia Mosque

Between the busy Avenue Mohammed V and the Koutoubia Mosque lies the Tomb of Fatima Zohra, a traditional white-washed domed mausoleum, popular with the local women who seek her blessing (*baraka*) to conceive children and to help cure illness. Like many of the venerated saints (or marabouts) of Morocco, not much is known about Fatima Zohra. The local myth is that she was the wife of a liberated slave who had become an imam. By day she is said to have been a woman, and by night a wondrous dove. The tomb is closed to non-Muslims, though it is unmissable right next to the pedestrian crosswalk to the Jemaa el-Fnaa and makes for a great meeting point.

KOUTOUBIA GARDENS

Koutoubia Mosque; daily 8am-8pm; free

On the other side of the minaret from the ruins of the mosque are the Koutoubia Gardens. These provide an excellent spot for picnicking and are often used by groups of Moroccan ladies looking for a shaded spot, perhaps after a visit to Fatima Zohra. The gardens are small, though well laid out, and offer plenty of opportunities for photos, but be respectful because local women can be very superstitious about having their photos taken.

Hotel Mamounia Gardens

Avenue Bab Jdid; 8am-8pm; free

The most elaborate gardens to tour within walking distance from the medina are the Hotel Mamounia Gardens just west of the Koutoubia Mosque, down Avenue Houman el Fetouaki. A nice circuit to do is to pass the Koutoubia Mosque and cut through the Koutoubia Gardens to where the horse-drawn carriage stand is outside the Hotel Mamounia. You can walk through the hotel, taking in the palatial spread, to the gardens out back. In the heat of the day, the hotel's gardens make for a shaded distraction. The well-cultivated garden always provides a fresh, green respite from the dusty medina and heavy roar of traffic. The gardens and hotel can be found directly through Bab Jdid on the west wall of the medina.

Place de la Kisseria

North of the souks is the Place de la Kisseria. This central square houses a few of the more interesting sites in Marrakesh, including the **Marrakesh Museum** and **Medersa Ben Youssef.** Directly across from the museum is the **Ben Youssef Mosque.** This mosque was originally built during the Almoravid dynasty in the 12th century and is the oldest mosque in Marrakesh, though not the best preserved—that distinction belongs rightly to the Koutoubia Mosque. Though the Almoravids built the mosque, nothing is left of their original design. The Almohad dynasty took over, declared the mosque was oriented poorly, had it destroyed, and built another mosque atop the rubble. This mosque fell into disrepair and was completely rebuilt in the 19th century,

Marrakesh Medina

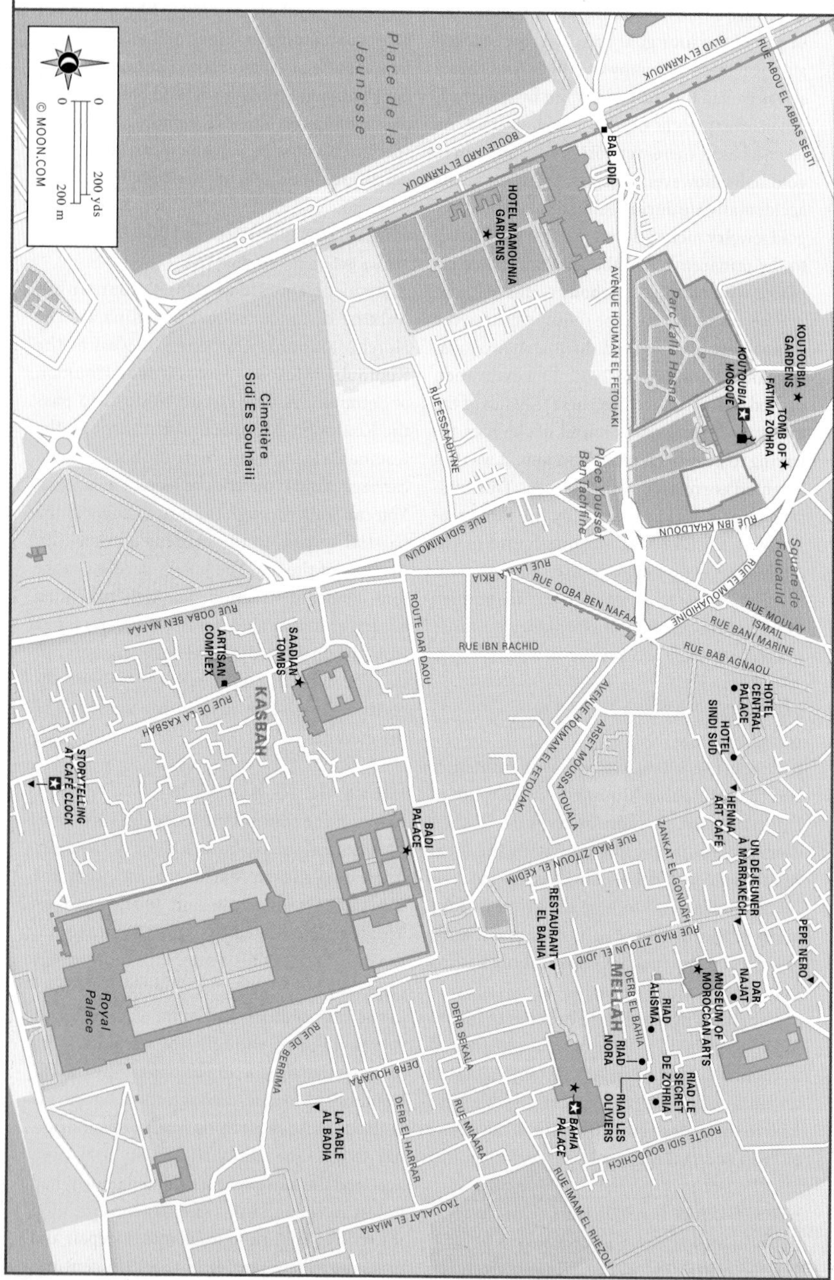

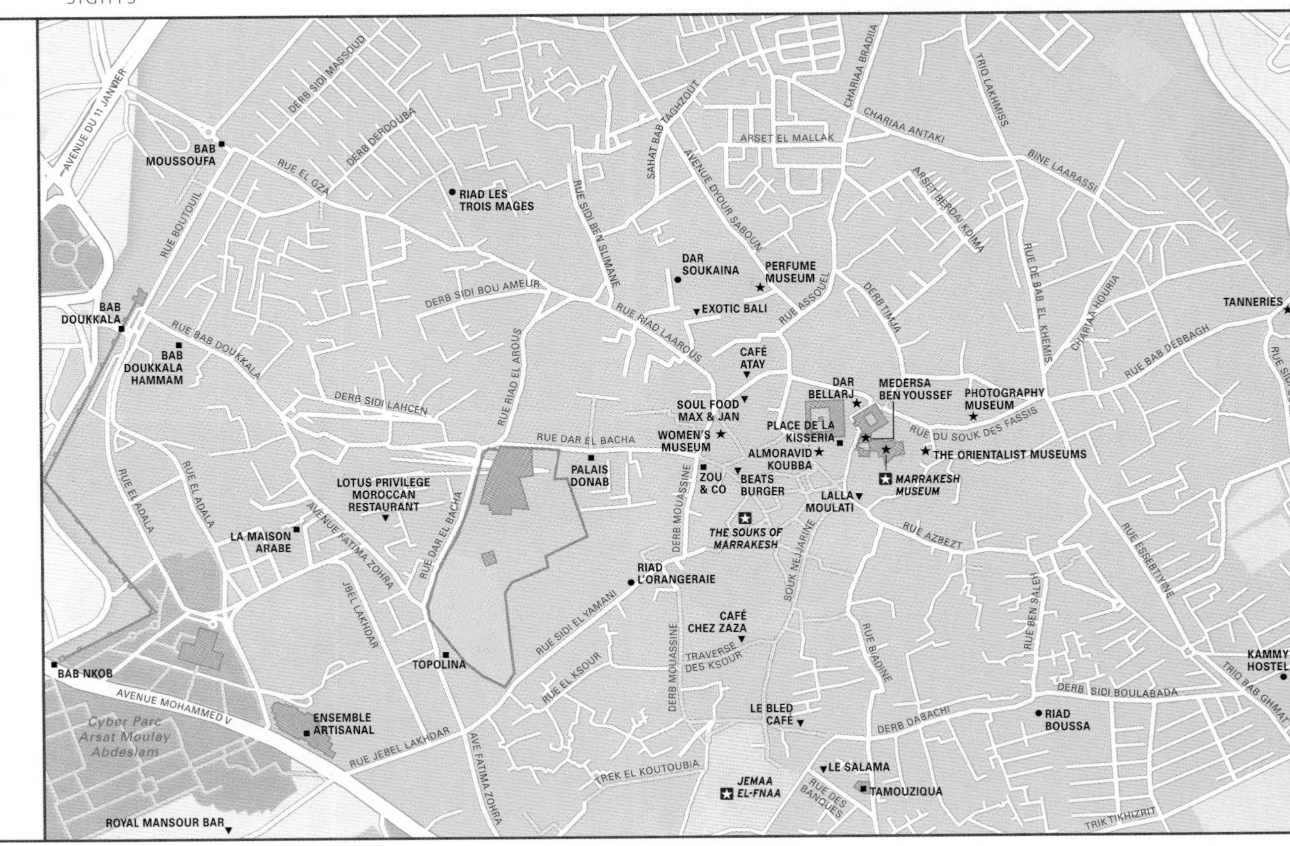
AVENUE DU 11 JANVIER
DERB SIDI MASSOUD
DERB DERDOUBA
BAB MOUSSOUFA
RUE EL GZA
RUE BOUTOUIL
RIAD LES TROIS MAGES
RUE SIDI BEN SLIMANE
SAHAT BAB TAGHZOUT
AVENUE DYOUR SABOUN
CHARIAA BRADIIA
CHARIAA ANTAKI
ARSET EL MALLAK
TRIQ LAKHMISS
BINE LAARASSI
ARSET BERDAI KDIMA
DAR SOUKAINA
PERFUME MUSEUM
DERB SIDI BOU AMEUR
RUE RIAD LAAROUS
EXOTIC BALI
RUE ASSOUEL
DERB TIMJA
RUE DE BAB EL KHEMIS
CHARIAA HOURIA
TANNERIES
BAB DOUKKALA
RUE BAB DOUKKALA
BAB DOUKKALA HAMMAM
RUE RIAD EL AROUS
CAFÉ ATAY
RUE BAB DEBBAGH
RUE SIDI SOUSSAN
DERB SIDI LAHCEN
DAR BELLARJ
MEDERSA BEN YOUSSEF
PHOTOGRAPHY MUSEUM
SOUL FOOD MAX & JAN
PLACE DE LA KISSERIA
RUE DU SOUK DES FASSIS
RUE DAR EL BACHA
WOMEN'S MUSEUM
ALMORAVID KOUBBA
THE ORIENTALIST MUSEUMS
RUE EL ADALA
PALAIS DONAB
ZOU & CO
BEATS BURGER
MARRAKESH MUSEUM
LOTUS PRIVILEGE MOROCCAN RESTAURANT
DERB MOUASSINE
LALLA MOULATI
RUE DAR EL BACHA
THE SOUKS OF MARRAKESH
AVENUE FATIMA ZOHRA
LA MAISON ARABE
RUE AZBEZT
SOUK NEJJARINE
RUE ESSEBTIYNE
RIAD L'ORANGERAIE
JBEL LAKHDAR
RUE BEN SALEH
RUE SIDI EL YAMANI
CAFÉ CHEZ ZAZA
RUE BIADINE
TOPOLINA
RUE EL KSOUR
TRAVERSE DES KSOUR
KAMMY HOSTEL
BAB NKOB
TRIQ BAB GHMAT
AVENUE MOHAMMED V
DERB SIDI BOULABADA
ENSEMBLE ARTISANAL
LE BLED CAFÉ
DERB DABACHI
RIAD BOUSSA
Cyber Parc Arsat Moulay Abdeslam
RUE JEBEL LAKHDAR
AVE FATIMA ZOHRA
TREK EL KOUTOUBIA
LE SALAMA
JEMAA EL-FNAA
RUE DES BANQUES
TAMOUZIQUA
ROYAL MANSOUR BAR
TRIK TIKHIZRIT

1
2
3

leaving nothing behind of the Almoravid or Almohad design. Today, the mosque is largely indistinguishable from many of the mosques in Morocco, though it is still one of the most important in Marrakesh and houses the *kadi* (the judge of the region). It was once the center of Marrakesh. Like other mosques, it is closed to non-Muslims.

On the square next to the mosque is another site of interest, the recently excavated **Almoravid Koubba,** which features an intact dome and latrines dating from AD 1117. It is the oldest building in Marrakesh, and although it's currently closed indefinitely for renovation, visitors can still view the *koubba* (shrine). Located below the current ground level of Marrakesh, this fenced-in ornate domed structure was built at the same time as the original Ben Youssef Mosque for Muslims to do their ablutions before entering the mosque. The interior is richly decorated with floral patterns, including pinecones, palms, and acanthus leaves, though much of this will have to be left to the imagination until it reopens. In the meantime, it's worth looking at if for no other reason than it is the best-preserved piece of Almoravid architecture in all of Morocco.

★ MARRAKESH MUSEUM (MUSÉE DE MARRAKECH)

Pl. Ben Youssef; tel. 0524/441 893; www.musee.ma; daily 9am-6:30pm; 50Dh

Housed in the restored Dar Menebhi Palace, the Marrakesh Museum was opened in 1997. The Omar Benjelloun Foundation generously financed the elaborate restoration. Today, photos near the museum entrance showcase this restoration work. One wing hosts Moroccan textiles and embroidery as well as Amazigh jewelry. The traditional hammam has been transformed into a rotating exposition gallery featuring many more contemporary Moroccan and international artists. You'll also find a collection of decorative ceramics and ornate daggers. Though there is a lot on display, half of the fun of this museum is walking around the restored palace and taking in the attention to details, such as the *zellij* tile work, enormous carved wood doors, and fine stucco work. Anglophones will likely be disappointed to find most signs and postings only in French, though for museums in Marrakesh, this is still the standard and should be visited to get a feel for the history and culture of the region.

MEDERSA BEN YOUSSEF

Kaat Benahid; tel. 0632/251 164; www.medersa-ben-youssef.com; daily 9am-5pm; 70Dh (closed until 2020/21)

The Medersa Ben Youssef was a functioning Quranic school originally built during the Almoravid period in the 12th century. It was in use as a school until the 19th century. During the French protectorate it fell into disrepair and disuse before being restored by the same Omar Benjelloun Foundation that restored the Dar Menebhi Palace. Throughout the *medersa* you'll find photos of the recent restoration as well as beautiful woodwork carved from the cedar trees of the Atlas Mountains throughout the vestibules, cupolas, and main prayer room. Marble, imported from Italy, and the local stucco work provide most of the rest of the decoration, with some complex *zellij* (mosaic) work of various shapes, techniques, and arrangements keeping the eye busy. The *medersa* will be closed until sometime in 2020/21 for a major renovation.

DAR BELLARJ

9-7 Zaouiate Lahdar; tel. 0524/444 555; daily 9:30am-12:30pm and 2pm-5:30pm; free

Just outside the Medersa Ben Youssef, the Dar Bellarj, literally meaning "Stork House," is a beautifully restored animal clinic that now serves as a business front for local artisans. Exhibits vary and entrance is usually free, though sometimes a small fee of 15Dh or so might be charged depending on the exhibit. Exhibits are chosen every few months and are generally themed around something like

1: the Koutoubia Mosque **2:** a scooter zips through the medina **3:** a musician on the Jemaa el-Fnaa

photography or textiles. Check out the gift shop for some wonderful ideas for presents to take back home and to support local artisans. Even with the posted hours, this is one place that is sometimes closed for apparently no reason.

ORIENTALIST MUSEUM

5 Derb El Khamsi; tel. 0524/447 379; daily 9am-7pm; 50Dh

Opened in 2018 in a restored *riad,* this is a small, curious museum that "owns" the orientalist expression generally derided by those sensitive to the "othering" of people. It isn't an overly large collection and mostly features the work of Europeans depicting African and Asian subjects. However, with one work each by the French great Eugène Delacroix and the Spanish master of surrealism Salvador Dalí, as well as a few by the Marrakesh French expat icon Louis Majorelle, I would be hard-pressed not to recommend stopping in to enjoy this collection for any lover of art. Unfortunately, the museum does not currently feature explanatory plaques. Instead, the manager encourages visitors to walk around, guided by their sense of the aesthetic.

PHOTOGRAPHY MUSEUM (MUSÉE DE PHOTOGRAPHIE)

46 Rue Bin Lafnadek; tel. 0524/385 721; www.maisondelaphotographie.ma; daily 9:30am-7pm; 50Dh

Following Zaouiate Lahdar from the Dar Bellarj west toward Place du Maoukef will bring you to the Photography Museum. Photographers and those interested in Moroccan history will enjoy the collection of black-and-white photos dating from 1870 to 1950. The curator has so many photos, over 5,000 original prints, that they can't all be shown at once, so they are exhibited by theme, which changes every three months. A short documentary from 1957 about the Amazigh, *Chez les Berbères du Haut-Atlas,* by Daniel Chicault, screens every hour. This was the first time that the Amazigh were filmed in color, and the scenes, even if you don't understand the French narration, are breathtaking. The rooftop terrace has views over Marrakesh with the distant snowcapped mountains of the High Atlas serving as a backdrop. The terrace is open for lunch and serves traditional Moroccan cuisine (80Dh), though a short break for coffee or tea is likely sufficient for most guests.

PERFUME MUSEUM (MUSÉE DU PARFUM)

2 Derb Chérif, rue Diour Saboun; tel. 0661/095 352; www.benchaabane.com/lemuseeduparfum; daily 9am-6pm; 40Dh

Unlike so many museums that are interested in showing you something, the Perfume Museum wants you to experience something—namely, your sense of smell. Housed in a restored 19th-century *riad,* the museum will immerse you in the world of perfume. By far the most interesting room in this small museum is the darkened room where you inhale the seven scents of Morocco, including saffron, cedar, rose, and other natural fragrances that are all indigenous to the country. Amina is usually around and can tell you a lot about the history and art of perfume-making in Morocco. You'll also have the option of making your own perfume to take home with you (400Dh), which makes for an incredible personalized souvenir. This is an unforgettable olfactory experience, unique in Morocco, that should be on a "must do" list for any visit to Marrakesh.

WOMEN'S MUSEUM (MUSÉE DE LA FEMME)

19 rue Sidi Abdel Aziz, Souk Jeld; tel. 0524/3811 29; www.museedelafemme.ma; daily 9:30am-6:30pm; 30Dh

A few minutes by foot north of the Jemaa el-Fnaa along one of the busier souk roads you'll find the wonderful Women's Museum. This

---

1: the Almoravid Koubba, the oldest building in Marrakesh **2:** travelers exploring the Bahia Palace **3:** The Marrakesh museum is an excellent example of Islamic architecture. **4:** decorative Arabic script in the Medersa Ben Youssef

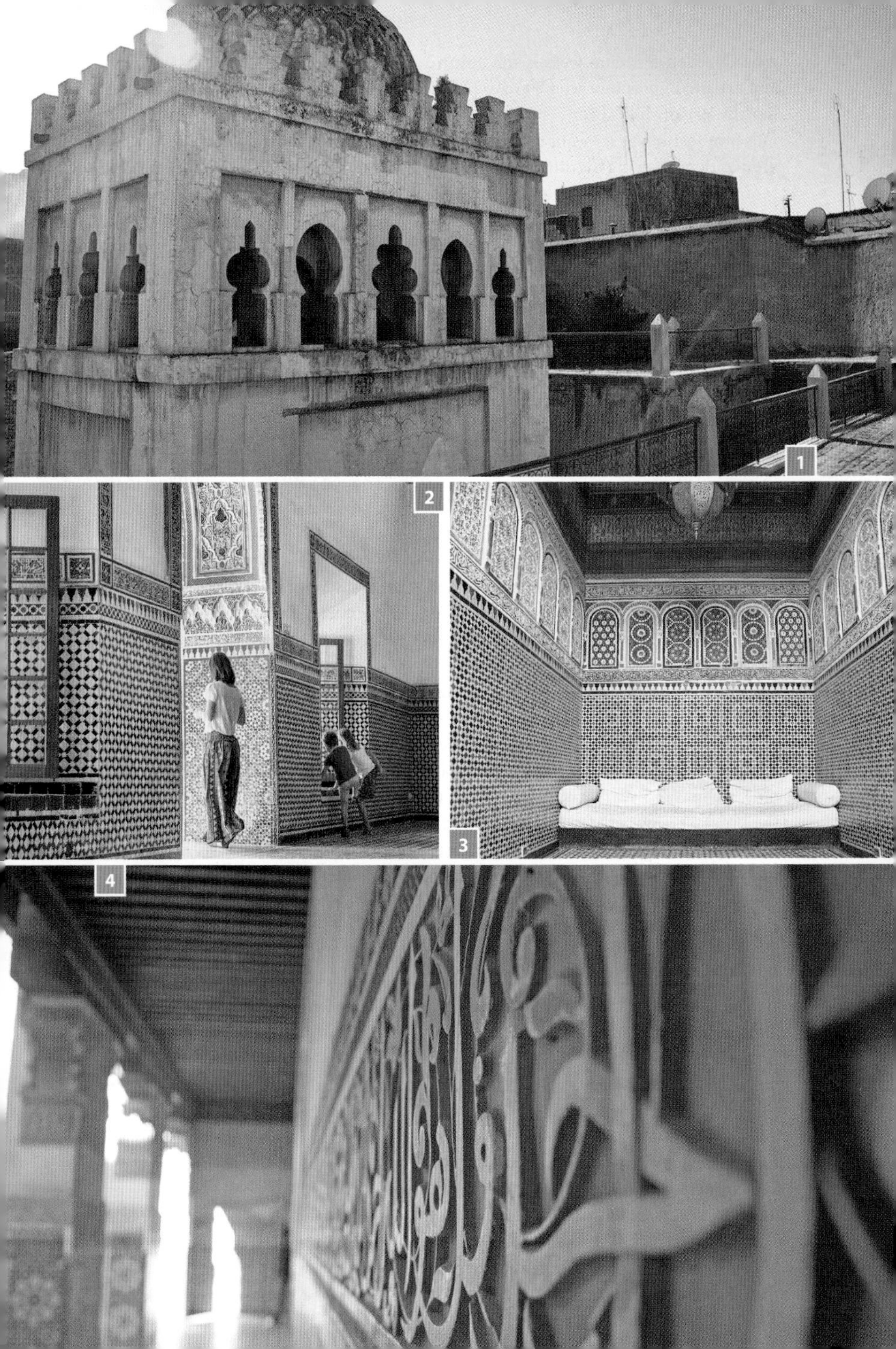
1
2
3
4

much-needed museum weaves the culture and artistic importance women have played in "the art of daily life." The three-story museum features a series of carpets on the ground floor showing the different regions of Morocco while introducing how women incorporated their lives into their art. On the next two floors are ornate shoes from the beginning of the 20th century as well as a selection of pottery, jewelry, *handiras* (highly decorative capes), and other traditional clothing. A series of black-and-white photographs from the French painter Jean Besancenot from the 1930s helps to bring the past of these women to life. The exposition changes every six months, with a terrace café slated to open in early 2020.

TANNERIES

Bab Debbaugh; 10am-sunset; free

Farther west along the same road that led from the Place de la Kisseria, past the numerous shops selling everything from bottled water to recycled metal sculptures, and all the way to the exit of the medina near Bab Debbaugh, you'll come to the tanneries of Marrakesh. Marrakesh tanneries have been working leather hides traditionally for almost a thousand years with little change to the process. Hides are first left to soak in a vat of quicklime, salt, water, and cow urine to make hairs and fat easier to remove. Tanners then leave the hides out to dry. Once dry, they are transferred to a vat of pigeon excrement, which makes the leather softer, before being dipped into a final vat of colored dye. The hides are left to dry in the sun once more and then cut and sold to leatherworkers, who make slippers, bags, purses, belts, wallets, and other products with them. With all the poop, pee, bloody animal hides, and hot sun, it's no wonder that the tanneries smell as rank as they do, and it's obvious why they are so far away from the rest of the medina. You'll likely be given a mint leaf cluster to shove up your nose. This will make the smell more bearable. It's an impressive sight, all the same, and a truly medieval experience.

Mellah

The **mellah,** or old Jewish Quarter, is a neighborhood now called Hay Essalam that is spread out to the south of the Jemaa el-Fnaa. To get to the mellah from the Jemaa el-Fnaa, you can either take the southwest passage, Rue Riad Zitoun el Kedim, across from the orange juice stands, and follow the crush of traffic for 15 minutes, or take the infinitely more pleasant Rue de Banques starting near Café de France—keep to the right where it merges at the Café Bakchich and continues on as Rue Riad Zitoun el Jdid. Follow this café- and shop-lined pedestrian thoroughfare until you come to a small park with a few cafés around it. This is the mellah.

Though very few Jews still live in the mellah, there are still several shops dedicated to classically Jewish crafts, including jewelers and a few tailors. After coming to the park, stay to the right to arrive at Place des Ferblantiers, which was once better known as Place de Mellah and the center of the Jewish Quarter. There are several synagogues, some of which have gardens you can visit, though you will likely need a guide to find most of them. The majority are spread to the east of the Place de Ferblantiers around the Jewish Cemetery.

★ BAHIA PALACE (PALAIS DE LA BAHIA)

5 Rue Riad Zitoun el Jdid; tel. 0524/389 511; www.palais-bahia.com; daily 9am-4:30pm; 70Dh

You'll find the Bahia Palace in the midst of the mellah, just off the Rue Riad Zitoun el Jdid. This ornate palace was given to the concubine Bahia, a favorite of the wealthy vizier Si Moussa Ba Ahmed's harem. The exact dates of the construction are unknown, but it is thought to have been built in two parts. The first section of the palace, known as Dar Si Moussa, was constructed by Ba Ahmed's father between 1859 and 1873, and the palace as it is known today was completed by Ba Ahmed while he was the grand vizier to the sultan by the end of the century.

Be prepared to strain your neck looking up

at the beautifully maintained woodcarving, geometric painting, and stucco work throughout the ceilings of the palace. Materials for decorating the Bahia Palace were sourced from across North Africa. Marble was brought from Meknes and was probably originally extracted from Carrara, Italy. This same marble may have previously decorated Moulay Ismail's palace in Meknes and perhaps the ancient city of Volubilis. Marble was also stripped from the nearby Badi Palace. Cedar for the painted ceilings of the palace apartments was commissioned from the Middle Atlas, and glazed terra-cotta tiles arrived from Tetouan. Artisans across North Africa and Andalusia were used in the construction of the palace, though the end result is less geometrically harmonic than spatially organic.

The palace is still used by the government, with the current Minister of Culture Affairs residing in a small section of the palace. A few scenes from the Alfred Hitchcock film *The Man Who Knew Too Much* were filmed in the palace. Get here early to avoid the crowds and have a more tranquil stroll through the palace and its gardens.

MUSEUM OF MOROCCAN ARTS

Derb Si Saïd; tel. 0524/389 564; Wed.-Mon. 9am-4:45pm; 20Dh

Confusingly also known as the **Dar Si Saïd Museum,** this spacious museum near the Bahia Palace is housed in the remodeled house of Si Saïd, brother to the grand vizier Ba Ahmed. You'll find it behind the Préfecture Medina on Rue Riad Zitoun el Jdid. The museum has transformed from an "arts and crafts" museum to one that really specializes in Moroccan carpets. Though you'll be able to find carpets from all around the country, it is the spectacular carpets from Haouz and High Atlas tribes that are truly worth the price of admission. Also be sure to check out the intricate mosaic work upstairs in this remodeled palatial house.

Kasbah

The **kasbah** comprises the southwest corner of the medina, on the other side of the expanse of the king's palace from the mellah. The **Saadian Tombs** are the most interesting site here. There is also an interesting **Artisan Complex** on the main road cutting through the kasbah (aptly named "Rue de la Kasbah"), as well as several quieter boutique *riads* that are away from the hustle and bustle of the rest of the old medina.

There are a few ways to get to the kasbah from Jemaa el-Fnaa. To take the most direct way, follow the busy Rue Riad Zitoun el Kedim until it ends, and then take a right past the small covered market and follow the road to the horse-drawn carriages. From the horses, you can turn left into the kasbah, though this will cut through a neighborhood where there is a good chance you might get a little turned around. An easier way to navigate, though a bit longer, is to follow Rue Riad Zitoun el Kedima as above, but this time, keep going straight past the horse-drawn carriages until this dumps you out of the medina walls at Rue Sidi Mimoun. You'll see a little post office. Take a left and then another left to immediately enter back through the medina walls, beneath the elaborately arched Bab Ananou and into the kasbah.

SAADIAN TOMBS

Rue de la Kasbah; daily 8am-4pm; 70Dh

Originally walled in by Moulay Ismail in the late 17th century and then "rediscovered" by French in 1917, the Saadian Tombs are some of the most ornate tombs in all of Morocco. It is the sheer beauty—or, some might argue, audacity—of their decoration that drives so many tourists here to gape at the gaudy mesh of stucco work, *zellij* tiles, inlaid gold, and Italian marble. The mausoleum consists of three rooms, while the elaborate graves and gravestones spill out into the courtyard and its gardens. About 60 members of the Saadi dynasty (1554-1659) are buried inside the mausoleum. The most famous room is the Room of the 12 Columns, which houses the grave of Ahmad al-Mansour, the best known of the Saadi rulers. He ruled from 1578-1603

1
2
3

and built the nearby Badi Palace. It is rumored that French authorities found the tombs while conducting an aerial survey of Marrakesh. The locals say otherwise, and that they have always known they were here.

BADI PALACE (PALAIS EL BADI)

Ksibat Nhass; tel. 0661/350 878; daily 8:30am-12:30pm and 2:30pm-4:30pm; 70Dh

The Badi Palace is the ruined palace of the Saadian sultan Ahmad al-Mansour. Al-Mansour began construction of the palace in 1578 to celebrate his victory over the Portuguese at the famous Battle of the Three Kings in the town of Ksar el-Kbeer near Tangier. The empty palace grounds are a bit more interesting after a tour of the Bahia Palace, where you will see a window into the history that has been preserved and then, when visiting the Badi Palace, see that which has been left to ruin. The ramparts serve as great spots to photograph Marrakesh, and the general lack of crowds ensures a little peace and quiet after the busy medina crowds.

The palace has a long history of being looted and sacked. In the 17th century, after the fall of the Saadian dynasty, the palace was stripped of materials and marble was taken, perhaps to Moulay Ismail's palace in Meknes. Today, the coos of pigeons and clacking bills of mating storks enliven this place. There are some projects underway in the palace to renovate some areas and develop gardens.

Admission price does not include access to the small museum (10Dh) and the excellent *minbar* (a type of pulpit sometimes used by imams to deliver their Friday sermons) housed there. The *minbar* is an excellent example of the artistry of the 12th century and has been faithfully restored. The museum is the best preserved indoor area of the expansive palace grounds. The token admission is worth it for those interested in glimpsing what has been preserved of the palace and for a look at the *minbar*.

VILLE NOUVELLE

The Ville Nouvelle is a place to live, shop, dine, and party, but not so much for sightseeing—with the exception of a few unique gardens, namely the Majorelle Gardens and the Palmeraie, which should be high on everyone's list of things to see in Marrakesh. If time allows, consider swinging through the Menara Gardens, though perhaps the most animated walk is along Avenue Mohammed V, the main promenade for shopping. Here, everything becomes lively right around sunset as the heat cools and the fragrant trees lining the promenade give off their perfume.

★ Majorelle Gardens (Jardin Majorelle)

Rue Yves Saint Laurent; tel. 0524/313 047; http://jardinmajorelle.com; daily 8am-6pm May-Sept., 8am-5:30pm Oct.-Apr., 9am-5pm during Ramadan; 70Dh for gardens, additional 30Dh for Berber Museum

The wonderfully art deco Majorelle Gardens is the loving creation of French painter Jacques Majorelle, who began working on the gardens in the 1920s. Majorelle cultivated this garden over 40 years, first opening it to the public in 1947. However, because of health issues, he had to abandon the gardens. The gardens suffered without a caretaker and were nearly destroyed; at one point, there was thought of turning the space into a hotel. Luckily, in 1980, fashion designer Yves Saint Laurent and his partner, Pierre Bergé, purchased the gardens and set about a restoration effort.

Today, the intense cobalt blue walls (incidentally, this particular intense shade of blue is called "Majorelle blue" after the French painter), water lilies, lotus flowers, and numerous cacti tucked beneath the shade of the towering palm trees make this a heaven for people and birds alike. However, because of its popularity, the gardens are not quite as relaxing as one might imagine, particularly when buses full of tourists descend onto the

1: lavish decoration in the Saadian Tombs **2:** the tropical Majorelle Gardens **3:** the ruins of the Badi Palace

property. It is best to go early in the morning, when the crowds are away, the air is fresh, and the blackbirds, house sparrows, warblers, and turtledoves who call these gardens home are at their most active.

There is a small café with a terrace inside the gardens, but it's expensive for what it is. The small **Berber Museum** houses an interesting look at the neighboring culture of the High Atlas mountains and includes a review of textiles and jewelry. The gift shop has original period photographs for sale, some of them decades old and nearly all of them fascinating, though not cheap. If you've made it all the way to the Marjorelle Gardens, it's probably worth your time to pop in for a quick look, though there are better museums in Marrakesh.

During Ramadan, the gardens are open 9am-5pm. The attached Berber Museum is open from 10am-garden closing time. The gardens and museum typically close at 6pm, though from Oct. 1-Apr. 30, they close at 5:30pm. It's best to consult the Majorelle Gardens website to be sure of opening and closing hours ahead of your visit and to plan on getting there as early as possible.

Menara Gardens

Ave. de la Ménara; daily sunrise-sunset; free

The Menara Gardens are an expansive olive grove southwest of the old medina and directly south of the Hivernage neighborhood, abutting the olive groves of Bab Jdid. In 1985, UNESCO declared the 12th-century Almohad gardens, along with the Agdal Gardens of the king's Royal Palace, a World Heritage Site. The 100-hectare (250-acre) grounds are ideal for picnics, where quiet and shade are easily found.

The **Saadian Garden Pavilion** (20Dh) at the edge of a pool, dating from the 16th-century Saadian dynasty, can be entered from roughly 7am-5pm, with proceeds going to the Cultural Foundation for Restoration. There is a terrace view from the garden pavilion overlooking the pool to Marrakesh, while behind the pavilion the High Atlas mountains soar up over the plain. The pool dates from the Almohad era. It was a favorite with soldiers, who used to train in it, though swimming is not allowed any longer. Camel rides are usually available in the gardens for 40-100Dh, depending on how long the ride is and how good your bargaining skills are.

Palmeraie

To the northeast of the medina lies the expansive **Palmeraie,** or palm groves, spread over 12,000 hectares (30,000 acres). This impressive spread of palm trees is the only oasis north of the High Atlas mountains and is considered throughout North Africa as the most stunning garden in all of Marrakesh, with palm trees seemingly without end. During the Almoravid dynasty in the 11th and 12th centuries, the elaborate underground network of irrigation that allows the vegetation to thrive in this otherwise arid environment was constructed. Several golf courses dot the Palmeraie, along with a few larger resort complexes. For the best view of the Palmeraie, take the double-decker tour buses (tel. 0663/527 797, bustouristique@also.ma, 145Dh), which you can catch at the Jemaa el-Fnaa just outside the Tourist Information Center on Avenue Mohammed V in the Gueliz neighborhood. The views from the top of the bus really allow you to take in these expansive gardens—just don't forget your sunscreen.

PALMERAIE MUSEUM (MUSÉE DE LA PALMERAIE)

Dar Tounsi; tel. 0628/031 039 or 0661/095 352; www.benchaabane.com/musee_palmeraie; daily 9am-6pm; 40Dh

Supported by a generous donation of over 100 pieces of contemporary art by the Benchaabane Foundation, the airy Palmeraie Museum is a surprisingly great museum for families. Housed in a reclaimed French protectorate-era 1940s farm, with lots of green space and a large Andalusian garden, there is lots of room to roam around. There are also art workshops for children as well as educational workshops where children can

Arabic Storytelling

Morocco has long been a land of stories and storytellers. Oral storytelling is an art that is passed from generation to generation, with storytellers becoming masters of the form, of keeping an audience hypnotized and on-edge, before delivering the final revelation, moral, or lesson. Stories are often told by women in the privacy of their homes, but in public, it is a craft of men and it is a high art. However, it is also a dying art. Aging storytellers are anxious to find young people to take over their craft.

Oral storytelling, or *hiyakat,* can trace its roots far back, before the written word, in the cradle of civilization on the Persian Peninsula. In Morocco, the roots trace back to the storied Jemaa el-Fnaa. Storytellers have sat in this popular square, plying their trade late into the night, for generations. They spin their tales among the snake charmers, musicians, and fortune tellers as their fathers and forefathers have, telling stories of intrigue, of sultans and harems, adventures of Sindibad, and genies that arise from bottles with little more than a dusting off, often with disastrous results.

Storytellers generally apprentice for five or more years, learning how to charm an audience, how to work on their breath and speech cadence, to understand when to lower their voice to a whisper and then when to unleash the wrath of the heavens with a thunderous roar. Professional storytellers have a thousand or more stories, not unlike their muse, Scheherazade, perhaps the most famous story of them all. You'll hear versions of the famed stories of *1,001 Nights,* as well as tales of the birth of the Sahara and of Aicha Rmada, a local version of Cinderella. There is a rekindled interest in Moroccan storytelling, particularly in Marrakesh, with Café Clock leading the revival.

learn about the environment, the dangers of climate change, and what they can do to help protect it for the future. Workshops are run by Rachida Touijri, a popular local artist. The museum also has a rotating exhibit featuring (usually) contemporary Moroccan artists as well as a permanent collection of contemporary and modern Moroccan artists.

Entertainment and Events

On arriving, pick up a copy of ***Marrakech Pocket*** from your hotel or the Tourist Information Center. This monthly publication lists all of the upcoming events in the city, though only in French. There seems to be a festival at least once a month, some larger than others. It's also worth knowing that some of the nightclubs, particularly 555 (tel. 0678/181 085, www.beachclub555.com) occasionally host concerts.

★ STORYTELLING AT CAFÉ CLOCK

224 Derb Chtouka; tel. 0655/210 172; www.marrakech.cafeclock.com; free

Every Thursday night at 7pm, Café Clock hosts one of the most culturally interesting events around town. Professional storytellers from the Jemaa el-Fnaa come and weave their tales for audiences in English and Moroccan Arabic. Other weekly events include traditional music on Sundays (6pm), jam sessions on Wednesdays, where you can bring an instrument and play with a cast of characters from around the world (7pm), and Saturday night live local music (6pm).

INTERNATIONAL FESTIVAL OF CONTEMPORARY DANCE

various locations around the city; Mar.; free

Contemporary dance has really taken hold throughout North Africa and the Middle East. The love for dance is expressed in the annual

International Festival of Contemporary Dance, held every March throughout the city. For a few days, the city is transformed by bobbing heads, swaying hips, and twisting torsos spinning like dervishes in the Jemaa el-Fnaa. Most events are public and free, though some private shows in theaters have a cover charge.

POPULAR ARTS FESTIVAL

various locations around the city; June or July; free

The Popular Arts Festival showcases talents typically seen in the Jemaa el-Fnaa and exports them into the palatial digs of the **Badi Palace** (Ksibat Nhass, tel. 0661/350 878) and **Royal Theater** (Ave. Hassan II, tel. 0524/431 516) every June or July. The energy around this festival is palpable, and it seems to be all anyone talks about for the weeks leading up to it. Performers of all stripes—storytellers and snake charmers, fire eaters and Gnawa musicians—descend on the city to swallow flames in the famed city square and belly dance in the transformed ruin of the Badi Palace in the plush confines of the Royal Theater. Those lucky enough to be in Marrakesh over the course of this festival are in for a carnival treat.

INTERNATIONAL FILM FESTIVAL

www.festivalmarrakech.info/en; Nov. or Dec.; free-200Dh

The International Film Festival, held late November or early December every year, brings a diverse collection of filmmakers together from around the world in late fall to screen films in English, French, Arabic, and other languages. The festival honors strong performers, with a list of recipients including Sharon Stone, Juliette Binoche, Hirokazu Kore-Eda, Mohamed Khouyi, Fernando Solanas, and Jeremy Irons. The festival works with local Moroccan film studios, such as Atlas Film Studios in Ouarzazate. Inquire at your accommodations for ticket availability.

Shopping

One of the charms (and hassles) of Morocco is having to barter. Prices are nearly always negotiable. The entire act is a great dance with partners taking turns with the lead, spinning one another around until a final price is agreed upon. Moroccan dancing partners, at least when it comes to the realm of shopping, are notoriously aggressive and demanding. Like in a good dance, you are expected to be equally aggressive and demanding. Don't be rude, but be firm with a price you think is fair. Whatever prices you and the shopkeeper start out at generally signal that a "fair price" will be arrived at somewhere in the middle.

MEDINA

★ The Souks of Marrakesh

If crowds aren't your thing, consider going to the souks on a Friday afternoon, when the medina is much more subdued and many, though not all, of the stores are closed. Otherwise, be sure to slip on your best pair of walking shoes and shop till you drop.

SOUK ABLEUH

From the Jemaa el-Fnaa, head north past the Café de France and keep to the left past the Terraces de l'Alhambra restaurant, where you'll enter the Souk Ableuh, the first of the many souks of Marrakesh. This souk is relatively tame, with a selection of bazaars, and it's mostly a busy **thoroughfare** to the main souks beginning with the longer Rue Smarine. You'll see a row of **olive sellers** with mounds of deliciously spicy olives, reflecting the Souk Ableuh's predominant historical trade.

SOUK SEMMARINE

Past the Souk Ableuh you'll duck through archways and come to the clearly marked

TOP EXPERIENCE

Souk Shopping 101

Here is a quick list of souk goods and a considerably fair price for each, though some souk items are of notoriously poor quality, and that's something to watch out for. As they say in Morocco, "Not everything that sparkles is gold."

a stylish bazaar in the souks

- **Carpets:** Prices vary with size; three-meter by four-meter (roughly 10-ft by 13-ft) carpets are typically around 1,000-3,000Dh, though certain more ornate carpets, such as carpets from Tazenakht and Rabat, can fetch 2-4 times as much. Of all the sellers in the souks, carpet sellers are notoriously the most aggressive and often start with outrageous prices, like 20,000Dh.
- **Ceramics:** Decorative plates and bowls, typically from Fez and Safi, will cost anywhere from 40Dh (small plate or bowl) to 200Dh (large plate or bowl). Some bowls from Fez, distinguished by the heavier gray clay and blue-and-green flower motifs, can cost up to 400Dh.
- **Moroccan slippers (*belghas* or *babouches*):** These cost 50Dh for indoor slippers, 90Dh for outdoor versions with rubber soles. Beware of paper-soled indoor *belghas,* which will quickly wear out. The embroidered slippers from Tafraoute will generally cost 150Dh.
- **Scarves:** Light scarves range from 40-100Dh.
- **Shisha pipes:** It costs 150Dh for a small one, though large ones can cost as much as 500Dh, depending on ornateness.
- **Silver jewelry:** The price is always negotiable, but silver jewelry is sold by the gram, and 20-25Dh a gram is reasonable. Sterling silver will be stamped with the number 925. All other silver is of mixed quality and should be substantially less.
- **Spices:** Cost varies with type and quality. Good **saffron** can be had for less than 10Dh a gram. Most other spices are less than 50Dh for a kilogram. It's best to say how much you want in dirhams. Order 5Dh of one spice or 10Dh of another. Often, you will be surprised by the quantity.
- **Tajines:** You'll pay 25-40Dh for a plain clay tajine. Beware of the decorative glazed tajines, as they may contain lead; these should not be used to prepare or serve food. The two- or three-piece tiny tajine pinch pots for spices are typically 20-30Dh.
- **Teapots:** Cost runs 100Dh (small) to 200Dh (large).

Souk Semmarine. This is basically a road that turns into two other souks: **Souk Nejjarine** and **Souk el Kebir.** Most of the smaller souks run off of this **main artery** formed by these three souks. Above, slats in the bamboo covering over the souks let in slivers of sun, the bamboo providing just enough shade to keep shoppers cool throughout the long, hot afternoons. These main three souks are filled with **pottery and pastry sellers,** as well as larger bazaars catering to tourists with all manner of traditional Moroccan goods. At the junction where the souk road forks, you will find the **Souk Attarine** complex just through Souk

Stalia to the left. If you continue straight ahead, you will find the **Souk Laghzel** (the wool and former slave market), as well as the **Souk Zrabia** (the carpet souk) on the right, before arriving at Souk Cherratine, which connects with the Souk Attarine, forming a connected circuit.

SOUK CHERRATINE

The Souk Cherratine connects with the main Souk Semmarine road, at this point now called Souk el Kebir. This area is the primary reserve of **leatherworkers** and their goods. Camel-skin bags and goat-hide coats are all on offer here, though prices can be outrageous. Some smaller items, such as wallets and belts, are 20-100Dh, while purses and clutches typically run 100-300Dh, depending on the type of leather used and the decoration. Camel leather is the most expensive, with goat and sheep being a close second and cow the cheapest and most common. A well-made leather bag big enough for your laptop should cost 200-300Dh, though you will almost always have to bargain to get that kind of price. Like carpet dealers, leather sellers can be notoriously aggressive with their pricing. Don't be surprised if you hear 2,000Dh for a leather jacket that should be half that price.

SOUK SMATA

Running nearly parallel to the Souk el Kebir, south about midway through Souk Cherratine, is the Souk Smata or the Souk des Babouches, a series of shops dedicated to the lovely **Moroccan slippers** you've likely seen everywhere. The traditional slippers of Marrakesh are cream, while saffron yellow ones are favored by the people from Fez. Today, you can find slippers in a wide range of styles and colors. Some slippers are meant to be worn indoors, while others have rubber soles, making it possible to wear them outside of the house. The shop owners in this souk are typically friendly and mostly honest with pricing. If you're buying multiple pairs of slippers, discounts will be available.

SOUK ATTARINE

Located in the northwest of the souk complex, the Souk Attarine now houses shops selling silver teapots, brass lanterns, and other metal works. However, the few **spice stands** that are still around, with their fragrant pyramidal towers of spice, give a hint to the real historical importance of this souk. Spices were, and still are, one of the more valued commodities in the Moroccan household kitchen.

SOUK DES TEINTURIERS

Down the busy street leading to the decorative Moussine Fountain from Souk Attarine is Souk des Teinturiers, or the **Dyers Souk.** Traditionally, this is where wool and silk were naturally dyed into bright reds, indigo blues, saffron yellows, and a kaleidoscope of other colors. Historically, this was a well-known souk for its rich, deep purple dye, sourced from nearby Essaouira. Today, the dyes are largely chemical, though a few keep to tradition. The wool is likely imported from Australia, and the "silk" is more rayon than anything else, though shopkeepers will insist on calling it cactus silk. This is the best souk to find a light scarf to wrap around your head. If you're lucky, one of the owners or boys in the neighborhood will show you to a rooftop for a spectacularly colorful view of the souk. A tip of 5-10Dh is customary for this unbeatable photo op.

SOUK DES CHAUDRONNIERS

You can still hear the pounding of hammers on metal at the Souk des Chaudronniers, or **metal workers' souk,** just north of the Souk Attarine. Here, copper and bronze are still pounded into bowls, plates, spoons, and all manner of shapes to be used around the home. Workers can be particularly sensitive to having their photos taken, so be careful. After a few minutes in the heat of the action

---

1: the popular orange juice stands of the Jemma el-Fnaa **2:** bright dyes in the Dyer's Souk **3:** Moroccan lamps in the Souk des Chaudronniers **4:** the iron monger souk in Marrakesh

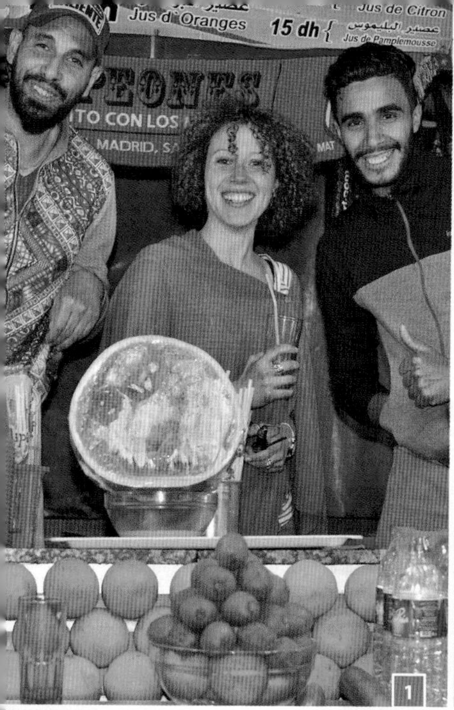
Jus d' Oranges
15 dh
Jus de Citron
عصير البليموس
Jus de Pamplemousse
1

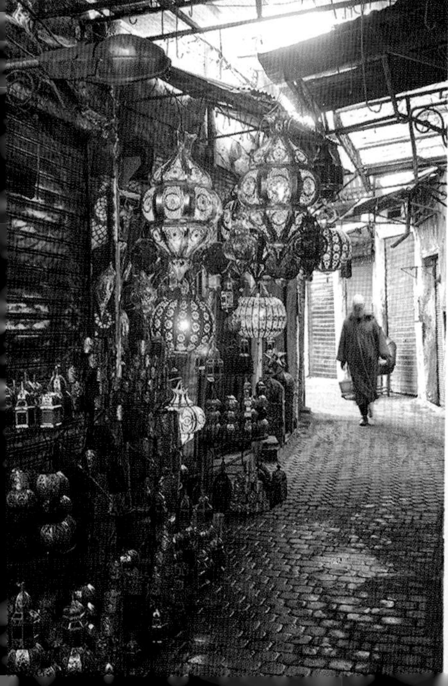

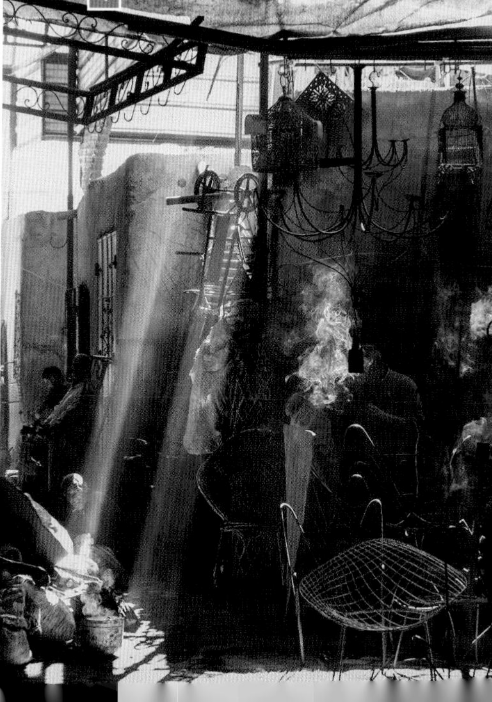

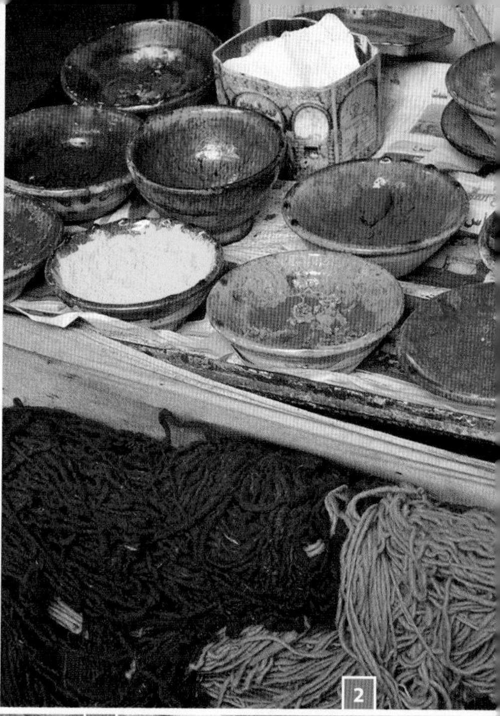
2

3

4

when the workers are at their most furious, pounding and tapping incessantly into the metal, the overwhelming orchestra can induce headaches. Perhaps this is where metal music got its start? Though headache-inducing, a stop by the Souk des Chaudronniers provides a fascinating glimpse into the art of metal sculpting.

SOUK KIMAKHNINE

Farther north from the Souk Attarine, along Souk Kchachabia in the quietest area of the souk complex, you'll find the Souk Kimakhnine, a souk still dedicated to making traditional Middle Eastern **musical instruments** such as ouds (lutes), *watars* (a type of acoustic guitar), *tarboukas* (goblet drums), and all manner of Moroccan-specific instruments. This is an absolute must-stop for musicians and one of the favorite souks for kids, where the owners will happily let them bang on drums or try their hands at plucking notes on the *watar.*

SOUK HADDADINE

Next to Souk Kimakhnine is Souk Haddadine, another one of the lesser-visited souks in Marrakesh. This souk and the smaller **Souk Chouari** form the **Woodworker and Blacksmith Souks.** The alleyways here smell of freshly cut pine wood and are some of the quietest places in the medina, making a stroll through here surprisingly relaxing. Peek into the shops, where some workers are cutting wood to fit while others are painting decorative motifs. Meanwhile, the blacksmiths forge wrought iron into window grates and coat hangers.

SOUK HARRARINE

Formerly the silk market (from whence it gets its name), today's Souk Harrarine has become a market for popular, geometrically intricate light fixtures. There are light fixtures of all types, from those that wouldn't look out of place in a grand palace to smaller lights that would be at home on a nightstand, cozily illuminating your bedroom.

Other Shopping in the Medina

ENSEMBLE ARTISANAL

Ave. Mohammed V; tel. 0524/443 503; Mon.-Sat. 9am-7pm, Sun. 9am-1pm

If you're looking for traditional Moroccan goods but find shopping in the souks intimidating—and rightfully so—make your way to the Ensemble Artisanal. You'll find well-made Moroccan products, such as leather bags and decorated pottery, for government-established prices. If you want to be a little more familiar with standard prices, it's a good idea to duck into the Ensemble Artisanal to see the prices of goods before attempting haggling in the souks. You can window shop all you like, wonderfully hassle free. The Ensemble Artisanal is a short five-minute walk from the Jemaa el-Fnaa, north from the Koutoubia Mosque on Avenue Mohammed V across from the Cyber Park.

ZOU & CO

11 Souk Jeld Sdid Abdel Aziz; tel. 0524/428 662; daily 10am-8pm

This upscale concept store in the medina offers a contemporary take on many Morocco classics, from plates fashioned from olive and walnut wood to stylish ceramics, fashionable linens, and one-of-a-kind mirrors. This is a great stop for shoppers who are looking for something that wouldn't be out of place in a Parisian apartment.

TOPOLINA

134 Dar el Bacha; www.topolina.shop; daily 10am-8pm

For funky, Japanese-Moroccan-fusion fashion, check out this boutique shop not far off the Jemaa el-Fnaa. You'll find hip takes on Moroccan shoes with prints that will leave your feet dizzy to big sacks with matching kimono-style robes that would look great on the street or on the beach.

TAMOUZIQUA

84 Kennaria Touala; tel. 0671/518 724; daily 10am-9pm

Tamouziqua is easy to miss. It's one of the many stores dealing in musical instruments, though where many of the other shops along Kennaria Touala also sell flamenco guitars from Spain and Fender knock-offs from China, Mustapha Mimani is still making *watars, gimbris,* and Moroccan drums the old-fashioned way, with carved, notched wood and stretched animal hides. Look for the cubbyhole shop raised a couple of feet off the street and listen for the banging of drums. Mustapha also gives music lessons for those looking to find their Gharnati or maybe Gnawi soul.

VILLE NOUVELLE AND GUELIZ

Gueliz has quickly become the go-to shopping district in Marrakesh, with the popular Avenue Mohammed V lined with shopping centers. There is a sort of **outdoor shopping mall** along the Place du 16 Novembre, which features many brand names familiar to Europeans and North Americans. Farther up Avenue Mohammed V is the new **Carre Eden** shopping center, another popular stop for name-brand goods, as well as the Marrakesh branch of Starbucks. For traditional Moroccan goods, duck through the alleyway across from the Carre Eden for a selection of bazaar goods, including handsome

pottery, embroidered kaftans, and decorative Moroccan pottery, often for prices far less than you'll find in the medina.

BEN RAHAL

24 Rue de la Liberté; tel. 0524/433 273; www.benrahalart.com; Mon.-Sat. 9:30am-1pm and 3pm-8pm

If carpets are your thing, head to the reputable Ben Rahal. This is one of the best shops in Marrakesh and maybe in all of Morocco. The service is informative and friendly, without being pushy. Bruce Willis, Bill Murray, and Kate Hudson have all shopped here. Carpet selection includes some Moroccan standards as well as some of the most diverse, truly unique pieces you'll find anywhere. The prices are higher than in some of the smaller villages, but quality will be assured. You can get a spectacular piece for around 5,000Dh.

MY ART

Pl. du 16 November at Rue Tarek Ibn Zyad; tel. 0524/449 181; Mon.-Sat. 10am-1pm and 3pm-7pm

For upscale, handcrafted artisan furnishings, such as tables, lamps, and leather sofas, as well as some other handicraft items, check out My Art. It features exceptional home decor crafted by Moroccans to contemporary European tastes.

MENZIL EL FAN LIBRAIRIE D'ART

55 Blvd. Zerktouni, next to the restaurant Al-Fassia; tel. 0524/446 792; Mon.-Sat. 9am-12:30pm and 3pm-7pm

One of the best bookstores in Marrakesh is the eclectic Menzil el Fan Librairie d'Art. Shelves of coffee-table books—mostly dedicated to Moroccan handicrafts—line the walls. Some great art deco posters from the French protectorate era go for 70Dh.

Sports and Recreation

★ MOROCCAN COOKING CLASSES

One of the best ways to dive in and really experience the culture of Morocco is to learn how to prepare the various salads, tajines, and couscous dishes that you will undoubtedly become familiar with during your travels. Expect to spend at least half a day with any cooking class, as Moroccan cuisine tends to take a while to prepare.

CAFÉ CLOCK

224 Derb Chtouka; tel. 0524/378 367; 300-600Dh

Café Clock runs a varied cooking course in English that includes different salads and tajines, though their course on baking Moroccan breads is perhaps the most interesting. It's a shorter, two-hour course that involves a trip to the 600-year-old neighborhood *farran*, a local oven that is used by the community every day for baking, and the price is considerably less than the asking price for the normal cooking classes at 300Dh.

FAIM D'EPICES

Douar Old Ali Ben Aich; tel. 0600/048 800; www.faimdepices.com; 550Dh

Discover the secrets of Moroccan spices and a few kitchen shortcuts at Faim d'Epices. The kitchen is about a 20-minute drive from Marrakesh; your tuition for the class includes transportation to and from Marrakesh. The courses include instruction in English on making traditional breads, as well as couscous and various salads, tajines, and sweets. Throughout the day, chef Nezha will tell you about storing all those wonderful spices you'll likely be packing home and give you some culinary history. You'll sip on artisan coffee or mint tea while preparing your meals and finish the afternoon on the terrace among the citrus trees digging into your day's work. It's a full day, with pickup around 10am and drop-off at 4pm, and one of the most enjoyable days you could hope for. A relaxing spa package can be added on to your day; it runs 5pm-8pm and is a nice way to unwind.

LA MAISON ARABE

1 Derb Assehbé, near Bab Doukkala; tel. 0524/387 010; 600Dh

For classes in the medina, check in with the *dada* (Moroccan Arabic for a woman who manages the cooking and children of a house) at the chic La Maison Arabe. Geared toward both amateurs and professionals, classes work with translators and use modern equipment. Classes start with an explanation of the seasonal menu, typically with one of the Moroccan salads and a tajine of your choice (or forgo the salad and make a dessert instead). You'll take a tour of the local market to pick fresh ingredients, make a quick stop at the spice market, and then get to work. After slaving away, you'll eat the fruits of your labor poolside in the elaborate setting of this upmarket *riad*.

BIKING

Bike tours have become increasingly popular over the last few years. They can be a wonderful, eco-friendly way to get out and explore the surrounding palm groves and the further reaches of Marrakesh. E-bikes have become increasingly popular. For those looking to bike into the mountains, this is the e-ticket.

★ MARRAKESH BIKE TOURS

44 Rue Tarik Ben Ziad; tel. 0667/797 035 or 0661/240 145; www.marrakech-city-bike-tour.com; 250Dh for group city tour, 400Dh for private guided city tour

Located next to the Carre Eden shopping center, this outfit has become the go-to company for those looking to explore the Red City on two wheels. By far the best deal is the friendly group city tour, though private tours are also available. You'll want to make sure to book the morning tour (10am) on hotter days, as tours are around three hours long. The afternoon tour (3pm) is in the hottest part of the day and should only be attempted in hot months by those with a predisposition for self-harm. Otherwise, the guided tours will keep you safe on the busy Marrakeshi roads while showing off some of the best that the Red City has to offer.

ARGAN XTREME SPORTS

Rue Fatima al Fihria; tel. 0524/400 207; www.argansports.com; bike rental 200Dh/day, tours from 300Dh

To rent a bike, check in with Argan Xtreme Sports, who can set you up with a bike to get around the city for around 200Dh a day. They also arrange more extreme bike tours throughout the High Atlas mountains and around Morocco. The Palmeraie Tour (300Dh) is a great way to circuit through the vast palm groves of Marrakesh. For those looking to really challenge themselves, perhaps imagining a future outing with the Tour de France, this is your outfit.

GOLF

SAMANAH

Menara, tel. 0524/483 200, www.samanah.com, 650Dh

Marrakesh has quickly become the European golfer's destination of choice, with a growing number of world-class courses to choose from. The near-constant sunshine, distant snow peaks of the High Atlas, unbeatable culture, and relative inexpensiveness all add up to unforgettable days on the links. Most courses are at resorts, with multiday golf packages available for about 4,000Dh. However, the stress that these courses put on Morocco's unstable water resources is something to be concerned about, despite what good they do for the economy and preservation of green spaces. The 18-hole Samanah Golf is a Jack Nicklaus-designed course and is surprisingly one of the less busy golf courses in Marrakesh, despite winning the International Golf Development of the Year award in 2011.

PUBLIC POOLS

When the heat turns up, and your accommodation doesn't have a plunge pool or swimming pool, there's only one thing to do: search for water. In the summer, temperatures can soar to 50°C (120°F), making a refreshing dip in a swimming pool something of a midday ritual ... or necessity. The most convenient pools will be in your accommodation. Many, but not all, accommodations in Marrakesh have pools. Be sure to ask ahead to see if your accommodation has a pool. If not, check into some of these public options.

PALAIS DONAB

53 Dar el Bacha; tel. 0524/441 897; www.palaisdonab.com; daily 11:30am-3pm; 150Dh pp

If your accommodations don't have a pool or you're just looking for a place to chillax, pop into the Palais Donab. There is an attached hotel, restaurant, and lounge, but the real draw here is being able to be poolside in the middle of the medina for 150Dh (per person). The price of admission includes towels and sun beds, but you'll have to pack your own sunscreen.

PALMERAIE RESORTS

Circuit de la Palmeraie; tel. 0524/334 343; www.palmeraieresorts.com; 150Dh pp

If you're looking to enjoy some sun, party a bit, shake your moneymaker, and sit down to a luxe meal, check out the pool at Nikki Beach in this resort tucked into the palm groves. It boasts three swimming pools, tennis courts, lounge spaces, and a DJ that spins the latest cuts all day long. This is not a great place for kids, but ladies might be interested in the resort's midweek escape on Tuesdays with a complementary pool bed and open bar from 11am to 1pm. Gentlemen, don't worry, you have your own deal on Thursdays from noon-1pm.

HAMMAMS

There are still traditional hammams throughout the medina of Marrakesh. These are simple affairs, with a steam room and scrubbing available for 10-20Dh. Though they're intended for locals, many travelers find an experience in a real Moroccan hammam something memorable. You can ask at your accommodations for the closest neighborhood hammam.

BAB DOUKKALA HAMMAM

southeast corner of the Bab Doukkala Mosque; daily, men 8pm-midnight; women noon-7pm; 10Dh

The Bab Doukkala Hammam is a great option to experience a local hammam for the centrality to many of the *riads* in the north part of the souks. This is one of the largest local public hammas, though as all of the public hammams tend to be, it seems like it could use a big scrub-down itself. Scrubbing (20Dh) and massages (50Dh) are usually available, and the attendants understand enough English so communication, though limited, it better than at most other local hammam options.

ES SAADI PALACE SPA

Rue Ibrahim el Mazini; tel. 0524/337 400; www.essaadi.com; daily 8am-9pm, by appointment only; 400Dh

A considerably less traditional, though completely enjoyable, spa experience can be had at some of the palatial hotels in Hivernage. The cream of the crop is the Es Saadi Palace Spa. The grounds of this spa are enormous, featuring a thermal spa, high-tech swimming pool with multiple water pathways, thermal heat baths, dedicated rooms for massage, open terraces for yoga, a total workout gym, and a mirrored room for indoor yoga or dance. This is holistic body care at its finest.

ROYAL MIRAGE DELUXE

Rue de Paris; tel. 0524/425 400; daily 8am-9pm, by appointment only; 400Dh

One of the better excuses to make your way into the Royal Mirage Deluxe is to make a reservation at their spa. Indulge in a California or Thai massage, and while you're at it, add in a facial, body scrub, and a relaxing 30 minutes in the traditional Moroccan steam room. With all the heat and humidity, your body will feel refreshed and your skin wide open, and when you make your way out of the spa and back into the opulence of the hotel, you'll be sure to leave feeling like spoiled royalty.

Food

Inspired by the taste buds of the millions of people from hundreds of nationalities that visit the city each year, Marrakesh is the place to dine out on great fusion-fueled menus. French bistros and Italian pizza joints cozy up with sushi restaurants, Chinese noodle dives, and Balinese cuisine, lending the entire culinary vibe of Marrakesh somewhat surprisingly, for first-time visitors, truly international. It wouldn't be a mistake to say that the food scene in Marrakesh is perhaps the most eclectic in the entire country. If you're spending a long time in Morocco, you would be wise to check out a few of the international options as, outside of some of the bigger cities, your options throughout the rest of the country are generally limited to Moroccan fare.

For traditional Moroccan food in Marrakesh, though there are some really nice Moroccan restaurants, the functioning restaurants in high-end *riads* are well worth checking out, as the atmosphere of dining in beautifully restored *riads* is part of the Marrakesh experience. For couples and close friends, these cozy restaurants often make for the most memorable nights out.

MEDINA

There are several places to eat around the medina, though an evening snack on the Jemaa el-Fnaa itself is an experience not to be missed. Most cafés in the busier parts of the medina and around the city serve some sort of breakfast, lunch, or dinner from around 8am until 10pm or so, while reservations will be needed for most of the fine-dining establishments tucked into the numerous *riads* and hotels. If you don't have a phone, you can either have someone at your lodging make a reservation for you or stop by the restaurant the day before and make a reservation in person.

LE BLED CAFÉ

6 Kennaria Dabachi; tel. 0524/368 346; daily 10am-10pm; 40Dh

Just a short walk off the Jemaa el-Fnaa, Le Bled Café is one of the quieter options, where hearty tuna sandwiches and veggie pizzas are made with a smile, along with coffee and freshly squeezed juice. The terrace of this café, and the popular **Bakchich Café** next door, make for great people-watching just off the plaza with a light lunch or just a tea or coffee.

LALA MOULATI

1 Talaa Ibn Youssef, Souk Chaaria; tel. 0524/385 012; daily 9am-10pm; 70Dh

For people-watching, it doesn't get any more comfy than this bakery cafe. For a coffee and cookie, stick to the downstairs window front bar and take in the busy medina street outside. Head upstairs or to the terrace for a quick breakfast or lunch. The menu is full of familiar favorites to keep the kids happy, from spaghetti bolognese and cheese pizzas to burgers and pancakes. Though tajines and *pastillas* are on the menu, you can find better elsewhere for half the price.

UN DÉJEUNER À MARRAKECH

corner of Rue Kennaria and Douar Graoua; tel. 0524/378 387; daily 11am-10pm; 50Dh

Un Déjeuner à Marrakech has favorites for a late breakfast, lunch, or light dinner. The menu includes omelets, salads, and fresh juice mixes, including beet root, cucumber, and mint. Vegetarian and gluten-free options are available. Seating inside can be a smoke-free reprieve from the hot sun, but the shaded terrace views on the roof over the medina and to the High Atlas are worth the climb.

BEATS BURGER

35 Souk Jeld Kimakhine; tel. 0524/391 213; www.beatsburger.com; daily noon-10pm; 100Dh

After a long morning in the souks, sometimes

you just want a burger, and Beats Burger fills that craving. From classic cheeseburgers and homemade chicken nuggets to vegetarian-friendly bagels slathered with cream cheese and stuffed with cooked tomatoes, eggplant, zucchini, and peppers, this is a stop that has a little something for everyone. Stop in for an easy lunch in the medina with bright, Beat-era inspired decor. Free Wi-Fi is available. For a little more quiet, brave the spiral staircase to the intimate terrace, and if you like spicy foods, make sure to order your sandwich with the harissa mayonnaise. No alcohol is served.

SOUL FOOD BY MAX & JAN

16 rue Amsefa, Sidi Abdelziz; www.maxandjan.com; daily 10am-11pm; 150Dh

Americans shouldn't be fooled by the name. This is Moroccan-style "soul food," with a slow cooked beef *tangia* taking center stage. There is only rooftop terrace dining here, so for rainy days or particularly hot days, it's perhaps better to look elsewhere. Otherwise, a charming, expensive terrace greets you decorated with *bouchourette* carpets from around Morocco, adding to the hip, funky vibe Soul Food carries over from the Max & Jan Concept Store on the ground floor. If you're in the neighborhood, consider stopping in between 4pm-6pm for a tea or coffee with a pastry (80Dh).

★ EXOTIC BALI

56 Derb Chentouf; tel. 0666/044 882; http://exotic-bali.com; daily noon-10pm; 200Dh

If your hunger pangs steer you toward something farther east, look no further than Exotic Bali. Located on the far end of the souks, the tranquil, moonlit terrace is the perfect spot to unwind while Balinese chef Andy Gustiandi whips up some fresh mint-infused spring rolls to get you started. You'll likely be surrounded by in-the-know French travelers who always seem to have a nose for the hottest restaurants in town. Though the *ikan kukus sumedang* (steamed white fish with *sumedang* sauce or coconut cream) is the chef's specialty, you'd be forgiven for digging into the succulent *daging rendang padang* (slow-cooked beef with coconut and veggies in a creamy *padang* sauce) that just falls apart, not unlike a perfect pot roast. As you might expect from an Indonesian restaurant, there are also tons of options here for vegetarians and vegans alike. This is a can't-miss restaurant for those interested in Marrakesh's burgeoning international dining scene and for those seeking something a world away from the neighborhood *tajine*. No alcohol is served.

★ PEPE NERO

17 Derb Cherkaoui Douar Graoua; tel. 0524/389 067; www.pepenero-marrakech.com; daily dinner seating at 8pm; 200Dh

For an upscale *riad* dining experience, Pepe Nero is just the trick. An Italian-Moroccan fusion menu is served in this beautifully restored *riad*. Dine outdoors beneath a cover of stars; the long central pool and fountain are lit up at night, surrounded by candlelit dining tables. Choose from two menus created by the friendly Cordon Bleu-trained chef, Khalid: The Il Bel Paese menu features Italian dishes, such as mouthwatering saffron carnaroli risotto. The Ville Rouge menu focuses on Moroccan classics revisited, such as pigeon *pastilla* and slow-roasted shoulder of lamb. If you were going to splurge on one restaurant in the medina, it would be this one. Call ahead for reservations.

CAFÉ CHEZ ZAZA

21 Bab Fteuh; tel. 0673/081 716; daily noon-midnight; 80Dh

Just a bit north of the Jemaa el-Fnaa you'll find Café Chez ZaZa. The lively terrace looks over the rooftop of the medina, and the waiters, most of whom know more than just a bit of English, will make sure you are well looked after. The menu is traditional Moroccan. Vegetarians will delight in the veggie *pastillas,* a rare find in Morocco, as well as the fresh, clean salads. This is perhaps the best place around the souks for lunch, so the terrace tends to fill up by 2pm.

Dining Out on the Jemaa el-Fnaa

It might seem overly touristy, but the food stalls in the Jemaa el-Fnaa actually existed long before tourism ever took root. The smoke from the grills wafting over the carnivalesque square is as familiar a sight to the locals as the nearby Koutoubia Mosque. Prices will fluctuate wildly depending on your negotiation skills. In principle, you should agree to a price for everything before eating. A typical meal costs 30-50Dh, and a plate of grilled meats large enough for 3-4 people to share can run 100-150Dh. Other options include a small bowl of snail soup (5Dh), *harira* (5Dh), and one of the most refreshing glasses of freshly squeezed orange juice you've ever had (4Dh).

Feel free to walk around the stalls and inquire about the food on offer; high-pressured sales are the name of the game, with everyone promising to feed you "the best" in Marrakesh, but it's all largely friendly. Several stands have been featured in travel guides and on websites, though in practice, the food is pretty much the same across the board. The only real issue you might run into is the occasional owner trying to charge more for olives and bread, which are typically free, or having you pay for a full plate instead of half plate, though if you agree on a price ahead of time, this can be avoided.

The stands are controlled by the Moroccan government, so cleanliness is generally okay, though as a rule stick to the soups, fried foods, and meats, and stay away from the seafood or anything uncooked, as there are no refrigerators to keep food cold, and in the heat bacteria can be a problem if anything is undercooked. It might be a good idea to forgo the silverware, as it is often washed with the same water all day long; instead, eat with your hands. For sauces, use a piece of bread to scoop up your food, just like the locals.

CAFÉ ATAY

62 Rue Amsefah; tel. 0661/344 246; daily 10am-10pm; 60Dh

Another option around the souks is Café Atay, which serves tea. (*Atay* is "tea" in Moroccan Arabic.) The menu includes a variety of simple sandwiches and pastries, but it's a surprisingly competent coffee, which can be just the sort of caffeine jolt you might need after a day in the souks. The double-decker terraces serve to elevate above the hum of activity below, giving some great views over the medina, and the free Wi-Fi is handy.

★ HENNA ART CAFÉ

35 Derb Sqaya, off Rue Riad Zitoun el Kedim; tel. 0666/779 304; www.marrakechhennaartcafe.com; daily 11am-8pm; 60Dh

South of the Jemaa el-Fnaa you'll find the wonderful Henna Art Café, a veritable haven for vegetarians and vegans. Offerings include copious simple yet delicious salads and falafel (how is this not more popular around Morocco?). The service is friendly, and the entire café really does its best to show off local artists; American artist Lori Gordon curates the gallery's rotating exhibitions. It's best to come in early or mid-afternoon for the best terrace seating.

Kasbah

LOTUS PRIVILEGE MOROCCAN RESTAURANT

9 Derb Sidi Ben Hamdouche; tel. 0661/997 919; www.restaurantlotusprivilege.com; daily 7pm-1am; 250Dh

Book at least one or two days ahead of time for a seat at Lotus Privilege Moroccan Restaurant. You might even need to hire a guide to lead you to the restaurant, buried in the kasbah neighborhood. Dinner is served in the cool confines of the starlit patio pool. At 8pm, live Tarab Al-Andalusi (Moroccan music with Andalusian roots) stirs the soul while whirling dervishes spin to the beat. The menu features traditional Moroccan food revisited, such as a succulent John Dory fish tajine with spicy Moroccan *charmoula*. The food is good, but make no mistake—this is a place you come to for the show.

Mellah

As in the kasbah, the choices in the mellah are pretty limited outside of the individual *riads*, which will usually make lunches or dinners on demand, even for non-guests. This can be a great way to see a few different *riads*. You can expect a well-done tajine for around 100Dh, and possibly, depending on the restaurant and *riad*, a good wine might be had.

RESTAURANT EL BAHIA

Ansa el Bahia; tel. 0524/378 679; daily noon-4pm and 7:30pm-11:30pm; 150Dh

The Restaurant El Bahia near the Bahia Palace serves competent, though overpriced, tajines. This place is popular with tour groups; when they arrive, it can make service crawl to a halt. The palatial digs are nice and worth skipping the terrace for. Grab a courtyard seat and snack on some spicy olives while your tajine simmers. The menu features Moroccan wines, and let's be honest, after a hot day of touring the souk, sometimes a glass of crisp white wine is all you really need.

★ LA TABLE AL BADIA

135 Derb Ahl Souss; tel. 0524/390 110; www.riadalbadia.com; daily 7:30pm-11pm; 300Dh

For authentic home-cooked Moroccan cuisine, check out La Table Al Badia in the Riad Al Badia. Samira, the chef, heads to the souk every day to hand-pick fresh meat and produce. Succulent lamb that falls off the bone and crispy meat-stuffed pastries are just a couple of the tricks up Samira's sleeve. During the few cold months, you'll dine fireside, as the Marrakesh nights can get cold. Otherwise, you'll dine outside on the palatial terrace under the dim lights and the stars. Reservations are required the morning of your intended dinner at the very latest. Most dietary needs, such as vegetarian or gluten-free, can be accommodated.

GUELIZ

The dining options here, as at the hotels, are largely budget and midrange choices with a few more upscale dining options available. Some cafés have a real European feel. If you're looking to pass some time people-watching or digging into a vacation read, there are far fewer hassles with sellers and beggars, making this a good place to relax or meet up with friends.

Café les Négociants, Café Atlas, and **Café la Renaissance** are all at Place Abdelmoumen. Their competing positions across from each other evoke Parisian cafés, such as the well-known Café Flore and Deux Magots. Café Atlas, recently remodeled, is the clear winner of this art deco showdown. The wide patio and renovated interior make for a pleasant late-morning coffee or light early-evening snack. Café les Négociants is the local favorite, and the Renaissance is a tad more upscale with a diverse clientele, many from the attached hotel.

LE 1ER BOULEVARD

19 Immeuble Jakar, Ave. Mohammed V; daily 7am-10pm; 25Dh

If you're staying around Gueliz and need a place to go out for breakfast or a light lunch, Le 1er Boulevard is a good, clean café. Nothing on the menu will knock your socks off, but sometimes simple is good enough. Service starts at 8am. Continental breakfast, including a freshly squeezed orange juice, is the staple here.

CAFÉ DU LIVRE

44 Rue Tariq Ibn Ziad; tel. 0524/446 921; Mon.-Sat. 11am-midnight; 20Dh

A tour of the Marrakeshi café scene wouldn't be complete without mentioning the haven of English-speakers, Café du Livre, near the Carre Eden shopping center. Whether you're looking for other Anglophones to hang out with, want to curl up among shelves of familiar books, or plan to drop in on the popular quiz night, the newly remodeled café is a gem of modern Marrakesh, with light sandwiches served throughout the day.

★ LIBZAR

28 Rue Moulay Ali; tel. 0524/420 402; daily noon-3pm and 7pm-11:30pm; 250Dh

There are a few restaurants where you can find really excellent Moroccan food outside of a Moroccan house. Libzar is one of them. If this is your first Moroccan dining experience, most others will likely pale in comparison afterward. The elaborate menu features seven traditional starter salads, as well as classic tajines such as beef and prune, done to perfection. There's great attention to detail throughout the expansive dining room and in the *zellij* and stucco work. The menu includes a list of local Moroccan wines to pair with dinner.

AL FASSIA

Blvd. Mohamed Zerktouni; tel. 0544/434 060; daily 8pm-midnight; 300Dh

Another excellent option for Moroccan dining is Al Fassia. It's nearly always busy, and deservedly so. The menu features tajines and couscous dishes, but the setting inside this restored palace, the all-female service, and the ability to order à la carte (instead of an entire five-course meal) set it apart from the crowd. The restaurant can be a bit hard to find. It's a short walk down a shopping alley just off the boulevard, across from the Franco-Belge hotel by Café SBJ. If it's on the menu, go for the lamb with roasted plum.

VITA NOVA

36 Rue Ibn Aïcha; tel. 0524/423 939; daily noon-3pm and 7pm-midnight; 80Dh

Sleek Vita Nova features favorite Italian classics, such as spaghetti alla carbonara, as well as some of the best pizzas in Marrakesh. The Diavoli is a spicy, devilishly good pizza. The wine list isn't as extensive as at some of the other restaurants in the neighborhood, but the homemade ice cream makes up for it. Make no mistake, though, you are coming here for the food and not the service ... which can be a hit-or-miss affair.

MAMMA MIA

18 Rue de la Liberté; tel. 0524/434 454; daily noon-3:30pm and 7pm-11:30pm; 150Dh

The Marrakeshi Italian restaurant staple Mamma Mia serves up pastas, as well as Italian lamb shank. Of course, it's the homemade, wood-fired pizzas that tend to steal the show. They're a big hit with the kids. Thankfully, the first floor is nonsmoking in this rustic local favorite. The red-and-white checkered cloths seal the Italian authenticity. If you're looking for an Italian *séjour* from couscous, look no further.

LE LOFT

20 Rue de la Liberté; tel. 0524/434 216; www.restaurant-loft.com; daily noon-midnight; 140Dh

Le Loft keeps the distressed-elegance vibe of the neighborhood with lots of exposed wood and brick. The contemporary French bistro menu serves easy-to-like favorites, such as a chicken cordon bleu and a cheeseburger that would be right at home in the Marais in Paris. There is a nonsmoking section upstairs. With the rotating indie-favorite and international music jams, the vibe is definitely European. All in all, a great escape from the fare of the medina and the standard Moroccan plates.

KECHMARA

3 Rue de la Liberté; tel. 0524/422 532; www.kechmara.com; Mon.-Sat. 10am-1am; 130Dh

Down the street from Le Loft and Mamma Mia is Kechmara, an industrial joint that wouldn't look out of place in Brooklyn or Camden Town. The menu is upscale pub food, including fish-and-chips and sizzling duck-sausage hot dogs. The indoor smoking can be a problem for some. Luckily, there are a few seats on the street and an upstairs terrace.

Nightlife

Nightlife in Marrakesh is the best in Morocco and famed around the world. Its reputation is fully earned. The nightclubs are as good, if not better, than clubs you might find in London, Paris, Tokyo, New York, or other world capitals. The DJs spinning are generally some of the best in the world, many of them international, though there are fantastic home-grown DJs as well. However, fun does come at a price, often in the form of exorbitant drink prices and high cover charges, usually 250Dh or more. Most cover charges include a drink. If you reserve table or bottle service before coming, cover is free. Keep in mind that though the doors typically open in most nightclubs around midnight, the party never gets going until about 2am.

Prostitution (both male and female) is rampant. Beware of engaging in any suspicious conversation. The local police force does take prostitution seriously, and there are efforts to curb this. If going out, use a reasonable amount of caution, particularly with strangers.

555

Hôtel Ushuaia, Blvd. Mohammed VI; tel. 0678/181 085; www.beachclub555.com; 10pm-late; 200Dh

Continuing the party is never a problem at 555. Guest DJs are drawn from around the world, with a heavier emphasis on the American hip-hop and rap scene. Snoop Dogg and Jay-Z have even thrown down here. There is also a dinner spectacle worth checking out, with flashy dancers and outrageous costumes. Doors open at 11:30pm. Every night, groups of four or more ladies get in free, with free drinks all night long, making it a good stop for girls' night out.

LE SALAMA

40 Rue des Banques; tel. 0524/391 300 or 0657/733 879; www.le-salama.com; daily noon-midnight; 200Dh

This is one of very few places around the Jemaa El-Fnaa square that offers beer, wine, and spirits. You could have dinner here (300Dh), but the real gem is the rooftop terrace, dubbed the Skybar. While overlooking the medina of Marrakesh, you can enjoy hookah and cocktails. In fact, these are some of the best cocktails in town, including strawberry mojitos. Local DJs spin some contemporary favorites, while most nights belly dancers will also perform.

PACHA

Blvd. Mohammed VI; tel. 0566/110 288; www.pachamarrakech.com; 11pm-4am; 200Dh

Pacha holds claim to being the biggest nightclub in Africa. If your favorite big-name European DJ is spinning in Morocco, this is likely the place. Doors open at 11pm, but the party doesn't start until well after midnight. Drinks are more overpriced than usual. Thursday night is ladies' night with free entry for women.

ROYAL MANSOUR BAR

Rue Abou Abbas El Sebti; tel. 0529/808 282; www.royalmansour.com/en/dining/bars; daily 11am-1am; 250Dh

This might be the most elegant bar in the world, where British style is livened up with a bespoke Moroccan touch. Whether you're wanting to chat with friends, take part in exquisite tastings, or just enjoy some soothing piano music, this is something of a dream bar, though your pocketbook won't think so. It's the sort of place you can imagine James Bond swaggering down the balustrade to order a martini—shaken, of course. Drinks here are expensive, often 150Dh or more. The bar closes at midnight, making this a romantic stop for a nightcap or a calm start to the storm of the local nightclub scene.

TOP EXPERIENCE

★ Choosing a *Riad*

To get all the way to Marrakesh and not experience at least one or two nights in one of the estimated 1,600 renovated *riads* and *dars* that have been retrofitted into unique guesthouses would be a mistake. Each one of these guesthouses, once a home to generations of Moroccan families, reflects its wonder in a distinct way.

Many owners, both foreign and Moroccan, have decided to maintain a rustic charm to their guesthouses, while still others have stripped the houses down to their barest essentials, lending a minimalist appeal that highlights the architecture of these old homes. Generally speaking, each of these *riads* and *dars* offers a sort of Orientalist fantasy, fused with European decadence, that meets warm Moroccan hospitality. The staff of these *riads* are nearly always friendly, and for most travelers, the real highlight of their trip to Marrakesh is staying in one of these renovated *riads*.

You'll find these guesthouses spread throughout the medina, tucked down the pedestrian side streets, often in the quieter corners of the sprawling old city. As you walk down run-down medina streets and approach the aged door for the first time, you'll have no hint as to the wonders waiting for you just on the other side. Here you'll find some of my personal favorites for staying in the Red City, though truthfully with so many choices for guesthouses in Marrakesh, it's hard to go wrong. Nearly every single one I've stayed at, even ones I'm not listing in this guide, have provided good or even excellent value.

THEATRO MARRAKECH

Rue Ibrahim El Mazini; tel. 0524/448 811; www.theatromarrakech.com; daily 11:30pm-5am; 250Dh

If Pacha seems overwhelming, try the slightly more intimate TheatrO. With some of the bolder art directions—circus-style acrobats and fire-spitting dancers—this is the spot for many European partygoers. The owners have an inspired philosophy of "reinventing the party each night," which is based on the original Theatre Es Saadi, Marrakesh's first dance hall, established over 60 years ago. The weekly calendar features a rotating ladies' night. Table reservations with champagne service are available starting at 10,000Dh.

Accommodations

MEDINA

Under 400Dh

★ KAMMY HOSTEL

26 Derb Sekkaya; tel. 0654/215 440 or 0623/143 375; 55Dh for a dorm-style bed

For those looking for a down-home budget experience, the Kammy Hostel is an absolute gem. The rooms are a little cozy, with 4-8 sleeping in bunks. There are four rooms, with one room reserved for only women (85Dh). The management team of Shakira (from the US) and Nacer (from Marrakesh) are a superb team, happy to look out for you and to make sure that you'll find the best deals in town. There is an upstairs terrace to chill out on. This is a quieter hostel than most in Morocco, making it a welcome reprieve from the cacophony of the souks outside. Breakfast and Wi-Fi are included, though like most hostels you'll want to remember to pack your own towel (though you can rent one for 10Dh if needed) and soaps. Lunch and dinner are also available, with Karima whipping up one of the most delicious *tangias* in all of Morocco.

HOTEL SINDI SUD

109 Derb Sidi Bouloukate, just off Riad Zitoun Lakdim; tel. 0524/443 337; 100Dh d

There are few really outstanding budget accommodations in Marrakesh, but the Hotel Sindi Sud is one of them. Just a short walk south from the Jemaa el-Fnaa, the lodgings are simple, and for shoestring travelers, it's possible to sleep on the terrace for just 30Dh a night. The *riad* is impeccably clean, making it a real steal at this price range. Bathrooms are shared, and there is Wi-Fi. The staff here are incredibly friendly, and, if they have a moment, will help you find your way around the confusing environs of the Marrakesh medina.

HOTEL CENTRAL PALACE

59 Sidi Bouloukate; tel. 0524/440 235; 150Dh d pp

A long-time backpacker favorite is the Hotel Central Palace. Just a five-minute walk south of Jemaa el-Fnaa, this remodeled *riad* features simple rooms with comfortable beds and shared bathrooms, though cleanliness can sometimes be an issue. There is no air-conditioning or heating in the simple rooms, so nights tend to be hot in the summer and cold in the winter—pack accordingly. The bathrooms are cleaned every day but can become filthy quickly; some might want to pay the extra 50Dh for the rooms with en suite bathrooms.

400-800Dh

DAR SOUKAINA

19 & 24 Derb Lhammam; tel. 0524/376 055; 400Dh d

There are two houses here, directly across the street from each other, with the same name ownership. Each has its charm, with verdant open-air patios and helpful staff. A great-value proposition with all the charm of a Moroccan *riad,* and usually available for much less than other *riads* closer to the Jemaa el-Fnaa. Avoid the ground floor rooms as they can be a bit humid. Families might consider renting two rooms close together, such as the Cumin and Cannelle rooms. Breakfast, air-conditioning, and Wi-Fi are included.

RIAD ALISMA

50 Rue de la Bahia; tel. 0524/378 935; www.riadalisma.com; 500Dh d

The 18th-century Riad Alisma has been renovated to great effect with *mashrabiya*—latticed woodwork that covers the windows and hints at the splendor inside. There is a lot to like about this boutique *riad.* It's a favorite with French travelers passing through Marrakesh, and it's easy to see why. Lining the central patio, rooms are calm with plenty of beige and brown. The *riad* is large enough so that there are plenty of private nooks to curl up and enjoy a quiet stay. Wi-Fi, air-conditioning, and breakfast are included with your stay.

RIAD LES OLIVIERS

47-48 Rue de la Bahia; tel. 0524/386 368; 500Dh d

On the strip alongside the Bahia Palace is the Riad Les Oliviers. The tastefully elaborate entry that greets you upon opening the doors is a pleasant surprise after ducking down the arch-covered passageway outside. This is a classically renovated *riad* that keeps many of the arabesque charms of the Bahia-era construction, with wall tiles throughout. The rooms might be a little small for some, but the location, price, and wonderful nights spent on the terrace more than compensate for it. Wi-Fi, air-conditioning, and breakfast are all included with your stay.

DAR NAJAT

18 Douar Graoua, Derb Lalla Chacha; tel. 0524/375 085; 650Dh d

The owner of the Dar Najat has channeled the desert heritage of Morocco's Sahrawi tribes throughout this quaint *riad.* There's plenty of beige mudbrick, plus masks imported from Mali, though bathrooms are more traditional *zellij* work. Though a bit off

---

1: the interior garden of Dar Soukaina **2:** a local woman walking into the Marrakesh medina **3:** most hotels in the Ville Nouvelle feature swimming pools **4:** Rue de la Liberté in the Ville Nouvelle's distinctly European-feeling Gueliz quarter

1
2
3
4

the beaten path, it is in a quiet part of the medina, which ensures a restful night of sleep. The staff is friendly, the service prompt, and your every need seen to in this wonderfully relaxing little slice of the Sahara. Wi-Fi, air-conditioning, and breakfast are all included with your stay.

RIAD LES TROIS MAGES

11 Derb Jamal Riad Laarousse; tel. 0524/389 297; www.lestroismages.com; 800Dh d

For the price point, this is probably one of the best deals in Marrakesh. The English-speaking staff, including the ever-hospitable Aziz, will help you around the medina if you need to find a restaurant or particular shop. For budget-minded travelers and those who abhor waste, you'll be happy to know that if you have dinner in the *riad*, they'll keep your leftovers and reheat them for you the next day for lunch. The *riad* itself has a few different lounge areas, an open-air interior patio, a heated pool, and even a baby grand piano. Lush fabrics, fluffy towels, and carpets form part of the ambiance. But what really sets this *riad* apart is Saïda, the French-trained cook who can not only whip up some of the finest Moroccan food in the city, but who has a flair for international cuisine made with the freshest ingredients selected that day from the market. Saïda's cooking ranks among the best in the city. Wi-Fi, air-conditioning, and breakfast are included with your stay.

★ RIAD BOUSSA

192 Derb Jdid; tel. 0524/380 823; www.riadboussa.com; 800Dh d

Just off the main thoroughfare of Derb Derbachi, Riad Boussa is a classic *riad*, full of understated elegance. The welcoming staff and delicious homemade breakfast add up to making this an easy choice to settle in for a few nights. The property itself is intimate, with five bedrooms, an outdoor patio, and rooftop terrace that is perfect for sun worshippers, adding to a feeling of exclusivity. All of this is thanks to Brigitte, the tireless owner, a resident of Marrakesh for nearly 15 years. Brigitte has made this a popular choice for solo female travelers and has a way of helping you feel right at home while also guiding you around the confusing medina. You will sleep and eat like royalty while staying here, but what really makes this a can't-miss *riad* in Marrakesh is Brigitte's incredible wealth of information about her adopted hometown, which she happily shares with anyone. There are few foreigners who know the medina and love it as much as she does. Probably the best value is the Tehmara room with its splendid bathtub, while the Limoun suite with its double bed on the mezzanine is perfect for a small family. Wi-Fi, air-conditioning, and breakfast are all included with your stay.

Over 800Dh

★ RIAD LE SECRET DE ZOHRIA

32 Jnane ben Chegra; tel. 0673/656 552; http://riadlesecretdezoraida.com; 900Dh d

The ladies running the Riad le Secret de Zohria deserve some sort of award for one of the most charming *riads* in Marrakesh. Besides the wonderful and kind service, the taste in Moroccan-style decor is unmatched in Marrakesh. Touches such as fresh flowers in the rooms and the heated swimming pool, one of the very few in the medina, add up to a special stay. Accommodations include air-conditioning, Wi-Fi, and breakfast, as well as mint tea on arrival. If you're looking to complete your relaxing stay with a nice long bath, consider upgrading to one of the suites for 400Dh or so more.

RIAD NORA

29A Rue de la Bahia; tel. 0655/289 417; www.riad-nora.com; 900Dh d

Once part of the complex that included the nearby Bahia Palace, the 19th-century Riad Nora has retained much of the floral charm of the palace, with flowers seemingly always in bloom around the traditional courtyard. While the standard bedrooms are perfectly fine, with soft beds and color-themed rooms, it's worth paying the extra 100Dh a night for the suites, with their sprawling bathrooms and Jacuzzi-size tubs. Air-conditioning, Wi-Fi, and breakfast are all included with your stay.

RIAD L'ORANGERAIE

61 Rue Sidi Yamani; tel. 0661/238 789; www.riadorangeraie.com; 1,400Dh d

The two brothers running Riad l'Orangeraie have thought of seemingly everything, including giving guests prepaid cell phones to use during their stay. Rooms all have top-of-the-line beds nestled in the clean lines and elegant decor of Moroccan-European fusion. The staff will happily walk you to any place in the medina, making getting to and from restaurants less stressful. If you were going to splurge on one *riad* in Marrakesh, this would be it. Rooftop terraces give views over the High Atlas mountains, and below there are two courtyards, one with a shaded swimming pool.

VILLE NOUVELLE AND GUELIZ

Under 400Dh

HOTEL TACHFINE

corner of Blvd. Zerktouni and Rue Mohamed El Beqqal; tel. 0524/447 188; 270Dh d

For a no-nonsense stay, the reasonable Hotel Tachfine, though outdated, is a good spot for active travelers who are going to spend most of their time out of their rooms. Beds are comfortable, rooms clean, and showers hot. Most of the rooms feature small terraces. Street-side rooms can be noisy, as the Tachfine looks right over some of the more popular neighborhood restaurants and bars. For nonsmokers, the smoking can be an issue here.

★ HOTEL AMALAY

87 Ave. Mohammed V; tel. 0524/448 685; www.amalay-hotel.com; 350Dh d

With comfy beds and cozy rooms, the Hotel Amalay is one of the better options outside of the medina for its price range. The rooms, though seemingly trapped in the 1970s-era decor, are cleaned every day and include fresh towels and soaps. The staff is friendly; they occasionally have problems with other booking agencies, so it's best to book direct if possible. The restaurant downstairs is forgettable, though a light breakfast is served with your stay. Streets along the avenue are a bit noisier than the ones out back. Air-conditioning can be hit-or-miss, something to think about in the hot summer months. Wi-Fi and breakfast are all included with your stay. This is one of the better deals in Marrakesh.

400-800Dh

BY HOTEL

Rue Ben Aïcha; tel. 0524/339 151; http://by-marrakech.hotels-marrakesh.com; 710Dh d

The By Hotel is a touch of modern amid the 1970s architecture of the Gueliz district. The large glass doors give way to a chic salon with clean lines and a baby grand piano at your disposal. Youssef, the manager, is friendly and can help you with anything from taxis to restaurant recommendations. Rooms feel a bit cramped with no real views, but the beds and linens are all brand-new. The small, shaded pool on the back patio is perfect for cooling off on those hot Marrakesh afternoons. If you are looking for more modern accommodations, this is the best value for the money. Air-conditioning, Wi-Fi, and breakfast are included with your stay.

Over 800Dh

BAB HOTEL

corner of Blvd. El Mansour Eddahbi and Rue Mohamed El Beqqal; tel. 0524/435 250; http://babhotelmarrakech.ma; 1,100Dh d

For a boutique B&B experience, the Bab Hotel might be just the ticket. The swank sky bar, chill poolside, and Los Angeles feel to this hotel make it something a bit different in Gueliz. The sky terrace provides lots of shade, while the rooms are as sleek as the contemporary-design coffee-table books lying about. The all-white rooms with solid black-framed beds and colored throw pillows will provide a comfortable, hip place to crash for a few nights. Air-conditioning, Wi-Fi, TV, and breakfast are included with your stay.

HOTEL LE RENAISSANCE

89 Blvd. Zerktouni, corner of Ave. Mohammed V; tel. 0524/337 777; www.renaissance-hotel-Marrakech.com; 1,500Dh d

The recently remodeled Hotel Le Renaissance, in the middle of the Gueliz shopping district, offers standard, modern rooms. There was little done to keep the protectorate-era architecture and design, though the art deco 1970s suite (room 503) is worth considering splurging for; it has a spacious living room, a separate dressing room, and curvy furnishings that will make you feel groovy. Some balconies have views over Marrakesh to the High Atlas. The on-site spa has a full-service Moroccan hammam, with *gommage* exfoliation, massage, and body scrubbing. Air-conditioning, Wi-Fi, TV, and breakfast are included with your stay.

Information and Services

The city code for Marrakesh and the area is 24.

TOURIST INFORMATION CENTER (DÉLÉGATION RÉGIONALE DU TOURISME DE MARRAKECH)

Pl. Abdelmoumen Ben Ali; tel. 0524/436 131; www.visitmorocco.com; Mon.-Fri. 8:30am-4:30pm

The Tourist Information Center can be found at the plaza where Avenue Mohammed V and Boulevard Mohamed Zerktouni meet. The office has some maps and updated information about city events, particularly about the numerous festivals, concerts, and gallery showings. If you're looking for the latest pulse for events while you're in town, be sure to stop by. Service is friendly and incredibly helpful.

POST OFFICES AND COURIER SERVICES

The **main post office** is at Place du 16 Novembre in Gueliz. In the medina, you can find a convenient post office on the south side of the Jemaa el-Fnaa near the horse-drawn carriages. There are also post offices at the train station and airport. Post offices keep the same hours (Mon.-Fri. 9am-4:30pm, Sat. 9:30am-noon, abbreviated during Ramadan). **FedEx** (Blvd. 113 Ave. Abdelkrim El Khattabi, tel. 0524/448 257, Mon.-Fri. 8am-noon and 2pm-6:30pm, Sat. 8am-12:15pm) has a branch in Gueliz, east of Place Abdelmoumen Ben Ali.

MONEY

Cash machines are ubiquitous around Marrakesh, though they distribute only 100- and 200-dirham notes. Most large hotels will change currency at the bank rates. Most Moroccan banks now charge a 20-25Dh withdrawal fee.

In the **medina,** you'll find several banks with ATMs conveniently located on the south side of the **Jemaa el-Fnaa,** including ***Banque Populaire*** (Mon.-Fri. 8:15am-4:30pm), **Bank Al Maghrib** (Mon.-Fri. 8:15am-3:30pm), and **BMCE** (Mon.-Fri. 8:15am-6:30pm, Sat.-Sun. 9am-6pm, Ramadan 9am-5pm). For travelers checks, foreign currency exchanges, and other services, it's best to use BMCE. Banks are also found in **Gueliz** along Avenue Mohammed V. You'll find **Attijarwafa Bank** (Mon.-Fri. 8:15am-3:45pm, Ramadan 9:15am-2:30pm) and **Wafacash Currency Exchange** with **Western Union** (Mon.-Fri. 8am-7pm and Sat. 9am-4pm), as well as the Banque Populaire and BMCE.

Credit cards are accepted more widely around Marrakesh than in some other cities, though there will often be a surcharge of 5 percent added on to any sale. In principle, it's best to use cash whenever possible.

SAFETY

Marrakesh is a very safe city and is patrolled by police, both uniformed and undercover, in part to protect tourists and also to combat prostitution, drug use, and petty crimes, which do unfortunately remain an issue. Most nightclubs have a number of prostitutes working, both male and female. Single partygoers, as usual, should keep a close eye on their drink. Pickpocketing and petty theft can be a concern. Keep valuables locked up in your lodgings or tucked away someplace safe.

HOSPITALS, CLINICS, AND PHARMACIES

In dire circumstances, head directly for the private clinic **Polyclinique du Sud** (2 Rue Yougoslavie, tel. 0524/447 619) in Gueliz for emergency services.

Pharmacies are spread throughout the city on seemingly every street corner. They can prove to be indispensable in Marrakesh, particularly after a little too much sun, when the need for SPF 140 sunscreen and lip balm arises. Most pharmacies are open daily 8am-6pm, though they sometimes close for lunch.

In the **medina,** the easiest pharmacy to find is the **Pharmacie la Place** on the south side of the Jemaa el-Fnaa next to the Banque Populaire. **Pharmacy Jnane Benchagra** is on Derb el Hammam, and **Pharmacy Ksar Al Hamra** is near Bab Agnaou.

In **Gueliz,** you'll find the **Pharmacie Centrale** on the corner of Avenue Mohammed V and Rue de la Liberté near the Carre Eden. The **Pharmacie Ibn Rochd** (36 Rue Ibn Aïcha) is another good neighborhood pharmacy.

In **Hivernage,** you can find **Pharmacie Natura** on the corner of Avenue El Kadissia and Avenue Echouhada, across from Café Extra Blatt.

Getting There

BY PLANE

Marrakesh-Menara International Airport

about 5 kilometers (3mi) west of the city center; tel. 0544/447 910

The **Marrakech-Menara International Airport** offers direct flights to London, Dublin, Oslo, Copenhagen, Stockholm, Paris, Madrid, and other European hubs with various carriers, including low-budget carriers such as **Air Arabia** (www.airarabia.com), **Easy Jet** (www.easyjet.com), **Transavia** (www.transavia.com), and **Ryan Air** (www.ryanair.com). Travelers arriving direct from North America and other non-European regions will have to transfer planes at the Mohammed V International Airport in Casablanca. **Royal Air Maroc** (www.royalairmaroc.com) offers direct in-country daily flights to Casablanca and Fez as well as in-country flights to **Agadir, Dakhla, Ouarzazate,** and **Tangier.**

You can usually get a SIM card for your phone for free with Orange, INWI, or Maroc Telecom next to baggage claim. You'll be able to charge this while you're on the go around the entire country. There are money exchange offices and ATMs just beyond the customs area. It's a good idea to exchange some local currency before heading out of the airport.

The local **19 Airport Bus** runs daily every 30 minutes 7am-9:30pm (30Dh single, 50Dh round-trip), with service to the Jemaa el-Fnaa. Exit from the main exit of the airport and cross the parking lot. There is usually a bus parked, but if there isn't, just wait next to the entrance to the paid portion of the parking lot. There are no other stops on the route, but if your hotel is along the route, just ask the driver to drop you off. Most drivers know the hotels along the route and can tell you if your hotel is one of them. If you're staying in the medina, this is the best option to and from the airport. Taxis will often try to charge exorbitant fares; 50Dh is a good price to/from the airport (though the metered fare is usually around 25Dh), and you can expect to pay a surcharge of 50 percent after sunset.

From the UK and Europe

Marrakesh is extremely well connected with nearly all major airports in Europe. Most European cities are 3-4 hours away, often connecting via low-cost airlines such as **Easy Jet** (www.easyjet.com), **Ryan Air** (www.ryanair.com), **Transavia** (www.transavia.com), and **Vueling** (www.vueling.com). If you're looking to get out of Marrakesh and travel around the country, consider booking a one-way ticket into Marrakesh and then your return ticket from another city, such as Fez or Tangier. This way, you can maximize your travel time in-country and make a circuit with Marrakesh as your southernmost destination.

From North America

All direct flights into Morocco from North America arrive first in Casablanca via **Royal Air Maroc** (tel. 0522/489 751, www.royalairmaroc.com) and have a short layover before connecting with a brief flight (45min) to Marrakesh. From the Casablanca airport, it's also possible to take the train to Marrakesh. Often, it's quicker to take the train as the layover in Casablanca can be lengthy. It's possible to avoid Casablanca altogether and travel through a European hub, such as Madrid or London, or a Middle East hub. Typically, flights through Europe are less expensive than direct flights from North America to Casablanca, and are highly recommended. Flights from Europe (see above) can land directly in Marrakesh, making this a preferable alternative to landing in Casablanca.

From Australia, New Zealand, and South Africa

It's possible to avoid Casablanca altogether and travel through a European hub, such as **Madrid** or **London,** or a Middle East hub, such as **Dubai,** by choosing a ticket directly to Marrakesh. This is a preferable alternative to landing in Casablanca.

A great travel strategy is to break up your trip to Morocco with weekend layovers in and out of Europe. Consider booking a round-trip ticket from a European hub, such as **Paris,** and then purchase a second round trip from the European hub of your choice with one of the low-cost carriers. Just make sure to leave yourself a day or two on either end of your Morocco trip to explore the European city of your choice and to give yourself plenty of time in case one of your flights is delayed or canceled.

BY CAR

Coming by car, Marrakesh is an easy drive along the autoroutes.

From Casablanca: Follow the A1 autoroute south for 243km/151mi, about 2.5 hours. The toll is 80Dh for a regular four-door sedan.

From Rabat: Follow the A1 autoroute south for 328km/204mi, about 3.5 hours). There are two tolls, one on the Casablanca-Rabat part of the A1 autoroute (23Dh) and another at Marrakesh (80Dh).

Agadir (242km/150mi via the A1 autoroute, 2.5hr, 91Dh toll) and **Essaouira** (177km/110mi via the R207 road, 2.5hr) are popular day trips outside of Marrakesh. **Ouarzazate** (198km/123mi via the N9 national road, 3.5hr), **Meknes** (469km/291mi via the A1 to the A2 autoroutes, 5hr, 88Dh olls), **Fez** (529km/329mi via the A1 to the A2 autoroutes, 6hr, 120Dh tolls), and **Tangier** (572km/355mi via the A1 autoroute, 6.5hr, 169Dh tolls) are longer drives requiring half a day to a full day. The mountain pass to Ouarzazate should be driven with extreme caution, particularly during winter months and during storms. Night driving is always dangerous, though the roads to Ouarzazate and Agadir are particularly accident prone.

BY BUS

The new **CTM bus station** (tel. 0800/0900 30, www.ctm.ma) is just south of the train station on Rue Abou Baker Seddik and Rue Ibn el Cadi in Gueliz. Check the scheduled information online or at the station for specific departure information and for "premium" coach buses that are a bit more comfortable and come with onboard Wi-Fi. Some of the more popular bus runs include: **Agadir** (3hr, 18 daily, 105Dh, premium available), **Essaouira** (2.5hr, 2 daily, 75Dh), **Fez** (5.5hr, 6 daily, 170Dh, premium available), **Casablanca** (4hr, 16 daily, 80Dh, premium available), **Ouarzazate** (4.5hr, 47 daily, 85Dh), **Rabat** (4.5hr, 10 daily, 140Dh, premium available), and **Tangier** (9.5hr, 3 daily, 230Dh).

Supratours (tel. 0890/203 040, www.oncf.ma) is popular, particularly with those traveling by train. Supratours operates in conjunction with ONCF, the train company, and the **bus station** is directly behind the Marrakesh train station (due west just off Avenue Hassan II) in Gueliz, making connections easy. Popular runs include **Agadir** (3hr, 12 daily, 110Dh), **Essaouira** (3hr, 6 daily, 80Dh), and **Ouarzazate** (4.5hr, 3 daily, 90Dh).

BY TRAIN

Marrakesh serves as the southern terminus for the national train run by **ONCF** (tel. 0890/203 040, www.oncf.ma). The **train station** is along Avenue Hassan II in Gueliz, turning west from Avenue Mohammed V at Place du 18 Novembre. From Marrakesh, some of the more popular train lines run to and from **Casablanca** (3.5hr, 9 daily, 2nd/1st-class 90Dh/140Dh), **Rabat** (4.5hr, 9 daily, 120Dh/185Dh), **Meknes** (7hr, 8 daily, 174Dh/265Dh), and **Fez** (8hr, 8 daily, 195Dh/295Dh).

Trains also leave to **Tangier** (9.5hr, 7 daily, 205Dh/310Dh), though most trains change at Casa Voyageurs or Sidi Kacem. Conveniently, the only direct train to Tangier is the **overnight train** that leaves Marrakesh at 8:45pm and arrives in Tangier at 7am without a change. It's best to book the "*voiture-lit single/double*" or "*couchette*" sleeping cars at the train station a day or two before departure. These cannot be purchased online but must be purchased at the train station. Prices per bed start at 350Dh, and beds can sell out quickly during peak summer travel season.

a kilometer marker on the road to Marrakesh

Getting Around

BY WALKING

Pack a good pair of walking shoes. The majority of the sprawling Marrakesh medina is only navigable **by foot,** and that's how you'll experience the myriad souks, twisting alleyways, and upbeat medina life. Avenue Mohammed V, with its wide sidewalk and continuous traffic, is the main thoroughfare between the medina and the animated strip in Gueliz. For quieter walks, consider an outing through the guarded palaces breaking the sidewalks of Hivernage.

BY PETIT TAXI AND CARRIAGE

The sand-colored ***petits taxis*** of Marrakesh are the quickest way around town. Fares typically run 10Dh-40Dh, depending on the length of the drive. Always ask the driver to use the counter, and keep in mind that prices go up by 50 percent at night. Most drivers are friendly and will use the meter, though they have been known to take advantage of tourists late at night, particularly if they think the tourist has had a few drinks. Taxis are easy to spot outside of most medina gates. During the day they will even cut across the Jemaa el-Fnaa looking for fares. In general, it is best to try to flag down a moving taxi, as the taxis waiting for fares are more likely to try to extort you by charging for any baggage you might have, by not using the counter, or by claiming that they don't have change. In general, in Marrakesh, the older and more beat-up the taxi (and driver!) look, the more honest they typically are.

A **horse-drawn carriage,** or ***calèche,*** is a fun way to get around, with a tour typically taking you on an hour-long trip around the medina walls. Prices are typically 150Dh per hour but are always negotiable. Make sure you agree on a price before taking off. There are stands for *calèches* around the medina at the Koutoubia Mosque, just off the Jemaa el-Fnaa, near Bab Doukkala, and inside Bab Agnaou along Rue Arset el Maach. You'll also find stands in Hivernage across from the Hotel Al-Andalous on Avenue du Président Kennedy and along Place de la Liberté.

BY LOCAL BUS

The public bus run by **Alsa** (tel. 0524/335 270, www.alsa.ma, 4Dh) is an option for getting around, particularly between Gueliz and the medina. Nearly all of the local bus lines converge around the Koutoubia Mosque. From here, you can take **bus 1** or **15** to Gueliz or the **19** to the airport (30Dh). If you want to cut quickly across the medina, take **bus 2** to Bab Lahkmiss. The other two convenient buses are the **11** and **7,** which will take you pretty close to the Majorelle Gardens. Interestingly, Marrakesh is the first city in Africa to have 100 percent electric buses. The transition is slow but encouraging.

BY GRAND TAXI

For destinations outside of Marrakesh, such as day trips into the nearby High Atlas mountains, consider taking a ***grand taxi.*** It is always possible to negotiate the price for the entire taxi, which is a good idea for small groups traveling together. Night prices often increase by 50-100 percent. Fares to less popular destinations vary, and you'll likely have to negotiate with the driver and agree to pay for a partial rate for his return.

Most *grands taxis* for the High Atlas leave from the **Route Secondaire N501** outside of the kasbah. Follow Bab Agnaou and Bab er Rob past the Sidi Es Souheïli Cemetery, or take a *petit taxi,* asking the driver for the "Imlil *grand taxi.*" From this station, you can catch *grands taxis* to **Asni** (1hr, 51km/31mi, 30Dh), **Imlil** (1.5hr, 66km/41mi, 40Dh), **Ourika Valley** (Setti Fatma, 1hr, 65km/40mi, 40Dh), and **Oukaïmeden** (1.5hr, 79km/49mi, 60Dh). Taxis for other destinations leave from the *gare routière* outside of Bab Doukkala.

BY CAR

Driving in Marrakesh is hectic all times of the day. Many forms of traffic will be generally unfamiliar to drivers from North America, Europe, and Australia. Notoriously aggressive scooter drivers bob in and out of streets packed with four-door sedans, horse-drawn carriages, donkeys, and kamikaze pedestrians. Streets are not well marked. Even with GPS guidance, the going can be difficult and it's all too easy to get lost in the chaos. That said, somehow everything works out and most travelers chalk up this frantic driving to something that adds to their unforgettable experience.

Most hotels in the Ville Nouvelle offer **free parking** for guests, and around the medina there are **guarded parking lots.** Across from the Koutoubia Mosque along Trek el Koutoubia is one of the more convenient guarded parking lots near the Jemaa el-Fnaa. There is also parking through Bab Doukkala along Rue el Adala near the horse-drawn carriages and through Bab el Khemis off Rue Assouel. Parking is typically 50Dh a day, including overnight. You can pay in advance, but always request a ticket.

Car Rentals

Car hires are best reserved before you depart. Unless you're really in a pinch, stick with international companies like Hertz or Avis. The local outfits are often hit-or-miss with the level of service, and their cars are often a bit worse for wear. **Avis** (www.avis.com), **Budget** (www.budget.com), **EuropCar** (www.europcar.com), **Right Cars** (www.right-cars.com), and **Sixt** (www.sixt.com) all operate directly from the airport. You can find the **Hertz** branch office (154 Ave. Mohammed V, tel. 0663/614 209) in Gueliz, near the Carre Eden.

Basic car insurance will be provided by the supplier, limited to covering theft, third-party damage, and liability, but with a 10,000Dh (around £800/$1,000 USD) deposit that will be blocked on your credit card until you return the car. Check with your credit card company to see if they provide rental car insurance. Many companies do this as part of a normal rental transaction when traveling. If your credit card provider does not, consider taking out a separate insurance policy. You will want to make sure you keep all of your paperwork easily accessible, as you'll likely be stopped by the local police at least once to make sure all of your paperwork is in order. It goes without saying that you should remember your driver's license. You won't need an international driver's license. A valid driver's license from your country of residence will do.

Small groups might consider a van with a driver. This can be an easy way to get around and, if splitting the cost, can be quite affordable. Typical transports cost 500-800Dh a day, and a driver an additional 200-300Dh. **Ourha Transport Touristique** (129 Ave. Imm el Bakouri, Khalid ibnou el walid Gueliz, tel. 0524/446 345 or 0666/164 173, transportouhra@menara.ma) offers new, comfortable vans for rent.

The High Atlas

Above the palm-lined streets of Marrakesh loom the snowcapped High Atlas Mountains—the tallest mountains in North Africa. At 4,167 meters (13,671ft), Jbel Toubkal marks the highest peak of this range.

Adventurous travelers can climb Toubkal year-round and look down on the Marrakesh plain from the top of the world, bike across the mountain passes and into the Sahara, or go white-water rafting through the national park. Those looking for something a little less pulse-pounding should be content with long walks in the fresh mountain air, plenty of alpine trees, and rustic mountain towns.

The High Atlas is a year-round destination. In the hot summer months, travelers can follow Marrakeshis into the popular Ourika

Highlights

Look for ★ to find recommended sights, activities, dining, and lodging.

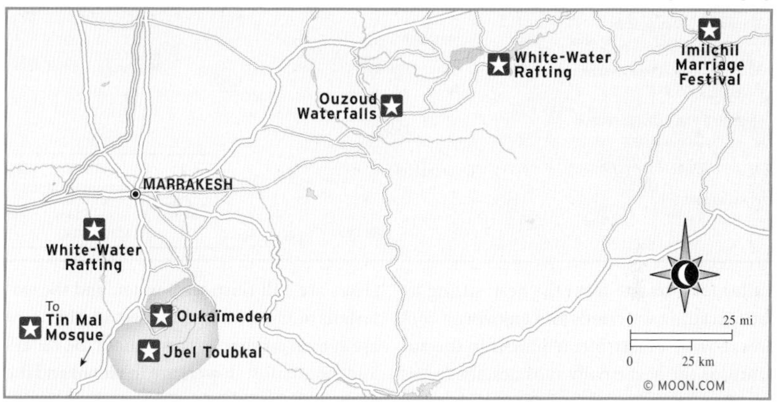

★ **White-Water Rafting:** Splash down the Ahansal or N'Fis River and experience the ride of your life (pages 359 and 385).

★ **Oukaïmeden:** Hit the slopes in Africa's premier ski resort. While you're there, don't forget to check out the 5,000-year-old rock carvings (page 369).

★ **Jbel Toubkal:** Summit the tallest peak in North Africa and hike around Morocco's most visited national park (page 371).

★ **Tin Mal Mosque:** This Almohad-era mosque is one of the very few that non-Muslims are allowed to visit in all of Morocco (page 378).

★ **Ouzoud Waterfalls:** These dazzling waterfalls are Morocco's tallest and are one of the most impressive natural phenomena in the country (page 383).

★ **Imilchil Marriage Festival:** Locals gather every summer at this ancient, festive fair to find their life partner and declare their wedding vows (page 386).

The High Atlas

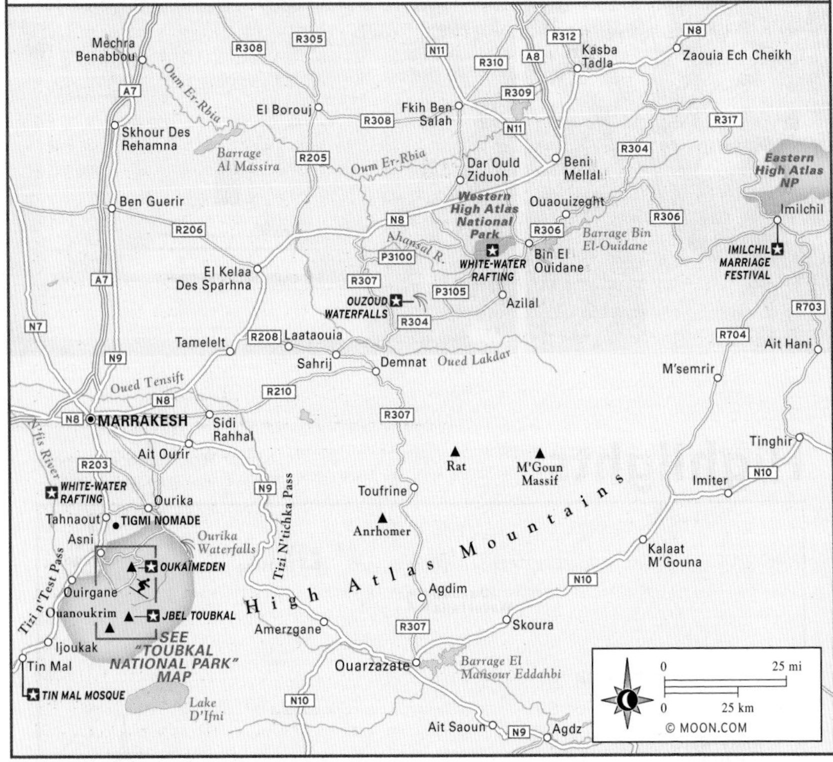

Valley for a respite from the heat, sitting by the cascading waterfalls and enjoying a cool breeze with a tasty picnic lunch. In the autumn, as the heat finally subsides, the leaves are shed from deciduous trees lining the roads in the Ouirgane Valley, making this an excellent time to visit the mosque at Tin Mal and hike the surrounding environs. In the winter, nearby Oukaïmeden is usually flush with snow, providing skiing and snowboarding opportunities for those wishing to cross Africa off their list of continents whose slopes have been carved, shredded, and slalomed. Springtime is the best time to visit, when the winter snows have thawed, the rivers are still flush with water, and the waterfalls at Ouzoud (the highest in Morocco) are at their strongest. Throughout the valleys and mountains, flowers are in bloom and the entire region is alive.

Birders will have their eyes full. Alpine choughs, blue jays, golden eagles, alpine accentors, Atlas shore larks, warblers, and rock sparrows all call the High Atlas home. Keep a sharp eye out and binoculars at the ready around the Ouzoud Waterfalls and Oukaïmeden. In the higher elevations you'll find mostly evergreen alpines with some occasional undergrowth, while the lower elevations have diverse valleys of almond, olive,

Previous: men descend the mountains into the weekly market; two men greeting one another in the High Atlas; Tin Mal Mosque.

cherry, and other fruit trees as well as mountain orchids, poppies, and irises.

Though some of this region is touristed by trekkers from Marrakesh, much of it remains isolated. You'll be less likely to hear French or Arabic spoken and more likely to hear Tashelhit, the local Amazigh dialect, everywhere you go, though people have been quick to adapt to global trends, with English quickly taking hold for businesses and guides.

ORIENTATION

The High Atlas mountain range extends across central Morocco from southwest to northeast, stretching for 740 kilometers (460mi) from the Atlantic Coast all the way to the Algerian border. The mountain chain runs south of Marrakesh, dividing it from Ouarzazate and the rest of southern Morocco, and provides protection to the Marrakesh plain from the harsh climate of the Sahara. The mountains feature the highest peaks north of the Sahara and some of the highest peaks in Africa, with Jbel Avachi at 3,737 meters (12,260ft), Jbel M'Goun at 4,071 meters (13,356ft), and Jbel Toubkal, the highest peak in Morocco and North Africa, at 4,167 meters (13,671ft).

The High Atlas region can be roughly divided into three, loosely connected sections: **Toubkal National Park, Ourika Valley,** and the **M'Goun Massif.**

Toubkal National Park in the west of the range is the primary destination for most travelers. It includes the Ouirgane Valley and the town of Tin Mal on the western border of the park, as well as the town of Imlil, the Jbel Toubkal summit, and the ski resort of Oukaïmeden in the middle of the park. It's a good strategy to choose one or two **gateway towns** to use as a base from which to explore the rest of the park.

The **Ourika Valley,** which runs through the middle of the range, just east of Toubkal, follows a series of villages along the Ourika River. This is the most popular day trip from Marrakesh, with numerous riverside cafés for lunch and a small series of waterfalls and shops.

Farther east from Ourika is the much less touristed **M'Goun Massif,** which includes the stunning **Ouzoud Waterfalls** and offers opportunities to hike through some of the most untouched landscape in Morocco. Experienced backpackers should consider picking up a good topographic map before going it alone in this region.

Several **mountain passes** cut through the High Atlas. The **Tizi n'Tichka pass** is the most well-known of the routes across the High Atlas and the most trafficked. It connects Marrakesh with Ouarzazate via National Road 9 (N9), cutting to the east of Toubkal National Park and crossing through Ait Ourir before ascending to 2,267 meters (7,438ft) to make the crossing. This road can be particularly dangerous when crossing during rains and the winter season. Night driving should be avoided at all costs.

The **Tizi n'Test mountain pass** borders the west of Toubkal National Park along a secondary road (R203) that links Marrakesh with Taroudant via the **Ouirgane and N'Fis Valleys** while also passing by Tin Mal. The pass reaches heights of 2,225 meters (7,300ft). Rockslides can be a real concern here, and during the winter and early spring, driving can be slow going.

PLANNING YOUR TIME

Of all the destinations in Morocco, traversing the High Atlas typically requires the most preparation and planning. There is not one major road connecting the region. Along the mountain range are hiking trails and a few treks that can only be taken by **four-wheel drive** or **mule.** Thus, most travelers will see just part of the High Atlas as a day or a weekend trip from **Marrakesh,** or perhaps while crossing one of the two major passes from Marrakesh to **Ouarzazate** or **Taroudant.** Day trips to **Ourika** and the **Ouzoud** waterfalls can be done easily enough by **bus;** however, a day trip farther into the High Atlas is much easier if you **rent a car** or if you **book a hike with a mountain guide.**

Hiking **Jbel Toubkal** generally takes two days from **Imlil,** including a stay at the base camp. Of course, those wishing to spend longer in this region will experience some of the kindest **hospitality** in Morocco at the numerous humble refuges and *gîtes* dotting the trails. Temperatures plunge well below freezing during the winter months at the higher altitudes, while summers can get hot in the afternoons. Pack accordingly.

For longer treks, either a guide or a good detailed **map** is required. Experienced mountaineers will have no problem with the ascent at Jbel Toubkal, as there is clear visibility and the trek is a light grade, though axes and crampons will likely be needed in winter months. Other possibilities for longer excursions include hiking and cycling through the region, which can be done year-round, though in winter months, delays because of rain and snowstorms are more likely.

GUIDES

Of all the places you might visit in Morocco, the High Atlas is one of the few regions where you really should consider a guide. The guides recommended here are reputable, English speaking, and certified wherever certification is possible, all locals who know the region incredibly well. They have families and friends scattered throughout the mountain range, offering you a chance to glimpse some of the proud Amazigh history that you might otherwise miss, as well as allowing you the chance to safely climb through the mountains and see the sorts of landscapes that will leave you short of breath.

It is possible to do many activities in the High Atlas without a guide, such as hiking around the Ouzoud Waterfalls or through the Ourika Valley. However, guides speak the languages and know the terrain. They can be of assistance, give you cultural insights, and provide direction for trails and roads, as well as provide equipment, all at a reasonable cost. Because of the complexity of the roads and occasional hazards, having a knowledgeable guide in this region is beneficial, even for experienced, die-hard mountaineers, trekkers, climbers, and bikers.

Hiking and Trekking

TOUBKAL PEAKS

tel. 0661/283 086; www.toubkal-peaks.com; from 900Dh

For all-inclusive day treks into the High Atlas,

a village in the High Atlas

contact **Omar Jellah** with Toubkal Peaks. This is the most respected tour company in the region. Prices start at 900Dh per person, including transportation from Marrakesh. Of the numerous companies running day trips and hikes into the High Atlas, this company has the most interesting hikes for every fitness level, and the guides are all certified and incredibly friendly. They can also arrange tours on camel along the beaches and horse-riding adventures along the breathtaking coastline of the Atlantic, which are legendary. All-day excursions include lunch in a traditional setting.

TOUBKAL GUIDE

tel. 0661/417 636; www.toubkalguide.com; from 1,750Dh for 2-4 people

If you want to make your way deep into the mountains, get in touch with **Jamal Imerhane** with Toubkal Guide. He is a certified guide, well-respected by other local guides, and runs a very cozy lodge in Imlil. Most of his better excursions into the mountains are based from here. Two-day treks for Toubkal start at 1,750Dh for a small group of 2-4 people and include transportation from Marrakesh, accommodations, and all meals.

MOUNTAIN TRAVEL MOROCCO

tel. 0668/760 165; www.trekkinginmorocco.com; from 1,250Dh

The team at Mountain Travel Morocco is led by Mohamed and Ibrahim, who are well respected and offer breathtaking hikes around the region. All of their guides are certified, and most speak English. Prices typically start at 1,250Dh per person and include the guide, mules, meals, and accommodations.

★ White-Water Rafting

MOROCCO RAFTING

tel. 0661/775 251; www.rafting.ma; from 1,000Dh

A few rafting and kayak tour companies now operate out of Marrakesh. Hamich with Morocco Rafting is one of the more established guides. Half-day excursions cost 1,000Dh and three-day excursions are 6,400Dh, including pickup and drop-off in Marrakesh as well as meals.

SPLASH MOROCCO RAFTING

tel. 0618/964 252; http://moroccoadventuretours.com; 900Dh

Splash Morocco Rafting has great gear and may be the most family-friendly outfitter for rafting. They have a wonderful route down the **N'Fis River.** Rafting this river is suitable for beginners. This can be done as a day trip from Marrakesh, and can be an exciting way to interact with the locals who live along the river. The tour stops for lunch, to chit-chat, sip on a tea, or barter for goods.

MOSTAPHA OUTILI

tel. 0670/924 413; from 1,000Dh

If you're looking to paddle down the raging waters of the **Ahansal River** for an unforgettable journey through some of the most untouched, breathtaking landscape in Morocco, give Mostapha a call. His trips start at 1,000Dh per person. This particular route is not for the faint of heart, though if you've rafted in Colorado or Washington, you've likely experienced stronger currents.

Mountain Biking

ARGAN XTREME SPORTS

tel. 0622/278 610; www.argansports.com; from 1,000Dh

This friendly Marrakesh-based outfitter can arrange for tours for anything from beginner to advanced riders through the High Atlas. They offer complimentary argan-ic smoothies for day tours. The equipment is all Giant Bicycles with lightweight Giant Realm helmets. All trips include full mechanical backup with support vehicle and driver, as well as fresh seasonal fruit, all-natural snacks, and authentic Moroccan meals. Students receive an extra 10 percent off with a valid student ID, and there are discounts for large groups. Prices start at 1,000Dh per person.

BIKE ADVENTURES IN MOROCCO

tel. 0524/485 786 or 0666/238 200; www.bikeadventuresinmorocco.com; 700-1,400Dh

Lahcen Jellah, one of the most knowledgeable certified mountain guides in the region, is now based out of Marrakesh. He started this company that offers a wide range of High Atlas tours, though they specialize in mountain biking with cross-country, free-ride mountain, and road biking all possibilities. Treks run from one-day outings to two-week excursions, with rates ranging from 700-1,400Dh per person a day, depending on equipment requirements and group size. Bike Adventures carries the latest Cannondale bikes, and new equipment is purchased every year. For multi-day bike trips, all meals are included—and Lahcen happens to be one of the better chefs in the mountains, too!

MARRAKECH BIKE ACTION

tel. 0667/797 035 or 0661/240 145; https://marrakechbikeaction.com; 1,490Dh pp 2-3 people; 1,090Dh pp 4-8 people

Based out of Marrakesh, this outfit has become a go-to company for those looking to explore the High Atlas Mountains on two wheels. They were the first company to have electronically assisted biking (e-biking), which is great if you're not a hard-core biker but still like the idea of venturing through the mountains more romantically than by car. The e-bikes have a motor that kicks in to help you on those long, tough hills. The bikes are totally customizable, and the motor isn't heavy and can be turned on and off, making it a great solution for couples or families with mixed levels of abilities.

Rock-Climbing

Perhaps unsurprisingly, Morocco's tallest mountain range also offers some of the best rock-climbing in the country, though rock-climbing in the High Atlas is for serious climbers only. World-class climbs can be found at Taghia in the M'Goun Massif to the east. Though climbers don't generally need guides, they might want to consider picking up the French-language rock-climbing guidebook for Taghia by **Christian Ravier** (www.christian-ravier.com/taghia.html). This is a good guide for climbing the faces of the Taghia Gorge and can be helpful even for non-Francophones.

Itinerary Idea

DAY TRIP FROM MARRAKESH

With such close proximity to the vibrant city of Marrakesh, it's no wonder that a day trip to the High Atlas is one of the most popular ways to see this region of Morocco. In one day you won't be able to see everything, but you can get a nice taste of what this part of the country has to offer. Be sure to consult the "Packing List for the High Atlas" (page 368) to make sure you are well-equipped. Before you start this itinerary, grab a quick breakfast, pack a picnic lunch, and head to the *grand taxi* station to get a taxi to Asni.

1 If you're traveling on a Saturday, check out the local **Asni market.** If you want to add some fresh fruits or veggies to your picnic, this is where you stock up.

2 Hop into the next *grand taxi* to **Imlil** and enjoy the short ride that twists up into the High Atlas and Toubkal National Park.

3 To make sure you are full of energy for your hike, stop in for a steamy bowl of *bissara* at **Café Restaurant Le Grand Atlas.**

Itinerary Idea

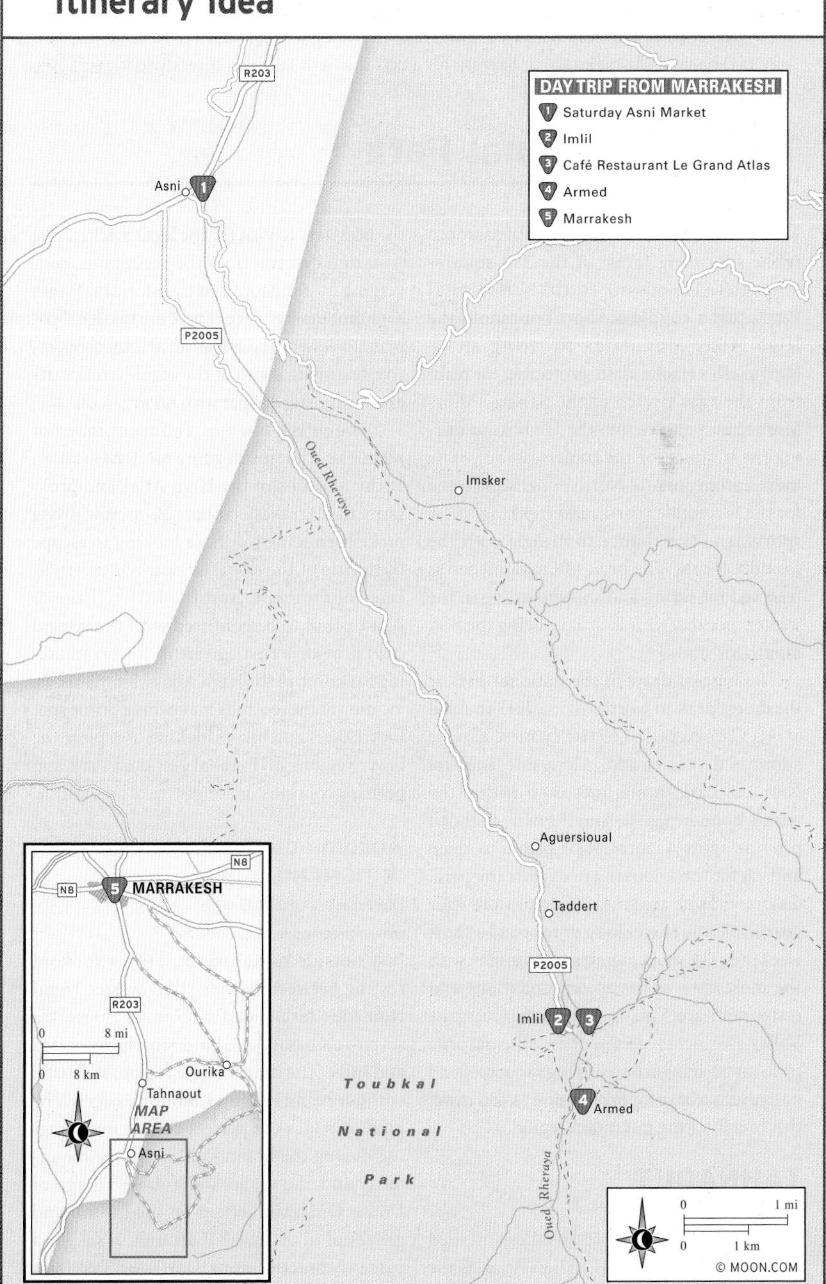

4 Start the ascent of your day hike to the village of **Armed.** Above the village of Armed, take in the view over the village, valley, and High Atlas Mountains.

5 Descend back to Imlil before dark and take the first *grand taxi* back to Asni to link with a taxi back to **Marrakesh,** or bargain for a taxi that will take you directly to Marrakesh.

Toubkal National Park

The most touristed national park in Morocco is the sprawling forest of the 380-square-kilometer (146-sq-mi) **Toubkal National Park,** just a couple of short hours into the High Atlas Mountains towering above Marrakesh's Haouz Plain, protecting the plain from the vast stretch of the Sahara. Many Moroccans venture into the High Atlas during the summer for the cool, clean air, while most Europeans and North Americans come for the incredible year-round trekking, snow sports, and the chance to mingle with the friendly locals. The peak of Oukaïmeden is reserved for skiing and snowboarding in the winter months, with February being the best month for snow.

The biggest draw in the national park is the tallest peak in North Africa, Jbel Toubkal at 4,167 meters (13,671ft), which can be summited year-round. Alongside Toubkal National Park, sometimes even within the park's boundaries, lie small towns that can provide spots of interest or places to sleep and eat for those looking to explore the park. Gateway towns are good places to store your gear while you're trekking or to spend a short weekend. The most popular spots to stay with the most choices for accommodations and restaurants are Asni, Imlil, and the Ouirgane Valley. I've included a few of my other favorite little towns in which to unplug for a weekend or to use as a base for exploration as you travel this breathtaking mountain region.

TAHNAOUT

تحناوت

Just 30 minutes south of Marrakesh, nestled against the foothills of the High Atlas, is the sleepy little town of Tahnaout. Tuesdays are the best days to visit for the local market. The Amazigh descend from the mountains, converging on Tahnaout and transforming it into a vibrant marketplace. There are two local co-operatives here of interest: an artisan cooperative featuring some of the local handicrafts and a women's cooperative for argan oil.

Though the town of Tahnaout may not seem like it has much going for it, its location at the foothills of the High Atlas and proximity to Marrakesh (a short 30-minute drive) make it enticing for those looking to escape the bustle of the city. The nearby Berber villages of Ouirzane and the little village of Agadir (not to be confused with the coastal city) provide a rustic heart to the breathtaking backdrop of the High Atlas Mountains. Its location at the foothills make this a prime spot for trekkers and hikers looking to explore the lower regions of Toubkal National Park and perhaps continue on longer treks up to Imlil.

Accommodations

★ TIGMI NOMADE

Ouirzane; tel. 0662/105 600; www.tigminomade.com; 600Dh d

Just outside of Tahnaout, atop a lookout resting between Berber villages, sits Tigmi Nomade (Tashelheit for "Nomad House"), a seven-room boutique hotel simply decorated and full of the charm of the region. It's rustic without being rough around the edges. The pool provides the perfect respite for lounging during the hot months, with the mountains and the stone-and-rubble village of Douar Ouirzane settled on the far hill and groves of olive trees all around. It's a good place to practice your Darija or Tashlheit with the friendly, local service. Guided treks

Toubkal National Park

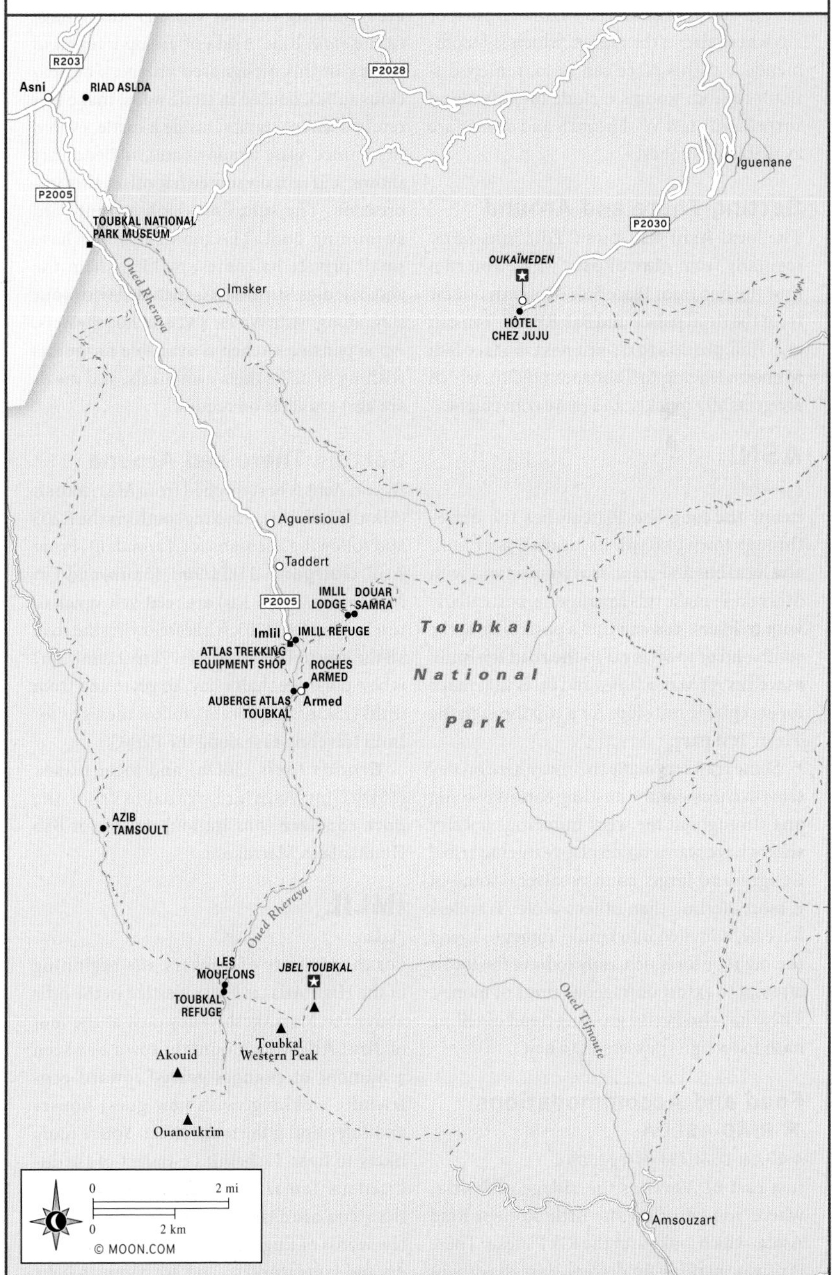

and excursions by donkey or horse are available, starting from 100Dh, as well as transport to and from Marrakesh, the airport, or anywhere else in the region, which is recommended, as this place can be extremely difficult to find. Rooms include breakfast and surprisingly fast Wi-Fi; lunch and dinner are available on request.

Getting There and Around

The local **Asni #35 bus** (7Dh) runs fairly regularly from **Marrakesh,** where you ca n find the bus from Place Sidi Mimoun not far from the royal palace and Bab Rhoub. You can also find ***grands taxis*** just next to Place Sidi Mimoun leaving to Tahnaout (20Dh), which are generally quicker and more convenient.

ASNI

أسني

Below the long Kik Plateau lies the drive-through town of **Asni.** Its location near Imlil and local bus and *grand taxi* connections with Marrakesh make this a main stop, particularly with trekkers. You can find a post office at the south end of town, next to the road for Imlil, as well as ATM machines and cafés that make for acceptable rest stops for a trip through the Tizi n'Test pass.

Some travelers make their way here on day trips to check out the bustling Saturday souk, and throughout the week numerous jewelry sellers have wares on display featuring tribal designs and large, chunky silver—some of it more sterling than others. Note: Travelers have been invited into family homes to spend the night or for lunch, only to have the locals attempt to extort outrageous sums of money. There has also been a growing trend of selling hash to foreign travelers. Be wary.

Food and Accommodations

★ RIAD ASLDA

Aslda; tel. 0524/484 044; 300Dh d

Just east of Asni lies the village of **Aslda,** where you can find the little-known Riad Aslda, which looks over the Kik Plateau. There is private parking for drivers, though without a guide the *riad* will likely prove difficult to find. Once in Aslda, look for the yellow placards marking the way through the village to the *riad.* Riad Aslda offers up a touch of luxury in this oft-ignored village. The spacious suites, housed in stone walls, make this reminiscent of staying inside a castle, even if the stained-glass windows and rubber ducky shower curtain do somewhat offset this impression. The suites overlook a front-yard swimming pool. The rooms upstairs have small private balconies, making them the choicest digs. Breakfast is included with your stay, along with Wi-Fi, TV, and hot showers. An expansive kitchen is available for guests wishing to make their own meals, and meals are also available on request.

Getting There and Around

By car, Asni is best reached from **Marrakesh** (51km/32mi, 1hr), traveling south via the R203 and following the signs for Taroudant. From Asni, **Ouirgane** (15km/9mi, 15min) and **Tin Mal** (55km/34mi, 1hr) are relatively quick to reach along the R203, while following the road all the way to **Taroudant** (177km/110mi, 3hr) is best done over half a day. To get to and from **Imlil** (15km/9mi, 25min), follow the signs for Imlil traveling east along the P2005.

Grands taxis (30Dh) and local **buses** (15Dh) for Asni are available from the ***gare routière*** (bus station) outside of Bab Doukkala in Marrakesh.

IMLIL

إمليل

For the majority of trekkers, the beginning of the High Atlas is Imlil. Nestled in the hills above the Marrakesh valley, just at the foot of **Jbel Adj,** this mountain town has seen a number of changes geared toward eco-friendly trekking, with new guest houses and cafés lining the main street. You're more likely to hear Tashelhit (a dialect of the indigenous Tamazight language) spoken here than you are Darija. Many people know a few words of English, particularly shop owners and hotel workers, and are happy to help.

The accommodations, restaurants, and shops make this a good place to settle in for a few days. As in the rest of the High Atlas, the feel is noticeably more conservative, though perfectly friendly. Imlil begins a series of mountain villages whose primary source of income revolves around the tourist industry and, as such, they are welcoming hosts.

The large kasbah you pass on your way into town is **Kasbah Tamadot,** owned by Richard Branson, the billionaire founder of Virgin Records, who is famed among the locals for having this kasbah restored. The philanthropist and his mother established a foundation aiming to improve the living conditions of the women of the region. Their work can be seen throughout the valley, though there is talk locally suggesting that not all the proceeds of the cooperative next to the kasbah find their way to the women. Sadly, it is perhaps another sign of the corruption endemic in some spheres of Morocco.

Sights

TOUBKAL NATIONAL PARK MUSEUM (MUSÉE DU PARC NATIONAL DE TOUBKAL)

tel. 0629/275 463; Mon.-Fri. 8am-noon and 3pm-6pm; 50Dh

Toubkal National Park Museum, across from the Richard Branson hotel, features displays and information on all of the naturally occurring plants and animals of Toubkal National Park, which should interest most hikers, trekkers, and naturalists visiting the region. The caretaker, who talks with you as you circle the museum, provides information in English, French, or Arabic. This service is included with admission. Signage is minimal and in Arabic and French. The hours vary quite a bit depending on the season, the weather, and, apparently, the caretaker's whims.

Equipment Rentals

There are several places to rent equipment for summiting Jbel Toubkal, such as crampons, ice axes, sleeping bags, stoves, and rain jackets, as well as walking poles for trekkers.

AMAOZOZ SHOP

Imlil Center; daily 9am-noon and 2pm-6pm

The Amaozoz Shop has rentals for climbing and mountaineering, including crampons and ice axes, for 20-50Dh a day.

ATLAS TREKKING EQUIPMENT SHOP

Imlil Center; tel. 0668/760 165 or 0661/953 407; www.atlastrekshop.com

The Atlas Trekking Equipment Shop has all the gear you could want for 20-50Dh a day, and the staff speaks English, making requests a bit easier over the phone if you're trying to reserve gear from Marrakesh.

Shopping

COOPERATIVE FEMININE AFRA D'HUILE D'ARGAN

daily 9am-noon and 3pm-6pm

In the tiny stretch of the road that serves as the downtown of Imlil you can find the Cooperative Feminine Afra d'Huile d'Argan. This is a friendly co-op with plenty of cosmetic and alimentation oil, though as at most other cooperatives it's impossible to tell if you're getting the "pure" argan oil. Typically, cosmetic oil is diluted while the oil for cooking is more pure. The oil here seems to be of better quality than at many of the other cooperatives in the region.

Food

Cafés in Imlil serve *bissara,* lentils, tajines, and sandwiches. A typical bowl of *bissara* or lentils served with bread will run around 10Dh, while tajines typically run 30-40Dh.

CAFÉ DJEBEL OUABKRIM

on the corner, by the big rock, across from the parking lot; daily 10am-8pm; 35Dh

The Café Djebel Ouabkrim serves some deliciously hearty mountain tajines for 35Dh. This is about as humble of a restaurant as you'll find. Best for small groups looking to fill up before hiking. Tajines are made on command, with plenty of root vegetables and hunks of meat. You'll likely be waiting 30

1

2

3

minutes or longer for your tajine to cook, so plan on writing those postcards back home while you're taking in the mountain air.

CAFÉ RESTAURANT LE GRAND ATLAS

Imlil main road, before the parking lot; daily 8am-10pm; 40Dh

The Café Restaurant Le Grand Atlas is easily missed along the main road, across from Les Mouflons Refuge and Restaurant (not to be confused with the base camp of Jbel Toubkal of the same name) before the parking lot. Breakfast is the best time to come to this little hole in the wall. Pull up a seat on the small shaded terrace and enjoy a steaming bowl of *bissara* or lentils (10Dh) while watching the kids, trekkers, and donkeys make their way up the road and into the mountains.

Accommodations

★ IMLIL REFUGE

next to the parking lot; tel. 0661/873 771; 70Dh d

Opened in March 2015, the Imlil Refuge is one of the newer guesthouses. The lodgings are no-frills, though amenities include Wi-Fi, hot water, and a chimney to warm the cozy living room. Kitchens are open for use by guests; you just have to clean up after yourself and pay for whatever gas was used. Breakfast and dinner can be made for you, at an additional cost. This is the best budget accommodation in Imlil, made better by the gracious hosts (a couple of mountaineers) and whoever else happens to be passing through on their way up or down the mountain.

GITE CHEZ MOHAMED AÏT IDAR

Imlil Center, after the rock; tel. 0668/045 140; 350Dh d

When the original owner of Gite Chez Mohamed Aït Idar died, his two wives and daughters took over running it. Today, this is the only *gîte* in the national park run solely by women, and it's a great budget option, particularly for single women or groups of young women traveling on a budget. There are two sets of rooms. The less expensive rooms of the *gîte* are all on the ground floor and, in the winter, can be quite cold. The second floor has refurbished standard rooms with heating and en suite bathrooms, though it's not quite a budget option at 350Dh a night. Meals can be had on request.

★ IMLIL LODGE

Tamatert; tel. 0661/417 636 or 0671/157 636; www.imlil-lodge.com; 350Dh d

The cozy Imlil Lodge is full of rocky rustic mountain charm, with Tazenakht rugs, exposed wood, and stone throughout the lodge. All rooms feature air-conditioning, Wi-Fi, and en suite bathrooms. A room with three bunk beds is perfect for small groups and families. A sprawling terrace offers views over the valley and the twin peaks of Jbel Adj and Jbel Toubkal. The owner, Jamal Imerhane, is a certified guide, well respected in the region, and can lead treks or suggest routes. There's also convenient storage hikers can use to leave unneeded stuff behind, like maybe that carpet you just bought. Meals are available on request, while breakfast is included with your stay.

DOUAR SAMRA

Tamatert; tel. 0524/484 034 or 0636/048 559; www.douar-samra.net; 500Dh d

A self-described treehouse, the funky Douar Samra has a distinct touch, with hand-woven beige linens, bamboo shelves, and lots of exposed rock in this whimsical little guesthouse. The hot-water bottles tucked into the beds on cold nights are a nice touch, and the restaurant is one of the absolute best in Imlil, with a varied seasonal menu that includes traditional favorites, such as chicken and lemon tajine, done exquisitely well. Call ahead for reservations. This particular guesthouse is a little difficult to reach, tucked up the hill from the main road and accessible only by foot or mule, but a guide will meet you on the main road to lead you up to the guesthouse.

1: a spring rain in Imlil **2:** trekkers in Imlil striking out on a March morning **3:** local mountain homes

Packing List for the High Atlas

Nights in the High Atlas, particularly from October to March, can be surprisingly cold, with the weather often differing drastically from nearby Marrakesh. Remember to pack the following pieces to make your adventure through the High Atlas memorable for all the right reasons. If you forget to pack something, most items are available in Imlil for rent or purchase.

- Waterproof walking boots or sturdy walking shoes
- Long-sleeved shirts
- Walking/waterproof pants
- Thin fleece (summer) or thick fleece (winter)
- Lightweight waterproof jacket (summer) or warm waterproof jacket (winter)
- Warm hat and gloves (winter)
- Sunhat (styled to cover face, ears, and neck)
- Lightweight daypack
- Sleeping bag
- Sunglasses
- Insect repellent
- Sunscreen
- Flashlight and batteries
- Bathroom kit (with toilet paper, wet wipes, antibacterial hand wash)

Getting There and Around

Imlil is a quick but twisting drive east from **Asni** (15km/9mi, 25min) along the P2005. To get to Imlil, follow the turnoff from Asni and climb east through the **Ait Mizane Valley.**

Most directions around Imlil revolve around the well-signed **parking lot** and large rock at a bend in the road in the middle of town. Directly next to Imlil, just a couple of kilometers east up the road and after the downtown, is the area known as **Tamatert,** where there are a few other lodging options. About 15 kilometers (9mi) east of Imlil is the small mountain village of **Tacheddirt** (pronounced "tash-deert"). This is the end of the road. It's not possible to cross by car to Oukaïmeden no matter what the maps tell you. Tacheddirt is another place to consider for staying a few days and making day hikes, though nearby **Armed** is more easily accessible and provides better lodgings.

Grands taxis (15Dh) are always running to Imlil from Asni.

ARMED

أرمد

A few kilometers uphill from Imlil is the sleepy mountain village of **Armed** (pronounced "ar-MED" and often written "Aroumd" on maps). Tucked into the folds of the High Atlas in the Ait Mizane Valley, with Jbel Adj and Jbel Agelzim towering overhead, Armed is the last in a series of typical Amazigh villages in the area. It's not nearly as touristed as nearby Imlil, making for a more authentic cultural experience for those looking for a base to start their High Atlas adventure. This is an excellent, preferable alternative in some ways to Imlil for trekkers and mountaineers who wish to keep away from the crowds. That said, you'll want to gear up elsewhere. There are a few small stores selling bottled water and chips, but that's about it. All accommodations offer meals throughout the day on request, with the service typically friendly as well as above and beyond.

Food and Accommodations

AUBERGE ATLAS TOUBKAL

tel. 0524/485 750; 150Dh d

Before crossing the river into Armed, you'll see the rustic Auberge Atlas Toubkal across from the small dirt parking lot. The rooms here are adequate, but of good value and with en suite bathrooms. For travelers without a guide, this is quiet and easier to find than the other options up the winding pathways of Armed. Accommodations are half board, with breakfast and dinner included. It also has Wi-Fi and, thankfully, hot showers.

ROCHES ARMED

tel. 0667/644 915; 120Dh s, 200Dh d

The Roches Armed offers views of the dominating peaks of Jbel Adj and Jbel Agelzim. The rooms are understated and comfortable, with plenty of heavy blankets to keep you warm. Breakfast and Wi-Fi are included with your stay. Options for half board (200Dh per person) and full board (300Dh per person) are also available. Meals are generally plucked straight from the on-site garden, making it an eco-friendly option, with vegetarian meals available on request. The friendly manager Samir can help you out with anything you need. Though he's not certified (yet!), he knows the mountains well and can guide you, or, if you want, find an available certified guide. Prices for guided tours range from 240Dh per person and include guides, mules, and meals.

Getting There and Around

Armed is 5 kilometers (3mi) uphill from **Imlil** (20min) and is reachable by a normal car, though **four-wheel drive** would be preferable, as it is a climb along a narrow, unpaved road that hugs the mountainside. This drive should not be attempted during the winter months. There is free **car parking** on the edge of town, down a short slope near the river on the east side, on your left, as you arrive in Armed from Imlil. Park your car and walk across the river and up through the steep, pedestrian-only passages of the hillside village.

There is no public transportation for Armed, though often you can ask in Imlil and transportation can be arranged for a modest fee (20Dh or so). Or, if you are staying in Armed, you can ask your accommodation to arrange for transportation.

★ OUKAÏMEDEN

أوكايمدن

If you've ever wanted to hit the slopes in Africa, the ski resort of Oukaïmeden provides a golden opportunity, though with a short, and often unpredictable, season. The best time for mountain sports begins in mid-late January, and by the middle of March, the snows are typically melting into slush. There are five ski lifts with a few different routes, the longest being a 1,000-meter (3,200-ft) descent. This isn't world-class skiing, but it is a pleasant outing, and the bragging rights of slaloming African slopes shouldn't be missed by avid skiers and snowboarders.

The town itself is subdued, with a few cafés and snack huts, typically busy throughout the ski season, though notably quieter in other months. A few ski lodges offer rental equipment, and plans are in the works to develop this into a more high-profile destination with five-star resorts and snow machines to extend the season, though as of now it is a quiet village with humble accommodations.

Rock Carvings

One of the more interesting diversions is with **Hassan Hachouch** (tel. 0678/551 527), who can explain some of the **rock carvings** in the area. Hassan speaks French and Arabic, but his English is very limited. Still, it makes for a pretty incredible hour or two alongside the

1
2
3
4

road examining the different carvings. There are other carvings around the mountain, and with full-day treks (300Dh) it is possible to explore the various carvings of the region.

A French professor living in Marrakesh, Jean Malhomme, began to document the carvings in 1949. The carvings date all the way back to 3000 BC and display many different animals, settings, and weapons common to the Iron Age and Bronze Age. This is an incredibly important petroglyph series that shows evidence of contact with similar European petroglyphs from the Iberian Peninsula and, in particular, the series found at Mount Bego in southern France.

Ski Passes and Rentals

Ski passes cost around 80Dh for the day. Several places rent equipment, but have a look around before agreeing to rent. The quality of the equipment and the prices fluctuate highly, though you should be able to get outfitted for the day for 100-200Dh. Ski instructors are available for half days and full days (typically 200-300Dh). It's best to ask at Hotel Chez Juju for available instructors.

Food and Accommodations

CLUB ALPIN FRANÇAIS

Oukaïmeden; tel. 0524/319 036; 120Dh summer, 170Dh winter

The Club Alpin Français is one of the more established retreats, open year-round, catering not only to skiers and snowboarders but also to trekkers, mountaineers, and mountain bikers. The dormitory-style rooms have shared bathrooms. During the ski season it's best to avoid the weekends, as the club can be overrun with children from the local schools learning how to ski. Lodging does not include breakfast (30Dh) or other meals (100Dh). However, beer, wine, and alcohol are served, and there is air-conditioning, heating, Wi-Fi, and hot showers.

1: snow-covered Oukaïmeden **2:** mountain guide Omar Jellah explains his culture **3:** rock carvings near Oukaïmeden **4:** the man-made lake in Ouirgane

HOTEL CHEZ JUJU

Oukaïmeden; tel. 0524/319 005; 900Dh d

The Hotel Chez Juju offers slightly more upscale, private lodgings—some rooms have been renovated, while others are in dire need of a remodel. Amenities include air-conditioning, heating, TV, and Wi-Fi, and all rooms have en suite bathrooms. This hotel is expensive for what it is, but it is the most comfortable lodging in Oukaïmeden. Some of the suites feature wood paneling, and for this price range, the upgrade may be worth it. The **French bistro-style restaurant** is the best in town; the menu features *tartiflette* (potato and cheese gratin) with turkey bacon, rotisserie chicken with lemon, and duck confit (150Dh).

Getting There and Around

Oukaïmeden is easy enough to reach by car. From **Marrakesh** (79km/49mi, 1.5hr), follow the road (P2017) from the south of the city, near the Marrakesh Airport, that leads to Ourika. A well-signed turnoff from the road winds up to Oukaïmeden.

Grands taxis leave near **Bab er Rob** in Marrakesh (1.5hr, 79km/49mi, 60Dh), though you'll likely have to purchase the entire taxi and negotiate. A fair price is around 350Dh.

★ JBEL TOUBKAL

Summiting Jbel Toubkal is one of the true peak moments of an adventure through the High Atlas. (Pun fully intended. Sorry.) At 4,167 meters (13,671ft), this is the tallest summit in Morocco and North Africa. On a clear day, you can see down the Haouz Plain to distant Marrakesh and perhaps make out the thin blue line of the Atlantic. On cloudy days, the summit generally provides outstanding views over the clouds. Summiting the mountain can be done year-round, though in winter months, mountain climbing gear, such as crampons and ice axes, will be necessary, while in the summer all you'll need is a good pair of shoes. It is possible to summit Toubkal from Imlil in a single day (35km/22mi, about 14hr round-trip), though at some risk of

Getting to the Top of Toubkal

A climber pauses on the ascent to Jbel Toubkal.

Because of the real danger of altitude sickness in summiting Jbel Toubkal, experienced guides and trekkers in the region recommend approaching the mountain more slowly and following a trek that ascends from Imlil (at 1,740m/5,708ft) through a few of the more picturesque mountain valleys and villages before reaching the summit on the third day. Here is an example of a trek:

- **Day 1:** Leave Imlil after breakfast, around 9:30am, and trek up through Tizi n'Mazik pass to the village of Tamsoult (2,250m/7,381ft), where dinner and a comfortable bed await your arrival.
- **Day 2:** From Tamsoult, hike to the stunning Irhoulidene Waterfalls, have lunch, and then take mules to Aguelzim before continuing a trek to the mountain base camp (3,207m/10,522ft) to spend the night at elevation.
- **Day 3:** After breakfast, ascend Toubkal. Picnic atop the summit or descend and have lunch at the base camp before continuing back to Imlil or Armed.

Though most people are able to summit the mountain, altitude sickness is a real concern. Symptoms of altitude sickness include dizziness, shortness of breath, fatigue, and insomnia. The cure is easy enough and requires slowly descending below 2,450 meters (8,000ft). If it's untreated, high altitude pulmonary edema (HAPE) or high altitude cerebral edema (HACE) may occur. This is a buildup of fluid in the lungs (HAPE) or brain (HACE) and can lead to death if untreated. If you or a member of your group begins showing signs of altitude sickness, descend immediately.

altitude sickness. From Imlil, it's best to take a three-day climb to see more of the region and allow your body to acclimate. Skiers and snowboarders willing to pack their equipment to the top will have a nice ride back to the base camp. Guides are not necessary, though they're highly recommended for inexperienced mountain climbers. (See the beginning of this chapter for information on guides, and look for equipment rentals in Imlil.)

Jbel Toubkal Base Camp

TOUBKAL REFUGE

tel. 0661/695 463; www.refugedutoubkal.com; 120Dh

The Toubkal Refuge run by Club Alpine

Français is better known locally as **Nelter,** named after Louis Nelter, the French mountaineer who established this refuge as well as the nearby Lepiney ski camp. The club is dormitories only, though the food is notably a notch better than the competition. Breakfast (30Dh), lunch (50Dh), and dinner (70Dh) are all available and include tajines as well as warm vegetarian-friendly soups.

LES MOUFLONS

tel. 0524/449 767; www.refugetoubkal.com/uk; 820Dh

Les Mouflons is the more comfortable of the two options, with double rooms and en suite bathrooms. Dormitories are also available (280Dh). The refuge is named after the type of deer found on the surrounding mountain slopes. The price of lodging is for two people and includes breakfast and dinner, with lunch also available on request (110Dh).

Accommodations in Tamsoult

AZIB TAMSOULT

tel. 0661/695 463; www.refugetamsoult.com; 100Dh dorms, 600Dh private rooms

In Tamsoult, before the Irhoulidene Waterfalls, you can find Azib Tamsoult, a refuge that takes its name from the local term for "goat hold," as Tamsoult is the place where shepherds spend the summer with grazing goats and sheep. Accommodations here are some of the friendliest around. The dormitories are good for groups, while couples might want to opt for the cozy double beds in the private rooms that have en suite bathrooms. Breakfast (30Dh), lunch (60Dh), and dinner (70Dh) are available on request.

Getting There and Around

The only way to get to the Jbel Toubkal base camp, Tamsoult, and the summit is by going to **Imlil** and trekking up the mountain from there, so dress accordingly and plan for cold weather at the top.

Ouirgane Valley

The **Ouirgane Valley** is known for being green year-round with acres of olive groves and almond trees. This is the first valley you cross on the road leading through the N'Fis Valley, Tin Mal, and more distant Taroudant. Because of its excellent location just an hour away from Marrakesh, this is a wonderful day trip outside of Marrakesh and is less touristed than the Ourika Valley to the east. Adventurous travelers should consider spending 2-3 days in the valley. There are plenty of good treks for hiking and mountain biking in the region and into the slopes of the nearby Toubkal National Park.

Ouirgane Valley is a strategic base for exploration of the region. Day trips can include ventures to Imlil, horseback riding to Tin Mal, or even a day trek to the picturesque Kasbah Tamadot (better known locally as the Richard Branson Hotel) in the Ait Mizane Valley. It's also possible to tour many of the local villages and have cultural encounters with some of the friendliest people in Morocco.

OUIRGANE

ويركان

In the middle of the valley you'll find a small town by the same name, **Ouirgane,** with a few cafés and some humble lodgings. Around the town are some of the choicest lodgings outside of Marrakesh; Moroccans and foreigners, mostly French, have established guesthouses on sprawling acreage. Most feature gardens and swimming pools. One of the features of Ouirgane is a small lake that has formed to the northwest edge of the town. This is a manmade lake created by the dam built by the state to regulate the much-needed water for Marrakesh.

Sights

OUIRGANE MUSEUM

Ouirgane center; daily 9am-sunset; 10Dh

The ramshackle Ouirgane Museum is alongside the road in Ouirgane. If you've never seen an old olive press, now is your chance. There is one giant press on display here, dating from the 19th century. It was traditionally powered by a donkey, which would circle around the press to operate the wheel that extracted the oil from the locally grown olives. Pots, tools, and other accessories used for the job hang in this little museum, though there is no posted information and the caretaker's English, French, and Spanish are limited. The olive press once served many of the olive trees that were flooded when the local dam was built. This is a somewhat interesting diversion for a few minutes, but no more.

FOOD AND ACCOMMODATIONS

All listings in the High Atlas include a demi-pension (breakfast and dinner) unless otherwise noted. Restaurants are all of the rustic cafe variety with hearty meals for a fraction of the price in other parts of Morocco, with a standard tajine generally running 25-40Dh. For the best meals, it's best to reserve at one of the accommodations listed below the day before for lunches and/or dinners.

★ GITE BRAHIM BOUTFOUNASTE

tel. 0676/622 790 or 0524/485 937; 150Dh per person

In the middle of the town of Ouirgane lies Gite Brahim Boutfounaste. The most notable feature of this *gîte* is the traditional public hammam (20Dh), which offers you a chance to scrub down after a few days of hiking through the park and valley. You'll find terrace views over the valley and unsophisticated, though friendly, service. The showers have hot water, and Wi-Fi is available throughout the grounds. The owner, Hamid, will make sure you're well taken care of. Lodging includes breakfast and dinner. The small fireplace in the salon does a surprisingly good job of warming the place up on cold winter nights.

LE MOUFLON

Souk l'Hamis; tel. 0524/484 371; 400Dh d

A short turn off the main road will bring you to the door of this rustic café, restaurant, and hotel. Perhaps the best budget option in the region, the restaurant is a local staple, a family tradition that has been serving up hearty tajines since the 1950s. Chef Rachida has followed in her father's footsteps in the restaurant, with meals served outside in the stunning backyard garden when the weather allows (45Dh). The couscous is recommended, though you'll need to call ahead and reserve. They only make it in Moroccan family-style, meant to serve four people (50Dh per person, 200Dh for the plate). Rooms here are simple, but warm enough for the cold nights so you can snuggle down before hitting the trails. Couples not taking advantage of the included breakfast and dinner can deduct 150Dh per night for the cost of meals. All in all, a great bargain for couples and good friends.

KSAR SHAMA

58km from Asni on the Taroudant road, Marigha; tel. 0524/485 032; www.ksarshama.com; 800Dh d

The Ksar Shama is another option for those seeking refuge in the mountains in a cultivated garden. The property is quieter than some of the other options, with fewer tour groups and day-trippers from Marrakesh. The rooms are notably larger, as are the beds, making it a good option for those in need of more space. Some of the rooms feature separate salons that have two banquettes, perfect for kids, while other rooms are darker, with fewer windows and a combined salon/living room. Breakfast, Wi-Fi, and air-conditioning are included with your stay. The service can be a little slow, though perfectly friendly. The on-site restaurant and spa are serviceable and can be visited by non-guests, though reservations are needed.

L'OLIVERAIE DE MARIGHA

59km from Asni on the Taroudant road, Douar Imarigha; tel. 0524/484 281; www.oliveraie-de-marigha.com; 900Dh d

The expansive L'Oliveraie de Marigha features plenty of room to spread out, even with the tour groups that stay in the numerous bungalows occasionally. The cabana bar and poolside seats sprinkled throughout the olive grove all add up to the feeling of really being away from it all. The restaurant has a varied seasonal menu with a mix of French classics and Moroccan favorites (220Dh, reservations required). A lunch next to the pool is particularly welcome. Breakfast is included with your stay, and discounts are sometimes available, particularly outside of the busier seasons.

★ DOMAINE MALIKA

59km from Asni on the Taroudant road, Marigha; tel. 0524/485 921 or 0661/493 541; www.domainemalika.com; 1,550Dh d

Tucked just half a kilometer off the main road, Domaine Malika is a charming luxury guesthouse nestled into the Ouirgane Valley. The property features large, modern salons with a rustic touch for groups to gather. There is plenty of natural light, with windows everywhere you turn. In the rooms, beds have lush linens and you'll find plush towels hanging in the bathroom. The bathtubs are big enough for two, making this a perfect location for a romantic mountain getaway. Lodging includes breakfast, air-conditioning, TV, and Wi-Fi, as well as access to the swimming pool. The private hammam on-site offers facials, scrubs, massages, and other services on reservation. If the budget allows, the splurge is well worth it.

GETTING THERE AND AROUND

There is no public transport outside of the *grands taxis* into the Ouirgane Valley. The easiest way to get to the valley is **by car,** along the secondary road (R203) that leads between **Marrakesh** (63km/39mi, 1hr) and **Taroudant** (162km/101mi, 2.5hr). ***Grands taxis*** are available regularly from **Asni** (20min, 15km/9mi, 10Dh).

CTM (tel. 0800/0900 30, www.ctm.ma) connects directly with Taroudant (5hr, 1 daily, 100Dh) from Marrakesh. It's possible to pay for the complete fare to Taroudant and ask the driver to stop in Ouirgane, though that's not the most practical solution given that the only bus for Taroudant leaves at 2am.

N'Fis Valley

The **N'Fis Valley** is a wide, relatively unexplored gorge that lies beyond the Ouirgane Valley along the same route (R203) that cuts through the Tizi n'Test Pass on its way to Taroudant. The N'Fis Valley is well known locally for its olive groves and almond trees. The land here is largely rural, with few landmarks of note and still even fewer towns, though it's in this region that you will find the **Tin Mal Mosque,** one of the finest attractions in the High Atlas. Life here is primarily agricultural. Tourism hasn't made its impact felt here, as it has in other parts of the High Atlas. However, it is still possible to find lodging, hike into the Toubkal National Park, or use this area as a stopover on the way to Taroudant.

Heading south from Marrakesh on R203, you cross the Ouirgane Valley before entering the N'Fis Valley. The entrance to the valley is marked by a relatively humble town on the opposite bank of the N'Fis River from the road. This is the town of **Iguer n'Kouris.** The local legend tells us that this was originally a farm owned and run by a French man by the name of Kouris some 300 years ago. He worked with 15 men and in his will left the land to the men, who divided the land equally among them. Over time, the men married and had families. Today, there are nearly 200 people living in the village, all descendants of the original 15 men who worked for Kouris.

After Iguer n'Kouris, you pass the mountain town of **Ijoukak** and then the **Kasbah Goundafa,** a picturesque fort built by the Kaid Goundafi, a once powerful leader in the High Atlas. The kasbah stands atop a hill alongside the road, commanding views of the entire valley. Supposedly the kasbah has been purchased by a foreigner to convert into a hotel, though construction has yet to begin. Finally, you reach the town of **Tin Mal** before the road continues south, out of the High Atlas, to join with Taroudant.

The living conditions are notably more rustic throughout the N'Fis Valley than in the relative cushy confines of the neighboring Ouirgane Valley. Those seeking more comfort in their accommodations would be well served to sleep in the Ouirgane Valley and visit the sights in the N'Fis Valley as a day trip or on the way to or from Taroudant.

IJOUKAK

إجوكك

If you are driving south from Marrakesh and the Ouirgane Valley, the first village you'll enter is Ijoukak. This is one of the primary towns of the region. Cafés and the ubiquitous Moroccan grillades dot the main road. They all serve hearty mountain tajines. There are a few shops selling packaged goods and bottled water. The Agandiz River, a tributary of the N'Fis River, runs ice cold down from Toubkal, providing babbling brooks throughout the year to picnic beside. Along this river, on the south slope, potters spin earthy mountain pottery that Ijoukak is known for locally.

Trekkers with a good topo map can use Ijoukak to explore the area. Day hikes to Tin Mal and up the Agandiz River are two of the easier options. Experienced hikers can start a four-day trek into Toubkal National Park and to Imlil.

Accommodations

TAMAZIGHT HOUSE

near Tigmmi n'Tmazirte; tel. 0668/253 421 or 0633/552 129; 260Dh s, 500Dh d

For overnight stays, the Tamazight House is a simple, homey option. The staff is friendly and the beds, though a bit old, are clean and comfortable with secondhand bedding. The rooms are all nonsmoking. The location makes it a good stopover for hikers, independent budget travelers, and small groups, and breakfast and dinner are included. The property uses solar power for the hot water, making it somewhat eco-friendly. Interestingly, there are pottery lessons available with classes of up to five people (50Dh an hour per person). Lessons usually run three hours. Lunches and dinners can be reserved and are highly recommended.

Getting There and Around

Ijoukak lies along the R203 and is easily reached **by car** heading south from **Marrakesh** (99km/62mi, 2.5hr), **Asni** (48km/30mi, 1.5hr), and **Ouirgane** (33km/21mi, 45min). ***Grands taxis*** are always a possibility, though you'll have to bargain hard, with your best chances for a good price at **Asni** or **Ouirgane.** A good price would be 30Dh per seat (or 150Dh for the entire taxi).

TIN MAL

تين مال

The distant town of **Tin Mal** (often spelled Tinmel) is a small, easygoing town nestled in the dry foothills of the High Atlas Mountains. There is a relatively small population here and, somewhat surprisingly, no guesthouse to speak of, though it's possible to ask locals to spend the night as a guest.

There is some difference of opinion as to what the name Tin Mal originally signified. Some believe that it was intended to mean a school, while others believe it means to take a hajj, a holy Muslim pilgrimage. Still

1: Ijoukak is the place for rustic mountain pottery. **2:** Kasbah Goundafa makes for a good hiking reference.

1

2

others say that Tin Mal referred to a rendezvous point; they believe the famous Tin Mal Mosque was built here due to the history as a meeting place, and because of the mosque, the town thus had the only Quranic school in the region. The Almohad rulers came from this region. Their tombs are in the adjacent cemetery.

Sights

★ TIN MAL MOSQUE

daily 9am-5pm; 10Dh

The historically important and wonderfully ornate Tin Mal Mosque is one of the very few mosques in Morocco that non-Muslims can visit. Dubbed Timguida Toumlilt (White Mosque) by the Soussi tribes in the area, it was built by the powerful Abdelmoumen Ibn Ali in 1156, during the Almohad dynasty. The prototypical Moroccan mosque is based on the Tin Mal Mosque, making it an important architectural and historical monument and the reason why it is listed tentatively with UNESCO as a World Heritage Site. Some restoration work was done in 1991, though throughout the mosque there is still no roof.

The mosque lies just off the main road, a short drive uphill at the edge of town. It is customary to honk your horn as you approach the site to let the guardian know that there are visitors in case he isn't at the site.

The layout of the mosque is a classic of Almohad design. Curved archways form a series of decorative naves that connect with a central aisle, which leads to the decorative *mihrab* (a niche in the wall that indicates the direction to Mecca, toward which the faithful pray) and to the fountain where ablutions would have been performed. The mosque was originally divided into two halves, one for women and the other for men, likely with a muslin veil dividing the fountain so that both men and women could perform their ablutions prior to prayer. The mihrab is the most well-preserved part of the mosque, with decorated archways radiating from it as well as ornate stucco work original to the period of construction. At this mihrab you can see the typical designs of the Almohad era, such as the scallop and rosette, which are repeated on the Koutoubia Mosque and the Giralda in Spain. However, the mihrab (and the rest of the mosque) is oriented to the southeast, many degrees away from Mecca. This is a possible reason why the mosque is no longer in use.

Food

CAFÉ RESTAURANT BA ADAM TINMEL

Tinmel, near the mosque; Sat.-Thurs. 8am-6pm; 10Dh

At the start of town just after the bridge, you can get a coffee, tea, or tajine lunch at Café Restaurant Ba Adam Tinmel. More importantly, it has clean bathrooms, which are sometimes needed when crossing through the valley.

Getting There and Around

Tin Mal lies along the R203 and is easily reached **by car** heading south from **Marrakesh** (107km/67mi, 3hr), **Asni** (56km/35mi, 1.5hr), and **Ijoukak** (8km/5mi, 15min). ***Grands taxis*** are a possibility from Ijoukak (12Dh).

Ourika Valley

The most popular day trip from Marrakesh is the **Ourika Valley.** The valley follows a series of villages—**Ourika, Oualmes,** and **Setti Fatma**—up the Ourika River into the High Atlas Mountains. Because of the altitude and the location in the protected cover of the mountains, locals often come here to catch a break from the hot Marrakesh summers. Just a short two-hour drive from Marrakesh heading east along the P2017 following the signs from Ourika, this day trip can be done with a group, with a guide, or all by your lonesome. There are several hotels, cafés, and shops along the route, as well as some light hiking in the region, making for plenty of activities for just about everyone.

SIGHTS

La Paradis du Safran

Km31 from Marrakesh; tel. 0628/796 979; Wed.-Mon. 11am-7pm; 50Dh

Just a few kilometers before reaching the Ourika Valley, La Paradis du Safran is worth a short detour, especially if you won't be able to make it to Talouine during your stay in Morocco. This garden, curated by Swiss-born Christine Ferrari, is a little oasis dedicated to harvesting the extraordinary saffron flower, as well as a few other exotic fruits. The best time to visit is during October and early November when the saffron is harvested, though even outside of this season, Christine will be more than happy to explain to you the painstaking process of harvesting saffron over a deliciously floral tea. Follow the bright orange signs about 30 kilometers (18mi) outside of Marrakesh to find this veritable paradise.

Le Savo'art Fer

Km43 from Marrakesh, Asguine; tel. 0676/561 799; hours vary; free

One of the more interesting stops to make along the way to or from the Ourika Valley is the strange gallery of Le Savo'art Fer. The gallery features sculptures of recycled metal crafted by Abdelhaq Elyoussi, a local artist. Sculptures of recycled metal—featuring bolts, nuts, screws, car parts, tin cans, spatulas, and other discarded waste—have been gaining traction in Morocco with several practitioners

the steep mountain faces around Ourika

now in nearby Essaouira. The sculptures are whimsical while at the same time commenting on the state of the rusty decay of our civilization, adding a sort of melancholy to their twisting forms. One can easily imagine these figures crawling out of the local trash heap and into the living room.

SPORTS AND RECREATION

Setti Fatma Waterfalls

The last village along the road is **Setti Fatma** (64km/40mi, 2hr from Marrakesh), which provides for a base to hike to the Setti Fatma Waterfalls. The trailhead is well marked and lies just across the river.

There is well-signed **guarded parking** in the middle of town (10Dh). Every August a *moussem* for Setti Fatma takes place, typically August 11-13. This can be a crowded, though festive, time to visit.

Travelers should note that the **hike to the waterfalls** (2km/1.2mi, 30min) requires some scrambling up rock faces, though most of the hike is easy. This is a safe climb, and those in moderate physical condition shouldn't have a problem. At times the elevation might get to some who are nervous climbing heights, though the largest rock face is only three meters (10ft). There are stunning cliff faces and rocky outcrops around the waterfalls and into the nearby mountains. There is only one well-traveled path, so a guide is unnecessary.

FOOD AND ACCOMMODATIONS

LA KASBAH DE L'OURIKA

Km48, Arbalou; tel. 0524/484 536; daily 11am-9pm; 150dh

Restaurant La Kasbah de l'Ourika is a sprawling complex just a couple of kilometers after the turnoff for Oukaïmeden. On a chilly day, the ornate salons provide comfort, while most days, the terrace is the best seat in the valley to dine. (Those not interested in the views are best off going to one of the small cafés lining the road for an equally delicious tajine for less than half the price.)

★ OURIKA GARDEN MOUNTAIN VILLA

Km50, Aghbalou; tel. 0524/484 441; www.ourikagarden.com; 660Dh d

You can literally drink up the herb garden at the relaxing Ourika Garden Mountain Villa. Located just far enough off the main road to be immersed into the spacious terraced gardens and towering peaks surrounding the valley, this is far and away the best overnight stay one could hope for in Ourika. The traditionally built mountain retreat features lots of craggy stonework and pinewood beams around a curvy swimming pool that will take the heat off any summer afternoon. The rooms are heated by fireplace or a mechanical unit, if you prefer, with TV, air-conditioning, Wi-Fi, and breakfast all included with your stay. The on-site restaurant is open to travelers making a day trip in Ourika, though you will need to call at least two hours in advance. The menu features tajines, reputed as the finest in the valley, starting from 200Dh.

GETTING THERE AND AROUND

The town of Ourika lies at the junction of the P2017 and P2010 and marks the beginning of the Ourika Valley. It is easily reached **by car** heading southeast from **Marrakesh** (64km/40mi, 1.5hr). The valley continues, with the P2017 serving as the only through road until it ends about 45 minutes later (28km/17mi) at Setti Fatma. For those willing to chance public transportation, **local minivans** leave from Marrakesh for Setti Fatma (2hr, 50Dh) from just outside the Jemaa el-Fnaa, near the Koutoubia Mosque, though times vary widely, with buses waiting until they are near full capacity to leave.

M'Goun Massif

The least-visited area in the High Atlas is the **M'Goun Massif.** Located in the northeast of the High Atlas, the massif includes the confusingly named **Western High Atlas National Park,** where rafting is available, as well as high-end luxury on the edge of pristine **Lake Bin El Ouidane.** For those looking to get off well-trodden circuits, this is the area to explore, with trails running around the national park and through the Ahansal Valley, which is also a popular rafting destination.

Connecting from the M'Goun Massif region to the tourist-friendly confines of the **Dades Gorge** or **Todra Gorge** is relatively easy with the small mountain towns of **M'semrir** and **Imilchil** at the northeast of the region serving as stops for *grands taxis* and local buses that can shuttle you down into either gorge. (See the Ouarzazate and the Southern Oases chapter for more information about the Dades Gorge, Todra Gorge, and M'semrir.) Hikers and trekkers will find traversing the massif rewarding, particularly in the springtime when the fields erupt with blooming foliage.

The **Western High Atlas National Park,** approximately 244 square kilometers (94 square miles), is the primary destination for most travelers to this region. Lake Bin El Ouidane provides a border to the northeast with a massive dam that makes for a pristine lake setting. From the lake, the Ahansal River cuts and twists south through the park, offering 80 kilometers (50mi) of rafting in the spring and early summer. The village of Ouzoud, southwest of the park, houses the largest waterfalls in Morocco, which are best visited in spring when the waters are at their roaring finest.

The jagged mountain peaks and rocky outcrops making up the national park's rough terrain are dusted with valleys full of alpine trees and, in the lower altitudes, the endangered thuya. Hiking solo through the park is for the brave of heart and should be avoided in winter, when it is colder and the unpredictable weather patterns often bring in sudden storms. It is best to tackle the Western High Atlas with a good guide or a good topo map—ideally both.

Many small villages are dotted throughout the park, with farmers and their families making a humble living from the land. As in most places in Morocco, the people met are more friendly than not, and offers to share an afternoon tea or lunch are common. Most travelers arrive to the park at one of the primary towns within the park's perimeter, such as Azilal, Ouzoud, or Ouaouizeght.

This is a prime area for independent travelers, nature lovers, and adventure seekers. The towns and cities in this region don't provide much in the way of tourist sights or activities, though they are necessary travel hubs for those without cars, as buses and *grands taxis* provide service. Hikes are not well marked. Travelers will want to come prepared with a good topo map or a knowledgeable guide. For a guide around the massif, contact the team at **Mountain Travel Morocco** (tel. 0668/760 165, www.trekkinginmorocco.com), led by Mohamed and Ibrahim. Their guides are certified and speak English. Prices typically start at 1,250Dh per person.

BENI MELLAL
بني ملال

Beni Mellal is the largest transportation hub for travelers connecting via bus or *grand taxi* to other destinations in the region. The city is a growing metropolis, with wealth gained from the enormous tracts of farmland on the wide, well-irrigated plain between the Middle Atlas and High Atlas ranges. If you're spending a day here, consider visiting the **Borj de Ras el Aïn,** an old fortress at the top of the mountain above Beni Mellal that offers panoramic views of the city and valley. Close to the fortress are the **Aïn Asserdoun springs.** The name, strangely, translates to the "eye" or "source" of the mule. This old spring feeds into the city. It's thought that the fortress was originally built to protect this spring, as well as the fertile valley below.

Hotels such as the **Hotel Ouzoud** (Km3, Marrakesh road, tel. 0523/483 752, 450Dh) and the **Hotel Oum el Fadl** (309 National Rd., near the Bin Saleh al-Faqih, tel. 0523/426 498, 300Dh) offer modern accommodations, including Wi-Fi, pool, and bar, though they are more geared toward business travelers.

Getting There and Around

Beni Mellal is well connected along National Road 8 (N8), which feeds directly to **Marrakesh** (195km/121mi, 3hr), **Khenifra** (125km/78mi, 2hr), **Azrou** (205km/127mi, 3.5hr), and **Fez** (289km/180mi, 5hr). A beautiful, twisting gorge road (R304) leads to **Ouaouizeght** and **Bin El Ouidane** (43km/27mi, 1hr), as well as more distant **Azilal** (82km/27mi, 2hr).

You can get here easily by bus. **Supratours** (tel. 0890/203 040, www.oncf.ma) connects with **Fez** (5.5hr, 1 daily, 90Dh), **Marrakesh** (3.5hr, 3 daily, 60Dh), and **Meknes** (4.5hr, 1 daily, 80Dh). **CTM** (tel. 0800/090 030, www.ctm.ma) connects with **Casablanca** (4.5hr, 4 daily, 90Dh), **Fez** (6hr, 2 daily, 100Dh), **Marrakesh** (3.5hr, 3 daily, 60Dh), and other destinations.

By ***grand taxi*** other local destinations are available, making taxi-hopping one of the quickest ways to get through this part of the High Atlas. A popular taxi run is to and from **Azilal** (1.5hr, 82km/51mi, 45Dh).

AZILAL

ازيلال

The provincial capital of **Azilal** feels more provincial than capital. Besides a small main street with a few cafés and ATMs, there is little to see or do. Azilal functions more as a transportation hub for the region. It's easy to find taxis or local buses to nearby **Ouzoud** or **Imilchil,** or find passage to Zaouiat Ahansal to hike to the **Taghia Gorge** for **rock-climbing** or to Bin El Ouidane and the small town of Ouaouizeght for some **white-water rafting** down the Ahansal River.

The weekly souk in Azilal takes place on Thursday, making this a prime time to stock up on provisions for longer hikes. The **Delegation du Tourisme d'Azilal** (Ave. Hassan II, tel. 0523/458 722, Mon.-Fri. 9am-noon and 3pm-6pm) has some information on local happenings and some basic hiking materials, and the **Ensemble Artisanal** (Ave. Hassan II, Sat.-Thurs. 9am-6pm, though hours vary) on the outskirts of town on the road to Tabant is worth stopping in if you're looking for handcrafted souvenirs.

Taghia Gorge

You would be forgiven if you thought this difficult-to-find gorge was a private reserve for rock climbers looking to do some serious peak bagging. There is some trekking to be had in the region, but the local tourist economy here is nearly all focused on rock climbing. Europeans have been coming here since 2005 or so, though there is still plenty of exploration to be had and the area is hard enough to reach that there are seldom more than a few climbers at any given time. The gorge itself sports some impressive sheer rock walls and formations with hikes in the area largely following local horse and donkey trails.

Getting There and Around

Most travelers arrive to Azilal via the R304, which winds south through the mountains, past Ouaouizeght, **Bin El Ouidane** (28km/17mi, 45min), and **Beni Mellal** (82km/51mi, 2hr). Azilal is also reached from the popular waterfalls of **Ouzoud** (38km/24mi, 45min) by following the P3105 south from Ouzoud until it meets with R304, taking the road east.

From Azilal, ***grands taxis*** and local buses run to **Ouaouizeght** (1hr, 42km/26mi, 35Dh) and **Bin El Ouidane** for rafting and hikes through the Western High Atlas. For rock-climbing in the Taghia Gorge, hire a *grand taxi* to **Zaouiat Ahansal** (2hr, 82km/51mi, 60Dh). You'll likely have to negotiate for the price and rent the entire taxi. Expect to pay around 500Dh.

OUZOUD
أوزود

The small village of **Ouzoud** is an easy day-trip getaway from Marrakesh, though one or two days allows for a more relaxing exploration of the area. Hikers should plan on spending a day or two here before or after a long trek to catch your breath.

Outside of the village is a large parking lot for buses. Daytime and overnight parking for cars and campers is 10Dh. From the parking lot, it is a five-minute walk through the village, past cafés, restaurants, and souvenir shops, to the waterfalls.

★ Ouzoud Waterfalls (Cascades d'Ouzoud)

The primary draw in the entire region are the impressive 110-meter-tall (330-ft-tall) Ouzoud Waterfalls. The waterfalls pierce through a buttress of tufa rock before plunging into a cold, clear pool of mountain water below. The mists from these pools are thought to have given rise to the name of the village, Ouzoud, which is a Tashelhit word for "mill." This is due to the impression that the mist filling the air gives off "fine flour dust." The rocky outcrops break the waterfall at several points, filling the air with a fine mist and creating a near-permanent rainbow. The surrounding thuya forest is a haven for a small troop of friendly Barbary macaques and eagles, hawks, and lesser kestrels, though of course the monkeys and birds should never be fed. At the bottom of the falls, a boat will take you across the river for 20Dh.

There are several well-marked **hikes** around the waterfalls. Most are 2-3 hours, with some leading into nearby villages where it is sometimes possible to have lunch with one of the old families from the region, making a spontaneous Amazigh cultural encounter likely. The hikes are all relatively easy. Hiring a guide or carrying a map, though somewhat helpful, isn't necessary. In the summer, heatstroke can be a real concern, so it's better to set off early in the morning.

Food and Accommodations

★ HOTEL CHELLAH

Le Chemins de Cascades; tel. 0523/429 180 or 0672/384 791; www.hotelchellalouzoud.com; 250Dh d

Travelers spending just a night or two would do well to make their way down the pedestrian path to the falls and stay at Hotel Chellah. The rooms are austere, but the food is some of the best around the waterfalls. Breakfast is included with your stay. The terrace is relaxing, and the staff is friendly and very knowledgeable about the area. They'll happily direct you to some of the better hikes you can take in the area without needing to hire a guide. Even if you don't stay the night, this is hands-down the best place for lunch. A good tajine lunch will set you back around 60Dh.

LA KASBAH D'OUZOUD

Ouzoud road; tel. 0523/429 210; https://kasbahouzoud.com; 760Dh d

For a swell retreat, consider La Kasbah d'Ouzoud. This traditionally constructed kasbah features charming wood-beam ceilings and carved doors with tribal touches all around an open courtyard with plenty of twittering birds. The grounds include a swimming pool, garden, and lush palms. Wi-Fi, air-conditioning, and heating are all standard, and breakfast is included. Other meals are available on request. Bungalows are a bit less at 600Dh and charming in their own right. However, the kasbah is a walk up the hill, away from town by the main parking plaza.

Getting There and Around

Ouzoud is just a short drive from **Azilal** (38km/24mi, 45min) following the R304 west from Azilal and then turning north on the P3105 toward Ouzoud. Azilal is the local transportation hub, though; except for tour buses, there is no local bus service to Ouzoud.

1
2
3

From Azilal you'll have to catch a *grand taxi* (25Dh).

Tour buses make their way here from the ***gare routière*** in **Marrakesh** (3hr, 160km/99mi, 300-400Dh, depending on bus carrier) for day-trippers, though the drive from Marrakesh makes for a long day trip. An overnight stay is possible. Check with the tour bus to purchase tickets returning to Marrakesh the next day.

OUAOUIZEGHT AND LAKE BIN EL OUIDANE

واويزغت and بن الويدان

Ouaouizeght is a remote mountain village that is used as a base for most rafting tours in the region. Hikers can use this as a stop while circling the M'Goun Massif region. If you're looking to get away from it all and really unplug, consider a long weekend along the shores of the crystal-clear **Lake Bin El Ouidane.**

★ White-Water Rafting

MOSTAPHA OUTILI

tel. 0661/313 761 or 0670/924 413, https://tafouitevoyage.wordpress.com; 1,300Dh pp

White-water rafting on the **Ahansal River** is good March-June and typically is done as a four-day trip from Marrakesh. Mostapha is one of the better-known rafting guides in the region and can plan trips, no matter the number of days you have (or don't have!) for your vacation. Buried in the High Atlas, the river in this region carves through 80 kilometers (50mi) of soft rock, winding through vertiginous gorges and the Western High Atlas National Park. The mountain scenery provides an unbelievable backdrop of sawtoothed peaks that jet into the sky, while forests of alpines provide some shade along the way. The river itself is suited to beginners and intermediates, although there are some occasionally challenging white-water stretches.

1: the Ouzoud Waterfalls 2: a Barbary macaque at the Ouzoud Waterfalls 3: the expansive Lake Bin El Ouidane

Food and Accommodations

HOTEL OUAOUIZEGHT

Ouaouizeght, near the mosque; tel. 0612/097 737; 250Dh d

In Ouaouizeght, Hotel Ouaouizeght offers plain accommodations. The beds are stiff, though comfortable enough, and the hosts are extremely kind. Breakfast is included, and lunch and dinner are available. There are not too many options in town for those arriving without a guide. The hotel reflects the area, with a slight dust over most things and very, very rustic. It's not for those uncomfortable with camping.

WIDIANE SUITES AND SPA

Chemin du Lac Bin El Ouidane; tel. 0523/442 776; www.widiane.net; 2,800Dh d

Right on the lake is the decidedly upscale, luxury award-winning posh digs of Widiane Suites and Spa. Constructed as a terraced kasbah sitting right at the edge of the lake, this is a choice getaway for expats and Moroccans in-the-know. The rooms are color coded in teals and yellows with expansive terrace views out over the lake and neighboring mountain peaks. The infinity pool is a warm place to relax with a cocktail from the poolside tiki bar. Boats are available to explore the lake. Multiple restaurants on-site include, somewhat bizarrely, a Thai restaurant. Air-conditioning, TV, Wi-Fi, and breakfast are all included, and there is a full-service spa on-site as well. This may be just the thing after a long trek through the M'Goun Massif, if your wallet allows.

Getting There and Around

Those driving will likely come to Ouaouizeght and Lake Bin El Ouidane via **Beni Mellal** (43km/27mi, 1hr) along a beautiful, twisting gorge road (R304), though others will be arriving from the south via **Azilal** (42km/26mi, 1hr).

There are local **buses** (1.5hr, 42km/26mi, 20Dh) and ***grands taxis*** (1hr, 42km/26mi, 35Dh) to and from **Azilal.**

IMILCHIL

إملشيل

Famous throughout Morocco for its celebrated Marriage Festival that takes place at the end of every summer or early fall, the small mountain town of **Imilchil** is relatively quiet throughout most of the year. There are several cafés, small guesthouses, grocery stores, and pharmacies along the main road that curves through town. Saturday is the souk day. Picturesque **Tislit Lake** lies just a kilometer north of town.

Festivals and Events

★ MARRIAGE FESTIVAL

One of the most anticipated festivals in Morocco is the renowned Imilchil Marriage Festival (called locally the "Souk Aamor Agdoud N'Oulmghenni"), which takes place in late August or September and lasts for about a week. The festival has a romantic history that would make Shakespeare proud. Once upon a time, there lived a young man and a young woman from two different tribes, the Capulets and Montagues of the region. Like Romeo and Juliet, the two young people fell madly in love, but were prevented from seeing each other by their warring families. In their grief, the lovers wept. Their tears formed two neighboring lakes: Tislit and Isli, or "bride" and "groom." The young lovers died of grief and, in mourning their loss, the families came together and sought a way for the young people of their tribes to find marriage partners. Thus, the marriage festival was born.

The purpose of this festival is for parents to show off their daughters in the hopes that they might secure their future in a good marriage partner. These partnerships are often struck up at the beginning of the festival, and by the end of the festival, 30-50 new couples become married. They perform the complex marriage ceremony over the course of the week-long fête, becoming husband and wife after knowing each other for only a couple of days and, in some cases, meeting for the first time on the day of their wedding!

The festival is a joyous occasion, with local music playing throughout the day and lively dancing. Locals dress to the nines in their best jellabas and most colorful kaftans.

Though tourism has affected this festival, largely positively, there has been some talk locally of the purity of the festival being contaminated and even the historical accuracy of the festival being compromised. Rumor has it that now a secondary marriage festival takes place solely for the locals that is kept highly secret by the community. Some Amazigh scholars even question the origin of the festival, as it may have begun as a festival to mark the end of the harvest, where already married couples could then gather and obtain their marriage certificates. Regardless, this event is still one of the most entertaining festivals around Morocco.

Food and Accommodations

Cafés and restaurants in town serve lunch for around 35Dh. Most accommodations offer lunch and dinner, though you will need to request ahead of time. These are often the best meals to be had. The few accommodations in Imilchil fill up quickly during peak travel seasons over the summer and, as to be expected, during the Marriage Festival. Prices often double or triple during the festival. Make sure you book your stay and plan accordingly.

★ AUBERGE TISLITE

Lake Tislit; tel. 0622/039 682; www.auberge-tislite.com; 300Dh d

Just north of Imilchil along Lake Tislit (Bride's Lake) are the splendidly Zen digs of Auberge Tislite. The host, Malika, will see to it that you have everything you might need, and is something of a grandmotherly figure. The nights can get cold, and there is no central heating, so you'll have to bundle up. At night a central fire is usually built; it also heats up the water, making hot showers in the common bathroom possible. The inn has a wonderful location and wonderful people, but it's for those who don't mind roughing it a bit for a day or two, as bathrooms are shared and the beds can be a bit rough. Camping is also available on the grounds (50Dh), making this a possible stop for those trekking through the region.

HOTEL IZLANE

Imichil Center; tel. 0661/224 882; 400Dh d

In the middle of town, Hotel Izlane is a basic hotel, though clean and with friendly service. The restaurant can do vegetarian meals on request, though these are usually somewhat bland, as is the custom. As at Imilchil's other hotels, there is no heating, so dress accordingly, particularly during the colder months. Your stay includes a simple, though appreciated, breakfast.

Getting There and Around

The drive to Imilchil is rewarding. There are plenty of well-paved roads and spectacular scenery. The easiest routes are from National Road 8 (N8) at **El Ksiba** (114km/71mi, 1.5hr), just northeast of Beni Mellal, where you follow signs for Imilchil and start a winding road into the mountains, and the route from **Tinghir** (122km/76mi, 2hr) through the Todra Gorge. Though these routes are perfectly safe during the day, night driving should be avoided.

More distant passageways into the desert, including the palm groves of the **Ziz Valley,** snaking **Dades Gorge,** and the towering cliffs of the **Todra Gorge,** are just a couple of hours by car.

For public transportation, getting to Imilchil is a little trickier. The village is reached only by local buses and *grands taxis.* ***Grands taxis*** to and from **El Ksiba** (near Beni Mellal, 1.5hr, 114km/70mi, 40Dh) and **Tinghir** (Todra Gorge, 2hr, 122km/76mi, 50Dh) are frequent, and typically **buses** (20Dh) depart for Imilchil in the early mornings. The going can be tough; many local passengers become carsick.

Ouarzazate and the Southern Oases

A trip to Morocco feels somehow incomplete

without spending at least one night in a desert oasis.

Here, paved roads give way to packed dirt and sand. If you're lucky, just over the next great dune is a fresh, quiet palm grove.

Moroccans and foreigners alike come to take in the great expanse of the Sahara and experience the warm hospitality that this region is known for. In the popular oases of Skoura and Zagora, travelers can wake in the midst of a palm grove feeling the calm at the edge of the great Sahara.

Ouarzazate is the largest city in the region and also serves as the country's film hub, often called the "Moroccan Hollywood" by locals, coming to life with the buzz of film crews under clear skies and

Highlights

Look for ★ to find recommended sights, activities, dining, and lodging.

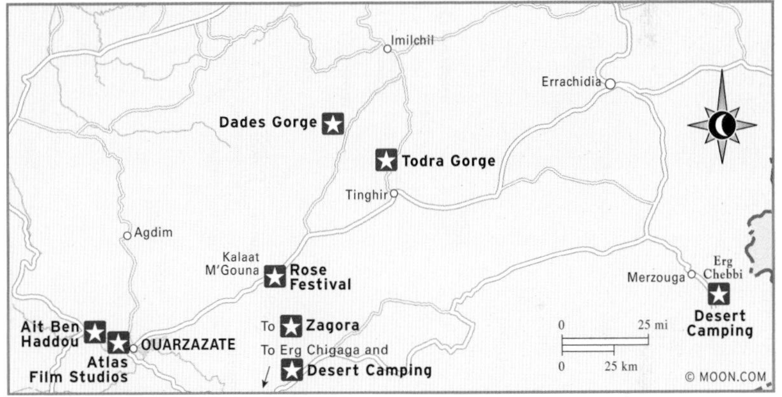

★ **Atlas Film Studios:** Spend an afternoon touring Morocco's most famous movie studio and go behind, and into, the scenes of some of your favorite Hollywood productions (page 396).

★ **Ait Ben Haddou:** This is the most impressive kasbah in Morocco. The stunning High Atlas range serves as a backdrop for some very memorable photographs, particularly as the sun rises over the Sahara, lighting the snowcapped mountains in hues of pink (page 401).

★ **Rose Festival:** Held every spring in Kalaat M'Gouna, this festival brings together traditional dance and music as a veritable ode to the rose (page 407).

★ **Dades Gorge:** The famed "Road of 1,000 Kasbahs" peters out in this wide gorge full of date palms, crumbling kasbahs, and a winding road that gives San Francisco's Lombard Street a run for its money (page 409).

★ **Todra Gorge:** For novice climbers, dirt baggers, and trekkers, a few days climbing the steep rocks of the Todra Gorge and hiking around the villages throughout is a highlight of any trip to Morocco (page 411).

★ **Zagora:** A night in the calm of a date palm oasis, a quintessential Morocco experience, is just the thing to relax the mind and body after the often-grueling trip through the desert (page 417).

★ **Desert Camping:** The two great *ergs* (sand dunes) of Morocco, Erg Chigaga and Erg Chebbi, play host to nights camping in Bedouin tents beneath the crystal-clear desert sky (pages 423 and 432).

Ouarzazate and the Southern Oases

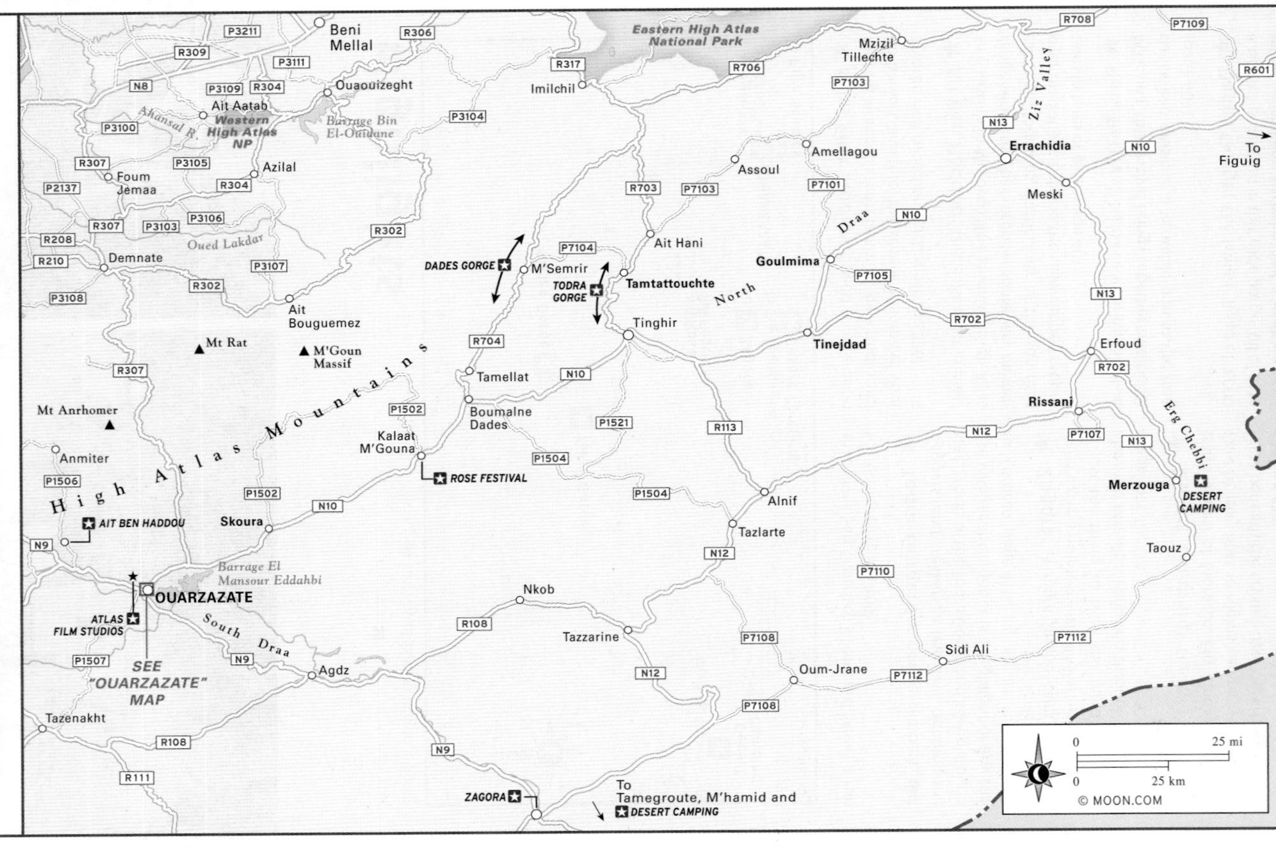

the beautiful mountain backdrop of the High Atlas. There are several kasbahs nearby to explore, including the famed Ait Ben Haddou, which strikes a majestic scene with the snow-capped peaks hovering in the not-too-distant background.

From Ouarzazate, you can continue northeast, along the famed "Road of 1,000 Kasbahs" through the Skoura oasis, surrounded by numerous mud-bricked fortresses, and up to the breathtaking Dades Gorge. The road up the Dades Gorge continues into the High Atlas Mountains, the road littered with picturesque crumbling kasbahs and death-defying hairpin turns. There is a lot of hiking and camping in this area. From Boumalne Dades, most people continue up the national road through the North Draa Valley to the Todra Gorge, popular with hikers and rock-climbers, and on to the desert at Erfoud and Merzouga to venture into the Sahara.

Southeast along the N9 is the largest and most impressive palm grove in all of Morocco, the South Draa Valley. This palm grove hosts over two million trees and stretches from the relatively nondescript drive-through town of Agdz, through the oasis town of Zagora, formerly the start of the Caravan Route to Timbuktu, and on to the end of the road, M'hamid. From M'hamid, the paved road ends and the real adventure begins. Traverse the desert—by foot, camel, or four-wheel drive—to the distant Erg Chigaga, where you stargaze beneath the clear desert sky and watch as the sun rises over the golden Saharan sands.

Another palm grove in the Ziz Valley through Errachidia road gives way to Erfoud and Merzouga—where you can hop on a camel to trek into the desert for a quiet night in a Bedouin tent, sipping mint tea on the great Erg Chebbi, eating a wood-fired tajine, and waking to watch the sun rise in hues of pink and crimson.

ORIENTATION

The Southern Oases and Sahara Desert stretch northeast to southwest along Morocco's eastern border with Algeria. For the purposes of this guidebook, I've divided this region into three sections: **Ziz Valley, North Draa Valley,** and **South Draa Valley.**

The Ziz Valley and small city of **Errachidia** mark the northernmost area of this section, while the South Draa Valley and less-touristed towns of **M'hamid** and **Foum Zguid** mark the southernmost region. **Ouarzazate** is the largest city in the region, though small in comparison with other cities in Morocco. **Erg Chebbi** and **Erg Chigaga** are the two largest formations of sand dunes in Morocco. Erg Chebbi towers over the touristic town of **Merzouga,** 130 kilometers (81mi) from Errachidia, while the more distant Erg Chigaga is only accessible via 4x4 (or camel) from M'hamid, 260 kilometers (162mi) from Ouarzazate.

Most travelers will likely enter this region via the mountain pass connecting **Marrakesh** with Ouarzazate, the largest city in the region. Another route starts from Fez through the Ziz Valley to the north.

PLANNING YOUR TIME

There are no trains in this region, so you will be traveling by either **bus,** ***grand taxi,*** or **car.** The roads are generally passable and much work is being done to improve the infrastructure, though heavy rains (typically during winter months) can sometimes wash roads out and make some areas unreachable. For most major destinations, the road is paved and perfectly drivable, though for off-piste roads, such as the roads past **Merzouga** or **M'hamid** into the more remote regions, you will need **four-wheel drive.** If you are not renting a car or have not arranged a driver, then the buses are your best option.

From **Marrakesh,** you most likely will come via the **N9** through **Ouarzazate.**

Previous: the traditional green pottery of Tamegroute; the winding drive through the Dades Gorge; Ait Bin Haddou, the site of many movies.

From **Fez** or **Meknes,** you will arrive from the north via the **N13** by way of **Midelt** and through the **Ziz Valley.** It's best to drive this region with a **map,** as roads are often unmarked or marked only in Arabic. Before setting out, it's best to have an idea of the roads you will take and possible circuits you might do. Roads are all two-lanes, which means that traffic can sometimes get backed up because of farm equipment and herding animals. Buckle up for some long drives.

From Marrakesh, it's possible to take a trip into the Sahara via Ouarzazate in three days, though this will mean a lot of travel time. Four days is preferred: one day to get to Ouarzazate and from there another half day to explore the famed **kasbah** of Ait Ben Haddou, and then a half day to continue out to the first *erg* of the Sahara outside of Zagora (or to Erg Chebbi at Merzouga). Count one day for the Sahara and then another for the return trip. It's possible to continue from Marrakesh all the way to Zagora in one day, though this is a lot of driving.

From Fez or Meknes, it will take a full day of driving to get to **Erfoud** or Merzouga, the two closest stops to the Sahara. If you leave early enough, it's possible to take a **camel** or four-wheel drive out to a **Bedouin tent** and then return the next day, though three or four days is a more relaxing pace.

It is possible to visit the **Dades** and **Todra Gorges** as well as the **Zagora** and **Skoura oases** during the summer months, but the desert itself is generally much too hot for most people. The spring and fall are thought to be the best months to visit, though temperatures can still be hot during the day and quite cool at night. Winter can be an excellent time to visit, though rainstorms and flooding can be a concern, and at night temperatures will dip below freezing in some parts.

Most travelers to this region prioritize a night under the stars in the remote sand dunes of either **Erg Chebbi** or **Erg Chigaga.** Depending on whether you're coming into the region from Fez, to the north, or Marrakesh, to the south, you might want to consider which sand dune to visit. For travelers making a larger tour of Morocco that includes both Fez and Marrakesh, it makes a lot of travel sense to choose Erg Chebbi near Merzouga for your night in the Sahara. No matter the circuit you choose, expect some long drives. Travelers using public transportation in this region, particularly buses, should expect delays and be ready for some early mornings. This is a region that makes the most sense to explore with a **rental car,** giving you more flexibility for exploration. If you have more than three days, explore the Dades Gorge, Todra Gorge, and Erfoud in the **North Draa Valley,** or make for **Zagora** and **M'hamid** in the **South Draa Valley.** For travelers coming from Fez, consider doing the following in reverse.

GUIDES

In the oases and desert it is generally easier to hire a tour company than to go it alone, though you should be selective and use care in choosing companies. Many companies will tell you that they know the region, only to easily get lost in the difficult-to-navigate desert. I've used the following well-reputed companies.

AMAZING JOURNEY MOROCCO

tel. 0665/952 465 or 0661/354 093; www.amazing-morocco.com

Amazing Journey Morocco is perhaps the best tour company headquartered in southern Morocco. Their English-speaking tour guides all have four-wheel drives and know the area extremely well. Not only can they do tours around the desert and Erg Chigaga, but they also lead treks by foot and camel through the picturesque Draa Oasis to the Jewish Dunes (Erg Lehoudi) at the edge of the desert. They also have a campsite in Erg Chigaga with rustic Bedouin-style tents complete with bathrooms and a restaurant.

JOURNEY BEYOND TRAVEL

tel. 0610/414 573, US toll-free tel. 855/687-6676; www.journeybeyondtravel.com

For those looking for a culturally immersive, fully customized tour, the team at Journey

Beyond Travel have established themselves as far-and-away the best tour operator in Morocco. They create custom packages and tours while working to maintain an eco-friendly, socially sustainable business model that strives to fully offset the carbon footprint of their tours. They are true leaders in the industry, continuously inventing new itineraries and discovering little hidden gems that really make a journey through Morocco with them something special. They arrange trips throughout this region with reliable, friendly drivers and the best accommodations the area has to offer.

Itinerary Ideas

DAY 1

1 For this day, leave **Marrakesh** directly after breakfast. The drive to Ouarzazate is long, about five hours. Don't forget the road snacks.

2 Take the N9 in the direction to Ouarzazate. Take a break atop the **Tizi n'Tichka** pass, the highest major mountain pass in North Africa, clocking in at 2,260 meters (7,415ft). You'll easily spot the "Col du Tichka" with several snack shops marking this summit.

3 Descend into the desert and spend the late afternoon stretching your legs and exploring **Kasbah Aït Ben Haddou.**

4 Check into your accommodations in **Ouarzazate** and then head out for dinner.

DAY 2

1 Today, you'll have about six hours of driving north along the **N10.** Known as the "Road of 1,000 Kasbahs," this road takes you through the North Draa Valley and makes for a relaxing drive with plenty of opportunities to pause in the palm groves and small desert towns.

2 As you head north from Ouarzazate, stop in at **Kalaat M'gouna** to smell the flowers. The local roses are used worldwide for perfumes and essential oils.

3 For lunch, get off the N10 at Tinghir and take a little detour into the **Todra Gorge.** This is a good opportunity to stretch your legs and take a little hike.

4 You'll want to be in Merzouga before sunset, so make sure to give yourself three hours of drive time between Tinghir and Merzouga, just in case. Once in **Merzouga,** you will meet your desert guide.

5 At the foot of **Erg Chebbi,** pick your favorite camel and ride out for a night in the Sahara under the stars. If time allows, climb the nearest dune to take in the sunset. You'll have dinner in a desert encampment of **Bedouin tents.** This is one of the best places in the world to stargaze and do a little astrophotography.

DAY 3

1 This is a long driving day to Fez (463km/288mi, 8hr), so you'll want to leave as early as possible on the **N13.** Road snacks are a good idea, as well as making sure you have a full tank of gas. Rise early to watch the sunrise at the **camp.** After sunrise, you'll have a quick breakfast before heading back to civilization on your camel.

Itinerary Ideas

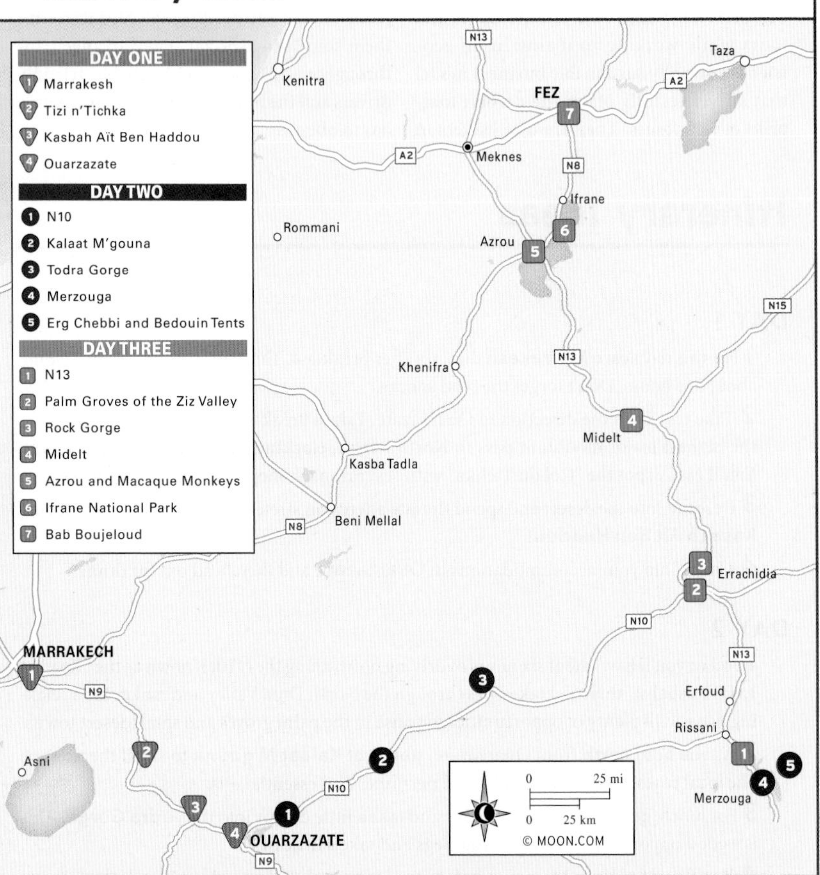

2 Today's drive will take you through Erfoud and Errachidia. Just after Errachidia are the **palm groves of the Ziz Valley,** the most picturesque place to stop for lunch on this drive.

3 After leaving the Ziz Valley, you'll enter a **rock gorge** with a few turnoffs for views down the gorge and the Ziz River.

4 **Midelt** is the best stop for a quick bite to eat and for a bathroom break.

5 Just outside of **Azrou,** stop to observe the local **Macaque monkeys** that are ubiquitous in the region.

6 If time allows, a walk through Ifrane or the **Ifrane National Park** can be a great way to wind down from a long road trip. From Ifrane, Fez is about a one-hour drive.

7 Park outside of **Bab Boujeloud** in Fez. Consider having a porter from your accommodations meet you as, after a long trip, you'll probably not want to navigate this confusing old city as night falls. Settle in for a great night of sleep after your desert adventure.

Ouarzazate

ورزازات

Originally built by the French during the protectorate era in 1928 as a military installation, Ouarzazate serves as the gateway to the desert for most travelers today. Ouarzazate comes from the Tashelhit expression *aourz nfzat,* or "ankle of Zat Mountain." Located where the Ouarzazate and Dades Rivers join to form the head of the Draa River, Ouarzazate has become the chief town and administrative capital of the region. The massive production of *Lawrence of Arabia* in the 1960s gave rise to the film studios here and Ouarzazate's new nickname, the "Hollywood of Morocco."

Many movies and TV series are shot here throughout the year, giving Ouarzazate a particular buzz of big-name directors, busy camera crews, and movie stars.

Most of the few sights in Ouarzazate can be seen in a day. The **Taourirt Kasbah** has been given some restoration efforts by UNESCO, and next to it lies a relatively unexplored old medina. There are a few bazaars in the medina, along with cafés and *riads*. The small **Cinema Museum of Ouarzazate** and the **Ensemble Artisanal** are across the street from the kasbah. Otherwise, there are the two

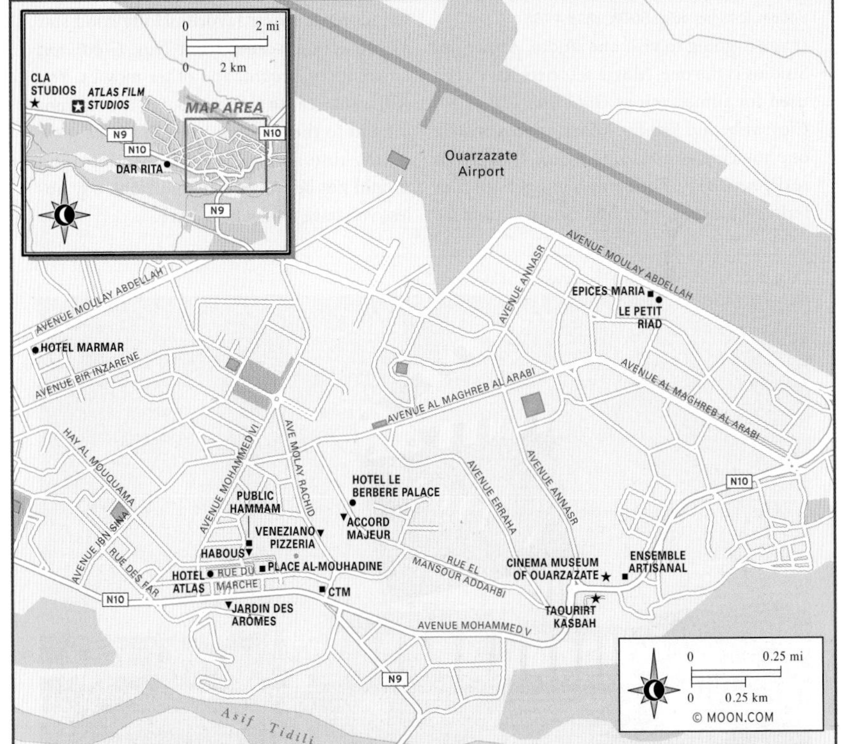

movie studios (Atlas and CLA) along the road to Marrakesh. Most travelers will want to make their way to nearby **Ait Ben Haddou,** the most interesting *ksar* (connected series of fortresses) in the area, to wander around and take photos for a half day at least. Lodging is possible in the *ksar* and can be a nice alternative from a city—plus, you'll be treated to incredible sunrises.

Most travelers will likely spend just one day in Ouarzazate before continuing on to the region's more scenic locations, including the numerous palm groves, ancient kasbahs, winding gorges, villages constructed from ocher-colored earth, and the majestic Sahara Desert.

SIGHTS

★ Atlas Film Studios

Rte. de Marrakech Tamassinte; tel. 0524/882 166; Oct.-Feb. daily 8:15am-5:45pm, Mar.-Sept. daily 8:15am-6:45pm; adult 50Dh, child 40Dh

If you're going to visit one studio, Atlas Film Studios is the one. Movie sets here have been used for films such as *Gladiator, King Tut, Cleopatra,* and *Exodus.* Tours, approximately one hour, are available in English, though not really necessary. The many highlights for film buffs include the set of "old Tangier," used for many medina shots in movies, and the gaudy Egyptian throne room used in *Asterix & Obelix.* Tours are not usually available during film shoots. In the distance from the back lot, you can see the looming castle structure from nearby CLA Studios set against the snowcapped backdrop of the High Atlas. Be sure to have your camera ready. Action!

CLA Studios

Rte. de Marrakech Tamassinte; tel. 0544/882 053; www.cla-studios.com; daily 8am-6:30pm; adult 50Dh, child 30Dh, under 12 free

The nearby CLA Studios offer a chance to visit the site of the city of Astapor from the popular *Game of Thrones* series (or if you prefer, the castle from *Kingdom of Heaven*). There are no English-language tours available. However, you do have free run of the castle and can climb up and down the vast set, examine the catapult, and picture yourself alongside your favorite Hollywood star as you act out scenes from *Troy, Gladiator, Lawrence of Arabia,* and other movies. You will want a car to take you out to the Astapor set and to the set of *Journey to Mecca,* now falling into ruin. The road is bumpy and should not be traveled if it's a rainy day unless you have four-wheel drive.

Ouarzazate is known as the "Hollywood of Morocco."

Taourirt Kasbah

Ave. Mohammed V; tel. 0666/940 302; daily 8am-6pm; 10Dh

The 19th-century Taourirt Kasbah has been partially renovated, though perhaps not for the better. Many rooms in the maze-like fortress of Taourirt have been reinforced with concrete and tiles not typical of the era. Still, it's worth the price of entry if this is the only kasbah you are going to see. Guides compete for customers, so you might find them fighting over you; a few speak English, and having a guide will make the tour infinitely more interesting, so it's worth hiring one. Guides will explain the history of the inner sanctum; the process of constructing the traditional *tataoui* ceiling, a sort of thrush-reinforced ceiling, still visible in some parts; and the history of the notorious Pasha of Marrakesh, El Glaoui, who had control of this region and the camel trade over the Sahara in the early part of the 20th century. The going rate for a guide is 70Dh, which will include a 30- to 60-minute tour of the kasbah and, if you choose, the small medina within the kasbah walls. If you're on the tall side, be sure to watch your head. There are numerous short ceilings that can give you a surprising bump.

Cinema Museum of Ouarzazate (Musée du Cinéma de Ouarzazate)

Ave. Mohammed V; tel. 0524/882 166; daily 8am-5:30pm, closed Fri. noon-2pm; 30Dh

For cinema buffs, the Cinema Museum of Ouarzazate, just across the street from the Taourirt Kasbah, is a great look into the history of the various landmark movies and TV series that have been filmed in and around Ouarzazate. Discover how the local film industry began with *Lawrence of Arabia,* and learn about the progression of the industry through today and the outlook toward the future. Props from movies such as *Asterix & Obelix* and *Kingdom* can be found here. It's not nearly as interesting as a visit to either of the studios, but it can be a pleasant diversion in the middle of town to escape the afternoon heat.

EVENTS

MARATHON OF SAND (MARATHON DES SABLES)

www.marathondessables.co.uk; Apr.

Described as the most difficult footrace on the planet, the Marathon of Sand is an international event that brings long-distance runners from around the world at the beginning of April every year. The runners must carry all of their water, food, and other needs through a course that will take them 250 kilometers (155mi) through the dunes of the Sahara, across the springtime babble of rivers, across the vast palm groves, up into the mountains, and all beneath the scorching Moroccan sun. Started in 1986 by Patrick Bauer, the race continues to grow in popularity with places now much sought after. For those craving extreme sports, it doesn't get any more extreme than this.

SHOPPING

ENSEMBLE ARTISANAL

Ave. Mohammed V; daily 9:30am-12:30pm and 1:30pm-6pm

Worth a glimpse is the Ensemble Artisanal, where you can find local crafts on display for a fair price, including inlaid daggers, Amazigh carpets, and lamps of all shapes and sizes. Of particular note is Said's shop. Said is one of the few remaining stoneworkers handcrafting traditional tribal Tashelhit designs of the High Atlas, alongside some more commercial pieces, in white and black alabaster. Said's pieces range from something to tuck into your pocket to much larger objects that will have to be carefully wrapped and shipped back home.

HAMMAMS

The perfect end to a taxing, sweaty, sand-filled journey through the desert is a relaxing, steamy hammam. Take a moment to wash the sand out of every nook and cranny and, while you're at it, pamper yourself a bit. Ouarzazate has several Moroccan hammams, ranging from high-end luxury to something less elaborate but still relaxing.

OASIS SPA AND JACUZZI AT THE HOTEL LE BERBERE PALACE

Rue El Mansour Addahbi; tel. 0524/883 105; daily 10am-8pm by appointment only; 150Dh

Oasis Spa and Jacuzzi at the Hotel Le Berbere Palace offers the type of scrubbing, exfoliation, and massage meant to make you feel like Hollywood royalty. This is the epitome of luxury. You could easily imagine Gwyneth Paltrow or Keira Knightley emerging from the steam clouding the Moroccan *zellij,* taking a moment to indulge in some self-care after a long day of shooting.

EPICES MARIA

1579 Ave. Moulay Abdellah; tel. 0524/883 776; Sat.-Thurs. 10am-8pm by appointment only; 150Dh

The less elaborate Epices Maria, next to Le Petit Riad, offers a chance to have the sand of the desert scrubbed off you with traditional Moroccan soaps and essential herbs. For those of us not necessarily comfortable rubbing elbows (or knees, for that matter) with Hollywood royalty, this is a more humble place for mere mortals.

PUBLIC HAMMAM

Pl. Al Mouhadine; 10Dh

Another option is the newly built public hammam near the Patisserie Habouss, where you can mingle with locals. For those looking for an authentic experience, this is where you can go to hear all the women trading the latest tales and the men talking up the latest football (soccer) match. Don't worry if you don't have soap—they sell it at the door. You will want to remember a pair of flip-flops and a towel, though.

FOOD

For breakfast, lunch, or a light snack, head to **Place Al-Mouhadine,** which has numerous indistinguishable cafés and food joints. The meals are all pretty standard, but these are great spots for grabbing a little sun while people-watching on the sprawling patio that feeds out onto the plaza.

HABOUS

Place Al-Mouhadine; daily 7am-9pm; 35Dh

Popular with locals and travelers, this Ouarzazate staple serves up a lunch menu with a variety of fast-food style plates, like burgers and chips (fries) and pizzas. These are good in a pinch, and the service is usually fantastic. If your accommodations don't offer breakfast, consider making this your breakfast stop. Sip on a coffee and nibble on a pastry while doing a little late-morning people-watching ... just like the locals.

VENEZIANO PIZZERIA

Ave. Moulay Rachid; tel. 0524/887 676; daily noon-9:30pm; 40Dh

Veneziano Pizzeria serves up standard, if not a little disappointing, Moroccan-style pizzas, salads, and tajines. Stick with the thin-crust pizzas. Varieties include a spin on the Hawaiian Pizza, with salami substituted for ham, and the Pizza Américaine, with seasoned ground beef, mushrooms, and cheese. Vegetarian options are available, as is Wi-Fi. It's well located close to Place Al-Mouhadine, across from the large Banque Populaire.

★ ACCORD MAJEUR

Rue El Mansour Addahbi; in front of the Berbere Palace; tel. 0524/882 473; Mon.-Sat. 11am-10pm; 200Dh

If you're looking to brush shoulders with the Hollywood crowd and nibble on delicious French cuisine, Accord Majeur is the place to be. Expect crowd favorites such as escargot and duck confit alongside seared salmon or grilled haddock covered with saffron-butter sauce. Though the food is delish, the real draw is the setting, replete with the film industry crowd chatting about the day's shoot in the warm, Moroccan-chic salon. The French bistro vibe and a fully stocked bar serve as the backdrop to your own Hollywood dream. Reservations are recommended for dinner; the restaurant will fill up at night, especially if there is a film shoot in town, and there often is. Best for couples and those looking for a break from Moroccan fare.

LE JARDIN DES ARÔMES

69 Ave. Mohamed V; tel. 0524/888 802; Tues.-Sun. noon-2:30pm and 7pm-midnight; 200Dh

While you might think of stopping in exclusively for the fantastical decor—a blend of lush gardens and Arabian kitsch, like something described in the pen of Sir Richard Burton—that would be missing the main attraction. And what is the attraction of this new up-and-coming player in desert cuisine? The food, of course! Come here for crispy vegetarian *bastilla* (vegetable pie), perfectly spiced *meshoui* (roast lamb), and a mosaic of Moroccan salads. Service is friendly, as expected. Great for couples and families.

ACCOMMODATIONS

Accommodations in Ouarzazate range from pensions and auberges to larger hotels catering to tour groups and smaller boutique hotels located in quaint (though nearly impossible to locate) neighborhoods dotted around the downtown. They all have their good and bad qualities. Similar to Casablanca, Ouarzazate functions more as a travel hub for the area than as a destination in its own right. There are more interesting and picturesque accommodations available in towns around Ouarzazate, particularly in Ait Ben Haddou, the Dades and Todra Gorges, and the oases of Skoura and Zagora.

HOTEL ATLAS

13 Rue de Marche, just off Pl. Al-Mouhadine; tel. 0524/887 745; 50Dh s, 180Dh d

For travelers on a shoestring budget, the brightly painted Hotel Atlas has simple, functional rooms. It's a good spot for student groups and backpackers. The front desk is friendly and knowledgeable about the area. The location, right off the Place Al-Mouhadine, is ideal for exploration and close to many cafés and snack places. Bathrooms are generally shared. Hot showers are 10Dh.

HOTEL MARMAR

16 Ave. Le Prince Moulay Abdellah; tel. 0524/888 887; www.hotel-marmar.com; 160Dh s, 250Dh d

Just a short walk from the *gare routière*, **Hotel Marmar** is the cleanest, though perhaps most characterless, option in Ouarzazate. The helpful, knowledgeable staff will gladly call for taxis and arrange transportation for you to continue your journey. The café downstairs is handy for a quick breakfast and freshly squeezed orange juice. If you're just arriving and the hotel isn't full, it is sometimes possible to negotiate prices.

DAR RITA

39 Rue de la Mosquée, Hay Tassoumaât; tel. 0654/164 726; www.darrita.com; 550Dh d

If off-the-beaten-track-in-a-big-city is your thing, consider the guesthouse Dar Rita, in the midst of the Tassoumaât neighborhood, a popular neighborhood in Ouarzazate a bit far from the main square and sights. Consider having someone meet you to take you to the guesthouse, as it is buried in a short maze of unnamed streets that can be daunting to navigate for the uninitiated. The decor is a bit cluttered, but it retains a sort of family charm. The staff is friendly to a fault, Wi-Fi is available, and breakfast is included.

★ LE PETIT RIAD

1581/1582 Hay Al Wahda; tel. 0524/885 950; www.petitriad.com; 650Dh d

Le Petit Riad is a charming house on the edge of the Al Wahda neighborhood southeast of the airport along Avenue Moulay Abdellah. Though taxis are possible from this location, it is better if you have your own car. The newly constructed house has lots of artistic charm, featuring adaptations of tribal Amazigh motifs, comfortable beds, an outdoor patio garden with a pool, and lots of space to spread out. Fatima, the owner, was the first licensed female guide in southern Morocco and will happily point you in the direction of some of the more interesting spots in and around Ouarzazate. Dinner here shouldn't be missed, whether dining poolside or indoors in the artsy dining hall; meals are served with a local spin on traditional Moroccan cuisine.

HOTEL LE BERBERE PALACE

Rue El Mansour Addahbi; tel. 0524/883 105; www.hotel-berberepalace.com; 2,000Dh d

Hotel Le Berbere Palace is the accommodation of choice for most film crews, directors, and actors working at the nearby Atlas or CLA studios. This large-scale hotel is littered with movie memorabilia from films that have been shot at the studios. The rooms are top-notch, with fluffy pillows and cozy beds. There is a surprisingly good buffet-style breakfast, and dinners are typically excellent, with tajines, salads, and, of course, couscous. The staff can seem aloof, but perhaps that's a small price to pay to possibly bump into a Hollywood star! The grounds are open to non-guests and are worth wandering around to take a look at the memorabilia and grandeur of this hotel.

INFORMATION AND SERVICES

The city code for Ouarzazate and the area is 24.

Post Offices and Courier Services

POST OFFICE

Ave. Mohammed V; Mon.-Fri. 8am-4:15pm and Sat. 8am-11:45am

The main post office, along the main road to Marrakesh, at the corner of the Rue de la Poste, has Western Union services. At higher-end hotels it is also possible to ask for postal service.

Money

Most banks are around the **Place Al-Mouhadine. Attijariwafa Bank** and **Banque Populaire** both have branches with 24-hour ATMs and exchange services (Pl. Al-Mouhadine, Mon.-Fri. 8:15am-3:45pm). There is another **Banque Populaire** (Ave. Moulay Rachid, Mon.-Fri. 8:15am-3:45pm) across from the Hotel La Palmeraie, down the street from the Hotel Le Berbere Palace. It will exchange travelers checks.

Hospitals, Clinics, and Pharmacies

The **Sidi Hssayne Ben Nacer Hospital** (Ave. Bin Sina) is equipped to deal with emergencies, though English is not commonly spoken. Pharmacies are found easily throughout Ouarzazate, especially around the Place Al-Mouhadine. All pharmacies have a list of after-hours and weekend pharmacies posted on their front door. For service outside of regular business hours, keep an eye out for "Le Pharmacie de Garde" posted on all pharmacy doors, with information in Arabic and French. **Pharmacy l'Aeroport** (151 Cité Al-Wahda, Mon.-Fri. 8:30am-noon and 3pm-7pm, Sat. 8:30am-12:30pm) and **Pharmacy Ouarzazate** (Mohammed V, just across from Pl. Al-Mouhadine, Mon.-Fri. 8:30am-noon and 3pm-7pm) are two of the more convenient pharmacies around.

GETTING THERE

By Plane

OUARZAZATE AIRPORT

north end of Ave. Mohammed VI, tel. 0524/887 340

Most visitors will arrive by bus or car, though the Ouarzazate Airport does have regular direct flights connecting with Casablanca, Marrakesh, and Paris via **Royal Air Maroc** (www.royalairmaroc.com), while budget carrier **Ryan Air** (www.ryanair.com) began direct connections with Bordeaux, Madrid, and Marseilles in April 2019. The airport is attached to the north end of the city, and taxis are the only option into town (15-20Dh), though if you're traveling light, you can consider walking the 2 kilometers (about a mile) into town through a residential neighborhood.

By Grand Taxi and Bus

The ***gare routière*** is just off Avenue Moulay Abdellah and is the primary hub for *grands taxis* and buses. ***Grands taxis*** regularly head to **Ait Ben Haddou** (30min, 32km/20mi, 100Dh, entire taxi only), **Kalaat M'Gouna**

(1.5hr, 90km/56mi, 30Dh), **Tinghir** (3hr, 165km/102mi, 70Dh), **Skoura** (40min, 40km/25mi, 15Dh), **Marrakesh** (4hr, 200km/124mi, 100Dh), **Casablanca** (6hr, 440km/273mi, 1,500Dh, entire taxi only), **Agadir** (5.5hr, 360km/223mi, 1,000Dh, full taxi only), and **Zagora** (3hr, 162km/100mi, 70Dh). There is a smaller *grand taxi* stop just off Place Al-Mouhadine with service mainly to Skoura.

Supratours (tel. 0524/888 566 or 0524/885 632, www.oncf.ma) is the bus line that extends the rail network. There are no trains in this region, but the Supratours bus does connect directly with **Marrakesh** (5hr, 1 daily, 75Dh), **Agdz** (1hr, 1 daily, 30Dh), **Zagora** (2.5hr, 1 daily, 50Dh), **Tinghir** (4hr, 2 daily, 55Dh), and **Merzouga** (8hr, 1 daily, 200Dh). There is a handy **Supratours office** (Ave. Mohammed V, Mon.-Fri. 9am-5pm) in the Tassoumaât neighborhood in the roundabout with the *Movie* monument.

The reliable **CTM** bus (tel. 0800/0900 30, www.ctm.ma) connects directly with **Marrakesh** (5hr, 4 daily, 80Dh), **Zagora** (2.5hr, 3 daily, 50Dh), and **Agadir** (6hr, 1 daily, 140Dh, overnight bus). For travelers continuing north along the N10, the daily 12:15pm bus starts in Ouarzazate and serves Skoura, Kalaat M'Gouna, Boumalne Dades, Tinghir, and Goulmima before arriving at **Errachidia**, making it an indispensable bus route for those exploring this region. The **CTM station** is at the corner of Avenue Mohammed V and Rue de la Poste.

By Car

If you are brave enough to drive in Morocco, be wary of the **Tizi n'Tishka pass** along the **N9** while coming from Marrakesh. Though an extraordinarily beautiful drive, this is also an extraordinarily dangerous one, with hairpin turns, blind corners, steep cliffs, and drivers rambling through without a sense of fear or safety. The pass should be avoided in winter, as the road will ice over, and after heavy rains, when landslides are a real threat. From **Agadir,** the **N10** is a picturesque road through the Souss and Anti-Atlas. Rains can be a problem, though the road is in generally good condition. From the north, the N10 also connects **Ouarzazate** along the northern scenic **"Road of 1,000 Kasbahs"** past the Dades and Todra Gorges through to **Errachidia.**

GETTING AROUND

Yellow ***petits taxis*** can shuttle you around the city for around 10Dh. Taxis here don't use counters, but anything over 20Dh is likely exorbitant. Most drivers are friendly and know most major hotels and restaurants.

Green **Lux Transport buses** (5Dh) also crisscross the city. Bus 4 conveniently runs along Avenue Mohammed V to Place Al-Mouhadine and the Taourirt Kasbah, usually every 30 minutes from sunrise to until midnight or so, though schedules are sporadic. Buses 1 and 2 pick up directly across from the CTM station (corner of Ave. Mohammed V and Rue de la Poste).

★ AIT BEN HADDOU

آيت بن حدّو

Just 32 kilometers (20mi) west of Ouarzazate lies the *ksar* of Ait Ben Haddou, one of the most impressive in all of Morocco. If you could only see one *ksar* in Morocco, this would be it. Set alongside a palm-lined hillside with the towering, oft snow-capped High Atlas Mountains servings as the backdrop, this crumbling series of six joined kasbahs and nearly 50 palaces has been a UNESCO World Heritage Site since 1987. Though the seasonal rains perpetually damage the buildings, the oldest of which date back to the 17th century, a nominal entrance fee to the *ksar* (10Dh) goes toward restoration efforts and maintenance.

For many years, Ait Ben Haddou was one of the great economic and cultural crossroads of the region and served travelers after their long journey through the desert along the caravan road to Marrakesh. Today, it is perhaps most famous as a filming location for a number of movies. *Gladiator, The Mummy, Kingdom of*

1

2

Heaven, Prince of Persia, and many, many other movies have used Ait Ben Haddou as a setting for their sprawling epics. Its sheer size, the winding medina roads, the clay brick walls, and the lingering calm that descends on travelers once they enter the gates to the sprawling *ksar* are all part of the magic. Be sure to pack an extra battery for your camera. It's irresistible not to take as many photos as possible of this photogenic gem.

Getting across the river to the *ksar* can be a challenge for some. There are sandbags in the river, which generally runs low enough that you can step across the sandbags to the entrance. A new footbridge built farther upstream runs across to the town gate farther uphill. Those staying in the calm confines of Ait Ben Haddou should keep this in mind, as cars cannot cross, and you'll have to carry across the river whatever you don't want to leave in the car.

Across the river from the *ksar* is a newer town that has sprung up in recent years, with hotels, cafés, and shops catering to tourists.

Food and Accommodations

For travelers wishing to stay at the *ksar,* there are several okay options. Some might consider this as an alternative to Ouarzazate on the way to the oases, gorges, or desert, as the *ksar* is a much more picturesque stopover for a night, though the lodgings are a bit rougher around the edges. There are several places to get a quick bite along the roadside, however the food on offer is not particularly savory. It's generally better to eat at your lodgings.

AUBERGE CAFÉ RESTAURANT TAMLALTE

Asif Ounila; tel. 0524/890 302; 200Dh d

The conveniently located Auberge Café Restaurant Tamlalte, just across the new walking bridge to the *ksar,* offers clean, simple rooms along the riverbank, with fantastic views looking out over the *ksar.* Wi-Fi and breakfast are included. Lunch and dinner are available on request.

MAISON D'HÔTE HAJJA

Ait Ben Haddou; tel. 0524/887 222; www.hajja-aitbenhaddou.com; 700Dh d

Maison d'Hôte Hajja offers stylish rustic lodgings right in the middle of the old *ksar,* with decorated clay-brick walls touched with traditional Moroccan *zellij* (mosaic tile work). Rooms are a bit on the tacky side but include en suite bathrooms and breakfast. Dinner is available on demand (60Dh). This is a good option for those looking to disconnect. It can be very, very quiet at night because of limited cell phone reception and no Wi-Fi. The terrace looks out over the valley, giving you a sense of what it must have been like to live here 200 years ago.

★ KASBAH TEBI

Kasbah Ait Ben Haddou; tel. 0661/941 153 or 0622/536 522; www.kasbah-tebi.com; 800Dh d

For a more romantic stay in the medina, Kasbah Tebi offers a unique experience in that everything is candlelit and there is no electricity, Wi-Fi, or TV. Set amidst the beautiful *ksar* of Ait Ben Haddou, this house has been in the family for 300 years, and your hosts will happily show you around and share stories of growing up in their family home with you. This is another wonderful option for those looking to connect with the incredible night sky and turn off their screens. Rooms are cozy, if a bit on the small side, but the beds are comfy and the experience is once-in-a-lifetime.

Getting There and Around

If you're driving to Ait Ben Haddou, head west from **Ouarzazate** via the **N9** before following the signs for the turnoff on **P1506** (30min, 32km/20mi).

Travelers without their own vehicles will have to come from Ouarzazate. The ***gare routière*** in Ouarzazate is just off Avenue

1: the Anti-Atlas Mountains, en route from Agadir to Ouarzazate **2:** a guide walking the streets of Ait Ben Haddou

Moulay Abdellah and is the primary hub for *grands taxis* and buses. ***Grands taxis*** regularly head to **Ait Ben Haddou** (30min, 32km/20mi, 100Dh, entire taxi only). There is a smaller *grand taxi* stop just off Place Al-Mouhadine, where you can also hire taxis to take you to Ait Ben Haddou.

Around Ait Ben Haddou, there are several places to park along the main road. The *ksar* is accessible only by foot.

North Draa Valley

The route through the **North Draa Valley** will take you through the scenic **"Road of 1,000 Kasbahs"** along the N10. Stops are possible at the Dades Gorge, Todra Gorge, and several smaller towns and palm groves along the way. For **hikers** and **trekkers,** the Dades Gorge offers some wonderful day hikes as well as a longer multi-day hike around Jbel Saghro. **Rock-climbers,** beginners, and dirt baggers, will want to spend a few days scaling the famous rock cliffs of the Todra Gorge. For those traveling from Ouarzazate to Fez or Erfoud and Merzouga, this is the best route to travel.

SKOURA

سكورة

Skoura has become something of an "it" spot for the well-to-do and Hollywood crowd. The palm groves here are stunning, and the kasbah, in crumbling reds and ochres, is breathtaking. It's easy to see why Skoura is on the radar of those in the know.

There is a *moussem,* or festival, held over the week before the Prophet's birthday, Eid Mouloud, culminating in the **Souk dial Am** (Yearly Market), the largest market of the year, which is a source of entertainment and commerce for families and businesses alike. This festival will fall in the last week of October in 2020 and be approximately two weeks earlier every year thereafter owing to the fact that the Prophet's birthday is celebrated according to the Lunar Calendar.

Sights

MUSÉE THEATRE: MEMOIRE DE OUARZAZATE (THEATER MUSEUM: MEMORY OF OUARZAZATE)

Dar Bahnini; tel. 0661/572 638; daily 8am-5pm; 20Dh

Just off the main road on the western side of Skoura is the Musée Theatre: Memoire de Ouarzazate, a small ethnographic museum dedicated to the preservation of the history and people of the region. The collection of artifacts is relatively small, but the collection of ancient manuscripts in beautiful Arabic calligraphy is worth the price of admission. Most explanation is available in English by Abdelmoula El Moudahab, the founder of the museum, who is usually around to conduct tours. Abdelmoula is a former English teacher who, because of his love for the region, created this museum in 2006 as a way to give back and preserve a bit of his heritage.

KASBAH AMRIDIL

Skoura Palmeraie; tel. 0524/852 387 or 0616/101 604; daily 8am-sunset; 20Dh entry

The elaborately decorated Kasbah Amridil is the most famous of all the kasbahs along the "Kasbah Road." It is even featured on the Moroccan 50-dirham note, as every English-speaking guide will be eager to tell you. There are two entrances for two different parts of this 17th-century kasbah. Because of a small family feud, the kasbah has been divided into two parts, with each charging its own entrance fee.

The Cunning Construction of Kasbahs and *Ksour*

mud bricks used in constructing the kasbahs

For hundreds, possibly thousands, of years, the people of southern Morocco have constructed an ingenious type of housing that is both eco-friendly and suitable to the harsh desert climate: the kasbah. Some of the finest specimens of these remarkable adobe constructions are found along the Dades Gorge and Draa Valley, making a famed stretch of road known locally as the "Road of 1,000 Kasbahs."

A **kasbah** (or *tighremt* in Tashelhit, the local Amazigh dialect) is a fortified house with corner towers built of adobe, a mixture of earth and straw. The material allows for cool air or warm air to flow, depending on the season. Originally, these structures were made by nomadic families seeking something better than their tents to protect them from both humans and nature. The center of a kasbah is a patio that opens toward the sky, specifically designed to allow in light. Typically, salons surround the bottom floor, and living quarters are upstairs. The intricate tribal motifs decorating the outside of the kasbah denote the wealth of the patron, with more decorations generally indicating more wealth.

If the kasbah has a single door with a rampart, it is then called a ***ksar*** (castle, or *imghrem* in the local Amazigh dialect; plural ***ksour***), though this distinction has been lost as *ksar* is now used to denote a walled village. The walls of these kasbahs and *ksour*, if not kept up, deteriorate quickly with the seasons. It only takes a few short decades or sometimes just a strong rain for them to reach a ruinous state.

These fortified houses were the seats of the lords of the region, one of the more famous being the Pasha of Marrakesh, El Glaoui. Generally, these houses are located on the edges of cliffs, tops of hills, or on the many rocky peaks of the region so that the lords could control the oasis, including the supply roads, and protect the inhabitants and passing camel caravans from invading bandits and looters.

Food and Accommodations

MUSÉE THEATRE: MEMOIRE DE OUARZAZATE (THEATER MUSEUM: MEMORY OF OUARZAZATE)

Dar Bahnini; tel. 0661/572 638; daily 8:30am-6pm; 65Dh

If you're looking to avoid the popular barbecued meats (*grillades*), call in the morning to arrange a delicious Moroccan lunch at the Musée Theatre: Memoire de Ouarzazate. There is little here aside from tajines, but the chef is originally from Agadir, which means that seafood is generally an option. The sardine-meatball tajine is warm, spicy, and will keep you going as you tour along through Skoura's expansive palm grove. Otherwise, the guesthouses listed also serve lunch and dinner by reservation, typically 100-150Dh for a fixed menu.

KASBAH FAMILLE BEN MORO

N10 Skoura; tel. 0524/852 212; 400Dh s, 600Dh d

Interestingly, the Kasbah Famille Ben Moro is a quaint guesthouse that serves as a sort of knockoff to the restored Ait Ben Moro next door. The service is perfectly friendly, if a little rough. This is a good option for those wanting to save a few dirhams and if everywhere else is full or you're arriving to town without reservations. Breakfast is included. Dinner is available on request (100Dh), though not recommended. There is Wi-Fi in the main lobby, and the pool is a great spot to relax.

AIT BEN MORO

N10 Skoura; tel. 0524/852 116; 700Dh s, 1,000 d

The refurbished kasbah Ait Ben Moro sits alongside the palm grove, right off the main roads. The rustic, minimalist decor, with lots of stone, wood, bamboo, and white linen blankets, puts you immediately at ease. The views over the oasis and to the distant High Atlas Mountains will reinvigorate the spirit, especially during warm springs as you soak in the pool, taking it all in. Accommodations include breakfast and dinner. There is a discount available if you don't want dinner, though dinner here is recommended. The chef can work with all of your dietary needs, including gluten-free and vegetarian.

LES JARDINS DE SKOURA

Skoura Palmeraie; tel. 0524/852 324; www.lesjardinsdeskoura.com; 1,200Dh d

In the summer, consider relaxing poolside beneath the olive trees at Les Jardins de Skoura. With plush beds and friendly service, this is an über-comfy stop for those seeking a little peace and quiet. The restaurant features Moroccan and Mediterranean specialties, such as cool beetroot gazpacho, *charmoula*-marinated zucchini, melon with ginger zest, or a coriander-flavored citrus fruit terrine. On winter nights, the dining room is warmed up by fellow travelers and a cozy chimney. If you're looking for a place to disconnect, or maybe reconnect with yourself, this is the spot.

Getting There and Around

If you're driving, Skoura is 40 kilometers (25mi) north of **Ouarzazate,** about an hour's drive on the **N10.**

Travelers without their own vehicles will have to come from Ouarzazate. The ***gare routière*** in Ouarzazate is just off Avenue Moulay Abdellah and is the primary hub for *grands taxis* and buses. ***Grands taxis*** regularly head to Skoura (40min, 40km/25mi, 15Dh). There is a smaller *grand taxi* stop just off Place Al-Mouhadine, where you can also hire taxis to take you to Skoura. The trusty **CTM** bus (tel. 0800/0900 30, www.ctm.ma) leaves Ouarzazate at 12:15pm (1hr, 1 daily, 20Dh). This same bus continues all the way to **Errachidia** and is a good line to know for those traveling north on the N10 past the Dades and Todra Gorges.

KALAAT M'GOUNA

قلعة مغونة

The tranquil little city of Kalaat M'Gouna (also: Kelaat M'Gouna and Kelaa M'Gouna), tucked at the foothills of the High Atlas, has long been the economic, social, and cultural capital of the area known locally as "The Valley of Roses"—named not only for the roses, for which this area is well known in perfume circles, but also for the color of the rocks, a sort of dusty pink color. The population is primarily Amazigh, so if you are working on learning the local dialects of Morocco, this is a great place to practice! The city gets its name from the nearby **M'Goun Massif**, which offers some wonderful hiking. Otherwise, most travelers will likely continue on to spend the night in the nearby **Dades Gorge**. However, for a few weeks in May, Kalaat M'Gouna is the most popular destination east of the High Atlas, with the annual **Rose Festival** transforming this otherwise quiet little city into a center of festivity.

Lining the roads are stalls of cooperatives, some more honest than others, who sell **rose water**, the famed derivative from the local roses. The deliciously pink damask roses, originally imported from Damascus, are known worldwide for their fragrant blossom, with the roses of this region generally thought of as being the best. Rose water is not cheap, even in Morocco, because it takes around 60,000 roses to produce one ounce of rose oil. The best time to visit this region is in April, when the roses are all in bloom, erupting in shades of pink for miles around.

Shopping

AZLAG DAGGER COOPERATIVE

N10 Kelaat M'Gouna; tel. 0524/830 000; daily 9am-6:30pm, closed Fri. afternoon

The Azlag Dagger Cooperative, at the entrance of town, past the rose sculpture roundabout, is the last place in Morocco where traditional daggers are made as they have been for seven centuries. Artisans work with traditional methods and tools to create these important pieces of Moroccan history, which you can take away for a song. Expect to pay 100-200Dh for a dagger using some good bargaining skills. Proceeds all go to support over 100 families in the region.

Festivals and Events

★ ROSE FESTIVAL

May

During the annual Rose Festival, held every May, the population of Kalaat M'Gouna doubles. The exact time of the festival varies year to year, but it is generally held over the first weekend in May. The families that arrive from around the country dance and sing long into the night, celebrating the harvest and the security of their loved ones. Rose petals seemingly float everywhere, over the souks, street vendors, and boisterous crowds, dancing on the light winds blowing down the High Atlas, drenching the scene in pinks, reds, and whites and gifting the parade procession with its fragrant blossom. A Rose Queen is selected to watch over the crop. Accommodations are limited in this region, so if you're planning on attending the festival, it is best to plan well in advance.

Getting There and Around

If you're driving, Kalaat M'Gouna is about 45 minutes north of **Skoura** (50km/31mi) on the N10.

Travelers without their own vehicles will likely have to come by **bus** or ***grand taxi*** from **Ouarzazate**, with the best option being **CTM** (tel. 0800/0900 30, www.ctm.ma). The bus leaves Ouarzazate (2hr, 1 daily, 35Dh) at 12:15pm and stops in Skoura before arriving in Kalaat M'Gouna. This same bus continues all the way to **Errachidia** and is a good line to know for those traveling north. In the other direction, the CTM bus leaves Errachidia (3.5hr, 1 daily, 75Dh) at 6pm and continues south to Ouarzazate, making it a solid option to travel south.

For those making use of the ***grand taxi*** from Ouarzazate to Kalaat M'Gouna (1.5hr, 90km/56mi, 30Dh), it's a good idea to sit in the most shaded part of the taxi or pay for two seats and take the front seat; in the hot months, roll the window down because the taxis are not usually equipped with air-conditioning.

1
2
3
4

★ Dades Gorge

مضيق دادس

Continuing the long, winding drive of the famed "Road of 1,000 Kasbahs," the **Dades Gorge** is a seemingly never-ending series of switchback turns that snake up from the small town of **Boumalne Dades** (also: Boumalene), through a gorge brimming with date palms, to the village of **M'semrir,** which serves as the current end of the paved part of the main road that continues on, unpaved, and leads to distant Imilchil. The sudden beauty of an ancient kasbah rising almost magically from a lush palm grove feeds the imagination like almost no other place in Morocco.

As at the nearby Todra Gorge, there has been more tourism to the Dades Gorge in recent years, resulting in a series of nice accommodations in the Dades, along with perhaps the best restaurant this side of the High Atlas, the family-run Auberge Chez Pierre. But it's still not hard to get off the beaten track and find places to hike after the string of hotels along the steep slopes at the beginning of the gorge.

The sunrises throughout the gorge are incredible, quickly casting sharp shadows over the looming, dusty rock face, worn slowly away by the river over the course of thousands of years. Nights can be chilly, freezing in winter, and in the warmer months the sun can be strong, so pack accordingly. The best time to visit is outside of the winter months, as rockslides and floods can be a concern.

There is a lot of **hiking** and **trekking** in this region, making this a popular stop with day hikers, families, and seasoned backpackers. Trout fishing is also a possibility for those looking to unwind, though you'll have to stock up on gear at Boumalne Dades before heading into the gorge. If possible, a drive all the way to M'semrir shouldn't be missed. Stop in at the Hotel and Restaurant Timzzillite after some of the most intense switchback driving in the world, take a deep breath, and continue on, stopping at the numerous turnoffs and viewpoints along the way to take a photo or stretch your legs with a short hike through the gorge.

1: sunset at a kasbah in the North Draa Valley 2: the Kasbah Amridil in Skoura 3: snapping photos in the Dades Gorge 4: the distant Monkey Fingers along "The Road of 1,000 Kasbahs"

Hiking

The Dades Valley is renowned for its hiking and trekking, and rightly so. There are hikes available for all fitness levels, each offering jaw-dropping scenery.

MONKEY FINGERS HIKE

Trailhead Immzoudar; 5 kilometers (3mi); easy; 1.5 hours

The most popular day hike takes you past the Tamlalt cliffs and the unique cliff formations nicknamed the Monkey Fingers, past a beautiful kasbah perching over the river (Ait Arbi), and through the Sidi Boubkar Gorge. This hike is 3-6 hours round-trip, depending on if you loop all the way around or hike to the Monkey Fingers and backtrack from there (5km/3mi, easy to the Monkey Fingers; 11km/3mi, medium difficulty for the loop). The head of this trail is unmarked, but lies at the small town of Immzoudar, about 17 kilometers (11mi) from Boumalne Dades. The trail isn't particularly well marked, but the path is clear enough with the cliff formation serving as reference to make a ½ day of self-guided exploration.

CANYON WALK

Trailhead at Dades Gorge entrance; 16 kilometers (10mi); difficult; 8hrs

Another popular hike, the canyon walk, sets off at the foot of the Dades Gorge. This will take most hikers 6-8 hours round-trip, depending on fitness levels and the length of your lunch break (35km/22mi, difficult). You'll climb up through incredible canyons and atop high plateaus, where you can take in superb views of the gorge and the many crumbling kasbahs along the way. This hike is best done with a guide and a big lunch.

JBEL SAGHRO

Trailhead at Boumalne Dades; 56 kilometers (35mi); difficult; 5 days

For more experienced trekkers, a long, sometimes difficult, 56-kilometer (35mi) circuit leaving from Boumalne Dades loops around the mountain of Jbel Saghro (also: Jbel Sarhro) and will take you from the gorge and its lush date palms through pine forests and steep, rocky cliffs. The path is not very well marked, so a topographical map is a necessity. You can pick one up in Boumalne Dades (look for the *Randonnée culturelle dans le Djebel Saghro* map); though the only map available is in French, it is easy enough to understand. This trek can be done in as little as 3 days, but with possibilities for overnight stays with locals as well as camping, it makes more sense to include 1-2 days for camping and giving time for cultural opportunities such as lunch with locals. A guide is recommended, though not necessary, and can easily be found by asking at any local hotel.

Food and Accommodations

Nearly all accommodations are packed alongside R704, so keep an eye out for signs—they're sometimes hard to spot, even in daylight. It's best to arrive before dark for this reason.

RIAD DES VIELLES CHARRUES

Km23, Ait Oudinar; tel. 0670/634 176; www.riadvieillescharrues.com; 250Dh pp

Riad des Vielles Charrues is a cozy guesthouse, well-lit, constructed the traditional way using adobe and lime-rendered *tadelahkt* (a traditional type of anti-humidity wall coating). Ambient music relaxes you throughout your stay, and the various magazines and books strewn about, left over from previous guests, add a sense of being at home the moment you step in the door. The rooms are natural and cozy, while the terraces give out to wonderful views over the gorge, day or night. Chef Aziza cooks up some delicious local cuisine, including various soups, seasonal vegetables, and, of course, couscous and tajines. Price includes Wi-Fi access and breakfast. This is one of the better deals in the gorge.

HOTEL AND RESTAURANT TIMZZILLITE

Km29; tel. 0677/264 347; 250Dh pp

At the top of the infamous winding road lies the well-located Hotel and Restaurant Timzzillite, with commanding views over the gorge. Rooms are basic, though the ample terrace space and windows facing the gorge, plummeting below, ensure great views from every room. Otherwise, there are more comfortable lodgings to be had. The restaurant (lunch 50Dh) and the on-site café are popular with road-trippers and hikers making their way through the gorge to stop for a quick tajine or coffee before taking off.

★ AUBERGE CHEZ PIERRE

Km26, Douar Ait Ouffi; tel. 0524/830 267; www.chezpierre.org; 900Dh s, 1,200Dh d

One of the most charming guesthouses in the entire region is Auberge Chez Pierre, 26 kilometers (16mi) from Boumalne Dades along the R704 in the middle of the Dades Gorge. This veritable stone palace rises up alongside the road to the Dades Gorge. After a short walk through arched tunnels, you arrive at a courtyard and a series of terraces, each looking over the Dades. The rooms are simple, rustic, and decorated tastefully with modern and tribal touches. In the cold winters, there is central heating or wood stoves to warm your room, while in the summer you can cool off in the pool. Suites are available. Wi-Fi and breakfast are included. The on-site restaurant features a seasonal European-Moroccan fusion menu. Dinner here should not be missed. Vegetarian, gluten-free, and other options are available to meet your dietary needs, though you will need to contact them ahead of time.

Camping

★ BERBERE DE LA MONTAGNE

Km34; tel. 0524/830 228; 15Dh pp, 15Dh tent, 12Dh car

This is a quiet, fantastic camping spot tucked farther up the gorge, just past where the road narrows, run by Berbere de la Montagne. The camping is situated next to the bubbling river. There is plenty of hiking nearby. Showers are available, along with Wi-Fi and meals. The hotel next door to the camping spot has small rooms suitable for a night's sleep (310Dh per person); though they're a touch expensive for what you get, it's a bargain for a place to stay in the gorge. However, this is best suited for those with a camper van or tent.

Getting There and Around

Boumalne Dades is an utterly photographic drive through the palm groves along the **N10** northeast of **Kalaat M'Gouna** (23km/14mi, 30min), **Skoura** (72km/45mi, 1hr), and **Ouarzazate** (116km/45mi, 2hr). If coming from the north, Boumalne Dades is southwest on N10 and is easily reached from **Errachidia** (187km/116mi, 3hr), **Erfoud** (follow the R702 until it meets the N10 at **Tinejdad,** 194km/121mi, 3hr), and **Tinghir** (53km/33mi, 1hr).

Travelers without their own vehicles will likely have to come by ***grand taxi*** or **bus** from **Ouarzazate,** with the best option being the **CTM** (tel. 0800/0900 30, www.ctm.ma). The bus leaves Ouarzazate (2.5hr, 1 daily, 40Dh) at 12:15pm and stops in Skoura and Kalaat M'Gouna before arriving at Boumalne Dades. This same bus continues to **Errachidia** and is a good line to know for those traveling north. In the other direction, the CTM bus leaves Errachidia (3hr, 1 daily, 60Dh) at 6pm and continues south to Ouarzazate, making it the best way to travel south.

In the Dades Gorge, all addresses are denoted by the number of kilometers along the route R704 from the town of **Boumalne Dades.** The town sits at the beginning of the gorge, where the N10 forms a T intersection with the R704, which starts into the gorge, following the river. If you're driving, start counting kilometers from here to find your accommodations.

★ TODRA GORGE

مضيق تدرة

The Todra Gorge is an incredible, once-in-a-lifetime-type drive that follows the route R704 through the lush palm grove and into the towering red rock cliffs that soar 300 meters (980ft) into the air. This booming tourist hot spot has seen much change over the last few years. The beginning of this relatively short drive is dotted with placards advertising restaurants and hotels, as well as newer houses, which stand testament to this recent

Catch a ride through the oasis with Said and his camel, Jimi, based in Tinghir.

boom. Despite these developments, the gorge has held onto its natural beauty, marked by the towering rock faces that widen and then narrow to a space just a few yards apart, as the road follows the trickle of the river up to the nearby village of Tamtattouchte and eventually to Imilchil farther into the High Atlas.

The nearest town is Tinghir, which doesn't offer much for tourists, though it is possible to park your car and **walk through the palm grove** or take a **camel ride through the oasis,** starting from the lookout point at the oasis along the R703, the route to the Todra Gorge. Keep an eye out for **Said** and his two camels, Jimi Hendrix and Bob Marley—rides are anywhere from 50Dh on up, depending on the length of the ride you want to take and your bargaining skills. There are numerous ATMs and a post office along the main road, which can come in handy.

Rock-climbers have taken to this area with unbridled passion, making it one of the premier spots to scale some rock. The high cliff walls offer hundreds of routes for sport and multi-pitch climbing routes, all on solid, reddish limestone. The numerous climbing routes cover a wide range of difficulty; this is a great place for beginners to learn the basics of climbing. **Hikers** will find plenty of well-marked (and not so well-marked) trails through the surrounding countryside.

This is an area best visited outside of wintertime, as flooding and rockslides can be a major concern during winter and the temperatures can drop below freezing. Even in the spring and fall, the afternoons can be cold as soon as the sun drops, casting the gorge in shadow.

Rock-Climbing

For rock-climbing, if you have your own gear, you can go it on your own through numerous bolted climbs that have been established, though most likely you will need to rent some gear and possibly climb with one of the local rock-climbing companies or guides. Whatever you do, be sure to check for the most recent topos for the most up-to-date information. **Hassan Mouhajir** keeps a hand-drawn topo guide, the most authoritative in the area. He doesn't keep an office or have a phone, so it's best to ask for him at a hotel, café, or just on the street. He is a small man, in his 40s, and usually wears a Mammut T-shirt so people recognize him. He usually will invite you to his family home in the kasbah, where you can sit down with him over a mint tea to learn the latest news on the rock before you begin climbing. He sells handwritten, colored guides that he photocopies for climbers.

The rock itself offers plenty of sport, pitch, and single-trad climbing opportunities, with hundreds of different routes throughout the gorge for climbers of all levels. New routes are constantly being established. The diverse grades, rock formations, and skill levels make the Todra Gorge the premier rock-climbing spot in Morocco.

ADVENTURES VERTICALES

Tizgui commune de Todgha el Oulia; tel. 0524/895 727 or 0678/953 592; Spain tel. 34-0663/193 689; www.escalade-au-maroc.com; 40Dh pp (1-3 people 120Dh total)

Adventures Verticales has a great rope course they can take you on as well as rock-climbing guides with Spanish and English usually available, depending on what guide is available. If you need an English-speaking guide, it's best to arrange before arrival. Their shop at the beginning of town rents and sells gear. You can also check out routes and topographic maps from here. All climbs are done with one monitor for every three climbers.

CLIMB MOROCCO

http://climbmorocco.com

With Climb Morocco, all guides are certified Wilderness First Responders with the American Mountain Guide Association and specialize in single-pitch climbs, courses for beginners, and bouldering. They have numerous climbing locations around Morocco, including the Todra Gorge, as well as native English speakers. The company is based out of Marrakesh, so it's best to contact them ahead of time to arrange for guides or instruction. They provide all of the needed equipment (including harness, helmet, and shoes), so all you have to do is just tie in and start scaling some rock. They are best contacted through their website.

Hiking

You won't need a guide to hike around the Todra Gorge, though a topographic map (such as the one available from Hassan Mouhajir) might help for those looking to do longer excursions. Several day hikes are easily accessible at the foot of the gorge and there are several more trailheads farther into the gorge. Addi Sror, the owner of the Auberge le Festival in the middle of the gorge, beyond the Hotel Yasmina, has marked several trails in this part of the gorge that offer different grades of hiking.

Horse Riding

ASSETTIF AVENTURE

tel. 0524/895 090 or 0668/357 792; www.assettif.org; 150Dh

If you're looking to cover more ground in an eco-friendly manner without the use of four-wheel-drive, Assettif Aventure offers day and overnight trips by horseback. Short trips range from a one-hour ride for 150Dh to a longer day trip with a picnic lunch included for 500Dh. Trips leave from the nearby village of Tizgui, through the gorge 12.5 kilometers (8mi) from Tinghir. This is a wonderful way to explore the nearby mountains and meet with locals.

Food and Accommodations

LE PETIT GORGE

Km2, Todra Gorge; tel. 0524/895 726; daily 9am-10pm; 70Dh

Several indistinguishable eateries and cafés line the street through the gorge, all standard but serving acceptable local cuisine. Keep an eye out for Le Petit Gorge, which offers a set menu for 120Dh that's large enough for two people to split. The Berber Pizza on offer is best shared on the shaded terrace after a long day-hike, with the crumbling kasbah, trickling river, and afternoon call to prayer echoing down the valley providing the lunchtime backdrop. Wi-Fi is available, though this is a place best enjoyed sans Facebook updates.

HOTEL VALENTINE

Douar Tizgui Ait Baha; tel. 0524/895 225; www.hotel-valentine.net; 500Dh d

Just up from the main gorge, the Hotel Valentine is in the middle of the bustle of the gorge, for those wanting cafés, eateries, and shops nearby. The service is friendly and the guesthouse is a couple of blocks off the main street, facing the river. Rooms are clean and decorated in earthy reds and browns, with the rooms facing the river more ideal for their wonderful views out over the nearby kasbah. The pre-dawn call to prayer (*fajr*) in the nearby mosque can be unsettling for some and wondrous for others.

RIAD TIMADROUINE

Douar Timadrouine Ouaklim; tel. 0615/933 980; www.riadtimadrouine.com; 500Dh d

Riad Timadrouine, 22 kilometers (14mi) southwest on the N10 from downtown Tinghir, is a gem of an establishment. Located just between the Dades and Todra Gorges, this quiet establishment is just the thing for those looking for a more luxurious retreat in the region. This adobe mansion manages to respect the traditional kasbah-style architecture of the region while infusing it with just a hint of modernity. It has a pool and an on-site hammam that you can use free of charge, as well as a generous terrace to lounge on and take in the Moroccan sun and nearby Jbel Saghro. Breakfast is included. Dinner and lunch are available on request and consist of well-done traditional Morocco tajines, couscous, and a nice variety of salads.

★ AUBERGE LE FESTIVAL

Km5, Todra Gorge; tel. 0661/267 251; www.aubergelefestival-todragorge.com; 800Dh pp

For a wonderful Todra Gorge experience, the Auberge le Festival offers a chance to stay in an eco-friendly environment. The auberge is built from local stone and features five surprisingly comfortable, chic rooms nestled in the natural caves, alongside more traditional options spread throughout the guesthouse. The stay includes all meals, with most ingredients harvested from the on-site garden. Electricity is solar powered with a backup generator. The auberge lies in the middle of the gorge in a tranquil spot past the clutter of traders and hustle of street sellers. Addi Sror, the owner, is always around and is an avid hiker who can lead you to some trails. Other members of the staff are licensed rock guides and can lead you on climbs in the area.

Getting There and Around

The drive through the Todra Gorge follows the **R703** north from **Tinghir.** The towering cliff face of the gorge begins almost as soon you exit Tinghir and meanders along the riverbed at the bottom of the gorge past several small villages and encampments. **Parking** is generally available along the side of the road near the hotels and cafés.

Travelers without their own vehicles will have to come by **bus** or ***grand taxi*** and be dropped off at nearby **Tinghir,** where ***grands taxis*** will take you into the Todra Gorge for 15Dh a seat. The taxi will drop you off at your lodging. While in the gorge, you'll likely be walking everywhere, so pack a good pair of shoes.

TINEJDAD

تينجداد

For those continuing north along the N10 to the Ziz Valley, Erfoud, or Merzouga (or conversely, those traveling south on the N10 from Errachidia or Erfoud), a stop by **Tinejdad** can be a welcome treat.

Sights

OASIS MUSEUM (MUSÉE DE OASIS)

Ksar el Khorbat; tel. 0555/880 355; www.elkhorbat.com; 20Dh

Though it's not much more than a drive-through town, the wonderful Oasis Museum is located here. Housed in the restored Ksar El Khorbat, this museum is a great way to break up a long drive. It was created by Juan Romero, who also restored the Kasbah Ait Ben Moro in Skoura and has a passion for this region of Morocco. The museum covers the diverse artisans of the area, different styles of pottery, kitchen utensils, agricultural tools, and the building of the many *ksour* and kasbahs of the region. An hour in this museum is like a

a cozy, surprisingly chic cave-room at the Auberge le Festival in the Todra Gorge

university crash-course ethnographic seminar on the history and people of this region.

LALLA MIMOUNA SPRINGS MUSEUM (MUSÉE DES SOURCES LALLA MIMOUNA)

2km west of Tinejdad on the N10; tel. 0535/786 798; daily 8am-7pm; 50Dh

Another interesting stop for those driving is the Lalla Mimouna Springs Museum. Constructed around a series of rejuvenated springs, this ethnographic museum covers the history of the region and features a small gift shop full of locally made goods. Tours are available in English, though most signage is in French.

Getting There and Around

Tinejdad lies at the crossroads of the **N10** and the **R702.** From the north, Tinejdad is reached via the N10 through **Errachidia** (86km/54mi, 1.5hr) and from the south via **Tinghir** (54km/34mi, 45min), **Boumalne Dades** (106km/66mi, 2hr), and **Ouarzazate** (222km/138mi, 3.5hr). Conveniently for those travelers coming to or from **Erfoud** (104km/64mi, 1.5hr) and **Merzouga** (146km/91mi, 2.5hr) and the desert, the R702 connects directly with Erfoud.

GOULMIMA

كلميمة

Whether you're driving from the north via Fez or from the south via Ouarzazate, the ancient kasbah of **Goulmima** provides an interesting diversion and is a great place to stop for lunch. The kasbah, called Ighrem n'Iguelmimen (Castle of Lakes) by the locals, is in the process of restoration and is still lived in by hundreds of people, making it a thriving, bright kasbah, not like the abandoned kasbahs left to ruin in the rest of Morocco. English-speaking guides are readily available for the kasbah (50Dh).

Festivals and Events

JEWS OF ASHURA FESTIVAL (UDDAYN N' ASHUR)

10th day of the Islamic month of Muharram, around Aug. 30, 2020, and Aug. 19, 2021

Celebrated here during the Islamic holiday of Ashura, two months after Eid al-Adha, this is a Judeo-Berber tradition originating in Goulmima's mellah, carried out today by Muslims who don masks and chant the stories of two popular Jewish protagonists, Moshe and Biha. Now, the festival gives opportunity for locals to shout their demands from the government and voice their opinions. Original, sometimes spontaneous plays are often performed by the locals, adding to the sort of strange mix of political festivity.

Accommodation

CHEZ PAULINE FERMES D'HÔTES

Tadighoust; tel. 0535/885 425; 400Dh d

There are not many options for sleeping in Tadighoust, though Chez Pauline Fermes d'Hôtes, a guesthouse farm about 20 kilometers (12mi) from Goulmima in the Tadighoust Palmeraie, is a very interesting option in the area. The rooms are warm, feature en suite bathrooms, and are decorated stylishly with African masks, plenty of plants, and wood furniture. This is one of the more unique places to rest your head in this part of Morocco. Breakfast is included.

Getting There and Around

Goulmima is a quick drive from **Tinejdad** (22km/14mi, 20min) north along the **N10.**

Travelers without their own vehicles will likely have to come by ***grand taxi*** from either **Errachidia** (1hr, 60km/37mi, 30Dh) or **Tinghir** (1.5hr, 77km/48mi, 35Dh). A **CTM** bus (tel. 0800/0900 30, www.ctm.ma) leaves from Errachidia (1hr, 1 daily, 20Dh) at 6pm and continues south to **Ouarzazate.**

South Draa Valley

The route through the **South Draa Valley** will take you through the largest palm grove in Morocco, the Draa Valley Palmeraie, which has an estimated two million date palms, including the incredible oasis of **Zagora.** The well-paved National Road 10 (N10) climbs up through a pass cutting through the Anti-Atlas Mountains—a spectacular, dry, rocky chain of mountains thought to have once been taller than the Himalayas, though now little more than hills of crumbling rock—before ending at **M'hamid,** the literal end of the road and beginning of the great Sahara.

From Zagora it is possible to continue deeper into the **Anti-Atlas** following the N12 to **Foum Zguid,** a small oasis town about 1.5 hours from Zagora. From Foum Zguid, you can continue into the little-explored southeastern corner of Morocco alongside the closed border with Algeria, though this region is best traveled outside of summer (too hot) and winter (storms and cold nights).

Most will likely take the road from Foum Zguid toward **Tazenakht,** a beautiful 77-kilometer (48-mi) drive up through the Anti-Atlas, which will put you back on the N10, heading west to Agadir and the Atlantic Coast or back north to Ouarzazate and across the High Atlas to Marrakesh.

For **hikers** and **trekkers,** there are several good day hikes from Zagora. **Dromedary (camel) rides** and **four-wheel-drive excursions into the desert** are available from M'hamid. This is an area best explored by those wishing to get off the well-worn tourist track. Though there is tourism here, the area remains one of the least-visited regions in Morocco, particularly the road after Zagora.

AGDZ

أگدز

Those with a bit more time might consider stopping in **Agdz** (also: Agdez). Though seemingly little more than one of the numerous drive-through towns dotting the national roads of Morocco, Agdz is deceptively interesting. For **hikers,** the towering **Jbel Kissan** hovering toward the north provides numerous options for day hikes and, with a guide or a good topographical map, possibilities for longer treks in the area (it's best to inquire at your lodgings).

Sights

TAMNOUGALT KASBAH

9 kilometers (5mi) southeast of Agdz; daily, hours vary; 10Dh entry, 50Dh guide

Those interested in the architecture of the various kasbahs should take the opportunity to visit the Tamnougalt Kasbah just outside of the main town. The kasbah itself sits imposingly above the palm grove, with steep, red-rock hills providing an impressive backdrop. A guide to tell you about its hidden history is recommended for exploring the kasbah and its maze of corridors.

During the first week of October the **Ellama Tamnougalt** celebration (*moussem*) is held at the kasbah. This religious and cultural event brings together the villagers of the Draa Valley and helps the kasbah to maintain its long-held position as a preeminent village meeting place in this part of the valley. The kasbah makes a nice stop for those looking to break up the drive to Zagora.

Accommodations

FERME AUBERGE BERBÈRE OURIZ

Douar Aouriz in the Tanassift Commune; tel. 0524/843 960; 150Dh d

The Ferme Auberge Berbère Ouriz offers a chance at eco-friendly housing in the region. The rooms are simple, though the walls of this out-of-the-way guesthouse will leave some wondering at the bizarre patchy pink and orange color scheme. The price includes breakfast. This is a great place for those looking to give back a little and watch their carbon footprint. The farm encourages and practices ecological production of fruits and vegetables (including the local dates) as well as delicious goat cheese.

Getting There and Around

Agdz is well connected along the **N9** with **Ouarzazate** (74km/46mi, 2hr) to the northwest. The two-lane highway is easy enough to manage, though crossing the Anti-Atlas can be nerve-wracking, with a few sharp turns and usually one or two trucks slowing the crossing.

Travelers without their own vehicles will have to come by the local bus or the ***grands taxis*** that occasionally make their way here from Ouarzazate (1.5hr, 70km/43mi, 30Dh) and **Zagora** (2hr, 90km/56mi, 35Dh). The reliable **CTM** (tel. 0800/0900 30, www.ctm.ma) runs buses that leave Ouarzazate (2hr, 3 daily, 35Dh) in the afternoon (4pm-5pm) and stop here on the way to Zagora.

★ ZAGORA

زاكورة

Located in the middle of the Draa Valley oasis among literally millions of palm trees, **Zagora** once served as the gateway to the desert and the main city along the route to Timbuktu. This is a charming oasis quickly developing with guesthouses and boutique hotels scattered throughout the palms. Though increasingly popular with those traveling the south of Morocco, Zagora is still far enough away that it maintains the feeling of an oasis.

Most **hikers** and **trekkers** will be content to wander through the palm grove and, if feeling adventurous, make for some of the surrounding low-lying mountains. A trip up the mountainside rewards hikers with breathtaking views over the palm grove and, on a clear day, out to the sandy wastes of the desert. For longer hikes, it's best to check with your lodgings to arrange for a guide.

The famous painting of a blue-turbaned Sahrawi with a line of dromedaries that you will see countless replicas of, ***Tombouctou—52 Jours,*** once marked the beginning of the dromedary relay, which took traders from this important trading post all the way to Timbuktu. Though obviously altered over the centuries, the painting (or something like it) has marked this spot in Zagora from the 16th century, noting to passersby its strategic importance along the caravan route as well as the role the valley played in collecting tolls and taxes paid by traders along the route. The painting is still there, just outside the Province Building, at the head of the road to Foum Zguid (N12).

A lively souk is held on Wednesdays and Sundays, which can provide a nice diversion as well as cheap food and supplies for those looking to take a multi-day trek around the region. The **Hammam Al-Massjid** (10Dh, 12Dh for shower) is central, directly next to the big mosque. They have hours in morning and evening for men, while women have the hammam to themselves throughout the afternoon.

Camel Rides

In truth, there are no real camels in Zagora or the rest of Morocco. You'll only find **dromedaries** here. The difference between a camel and a dromedary is easy enough to distinguish: A dromedary has one hump on its back and a camel has two humps. In practice, everyone really calls the dromedaries of Morocco camels, and there are plenty to be had in Zagora to take you on excursions into the desert (though from Zagora the desert is still quite a distance, and four-wheel drive is a better option for most people wishing to ride into the Sahara sun). Dromedary tours are best arranged ahead of time with a reputable tour company, such as **Amazing Journey Morocco** (tel. 0665/952 465 or 0661/354 093, www.amazing-morocco.com), which also offers four-wheel-drive tours. However, other options are available in town for those

The Route to Timbuktu

Centuries ago, Zagora was an important stop for traders traveling by caravan through the long desert route between Timbuktu and Marrakesh. Traders carried valuable spices, manuscripts, gold, and other treasures along this route, paying tolls along the way as they passed from oasis to oasis. The most valuable of the treasure that was carried was the prized salt of the Sahara, from which this route took its name: the Salt Road.

With the advent of the salt trade in the 12th and 13th centuries, ideas began to travel back and forth, with Timbuktu rising in the middle of the desert as a distant, mythic center for scholarship and scientific and religious inquiry. The influence of this trade of ideas was felt strongly in Fez, the spiritual and educational center of Morocco, as well as in nearby villages such as Tamegroute. Libraries were constructed, manuscripts collected, and knowledge gained.

the beginning of the road to Timbuktu in Zagora

The Salt Road was often crossed more quickly by using posted dromedaries, so at each station riders would have fresh transportation that was watered, fed, and ready to cross the hot desert. Today, traders still use the southernmost part of this route in Mali as they take salt harvested from Taudenni, about 14 days from Timbuktu.

wishing to squeeze it in at the last minute, though you might have to negotiate hard for a good price.

At the roundabout where Boulevard Mohammed V (the main road) crosses the river and turns south to M'hamid is a stand of **local guides** who can arrange for trips by the hour (100Dh) or by the day (800Dh). This is a place to practice your negotiation skills. For larger groups, substantial discounts can be had.

Food

CAFE LITTÉRAIRE ZAGORA

Blvd. Mohammed V, next to the CTM station; tel. 0661/871 623; daily 8am-10pm; 10Dh

Jet past the drab-looking entrance and head straight back to the chill courtyard into the Cafe Littéraire Zagora, quickly becoming the meet-up spot for those who like music, art, and books. You can almost always count on a few musicians being around and the small collection of books to keep you company as you sip on one of the best espressos this side of the High Atlas.

KSAR TINSOULINE

45 Ave. Hassan II; tel. 0524/847 252; www.ksar-tinsouline.ma; daily noon-midnight; 50Dh (bar)

In a pinch, you could stay here. However, the real draw is the bar. Stop in for a nightcap after dinner out or to change pace from your other lodgings. These are modern digs in a decidedly unmodern setting. If you are staying the night, you'll be set back around 500Dh. The heating here is one of the most reliable in town for those cold desert nights. There is an on-site hammam (100Dh) as well as a swimming pool.

LE DROMADAIRE GOURMAND

Blvd. Mohammed V, by the Total gas station; tel. 0661/348 394; daily, hours vary; 40Dh

Le Dromadaire Gourmand, a cavernous Moroccan salon with a small patio along the main road, is a convenient stop along the route to Zagora, serving up a full Moroccan menu with a few vegetarian options, including *zallouk* (eggplant salad) and carrots with *charmoula* (a mix of garlic, olive oil, and parsley). Call ahead of time for camel meat, roast lamb (*michoui*), or the famous *tajine de mariage* (traditionally served for wedding feasts).

Accommodations

RIAD DE RÊVE

353 Hay Moulay Rachid; tel. 0677/191 337; 400Dh d

Abdesselam El Bali, the gregarious owner of the *riad*, will make sure you are well looked after. He can also arrange for your excursions to the desert in lesser-touristed environs for a perhaps more authentic Sahara *sejour* (1,500Dh per person for a night and day, all meals and transportation included). The stay at the *riad* includes a breakfast larger than you could possibly eat.

LA PERLE DU DRAA

Hay Amzrou, 3Km just after leaving Zagora; tel. 0524846210; 550Dh d

A large hotel on the south end of town on the road to Mhamid with 40 rooms. Though the property could use some updating, particularly the bathrooms, the rooms themselves are clean and all have a private terrace. For the price, there isn't a lot to complain about, particularly for families coming in at the last minute. Wi-Fi, air-conditioning, pool, and breakfast are included. The familial apartments are worth a look. If you come up with your Moon Guidebook, Hassan, the owner, will give you a 10% discount.

DAR SOUFIANE

Route de Nakhla BP 78; tel. 0524/847 319; www.riaddarsofian.com; 800Dh d

Dar Soufiane is well located on the edge of the palm grove. The style is eclectic: some Moroccan, some tribal, some Arabesque. Rooms are small but cozy, and there's a charming patio decorated with cacti and palms as well as a large swimming pool complete with pool-side bar, reminiscent of Hawaii. This is a great place to turn off and zone out for a few days. The price includes breakfast. Dinner is available, with select vegetarian options.

★ VILLA ZAGORA

Piste du Djebel; tel. 0524/846 093; 800Dh d

The charming, hospitable Villa Zagora is well located on the eastern edge of the oasis along the road leading up through the mountains (take a left at the roundabout at the end of Boulevard Mohammed V as it turns south to M'hamid). What sets this villa apart is the feeling that when you stay inside its walled garden, you feel at home. The traditional mudbrick construction, colorful bougainvillea, and smiling service all add up to a relaxing retreat in the oasis. Throw in Aisha and Naïma's stupendous cooking, and this is far and away one of the better accommodations in the region. Rooms are top-notch, with lots of natural linens and shelves dotted with books and memorabilia, and a small pool in the middle of the palm grove is perfect for a quick dip. For travelers on a tighter budget, there are a few rooms available with a shared bathroom for a hefty discount. Wi-Fi and breakfast are included with your stay. Dinner is available on request and highly recommended. Alcohol is available, as well as vegetarian options.

Camping

CAMPING SERDRAR

11km south of Tazarine near Zagora; 60Dh

Campers should consider Camping Serdrar. The camp is along an unpaved road northeast of Zagora, tucked into the folds of the breathtaking rocky hills endemic to this region, among a small grove of palm trees. Facilities are all modern, with hot showers available (10Dh) as well as bivouac-styled tents (350Dh). The staff can organize dromedary rides, hikes into the nearby hills, and fossil hunts, which can provide hours of entertainment for kids.

Getting There and Around

Zagora lies east on the **N9** from **Ouarzazate** (163km/101mi, 3hr) and **Agdz** (92km/57mi, 1.5hr).

1
2
3
4

Travelers without their own vehicles will have to come by ***grands taxis*** that make their way here from **Ouarzazate** (3hr, 90km/56mi, 70Dh) or by bus. The **Supratours** bus (tel. 0524/888 566 or 0524/885 632, www.oncf.ma) leaves from Ouarzazate (2.5hr, 1 daily, 50Dh) at 8pm. The reliable **CTM** (tel. 0800/0900 30, www.ctm.ma) also runs buses that leave Ouarzazate (2.5hr, 3 daily, 50Dh) in the afternoon (4pm-5pm). While in Zagora, yellow *petits taxis* will take you around town—though they are unmetered, most trips should run 10-15Dh.

TAMEGROUTE

تامكروت

From the 11th century, Tamegroute (also: Tamgrout) has served as the religious center of the region, making it a must-visit for Muslims traveling the region and those with an appreciation for ancient manuscripts. In this region, the Nasir family is one of the most revered. In the 17th century, Sidi Muhammad bin Nasir al-Drawi founded the Nassiriyya, a particular Sufi order that is still very influential in the region. Sidi Muhammad bin Nasir al-Drawi, a theologian, scholar, and physician, was particularly interested in mental disorders. Today people still descend on his shrine at the Zawiya Nassiriyya hoping to be cured of their mental ills.

Visitors might also be interested in taking a tour of the **Tamegroute Ksar.** You won't need a guide (though many will likely bother you if you don't have one). The small maze of streets are mostly covered and generally not well lit, which provides a nice sense of foreboding as you walk through where many of the local potters make the famed green pottery of this village in the semi-dark. This can be especially lively during the weekly **Saturday souk.**

The **green pottery** on display pretty much everywhere you look is native to this village. Many years ago, the elders of the village wanted to create more industry to make the village grow into a city and thus raise its status. They used Timbuktu and nearby Fez as likely models for the type of city it might become, a center for learning, culture, and pottery. The skill of the potters was imported from Fez, though exactly how the dark green hue, made of magnesium and copper, is created continues to be a closely held secret. Today, the entire industry of pottery has become an industry of solidarity, with the entire village working together and sharing the proceeds.

Sights

TAMEGROUTE LIBRARY

N9 Tamegroute center, look for a left turn at the roundabout; open daily, hours vary; free

At one time, the library attached to the Zawiya Nassiriyya, now known as the Tamegroute Library, housed one of the richest libraries in all of North Africa. It was a true center of learning. Over the years, thousands of manuscripts have been lost—some stolen, some sold, and some dispersed to other libraries around Morocco. There are still over 4,000 manuscripts well worth seeing. You can find an immaculate 11th-century Quran written in calligraphy on gazelle skin; Amazigh poetry transcribed into Arabic; a 15th-century Egyptian book of astronomy illustrated with signs of the zodiac, planets, and the solar system; ancient maps of the world; and other incredible treasures—though few of these are actually displayed. No photos are allowed. Entrance is free, though tips are appreciated to help upkeep the library as best as possible.

Shopping

POTTERY COOPERATIVE

N9 Tamegroute center, on the left just after the roundabout; open daily, hours vary; free

Just after the newer part of town and right after the roundabout, continue straight on to the beginning of the old town of Tamegroute to find the Pottery Collective. Abdellah is the

1: Tazenakht, just outside Ouarzazate in the South Draa Valley, is well known for its rugs. **2:** Abdellah, a proud Saharaoui and potter in Tamegroute **3:** a rug rolled out for a night in the desert **4:** an inviting suite in Dar Azawad

local potter who speaks great English. He is usually around, so you can just ask for him. He can lead you around and show you how the pottery is made from its earthy beginnings, the artisans wheeling bowls and plates to life, and the stoves where the pottery is fired and the mysterious greens of the famous Tamegroute pottery first reveal themselves. There is no official charge for the tour, but 25Dh per person is a fair price. Even better, take away a few pieces of pottery for yourselves as gifts or souvenirs. Even a small purchase does a lot for the local economy.

Getting There and Around

Tamegroute is a short drive east from **Zagora** (22km/14mi, 30min) along the **N9.**

Travelers without their own vehicles will have to come by either bus or *grand taxi* from **Zagora. *Grands taxis*** leave from downtown Zagora (30min, 20km/12mi, 35Dh), and a **CTM** bus (tel. 0800/0900 30, www.ctm.ma) leaves **Ouarzazate** (3hr, 1 daily, 60Dh) at 4:15pm. You can catch this same bus in nearby Zagora (20min, 1 daily, 20Dh) at 7pm as it passes through; it is always preferable to buy a ticket ahead of time, as spots are not always available. The CTM bus continues to the dusty drive-through town of **Tagounit** (4hr, 70Dh from Ouarzazate, 1.5hr, 30Dh from Zagora) and **M'hamid** (5hr, 80Dh from Ouarzazate).

M'HAMID

محاميد الغزلان

M'hamid (short for M'hamid al-Ghizlan) is at the literal end of the road. Historically, this was a settlement for Hassani-speaking nomads. It now serves as a tourist staging point for desert excursions, with a few cafés and snack restaurants. Some travelers might spend the night here or in the nearby village of **Bounou** before or after heading out into the desert.

Beyond M'hamid, the great **Erg Chigaga** rises, the largest sand formation in this part of the desert. Amid epic sand dunes, bivouac tents have been established near deep-water wells. Here you can spend nights beneath the stars, with constellations seen free from the light pollution of major cities, bringing the intricacy and immensity of the night sky alive. Erg Chigaga is five days round-trip by dromedary and four hours by car. **Erg Lehoudi** (Jewish Dunes) is an easier-to-manage day trip from M'hamid, though far more cluttered with tourists and trash and far less interesting. A relatively easy-to-drive road takes you north

a potter in Tamegroute

from M'hamid (8km/5mi) to Erg Lehoudi and can be driven without four-wheel drive.

Just before M'hamid lie the twin villages of Bounou and Oued Driss. While Bounou hosts a number of great options for accommodations, Oued Driss is the more interesting locale. This is a 400-year-old traditional village that hasn't changed. Shadowed corridors covered by palm fronds keep the passageways protected from the searing desert sun. Rays of light pierce through, alighting the mudbrick adobe walls magically, making for a wonderful exploration and to catch a glimpse of how day-to-day life has been lived out here for hundreds of years.

While in Oued Driss, make a quick stop by the **Oued Driss Museum** (20Dh for entry, 30Dh for guided tour of museum, kasbah, and tea). Though you'll find artifacts of Arab, Berber, and Jewish life from the region, the real treat is the 400-year-old house itself with its incredibly well-preserved Arab-Berber construction. Ibrahim, the owner and operator of the museum, is university educated and speaks English well enough for a quick tour (30 minutes-1 hour).

Most **desert wildlife** tends to be nocturnal, but keep on the lookout for sand fish (also known as the Berber skink), sand lizards, desert sparrows, the black-and-white *tamanghar* (a small bird said to bring the *baraka*, or "blessing"), the elusive fennec fox, and the endangered dorcas gazelle. Animals are generally found near water and their food source. Look for evidence of their passing by in the early mornings near your camp.

The souk of M'hamid is on Monday, making this a good day to stock up on fruits, vegetables, and supplies for those planning longer treks in the area.

★ Desert Camping

A quintessential trip through Morocco includes at least one night in the desert. Though it's possible, and generally easier, to check this off the "must-do" list in Merzouga at Erg Chebbi, it is infinitely more interesting and somehow conceptually closer to the idea of a night in the desert to do this at **Erg Chigaga.** The desert camps are more spread out and the trip out takes much longer, especially if done by dromedary, adding to the sense of being really disconnected and off the grid. Though it is possible to drive out to Erg Chigaga with your own four-wheel-drive, it is not really recommended. The desert shifts, often imperceptibly, and drivers have been known to get lost. For this reason, it is best to go with a guide.

AMAZING JOURNEY MOROCCO

tel. 0665/952 465; www.amazing-morocco.com; 700Dh

Amazing Journey Morocco has friendly, English-speaking tour guides with four-wheel-drive vehicles who know the area very well. Not only can they do tours around the desert and Erg Chigaga, but they also lead treks by foot and camel through the stunning Draa Oasis to the Erg Lehoudi at the edge of the desert. Their campsite in Erg Chigaga has rustic Bedouin-style tents complete with bathrooms and a restaurant worthy of Scheherazade.

Food and Accommodations

The small Amazigh village of **Ait Ghanima** nearby can provide some food and supplies. Besides desert camping, there are a few kasbah-styled lodgings along the road to M'hamid from Zagora. The village of **Bounou** (8km/5mi from M'hamid) is now basically a concentration of small hotels and provides the best lodgings in the area.

★ LA KASBAH DES SABLES

Bounou; tel. 0662/403 115; 250Dh d

One of the absolute best values in the region is La Kasbah des Sables, a wonderfully authentic guesthouse in the middle of the oasis. Palm trees cast shade from the hot Sahara sun and the swimming pool is cool and inviting. The barbecue is open for anyone to use, so it's possible to throw your own desert-front barbecue with food bought at the local souk. Wi-Fi is available, as are meals (on request). The staff is friendly and will be happy to find you a guide for the treks out in the desert and other more interesting, often out-of-the-way, gems that encompass the diverse nature of the region.

★ DAR AZAWAD

Bounou; tel. 0524/848 730; www.darazawad.com; 800Dh d

Dar Azawad was featured as one of the Top 10 most far-flung romantic getaways by traveller.com in 2016, and it's easy to see why. While some might be drawn to the on-site hammam (130Dh for a basic spa; a massage will set you back 400Dh with a full spa service including exfoliation), nearly everyone will dig the traditional Draa-style architecture with lots of touches from the desert and the local tribes, including wood doors, carpets, and traditional palm wood and reed ceilings. The property has an on-site bar, a pool, and Wi-Fi throughout. The rooms all have air-conditioning and en suite bathrooms. For a real treat, and if the budget allows, take the Sultan's Suite (2,500Dh). It will make you feel like a real pasha. The private terrace looks out into the palm groves and Sahara for a perfect night of private stargazing with your partner. Make sure to treat yourself to one of Salah's special juices while you're there. I'm partial to his homemade lemonade, a refreshing break from mint tea. A three-course dinner can be included with demi-pension for 180Dh per person.

CHEZ LE PACHA

Bounou; tel. 0524/848 696 or 0524/848 207; www.chezlepacha.com; 800Dh d

Chez Le Pacha is the local five-star, a sprawling complex featuring numerous restaurants and a lavish pool. The spacious rooms are romantically set around a beautiful flower garden, making this a veritable oasis beyond the oasis. Larger rooms are available. An on-site hammam offers full-body massages, perfect after a couple of days in the desert or a few days of trekking. Service is friendly, food is outstanding, and rooms have air-conditioning, which is practically a necessity. The hotel can arrange for trips to several different campsites in Erg Chigaga and the Sahara. The restaurant (Mon.-Fri. 8:30am-12:30pm and 2:30pm-6pm, Sat. 8:30am-1pm, 100Dh) requires reservations, though typically you can call just an hour or so before arrival and they should be able to have something prepared for you.

Getting There and Around

Getting to M'hamid is easy; just follow the **N9** east until the end of the pavement. It's possible to reach M'hamid in one day from **Ouarzazate** (261km/162mi, 5hr), though a more casual pace will have you stopping at either **Agdz** (190km/118mi, 3.5hr) or **Zagora** (100km/62mi, 2hr) overnight.

Travelers without their own vehicles will have to come by ***grand taxi*** from **Zagora** (2hr, 100km/62mi, 50Dh). The **CTM** bus (tel. 0800/0900 30, www.ctm.ma) that leaves **Ouarzazate** (5hr, 1 daily, 80Dh) at 4:15pm makes its final stop in M'hamid. It is possible to board this bus at its stops in Agdz, Zagora, and Tamegroute, though seats are not guaranteed. Book ahead of time. (Note that the CTM website uses an alternative spelling of M'hamid. It's listed there as "Lamhamid Ghozlane.") To continue from M'hamid, you need either a dromedary or a four-wheel-drive vehicle.

Ziz Valley

مضيق زيز

Travelers wishing to visit the desert from Fez or Meknes generally pass through the **Ziz Valley,** the northern palm grove that marks the historically important Ziz River (Oued Ziz) and the passage through the High Atlas Mountains to the Middle Atlas. The river begins around Er-Rich in the High Atlas and flows south through a craggy gorge and into the desert, providing the water for the palm grove as well as the cities of **Errachidia, Erfoud,** and **Rissani.** Most travelers now pass through the Ziz Valley without a second thought, snap a few photos, and continue on directly to **Merzouga,** the booming tourist town at the foot of the great **Erg Chebbi,** though those with a bit more time on their hands might want to slow down the pace and do a little more exploration along this route.

ERRACHIDIA

الرشيدية

There is little to do in Errachidia (also: Ar-Rachidia). It serves primarily as an administrative hub for those working in the area and a connection hub for travelers making their way to/from the desert. The newly paved streets lined with streetlights and palm trees give it an attractive air. Several snack shops dot the route if you need to break for lunch.

Food and Accommodations

Nearly every village along National Road 13 (N13) from Midelt has a few snack places for a quick bite to eat, and there are many in Errachidia. Decent accommodations, however, can be scarce. There are few places to stay along the way, and even in Errachidia the accommodations veer toward the Moroccan business traveler and other more lewd options where prostitution can be a real concern. Most travelers are best served by continuing past Errachidia to spend the night in the guesthouses outside of Errachidia or just pushing on to Erfoud, where the selection is more acceptable.

GITE D'ETAPE VALLÉE DE ZIZ

Aoufous, between Errachidia and Erfoud; 250Dh pp

The friendly Gite d'Etape Vallée de Ziz is a simple, frills-free guesthouse just off the main road. There is no telephone to make reservations. Accommodations are on a first-come, first-served basis. Rooms are exceptionally clean, and the breakfast spread is ample and included in your stay. Ask for a room off the main road in the back, where you will have your own private balcony. For a night away from it all, this can be a quiet precursor to a stay in the desert in Erfoud or Merzouga.

MAISON D'HÔTE ZOUALA

Aoufous, between Errachidia and Erfoud; tel. 0555/578 182; 350Dh d

Also a little off the main road is the cozy Maison d'Hôte Zouala, a relatively new guesthouse, though all the construction has been done using traditional materials. The service is excellent and the meals are breathtakingly delicious, including savory tajines that seemingly melt in your mouth. They also do some of the best vegetarian food around. The rooms are basic, though decorated with a local touch.

Getting There and Around

BY PLANE

The **Moulay Ali Cherif Airport** (off the N13 on the north end of town, tel. 0699/984 085) has direct flights with **Casablanca** via **Royal Air Maroc** (www.royalairmaroc.com), though most travelers will likely be traveling into Errachidia by bus, either CTM or Supratours, which arrive and depart from the ***gare routière*** on Rue M'daghra, just off the N13 in the center of town.

BY GRAND TAXI AND BUS

Grands taxis leave regularly to and from **Erfoud** (1hr, 73km/45mi, 20Dh), **Rissani** (1.5hr, 93km/57mi, 30Dh), and **Goulmima** (1hr, 60km/37mi, 20Dh) from Errachidia. Other destinations are possible, though you will likely have to bargain for your taxi rate and pay for the entire taxi.

The overnight **CTM** bus (tel. 0800/0900 30, www.ctm.ma) leaves Errachidia for **Fez** (7.5hr, 1 daily, 135Dh), **Meknes** (6hr, 2 daily, 120Dh), **Rabat** (7.5hr, 1 daily, 170Dh), and **Casablanca** (9hr, 1 daily, 200Dh). Overnight buses leave at either 9:30pm or 9:45pm. Those heading to **Ouarzazate** (5.5hr, 1 daily, 90Dh) will want to pay attention to this line, which follows the N10 south and calls on **Tinghir** (2hr, 1 daily, 50Dh) and **Kalaat M'Gouna** (3.5hr, 1 daily, 70Dh), making it indispensable for those using the bus to explore this region into the North Draa Valley. For those venturing into the desert, the bus for **Erfoud** (1.5hr, 1 daily, 35Dh) departs Errachidia at 5:30am and continues to **Rissani** (2hr, 1 daily, 40Dh). Getting to Errachidia is easy enough; buses leave daily from **Fez** (7.5hr, 1 daily, 135Dh) and **Ouarzazate** (5.5hr, 1 daily, 90Dh).

Supratours (tel. 0524/888 566 or 0524/885 632, www.oncf.ma) operates two daily buses out to **Merzouga** (2.5hr, 2 daily, 60Dh) with stops in **Erfoud** (1hr, 2 daily, 40Dh) and **Rissani** (1.5hr, 2 daily, 50Dh). The morning bus leaves at 5am and the evening bus at 6:30pm. A convenient overnight Supratours bus leaves **Fez** (8.5hr, 1 daily, 120Dh) every day at 8:30pm. Tickets must be purchased at the ONCF or Supratours booth at the *gare routière* or the train station, ideally a few days ahead of travel so you ensure getting a seat.

BY CAR

The **N13** passes through Errachidia and will take you all the way to **Erfoud** (74km/46mi, 1hr) and **Merzouga** (133km/83mi, 2hr). It is possible to join the N13 from **Fez** (336km/208mi, 6hr). Follow the **N8** into the Middle Atlas, past the towns of **Immouzzer, Ifrane,** and **Azrou,** before joining the N13 and following the road signs to Midelt and Errachidia. From **Meknes** (328km/204mi, 6hr), the route is a bit more straightforward, taking you directly through **El Hajeb** and **Azrou** on the N13. After crossing the Middle Atlas, the road treks through high mountain peaks and vast plains before plunging into the dramatic Ziz Valley.

From the North Draa Valley the drive is straightforward, following the **N10** north from **Ouarzazate** (303km/188mi, 5hr) through **Tinejdad** (82km/51mi, 1hr) to Errachidia.

ERFOUD

أرفود

Erfoud (also: Arfoud) was the longtime village at the edge of the desert and the palm grove when Merzouga was little more than a couple of nomad tents near a waterhole. Now, most tourists skip Erfoud and head directly for Merzouga, which is a shame. There is still a lot happening in the town of Erfoud, with a few restaurants, a lively daily market, the annual Date Festival, and the renowned fossil mines around the region. Hotels and *riads* are a little less expensive than those found in nearby Merzouga and offer predominantly the same services, though most are beginning to show their age. For alcohol, you will need to dine at one of the restaurants in the hotels or check out the lounge bar at Hotel Tizimi. Those looking to dive into the region and do more than a night in a desert should consider spending a night or two in Erfoud. This is a real edge-of-the-desert town with all of its whimsicalities and hardships.

Festivals and Events

AICHA DES GAZELLES

www.rallyeaichadesgazelles.com; Mar.

The annual Aicha des Gazelles is a unique event—it's the sole international off-road rally for women only. It takes place over 10 days every March, with the race beginning in Erfoud and ranging throughout the desert, ending in faraway locations such as Foum Zguid and Essaouira. This is a lively event featuring racing teams from all over the world who compete in this off-road rally without the use of GPS, support teams, cell phones, or even updated maps, though helping other racers is encouraged. The towns greet the racers as they pass through, making this a real spectacle for locals and travelers alike.

DATE FESTIVAL

Oct.

At the end of October, the annual Date Festival is held to mark the harvest season and the region's primary historic source of income. This is one of Morocco's richest regions for dates, with the local variety, Mejoul (also: Medjool), thought to be the best. This three-day festival offers lots of free local music, dancing, activities, and, of course, a load of dates. It has really gained in attraction over the last few years, so book hotels and other lodgings well in advance of the end of this month.

Food and Accommodations

CAFÉ PIZZERIA RESTAURANT DES DUNES

104 Ave. Moulay Ismail; daily 11am-11pm; 50Dh

There are few restaurants besides the ones in the hotels, but Café Pizzeria Restaurant Des Dunes is perfectly acceptable, with a large, cool dining space as well as a terrace to enjoy the more warm nights. Right on the main avenue, it is easy to find and is a nice change of pace from many of the heavier meals around. Ask for the specialty of the region: *kalia*, a meat buried in the hot sand to cook. Vegetarian versions are available but likely contain meat fat. Pizzas here are all wood-fired, simple but delicious.

HOTEL TIZIMI

Route de Jorf; tel. 0535/576 179; www.kasbahtizimi.com; 600Dh d

Of the midrange choices, a longtime favorite, Hotel Tizimi, is one of the cozier options, with a Bedouin-styled entry, swimming pool, restaurant, and fully stocked bar. Rooms are a bit dated, but for the price compared to the rest of the region, it's hard to nitpick. Rooms all feature en suite bathrooms and Wi-Fi, and rates include breakfast. A picture of Kate Winslet taken while she stayed here is proudly displayed at the desk. The nights here are quiet and just the thing after a stressful few days in one of the bustling Moroccan medinas. One of the better deals in the region.

LA ROSE DU DESERT

Route du Errichidia (off the main road just outside Erfoud center on the north end of town); tel. 0675/411 076, http://hotellarosedudesert.com, 800Dh d

For garden lovers wanting a respite in a true oasis, La Rose du Desert is well worth the price of admission. This hotel is popular with in-the-know Europeans looking for a high-end getaway desert experience. The adobe building has a large central swimming pool surrounding by a lush, palm-lined desert garden with lots of cozy nooks and corners for curling up with a book or sunbathing. The staff can arrange excursions to the desert, including luxurious overnight stays as well as four-wheel-drive options and camel caravans. Though the junior suites provide a good value, the private bungalows are a bit more private and spacious; however, avoid the bungalows in the winter months as heating for those cold desert nights can be difficult. Breakfast and Wi-Fi are included. Othmane, the manager, can be slow about answering emails, so it's best to follow up with a phone call to ensure your reservation.

Getting There and Around

Erfoud is reached from the north via the **N13** from **Errachidia** (74km/46mi, 1hr) or from the south along the **R702,** which connects with the **N10** at **Tinejdad** (104km/64mi, 1.5hr).

Both the **CTM** (tel. 0800/0900 30, www.ctm.ma) and **Supratours** (tel. 0524/888 566 or 0524/885 632, www.oncf.ma) buses have local offices on Boulevard Mohammed V by the Hotel de Ville (city hall) to arrange travel and purchase tickets (daily 9am-8pm).

The CTM bus leaves for **Errachidia** (1hr, 1 daily, 30Dh) at 8:10pm before continuing on to **Fez** (8.5hr, 1 daily, 155Dh). The bus to Erfoud departs Errachidia (1.5hr, 1 daily, 35Dh) at 5:30am. Book ahead of time to ensure a seat.

Supratours operates two daily buses from **Errachidia** (1hr, 2 daily, 40Dh) that stop in Erfoud; the morning bus leaves Errachidia at 5am and the evening bus at 6:30pm. The bus leaves for Errachidia (1hr, 2 daily, 30Dh) at 9:30am and 8:30pm.

Grands taxis are usually the quickest way to get in and out of town. From Erfoud, they leave from the local market. Prices to or from **Errachidia** (1hr, 73km/45mi, 20Dh), **Rissani** (30min, 25km/15mi, 8Dh), and **Merzouga** (1hr, 60km/37mi, 20Dh) can be negotiable if you purchase an entire taxi. Keep in mind, it is always possible to purchase multiple seats so that you can leave sooner or have more room. Single travelers should think about buying the front two seats, especially if it's hot out. This makes for a much more pleasurable journey.

RISSANI (SIJILMASSA) الريصاني

Directly on the road to Merzouga lies the historically important town of Rissani (also: El-Rissani and Sijilmassa). Though little more than a dusty large market town, Rissani does offer plenty of distractions for an afternoon. Those with more time might find themselves taking a tour around the ruins of Sijilmassa and visiting the famous Rissani Souk; both are interesting diversions for an afternoon, but as with many things in Morocco, timing is everything.

For trips to the desert, most travelers opt to stay in either Erfoud or Merzouga. In Rissani, there are not many options for lodging.

Sights

MAUSOLEUM MOULAY ALI CHERIF

off the P7101 near Ksar Abbar on the eastside of town; free

Muslim travelers may be interested in visiting Mausoleum Moulay Ali Cherif, one kilometer from the end of the main road near the exit for Merzouga. Moulay Ali was the founder of the current Moroccan Alaouite dynasty and is the most venerated saint in the region. The rebuilt mausoleum, constructed in 1965, is tastefully decorated and is a spot of pilgrimage for many Moroccans. The king visits occasionally. Non-Muslim visitors are welcome to tour the garden courtyard and take respite from the heat.

SCENIC DRIVE

Otherwise, there is a picturesque drive marked by a "Cirque Touristique" sign approaching Rissani from Erfoud. This 8-kilometer (5-mi) drive takes you past the ruins of **Sijilmassa**, through palm groves and several interesting kasbahs, many of them still lived in. Ksar Charfat Bahaj at Oulad Tineghras is interesting to stop at and tour. However, the most interesting kasbah to visit, Ksar Ouled Abd el Halim, toward the end of the circuit, is currently under restoration work; it features updated adobe work as well as several ruined palatial *riads* with original layouts, *zellij* work, and Arabic inscriptions, exuding a sense of what it must have felt like to live in this oasis at the end of the great Sahara.

Shopping

On non-souk days, the local market is still busy with shop owners, street vendors, local shoppers, tour groups, and others all winding their way through, shopping for goods and bargaining for fruits and vegetables, whole goats, and sheep, as well as traditional drums. Fridays and holidays are typically quieter than most other days.

RISSANI SOUK

Rissani center

The Rissani Souk, the largest souk in the

The Sijilmassa Empire

Historically, Rissani was an incredibly important town better known in the annals as Sijilmassa. The location of Sijilmassa at the terminus of the Ziz River made it the natural end for the northern terminus of the trans-Sahara trading route, and the abundant dates and water supply made conditions temperate and ensured food and water for the region. The wealth of the city grew, and by AD 771, it divided from the Abbasid caliphate, making itself the first independent kingdom in the region.

Several famous travelers, including Ibn Battuta in the 14th century and Leo the African in the 16th century, passed through Sijilmassa on their tours through the region and recounted the size and beauty of the city, elevating its legend to a near-mythic status. The city was falling into ruin until Sultan Moulay Ismail ordered it to be rebuilt in the 18th century. In 1818, the nomadic tribes of Ait Atta destroyed the city once and for all.

Today, Sijilmassa lies on the outskirts of Rissani, mostly destroyed, though a few kasbahs and *ksour* still stand in the midst of the palm grove, slowly crumbling into ruin. Though this area is protected by the World Monuments Fund as an endangered site and preserved by the Moroccan Ministry of Culture, little has been done in recent years to preserve the ancient city.

region, happens three times a week: Tuesday, Thursday, and Sunday. This is well known for being one of the better places in Morocco to shop for **silver,** though you will still need to bring your best bargaining cap to the table. Earrings, necklaces, brooches, rings, hairpins, and all manner of jewelry can be found, often with tribal and modern designs, though make sure that all jewelry has the required stamp reading 925. This stamped number denotes the quality of the silver and ensures you are purchasing real silver and not something else.

Food

CAFÉ RESTAURANT CHAKROUNI

off the P7101 near Ksar Abbar on the eastside of town; daily 8am-10pm; 25Dh

Just off the main road to Merzouga, at the turnoff for Mausoleum Moulay Ali Cherif, is the incredibly convenient Café Restaurant Chakrouni. It has free Wi-Fi and is one of the better spots around for a quick breakfast or lunch.

Getting There and Around

Rissani is a short drive south from **Erfoud** (23km/14mi, 30min) and north from **Merzouga** (42km/26mi, 45min) along the **N13.**

At the ***gare routière,*** on the outskirts of town at the western entrance, you can find the **CTM** bus (tel. 0800/0900 30, www.ctm.ma). CTM buses to Rissani depart from **Errachidia** (2hr, 1 daily, 40Dh) at 5:30am, stopping in **Erfoud** (30min, 1 daily, 20Dh) along the way. Buses leave for Errachidia (2hr, 1 daily, 40Dh) at 7:30pm before continuing on to Fez (9.5hr, 1 daily, 160Dh).

Supratours (tel. 0524/888 566 or 0524/885 632, www.oncf.ma) operates two daily buses from **Errachidia** (1hr, 2 daily, 40Dh) that stop in Rissani; the morning bus leaves Errachidia at 5am and the evening bus at 6:30pm. The Supratours bus leaves for Errachidia (1hr, 2 daily, 40Dh) at 8:30am and 7:30pm.

Grands taxis are usually the quickest way to get around this part of Morocco. They arrive and depart from Dar Atakafa, near the mellah in the middle of town. **Errachidia** (1.5hr, 93km/58mi, 30Dh), **Erfoud** (25min, 20km/12mi, 8Dh), and **Merzouga** (30min, 35km/22mi, 10Dh) are common runs in the region. It is always possible to purchase multiple seats so that you can leave sooner or have more room. Single travelers should think about buying the front two seats, especially if it's hot out, and, if possible, sit on the opposite side of the car from the sun. This makes for a much more pleasurable journey.

MERZOUGA

مرزوكة

Snug against the beginning of the vast Sahara desert, Merzouga was little more than a collection of a few Bedouin tents a few short years ago. The undeniable draw of the desert has proven irresistible for tourists, as evidenced by the number of new hotels and specialty *riads* that have recently sprung up, as well as the new paved road from Rissani and new boulevard. Merzouga exists largely for tourism, though this hasn't taken away from its seemingly magical pull.

For most travelers, Merzouga is the end of the road. With a four-wheel-drive you can brave the unpacked, sand-strewn route to **Al-Taous,** though this is largely an area exploited for its phosphorous mines. There are a few faded petroglyphs in the area, though the majority are knock-offs carved by industrious locals. Birders will want to look out for the lake, **Dayet Srji**—known as Dayet Tifert by the locals—that usually forms to the west of Merzouga, toward the mountains in the midst of the black-rock desert. During the winter, several migratory birds make their way here, including the **greater flamingo.**

Guides

The region is best explored with a guide for those who don't have much time but want to be able to experience a glimpse into the desert culture and are looking for something a bit more than just a night in the Sahara.

MOROCCO GEO TRAVEL

tel. 0661/503 500; www.moroccogeotravel.com

If you're interested in rocks and stars, this is the outfit to contact. For your trouble, you will get a superb lesson in desert astronomy as well as the geology of the area, which are, surprising for some (like me), intimately linked. While attending a short lecture, you'll learn how the Little Dipper is known throughout the Sahara as "the baby camel," while the Big Dipper is known as the "mama camel." Excursions are available into the outlying region to discover the geology of the region and some of the different fossils to be found, many of them remnants of when Morocco was buried in the last Ice Age. For families and young archeologists in the making, a must-do bit of desert erudition.

ABDELKARIM TATA

tel. 0662/294 386; www.tataziztrekking.com; email: abdelkarim.tata@gmail.com

The most dependable, honest guide in the region is Abdelkarim Tata. Tata can arrange for day trips in the region, including the nearby Ziz Valley, four-wheel-drives into the desert, overnight trips into reputable Bedouin nomad camps, and meals with a nomad locally famous for his *madfouna,* a local specialty of ground camel, chicken, or cow and onion seasoned, spiced, and folded, slow cooked beneath hot desert sands (a non-traditional but equally delicious vegetarian option is available). Tata has also plotted a hike with houses where trekkers can stay that cuts through the Tafilalt region.

M'HAMMED "HAMID" SERGOUI

tel. 0621/218 521; www.moroccodesertstargazing.com; email: contactastrohamid@gmail.com

Hamid has studied geology and astronomy for over 20 years and has done a number of lectures in the U.S., Europe, and even Japan. He is a veritable wealth of information about Bedouin and Touareg culture in the region. Hamid can arrange an excursion into the desert where you will be able to collect your own fossil to take home as truly one-of-a-kind souvenir.

Erg Chebbi

عرق الشبي

From a great distance, the ocher brilliance of Erg Chebbi rises high above Merzouga.

1: the black desert meets Erg Chebbi in Merzouga **2:** motorbikes in the sand dunes **3:** hitting the sandy slopes **4:** tea service in the desert in Merzouga

1
2
3
4

Though not as big as some of the great sand seas of the Algerian or Libyan Sahara, it is beautiful nonetheless and a stunning reminder of the sheer awesomeness of the Sahara. Throughout the day, the sands shift in shades of red and pink, making for breathtaking pictures and ever-changing scenery. As the French writer Antoine de Saint-Exupéry once wrote: "One sits down on a desert sand dune, sees nothing, hears nothing. Yet through the silence something throbs, and gleams."

A vast *hamada* (barren, rocky plateau) separates this piece of the Sahara from the rest of the desert, making it something of a curious sight in this otherwise rocky region. The dunes rise to heights of nearly 150 meters (500ft) and spread out over an area of more than 500 square kilometers (200 square miles). Though more touristed than the other great sand sea, Erg Chigaga outside of M'hamid, this *erg* is much easier to reach, and even with the increase of tourism, a quiet night beneath the stars with the hush of the desert is still very much a possibility.

There are several ways to tour Erg Chebbi. The easiest is to walk, though trekking through the dunes is tough work. Still, many people make it out on foot to the tallest sand dune to take in a sunset. ATVs are another possibility, but the noise and the pollution they create make this practice something highly discouraged. Not only are ATVs noisy, but they only serve to really ruin the beauty of this sand formation. For traveling into the desert, there are, of course, more natural solutions . . .

CAMEL RIDES

Numerous **guides** with their camels—sorry, *dromedaries*—hang out right at the base of Erg Chebbi. In the off-season, some deals can be had if you bargain hard. The typical going rates are 100Dh for a ride out to enjoy the sunset, 200-500Dh for an overnight stay with dinner and breakfast in a Bedouin tent, or 700-1,000Dh for a "luxury stay" overnight complete with en suite toilets. You've come all this way . . . it would be a shame not to ride that camel, or rather, dromedary, out into that wonderful Saharan sand and experience a bit of life in the desert.

As a rule of thumb, those looking for a quieter night beneath the stars should stick to the camel rides leaving directly from Merzouga right at the base of Erg Chebbi. Typically, these tours head south of Erg Chebbi into the quieter parts of the dunes. For those wanting a bit of luxury, this is the place to be, as all the luxury Bedouin tent camps are here. For those that don't mind the buzz of quads and dirt bikes, or those looking to save a few dirhams, head to Ksar Hassi Labied just 3 kilometers north of Merzouga. The tours here veer toward the northern half of Erg Chebbi and are usually a 100Dh or so less expensive.

SANDBOARDING

One of the new rages is to surf the sand. This is done with old snowboards, for rent at numerous spots throughout the village of Merzouga for anywhere from 50Dh to 100Dh for a full day. Rental includes boots, board, and bindings. These are all recycled goods, tossed-off snowboards that have been used and abused, though they are perfectly good for shredding some sand. Keep in mind that there are no "sand lifts" here, so you'll have to do the trekking up the dunes yourself. This is a fun diversion in the desert, though seasoned surfers, skiers, and snowboarders will likely get quickly bored from the lack of speed. Still, it makes for some good photo ops, and when is the next time you're going to be able to surf a part of the Sahara?

TOP EXPERIENCE

★ DESERT CAMPING

This is what you came all the way out here for, right? A night—or maybe a weekend—in the desert. There are many ways to spend the night in the desert, some more comfortable than others. Any of the guides at the edge of the *erg* will be able to arrange an overnight camping trip, usually including a tajine dinner, water, and tea as well as a light breakfast. Overnights typically range 200-500Dh per person. Bargain hard.

Gnawa Music

KHAMILA

The ever-rhythmic Gnawa music is popular in these parts, with many Gnawa musicians entertaining around the different hotels and even in the far-out villages. The music itself has a much more spiritual feel, and the most renowned musicians often fall into a trance as they communicate with the spiritual world through this ancient music. The village of Khamlia is home to an incredibly popular Gnawa musician group. Trips out to Khamlia to listen to the musicians, sip tea, and eat lunch can be arranged with any of the tour guides or through your accommodations. Khamlia is 7 kilometers (4mi) beyond Merzouga on the route to Taouz. For those without a car, it's sometimes easier to catch a taxi from Rissani (40min, 48km/30mi, 40Dh); although taxis can be had in Merzouga (20min, 7km/4mi, 20Dh), you'll likely have to pay the entire taxi fare.

Food

Besides the hotel restaurants, there are few options for dining around Merzouga.

CHEZ JORDI & NAIMA

N13 Merzouga; tel. 0661/631 591; daily early-late (hours vary); 50Dh

Just off the main road at the entrance into town, this is the best of the small snack stands and cafés. They serve cold beer, which can be a welcome reprieve after a hot day. Otherwise, the snacks in town offer the same fare (salads, meatballs, chicken tajines) without much variation.

CAFÉ FATIMA

R702 Hassilabied; daily, hours vary, generally 10am-9pm; 50Dh

You will also find Cafe Fatima, a nonsmoking cafe that is also a great hub if you are interested in renting snowboards or skis (100Dh), bicycles to tour the town (from 50Dh), and even quad rentals (from 300Dh). If you're feeling hungry, try the Berber omelette (35dh) deliciously spiced and cooked in a tajine.

Accommodations

Just outside of Merzouga the old village of **Ksar Hassi Labied** has developed over the last 20 years, adding to the number of boutique hotels and serving the popularity of desert excursion. Several smaller *riads* and hotels nestle at the foot of the dunes. Ksar Hassi Labied is a bit quieter than Merzouga, with fewer hotels and auberges, making this a little bit of a better spot to get a good night of sleep cozied up to the Saharan dunes. The easiest route into Ksar Hassi Labied is to take a left as you come into Merzouga on the asphalt road that makes a T-intersection with the main road right at the post office and Al Barid Bank.

RIAD OUZINE

Ksar Hassi Labied; tel. 0535/576 508; www.riadouzine.com; 300Dh d

Riad Ouzine offers comfortable lodging with breakfast and dinner included. The simple, clean lodgings are a real bargain in this part of the country. The staff is friendly, honest, happy to help you with anything you might need, and given enough notice will do their best to help with dietary restrictions. Though you are welcome to sleep in, the terrace views over the dunes at sunrise are incredible. There are nonsmoking rooms and Wi-Fi is available, in case you can't totally disconnect.

RIAD MAMOUCHE

Ksar Hassi Labied; tel. 0666/662 110; www.riadmamouche.com; 400Dh d

A good option for families because of the large rooms that can fit up to five people very comfortably, Riad Mamouche spreads out, circling around a small swimming pool, the perfect spot for a little tanning while the kids play in the water. There is a second courtyard, an Andalusian-style garden where birds happily chirp throughout the day, adding to the

Alhambra-esque allure of this *riad*. Alcohol is served in the restaurant, making this a popular stop. Air-conditioning, Wi-Fi, and a bountiful breakfast buffet are all included, and the rooms are all nonsmoking. Camel rides directly from the hotel can be arranged (350Dh per person) and include comfy lodgings, as well as campfire, music, and a tajine dinner for a slightly livelier night in the desert.

HOTEL YASMINA

Merzouga; tel. 0535/576 783; http://hotelyasminamerzouga.com; 700Dh d

Hotel Yasmina was one of the very first hotels in Merzouga. It started over 20 years ago as a series of Bedouin tents on the edge of the desert and has expanded to include standard rooms in a traditional mudbrick kasbah that sits on the edge of the desert lake. They are far enough away from the cluttered hotels and *riads* at the end of the paved road that, though not quite the experience of the Bedouin tents in the desert, spending the night here still gives the feeling of isolation expected from the great Sahara. Rooms are comfortable, with wonderfully hot showers, and breakfast and dinner are included. Bedouin tents, just next to the hotel, are also available (200Dh) and include breakfast. This is a fantastic option for those on a tighter budget.

★ RIAD DAR MADU

Ksar Hassi Labied; tel. 0535/578 740 or 0661/352 895; www.madu-events.com; 800Dh-1,100Dh d

For one of the most luxurious nights in the desert, reserve with Riad Dar Madu. Operated by the owners of the hotel by the same name, the tents are second-to-none. The Bedouin tents are solar powered and feature a Moroccan restaurant worthy of *1,001 Nights*. Keep in mind that prices are per person and, like everything else in Morocco, are negotiable. If you were to have just one night in the desert in your life, you would want it to be here. The *riad* also has a hotel in Merzouga constructed of eco-friendly mudbrick, romantically lit with hand-worked metal lamps resting beneath bamboo ceilings. For the cold nights, a crackling fireplace makes it a cozy spot to curl up with that vacation read you've been ignoring. The swimming pool looks out into the nearby Sahara. A scrumptious breakfast is included, and the restaurant (well worth checking out) uses only the freshest ingredients sourced daily from the nearby markets.

Information and Services

There is a post office with a cash machine right at the beginning of town at the T-intersection with the road for Ksar Hassi Labied. Several cash machines, a post office branch, and a seldom-open tourist office are found at the end of the road, near the edge of the dunes along the main commercial strip of Merzouga. Many hotels and nearly all tour operators accept only cash, so you will likely have to make liberal use of the cash machines. Keep in mind that the maximum amount most cash machines let you take in one transaction is 2,000Dh, which means you might have to do several transactions if you are paying for a larger group.

Getting There

Getting to the edge of nowhere can be a little tricky without a car, and even with a car you will likely want to rent a **four-wheel-drive vehicle** to further explore this edge of the Sahara.

BY CAR

From **Fez** (470km/292mi, 9hr), follow the **N8** into the Middle Atlas past the towns of **Imouzzer, Ifrane,** and **Azrou** before joining the **N13** and following the road signs to Midelt and **Errachidia** (133km/83mi, 2hr). From **Meknes** (462km/287mi, 9hr), the route is a bit more straightforward, taking you directly through El Hajeb and Azrou on the N13.

From **Ouarzazate** (368km/229mi, 8hr), follow the **N10** through the North Draa Valley, past the Dades and Todra Gorges. At

The Western Sahara

For travelers who have the time and who really want to explore the outer reaches of Morocco, the internationally disputed Western Sahara might be enticing. This region stretches along the Atlantic Coast, bordering Algeria to the east and Mauritania to the south. The border with Algeria is closed and should be avoided, as there is a large military presence and buried mines are still scattered along the border. Mauritania, however, is open and may be crossed for those looking to continue by land from Morocco and farther along the west coast of Africa. The two major cities of the Western Sahara are Laayoune and Dakhla.

Laayoune is the largest city in the Western Sahara, with over 200,000 inhabitants. Many pioneering businesspeople have relocated here because of the heavy subsidies given by the Moroccan government for new businesses located in this remote corner of the country. The overall feel of this beachside town is more akin to a Wild West frontier than anything else. Laayoune doesn't have the history of some of the other Moroccan cities. It was founded by the Spanish in 1940 under the name "El-Aaiún" and has a functioning Spanish cathedral, Saint Francis of Assisi, as a remnant of this era. Fishing and phosphates are the primary industries, though tourism has grown in recent years with Moroccans increasingly moving about and exploring their own country.

Dakhla is as far south as you can go without a visa. The border with Mauritania is just a few kilometers outside of the city. The camper van crowd has discovered Dakhla. They make their way here along desolate, but picturesque, National Road 1 (N1), which hugs the Atlantic Ocean, connecting Tangier with Dakhla. There is a growing surfer crowd, but for the most part this is a sleepy seaside town that goes about life at the hot edge of the ocean and desert at a very relaxed pace.

To get to the Western Sahara by land, follow the N1 south toward Laayoune from Agadir (644km/400mi, 10hr). There is really just this one road through this region, with side roads leading primarily to military installations. The **CTM** bus (tel. 0800/0900 30, www.ctm.ma) leaves directly from Casablanca all the way to Dakhla (27hr, 2 daily, 600Dh) with stops in Agadir and Laayoune. **Supratours** (tel. 0524/888 566 or 0524/885 632, www.oncf.ma) runs a bus from Agadir to Laayoune (10hr, 4 daily, 300Dh) and Dakhla (20hr, 4 daily, 400Dh). However, the quickest way is by plane. **Royal Air Maroc** (www.royalairmaroc.com) has daily flights to Laayoune and Dakhla (1.5-2hr, 1,500Dh).

Tinejdad (146km/91mi, 2.5hr), turn off the N10 and follow the **R702** (Route de Jorf) to **Erfoud** (60km/37mi, 1hr).

There is a convenient free **parking** at the end of the main road where the pavement meets the desert at the base of the largest single *erg*, Erg Chebbi, in the region.

BY BUS

The **Supratours** bus (tel. 0524/888 566 or 0524/885 632, www.oncf.ma) runs all the way to Merzouga from **Fez** (11hr, 1 daily, 190Dh) and **Marrakesh** (12.5hr, 1 daily, 200Dh). You can also catch this bus in **Errachidia** (2.5hr, 2 daily, 60Dh), **Ouarzazate** (8hr, 1 daily, 130Dh), **Boumalne Dades** (6hr, 1 daily, 90Dh), or **Tinghir** (5hr, 1 daily, 80Dh). Buy tickets a few days in advance to guarantee seating. The Supratours buses leave Merzouga at 8am and 7pm.

If you're heading south toward Ouarzazate and Marrakesh, you'll want to take the morning bus that passes through Rissani and Errachidia. This bus connects with the N10 and stops at Tinghir (4.5hr, 1 daily, 80Dh), Boumalne Dades (6.5hr, 1 daily, 100Dh), Ouarzazate (8hr, 1 daily, 120Dh), and Marrakesh (12hr, 1 daily, 175Dh).

If you're heading toward Fez, plan on taking the 7pm bus that runs through Errachidia before continuing overnight until Fez (11hr, 1 daily, 160Dh).

The **CTM** (tel. 0800/0900 30, www.ctm.ma) bus stops in nearby **Rissani;** after that, you'll have to get a ***grand taxi*** (42km/26mi, 45min, 10Dh).

Getting Around

From here, you can continue into the Sahara **on foot** or negotiate with the numerous **camel drivers** for a tour or overnight trip into the desert. The going rates are 100Dh for a ride out to enjoy the sunset, 200-500Dh for an overnight stay with dinner and breakfast in a Bedouin tent, but all prices are negotiable, so work on your bargaining skills.

FOUR-WHEEL-DRIVE RENTALS

In Merzouga, you can rent quads, buggies, or 4x4s at **Garage Ben Omar** (next to Chez Jordi & Naima at the entrance of town, tel. 0671/564 956). The garage also has a mechanic on-site, which can be handy if your car breaks down. Otherwise, if you want to drive yourself, it is best to rent a four-wheel-drive vehicle in **Marrakesh, Fez,** or other major city. In the south, a four-wheel-drive rental typically comes with a driver. The driver generally costs 100Dh a day and the car 300-500Dh a day. Renting with a driver can be beneficial, as the driver generally knows the area quite well and the risks of being lost in the desert are lessened.

TAFROUTE SIDI ALI

For those looking for something more undiscovered and maybe to escape from the crowds that can flood Merzouga, consider venturing to this little desert village, about an hour drive through the desert by 4x4 from Merzouga. Be careful to not confuse it with the "other" Tafroute that is nearer to Tiznit. If you are traveling by 4x4, the **Hostel Wilderness Lodge** (Ksar Hassi Labied, tel. 0661/591 297 or 0666/391 785) is your one stop along the way for a roof or a hot meal. It's an easier drive to Tafroute via the main road connecting Zagora with Er-Rossini and Merzouga. There are no fancy camps or 4-star lodgings here, only a few humble guesthouses, so you'll likely be roughing it for a night or two.

Food and Accommodations

AUBERGE LAC MAIDER

South Village; tel. 0555/884 656 or 0666/844 636; 300Dh d

Rustic, simple, traditional mud brick and straw construction with a palm frond roof right in the middle of the desert. What more could you ask for? There are only four rooms, though they have air-conditioning and Wi-Fi. This particular guesthouse is a popular stopover for those doing 4x4 tours of Morocco. You will want to call ahead to make sure rooms are available just on the off chance a tour is coming through at the same time you plan on making your way to Tafroute. Price also includes demi-pension (breakfast and dinner).

AUBERGE HAMADA KEM-KEM

South Village; tel. 0666/793 044; www.hamada-kemkem.com; 300Dh d

This is one of the larger options and should likely be the first one you try to book into if you're coming into the village without a reservation. There is an English-speaking staff member, which can help a lot, particularly if you're traveling with any sort of dietary requirements or anything else. The expansive property itself is encircled with a large stucco wall, which helps to cut down on the winds and sand as you're walking around. With air-conditioning, Wi-Fi, and friendly staff, what more could you ask for? Price also includes demi-pension (breakfast and dinner).

RIAD LES JARDINS DE TAFRAOUTE

East Village; tel. 0535/882 055 or 0662/291 504; http://lesjardinsdetafraoute.com; 900Dh d

Of all the options in the area, this is by far and away the most comfortable. The rooms are all generally fresh and cleaned, carefully protected from the inevitable sandstorms that sweep the area from the eastern hill. A large pool adds a touch of luxury for those hot desert days, and invites you to relax with a book and disconnect for a moment. This is the place where you come for a touch of luxury with your stay in the desert. Be sure to check out the on-site bar.

Getting There

Getting beyond the edge of nowhere is nigh impossible without a **car.** I traveled here stupidly in a 2-wheel drive, so it's possible to drive it from the main paved road, but you'll be much better off in a **4x4.** In places, the sand creates little dunes that wash over the pavement. There is a 4x4 path that arrives directly in Tafroute Sidi Ali from **Merzouga.** You'll want to ask for the road start if coming from Merzouga, but once on it, it's clear enough. Still, consider packing a GPS just in case. From the **N12,** you can easily arrive here from **Zagora** (2.5hr, 125km/78mi) and **Rissani** (2hr, 146km/91mi). The turnoff is clearly marked. Tafroute Sidi Ali is about a 30-minute drive down this road once you turn off the N12.

Background

The Landscape

Located on the northwest corner of Africa, the landscapes of this vast country are surprisingly varied. Long stretches of beach and craggy rock formations make up the Atlantic Coast. A second, shorter coast is to the north along the Mediterranean, with beaches tucked between the foothills of the Rif Mountains. Four mountain ranges form a spine arcing through the middle of the country: the Rif in the north, the Middle Atlas and High Atlas along the center of the country, and then the Anti-Atlas in the south. Jbel Toubkal, in the High Atlas Mountains, is the tallest mountain in Morocco, and at 4,167 meters (13,671ft) is

easily seen from Marrakesh. Lush coastal lowlands, primarily used for agriculture, rise between the coastal region and the plateaus of the mountain ranges. Beyond the mountain ranges to the east and to the south is the famed Sahara. Morocco shares land borders with Algeria to the east and Mauritania to the south, as well as the Spanish enclaves of Ceuta (Sebta) and Melilla on the northern coast.

GEOGRAPHY

The Coast

The little-known **Alboran Sea** continues from the easternmost port of the Strait of Gibraltar into its better-known big sister, the **Mediterranean**, from where the region takes its name. This region begins roughly at Tangier and runs across the foot of the Rif Mountains until the border with Algeria to the east. Several small islands, mostly unoccupied, dot the sea, including Isla de Alborán. Nearly all of these, including those close to the Moroccan shore, are controlled by Spain. To the west of Al-Hoceima a thin line of sand connects Peñón de Vélez de la Gomera, one of the Spanish *plazas de soberanía* (places of sovereignty), with the mainland of Morocco. Peñón de Vélez de la Gomera was an island, but a violent storm in the 1930s created a sandbar connecting the island with the mainland. Now, this thin tombolo is the world's shortest land border.

The long stretch of coastline running north-south along the **Atlantic** is largely a temperate zone, with long stretches of beach, incredible rock formations, and numerous ports and inlets. Generally, the weather is cooler and more moist toward the north and becomes warmer and drier farther south until the desert region of the Sahara. From the coast, the land rises to a series of coastal plateaus that are notably warmer, though still moderated by the influence of the ocean, and generally used for agricultural purposes. Some of the primary crops include wheat, barley, and other cereals in the northwest and olives, citrus fruits, wine grapes, and tomatoes just off the Atlantic.

Many of the largest cities in Morocco are dotted up and down this coastline, concentrating most of the population along this stretch. Casablanca and Rabat are in the middle of this region, with Tangier to the north and Essaouira and Agadir to the south. There are numerous other towns, some larger than others, and many of them, such as Larache and El Jedida, are primary fishing ports.

The Mountains

The **Rif**, as it is known to locals, lies just off the Mediterranean Coast and continues inland through the north, including the entirety of the Rif Mountains from which it takes its name, and continues east to the Algerian border. To the south, its borders are the gateway town of Taza and the Wergha River. The geography here is influenced by the mountains, desert, Atlantic Ocean, and Mediterranean Sea, making it one of the more biodiverse regions in the country.

The Rif Mountains (Arif, in the local Riffi dialect) are part of the Gibraltar Arc, along with Baetic Cordillera across the strait in Spain. Together, these are known to ecologists as the Baetic-Rifan complex. The highest peaks of the region, including Jbel Tidirhine (2,456m/8,059ft), are snowcapped in winter. They constitute one of the more diverse regions along the Mediterranean for flora and fauna because it forms a transitional zone between the Atlantic and Mediterranean. Many relict species in these mountains have been able to survive changes in climate over the last few million years because of the moderating influence of the ocean. Flora from the ancient laurel forests that once covered this area still thrive here, whereas in other spots around the Mediterranean basin they have gone extinct.

The western slopes of the mountains receive the most annual rainfall in Morocco at

Previous: Merzouga in the Sahara

about 203 centimeters (80in) per year. The forests are diverse and include tall cedars, oaks, and the last remaining Moroccan fir trees. To the east, the drier slopes are covered with different pines. Deforestation, due to forest fires, overgrazing, and clear-cutting for agriculture (predominantly cannabis farms), has unfortunately led to soil erosion in many regions.

The **Atlas Mountains** offer some of the most varied and stunning scenery in all of Morocco. Snowcapped jagged peaks, lush flowering valleys, and cascading waterfalls make this a nature lover's haven. The mountains extend for 2,575 kilometers (1,600mi) through Morocco, Algeria, and Tunisia and serve to separate the coastal regions from the Sahara. This region is not as populated as the coast, and most inhabitants live in smaller Amazigh villages.

The **Middle Atlas** runs approximately 349 kilometers (217mi) and forms the northwestern border of the Atlas Mountains. It is formed primarily of limestone, and the highest point, Jbel Bou Naceur, stands at 3,340 meters (10,958ft) high. The region holds extensive volcanic plateaus and craters as well as freshwater basins, such as the basins of Sebou and Bouregreg, that feed into the river system and provide irrigation and drinking water for the rest of the country. Deep valleys, caves, and gorges are etched into many parts of this region.

The **High Atlas** peaks are easily the tallest of this range, with Jbel Toubkal, the tallest mountain in Morocco and of the Atlas mountains, standing at 4,167 meters (13,671ft) high. This chain stretches west-east for 700 kilometers (435mi) below the Middle Atlas and serves to protect the region to the north from the harsh desert conditions of the south. Snow-fed rivers run through lush valleys and over rocky terrain. Gorges and box canyons dominate the middle of this chain, while Jurassic and Cretaceous-period formations stand watch over deep, erosion-carved valleys throughout the massif of Toubkal National Park.

The **Anti-Atlas** range extends south of the High Atlas for 500 kilometers (310mi), with peaks reaching over 2,400 meters (7,874ft). It is more barren and rocky and often resembles a lunar landscape more than a mountain range. However, there is evidence that this mountain range once reached heights greater than that of today's Himalayas. The Anti-Atlas peaks were formed at the same time as the Appalachians in the United States, when the continents collided 300 million years ago. This region receives less than 20 centimeters (8in) of rain a year and is considered part of the Saharan climatic zone. Low-water-demand plants, including rosemary, thyme, and the regionally famous argan plant, are spread throughout the region. The traditional inhabitants of this sparse region, the Chleuh tribes, mostly live in and around Tafraoute.

The Desert

Unsurprisingly, the **Sahara** is the most inhospitable region in Morocco. It includes the disputed Western Sahara and continues north through the eastern part of Morocco bordering Algeria. This region is the northwest corner of the Sahara, a vast desert approximately the size of the United States that spreads from Morocco to Egypt. Sand dunes, sand seas, and the occasional date-palm oasis dot this hyper-arid climate. Temperatures are extremely hot year-round, though often cold at night. During periods of heavy rainfall in the winter and spring, the region can experience flash flooding, such as the floods of 2014, which were deadly and washed out many of the more poorly constructed roads.

CLIMATE

Though it's generally classified as a "Mediterranean climate," the actual climate variation in Morocco takes many first-time visitors by surprise. The only true Mediterranean climate regions are the **northern Atlantic Coast** and along the **Strait of Gibraltar** across the **Mediterranean Coast** until the border with Algeria. Hot summers average around 30°C (mid-80s F) and winters are around

Morocco Geography by the Numbers

- 446,550 square kilometers (172,410 sq mi)—approximately the size and shape of California.
- 712,550 square kilometers (274,462 sq mi) including the Western Sahara, making in significantly larger than France (640,679 sq km/247,368 sq mi) and nearly the size of Turkey (783,562 sq km/302,535 sq mi) or Texas (696,200 sq km/268,820 sq mi).
- 17th largest country in Africa with the Western Sahara (25th largest without it).
- 39th largest country in the world with the Western Sahara (57th largest without it).
- 2,945 kilometers (1,830mi) of coastline, a bit more than South Africa (2,798 sq km/1,739 sq mi).
- 11 kilometers (7mi) across the Strait of Gibraltar from Spain. You can see Spain from Tangier.
- 4,167 meters (13,671ft) is the highest peak in Morocco, found at Jbel Toubkal.
- -55 meters (-180ft) below sea level is the lowest point in Morocco, at Sebkha Tah near Tarfaya.
- 35.74 degrees north latitude of Tangier, Morocco's northernmost city, is roughly 3 degrees lower than Washington D.C.
- 33.57 degrees north latitude of Casablanca, Morocco's financial capital, is roughly parallel to Los Angeles.
- 7.98 degrees west longitude, Marrakesh (and most of Morocco) is significantly west of London and Greenwich, though as of 2018 the country follows CET (Paris and Berlin).

16°C (low 60s F); spring and autumn fall in between. Winter is also the wet season. Tangier accumulates 10-13 centimeters (4-5in) of rain a month over the winter and around 5 centimeters (2in) per month in the spring and fall. Over the Rif in the east, it is notably drier, with Oujda averaging just over 2.5 centimeters (1in) of rain October-May and hardly anything during the summer. If you are traveling this area in the winter, remember to pack something for the nights. They can be chilly and sometimes (though rarely) dip below freezing.

Along the **southern Atlantic Coast,** you can expect cooler, wetter winters, and to the south it can feel like summer year-round, though with the occasional shower. The plateaus and valleys just off the Atlantic Coast are often humid with trapped condensation from the coastal region, though in the summers they become arid. This area is strongly influenced by the cold stream of the Atlantic, making extreme highs and lows unlikely. In Casablanca, temperatures vary 15-30°C (low 60s to 80s F), with an average of 17°C (62°F) in the winter months and 26°C (79°F) during the summer. At the southernmost end of this region, Agadir has even milder winters, with an average of 21°C (69°F), though similar summers. This semiarid subtropical climate can experience the *chergui* (hot, dry Saharan winds), which can push the temperatures over 32°C (90°F).

In and around the **mountains,** seasons are more diverse. This region experiences four seasons, with cold temperatures and occasional snow and heavy rain showers in the winter. Above 1,200 meters (4,000ft), nights often dip below freezing. The spring and fall months are the best for visiting these regions, with more moderate temperatures and a lower chance of rain showers. The summers are hot, sometimes unbearably so, particularly in cities at lower elevations, such as Fez and Meknes. With the dust and exhaust, temperatures spike to a sweltering 32°C (90°F) and can easily clear 40°C (104°F). In higher altitudes, temperatures dip to 21-30°C (70s and

80s), though the sun is much stronger, making sunstroke a real concern.

The **desert** regions are extremely hot during the summer months, and during winter months see occasional flooding and cooler, sometimes freezing, temperatures. Temperature swings are dramatic and average 16°C (30°F) or more between the day and night. The summers are unbearable, with an average daytime temperature well over 38°C (100°F) and nights around 20° (68°F). The winter months are a pleasant 21°C (70°F) or so during the day but dip to near-freezing temperatures at night. It is incredibly arid, as one would expect.

ENVIRONMENTAL ISSUES

Desertification

The drylands to the east of the mountains, as well as in some areas in the south of the country, are threatened by desertification due to overgrazing (particularly sheep), scarcity of water, and poor crop rotation. Recent policies have done little to help these regions, and the effects are apparent to the naked eye. In these areas, particularly, it is recommended to limit water and other resource usage.

Water

Morocco is challenged with occasional droughts that stress the fragile water system. Additionally, there is ongoing concern of industrial pollutants and raw sewage being introduced into rivers used for drinking water and irrigation. An estimated 35 percent of piped water is lost in the poor infrastructure, and water is a poorly managed resource throughout the country. The recent developments of heavy cyclical rains and snows, perhaps brought on by global climate change, have further stressed what resources there are and have resulted in tragic floods. Furthermore, many of the country's dams are silting up, causing an additional loss of water. Along with the poor management of farmable lands, all this has led to a steep increase in soil erosion. Along the coasts, the oil and sewage pollution of ocean waters has affected the fishing industry. The government has implemented policies, though many of the signs are still dire. As with many other ecosystems in the world, there is danger of an unpredictable ecological crisis that threatens the inhabitants and the fragile ecosystems of this biodiverse country.

Thuya Wood

Tetraclinis, better known as thuya, is a near-threatened species of evergreen conifer tree indigenous to Morocco (it is also found in Algeria, Tunisia, Malta, and Cartagena in Spain) and used in much of the ornate woodwork found in Morocco. The resin, sandarac, can be used to make a varnish or lacquer and is prized as a protective coating for paintings and antiques. With the rise of tourism and demand for thuya wood souvenirs, the Moroccan industry has been focused on extracting burls from the trunk of the tree, effectively killing the tree. With the addition of overgrazing of livestock in areas of potential regrowth, there has been a massive deforestation of this slow-growing conifer. The purchase of any souvenir made of thuya is discouraged, though today more sustainable methods of harvesting are being practiced.

Plants and Animals

Morocco is home to five distinct vegetation zones, with coastal regions along the Mediterranean and Atlantic, two mountain regions, and, of course, vast Sahara dunes. The biodiversity present in Morocco impresses many visitors.

MEDITERRANEAN

Running along the northeast coast, the Alboran Sea, the westernmost part of the Mediterranean, is a habitat for the largest population of bottlenose dolphins in the Mediterranean and lays claim to hosting the last population of harbor porpoises in the region. The fishing industry has done a lot of damage to these populations, but with new regulations, they look to be making a comeback. In the spring and summer months, you can spot the endangered loggerhead sea turtles, when they migrate here to feed and reproduce. These turtles, though endangered, are spread throughout the world and can be found in the Pacific, Atlantic, Mediterranean, and Red Sea. During reproduction, the females climb ashore to lay their eggs.

Cork oak, eucalyptus, and thuya trees are fairly common along the hills and cliffs that reach above the long stretches of beach. Al-Hoceima National Park, though still in the nascent stages, is a protective zone for this region and is a good place to take in its natural beauty. In Tangier, Perdicaris Park is something of a curiosity. Ion Perdicaris, among other things, was a plant lover and imported many species of plants to his home outside of Tangier. Some of these species have thrived and can be found alongside the native eucalyptus and cork oak.

ATLANTIC COAST

Morocco is a veritable paradise for birders. A wide variety of migratory birds travel between Europe and Africa. Combined with indigenous species, the total number you can witness in Morocco is over 450 species, with more than 150 species considered rare. Fifteen species, such as the northern bald ibis, are classified as globally threatened. In addition to the ibis, you can spot flamingos, slender-billed curlews, falcons, warblers, wrens, the incredibly rare black-browed albatross, and other distinct species. Saltwater flats and lagoons, as well as freshwater lakes, serve as feeding and breeding grounds and winter homes for many species. As such, late fall, winter, and early spring are the best for viewing migratory birds. Off the islands of Essaouira you can find Eleanora's falcon during breeding season. Species seen in Merja Zerga National Park include flamingos, black-winged stilts, avocets, and slender-billed gulls.

Most of the flora of this region is agricultural. Cork oak forests and olives are also found, though much of their ecosystem has been converted into farmland. To the south, indigenous argan trees can be seen, often with goats perched in their branches, munching on the prized nut that produces a special oil used in cooking and for beauty products. Oysters are also found along this stretch, notably around Oualidia and Agadir.

RIF MOUNTAINS

The western slopes of the Rif have more precipitation and tend to be more lush than the more arid eastern slopes that are influenced by Saharan climates. Because of this, the majority of the forest is on the western slopes, with the eastern slopes more of a dry highland with sage and brush and pine trees, including the Aleppo pine and maritime pine. The forests of the western slopes are predominantly made up of cork oak, holm oak, Atlas cedar, Moroccan fir, and quickly shrinking reserves of thuya wood.

The forests of this region are under threat from the continued expansion of cannabis plantations. Farmers have been clear-cutting

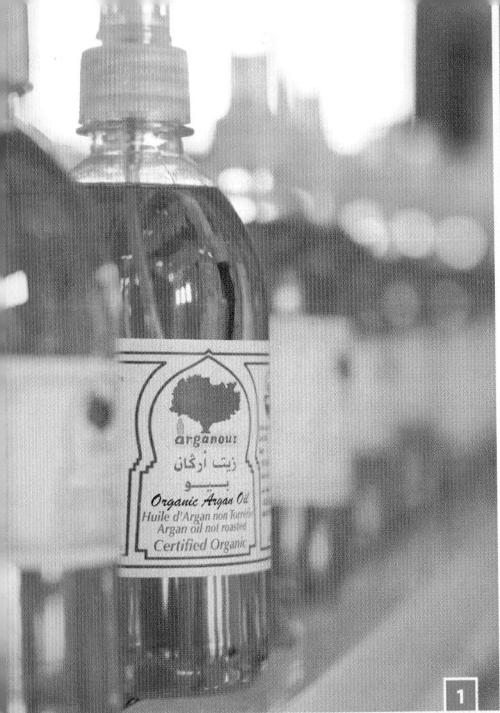
arganouz
زيت أرگان
بيو
Organic Argan Oil
Huile d'Argan non Torréfi
Argan oil not roasted
Certified Organic
1

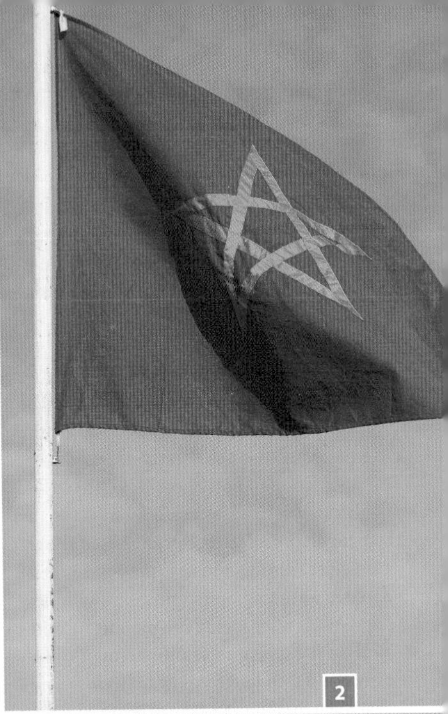
2

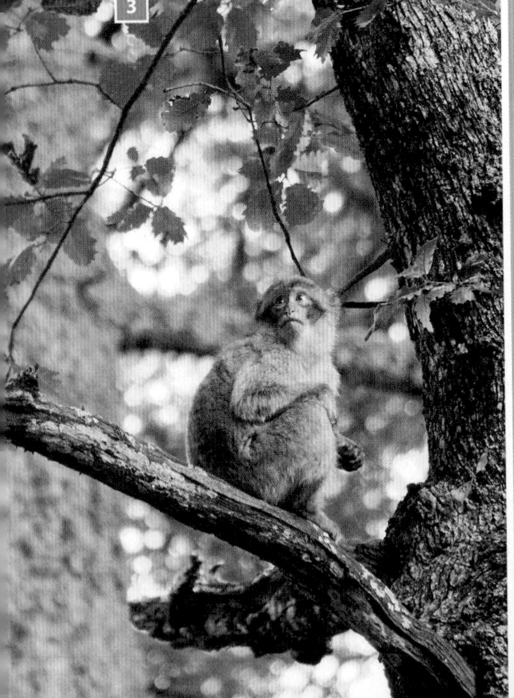

3

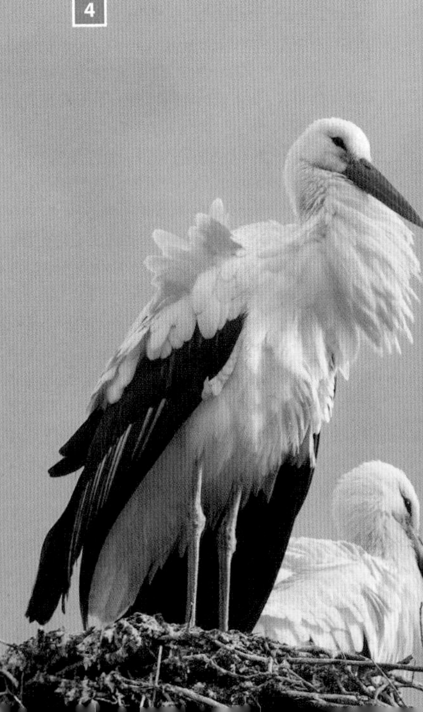

4

the forest to plant crops, and the subsequent soil degradation has led to massive deforestation over the past 40 years. Hashish, derived from the cannabis plant, is still in high demand, and though it is illegal, the Moroccan government has generally turned a blind eye to this highly profitable crop. Throughout this region, cannabis plantations are open and abundant.

This mountainous region serves as one of the few homes of the Barbary macaque, which can also be found in the neighboring Middle and High Atlas Mountains, and across the strait on the Rock of Gibraltar, as well as parts of Algeria and Libya. This endangered primate is one of the most well-known Old World monkey species. Boars, gazelles, ducks, and mountain birds can also be found.

MIDDLE AND HIGH ATLAS MOUNTAINS

Many of the indigenous mammals of this region, including the Barbary lion (also known as the Atlas lion), North African elephant, and Atlas bear, were hunted to extinction. The population of these animals, particularly the Atlas bear, was decimated during Roman rule. The Romans captured and used thousands of them for their gruesome sports. The Atlas bear is thought to have gone extinct in the 19th century. The Barbary lions, once thought to be the largest lion species in the world, were often captured and gifted as presents from the sultan of Morocco to overseas royalty. The last Barbary lion in the wild is believed to have been shot in 1942. Currently, there is a project to revive the Barbary lion from zoo lions and reintroduce it to this region. Other indigenous animals, such as the Barbary leopard, Barbary macaque, Atlas deer, Atlas red fox, and boar can still be spotted, though they are endangered and can be difficult to find. Barbary macaques, though endangered, are easily spotted outside (and sometimes inside) the towns of Azrou, Ifrane, and Ouzoud.

The national parks of Tazekka, Ifrane, and Toubkal serve to protect much of the forest and ecology of this region. The forests are mostly made up of holm oak and Atlas cedar, separated by the occasional extinct volcano crater and freshwater lake. Birders can spy ospreys, hoopoes, lesser kestrels, gray herons, storks, Eurasian eagle owls, and a variety of buzzards, eagles, ducks, tits, finches, sparrows, thrushes, and flycatchers in the lakes and forests of this region. Some of the unique species of the region include the woodchat shrike, alpine chough, and booted eagle.

In spring, the Atlas Mountains are in full bloom. Perennials such as snowcap, wolf's bane, wild peony, foxglove, and Spanish bluebell color the valleys and lakeshores, while colorful sedum and saxifrage grow from the sides of the mountains. Keep an eye out for bulbs and orchids, particularly the rare Atlas orchid.

SAHARA

For those unfamiliar with desert terrains, the biodiversity of the Sahara may come as a shock. Many animals, such as the all-too-familiar dromedaries (one-humped camels), have adapted to this harsh environment where the days are sweltering and the nights are often freezing. Fennec foxes, screwhorn antelopes, and jerboa (a type of rodent) have all adapted to desert life, as have jackals, hyenas, and the dreaded deathstalker scorpion. Of course, you will also find expansive oases of date palms with lush fronds that provide some much-needed shade and greenery to the miles of sand dunes and desert seas.

1: 100 percent natural argan oil **2:** the Moroccan flag **3:** a Barbary macaque in the Middle Atlas **4:** storks are revered throughout Morocco

History

AFTER THE ICE AGE

After the receding of the polar ice cap after the last ice age, Morocco was a fertile, attractive land with plenty of fish, game, wildlife, and edible plants to support the development of *Homo sapiens.* An excavation near Salé in 1971 turned up a fossilized hominid dated around 250,000 years old, making it the oldest such discovery in the country. Other findings around the country have sporadically occurred in recent years, including a beaded seashell necklace estimated at 82,000 years old, making it the oldest-known occurrence of personal adornment ever found.

During Mesolithic times, the country would have been more like a sub-Saharan savannah than its current landscape. Though not much is known about this period, it is thought that the environment would have been ideal for hunters and herders. Likely, as the climate began to change, these people became more sedentary and became part of the tribal history that followed.

THE AMAZIGH TRIBES

The peopled history of Morocco begins with the Amazigh (meaning "free" or "noble" people), a collection of different tribes that still inhabit much of the country. The Amazigh are thought to have inhabited this region since before 10,000 BC. Cave paintings dating from 12,000 BC have been found in the Atlas. They were the first people to develop domestication of livestock and substance agriculture in this harsh region (around 5,000 BC), though they often traveled into the mountains during the hot summer months and escaped to the valleys during the cool winters when the mountain regions were uninhabitable. Cave dwellings were common during this time and persist in some regions today.

The culture developed during this time was largely animist in belief. Writing had not yet been introduced, though oral poetry and song are thought to have been a large part of the culture during this time and provided the means through which tribes communicated news and entertained one another.

PHOENICIANS, CARTHAGINIANS, AND ROMANS

The Phoenicians originated from modern-day Lebanon and were some of the earliest explorers of the Mediterranean and North Africa. They were the first to explore the coast of Morocco and exploit the numerous ports to their advantage in order to take control of the trade of the region. The primary Phoenician settlement was Lixus, near modern-day Larache. They did not explore inland and were primarily interested in easily defensible ports for their ships to ease trade with Spain for valuable tin and silver. Other ports were set up in Tangier, Rabat, Asilah, and Essaouira.

With the rise of Carthage, the ports passed to control of the Carthaginians, who, like the Phoenicians, were primarily interested in keeping commercial trade routes open. Though little is left of these two societies, they formed the base for the Romans, who conquered the region after the fall of Carthage in 146 BC.

Rome claimed Carthaginian territories, ports, and other developments. As the Roman empire expanded, the region became more important. Much of the expansion in Morocco occurred from the 1st to 3rd centuries AD as the rich agricultural land was exploited for Rome. At one point, 500,000 tons of grain were shipped to Rome every year, nearly two-thirds of the city's consumption. During this time of prosperity, thousands of miles of roads were constructed, and cities such as Lixus, Chellah, and Volubilis saw massive growth as well as the introduction of Christianity to the

Berber Pride

An estimated 25-30 million people of various Amazigh tribes are spread throughout North Africa, from Egypt to Morocco. These people are not linked together through a common ancestry, history, or even language. Instead, they are linked by a term introduced by the Romans and Greeks as they fought and attempted to conquer North Africa. "Berber" was the term they used, stemming from the Latin *barbarus,* meaning "barbarian."

Over the centuries the title stuck, and now names like "Berber Palace," "Souk Berber," and "Riad Berber" are commonly seen around the region and throughout Morocco.

Of course, "Berber" is not the most accurate or politically correct word to describe these various people. However, it is often used, and parallels can easily be made with Native Americans of the various indigenous tribes of North America who once shunned the term "Indian" and who now take pride in the history, heritage, and suffering associated with the word. They are taking ownership of "Indian" as the Amazigh of Morocco take ownership of "Berber."

The Tamazight letter "Z" is used to show Amazigh pride.

The Amazigh are prideful people. This pride is made more apparent when you ask them not if they are Berber, but rather if they are Amazigh.

region. It wasn't until the 3rd century when Rome saw its downfall that the rule over much of Morocco was passed back to the Amazigh, with a chief named Iulius Matif named king of the region. Over the next few hundred years, the Vandals and Byzantines tried unsuccessfully to rule Morocco and were continually repelled by the Amazigh.

MOULAY IDRISS AND THE SULTANATES

During the 7th and 8th centuries, a great Islamic empire swept over North Africa and reached as far as Morocco. Morocco was briefly conquered and annexed as a small province under the realm of Ifriqiya. This was the beginning of the Arabization of the region and the introduction of Islam. However, this first Islamic empire was short-lived. The tribes rebeled and formed their own states across Morocco and Algeria.

Later in the 8th century, Moulay Idriss, a direct descendant of the Prophet Mohammed, fled would-be captors from the east. He was being pursued by the ruling powers, which persecuted him for his lineage. Idriss made his way across the Sahara, along the coast, and across the Atlas Mountains to the free land of the west. He was greeted in Volubilis by the ruling tribes and quickly established the Idrisid dynasty, recognized as the first true sultanate of Morocco. His son, Idriss II, moved the capital to Fez and began projects to make Fez a center of commerce, religion, and learning. Under the rule of Idriss II, the region prospered, collecting tariffs from the trans-Saharan trade route, which moved gold, silver, salt, and other precious materials across the Sahara and to the coast.

In the 10th century, the Fatimids conquered Morocco. They displaced the Idrisid dynasty and installed their own governors. However, their governors had problems controlling the populace. They shifted control to the Zenatas, who were unable to govern Morocco. The Fatimids concentrated their power in Cairo, the Zenatas were defeated, and Morocco fell into control of various chieftains of Amazigh tribes, many of whom had allegiance with the caliph of Córdoba.

The Almoravid dynasty was the first truly great Moroccan dynasty, though relatively short lived. The Almoravids were nomadic people. They came over the Sahara and began conquering the country from the south, joining forces with the princes of Al-Andalus in Spain to defend the territories from Christian armies. From 1060 to 1147, under Almoravid rule, Morocco was transformed by the first grand-scale mosques and *medersas* (Quranic schools). The Almoravids expanded their territories north, where expansion into modern-day Spain was made more permanent, as well as south and east, laying claim over the region and grabbing control over the profitable desert trading routes.

The Almoravids fell to the next great dynasty, the Almohad dynasty. The Almohads had their start in Tin Mal, where, under the direction of their fiery leader, Ibn Tumart, they formed pacts with other tribes and built a fortress and spiritual center from where they would launch their attacks on Marrakesh. For nearly 20 years they held the mountain passes across the High Atlas. When they finally conquered Marrakesh in 1147, Ibn Tumart had died and power had passed to an Algerian, Abd al-Mu'min al-Gumi, who prevailed in leading the Almohads over the Almoravids and declared himself caliph and amir of Marrakesh. The Almohad dynasty was another relatively short one, 1147-1248; it began in earnest when they took over Marrakesh. Under the Almohads' violent rule, territories continued expanding in Europe, reaching into Portugal, northern Spain, Algeria, and Tunisia. Though the Almohads had solidified leadership through the territories in both Europe and Africa, by the beginning of the 13th century, the Christian armies of Spain and Portugal had begun to take strongholds, and throughout Africa, tribes revolted, seizing back their lands, allowing for the rise of the Merenids.

The Merenids had wrested control of much of the empire by 1248, but it wasn't until they took Marrakesh in 1269 that they took complete control over the Maghreb. Like the Almoravids and Almohads before them, they expanded the territories east, to again control lands in Algeria and Tunisia, and fought unsuccessfully to wrest back control of the Spanish territories. They did, however, manage to take control of several important towns along the Strait of Gibraltar, giving them power over the seaway between the Mediterranean and the Atlantic and allowing them to support the faltering sultanate of Grenada. Slowly, the Merenid dynasty began to decay with the pressure of the Christian armies to the north and many of the tribes, leaders, and Sufis in their African territories declaring independence and refusing to support the sultanate. This decline began after the death of the powerful Abu Inan Faris in 1358. Viziers took the power, supporting different factions around the empire, and the sultans quickly succeeded each other, none able to establish their control. By 1459, with the empire in tatters, the Wattasid vizier Abu Abdallah sheikh Muhammad ibn Yahya declared himself sultan and began the Wattasid dynasty.

The Wattasids, however, controlled only the northern half of Morocco. During this time, the Spanish Reconquista came to a close with the final conquest over the Alhambra stronghold in Grenada in 1492. Many Muslims and Jews fled Spain, seeking asylum in Morocco, particularly in the towns of Tetouan, Chefchaouen, and Fez. Along the coast, the Portuguese with their powerful fleets began taking control of port towns and controlling the sea trade. Meanwhile, the south was in entire political disarray before the Saadians took control of Marrakesh in 1524. By the middle of the 16th century, Spain looked to spread south into Morocco.

The Wattasid dynasty was weak, militarily and economically, and in 1554, the Saadians wrested control of the country from the Wattasids. The Saadians were able to curb Portuguese and Spanish interest in Morocco. After the death of Ahmad al-Mansour in 1603, the Saadians engaged in a long, damaging civil war from which they never recovered. Morocco was fractured. Tribes retook their lands and a number of city-states emerged, each claiming part of the territory for their own.

Finally, in 1666 the Alaouite dynasty was founded. This is the current dynasty of Morocco. At the helm of Moulay al-Rachid at the end of the 17th century, the Alaouites took control of the country from their stronghold in the Tafilalt while the country faced pressures from Spain to the north and the Ottoman empire to the east. Though the empire was smaller, it remained wealthy. In 1684, control of Tangier was taken from the British while Larache was reclaimed from the Spanish a few short years later. Despite tribal revolts, the dynasty prospered, the country was unified, rebellions were quelled, and trading with Europe encouraged.

In 1777, under the leadership of the Sultan Mohammed III, Morocco became the first country to recognize the independence of the United States of America. The sultan granted safe passage to American supply ships to and from Europe and Africa in Moroccan waters during the American Revolutionary War. In 1786, the Moroccan-American Treaty of Friendship was signed and remains to this date America's longest unbroken relationship treaty.

FRENCH AND SPANISH PROTECTORATE

By the end of the 19th century, Morocco continued to bend under the power of Europe. Europe was quickly transforming under the steam of industrialism. It looked to Africa and began colonizing one region after the other, taking over tribal lands and countries, taking slaves and many of the continent's resources. Morocco was a strategic location for colonization, with shores on both the Atlantic and Mediterranean as well as fertile agricultural lands and overland connections with the rest of Africa. Spain provoked a war, retook Ceuta (Sebta), and created numerous enclaves in the north of the country. By 1884, Spain had declared much of the north and far south of Morocco a protectorate.

In 1904, France and Spain signed a treaty marking zones of influence, with Spain keeping its north and south pieces of Morocco and France taking the middle. Germany was provoked, and matters were not settled until a series of treaties and near-crisis between European powers ended in 1912 with the Treaty of Fez. This treaty made the area of French influence an official protectorate and sparked riots.

Over the next 40 years, colonialists flocked to Morocco, buying up cheap land, building harbors, and mining for precious minerals. The increased economic interest in Morocco, as well as the continual threat of revolt from the tribes in the Rif and Atlas Mountains, pressured Spain and France to build military presence in the region. General Hubert Lyautey was the French Resident-General of Morocco. He helped to create a successful French-Moroccan joint government. It is often recorded that he loved, respected, and admired Morocco. He set about creating extensive city plans for all of Morocco's major cities abutting the old Morocco cities. These new cities, or *villes nouvelles,* were built with wide boulevards, gardens, and parks. Lyautey also made plans to link the country by rail. By the time Lyautey left Morocco in 1925, the country had been transformed, quickly ushered into the 20th century with a series of public works, while leaving much of Morocco's architectural heritage intact.

During the 1920s, Abdelkrim El Khattabi from Al-Hoceima established the Republic of the Rif. A joint effort by Spain and France eventually quelled this rebellion. This wasn't

Morocco: A Timeline

250,000 BC	Earliest known hominid in the world (discovered near Salé in 1971)
12,000 BC (possibly earlier)	First known human inhabitants of Morocco: the Amazigh
1,200 BC	Phoenicians control the Moroccan coast, using Essaouira to produce Tyrian Purple dye derived from the shell of the Murex sea-snail. After the fall of the Phoenician Empire, the Carthaginians take control.
CE 40-285	Rome officially annexes the lands of Morocco into the Roman empire, establishing Volubilis as the regional capital. Eventually, the Amazigh overtake Volubilis, signaling an end to the Roman empire in Morocco.
711	Tariq ibn Ziyad crosses the Strait of Gibralter (named after him) with a large army, overtaking the Visigoths in Spain and helping to establish the Umayyad Empire.
788	Fleeing for his life, Idriss I, the great-great-great-grandson of the Prophet Mohammed, ends up in Volubilis and establishes the modern Moroccan state as the Idrisid dynasty, the first ruling dynasty of Morocco. The Idrisid dynasty ends around 200 years later and for many years, Morocco is under the power of the Umayyad dynasty.
1040	Almoravid Empire begins, establishing Marrakesh as the capital, expanding the Moroccan empire into Spain and south to Mauritania. Under the Almoravids, Fez was united and expanded.
1124	The Almohad Caliphate begins, taking over the former Almoravid lands. The landmarks of the Koutoubia Mosque in Marrakesh, the Giralda of Sevilla, and the Hassan Tower of Rabat are testaments to their art and architecture.
1244	The Marinid dynasty begins. They make Fez their capital city, expanding out into Fez Jdid (New Fez), thus making the entirety of the old Fez medina as we know it today. The Marinid rule marks Fez's Golden Age.

the last rebellion against the colonial forces of Spain and France, though. In the 1940s, the Istiqlal Party (Independence Party) was formed. From the confusing medina streets of Fez, they orchestrated and fought a long political war, with riots reaching as far away as Oujda. Their actions eventually managed to reinstate the deposed Sultan Mohammed V, setting the stage for Moroccan independence.

INDEPENDENCE

In 1956, King Mohammed V negotiated the peaceful settlement for the independence of Morocco from France. Spain was forced to follow, though they did not give up all of their possessions in the north. Notably, Spain held fast to a series of islands in the Mediterranean, as well as the Spanish exclaves of Ceuta and Melilla. Sidi Ifni, in the south, was also kept by Spain. King Mohammed V died a few years after independence due to a complication from surgery. Some say that his son and successor, King Hassan II, may have had a hand in his father's sudden death.

The reign of Hassan II consolidated Morocco and the king's power. Hassan II

1549	The short-lived Saadian dynasty begins, leaving some ornate art and architecture behind, including the recently discovered Saadian Tombs in Marrakesh.
1666	The Alaouite dynasty begins. This is the current ruling family of Morocco and the world's second-oldest continuous hereditary dynasty in the world just after the Yamoto dynasty of Japan.
1777	The Sultanate of Morocco, under Mohammed ben Abdallah, is the first nation to recognize the United States as an independent nation.
1912	The Treaty of Fez is signed, establishing much of Morocco as a French Protectorate. A separate agreement between France and Spain later in the year grants Spain protectorate rights in the north and south of Morocco.
1920-1927	The Rif War rages, pitting the local Moroccans, largely Riffian, against the Spanish, directly after WWI. The fierce Riffian warrior and judge, Abd el-Krim, establishes short-lived Republic of the Rif.
1956	The French and Spanish protectorate era come to an end under the stewardship of Sultan Mohammed V, transforming Morocco into what it is today: a constitutional monarchy.
1975	The Green March occurs, allowing Morocco to seize the Western Sahara, something still at debate in international politics today and something of an ongoing dispute between Spain, Algeria, and Morocco.
1999	Mohammed VI, the current king of Morocco, ascends to the throne following his father's death. Under Mohammed VI, large gains have been made in the realm of human rights, gender equality, tourism, and business, though there is still much work to be done.

survived two assassination attempts and a near coup by opposition parties. His response was heavy-handed throughout a time known as the "Years of Lead," stretching from the 1960s to the 1980s. Numerous secret prisons, the most infamous being Tazmamart, held political prisoners, dissidents, and citizens who denounced the throne. Hassan II quickly developed a reputation as a ruthless ruler and was charged with numerous human rights violations. During the 1970s, the Western Sahara was annexed to the country through the controversial Green March, adding a list of Sahrawis who have disappeared under the rule of Hassan II. The Green March was a peaceful protest arranged by the Moroccan government in 1975 that was comprised of 350,000 unarmed civilians and 20,000 Moroccan troops. The protestors and troops marched a few miles into the Spanish-controlled Western Sahara to reclaim it as part of Morocco. The international status of the Western Sahara has been at debate ever since.

MOROCCO TODAY

Since the ascension of Mohammed VI to the throne in 1999, Morocco has seen an incredible surge in development. The king is seen as more liberal than his father. He has worked to restitute families of political prisoners held captive under his father's rule and introduced new legislation, such as the *mudawana* (family law) of 2004, which gave women more rights in the law and in cases of divorce. Under his reign, the introduction of Tamazight (the language of the Amazigh) as a language of instruction and recognized state language, alongside Modern Standard Arabic, has been implemented. Following the February 20 uprising and the Arab Spring (2011-2012), reformation of the constitution to limit royal power and disseminate more power to the other branches of the government was undertaken.

Economic and political ties with France and Spain remain strong, with France being the largest financial partner to the region. However, ties with Spain have been strained as of late, with ongoing debates as to fishing rights along the Mediterranean and Atlantic coastlines. Drug trafficking (particularly in the north), prostitution, and pedophilia remain problems for the government, aided by widespread corruption at nearly all levels.

The press enjoys more freedom than it did under Hassan II. Opposition politics are regularly discussed and debated, though three issues—the status of the Western Sahara as part of Morocco, political Islam, and the absolute right of the king to govern Morocco—are subjects that are censored and not discussed publicly.

Economic progress is evidenced in the major cities with new housing developments, large-scale developments like the Morocco Mall, and government-sponsored projects, such as the development of high-end marinas in Casablanca, Rabat, and Tangier. The overall infrastructure of the country is undergoing a sort of revival under the current leadership. The Al-Boraq high-speed train, similar to France's TGV, now runs between Tangier, Rabat, and Casablanca. In a few years' time, hopefully by 2025, it will lead all the way to Marrakesh, connecting four of the country's most important cities.

These days, there is also a renewed interest in supporting the arts, with the construction of state-of-the-art theaters in Rabat and Casablanca underway. Cities are bustling with teens sporting some of the latest European designer brands, high-powered businesspeople in suits and ties, and the newest models from Porsche, BMW, and Lexus speeding past. This is contrasted greatly with the rural parts of Morocco, where life continues at a slower pace, largely revolving around the agriculture seasons, and where access to public health and education is notably more difficult to obtain. Life in the country is much poorer and generally more conservative than in the cities, as is the case in most countries.

Government and Economy

GOVERNMENT

Organization

Morocco is a parliamentary constitutional monarchy. The structure of the government is dictated by the Moroccan Constitution, which allows for a monarchy accompanied by a parliament and an independent judiciary. Thus, the government is separated into three primary branches: executive, legislative, and judicial. The executive branch is controlled by the prime minister. The legislative branch is divided into two parliaments: the Assembly of Councillors and the Assembly of Representatives. Finally, the judicial branch is considered independent.

In theory, the executive branch is controlled by the prime minister, but it is the king who appoints this position and has the power to terminate the role of the prime minister or any other minister serving in the government. In practice, the king holds extensive powers over the government, religion, and military. Nearly all real power in the government is held by the throne. In addition to being the chief of the military, the king is considered a direct descendant of the Prophet Mohammed and carries the title "Commander of the Faithful" (Amir al-Moomineen) as the religious leader of the country. The king is allowed to dissolve the parliament, suspend the constitution, and rule by decree.

Since the reforms of 1996, the legislative branch (parliament) has comprised two assemblies. The Assembly of Representatives of Morocco contains 325 members elected locally, 30 seats of which are designated for women, with each member serving a term of five years. The Assembly of Councillors has 270 members, divided into seats elected by local councils (162), professional chambers (91), and wage-earners (27), with each member serving a nine-year term. Parliament's powers have been increased in recent years and include budgetary matters, ad-hoc committees to investigate government proceedings, and the power to dissolve the government (though not the monarchy). Importantly, the constitution limits the power of any one party in the parliament such that any political party may hold a maximum of 20 percent of the total seats.

The judicial branch, though constitutionally separate, generally follows the wishes of the king. The Supreme Court is the highest court. There are 16 administrative regions, each governed by a wali (provincial governor) appointed by the king. The regional judicial branches are further divided into districts, with each district having a governor, also appointed by the king.

Politics

There are over 30 active political parties in Morocco, with several more that are nominally active, disbanded, or that refuse to take part in elections. In 2011, the PJD (Justice and Development Party), a self-described moderate-Islamist party, took control of the parliament. Istiqlal Party (Independence Party), National Rally of Independents, Authenticity and Modernity, and Socialist Union of Popular Forces all hold a significant number of seats in the parliament.

Elections

In 2006 there was an uproar over allegations of election fraud, and 67 people were arrested, 17 from the parliament, making this the first time in the history of Morocco that the government made arrests because of allegations of election fraud. Whether through fear or by other means, it seems that most of Morocco supports the monarchy. This was not always the case. As early as 1998, following popular elections, a band of members opposed to the monarchy, led by Abderrahmane Youssoufi, seized control of the parliament, marking the first occasion in modern history this has happened in the Arab world. Today, the king seems to embrace the opposition and has encouraged people to speak out.

Judicial and Penal systems

The Supreme Court, the final authority in the judiciary branch, is subject solely to the Moroccan Constitution. However, the king does have influence through his role presiding over the Supreme Council of the Judiciary. Beyond the Supreme Court, the country has two systems of courts. The first system is a secular one based on the French system. Beyond the Supreme Court, the secular courts include communal and district courts, courts of first instance, and appellate courts. There are 27 Sadad courts, courts of first instance that enforce Sharia and Jewish law. Criminal as well as civil cases may be heard here, with appeals moving to the regional court. Arabic is the official language of the courts and Moroccan law.

Bureaucracy

Morocco is a frustratingly bureaucratic country. Little is computerized, and most offices operate on a system of stamps, signatures, translations, and multiple copies. To complete the simplest task often takes multiple days, if not weeks or months, often in multiple cities and multiple offices. Very little in the system is transparent, and oftentimes offices ask for items that seem unrelated to the task at hand; documents may need to be translated to either French or Arabic, depending on the office.

ECONOMY

Morocco is considered a liberal economy based on the capitalist values of supply and demand. However, the influence of the king, through his projects around Morocco, is easily seen despite the state privatizing much of its infrastructure, such as the ever-growing telecommunications industry. The primary creditor to Morocco is France. Morocco has outstanding debts of around US$20 billion and around 10 percent unemployment. It is taking part in a joint effort by the International Monetary Fund (IMF) and World Bank to increase market competition and boost the economy.

Industry

Since the ascension of Mohammed VI to the throne, Morocco has seen an incredible surge in development. Ties (economic and political) with France and Spain remain strong. Phosphates, agriculture, and tourism are the three largest sectors, and the textile and fishing industries are also important contributors. Morocco counts for nearly two-thirds of the world's phosphate reserves, and even though this industry employs less than 2 percent of all Moroccans, it still counts for nearly 50 percent of the country's GDP. Morocco's total GDP cleared US$109 billion in 2017, counting 0.18 percent of the worldwide economy.

Agriculture

Agriculture remains the economic backbone of the country, accounting for nearly 50 percent of employment. The fertile valleys in the shadows of the Rif, Middle Atlas, and High Atlas mountains provide olives, wine grapes, tomatoes, apples, strawberries, cherries, melons, citrus fruits, grain, wheat, corn, potatoes, onions, and other crops. Most produce is exported to Europe. There has been an effort to introduce other types of cash crops, such as tobacco, into the region. Traditionally herded animals, primarily sheep and cattle, are raised for milk, cheese, and meat, and are largely sold in-country. The agricultural industry accounts for roughly 15 percent of the GDP—not counting hashish, grown primarily in the Rif, which is estimated to contribute as much as US$3 billion to the overall economy, though estimates vary widely. The hashish production is estimated to supply 80 percent of the hash for Europe, though figures are not readily available.

Tourism

Tourism is quickly growing, and the latest figures put it at 10 percent of the overall GDP of the country. Under a program titled Vision 2020, the king hopes to improve the tourism infrastructure such that the country will see a doubling of tourists visiting the country, from 10 million in 2010 to the goal of 20 million in 2020, while making Morocco one of the top 20 tourist destinations in the world and a model of social and environmental sustainability. This project is aimed not only at international tourism, but also national tourism.

A large part of Vision 2020 rests with the Azur Plan. This is a plan to develop six key coastal resorts in Morocco at Saidia, Larache, El Jedida, Essaouira, Taghazoute, and Plage Blanche. These resorts would add 70,000 beds and generate more than 200,000 jobs. Many Europeans are flocking to Morocco with the destabilization of nearby Tunisia and Algeria, as well as choosing Morocco over Egypt for political concerns. Growth with American, Chinese, Italian, and Scandinavian tourism has increased exponentially since 2012.

Distribution of Wealth

Though the wealth of Morocco has basically doubled since the ascension of Mohammed VI in 1999, most of this wealth has stayed concentrated among very few people in the elite classes. The king is now worth an estimated US$3 billion, with controlling power over much of the economy. He is the leading banker, agricultural producer, and landowner in Morocco, while the entire royal family has one of the greatest fortunes in the world. The budget to maintain the royal palaces is estimated to be nearly US$1 million *per day*, with much of that money going toward luxury cars, clothes, and personnel, all paid for by the state as part of the annual palace budget.

Even with the luxuries of the king there has been a rapid growth of the middle class, and it's estimated that 20-30 percent of all Moroccans now belong somewhere in the middle-class spectrum. The middle class takes home the third of the economy left over from the elite. Many of those on the higher end of this spectrum are using their newfound wealth to purchase brick-and-cement-walled villas outside of the major cities, while others slightly farther down the spectrum are purchasing large apartments in similar in-city constructions, fueling demand for very visible, poorly constructed eyesores around Morocco.

Whereas the middle classes are concentrated in cities, they make up less than 10 million of Morocco's 30 million inhabitants. Nearly 20 million people (two-thirds of the country) live at or well below the poverty line. These Moroccans are marginalized and have little access to education, health care, or public services. In some places, particularly in rural regions in the mountains and in the desert, running water and electricity are still unavailable. The gap between rich and poor is ever evident in Morocco and, unfortunately, continues to grow.

People and Culture

IDENTITY: AMAZIGH, ARAB, AND SAHRAWI

Within this relatively small country, a plethora of cultural identities and languages exist. Historically, this has long been a land of Amazigh tribes, along with the nomadic tribes of the desert, called Sahrawi, which often set up towns and encampments. With the arrival of Moulay Idriss, the country began a long process of Islamization that has continued to the present.

In many ways, the idea of a holistic national identity is still being constructed. In fact, most Moroccans identify most closely with the region or town in which they were raised. This gives rise to cities and regions having specific Moroccan-Arabic or Amazigh dialects and names. In Morocco, it is common for people to say they are from a region rather than from Morocco. For example, you may hear people say that they are "Tanjaoui" (from Tangier), "Fassi" (from Fez), "Marrkchi" (from Marrakesh) or "Soussi" (from the Souss Valley). Beyond regional differences, there is a more general identity of "Arab" or "Amazigh" (often "Berber"). Though "Berber" is often used throughout the country, the root stems from *barbarus*, meaning "barbarian," and some do, understandably, take offense at the terminology. "Amazigh" is not only preferred, it's actually more specific and appropriate, and more empowering, coming from the root for "free people."

Most Amazigh self-identify with the name of their tribe or, quite commonly, with the name of their region. There are three primary regions—the Rif, the Middle Atlas and High Atlas, and the southern Souss region—that tribes identify with, and each region holds a number of tribes. Perhaps the most notable change over the last few years is the reclamation of the term "Berber" to signify Amazigh heritage. There are now Berber pride movements as well as numerous restaurants and lodgings that use the term "Berber." Now, even though "Berber" is acceptable, you can go a long way by asking someone what tribe or group they are from. Most identify with Riffi (the Rif, in the north), Tamazigh (Middle and High Atlas), or Soussi. Other groups include the Gnawa and Haratin. The Sahrawi people identify with the nomadic tribes of the Sahara.

The influence of outside cultures is greatly apparent. Some Moroccans identify more with the cultures of the Middle East largely because of the religious link, though this has been supplemented in recent years with cable television broadcasts from Egypt, Saudi Arabia, Qatar, Syria, Turkey, and United Arab Emirates. Other Moroccans, particularly in rural areas, often feel stronger ties to their Amazigh heritage and identify most closely with what tribe they are from. Still others, particularly those who live in urban areas and have attended French, American, or Spanish schools, feel closer ties to the United States and Europe.

DEMOGRAPHICS

In 2019, Morocco had an estimated population of approximately 36.6 million, making it the 11th largest country by population in Africa and the third largest in North Africa, behind Egypt and Algeria. Nearly 5 million Moroccans live abroad, about 2 million in France, and 800,000 in Spain and Belgium, while others have emigrated to other parts of Europe, the Americas, the Middle East, and West Africa. The growth rate hovers just over 1 percent, and the median age is 26.9 years, making it a relatively young country. The life expectancy is steady at 76 years.

The majority of the population lives along the Atlantic and Mediterranean coast, protected from the Sahara by the mountain ranges. About 60 percent of the population lives in and around urban centers found here, with Casablanca being the most populated city at around 7 million inhabitants in the city and outlying suburbs. The cities of Fez, Marrakesh, Rabat, and Tangier each have a growing populations hovering around 1 million. Because of the relative lack of employment opportunities and more difficult life in the rural areas, the urban centers of Morocco are growing at an incredibly fast rate, making in-country migration a real concern.

Nearly all of the inhabitants of Morocco are Arab-Amazigh (99 percent), and the vast majority are Sunni Muslims (67 percent); others remain nondenominational Muslims (30 percent), and there's a very small, but growing, Shia Muslim following in parts of the Rif. The rest of the population is composed of Moroccan Jews (around 2,500) and immigrants from Europe, Africa, and the Middle East. There was once a much larger Jewish population, but with the creation of Israel, they have mostly emigrated. Today, over 1 million Moroccan Jews live in Israel, with other significant populations in France, Canada, and Spain.

ISLAM

A basic understanding of Islam is central to being able to make sense of Morocco, in both a historic sense and a contemporary sense, much like a basic understanding of Catholicism is central to understanding much of Italy. Of course, there was a time before Islam in Morocco, when the Prophet Mohammed lived in Mecca, receiving messages from God early in the 7th century AD. Though the Abbasid caliphate in Baghdad introduced Islam to Morocco while trying to expand their dynasty across North Africa toward the end of the 7th century, it wasn't until Moulay Idriss I (Idriss ibn Adbullah) was forced to flee from certain death at the hands of these same Abbasids nearly 50 years later that Islam took hold in Morocco.

Moulay Idriss I, the recognized great-great-great-grandson of the Prophet Mohammed, was a threat to the Abbasid caliphate, who derived much of their authority on the direct lineage from the Prophet Mohammed. He took refuge in Volubilis and founded the nearby town of Moulay Idriss after marrying the daughter of the chief of an Amazigh tribe, the Awrabas. He quickly became the recognized caliph of the region. This is the point when Morocco began following Islam. It would remain independent from the Abbasid caliphate, though the Abbasids would manage to finally assassinate Moulay Idriss by poison in 791.

Moulay Idriss's son, Idriss II, made Fez the capital of Morocco, and the practice of Islam quickly expanded, though it was somewhat different from the Islam practiced farther east. Perhaps because of an early local embrace of the Kharijite branch of Islam, a branch that differed greatly from the Sunni and Shia understandings and allowed for a non-Arab caliph, much of the turmoil that passed through the rest of North Africa and the Middle East because of the Sunni-Shia split left Morocco relatively unscathed.

The practice of Islam in Morocco differs from that of many other Islamic countries. One of the particular differences has been the adoption of various Sufi orders and holy men, or marabouts, which gave rise to a particular sort of worship that is fairly unorthodox and is generally frowned upon by much of the Muslim world.

A marabout is a type of saint, generally a religious scholar, leader, or a particular type of Sufi who has shunned the material world in a spiritual quest. Marabouts are generally buried in a domed shrine called a *koubba*. Morocco has numerous *koubbas,* with seemingly every old medina having at least one. Some of the more popular saints, such as Moulay Idriss, receive many visitors every day. These *koubbas* are refuges for those seeking the blessing, or baraka, of the marabout. Often, women visit these shrines looking for a kind of blessing that will help them to find a husband, ward off the evil eye, or become pregnant. These saints are seen as a sort of intermediary between the person praying and God, and it is thought that if the person prays well enough the saint may act on their behalf.

Marabouts are specialized, often depending on the type of religious study they accomplished or what sort of leader they were during their life. Some of the more storied marabouts in Morocco, such as Bouya Omar in the small town of Kalâat Seraghna, are said to heal the mentally ill. There are female marabouts as well. One of the better known is Leila R'Kia in Marrakesh next to the Koutoubia Mosque, who is often sought by women having trouble conceiving a child.

a busker on the street of Marrakesh

A *zawiya* (often spelled *zaouia*) often accompanies the burial spot of a particularly popular or strong Sufi leader as a sort of religious school, like a monastery, and these were some of the earliest places where literacy took hold. Sometimes entire towns, or even cities, sprang up around these *zawiyas*. These places are identified by their names, wherein the name of the saint is given the honorary titled of "Sidi," meaning "master." They are found throughout Morocco; Sidi Allal Tazi, Sidi Slimane, and Sidi Kacem are some of the larger towns named after their saints.

Today, Morocco is considered largely Sunni Muslim of the more liberal Maliki sect. There is an ever-shrinking Jewish population, mostly living in parts of Casablanca, as well as small Christian communities, primarily in the large cities and spread in the south. Islam, as it is practiced in Morocco, is much more liberal than in most of the countries of the Middle East and, generally speaking, promotes tolerance and acceptance among different faiths. Many Moroccans will gladly talk to you about their belief in Islam and how they see it as a religion of submission (the meaning of the word *islam*) and peace.

Even in the largely Europeanized big cities of Morocco, the daily impact of Islam can be seen and heard everywhere, from the morning call to the faithful chanted by the muezzin to the file of men sporting jellabas beelining for the nearest mosque for the Friday afternoon prayer. It is common to see men prostrating on the side of the road, performing one of the required five prayers of the day. To complete a prayer, a person must first cleanse themselves through ablutions (*wudu*) and then, depending on what time of day it is, perform 2-4 cycles of prayer (*raka*) with pure intention.

Along with the required five prayers a day, four other "pillars" compose the base of Islam: reciting the declaration of faith (*shahada*); charity (*zakat*); the month of fasting during Ramadan (*siam*); and the pilgrimage to Mecca (*hajj*). Islam, as it is practiced in Morocco, is based on the teachings of the Prophet Mohammed during his life (Sunna) and the Quran, considered to be the direct word of God. It recognizes Moses, Jesus, and other figures from the Jewish and Christian holy books as prophets, equal to Mohammed, but where their message was transformed by the interference of people, the Quran is considered untainted by the will of mankind and the unchallengeable, direct word of God.

WOMEN IN MOROCCO

Being a Moroccan woman comes with challenges. The society is heavily patriarchal. Though women are allowed to work, vote, and have education, Morocco has continually ranked near the bottom of the gender gap ranking done every year by the World Economic Forum. The forum ranks economic participation and opportunity, educational attainment, health, survival, and political empowerment among their criteria. Of 136 countries, Morocco perpetually ranks near the bottom, behind countries such as India, Egypt, and Tunisia. There are many reasons for this poor performance, not the least of which is the difficulties women face at home and in the workplace.

Traditionally, women in the Amazigh cultures of Morocco would, and still do, help with many of the hard tasks, including collecting firewood in the brush, as well as keep the home. With the spread of Islam, particularly in the cities, women found their outdoor roles reduced and in more conservative sects were rarely allowed out of the house. For these women in the cities, the ritual of going to the hammam to bathe was also a welcomed escape from the house, a chance to meet with other women in the community and to exchange news and gossip. The hammam also became a place where mothers talked of potential marriages for their sons and daughters and arranged the future of their families. To some extent, much of this tradition lives on, though times have changed and now the cities are a bustling mix of tradition and modernism. For women travelers, a trip to a hammam is a wonderful way to get a peek into the local culture.

With the strong economic and social influence of European countries, such as Spain and France, as well as the competing messages coming from television in Egypt, Qatar, and Saudi Arabia, the place of women in society in Morocco has perhaps never been more confusing. In 2004, the king enacted a new *mudawana,* or family law, that extended more rights to women, particularly in cases of divorce. Women are in the workplace, and a few have been elected to be part of the ministry and local municipal offices.

However, there is much backlash toward Moroccan women in the public sphere. They are often harassed by men, sometimes violently, with men grabbing, pinching, or even throwing stones at them. This harassment is unpunished by the police, who sometimes join harassers and generally engage in victim blaming, asking what the woman did to provoke the men. In many ways, even with the *mudawana,* women, particularly Moroccan women, are viewed by many Moroccan men as second-class citizens who should be at home baking bread and attending to the children. A walk by any Moroccan café, with its terrace lined with men ogling the women as they quickly pass, sometimes catcalling, is testament to how much further women have to go toward a semblance of equality and respect in much of the country.

LGBTQ IN MOROCCO

For many years, Morocco was a desirable escape for homosexuals from Europe. Tangier, particularly during the international zone period, had gay clubs, discos, and bars. In the 1960s and 1970s, Marrakesh began growing in popularity, and trendsetters found themselves spending lavish weekends sipping on cocktails under palm groves and, if they were lucky, attending parties at Yves Saint Laurent's exquisitely art deco gardens. Morocco was seen as more tolerant than the whole of Europe, and the LGBTQ population was largely left alone.

With the rise of conservatism, openly gay or "subversive" behavior is often derided, and under Article 489 of the Moroccan Penal Code, "lewd or unnatural acts with an individual of the same sex" are punishable by law. Under this article, any offender can find themselves in prison for six months to three years and charged with a fine. However, due to the nature of Moroccan tourism and the corrupt, sometimes whimsical, nature of the police force, tourists are rarely bothered. But any perceived "gay tourism" that involves locals, particularly if there is a large age difference, is likely to bring suspicion, inquiry, and possibly jail time; this has to do in part with the prevalence of prostitution in Morocco.

As Morocco's first outwardly gay writer, Abdellah Taïa, wrote, "Since individuals, whether heterosexual or gay, are not recognized or protected by laws, they are always in great danger." This is particularly the case with the LGBTQ community, where there are no laws to protect them, but there is a law to punish them, and the very discussion of sexuality and sexual orientation is a culturally taboo subject. In fact, lesbianism is seen generally as a sort of impossibility, gay men as an abomination, and transgenders remain unimaginable. There is a lot of confusion and miseducation, a good deal of it encouraged by the government, forcing most of Morocco's LGBTQ community to seek refuge in other countries when possible and, if not possible, then to somehow hide in their own country, often finding solace with open-minded travelers from other countries.

However, change, albeit slow, is afoot. The palace tolerates the publication of *Mithly,* a French-language LGBTQ publication geared for Moroccans, though published in Spain. The organization for LGBTQ rights, Kif-Kif (meaning "the same"), though not officially recognized by the state, has been allowed to hold several seminars and is the only advocate for equal rights in Morocco. In 2010, the very publicly gay Elton John performed as part of the Mawazine Festival. This was a controversial invitation by the palace and was condemned by more conservative elements of Morocco. Despite the conservative backlash, gay musicians and performers continue to come to Morocco, and Marrakesh remains one of the most popular destinations for the jet-setting European LGBTQ community.

LANGUAGES

To say that Morocco is linguistically diverse is somewhat of an understatement. Darija (Moroccan Arabic), Tamazight, French, Spanish, English, and other languages are all commonly spoken in different parts of the country. Though **Modern Standard Arabic** and **Tamazight** are the **official languages** of Morocco, Modern Standard Arabic is rarely spoken except for religious, administrative, and political purposes, while the indigenous Tamazight languages are primarily spoken in rural areas.

Darija (a Creole-type language with Arabic roots, often called "Moroccan Arabic"), though not an official language, is the most spoken language in the country, with over half of the populace speaking it as a first language. It is commonly used for everyday communication; however, the dialects between regions make for different pronunciations and sometimes different words. Darija is written, though not standardized, in both Latin script and Arabic script.

In the cities, you will likely see and hear some **French, Spanish,** and **English**—French is the most common second language in the cities, with a bit more Spanish spoken in the north. French is the de facto language of commerce and business, though English is seeing a sharp rise in use in recent years. English is quickly becoming known by many Moroccans as one of the languages of tourism, and many people in the tourism industry speak at least a few words of English.

An estimated 40-50 percent of the people, mostly rural, speak a **Tamazight** language as a first language. The languages of the Amazigh are highly varied and regionally centered, much like the dialects of Darija. The Tamazight languages most often spoken in Morocco are: Tarifit (often "Rifia") in the Rif, Tamazight (sometimes "Braber" or "Central Shilha") in the Middle Atlas, and Tashelhit (also called "Chleuh" or "Shilha") and Tasoussite (sometimes "Soussia") in the Souss Valley. Other spoken languages include Hassani-Arabic, particularly in the Western Sahara, and Figuig Shilha in the east.

The Arts

ARTS AND CRAFTS

Calligraphy

After touring one of the exquisitely renovated *medersas* (often called *madrasas*), such as the Medersa Bouanania in Fez, it is impossible not to admire the complex geometry of the knotted Kufic script adorning the walls of the *medersa*. In fact, this is one of just a few styles of calligraphy that have been practiced in Morocco over the last 1,000 years.

The practice of calligraphy is one of Morocco's highest art forms. One of the more popular styles is Naskh, a slanting script akin to cursive that is used particularly in recording holy texts, such as the Quran. This style was introduced by the Umayyads from far away Syria. In addition to the Naskh style, a number of decorative Kufic scripts are popular in Morocco. Besides the much-used knotted Kufic script, there are floriate Kufic and square Kufic as well, all brought from the Abbasids in Iraq. As the name implies, the knotted Kufic is made to look like a series of knots made by the calligrapher, while floriated Kufic is more floral in design, generally incorporating swirling patterns that look like a flower in bloom. Square Kufic is just that, more square in design, and growing in popularity for contemporary logos, such as the new logo for the Borj Fez shopping mall.

Henna

The usage of henna symbolizes centuries of tradition and is an act of embracing beauty. It is one of the most natural art forms and has slowly become a characteristic of Morocco's traditions and identity. Although the customs differ from one region to another, henna is mostly tattooed on the hands and feet, but it is also used as a natural hair dye for aging women.

Henna rituals have been traced back to the first Amazigh tribes of Morocco and have played an integral part in most major Moroccan celebrations, especially during important festivals such as circumcisions and marriages. During marriage ceremonies the *hennaya* or *neggafa,* a professional Moroccan henna artist, draws symbolic floral or geometric motifs on the hands and feet of the bride. The couple's friends and relatives involved in the ceremony will also have henna tattoos, because as with many Amazigh customs, the usage of henna is thought to bring good health and luck to the bride and protect her from harm.

Although the usage of henna is sacred in Morocco, you do not have to attend a festival or get married to enjoy its therapeutic effects. On a trip to any large city medina, like in Marrakesh, you will likely be approached by people with a book of patterns displaying examples of henna art. You can either choose from those or suggest your own design.

Designs vary quite a bit, depending on what part of Morocco you are visiting. In the north, it is common to see elaborate henna styles displaying intertwining leaves of Islamic art; in the south, be prepared to witness more bold and passionate designs of layered henna extended all the way to the fingertips, across the palms of the hands, and throughout the bottoms of the feet. Applying henna takes anywhere from 20 minutes to an hour, and when the work is complete the artist will most likely squeeze lime juice and sugar over the paste to help release the reddish-brown color in the powder and facilitate the peeling process once the henna is dry. Beware of anyone using black henna, as there are possibilities of allergic reactions, and it doesn't provide the same health benefits as the traditional red-brown henna.

Carpets

For many travelers, leaving Morocco without a hand-woven Moroccan carpet is a challenge. The numerous bazaars displaying piles of decorative wool carpets sprinkled throughout every medina are hard to pass up. Each

calligraphy is a revered art form

shopkeeper, with a wiliness that would make the most hardline capitalist grin, issues invitations and promises mint tea and no-pressure sales, while in fact the ritual often turns to a hard sale. The numerous cooperatives, where the women carpet weavers get a higher percentage of the sale, support sustainable initiatives. Carpets can be folded or rolled, shipped as an extra carry-on, or shipped directly home, making the unique designs found in Morocco nearly irresistible.

Carpet weaving in Morocco is a historically important tradition. Women would weave carpets for the home and often as part of a dowry. The designs used and style of the carpet varied from tribe to tribe. There are perhaps as many as 45 unique styles and untold variations. Every carpet is handmade, which makes it a truly unique piece. Generally, carpets are made out of wool, though nowadays the wool is imported from New Zealand, and increasingly cotton and synthetic fibers are being used. Shop owners might try to light the ends of a carpet on fire with their lighter. If the carpet does not catch fire, that is a good indication that it is made of wool and not synthetics. However, synthetics are often now used for the more colorful carpets. When shopping for carpets, it's best to use your judgment, to not succumb to high-pressure sales tactics, and to understand that the ritual, including drinking lots of mint tea and making small talk, can take up the better part of a morning or afternoon. Generally speaking, the carpet sellers in the medinas of Fez, Marrakesh, and Tangier have a wider selection, are more expensive, and employ pushier sales tactics, while the smaller towns of Asilah, Azrou, and Chefchaouen offer less selection but are far less expensive and the sales much more convivial. You should pay no more than 3,000Dh for a carpet measuring two meters by three meters (roughly 6ft by 10ft), with Rabati carpets being notable exceptions.

Here are some tips to recognize some of the more popular styles:

- **Beni-Mguild:** Generally red with a decorative centerpiece and ornate borders, featuring a type of X or diamond shape.
- **Beni-Ouarain:** Fluffy, predominantly white carpets with either a few black zigzagging lines or criss-crossing diamond shapes.
- ***Boucharouette:*** A contemporary rag rug made of recycled fabrics, generally very colorful and with outrageous designs. They are growing in popularity for collectors. Cost is generally 300-500Dh for a small carpet.
- **Rabati:** Considered the finest carpets in Morocco, they are the most like Turkish carpets, with ornate centerpieces and fine knotted construction. These carpets are some of the most expensive around, fetching around 10,000Dh or more for a room-size piece.
- **Tazenakht:** Located outside of Ouarzazate, the small village of Taznakht creates some of the most complex tribal designs using three techniques: flat weave, piled knot, and embroidery, generally in deep blues, saffron yellows, and crimson reds. These are often a bit more expensive than other carpets.
- **Zaine:** It is possible that this tribe is no longer making carpets, but their style involves many well-embroidered diamond patterns done in flat weave with occasional tufts of wool in narrow stripes.
- **Zanafi:** This is a newer type of flat-weave carpet, only made in the last 20 years or so. It is a reversible carpet that is sometimes referred to as the "river" for its flowing, complex design.
- **Zemmour:** Generally a red, white, and black flat-weave carpet that alternates patterned stripes. Often, cotton is used for the white.

Leatherwork

In the medinas of Fez, Marrakesh, and Meknes, leatherworkers are still treating and curing leather as they have for generations. Though chemical dyes have altered somewhat how workers treat the leather, most of it is done as it was hundreds of years ago. Fez offers the best example of this process. Tanneries there have existed since the 11th century. Fassi leather is known for its strength. Fez once produced leather shields and armor, reputed throughout the Mediterranean basin as the finest in the world.

The process of treating and curing leather is as follows: First, the skin is soaked in a diluted mix of pigeon excrement. This softens the leather. Next, the leather undergoes two dye soakings—traditionally these were vegetable dyes, including henna and saffron, though today, some colors have been exchanged for chemical dyes. The skins are then left to dry in the sun. Once they are dried, they can be cut to a pattern and used to make purses, bags, satchels, coats, pants, poufs, and other goods. One of the more popular souvenirs is the Moroccan *belgha,* an open-heel slipper, also commonly known by the French term *babouche.* Saffron yellow is the most traditional color, though there are many colors and designs available throughout the country. The remote Anti-Atlas town of Tafraoute is known for the complex embroidery added as a flourish to their *belghas.*

Leatherwork in Rabat and Marrakesh is considered some of the finest in the country. Though the tanneries are no longer in service in Rabat, workers purchase sheets of leather from the tanneries in Fez and Meknes and then make bags with fine details. Tanneries in Marrakesh often work with more supple leather, adding a sense of softness to the touch. Though more traditional bags are available in both Rabat and Marrakesh, leatherworkers also stitch iPad cases, laptop bags, and suitcases for the business class. In Meknes and Fez, the leatherwork tends to be thicker, perhaps not as fine of quality, but somewhat sturdier. Leather jackets and belts are some of the best-selling products.

Pottery

Morocco has a long, storied history of pottery, with several different types available. Fez has long been a producer of some of the world's finest pottery, and Safi, along the Atlantic Coast, is famed in its own right. Though these two cities are the better known sources of Moroccan pottery, two other styles are often seen. In the Rif, Atlas, and Anti-Atlas, many villagers still create their own pottery and fire it with smaller local kilns. This pottery is generally less fine, often adorned with geometric designs cut into the pottery, sometimes painted with black paint or just left raw. It's rarely glazed and generally more rustic in appearance. The other type of pottery is green and heavily glazed; it's produced only in the small town of Tamegroute, just outside of Zagora.

FEZ POTTERY

The famous blue color of Fez is used in almost all of the locally made pottery. The potters traditionally spin with fine, gray clay. There is a firm, heavy feeling to a well-spun bowl or plate from Fez. Designs are painted in Fez blue, soft greens, yellows, and other colors, all using various geometric forms, often incorporating flower motifs, a leftover influence from those who emigrated from Andalusia. Potters typically mark all of their work with a series of initials. Look for these on the bottom of the bowls, plates, vases, urns, and other pieces on offer. In particular, the initials "ACH" is one of the better marks to find and some of the highest quality pottery to be had. In recent years, many of the potters have been forced to relocate their kilns outside of the city limits to help curb pollution. This has caused prices to go up, and the average dinner plate or medium-size bowl now costs 60Dh or so. The best place to shop for pottery is the Henna Souk just off the Talâa Kbira. Sellers here are generally friendly and bargaining is easy.

SAFI POTTERY

Though less famous than the pottery of Fez, the pottery of Safi is no less interesting. Potter's Hill, just outside the medina, houses the workshops. The potters generally spin with red clay. Between the more brittle clay and the glazing technique, their dishes are more prone to chipping, so make sure they are packed well. Designs are typically geometric, though unlike the potters of Fez, who generally stick to strictly traditional motifs, Safi potters use motifs that are often experimental, sometimes commercial, and always fun to look at.

Silver

Because of its relative expense, not many Moroccans sport gold, whether wedding rings, bracelets, or anything else. Silver is often the metal of choice and is used for wedding bands, earrings, necklaces, and decorative pieces. It is regulated by the state, and any work of sterling silver will have the number 925 stamped on it if it is of good quality. The two best places to shop for jewelry are in Tiznit and Rissani, though medinas throughout the country have a jewelry souk, usually close to the palace in the mellah (Jewish quarter).

For generations, it was Morocco's large Jewish population that controlled the precious metals market in Morocco. They sourced gold from around Africa and even worked with local mines to produce silver. After the founding of Israel and the Jewish exodus in the latter half of the 20th century, the jewelry trade fell into decline, though now there are many enterprising Moroccans who are taking up this lucrative artisan trade.

Many Amazigh are fond of silver and use it for decorative jewelry. Chunky necklaces, bracelets, and earrings made of nickel-silver were, and still are, the fashion in mountain towns. Often, semiprecious stones, such as coral or turquoise, are used in making this jewelry. Designs such as the ornate, triangular fibula (generally used in necklaces and the ever-present Hand of Fatima, used to ward off the evil eye) are used as centerpieces. Jewelry is rarely worn except on celebratory days, such as Eid al-Adha or wedding celebrations.

Woodwork

In the mountains, wherever there are tall trees, you'll find wood bowls, serving utensils, sculptures, boxes, and ornate serving platters as well as larger pieces, such as dining tables, armoires, and bed frames. Traditionally, most of the woodwork in Morocco was done with **cedar,** though pine, lemon, and orange wood are also used. Cedar, a beautiful wood known for being naturally insect repellent, is used for numerous works, including the famed *moucharabi* panels that adorn many houses, providing for air flow and discreet places for women of the house to look out on life in the medina, as well as those ornate carved ceilings in most Moroccan palaces that make heads spin.

Much of Morocco's intricate woodwork was traditionally begun in mountain towns, such as Azrou in the Middle Atlas, where workers would cut trees, then make and cure boards. These pieces of wood would be delivered to the nearest large city, such as Fez or Meknes, and then woodworkers in the medina souk would finish products, taking slabs of cut wood, molding, sculpting, carving, and forming the wood into complex geometric patterns. Different processes of finish were developed, generally involving sanding and varnishing the wood, though some woodworkers began to specialize in painting floral and geometric designs on their finished pieces. Often, a simple furniture design, such as a cedar chest, set of drawers, or coffee table, is transformed in a colorful array of beautifully painted motifs.

On the southern coast, the complex natural designs of **thuya,** a slow-growing conifer tree, are prized by woodworkers and tourists alike. The resin, *sandarac,* can be made into a varnish and is used in some circles to preserve antiques. However, the largest demand made of the thuya is for wood souvenirs, typically bowls, which are made from extracting burls from the trunk of the tree, destroying the root systems and killing the tree. Because of its slow natural growth and the challenge it faces now from massive deforestation, this beautiful wood is becoming endangered. The purchase of thuya products is discouraged until a more sustainable way to harvest this natural resource is developed.

Maâlems: Morocco's Master Artisans

A *maâlem,* or master artisan, is a dying breed in Morocco, though with the influx of tourism and the interest in Moroccan handicrafts, a sort of revolution is in our midst, with many young men picking up paintbrushes, chisels, hammers, and screwdrivers to learn the ancient trade of their forefathers.

Historically, it was easy to spot a *maâlem.* He generally worked in a particular souk in the medina plying his trade. The *maâlems* working with wood gathered in the wood souk, while the *maâlems* working with metal plied their trade in the metal souk, and the tanners were in the tanneries. For the most part, this is still the case, though some *maâlems* have relocated from the growing expense of the medinas and often work in the outskirts of the cities, where rent is cheaper.

Maâlems, though generally men, are not always. Women have had roles as *maâlems,* particularly when it comes to the tradition of carpet weaving and knotting. A single carpet might take weeks or months to make. A woman would traditionally do this as a sort of dowry, though more often now, it is a side job to make some extra income for her family. Women also work to paint pottery and woodwork and can sometimes be glimpsed off the main streets plying this trade.

Zellij

Those picturesque mosaic fountains next to nearly every mosque in the old medinas, where children fetch a glass of water or women wash fruit, are constructed by master artisans who painstakingly chip away at individual pieces of tile, cutting them exactly to triangles, stars, squares, rectangles, and 360 other geometric forms, before cementing them into place. Most fountains take thousands of uniquely formed pieces, which are laid in a pattern according to the master artisan's whim. The overall effect is striking. Though most artisans now work on *riads* and historic restorations, fountains are still built, often in private homes, and tables, mirrors, and other more portable objects are also fashioned.

MUSIC

Chaabi

Chaabi, which translates in Moroccan Arabic as "popular," is a type of folk music exclusive to a few North African countries. It is widespread all around Morocco and is known for its use of informal or popular language (Darija in Morocco) and for its creative rhythms. This is the type of music mostly associated with festivals and weddings, and it is the most secularly festive of Moroccan music, though it often does incorporate religious aspects into the vocals. If you're taking *grands taxis* around Morocco, more likely than not you will hear a lot of Chaabi music.

Gharnati

Named for the region where it is thought to have originated, Granada, Gharnati music is a particular style of classical Andalusian music that made its way into Morocco during the time of the Spanish Inquisition, when Spanish Muslims fled into Morocco, forming large communities in Tetouan, Chefchaouen, and Fez, though now the practice of this form of music is largely preserved in Oujda, near the Algerian border. Gharnati is usually heard at more solemn occasions and, like classical music anywhere else, is notably more posh in its admirers. A small festival of Gharnati music happens each summer in Oujda.

Gnawa

Gnawa is, internationally, the most well-known type of Moroccan music. It has roots in sub-Saharan Africa, as is evidenced by the heavy stress on the unique rhythms the musicians keep. The music is often repetitive, providing background for the vocalist, who sings religious chants. The effect is meant to be trance-like, with listeners and musicians alike often falling under the spell of the song. An individual song might last for hours.

Musicians famously use iron castanets, or *krakebs,* and often drums, such as large *tarboukas,* to create the distinct Gnawa rhythm. A *gimbri,* or sometimes a *hajhuj* (basic stringed instruments, something like an acoustic guitar), is plucked along with the rhythm, while the vocalist, the most respected of the Gnawa musicians, chooses the particular chant to accompany the rhythm. Gnawa music today, in its purest form, is difficult to find in Morocco, because religious happenings occur only in the most distant, hard-to-reach places deep in the desert and the mountains. Most performers are now fusing Gnawa with blues, hip-hop, and even reggae, and often perform for tour groups in restaurants and hotels.

Rai

Rai music dates back to the beginning of the 20th century in Oran, Algeria. Even though it is not native to Morocco, it makes up a big part of the country's culture. In Arabic, *rai* means "opinion." Since the first appearance of this genre, the lyrics have been very controversial because they highlight social and racial issues such as immigration, diseases, and poverty, especially during the French protectorate. This form of popular Bedouin music was originally performed by young men or a group of men accompanied by traditional instruments, but with the evolution of music, women also adopted this style. The performers are usually referred to as "Sheikh(a)," or "Cheb(a)" for the younger generations. Some of the more famous Rai singers are Cheb Mami and Cheb Khalid, who is known as the "King of Rai." Both singers incorporate some reggae style into their songs and have French and Arabic lyrics. Despite the controversy behind Rai music, it has gained fans and followers from all around the world.

Essentials

Transportation

GETTING THERE

The **Mohammed V International Airport** is the primary international airport in Morocco, though it is small by international standards, with only a couple of terminals servicing flights in and out of the country. After arriving, you will be asked to fill out a customs form and likely have to wait for about an hour to make it through customs and sometimes even longer to retrieve your luggage. You may be asked to pass your luggage through a scanner for additional security measures.

There are money exchange offices and ATMs just beyond the customs area. It's a good idea to exchange for some local currency before heading out of the airport. There are taxis and an airport train that connect with Casablanca.

From North America

Most flights from North America connect with European travel hubs, with many of the least expensive flights connecting in Spain at either Madrid or Barcelona for a short layover via **Iberia** (www.iberia.com). Direct flights to and from North America are available only via **Royal Air Maroc** (tel. 0522/489 751, www.royalairmaroc.com), which provides non-stop service via Boston, Miami, Montreal, and New York City to Casablanca. For budget travelers and those looking to break up their trip in Europe, it's sometimes worth booking a less expensive round-trip ticket to and from Europe, like in Madrid, and then purchasing a separate ticket via one of the low-cost carriers directly into one of the other destinations in Morocco, such as Marrakesh, Fez, or Tangier.

From the UK and Europe

Europeans have a few modes of transport available to them beyond airplanes, though Morocco is extremely well connected with nearly all major airports in Europe.

BY PLANE

Most European cities are 2-4 hours away. Agadir, Casablanca, Essaouira, Fez, Marrakesh, Ouarzazate, Rabat, Tangier, and Zagora—all have direct connections with European transport hubs, often via low-cost airlines such as **Air Arabia** (www.airarabia.com), **Ryan Air** (www.ryanair.com), and **Transavia** (www.transavia.com). If you can, try not to arrive/depart from Casablanca. Other airports in the country generally involve a lot less waiting time with customs, check-in, and luggage retrieval, and are generally a better travel experience.

BY BUS

The **CTM** (www.ctm.ma) runs international bus lines that use the ferries between Morocco and Spain. Buses stop in major cities in Spain, France, and Italy. Tickets generally cost the same as a plane ticket and are sometimes more expensive. Buses leave from most major cities, as well as numerous small ones, generally once a week or more, and travel through Morocco via Tangier to Casablanca, generally making a stop in Rabat on the way south.

BY CAR OR CAMPER VAN

Ferries run services back and forth to Morocco, making it easy for people with their own vehicle in Europe to road-trip through Morocco. Drivers might be asked to provide proof of ownership and insurance that will cover any potential accidents while in Morocco. Check with your insurance company to purchase international driving insurance for the duration of your stay. If you are traveling in a car that is not your own, you must have a certified, stamped letter from the vehicle's owner. At the border, in Tangier, Ceuta, or Melilla, if you do not have international insurance, you will be able to purchase it from **Assurance Frontière** (59 Blvd. Bordeaux, Casablanca, tel. 0522/484 156) for 950Dh. This will cover driver and vehicle for one month. It is possible to renew this insurance at the headquarters in Casablanca. An International Driver's License is not a requirement for driving in Morocco, nor will you be asked for it. Your license from your home country will suffice.

BY BOAT

From Spain it's possible to take ferries over the Strait of Gibraltar into Morocco. Cars, camper vans, and walk-ons are all served by numerous ferry companies shuttling back and forth

Previous: the Marrakesh Airport

throughout the day. By far, the most effective crossing is between Tarifa, Spain, and Tangier, Morocco. This is the **quickest ferry crossing** at 35 minutes and will drop you off directly at the bottom of Tangier's old medina. However, this passage is occasionally closed if the seas are particularly stormy. **FRS** (www.frs.es), one of the longer-running ferry services, and the new **Intershipping** (www.intershipping.es) ferry service both have the same runs, alternating departure times across the strait. A typical four-door sedan with one passenger costs around 2,500Dh round-trip. It is not possible to cross the strait with a rented car.

Ferries also service Tangier across the strait from Algeciras and Gibraltar. These ferries take much longer to cross the strait and to load passengers and cargo. Additionally, they make port at the Tangier Med station (not Tangier Ville) about a 45-minute drive from Tangier. This port is also used by freight trucks and construction equipment, slowing the entire boarding process. The crossing from either Algeciras or Gibraltar will take an entire day with loading and unloading the ferry, customs, and additional drive times in Morocco. Prices are much the same as the crossing at Tarifa.

The Spanish exclaves of Ceuta (Sebta) and Melilla in the north of Morocco are also serviced by ferries from mainland Spain with prices and services more or less the same as the ferry service between Tarifa and Tangier, though with longer travel times.

You do cross an international border when arriving or departing Morocco via ferry and will be asked to fill out a customs form. When arriving, you will show this form along with your passport to a customs officer aboard the ferry. To avoid waiting in a long line, it's best to arrive immediately to the customs officer and present your passport and form. If a line has already formed by the time you enter the ferry, relax, enjoy the trip, and wait until the ferry has almost arrived to have your papers checked. There's no reason to spend the entire ferry ride waiting in a customs line.

From Australia and New Zealand

Unsurprisingly, there are no direct flights to Morocco available from the other side of the planet. Most flights will connect you with a travel hub, such as Doha or Dubai. Many travelers coming from Australia and New Zealand bookend their trips to Morocco with long stays in Europe. From Europe, it's a quick flight and easy to purchase a separate ticket via one of the low-cost carriers directly into Fez, Marrakesh, or Tangier, thus bypassing Casablanca. The quickest, most direct, and often least expensive flight into Morocco from Sydney or Auckland is via Qatar airlines with a stopover in Doha. This flight is still over 24 hours long, so be sure to pack a pillow.

From South Africa

There are no direct flights into Morocco from South Africa. Because you'll have to layover anyway, it's often worth it to book your round-trip ticket directly into one of the other destinations in Morocco, such as Marrakesh or Fez, to bypass Casablanca. Common cities for layover include Doha, Istanbul, Paris, and Rome. Like those coming from North America or Australia, it is an inviting proposition to bookend your holiday in Europe or the Middle East.

GETTING AROUND

By Plane

There are a few in-country flights worth thinking about to maximize time in Morocco. Direct flights between Fez and Marrakesh, Marrakesh and Ouarzazate, Tangier and Marrakesh, and Casablanca and Dakhla are the most interesting to cut down on some travel time. Flights within Morocco are operated by the state-run **Royal Air Maroc** (www.royalairmaroc.com).

By Train

For most travelers, the national train run by **ONCF** (www.oncf.ma) is the most convenient way to get around Morocco. Though limited, the train does stop in most major cities. There are two primary train lines, which meet at Sidi Kacem. One line travels up and down the Atlantic seaboard from Tangier south through Rabat and Casablanca before ending in Marrakesh. The other line begins in Casablanca and runs northeast through Meknes and Fez and crosses the mountains to distant Oujda.

Trains are inexpensive, and most travelers will want to purchase first-class tickets. These are a relative bargain, generally costing only 20-40Dh more, and ensure air-conditioning and a reserved seat.

During peak travel times, such as popular holidays like Eid al-Adha or school holidays, trains can quickly fill up, and sometimes first-class tickets are not available. If this is the case, be prepared for a long, stuffy ride standing in the side corridor walkway, avoiding the smell of the usually open and rarely cleaned toilet in second class.

Train stations are often unannounced. If you're unsure of what station you are at, ask around. Chances are that someone knows and will be willing to tell you when you've reached your station. Outside of the stations, be prepared to fight off taxi drivers and faux guides who will try to lure you into overpriced taxis or, even worse, overpriced lodgings. Simply walk out of the station and wait along the nearest busy street to hail a passing taxi.

The new Al-Boraq **high-speed train** makes getting to and from Tangier very quick, though requiring passengers from Fez and Meknes to change trains at Kenitra. From Kenitra to Tangier is now a short 45 minutes on the Al-Boraq, while Rabat to Tangier is now just over an hour and Casablanca to Tangier is about 2.5 hours. It's best to purchase tickets on the ONCF website a day or two ahead of your travel for the Al-Boraq, or in-person at the station.

By Bus

The network of privately run buses is a great alternative to riding the rails and is a safe, comfortable way to travel to destinations that are not serviced by the train. If traveling in the heat of the day, to avoid overheating make sure to sit on the side of the bus that will be the most shaded. Buses on trips of more than two hours make 15-30-minute rest stops at roadside cafés catering to the bus crowd.

CTM (www.ctm.ma) runs buses that crisscross the country. Most of their buses are comfortable, and there are even premier bus tickets available on buses with slightly more legroom and Wi-Fi—indispensable for some digitally tethered travelers. In larger cities, the CTM buses have their own stations, though in smaller cities they will be found at the main bus station or *gare routière*. During the busy travel seasons it is best to buy tickets a day ahead of time whenever possible, if not two or three days ahead of time, as these buses often fill up, making seats a scarce commodity.

The other recommended bus company is **Supratours** (www.oncf.ma), which has teamed with the ONCF train company. These buses pick up where the rails give out. The buses are comfortable, safe, and reliable, though, like the CTM buses, they will fill during peak travel times, so it is best to book ahead. When traveling by either CTM or Supratours, you will be asked to store any larger bags beneath the bus for a fee of 5-10Dh.

The Marrakesh Express

The "Marrakesh Express" was the nickname for the train ride between Casablanca and Marrakesh used by travelers to Morocco in the 1960s and 1970s. It was popularized by the Crosby, Stills & Nash song of the same name. Today's Marrakesh Express still runs between Casablanca and Marrakesh, but with a newer train and fewer hippies—though there are generally still a few lingering around, "traveling the train through clear Moroccan skies," just as the band sang 50 years ago. Plans are afoot to extend the high-speed train that runs from Tangier to Casablanca all the way to Marrakesh by 2025.

Other local companies also operate buses. These buses are generally less comfortable, less expensive, less punctual, and less safe. Buyer beware. The night services, though cooler, are subject to far more accidents, particularly in the mountain passes and along National Road 8 (N8) from Marrakesh to Agadir.

By Grand Taxi

The *grands taxis* relay passengers between cities and towns. Taxis are regulated by the local government, which sets the prices. Prices sometimes need to be negotiated (refer to relevant locations in this guide for average prices) with less-than-honest drivers, and the cost generally goes up by 50 percent after nightfall. Prices are per seat. Sometimes, *grand taxis* will ask one of the travelers for a passport to register travel outside of their normal jurisdiction with the local authorities.

It seems like almost every story of a traveler to Morocco involves some sort of a harrowing trip in one of these *grand taxis*. The seat belts often don't function and drivers are often exceedingly aggressive. However, many of the taxis now in service have been purchased since 2015 offering an infinitely more comfortable ride than their predecessors. By all means, when traveling by *grand taxi*, make sure you get one of the newer cars for your own story of a harrowing taxi ride.

By Petit Taxi

Petits taxis run in all cities and most midsized towns. Typically they use a counter in the cities and charge double rates after nightfall, though in some smaller towns a flat rate is common. Throughout Morocco, it is illegal for a *petit taxi* to travel outside of its city or town or to have more than three passengers at one time.

By Car

Driving in Morocco, though a bit more dangerous than in Australia, New Zealand, North America, or the UK, is perfectly doable for drivers who practice good defensive driving techniques. The roads are, for the most part, well paved, and road-tripping through Morocco can be a wonderful way to get off the path beaten by the trains and buses and find pieces of this stunning country that are less explored. Those who have driven in other parts of North Africa, India, or even around the Mediterranean will be right at home driving in Morocco.

Moroccan drivers, by and large, are some of the worst drivers in the world. The legal driving age is 21, and driving school, a comprehensive written test, and a performance test are all required by the government to earn a driving license. However, most Moroccan drivers have simply paid a small bribe to have their license issued, bypassing the school and test. Therefore, most drivers are unaware or care little for the basic traffic laws. Drivers sometimes pass on blind turns, run red lights, and will straddle two lanes on the paid autoroute. In the cities, the aggression is compounded, and streets are unmarked, adding to the confusion.

Driving at night should be avoided, as there are few street lights. Often, herders with camels, sheep, goats, and cows try crossing streets after dark, particularly in the countryside, making the possibility of hitting livestock a real concern. Keep in mind that the signage, generally in Arabic and French (though occasionally only in one or the other language) is not usually lit, making following turnoffs and other directions that much more difficult. Wherever possible, we've included the Arabic script for the names of the cities and towns appearing in this guide. Even if you can't read Arabic, you can match the script in this guide to the script on the signage. This could double as a fun road-trip game in the car for the kids.

However, daytime driving is perfectly fine. The speed limit on the autoroutes is typically 120 kilometers (75mi) per hour. Beware of speed traps and police who walk out onto the road, even the autoroutes, to stop speeding traffic. Keep your passport and driver's license on you at all times. A typical driving infraction will set you back 400Dh. You will be given a receipt for this and are expected to pay the fine on the spot. If you are unable to pay the fine, your ID may be confiscated and taken to the local court for you to pay the fine there.

Gasoline isn't exactly cheap in Morocco (12Dh a liter, around 25Dh a gallon), though it is subsidized by the government. Consider renting a newer, fuel-efficient diesel car. Diesel is slightly cheaper (less than 9Dh a liter, around 20Dh a gallon), and a new diesel engine can fetch nearly double the mileage of unleaded engines. Always fill your car up to the maximum whenever stopping at a station, particularly in the rural areas, as sometimes stations can be far apart.

CAR RENTALS

If you're renting a car in Morocco, to get the best deal and a wider variety of cars to choose from, it's best to arrange it before arrival. Be sure to request an automatic transmission if you need one, because the majority of rental cars are manual.

Rental insurance is required, and it comes included with car rentals. Check with your insurance provider at home to see if rentals are covered overseas. Some credit cards offer rental insurance if you use their card to rent a car. If your home auto insurance or credit card covers the rental insurance, you might be able to get the insurance that is included with the rental waived—it's worth inquiring. Spending a little extra on travel insurance is always a good idea.

Typical prices in Morocco for rentals with unlimited mileage range from 300Dh per day for a standard four-door sedan to 600Dh per day for four-wheel drive, with large discounts often available for weekly rentals. It's possible to find rentals for as little as 100Dh per day if you plan a bit in advance.

Hertz (www.hertz.com) and **Avis** (www.avis.com) have locations at Mohammed V Airport in Casablanca as well as airports in Agadir, Fez, Marrakesh, and Tangier. Large groups or families might consider the large vans available for rent through **GM2 Tours** (www.gm2tours.ma).

By Bicycle

Bicyclists share the road with the drivers and can be seen training throughout the Middle Atlas and High Atlas regions through the fall and spring seasons. Mountain biking has grown increasingly popular with European and North American travelers. It's a pleasant way to get around to otherwise inaccessible areas, and the roads are generally quieter than those found back at home. Biking is safe enough when sharing the road with vehicles, as long as bicyclists stick to the shoulder, though a helmet and lamp are highly recommended. However, biking is not regulated by Moroccan law, and in cities bikers are often seen without helmets. Bikes are welcomed on most buses for 10Dh.

Visas and Officialdom

PASSPORTS AND VISAS

Morocco is a tourist-friendly destination that doesn't require entry visas for visitors from most countries. Travelers from the UK, Europe, North America, Australia, and New Zealand are exempt from any form of visa and granted automatic 90-day entry. However, your passport should be valid for at least six months from the date of entry. On a customs form you will be asked to mark your profession. Journalists should consider writing in another profession, as customs officers have been wary of letting journalists into the country without extensive documentation.

South Africans do have to apply for visas, which they can do in their country of residency through the nearest Moroccan embassy. Otherwise, to extend your stay in Morocco, it is possible to exit to Morocco for a stamp via Ceuta or Melilla and reenter, sometimes on the same day, for another 90 days. However, some customs officers will ask you to travel to mainland Spain and spend at least one night there before returning for a 90-day extension.

CUSTOMS

Customs regulations are fairly lenient in Morocco. Hand luggage is rarely checked upon arrival, and while traveling across the borders between Ceuta, Melilla, and Morocco, customs officers almost never ask foreigners what they are taking with them. However, legally there are limits to what can be taken into the country. The limits are as follows: one liter of spirits (hard alcohol) or two liters of wine; 200 cigarettes, 50 cigars, or 400 grams (14 ounces) of tobacco; 150 milliliters (5 fluid ounces) of perfume or 250 milliliters (8 fluid ounces) of *eau de toilette*; one camera and one laptop for personal use; and gifts totaling no more than 2,000Dh.

Border controls are particularly weary of the smuggling of hashish. It and other controlled substances are forbidden. If you are traveling with many books or if you have a book that is controversial, prepare to be questioned. If the customs officers consider the text to be "immoral" or "liable to cause a breach of peace," it may be confiscated. Generally speaking, books condemning Islam, questioning the king, or questioning Morocco's right to the Western Sahara are banned throughout the country.

EMBASSIES AND CONSULATES

The **Canadian Embassy** (66 Ave. Mehdi Ben Barka, tel. 0537/544 949, www.canadainternational.gc.ca) in Rabat is generally open Monday-Thursday 8am-4:30pm and Friday 8am-1:30pm. It is closed for Canadian and Moroccan holidays. Australians traveling in Morocco who need assistance can be helped at the Canadian Embassy. For emergencies, **Canadian and Australian citizens** can call collect to reach the **Emergency Watch and Response Centre** (Canada tel. 613/996-8885).

New Zealanders will have to travel to Madrid, Spain for consular services (7 Calle del Pinar, tel. +34 915 230 226, email: madrid@embajadanuevazelanda.com).

The **UK Embassy** (28 Ave. S.A.R. Sidi Mohammed, Souissi, tel. 0537/633 333) in Rabat deals largely with political interests. It keeps **consulate** offices in Casablanca (Villa Les Sallurges, 36 Rue de la Loire, Polo, tel. 0522/857 400, Mon.-Thurs. 8am-4:15pm, Fri. 8am-1pm), Marrakesh (Borj Menara 2, Immeuble B, 5th fl., Ave. Abdelkrim El Khattabi, tel. 0537/633 333, appointment only), and Agadir (no address, tel. 0537/633 333, Mon.-Thurs. 8am-4:15pm, Fri. 8am-1pm, appointment only). For emergencies, UK citizens should call tel. 0537/633 333.

The **US Consulate** (8, Bd Moulay Youssef) in Casablanca is available for US citizens who need consular services or assistance, such as in the case of a lost or stolen passport. The consulate is closed on observed US and Moroccan holidays. For emergencies, contact the **American Citizen Services hotline** (tel. 0522/642 099 Mon.-Fri. 8am-5pm, tel. 0661/131 939 after hours). The **US Embassy** (Km5.7, Ave. Mohammed VI, Souissi, tel. 0537/637 200) in Rabat is strictly diplomatic without services for citizens.

The **South African Embassy** (34 Rue des Saadiens, Quartier Hassan) in Rabat has services for their citizens. It is best to call ahead for an appointment on one of the following numbers: 0537/689 159, 0537/700 874, or 0537/689 163, or you can email: safricamissionrabat@gmail.com.

Festivals and Events

RAMADAN

The holy month of Ramadan is one of the spiritual pillars of Islam, marking the first revelation of the Quran to the Prophet Mohammed. It is the ninth month of the Islamic calendar, a lunar-based calendar, so its dates according to the Gregorian calendar shift each year. Unlike other Muslim countries, Morocco does not use astronomic calculations to dictate the particular months of the lunar calendar and instead uses observation by authorities with the naked eye.

Ramadan is a period of abstention. Believers are required to fast from sunrise to sunset. Nothing is allowed to pass through the lips, including food, water, cigarettes, or even gum. Believers are also expected to abstain from sex and impure thought. It is illegal to disrespect Ramadan, as it is a pillar of Islam, and a few Moroccans are jailed each year, usually for eating or smoking in public during the daylight hours of Ramadan.

Non-Muslims are not required to fast, though they'll often be encouraged to, with Muslims telling them how good it can be for their health, both spiritual and physical. Pregnant women, women menstruating, children, the elderly, those sick or disabled, and non-believers are all exempt from fasting. However, those not fasting should be as respectful as possible, which includes eating, drinking, and smoking in private, away from crowds and off the streets.

Ramadan can be a beautiful time to travel the country. Because it is a period of heightened religious awareness, there are some unexpected benefits for single women travelers, who will rarely, if ever, be harassed, and throughout the daytime, because smoking is not permitted, cafés, restaurants, trains, and other public areas have improved air quality. Moroccans are often more convivial and are more likely to invite guests to *ftoor*, the breaking of the fast, which happens at sundown. In most cities, towns, and villages there is a particular signal to mark the end of the day's fast—often the sound of a siren, firing of a cannon, or lighting of a lamp atop a minaret.

A fast is traditionally broken with a glass of water, dates, and a bowl of *harira* (a soup typically made with lentils, chickpeas, and sometimes meat). The giving of alms, or *zakat*, is also a pillar of Islam, and during religious periods it is thought that the spiritual value of any *zakat* given doubles in value. Thus, much almsgiving to beggars happens during this period, particularly just after breaking the fast.

After sundown the party starts, with cities bursting into liveliness every night. Families will be out with children in tow, cafés and restaurants will open, and a seemingly endless promenade happens in major cities, such as Casablanca and Tangier, while in the countryside, many of the smaller villages break into religious song and dance.

Travelers will find many cafés and restaurants serving primarily Moroccan clientele closed for the month, and most businesses, including banks, post offices, and government offices, keep shorter hours. Restaurants geared toward tourists, particularly in heavily touristed areas, remain open during normal operating hours. Trains, buses, and other modes of public transportation are often delayed, and the entire pace of the country seems to slow to a crawl.

OTHER ISLAMIC HOLIDAYS

Besides Ramadan, the dates of other key Muslim holidays change on the Gregorian calendar each year. **Eid al-Fitr,** often called Eid es-Seghir or "the little holiday," marks the end of Ramadan. It is a period of festivity when things swing back to normal. Trains, buses, and *grands taxis* are often crowded just before and after this holiday.

The most important holiday during the Muslim year is **Eid al-Adha,** also known as Eid al-Kabir or "the big holiday." In French-speaking circles, this is also known as *la fête de mouton,* or "sheep festival." Eid al-Adha takes place two lunar months after the end of Ramadan, and it marks Abraham's willingness to sacrifice his son Ismael to God (similar to the Old Testament, though in the Old Testament it is Isaac who is offered as sacrifice). This is something like a multi-day Thanksgiving feast.

Just before the feast, you will likely see sheep being transported around the country and tethered to rooftops and balconies. Occasionally, kids take their new sheep out to play with them in the front yard.

The first day of the holiday is marked by the slaughter of a sheep—thus the French reference to the holiday. Outside, streets are generally barren, with people inside with their families, except for the butchers who go door-to-door, slaughtering each family's sheep. Meanwhile, it is customary to burn the heads of the sheep in cauldrons. These are found on the corners in most neighborhoods, with young men looking after this task. Generally speaking, these holidays are a time of great joy in Morocco, with many families reunited after the long year and friends coming together again, though some Moroccans are beginning to regret the commercialization of the holiday.

Even more so than during Eid al-Fitr, expect all modes of transportation to be congested and traffic to be at a standstill just before and just after the holiday, as families move back and forth across the country visiting relatives or returning home. During the holiday itself nearly everything is shut down, including most city buses, and taxi drivers are a scarce commodity. It is not advisable to schedule travel over this time, unless you are staying with a family in the country or sticking to metropolitan cities such as Casablanca or Marrakesh.

Other Moroccan holidays include **Ashoura,** a festival occurring one lunar month after Eid al-Adha. During Ashoura children will often ask for presents, which has given rise, with the help of Western influence, to the character of Baba Ashoura, or Father Ashoura, a Moroccan take on Father Christmas. Traditionally, children are given small toys, particularly little drums, during this smaller festival. **Moharem,** the Islamic New Year, happens two lunar months after Eid al-Adha. The **Mouloud,** which is the celebration of the birth of the Prophet Mohammed, is also observed in Morocco. A few important *moussems* (festivals) happen during the birthday of the Prophet, with a couple of the more interesting ones involving the arabesque fantasia during the **Moussem of Ben Aïssa** in Meknes and the **Candle Festival,** a candlelight promenade, in Salé.

OTHER FESTIVALS

Morocco is a festive country that knows how to have a good time, even if alcohol is in short supply. Many of the more popular festivals and events you'll find around the country are somehow tied to the agricultural calendar, almost always during a period of harvest. Because of this, the exact dates of these festivals are never known until the weeks and days leading up to them. Some of the most **popular agrarian festivals** include the Cherry Festival in Sefrou (end of June/beginning of July), the Rose Festival in Kelaat M'Gouna (mid-May), the Saffron Festival in Taliouine (end of October/beginning of November), and the Marriage Festival in Imilchil (end of September/beginning of October).

There are a number of **music festivals** that take place in cities across the country, as well. In Fez, you'll find the popular Sacred Music Festival (June), as well as the less-known but equally intriguing Festival of Sufi Culture (April). In the capital city of Rabat you'll discover the popular-music Mawazine Festival (end of June), while Essaouira plays host to the extremely energetic Gnawa Music Festival (mid-June) every year.

Spring

SUMMER FESTIVAL OF SUFI CULTURE (APR.)

Explores Morocco's Sufi culture through music and spiritual reflection. Held every year in Fez.

EID AL-FITR (MAY)

This bright festival is celebrated around the country as it marks the end of the month of fasting, Ramadan. Eid al-Fitr will be in the month of May in 2020, 2021, and 2022, though days change according to the Islamic calendar.

ROSE FESTIVAL (MAY)

One of Morocco's most pungent festivals takes place in distant Kelaat M'Gouna with a "rose princess" crowned after the festivities.

Summer

SACRED MUSIC FESTIVAL (JUNE)

One of Morocco's most popular music festivals held in Fez. Typically, this festival draws some world-renowned popular singers and songwriters.

GNAWA MUSIC FESTIVAL (JUNE)

With plenty of traditional Gnawa and lots of Gnawa-Blues fusion, this multiday music festival has become a staple of the Essaouira scene.

MAWAZINE FESTIVAL (JUNE)

Held in Rabat, this is the festival for pop and hip-hop lovers, with usually one or two big-name headliners.

CHERRY FESTIVAL IN SEFROU (JUNE/JULY)

Oft-neglected Sefrou transforms into the darling of the Middle Atlas for this week of celebration.

EID AL-ADHA (JULY)

Lasting three days, this is Morocco's largest holiday. Families travel across the country to celebrate with each other. In 2020, 2021, and 2022, Eid al-Fitr will be in the month of July, though days change according to the Islamic calendar.

Fall

IMILCHIL MARRIAGE FESTIVAL (SEPT.)

During one of the most storied festivals in Morocco, marriages are arranged and celebrated in the High Atlas town of Imilchil.

TANJAZZ FESTIVAL OF JAZZ MUSIC (SEPT.)

Tangier explodes into a syncopated, swing-time funk for a long weekend in September with Moroccan and international performers.

SAFFRON FESTIVAL (NOV.)

A must-do experience for foodies looking to get their hands on one of the world's most precious spices. Held in the little town of Taliouine in the Souss during the short saffron harvest season.

Winter

INTERNATIONAL FILM FESTIVAL (NOV. OR DEC.)

Marrakesh has one of the few winter festivals going in Morocco.

Conduct and Customs

By and large, Moroccans are some of the friendliest, most genuinely helpful people you can meet. Morocco is always ranked in the top 10 "friendliest countries in the world." Of course, a few bad apples may try to use this to their advantage and request something that seems unfair, such as an exceedingly high price for an item or service. But for the most part, people are friendly, curious about where you came from, and, if you've taken the time to master a few phrases in Moroccan Arabic, likely to invite you over for tea or dinner. That said, customs are different in Morocco than in many Western countries. Greetings are more elaborate. The importance of the family is heightened. The roles of men and women are more defined, in some cases rigidly. In many regions, even the clothing is significantly different. With this said, women have experienced harassment, typically in the form of persistent catcalls or, on rare occasion, being touched inappropriately. For the most part, tourists are left alone as they are an important part of the economy, though aggression does occasionally happen.

GREETINGS

Greetings in Morocco vary from region to region, though they are all elaborate. A typical greeting inquires about your health and the health of your family (often each individual member), and then finishes with "so everything is well, then?" before a conversation can be started. When women are meeting for the first time, it is generally customary to kiss once on each cheek, *á la française*. This is the case in most cities, though in some rural regions women kiss each other on the hands, arms, or foreheads as well. Men generally meet with a handshake, though often this handshake will be soft, even limp. Greetings between men and women are a bit more complex. For female travelers, it is best to stick with shaking hands with men, as some men might make the wrong assumption about your intention if you try to hug them or give them a friendly peck on the cheek. For male travelers, it is best to let the woman take the lead. Some Moroccan women kiss on the cheek, some shake hands, and some cannot be touched and will give you a deferential nod of the head, sometimes without even eye contact.

If traveling as a couple, you will likely be asked many times how many kids you have or, if you're younger, when you are expecting to have children. If you are older, you will be expected to have children, the more the better, and even grandchildren. You will be asked about your children—what they do, what they study, where they live, if they are married and have children. This is considered polite conversation. It's a great idea to have a few pictures of your family to share with people you meet along the way, even if just on your phone.

When invited for dinner or tea to a person's home, it is customary to take off your shoes at the entryway. Single women should be wary of any invitation to a man's house. If you are offered food and refuse, this is seen as very insulting. Vegetarians and vegans, in particular, are put in an awkward situation because nearly anything offered will contain some sort of meat product. Most Moroccans do not understand the concept of vegetarianism, let alone veganism or gluten allergies, and the host will feel bad, often for days and weeks on end, because he or she was not a good enough host. I find it best to swallow your morals in this rare instance in the name of cultural diplomacy. If you can't, then tell them you have an allergy. Your host will still feel bad, but less so.

Many friendly encounters happen in the context of public transportation. In this case, it is customary to share food. If being offered food, it is polite to take what is offered. Another semi-elaborate ritual between Moroccans involves offering and accepting food. A person should offer food three times. The first two times the food is offered, it should be declined out of politeness. The third time it is offered, this time more persuasively, the person being offered the food is then free to take it or refuse it.

BEGGARS

You will likely encounter quite a few people asking you for money. Keep in mind that as a foreigner visiting Morocco, you are considered wealthy. The country teems with poverty and there is no real social security. People, particularly the elderly, are entirely reliant on their families for support. Generally speaking, you will find older beggars outside of mosques and at gates into the old cities. A few dirhams will be appreciated, and you can expect some form of blessing for you and your family in return. If you do not have any dirhams to spare, master the phrase, *"Allah yejeeb tisseer,"* meaning "May God make it easy on you." This is a polite blessing for beggars to be used in lieu of giving them any cash.

If a beggar is being persistent, particularly younger beggars who are obviously able-bodied, it is best to ignore them. When possible, duck into the nearest shop or, if you're working on your Moroccan Arabic, tell them *"mandeesh whalloh, saafi, baraka."* This means, "I don't have anything. That's enough, really enough." If the beggar is being more persistent, you have permission to tell them, *"bahd mehni"*—literally, "get off my back," meaning "get lost."

Sadly, you will likely see quite a few children, sometimes begging and sometimes selling tissues near bus stations, train stations, and at busy intersections. It is best to never give children money. Better to give them pens, pencils, paper, or even candy. Gangs of street kids are known to use their money to buy glue and gasoline to huff. This is a very sad reality of contemporary Morocco.

CLOTHING

Generally speaking, the urban areas are Westernized, with jeans, T-shirts, tank tops, shorts, and skirts all being the norm. In the more popular beachfronts, such as Taghazoute and its environs, walking around in swimwear and flip-flops is generally acceptable. Otherwise, keep in mind that Morocco is generally more conservative. Men are expected to cover their chests, upper arms, and legs past the knees. Women are expected to be covered from the ankle to the wrist. It is best to wear loose-fitting clothes with natural fibers that allow your body to breathe. When traveling in the places in Morocco where the sun is stronger, such as the mountains and desert, you will be thankful for the extra covering.

MUSLIM ETIQUETTE

Religion is taken quite seriously in Morocco, and it is illegal to mock, deride, or otherwise insult Islam, the Prophet Mohammed, or the king, who is the religious leader, or "Commander of the Faithful," of Morocco. The mosque is a sacred space, and as disappointing as it might be for non-Muslim travelers, mosques, *zawiyas,* and other religious buildings are largely off-limits for nonbelievers. The exceptions are the guided tours at the Hassan II Mosque in Casablanca, the courtyards of some of the *zawiyas* (such as the Mausoleum of Moulay Ismail in Meknes and Mausoleum Moulay Ali Cherif in Rissani), and a couple of the mosques that remain unused, such as the Tin Mal Mosque in the High Atlas or the Spanish Mosque in Chefchaouen. Muslims dressed in western fashion will often be questioned at the doors of the mosque and, in some instances, be asked to prove that they are indeed believers through reciting the *shahada* (Islamic creed), particularly in the more superstitious *zawiyas.*

Street Food the Moroccan Way

For some delicious, inexpensive treats, the seemingly infinite number of snack carts you'll find in most medinas are a wonderful way to interact with locals and taste some fast food, Moroccan style. Street food generally ranges from 1-10Dh. This is a taste of true local flavor.

One of the more common street foods is a snail soup known as *babboosh* in most of Morocco and as *aghlal* or *ghoulal* in the North. Steaming bowls of this brothy treat are for the escargot lover. The snails are typically seasoned with a warm mix of spices, such as licorice, cinnamon, bay leaves, and the spice blend *ras el hanoot.*

In the North, you might see street vendors with large, round, flan-looking pies on hot plates. This is *caliente* (derived from the Spanish word for "hot"), a savory treat made of chickpeas. You can ask for more spices to shake on the *caliente* yourself.

Another chickpea treat is *hoomus*. This steamed chickpea snack is seasoned with generous amounts of salt and cumin. It's a bit like popcorn and made to be eaten on the go.

A more filling treat is *bissara,* generally made with fava beans, though sometimes with split peas as well. This is a thick, hearty soup, popular with sailors for its rumored qualities to help rheumatism. Usually this sailor staple is served with a half loaf of Morocco round bread and plenty of olive oil and chili pepper.

Popular barbecues sell brochettes of seasoned chicken and beef, and other vendors sell tropical fruits by the slice. For some energy on the go, consider the local nut roaster who'll be selling a variety of nuts—such as walnuts, almonds, and cashews—that can be had for peanuts, bad pun fully intended.

Food

Moroccan cuisine is widely considered one of the best cuisines in the world. While you can find good Moroccan food at restaurants, the best is made at home. This is largely because Morocco is not a dining-out country. Most of the meals happen at home, generally cooked by the wife or mother, and, as most Moroccans will tell you, made even more delicious upon the arrival of a guest.

MOROCCAN CUISINE

A typical **breakfast** in Morocco consists of different breads (such as *harsha,* a semolina flatbread), Moroccan pancakes (*m'smmen* or *miloui*), goat cheese, olives, freshly squeezed orange juice, and a hard-boiled or fried egg. Often, breakfast is served with a salad, just like lunch and dinner.

There are numerous Moroccan **salads,** nearly all of them involving steamed and cooked vegetables. Some of the better known salads include eggplant, beetroot, roasted peppers, onions, and tomatoes. These are served sometimes before, after, or with the **soup,** traditionally a *harira* (a tomato-based soup, often with chickpeas, lentils, or pasta noodles) or lentil soup, though sometimes *bissara* (a soup made of fava beans or split peas). In fact, in most Moroccan medinas and along the seaports you'll find sellers with vats of thick *bissara*. It is filling, inexpensive, and said to have properties that are great for the lungs. For vegan travelers, it often becomes a staple while wandering through the complex medinas.

The **tajine** is a main staple of Moroccan cuisine. Tajines are served in conical clay dishes (also called tajines), traditionally cooked over an open flame, and are something like a slow-cooked stew. Tajines generally involve some sort of meat. Some of the more common preparations include chicken, lemon, and olive; spiced meatballs and eggs; beef with honey, dates, and prunes; lamb with

1
2
3
10V
ONCF

prunes and olives; and spiced sardine meatballs. Vegetarian tajines are available, though invariably these lack many of the spices and are typically more bland than meat tajines.

Traditionally, families would gather around for **couscous** lunch on Friday after the imam gave his afternoon sermon. A lot of them still do, and to honor this tradition and make time for families, many businesses have shortened afternoon hours—many of the old medinas are closed for the entire day. Couscous, as it is known in Morocco, is quite different from its bastardized cousin in the West that comes in a box and is ready in less than five minutes. Couscous takes many, many hours to make. The small grains of pasta are hand rolled and steamed over the meat and vegetables in a special couscous maker. A traditional couscous is shared with the family from one large dish, with the meat, usually chicken, beef, or lamb, arranged in the middle of the plate. If you're eating with a Moroccan family, the portion in front of you on the plate is yours, and you will often be eating with your hands. Keep in mind that it is rude to eat with your left hand. This is considered the "dirty" hand as it should be used for performing your toiletries. Eat with your right hand only. You can either form balls of couscous and vegetables with your hand or use bread to scoop up the little grains and sauce.

Undoubtedly, you will have had enough **mint tea** by the end of your stay. Often jokingly called "Berber whisky" or "whisky Moroccan," mint tea is a customary ritual and something hosts offer to their guests. You will likely be offered mint tea at the many shops and bazaars in the medina, particularly at carpet sellers, where some time must be spent haggling over a price, as well as at most smaller hotels, guesthouses, and family homes. The tea is generally sweetened with copious amounts of sugar, making it a syrupy mint affair. It's okay to ask for only a little bit of sugar or no sugar at all.

1: Moroccan breakfast with *harsha*, a semolina flatbread 2: a tajine being cooked 3: the new Al-Boraq high-speed train

VEGANS, VEGETARIANS, AND GLUTEN-FREE

Veganism and vegetarianism are somewhat novel concepts in Morocco. Outside of major cities and high-end restaurants and *riads*, explanations about not eating meat or meat products are often met with confusion. Meat is a staple of the Moroccan diet. If invited to a Moroccan family's home for a meal, meat will invariably be the central feature. It is considered somewhat rude not to offer a guest meat and equally rude not to partake. Dishes generally served when a guest arrives are either tajine or couscous, each usually with some vegetables, though cooked or served with the meat. This leads to some true moral and ethical decisions for hardcore vegans and vegetarians. Is it okay to try to explain that you don't eat meat and pick at the vegetables around the dish or to refuse the dish altogether, thus insulting the host? In practice, it is best to pick at some vegetables, do your best to explain, and repent later.

While eating out, you will typically find seven-vegetable couscous (usually written in French: *couscous de sept legumes*) and vegetarian tajines and pizzas. Sometimes meat broth may be used for flavor, though, so beware. If asking for a dish without meat, you may be served something with fish, chicken, or turkey unless you are very clear, as these are often not considered meat dishes; the Moroccan concept of meat is generally confined to beef, goat, and sheep.

Good staples for vegans and vegetarians include Moroccan salads, generally vegan, as well as *bissara*, a kind of fava bean or split pea soup that is usually served with bread and plenty of olive oil and chili pepper. Plenty of shops in the medinas sell roasted nuts. Supplements, such as B12, iodine, iron, and calcium, should be packed with you, as you will likely not find them in Morocco.

The good news is that there are plenty of delicious fresh fruits and vegetables.

Though the use of pesticides and herbicides has grown and includes crop-dusting over some of the larger farms around Rabat and Casablanca, the vast majority of farmers are simply too poor to purchase these and rely on eco-friendly methods of growing their fruits and veggies. Fruits and vegetables should be washed thoroughly and be allowed to soak in vinegar for five minutes to kill unwanted bacteria.

Eating gluten-free is easy enough, though don't expect your waiter to understand what it means. Only the high-end restaurants and *riads* understand what a gluten-free food is. Couscous is decidedly not gluten-free and should be avoided, but rice and potatoes are plentiful in Morocco and make for easy substitutes.

BEER, WINE, AND HARD ALCOHOL

Though Morocco produces some fine wines (and has for over a thousand years) and now even produces beers, drinking alcohol is considered forbidden by Islam and is often an underground affair. In more liberal homes, wine might be served with dinner, but by and large this is a rarity. Drinking is not allowed within view of a mosque. In upscale restaurants, comprehensive beer, wine, and alcohol menus are available. Most local bars cater to men, and women seen drinking or smoking in these establishments will likely be considered prostitutes. Upmarket bars frequented by European and North American expats are generally okay, while nightclubs offer another type of scene, though again prostitution is often rampant and drinks are outrageously expensive.

In some medinas, such as in Tangier, alcohol sales are entirely banned. Before and after religious holidays, stores selling alcohol are required to close completely. During these holidays, nearly the only places to find alcohol are tourist-specific enclaves, such as big chain hotels.

Accommodations

Accommodations in Morocco are wide ranging—from the dingiest, dirtiest fleabag hostel in Tangier to the exquisitely luxurious seaside resorts found up and down the Atlantic Coast to nights in the Sahara wrapped snug in a Bedouin tent under the stars. Though it is perfectly possible to travel throughout most of the country using chain hotels and resorts, the more interesting options are generally found in the old medinas of Morocco. You will find traditional 18th- and 19th-century homes, known as *dars* and *riads*, renovated and converted into modern-day B&Bs replete with curvy stucco work, ornately carved woodwork, and imaginative tile work only found in Morocco. Because the homes are crammed into the medina, literally side by side, there is little (if any) attention paid to the exterior. Thus, rotting doors and rusty locks often give way to the welcome surprise of luxurious lodgings.

DARS, RIADS, AND MAISONS D'HÔTES

A *dar* is a traditional Moroccan home featuring a central patio and a series of surrounding rooms. The patio opens to the sky, allowing in fresh air. These homes were historically used by smaller families. Downstairs were the main living quarters, featuring a kitchen and one or two salons. Terraces were used primarily to wash and dry clothes, though they were also places for the children to play and for women to chat across rooftops.

Riads are much like *dars*, though considerably larger. The central patio often has a garden and almost always a fountain. Downstairs was traditionally the public space, with the quarters upstairs reserved for family and the terraces again used for laundry, play, and conversation. Some *riads* included a private hammam, a considerable luxury.

The French term *maison d'hôte,* meaning guesthouse, is used liberally throughout Morocco to refer to *dars, riads,* and new constructions outside of the medinas to house travelers. These are typically a bit less expensive than *riads,* as *riads* are considerably trendier. Many *dars, riads,* and *maisons d'hôtes* are foreign-owned or owned by Moroccans who have usually lived in Europe for some time.

In practice, *dars, riads,* and *maisons d'hôtes* are the best accommodations in the country, with locations generally near major tourist destinations and comfort often exceeding the best hotels in town. However, because the majority of these are remodeled homes from the 18th and 19th centuries, many have steep stairways that are not suitable for young children or mobility-impaired travelers. Because the market for B&Bs is loosely monitored, it is also worth taking a tour of the property, examining the beds, sheets, and bathrooms, before agreeing to stay at a property not recommended in this guide.

HOSTELS

The network of hostels throughout Morocco is quite good, particularly along the Atlantic Coast and at most of the major destinations. A typical bed will cost 40-100Dh a night, depending on availability, location, and season. Most Moroccan hostels are plugged into the **Hostel World** (www.hostelworld.com) network. It is best to book hostel rooms ahead of time, particularly around European holidays, as hostels will often be full of backpacking students.

GÎTES D'ÉTAPE AND REFUGES

Along popular hiking trails through the mountains of the Rif, Atlas, and Anti-Atlas, there are *gîtes d'étape* and refuges to keep you warm, dry, and safe from the elements. Refuges are generally little more than a rickety wood shack, though are occasionally something more of a low-end hotel, complete with a small café or restaurant. Bedding is of the bunkbed/army cot type. The *gîtes d'étape* sprinkled through many of the smaller mountain towns of Morocco are family homes where they welcome guests. Sometimes there are beds, but often you sleep like the family, on layers of wool carpets directly on the floor. Prices range from 100-300Dh a night, and often food is included.

Travel Tips

STUDY, EMPLOYMENT, AND VOLUNTEERING

Studying, working, and volunteering can all be wonderful ways to visit Morocco, meet locals, and become culturally immersed. With the growing economic sector and influence of North American, Chinese, and European companies, it is increasingly easy to find work in Morocco, particularly in the telecom and tourism sectors. Though French and Arabic can be useful in the work environment, they are often not necessary. People working for multinationals may want to check with their employers if there is a local office in Morocco, likely Casablanca, where they can be transferred. Employment is also sometimes possible with the American Language Center schools, which are located in most major cities. A TEFL certification is generally required in order to teach English.

Al Akhawayn University (www.aui.ma) in Ifrane offers enrollment to students in North America and Europe. It is Morocco's only university based on the liberal arts system generally used by US and Canadian universities. It partners with many American universities, large and small. Instructors are multinational, and English is the language of instruction. For many Anglophones, students, staff, and faculty, this is the best option in the country for university-related studies. There are work opportunities as well, not always advertised. It's best to contact individual departments with job-related inquiries and the Office of International Studies about possible study-abroad opportunities.

There are numerous language schools throughout Morocco, particularly for those interested in learning Arabic, whether the more universal Modern Standard Arabic (MSA) or Moroccan Arabic (Darija). Schools can be found in most major cities. The **Arabic Language Institute in Fez** (www.alif-fes.com) is one of the more renowned programs, and it's in the heart of the historic Fez medina, while **Qalam Wa Lawh** (www.qalamcenter.com) is in the more modern environs of Rabat.

For American citizens, perhaps the best way to volunteer and see the country is through the **Peace Corps** (www.peacecorps.gov). Morocco is one of the busiest countries with Peace Corps volunteers. The Peace Corps keeps a permanent staff in Rabat, and 180 volunteers are spread throughout the country, working mostly on youth development projects.

Besides the Peace Corps, many initiatives, both large and small, can benefit from volunteers. **Volunteer Morocco** (http://volunteermorocco.org) is a well-known outfit that works on developing poorer regions and villages and offers multiple trips every year.

ACCESS FOR TRAVELERS WITH DISABILITIES

Though many people in Morocco have disabilities, public assistance is scarce and they are reliant on their families and the generosity of strangers for support. Moroccans are quick to help people with disabilities, but the infrastructure to assist those with disabilities, such as wheelchair ramps and signs in Braille, is basically nonexistent. Even in the new cities, you cannot expect to find sidewalk ramps. Most of the *villes nouvelles,* found in Agadir, Casablanca, Marrakesh, and Rabat, and even the older medinas found in Marrakesh and Rabat, should be easy enough to navigate with assistance.

Buses and trains are comfortable enough, though boarding may prove difficult. The steep stairs and crush of people generally coming on and off will be worthy obstacles, to say the least. In this instance, *grands taxis* are generally a better idea. You can pay for two seats, having the entire front seat to yourself, and in the case you need help getting in or out or need any help with luggage, the driver and other passengers would normally be more than happy to help. Another option is to hire a driver for the course of your trip (200-300Dh a day) who can conveniently also double as a translator and guide through the country. Contact one of the tour companies if you're interested in hiring a driver. It may also be worth it to think about a packaged tour and put a company familiar with Morocco and its various challenges in charge of your travel in-country.

For the most part, remember that Morocco is predominantly a walking country, inside and outside. Outside, the old medinas generally have lots of slopes and narrow, often rocky, passageways, making the going tough for those with limited mobility. Most kasbahs, restored *riads,* and *dars* have oddly placed, often steep stairs, though some do offer lodgings on the ground floor, making stays possible. Some of the high-end lodgings, particularly in Agadir, Casablanca, Marrakesh, and Rabat, have made changes to cater to mobility-impaired travelers, including accessible rooms and toilets, wheelchair ramps throughout, spacious elevators, and even special vans to assist those who might require the use of one for their stay. Of course, this luxury comes at a cost.

TRAVELING WITH CHILDREN

Morocco is a child's dream come true. There are many fascinating sights and sounds, and the people are very indulgent to children. Children are kissed, hugged, caressed, and often blessed by total strangers. For children not used to this sort of attention, it can be disconcerting at first, though usually after a day or two, they've gotten the swing of it and are happy to meet all these smiling strangers. For parents, this unwanted and unasked-for attention might come as a shock, but it is meant to entertain the children as much as to compliment the parents. It is part of the social fabric of the culture and should be embraced.

As paramount as child safety can be, you'll see many children playing in the streets, often late at night, without a parent in sight. In many ways, this is akin to the time in Europe or North America when children were turned loose in the streets to run around until they were tired. Other than the occasional fight between kids, there are no real dangers. The only potential dangers children face while traveling in Morocco are the many, many feral cats in the streets and the wild dogs in the more rural areas. Rabies, though rare, can be a concern. If a child is bitten, then precautions should be taken and a vaccination gotten immediately. Otherwise, the chaotic traffic, particularly in the cities, is something to be aware of.

Children under four generally travel and are lodged for free. Notify your accommodations ahead of arrival if you will be needing extra beds in your room. Higher-end hotel chains and resorts often have children's playgrounds and even baby-sitting services. There are parks and other entertainments geared especially for children.

Babies will often be coddled, and as a parent you will be complimented on the beauty of your child more times than you will be able to count. However, traveling with a baby does pose certain challenges. Breastfeeding can be awkward. Outside of the airports, there are no changing stations. It is best to breastfeed as discreetly as possible. Some women are comfortable doing this in train cars and on park benches and just use a loose cloth or thin scarf to cover. In Morocco, this is perfectly acceptable.

You can find supplies, including disposable diapers and baby food, at local stores and at the larger grocery store chains, such as Carrefour and Marjane, both usually located on the outskirts of town. Outside of major cities, however, supplies can be more difficult to find, so stock up. If you need hot water or milk for formula, any restaurant or café will be able to help, and more than likely you'll find assistance a notch kinder than in North America or Europe.

The sun in Morocco can be particularly strong. Children are prone to sunstroke. It is best to keep children out of the hot afternoon sun, layered with high-SPF sunscreen (available at any pharmacy in Morocco), and hydrated with plenty of water. Kids can also be more sensitive than adults to the stressful effects that travel has on our bodies. This may manifest itself in a longer-than-normal period of jet lag, upset stomach, or cold-like symptoms. Because of this, light food and plenty of rest are recommended for the first 2-3 days in-country.

WOMEN TRAVELING ALONE

Overall, Morocco is a perfectly safe destination for women travelers. Adventurous single women travelers often make new friends, are invited to family homes, and bring back stories to share, along with a few souvenirs. That said, sexual harassment is a real issue in Morocco, though this is felt in some places more than others. In the cities, particularly Agadir, Casablanca, Chefchaouen, Essaouira, Marrakesh, and Rabat, women traveling alone are rarely bothered more than other tourists or foreigners. Women alone or in pairs can expect catcalls as well as more vulgar comments, though if you don't understand Moroccan Arabic, this will probably go unnoticed. Older men will sometimes flirt, though this is generally not meant to be taken seriously, while young men can be not only vulgar, but persistent. This is particularly the case in more rundown parts of cities and in less-affluent areas, as well as the medinas of Fez and Tangier. Be firm, though not aggressive, make it clear that you want nothing to do with them, and find a populated area or duck into a shop. Consider finding a pack of like-minded people, whether as part of a guided tour or at the local hostel, to accompany you through the medinas. Some ability in French or Arabic is recommended, and, as always, confidence is a must.

While in rural areas, keep in mind that a woman traveling alone, without the company of her husband, father, brother, or cousin, or even with a group of her friends, is viewed suspiciously. If you drink, smoke, or walk around remote towns at night, most people will think you are looking for companionship. At the very least, you will be seen as something *zeen*—that is, encouraging sinful behavior. Most Moroccan women appear diffident, if not snobbish, in public. This is for good reason. If you are seen as smiling easily in the company of men, too friendly, or too physical—that is, if you touch their arms or hands, hug them or kiss them on the cheeks when greeting—these are all seen as cues to the men that you are coming on to them.

Agadir and the beaches around it are the most touristed by Europeans and showing skin is the norm, though elsewhere in Morocco, particularly away from the beaches, it is discouraged. As a rule of thumb, the less skin you show, the better, which will also protect you from the sun. For visiting any religious monument, such as the Hassan II Mosque in Casablanca, you will need to cover your shoulders and have your legs covered beyond the knee. Some women feel most comfortable carrying a light scarf that can be used to cover their head to blend in with local women, though this is not necessary.

LGBTQ TRAVELERS

For many years Morocco was a haven for the LBGT community in Europe. Cities such as Marrakesh and Tangier developed a reputation for being liberated places that, despite the local culture, tolerated and even accepted practices that were derided, lampooned, and prosecuted in Europe. Today, the culture has swung more current conservative, and unfortunately Morocco is no longer quite the safe haven it once was. However, Marrakesh and other major destinations like Essaouira and Agadir are still popular with much of the European LGBTQ crowd. In general, LGBTQ travelers will feel most welcomed in the higher-end accommodations and should keep discrete in the public sphere.

Homosexual travelers, particularly men, should understand that engaging in homosexual behavior (such as kissing on the lips) is illegal in Morocco and punishable by a fine and/or jail time. (Same-sex friends kissing on the cheeks and holding hands is not uncommon, though holding hands is falling out of fashion among men.) For the most part foreigners are generally not bothered unless officials believe it to be possible that prostitution is happening. This is particularly the case if older foreigners are seen in the company of young Moroccans. Gay men should also be cautious if out on the town or using online dating sites. Moroccan men have been known to seduce foreign men to try to scam money from them. A common scam is to offer to go back home with you, only to steal stuff from your hotel room. When at nightclubs and bars, keep one eye on your drink and refuse drinks from strangers.

Around Marrakesh and in high-end hotels and *riads* around the country, particularly foreign-owned ones, same-sex couples shouldn't worry about sharing a bed. However, in budget and midrange accommodations or accommodations owned by Moroccans, caution should be taken and discretion is advised.

Navigating the Medieval Medinas of Morocco

Most Moroccan cities have an older neighborhood dubbed the *medina*. Literally, *medina* means "city" in Arabic, though in this context, it is meant to mean "the old city." Most medinas are smaller, usually only a handful of city blocks across, and are a fun distraction for a morning. However, the older, expansive, sprawling, labyrinthine medinas of Fez and Marrakesh—and to a lesser extent, Meknes, Tangier, and Rabat—are veritable mazes filled with sights and smells that can disorient even the most travel-hardened.

girls taking the family bread to the local bakery in Marrakesh medina

To most comfortably explore the medinas, be sure to be well rested and wear a suitable pair of walking shoes. Be sure to also have some small Moroccan money on you—5Dh and 10Dh coins will be invaluable for snacks or help along the way. Having a map, whether in this guide or downloaded on your phone, is also a good idea. Mark your starting point. Remember that people don't know street names in Morocco. It's better to know the name of your accommodation and a local landmark you can return to.

You will likely encounter fake guides and young boys along the way who will ask you if you are looking for something in particular, like the tanneries. A firm and persistent "no" is your only defense against these hustlers. Store owners can also be sticky, sometimes holding you by the elbow or arm to get you to visit their shop, sip a tea, and hopefully spend your money. For the most part, these are the only real dangers you'll face in the medinas.

To find your way out of the medina when you're lost, it's often a good strategy to follow a main thoroughfare until you find something you recognize or a door out of the old city, where you can find a taxi to take you somewhere you might be more familiar with, such as the "Blue Gate" in Fez or the Jemma el-Fnaa in Marrakesh. If all else fails, feel free to enlist the help of one of those pesky hustlers asking you where you want to go. 10Dh is usually enough, though they will always ask for more.

SENIOR TRAVELERS

Morocco is a country that still has a profound respect for its elders. This carries over to visitors from other countries, as well. Well-traveled, adventurous tourists of a certain age will feel right at home in Morocco. If you take medication or supplements, be sure to bring enough for the length of your stay. It can also be helpful to know the French equivalent of the generic medicine (unbranded) before you arrive so that you can likely track it down at a local pharmacy or notify a doctor if need be. You should also talk to your doctor at home about your trip and any dietary restrictions you should be aware of. For instance, if you're taking an ACE inhibitor, you will want to stay away from bananas. Travelers diarrhea is a real concern in Morocco. It helps to stick to fully cooked foods. You might want to consider packing some loperamide (Imodium A-D).

Keep in mind that Morocco is not a wheelchair-friendly country and lacks much of the infrastructure required for the mobility impaired. In larger cities, you may be more of a target for pickpockets and purse snatchers, so take care to keep your important documents on your body. It's a neat trick to leave the sign on the door of your hotel turned to "do not disturb." This can ward off potential intruders in your hotel room.

Otherwise, take care to protect yourself from the hot sun, apply liberal doses of sunscreen, pack your best pair of walking shoes, and stay hydrated. Morocco is very much a country to experience on your two feet, whether it's trekking through the High Atlas or wandering the medieval medina of Marrakesh.

TRAVELERS OF COLOR

Morocco is an incredibly diverse country, and Moroccans are used to travelers visiting the country from all over the world. However, physical traits can be a subject of comment. Black travelers might be asked if they are a popular public figure (like Barack Obama, Beyoncé, or Oprah) or somehow related. There may even be a request for a selfie; feel free to politely decline. This is all meant in good humor and not intended to offend. It's primarily a hustle to sell an item or service.

As wonderful as Morocco can be, there is some racism, though most Moroccans will not easily admit this. With the rise of immigration from Sub-Saharan Africa, tensions have risen between Moroccans and other African countries. If a store owner or taxi driver thinks you might be from somewhere south of Morocco, you might find yourself being entirely ignored, particularly in newer parts of Casablanca, Fez, and Tangier, where immigration is most prevalent.

Health and Safety

COMMON HEALTH PROBLEMS

Beyond the effects of jet lag for those crossing the Atlantic, there are few health problems to be worried about in Morocco.

Altitude Sickness

For those hiking the mountains, particularly the High Atlas, and particularly those peak bagging, altitude sickness can be a concern. It's best to wait until your body adjusts to being in Morocco before beginning any ascent. Altitude sickness generally occurs after 2,400 meters (about 8,000ft). There are quite a few peaks in the High Atlas well over this, including Toubkal at 4,167 meters (13,671ft), Immouzzer at 4,010 meters (13,156ft), and Timesquida at 4,089 meters (13,415ft). However, even the passes through the High Atlas climb well above the commonly accepted threshold for altitude sickness, reaching heights near 3,000 meters (about 10,000ft). Common symptoms of altitude sickness include headache, fatigue, stomach pains, dizziness, and an inability to sleep. Usually, effects subside in 1-2 days, though if they persist, you should descend. Avoid drinking alcohol, particularly when your body is first adjusting to the higher altitudes, as this can exacerbate symptoms and effects.

Tap Water

By and large tap water is okay to drink. In fact, many seasoned travelers suggest that drinking the local water helps to acclimate your body to the local bacteria normally found in the water that is used to clean fruits and vegetables, and can be an effective way to avoid upset stomachs and diarrhea. However, in the older medinas you should stick to bottled water, available everywhere. It's also possible to carry a refillable bottle and use the numerous local fountains.

Traveler's Diarrhea

By far the most common health complaint of visitors to Morocco is traveler's diarrhea. This is contracted through eating foods that have not been properly washed or cooked or water that has been contaminated with unfamiliar bacteria. This bacteria enters the body and acts like a mild food poisoning. Symptoms include a low-grade fever, stomach pains, loose stool movements, nausea, and sometimes vomiting. Usually within 1-3 days symptoms will go away. Eat only well-cooked and well-washed foods. Drink bottled water to stay hydrated. Locals recommend liberal doses of cumin coupled with a hot oregano infusion, as these both have antibacterial properties and help to flush unwanted bacteria from your system. Others recommend Coca-Cola. You could also pack loperamide (Imodium A-D).

HEALTH MAINTENANCE

Of course, you should travel with **medical insurance.** Check with your insurance agency to see about coverage in Morocco. Often major credit card companies offer travel insurance automatically or for a small additional fee when you use their credit card to book your plane ticket. Be sure to read the small print and contact your credit card company if you have any questions. Travel insurance generally covers any medical expenses, as well as theft, canceled or delayed flights, lost luggage, and any other manner of mishap, though extreme sports, such as kayaking, surfing, and rock-climbing, will only be covered if you pay a premium.

Of the hazards you may face in Morocco, **snakes** and **scorpions** are of a little concern. The Sahara is host to a few poisonous types of snakes, and scorpions are fairly common. It is best to wear thick-soled shoes (not flip-flops), walk with care through heavy brush, beware of turning over loose stones when in the desert, and be sure to shake out your shoes as a precautionary measure before putting them on. If bitten or stung, treat it as a medical emergency as it can be deadly if left untreated. **Dogs** and **monkeys,** though more of a nuisance, can be rabid. There are many wild dogs, particularly in the mountains, and they are pests to many hikers. Carry a few rocks in your pocket while hiking. You can slowly back away from the wild dogs' territory while threatening to throw a rock or, if they get too close, throwing it at their feet. If bitten, a rabies vaccination is required.

Sunstroke, heat exhaustion, and **dehydration** can be major concerns, even in the cooler mountains. Morocco's sun is strong, and the heat can be intense. Always travel with a light sunhat, drink plenty of fluids, and wear high SPF sunscreen. These are particularly important precautions for young travelers, who are more susceptible to the effects of the Moroccan sun. Symptoms of heatstroke include high body temperature, dizziness, and nausea. This is potentially fatal. Attempt to lower the body temperature through cool baths or showers before seeking help. Dehydration is always a potential problem. Make sure to drink plenty of fluids, especially if symptoms, such as headaches or lack of urination, are apparent.

MEDICAL SERVICES

For major medical emergencies, contact your consulate. Though all large cities in Morocco have public hospitals, often private clinics provide better, more hygienic service. If at all possible, make for Rabat, host to the best public hospitals and private clinics. Every major city and town will also have pharmacies, including the local *pharmacies de garde,* which are the all-night and off-hour pharmacies. You'll find a list of these posted at every pharmacy in the city. Pharmacists can often recommend local doctors. The **US Consulate** keeps a page of **recommended doctors and physicians** (http://morocco.usembassy.gov), including those who speak English.

SAFETY

Crime

The crime rate in Morocco is quite low and violent crimes are a rarity. As anywhere else, tourists are marks for thieves and pickpockets. Muggings are uncommon, even in the dark, twisting paths of the medina. Stealth is more likely, with pickpockets slipping hands into the purses of distracted pedestrians or perhaps breaking into hotel rooms, particularly in Agadir. Travelers have been known to have phones or laptops snatched from café tables, as well. Police are hesitant to file any paperwork for stolen goods or money, though they will always give you a form for a stolen ID or passport.

Harassment

Sexual harassment is often a problem experienced by women travelers, who are targeted by aggressive males. It is best to act confident, let it be known that you do not appreciate the lewd comments or suggestions, and if touched, grabbed, or fondled, feel free to yell at the offending man in public. A simple *"hashooma!"* (meaning "shame on you!"), said loudly, clearly, and confidently in a public space should be enough to attract unwanted attention to the man and cow him into submission.

Women might consider dressing so as to show as little skin as possible and avoid tight-fitting clothes. Baggy pants, long skirts, and long-sleeved shirts that cover as much skin as possible can deter much unwanted attention. Some women enjoy traveling with a loose scarf that can be shawled around the head and even the face, when they feel the stares are becoming too much. Though this might deter some men, the fact is sexual harassment is a real issue in Morocco.

Another form of harassment comes from street vendors and children. They can be sticky, to say the least. Street vendors generally won't leave their storefronts, so you won't have to worry about them following you, though faux guides and young children have made trailing tourists something of a bothersome art form in some of the medinas. Often when walking through the medina you may find yourself with a small group of children, usually young boys, asking for money or to guide you through the medina. You may have to repeat *"la"* (Moroccan for "no") many, many, many times before the boys get the hint. If they become aggressive or if you are particularly worn out, usually saying *"la, baraka, saafi"* (meaning "no, that's enough, really enough") is enough to deter them from bothering you anymore. The same goes for faux guides, many times found at the major entrances of the medinas.

Drugs

Hashish, kif, and majoun, all derivatives from marijuana, are by far the most seen, smelled, and used drugs in Morocco. Smoking marijuana is illegal, though tolerated almost everywhere in Morocco. Among the affluent, particularly nightclubbers and partygoers, cocaine and ecstasy are also commonly seen and used. Penalties for these drugs are severe. Tourists should beware of scams involving the police and bribery, particularly in the Rif. If arrested, contact your consulate. They cannot provide legal service, though they can recommend a lawyer.

Under no circumstances should you attempt exporting any amount of any drug to Spain or the rest of Europe. Border controls are tight and the penalties severe.

Smoking

Smoking is widely permitted in restaurants and hotels. There are occasionally nonsmoking areas, though the ventilation is often inadequate to make them truly smoke-free.

Women smoke in Morocco, more often in the cities, but there is still a cultural taboo against it.

During the holy month of Ramadan, Muslims are required to abstain from many things, including smoking. It would be very rude to smoke in the open during the daytime over the course of this month. If you need a cigarette, try to keep it to your accommodation, where the staff are trained to be much more tolerant toward those not abstaining.

EMERGENCY NUMBERS

For **police** in urban areas, dial 19. Outside of urban areas, dial 177 for the **Gendarmerie Royal.** For **firefighters** or **medical emergencies,** dial 15. For **roadside assistance,** dial 5050. For the **operator,** dial 160. Though sometimes you will find someone that speaks English, generally it is good to have someone who can speak French or Arabic call.

If you have a health, safety, or legal emergency, consider contacting the following numbers:

Australian and Canadian citizens can call collect to reach the **Emergency Watch and Response Centre** (Canada tel. 613/996-8885).

New Zealanders will need to call their consulate in Spain during working hours (tel. +34 915 230 226).

UK citizens should call their consulate emergency number (tel. 0537/633 333).

US citizens should dial the **American Citizen Services hotline** (tel. 0522/642 099 Mon.-Fri. 8am-5pm, tel. 0661/131 939 after hours).

South African citizens should contact their embassy (tel. 0537/689 159, 0537/700 874, or 0537/689 163).

Practical Details

WHAT TO PACK

Morocco is called a cold country with a hot sun. The cold is the most surprising element to travelers visiting Morocco for the first time. Outside of the summer months, temperatures can drop, particularly at night. Below-freezing temperatures in parts of the desert and the mountains are common and should be expected. Pack sweatshirts, hoodies, warm pants, thick socks, waterproof shoes, and a waterproof coat outside of the summer months—especially during the winter. Along the coasts, temperatures are regulated by the ocean and rarely get to freezing, but a light rain jacket should be packed along for all seasons for coastal exploration, along with a bathing suit.

All travelers should pack to protect against the sun. Bring a wide-brimmed hat, sunglasses, and waterproof SPF 100 or higher sunscreen (though this you can find at most pharmacies), as well as light long-sleeved shirts and pants, particularly if you plan on going to the desert or going into the higher altitudes of the mountain ranges.

Those interested in trekking through the mountains should pack collapsible trekking poles, waterproof hiking boots, and maps of the region whenever possible. Though not necessary, a good pair of binoculars for birding and spying wildlife should be considered.

A pair of earplugs, an eye mask, and a light scarf to use as a shade for bus, train, and *grand taxi* trips will make traveling through the country much more pleasant.

Morocco runs on the European 220-volt system, with electronics having two round plugs. Most electronics, such as laptops and battery chargers, require only a plug adapter from American to European and do not need a voltage regulator from 110 to 220, though check your device to be sure. Plug adapters can be easily purchased online or at your local electronics store and are a necessity for those looking to bring their cell phones, tablets, laptops, or cameras.

RESTROOMS

For the most part you'll find sitting toilets, though squatting toilets are common—particularly in poorer areas, less-expensive hostels, and in bathrooms at roadside cafés. Public restrooms are fairly easy to find, though often untidy (if not downright filthy), despite having an attendant. Tip attendants, particularly if the bathroom is fairly clean. 2Dh-5Dh is standard.

When traveling, it is a very good idea to bring your own roll of toilet paper. Many public restrooms in Morocco lack this basic necessity. It is customary for Moroccans to use water when cleaning in lieu of paper.

BUDGETING

Morocco is a country for almost any budget. True shoe-string budget travelers can find lodging for as little as 50Dh per night, if not free, in some limited cases. True 5-star lodgings can be found littered throughout the country, catering to Hollywood types, oil barons, and shipping magnates. Most travelers will want to be sure to spend at least a few nights in a restored *riad* in the old cities of Morocco. These can be had for as little as 200Dh per night, or as much as 800-1,000Dh per night.

Moroccans eat extremely well for very little. Travelers wanting to cook their own meals will find that they can pretty easily feed a family of four on 200-300Dh for an entire week by shopping at the local markets. Most fruits and legumes are sold by the kilo. Root vegetables are generally 2-5Dh a kilo (about 2.2 pounds), while most fruits are 5-20Dh a kilo. Small berries are usually sold in 150-gram (one-third of a pound) baskets for 8-22Dh.

There are a number of street vendors that sells kebabs and traditional Moroccan street food for pocket change, while a night out at a very nice restaurant in Marrakesh costs about the same as a bistro in Paris (budget 300Dh per person).

Most travelers will enjoy mixing up types of lodgings and dining experiences. Generally speaking, it's a fine strategy to spend a few nights roughing it at some of the nicer hostels in places like Chefchaouen and Essaouira and then splurge on a nice *riad* in Fez or Marrakesh complete with a feast. Most lodgings will include breakfast with your stay.

If you plan ahead, you will save money and get some of the best accommodations. Right now, Morocco is experiencing more tourism than they have room for in some locations, so the best lodgings fill up six months ahead of time. Renting a car is another great way to potentially save some money and will allow you freedom to explore.

There is no "one size fits all" budget. You'll need an absolute minimum of 100Dh a day to survive, though 500Dh a day will give you some more freedom to experience some of the attractions and history and take advantage of a few nice meals and better lodgings, particularly if you're traveling with a friend on the same budget. Travelers looking to have the best possible experience with the least amount of hassle should consider a substantially larger budget of 3,500Dh a day, which will allow for a hired driver the entire time you're in the country, some fantastic lodgings, incredible meals, guided treks, cooking classes, Sahara desert glamping, and more. Still other travelers will budget even more for royal suites at every property they enjoy, Moroccan spa treatments, private yoga lessons, surf classes, and hot-air balloon rides over Marrakesh.

MONEY

The unit of currency of Morocco is the Moroccan dirham, listed throughout this guide as "Dh" and written on official exchanges as MAD. Banknotes come in denominations of 20, 50, 100, and 200 dirhams. Coins are in denominations of 1, 2, 5, and 10 dirhams. There are smaller coins called *centimes* that are divisions of 1 dirham; these come in denominations of 1, 2, 5, 10, and 20 centimes.

In Morocco, cash is king. Many venues and services do not accept credit or debit cards as payment. If possible, order Moroccan dirhams from your bank, perhaps 500-1,000Dh, before traveling to take care of taxis and emergencies. It's also a good idea to keep smaller bills (20s and 50s) and change on you at all times, as it can be hard to find someone to break larger notes. Euros, and sometimes US dollars, will be accepted in lieu of local currency, though at a less-than-desirable exchange rate.

Exchange Rates

The Moroccan dirham is tied with the Euro and fluctuates accordingly. Check the exchange before your departure and keep in mind the difference between "buying" and "selling" a currency. Historically, exchange rates typically hover around 10Dh equal roughly to the following: 0.9 EUR, 0.8 GBP, 1 USD, 1.4 CAD, 14.5 ZAR, 1.5 AUD, or 1.5 NZD.

ATMs

Thankfully, ATMs are seemingly everywhere. You can find them at major banks throughout the *villes nouvelles* and near major transportation hubs, such as the airports and bus stations. ATMs all take credit and debit cards from around the world, though you should notify your bank that you are traveling. If you are unable to take money out of a machine, it is most likely because your bank or credit card company has issued a stop on your card. You will have to contact them to reactivate your card.

Most ATMs have options for instructions in English. North Americans should keep in mind that "current account" means "checking account." Most ATMs have a daily withdrawal limit of 5,000Dh, though you will only be allowed to withdraw a maximum of 2,000Dh at a time. This can make expensive purchases sometimes a hassle if the seller does not accept credit or debit cards because of the multiple trips required to the cash machine. Most Moroccan ATMs charge a small fee for the transaction—generally around 20Dh. If given the option to do your transaction in Moroccan dirhams or another currency, choose Moroccan dirhams, as this will be less expensive and save unnecessary currency exchange fees.

Credit and Debit Cards

The use of credit and debit cards is something new in Morocco. Many shops, particularly smaller bazaars, accept only cash. It is always best to check ahead of time, but most accommodations take plastic, except for budget lodgings, which often take only cash.

Make sure to notify your bank at home of your travel plans so that your debit and credit cards will not be blocked. It can be a hassle to attempt to call outside of Morocco to unblock cards. Cards without a chip will not work at some sellers. Generally, for purchases you will not sign but will enter your PIN number. It is a good idea to keep a separate card listing emergency numbers in your home country, including emergency bank contact numbers, in case of a blocked card. Keep this information separate from your wallet or purse.

In Morocco, there is sometimes a surcharge of 2-5 percent added to credit or debit card purchases. Often, credit card companies and banks also charge per usage and add a fee for currency conversion. Check with your company to see about exact charges and, as always, read the fine print to avoid unforeseen charges when returning home.

Tipping

Tipping is quickly becoming something of a norm in Morocco. For a quick coffee or tea, you can leave a couple of dirhams. For a meal, you can expect to tip 5Dh, though in upscale restaurants a typical tip is 5-10 percent of the bill. You will also be expected to give change to the parking attendant, gas attendants, and porters (5-10Dh). Otherwise, tipping is at your discretion.

OPENING HOURS

The opening and closing hours of many businesses and restaurants is fluid, to say the least. Don't be surprised to find a museum or restaurant opening half an hour or later after a stated opening time. National holidays and religious holidays (see Festivals and Events earlier in this chapter) will also affect opening and closing times for most local businesses.

Public Holidays

In addition to the observed Islamic holidays, some national holidays are fixed to the Gregorian calendar. Many of these holidays are observed by government institutions and banks, though otherwise it is business as usual. The dates and corresponding holidays are as follows:

- **January 1:** New Year's Day

- **January 11:** Proclamation of Independence (1944 declaration of independence from France)
- **May 1:** Labor Day
- **July 30:** Throne Day (King Mohammed VI ascends to throne)
- **August 20:** Revolution of the King and the People (King Mohammed V returns from exile in 1955)
- **August 21:** Youth Day and King's Birthday (King Mohammed VI's birthday)
- **November 6:** Green March (1975 demonstration that annexed Western Sahara into Morocco)
- **November 18:** Independence Day (independence from France in 1956)

COMMUNICATIONS AND MEDIA

The media throughout Morocco is controlled by the influence, or imagined influence, of the monarchy. Coverage on international events, and controversial national events, is somewhat limited. Topics criticizing Islam, the king, or the Western Sahara are routinely avoided, though most Moroccans will say that there is free press. The several journals and newspapers available are all in French or Arabic. *Le Matin, l'Opinion,* and *l'Economiste* are the major national newspapers in French. *Assabah* and *Almassae* are the two most popular papers in Arabic, though *Almassae* veers toward the sensational. You will find numerous Moroccan and French magazines in most newsstands in major cities. In some major cities, you can find the English-language *International Herald Tribune.*

TV, Radio, and Film

Moroccan television is limited to a few channels, with programs in Arabic, French, and Tamazight. However, satellite dishes are ubiquitous. Channels come in from around Europe, the Middle East, and North Africa. The Qatari-owned Al-Jazeera network is the most popular source for news, while many Moroccans tune into dubbed Mexican and Egyptian soaps for entertainment. During Ramadan there is always a new series that runs every day over the course of the month. Throughout the year, televisions are propped up in every café and most restaurants to lure patrons into watching football (soccer) matches.

The radio is fading in popularity, though it is still used by many Moroccans. Programs are typically in French or Arabic and feature a mix of music, from popular Moroccan Chaabi and more spiritual music to the latest in European and American rap, rock, and pop. Call-in shows are seemingly on every channel.

Though the Moroccan film industry is centered around Ouarzazate, most Moroccan films are shot in Casablanca. Films are typically of low quality, shot in Moroccan Arabic, French, and occasionally Tamazight, and not well distributed.

Phones and Cell Phones

Phone numbers in Morocco are 10 digits beginning with 05 for landlines followed by a two-digit city code. For example, the city code for Rabat and the area is 37. Thus, most phone numbers in Rabat begin with 0537. When in Morocco, it is generally not necessary to dial the 0 before numbers, though if your call does not work the first time, try it with the 0 prior to the number. Cellphones in Morocco start with 06 or 07.

To dial a phone number in Morocco:

From Australia, first dial 0011 (or + if using your cell phone), and then dial Morocco's country code (212), followed by the Moroccan phone number, omitting the 0 at the beginning.

From Canada or the US, first dial 011 (or + if using your cell phone), and then dial Morocco's country code (212), followed by the Moroccan phone number, omitting the 0 at the beginning.

From Europe, New Zealand, the UK, or South Africa, first dial 00 (or + if using your cell phone), and then dial Morocco's country code (212), followed by the Moroccan phone number, omitting the 0 at the beginning.

If you have an unblocked cell phone, it's worth purchasing a SIM card in-country for your travel to use for your phone. For about 20Dh you will have a local number with limited talk time and texts. For 200Dh, you will likely get enough Internet credit to use for a week or two on local 3g or 4g networks, which is sometimes faster than what you might find in London. **Maroc Telecom** (www.iam.ma), **Orange** (www.orange.ma), and **Inwi** (www.inwi.ma) are the major service providers in Morocco, with networks that operate around the country. Maroc Telecom features the widest network, though Orange has better download speeds in most metropolitan areas. You will find outlets for these providers along the main boulevards in the *villes nouvelles* of all the cities and in the Mohammed V Airport in Casablanca.

Having a smartphone can come in handy for all the usual tasks, and the GPS function can be a lifesaver when attempting to navigate unfamiliar city streets, follow winding medina paths, drive around the country, or look for a restaurant.

Internet

Internet access is widely available throughout the country. For some websites, the use of a VPN may be preferable. Wi-Fi is found at most accommodations, though sometimes only available in the public spaces, while Internet cafes can easily be found in all major cities and larger towns.

Shipping and Postal Service

One of the most common issues for shoppers is how to get all the special handwoven rugs and hand-spun pottery back home. In practice, nearly every shop in the medina can ship your items home for you. Even your new breakable will be expertly wrapped; shop owners are accustomed to providing this service. You will be informed of the cost of the shipping, though you will have to take care of customs if applicable in your home country.

Post offices are easily found around Morocco, often on the edges of the old cities and near tourist hubs, making sending letters and postcards easy and inexpensive. Visit the national post office website for more information: http://www.poste.ma.

WEIGHTS AND MEASURES

Morocco follows the metric system. Grams, liters, and kilometers are the primary units of measurement you'll be using on your trip. The country operates on the continental European 220-volt system, with electronics having two round plugs.

TOURIST INFORMATION

Tourist Offices

Tourist offices can be notoriously difficult to find and are generally not in the most touristed parts of town. I've included the addresses and hours of operation for the offices in major destinations. If you're interested in festivals and events, the local tourist offices will invariably have the most up-to-date information and nearly always have at least one person who speaks good English.

Maps

For most travelers, the maps in this guide should be sufficient to navigate the twisting and often confusing medinas and to get around the country without much trouble. In Morocco, maps can be difficult to find. Occasionally, bookstores, newsstands, or tourist information booths carry some sort of map, generally a free small map of the city and occasionally a road map. For the most part, it's better to purchase your maps outside of Morocco. Guidebooks and country maps that do not include the Western Sahara as part of Morocco are banned and liable to be confiscated upon arrival. This is something to remember when shopping for maps.

Drivers and cyclists should consider picking up the **Michelin road map** (1:4,000,000 with sectors of 1:600,000) or the waterproof **National Geographic Morocco map** (1:1,000,000). These maps include smaller roads between cities and towns and are essential for exploring some of Morocco's harder-to-reach places by car or bike.

Good topographical maps are essential for trekkers. The **Toubkal Trekking Map** (1:50,000) made by Cordee is the best topographical map. It's waterproof and should be the number one choice for hiking around Toubkal. The reverse side features a great map of Marrakesh. The second highest and arguably prettier range, M'Goun Massif, is highlighted in the **Central High Atlas Map** (1:100,000) produced by West Col.

Visit your local map specialist, travel bookstore, or independent bookstore, or browse maps and shop online with **Omni Map** (www.omnimap.com) for a great selection of Moroccan-specific maps and guides to help you on your journey.

If you're using your tablet or phone while traveling, be sure to download maps via the app Maps.me. Having a map of all the Moroccan cities you'll be exploring stashed in your pocket is a great idea.

Resources

Glossary

The terminology used in Morocco is often complex, adapted from various Arabic (A), French (F), Spanish (S), and Tamazight (T) sources. Here is a list of the more commonly used terms found in this guide.

A

agadir (T): a fortified communal granary

aïn (A): a spring or other water source

Al Andalus (A): Muslim Spain and Portugal (roughly 700-1500)

Alaouite: the current ruling family of Morocco (17th century-present)

Allah (A): God

Almohad: the powerful ruling family, originally from Tin Mal in the High Atlas, that overthrew the Almoravid dynasty, taking control of Morocco and the Iberian Peninsula (12th-13th century)

Almoravid: one of Morocco's great early dynasties that first spread Moroccan rule into the Iberian Peninsula (11th-12th century); also the founders of Marrakesh

Amazigh (T): the indigenous population of North Africa (see also Berber)

assif (A): a river or tributary

avenida (S): avenue

B

bab (A): a gate or doorway

babboosh (A): snail soup, typically served on the street; also known as *aghlal* or *ghoulal* in the north

babouche (F): the traditional leather Moroccan slipper (also *belgha*)

baraka (A): divine blessing, sometimes equated with luck or good fortune

Barbary (S): term used to describe much of the North African coast by Europeans from the 16th to early 19th centuries

belgha (A): the traditional leather Moroccan slipper (also commonly known by the French *babouche*)

ben (A): son of (also *ibn*)

Berber (F): indigenous inhabitant of North Africa, from Latin *barbarus* (see also Amazigh); some Amazigh consider the term offensive

bissara (A): a hearty soup made of fava beans and sometimes split peas

borj (A): a fort, tower, or other defensive construction

boucharouette (F): a contemporary rag rug made of recycled fabrics, generally very colorful and with outrageous designs

C

caliph (A): Islamic ruler; a descendant of or successor to the Prophet Mohammed

calle (S): street

caravanserai: an enclosed inn with stables for beasts of labor and quarters for merchants (see also *fonduq*)

Casaouia (A): resident of Casablanca

charmoula (A): a Moroccan olive oil sauce with coriander, cumin, garlic, and paprika

chergui (A): a hot, dry wind from across the Sahara

corniche (F): a coastal road or walkway

D E

dar (A): traditional Moroccan house with a small central courtyard

derb (A): a small, often narrow, street

dikr (A): prayer, often chanted or sung during holy days or periods such as Ramadan

douar (A): village

douche (F): shower

eid (A): a feast or festival, a term usually used with Islamic holidays (e.g., Eid al-Adha)

Ensanche (S): new, protectorate-era city; equivalent to Ville Nouvelle

Ensemble Artisanal (F): artisan shops supported by the government

erg (A): sand dunes, such as Erg Chebbi in Merzouga

F G

farran (A): traditional public wood oven

Fassi (A): resident of Fez

Fatimid: a dynasty originally from Syria that seized control of Morocco from the Idrisids (10th century)

faux guides (F): unofficial guides (literally "fake guides")

fonduq (A): an open courtyard surrounded by stables and shops (also *caravanserai*); sometimes used to mean "hotel"

ftoor (A): breakfast (literally "breaking the fast"); used for the meal to break fast during Ramadan (also *iftar*)

gare routière (F): transportation hub, generally for trains, buses, and *grands taxis*

garum (Latin): fish paste

gîte (F): hostel

Gnawa: unique musical form in Morocco that calls on influences from around Saharan Africa as well as the Middle East

grand taxi (F): long-distance taxi used in Morocco to get quickly from town to town

H I

hajj (A): the Islamic pilgrimage to Mecca and one of the pillars of Islam

hamada (A): a stony desert

hammam (A): the traditional Moroccan bath, akin to a Turkish bath, with cool rooms, scrubbing rooms, and steam rooms

haram (A): used to describe something that is not allowed (literally "forbidden")

harira (A): a tomato-based soup, often with chickpeas or pasta

ibn (A): son of (also *ben*)

Idrisid: Morocco's first Muslim dynasty (8th-10th century); named after Moulay Idriss I, the founder of modern-day Morocco

iftar (A): breakfast (literally "breaking of the fast"); popularly used to describe the meal to break the fast during Ramadan (also *ftoor*)

imam (A): Muslim religious authority, similar to a priest

J K

jbel (A): mountain (e.g., Jbel Toubkal) or hill (e.g., Jbel Kbeer in Tangier)

jdid (A): new

jellaba (A): traditional Moroccan garment for men and women (often spelled *djellaba*)

jemaa (A): mosque

kasbah (A): fort

kif (A): a smokable derivative of the marijuana plant

koubba (A): domed shrine

ksar (A): a fort, much like a castle, also used to denote a walled village (plural *ksour*)

Kufic: the most ancient calligraphic form of Arabic

M

Maghreb (A): the region of western North Africa comprising Morocco, Algeria, Tunisia, and Libya (literally "west")

maison d'hôte (F): guesthouse

majoun (A): an edible derivative of the marijuana plant

marabout: holy saint-like figure

mashrabiya (A): latticed woodwork

medersa (A): a school based on Islamic education that incorporates Arabic literature and grammar, as well as astronomy, law, physics, theology, and other disciplines

medina (A): old city; used to describe the older parts of cities (literally "city")

mellah (A): Jewish quarter of a city

Merenid: the dynasty that took control of Morocco after the dissolution of the Almohad dynasty (13th-15th century)

mihrab (A): a niche in the wall of a mosque that indicates the direction of Mecca

miloui (A): Moroccan crepes

minaret (F): tower of a mosque, from which the muezzin delivers the call to prayer

minbar (A): pulpit in a mosque, sometimes used by imams to deliver their Friday sermons

moucharabi (A): carved wooden latticework, typically seen in windows

moulay (A): prince or ruler

moussem (A): a celebration or festival often coupled with a pilgrimage to a marabout shrine

Mouloud (A): Islamic holiday celebrating the life of the Prophet Mohammed

muezzin (A): a man who sings the call to prayer from the minaret of a mosque

musée (F): museum

museo (S): museum

O P

oued (A): river

palais (F): palace

palmeraie (F): palm grove

pastilla (S): meat pie, with a paper-thin pastry coddling a blend of savory meat (chicken, fish, or pigeon), almonds, and eggs spiced with saffron, cinnamon, and fresh coriander (also *b'stilla*)

pensione (S): guesthouse, often much like a hostel

petit taxi (F): local city taxi

pisé (F): sun-dried clay or mud used for building, particularly in hotter regions around the desert

place (F): square or plaza

plage (F): beach

playa (S): beach

Q R

qiblah (A): the direction of the Kaaba shrine in Mecca toward which all Muslims turn in ritual prayer

Ramadan (A): the ninth month of the Islamic calendar year; the month of fasting; a pillar of Islam

ras el hanoot (A): a special spice blend unique to every spice vendor (literally "head of the shop")

rhassoul (A): a traditional Moroccan soap made from clay, often mixed with herbs, dried flowers, and essential oils, and popularly used in hammams

riad (A): traditional Moroccan house, larger than a *dar*, but similarly set around a courtyard large enough to incorporate a central fountain

S T

Saadian: a dynasty that wrested control of Morocco from the Wattasids (16th-17th century)

savon bildi (F/A): black soap

shahada (A): Islamic declaration of faith

shawarma (A): a mix of lamb and beef, usually slow cooked and shaved for sandwiches

shisha (A): a type of smoking device

sidi (A): a title given to men, similar to mister or sir (e.g., Sidi Hassan)

souk (A): market or marketplace; often used to refer to the weekly souks *(souks hebdomadaires)*

Sufism (A): a mystic, and often more liberal, branch of Islam with several schools

Syndicat d'Initiative (F): tourist office

tadelahkt (A): a traditional type of anti-humidity wall coating

tajine (A): a slow-cooked stew served in clay conical dishes, traditionally cooked over an open flame

talâa (A): road (e.g., Talâa Kbira)

Tanjaoui (A): resident of Tangier

V W

Ville Nouvelle (F): new city; generally begun during the French protectorate era next to the medina

Wattasid: a family that maneuvered their way to power before seizing it from the Merenids and taking control of Morocco (15th-16th century)

Z

zaalouk (A): roasted eggplant salad

zawiya (A): the place where the shrine of a holy man or marabout is located (often spelled zaouia)

zellij (A): decorative ceramic tilework

Phrasebook

There are few countries as linguistically complex as Morocco. The official languages, Classical Arabic and Tamazight, are not used nearly as often as Moroccan Arabic, otherwise known as Darija, a creole-type language that people from most other Arabic-speaking countries have a hard time understanding. Darija is not standardized, so even in different regions of the country people use different words for things and sometimes misunderstand each other. So don't feel too bad if you have a hard time understanding or speaking Darija! However, learning a few words of Darija will go a long way in making your stay in Morocco that much more enjoyable and, especially outside the major metropolitan areas, a little smoother.

If you know some French, Spanish, Italian, or German, you might find these languages useful as well. English is often spoken around heavily touristed areas, but French is more common. For those traveling in the north, Spanish is much more commonly used and can come in handy as well.

If you are really linguistically adventurous, you can try your hand at learning a few phrases in Tamazight, the language of the Amazigh, spoken mostly in rural areas. Of course, even this won't be easy, as the language has multiple regional dialects. Most Tamazight speakers also speak some Darija, if not other languages.

PRONUNCIATION

Some sounds in Darija (and Tamazight) do not have equivalents in English. They can only be explained phonetically or by finding the closest sound.

aa like the "ah" in "blah"

d an emphatic "d"; the closest pronunciation in English is "d" as in "dark"

gh close to the French "r" as in "Paris"

h a pharyngeal "h"; think of this as a "whispered h" sound, as no similar sound exists in English

j like the "s" in "illusion"

kh like the Spanish *jota* ("j") or the Scottish "ch" as in "loch"

q an emphatic uvular sound that doesn't exist in English; the closest pronunciation in English is "k" as in "key"

s an emphatic "s"; the closest pronunciation in English is "s" as in "massage"

t an emphatic "t"; the closest pronunciation in English is "t" as in "star"

y a stressed consonant "y"; sort of like the Chinese "y" in "Ying"

The **apostrophe** refers to a sound that does not exist in English called a pharyngealized glottal stop. In phonology, it is referred to as a creaky-voiced sound. Since the sound may be hard to pronounce, you can just skip the apostrophe sound and pronounce the vowel following it.

DARIJA AND FRENCH

Basic and Courteous Expressions

English	Darija (pronunciation)	French
Hello	assalaam 'alaykoom	Salut / Bonjour
Hello (response)	wa 'alaykoom assalaam	Salut / Bonjour
Good morning	sbaa*h* el kheer	Bonjour
Good evening	msa el kheer	Bonsoir
Good night	tesba*h* 'alaa kheer	Bonne nuit

English	Darija (pronunciation)	French
How are you?	labas? / keef nta (to a man)? / keef nti (to a woman)?	Comment allez-vous?
Very well, thank you.	labas, shokran	Très bien, merci.
Thank you.	shokran	Merci.
Thank you very much.	shokran bezzaf	Merci beaucoup.
You're welcome.	laa shokran 'alaa waajib / mar*h*ba / al 'afoow	De rien / Je vous en prie.
No problem.	mashi mooshkil / ma'alish	Pas de problème.
OK; good	mezyaan; bikhir	Bien
Not OK; bad	mashi mezyaan; 'ayyaan	Pas bien; mauvais
So-so	shwiyya	Un peu
And you?	we nta (to a man)? / we nti (to a woman)?	Et vous?
Goodbye	beslama	Au revoir
See you later	nechoofek men ba'ad (not commonly used unless you really mean it)	A plus tard
please	'aafak	S'il vous plaît.
yes	yeh / na'am	oui
no	laa	non
I don't know.	ma'arafetsh	Je ne sais pas.
Just a moment, please.	wa*h*ed dqeeqa, 'aafak	Un moment, s'il vous plaît.
Where are the restrooms?	Fin les toilettes?	Où sont les toilettes?
Excuse me, please (when you're trying to get attention)	sma*h*li, 'aafak	Excusez-moi, s'il vous plaît.
Excuse me (when you've made a mistake)	sma*h*li	Désolé (m.) / Désolée (f.)
I'm sorry	sma*h*li	Je suis désolé (m.) / Je suis désolée (f.)
All right (agreement)	wakha / mezyaan	D'accord
enough	baraka / saafi	assez / ça suffit
How do you say … in Darija?	keefash katqolo le … b darija?	Comment dites-vous … en Darija?
What is this?	shenoo hada?	Qu'est-ce que c'est ça?
Do you speak English?	katehdar b lingliziya?	Parlez-vous anglais?
Does anyone here speak English?	kayen shi wa*h*ed kayehdar b linglizia?	Est-ce que quelqu'un ici parle anglais?
I don't speak Darija well.	ana makanehdarsh b darija mezyaan	Je ne parle pas bien darija.
Please speak more slowly.	'aafak hdar b tqala	Parlez plus lentement, s'il vous plaît.

English	Darija (pronunciation)	French
I don't understand.	mafhametsh	Je ne comprends pas.
Please write it down.	'aafak ketbali	S'il vous plaît écrivez-le.
What is your name?	shenoo smitek?	Quel est votre nom? / Comment vous appelez-vous?
My name is …	(ana) ismi / (ana) smitee …	Je m'appelle …
I am from …	ana men …	Je viens de(s) …
I am American	ana mirikani	Je suis américain (m.) / Je suis américaine (f.)
Pleased to meet you.	metsharfeen	Enchanté (m.) / Enchantée (f.)
I would like …	(ana) bghit …	Je voudrais …
Let's go (to …)	zeed nemshiw (le …)	Allons-y (Let's go) / Allons à (Let's go to …)
That's crazy!	mayemkensh! (literally "impossible!")	C'est de la folie!
Congratulations!	mabrook!	Félicitations!
Welcome	mar*h*ba	Bienvenue!
Is there …?	kayen …?	Y a-t-il …?
Do you have …?	'andek …?	Avez-vous …?
Go away!	seer b-*h*aalek	Allez-vous en! / Vas-t'en!
this; these	hada (m.) / hadi (f.); hadoo	ce (m.) / cette (f.); ces
that; those	hadak (m.) / hadik (f.); hadook	ce (m.) / cette (f.); ces
and	oo	et
or	wella / awla	ou

Terms of Address

English	Darija (pronunciation)	French
I	ana	je
you (singular)	nta (m.) / nti (f.)	tu
he	hoowa	il
she	heeya	elle
we	*h*na	nous
you (plural)	ntooma	vous
they	hooma	ils (m.) / elles (f.)
my	diali	mon (m.) / ma (f.)
your	dialek	ton (m.) / ta (f.)
Mr.; sir	sidi	Monsieur
Mrs.; Madam	lalla	Madame
Miss; young lady	lalla	Mademoiselle
woman	mra	femme

English	Darija (pronunciation)	French
wife	zawja / mra	épouse / femme
man	rajel	homme
husband	zawj / rajel	époux / mari
friend	sadeeq (m.) / sadeeqa (f.)	ami (m.) / amie (f.)
girlfriend; boyfriend	sa*h*ebtee; sa*h*bee	petite amie; petit ami
daughter; son	bent; weld	fille; fils
sister; brother	okht; akh	soeur; frère
mother; father	oom / walida; abb / walid	mère; père
grandmother; grandfather	jedda; jedd	grand-mère; grand-père
aunt	khaalti (maternal) / 'amti (paternal)	tante

Transportation

English	Darija (pronunciation)	French
Where is …?	feen …?	Où est …? / Où se trouve …?
How far is it to …?	sh-*h*aal ba'eed …?	A quelle distance est …?
from … to …	men … le …	de … à …
Where (which) is the way to…?	feen Treeq dial …?	Où est le chemin vers …?
(intercity) bus station	ma*h*aTa dial keeraan / ma*h*aTa Toorooqiyya	gare routière
(city) bus station	ma*h*aTa dial Tobiss	station d'autobus
taxi station	ma*h*aTa dial Taxiyaat	station de taxis
Where is this (intercity) bus going?	feen ghadi had l-kar?	Où va ce bus?
Where is this (city) bus going?	feen ghadi had Tobiss?	Où va ce bus?
boat	babor / baaTo	bateau
airport	maTaar	aéroport
I'd like a ticket to …	bghit wa*h*ed biyyé le …	Je voudrais un billet pour …
reservation	rezervasion / *h*ajez	réservation
baggage	bagaj	baggages
next flight	l-vol lli men ba'ad	vol prochain
Stop here, please.	weqaf hena, 'aafak	Arrêtez-vous ici, s'il vous plaît.
entrance	dakhla	entrée
exit	kharja	sortie
(very) near	qreeb (bezzaf)	(très) proche
(very) far	ba'eed (bezzaf)	(très) loin

English	Darija (pronunciation)	French
in	fe	en / dans
to; toward	le	à; vers
by; through	men	par; à travers
from	men	de
right	limeen	droite
left	lisaar / shmaal	gauche
straight ahead	neeshan	tout droit
in front	qebalt	en face de; devant
beside	*h*da / qeddam	à côté de
behind	mor	derrière
corner	qent	coin
stoplight	Daw / Do	feu de circulation
turn (noun)	dawra	tour
here	hna	ici
somewhere around here	hna f shi jiha	ici quelque part
there	leheeh	là-bas
somewhere around there	qreeb leheeh	là-bas quelque part
road	Treeq	route
street	zanqa	rue
avenue	shaari'e	avenue
highway	otoroot	autoroute
kilometer	kilometr	kilomètre
bridge	qanTra	pont
toll	payaaj	péage
address	'oonwaan	adresse
north; south	shamaal; janoob	nord; sud
east; west	sharq; gharb	est; ouest

Accommodations

English	Darija (pronunciation)	French
hotel	oTel	hôtel
Is there a room available?	kayen shi beet khaawee?	Avez-vous une chambre disponible?
May I (may we) see it?	moomkin nshoofoo (nshoofooh)?	Pourrais-je (pourrions-nous) la voir?
room	beet	chambre
single room	beet dial wa*h*ed	chambre simple
double room	beet doobl	chambre double

English	Darija (pronunciation)	French
double bed	fraash doobl	lit double
single bed	fraash dial wa*h*ed	lit simple
with private bath	feeh *h*ammaam	avec salle de bain
television	telfaza	télévision
window	sherjem	fenêtre
view	menDar	vue
hot water	l-ma s'khoon	de l'eau chaude
shower	doosh / doocha (Northern)	douche
towel	fooTa	serviette
soap	Saboon	savon
toilet paper	papié twalet	papier toilette
pillow	m-khadda	oreiller
blanket	beTTaniyya	couverture
sheets	gh-Ta / sabana (Northern)	drap
air-conditioning	kleem	climatiseur / clim
fan	ferfaara	ventilateur
Turkish (or Moorish or Roman) bath	*h*ammaam	bain turque
swimming pool	piseen	piscine
gym	jym	gym
bike	beshkliTa	bicyclette
key	saroot / mefta*h*	clé
suitcase	baliza	valise
backpack	sak / sakado	sac à dos
lock	qfel	serrure
safe	kofr for	coffre-fort
manager	mes-ool / moodeer	gérant
maid	moonaDifa	femme de ménage

Food

English	Darija (pronunciation)	French
I'm hungry.	fiyya joo'e	J'ai faim.
I'm thirsty.	fiyya le'Tesh	J'ai soif.
Table for two, please.	Tabla le jooj de nass, 'aafak (rarely used in budget restaurants; in mid-scale or fine-dining restaurants, use French)	Une table pour deux, s'il vous plaît.
food	makla	nourriture

English	Darija (pronunciation)	French
menu	menoo	menu
order	Talab	commande
glass	kaas	verre
glass of …	kaas dial …	verre de / d' …
glass of water	kaas dial l-ma	verre d'eau
fork	forsheTa	fourchette
knife	moos	knife
spoon	me'elqa	cuillère
napkin	zeef / mendeel	serviette
soft drink	monada	boisson non alcoolisée
coffee	qahwa	café
coffee with milk	qahwa nuss nuss / qahwa bel *h*leeb	café au lait
tea	atay	thé
drinking water	l-ma dial shorb	eau potable
bottle (of)	qar'a (dial)	bouteille (de / d')
bottled carbonated water	qar'a dial l-ma ghaazi (or use "… dial walmas," after a brand name, Oulmès, turned generic)	eau gazéifiée en bouteille
bottled uncarbonated water	qar'a dial l-ma 'aadi	eau non gazeuse en bouteille
tap water	l-ma dial robiné	eau du robinet
beer	birra / servisa (Northern)	bière
wine	vin (French) / vino (Spanish/Northern)	vin
red wine	vin rouge	vin rouge
white wine	vin blanc	vin blanc
milk	*h*leeb	lait
juice	'aSeer	jus
cream	crem	crème
sugar	sookkar	sucre
breakfast	fToor	petit déjeuner
lunch	gh-da	déjeuner
dinner	'esha	dîner
cheese	jben	fromage
eggs	beeD	oeufs
bread	khobz	pain
(olive) oil	zeet (zaytoon)	huile (d'olive)
salad	shlaDa	salade

English	Darija (pronunciation)	French
lettuce	khaS	laitue
tomato	maTisha	tomate
onion	beSla	oignon
garlic	tooma	ail
hot sauce	Sos *h*arra / l-*h*arr / harissa (North African hot sauce)	sauce piquante
fruit	froTa	fruit
mango	mango	mangue
watermelon	della*h*	pastèque
melon	beTeekh	melon
banana	banaan	banane
apple	teffa*h*	pomme
orange	leemoon / lecheen (Northern)	orange
lemon	*h*aameD / leymoon (Northern)	citron
grapefruit	pamplemoos	pamplemousse
pomegranate	rommaan	grenade
grape	'eneb	raisin
fish	*h*oot	poisson
seafood	ferwi d-mer	fruits de mer
shrimp	crevet	crevette
tuna	Ton	thon
sardine	sardeen	sardine
meat	l-*h*am	viande
chicken	d-jaaj	poulet
turkey	beebee	dinde
pigeon	*h*maam	pigeon
pork	*h*alloof	porc
bacon	lardon	lardon
ham	jombon	jambon
mutton; lamb	ghanmi; khriyef	mouton; agneau
goat	ma'azi / 'anzi	chèvre
beef, calf	begree, 'ajel	boeuf, veau
canned meat	kasher / morTadela	viande en boîte
rabbit	lerneb	lapin
fried	meqli	frit
roasted	m*h*ammar	rôti
grilled	meshwi	grillé

English	Darija (pronunciation)	French
steamed; boiled	mbakhar; meslooq	à la vapeur; bouilli
Do you have vegetarian options?	'andek makla nabaatiyya? / 'andek makla bla l-*h*am?	Avez-vous des plats végétariens?
I'm vegetarian.	ana nabaati	Je suis végétarien.
I want to eat …	bghit nakool …	Je veux manger …
I want to buy …	bghit neshri …	Je veux acheter …
I don't eat …	makanakoolsh …	Je ne mange pas …
Does it have …?	feeh (m.) …? / feeha (f.) …?	Il y a …?
with; without	be; bla	avec; sans
without meat	bla l-*h*am	sans viande
without cheese	bla jben	sans fromage
to share	binaatna	à partager
Check, please.	le*h*saab, 'aafak	L'addition, s'il vous plaît.
tip	poorbwar / propina (Northern)	pourpoire
Is the service included?	wash poorbwar dakhel?	Est-ce que le service est inclus?

Shopping

English	Darija (pronunciation)	French
money	floos	argent
cash	kash	espèces
change	Sarf	monnaie
credit card	la karT (dial kredi)	carte de crédit
debit card	la karT	carte de débit
Do you have change for …?	'andek Sarf dial …?	Avez-vous la monnaie pour …?
money exchange office	ma*h*al dial Sarf	bureau de change
What is the exchange rate?	sh-*h*aal Sarf?	Quel est le taux de change?
How much is the commission?	sh-*h*aal komisyon?	Combien coûte la commission?
Do you accept credit cards?	kateqbel lé karT?	Acceptez-vous les cartes de crédit?
money order	ta*h*weel floos	virement d'argent
How much does this cost?	be sh-*h*aal hada (m.)? / be sh-*h*aal hadi (f.)?	Combien ça coûte?
Is there something cheaper?	kayen shi *h*aja r-khas?	Y at-il quelque chose de moins cher?
add in a bit more	zeed shwiyya	ajoutez un peu plus
value added tax	Tax	taxe sur la valeur ajoutée

English	Darija (pronunciation)	French
discount	sold / takhfeeD / rebakha (Northern)	réduction / soldes
small grocery store	*h*anoot	épicerie
large grocery store	soopermarshi	supermarché

Health

English	Darija (pronunciation)	French
Help me, please.	'aawenni, 'aafak	Aidez-moi, s'il vous plaît.
I am ill.	ana mreeD (m.) / ana mreeDa (f.)	Je suis malade.
Call a doctor	'ayyeT le Tbeeb	Appelez un docteur
Take me to …	ddeenee le …	Emmenez-moi à ...
doctor	Tbeeb	docteur
hospital	SbiTaar	hôpital
clinic	klinik	clinique
drugstore	farmasya / Saydaliyya	pharmacie
I have …	'andee … / fiyya …	J'ai …
pain; cramp	*h*reeq	douleur; crampe
burn (with fire)	*h*orqa (bel 'afya)	brûlure
fever	s-khaana	fièvre
headache	*h*reeq raas	mal de tête
belly ache	*h*reeq fe l-kersh	mal de ventre
stomach ache	*h*reeq fe l-ma'eeda	mal d'estomac
nausea	dookha	nausée
vomit (verb)	t-qiyya	vomir
medicine	dwa	médicament
antibiotic	antibiotik	antibiotique
pill	keena / pastiyya (Northern)	pilule
aspirin	aspirin	aspirine
ointment; cream	pomada; krema	pommade; crème
bandage (big/small)	binda (kbeera/segheera)	bandage (grande/petite)
Band-Aid	sparadra	sparadrap
cotton	q-Ton	cotton
sanitary napkin	serviet ijyenik / always (in Darija, the brand name Always refers generically to a sanitary napkin)	serviette hygiènique
birth control pills	hooboob man'e el *h*aml	pilules contraceptives
condoms	prezervatif	préservatifs
toothbrush	sheeta dial snaan	brosse à dents

English	Darija (pronunciation)	French
dental floss	kheyT dial snaan	fil dentaire
toothpaste	dontifris	dentifrice
dentist	Tbeeb dial snaan	dentiste
toothache	*h*reeq fe snaan	mal aux dents
vaccination	jelba / talqee*h*	vaccin

Communications

English	Darija (pronunciation)	French
Wi-fi	weefee	wifi
cell phone	(tilifon) porTabl	téléphone portable
username	nom dutilizator	nom d'utilisateur
password	mo dpas	mot de passe
laptop computer	(ordinator) porTabl	ordinateur portable
prepaid cellphone	telefon be karTa dial rosharj	téléphone avec carte prépayée
post office	bosTa	la poste
(phone) call	moukalama (haatifiyya)	appel (téléphonique)
I want to send …	bghit nsayfeT…	Je voudrais envoyer …
a letter	bra / briyya	une lettre
a postcard	karT postal	carte postale
a package; a box	koli	colis; boîte
stamp	Taaba'a / seeyo (Northern)	timbre

At the Border

English	Darija (pronunciation)	French
border	*h*oodood	frontière
customs	diwana	douane
immigration	hijra	immigration
inspection; control	tefteesh; mooraaqaba	inspection; contrôle
ID card	la karT / al-biTaaqa al-waTaniya	carte d'identité nationale / CIN
passport	paspor / jawaaz assafar	passeport
profession	khedma / mihna	profession
vacation	'oTla	vacances
I'm a tourist.	ana toorist / ana saa-e*h*	Je suis un touriste.
student	Taalib	étudiant (m.) / étudiante (f.)
marital status	al-*h*aala al-'aa-eliyya	situation familiale
single	a'ezab (m.) / 'aaziba (f.)	célibataire
married	mzoowej (m.) / mzoowja (f.)	marié (m.) / mariée (f.)

English	Darija (pronunciation)	French
divorced	mTellaq (m.) / mTellqa (f.)	divorcé (m.) / divorcée (f.)
widowed	armal (m.) / armala (f.)	veuf (m.) / veuve (f.)
insurance	ta-ameen	assurance
driver's license	permi / rokhSat assiyaaqa	permis de conduire

At the Gas Station

English	Darija (pronunciation)	French
gas station	bomba / sTasion dial leSanS	station d'essence
gasoline	leSanS	essence
unleaded	son plom	sans plomb
diesel	mazoT	diesel
full, please	l-plen, 'aafak	Le plein, s'il vous plaît.
tire	rweeDa	pneu
air	le-hwaa (differentiate between /h/ and /*h*/ in this word to avoid confusing with the word for "fornication")	l'air
water	l-ma	l'eau
oil (change)	(beddel) zeet	vidange
car	Tomobeel	voiture
RV	karavan	caravane
motorbike	moTor	moto
4x4	kaTkaT	katkat (colloquial)
battery	batri	batterie
repair shop	mikanik	mécanicien
Can you clean my window, please?	msa*h*li jaaj, 'aafak?	Pouvez-vous nettoyer ma fenêtre, s'il vous plaît?
My ... doesn't work.	... diali makhaddamsh	Mon ... ne marche pas.

Numbers

English	Darija (pronunciation)	French
zero	Sefer	zéro
one	wa*h*ed	un
two	jooj	deux
three	tlaata	trois
four	arb'aa	quatre
five	khamsa	cinq
six	setta	six

English	Darija (pronunciation)	French
seven	seb'a	sept
eight	tmenya	huit
nine	tes'ood	neuf
10	'ashra	dix
11	*h*edaash	onze
12	Tenaash	douze
13	tleTaash	treize
14	rba'aTaash	quatorze
15	khamesTaash	quinze
16	seTaash	seize
17	sba'eTaash	dix-sept
18	tmenTaash	dix-huit
19	tse'eTaash	dix-neuf
20	'oshreen	vingt
21	wa*h*ed oo 'oshreen	vingt et un
22	tenayen oo 'oshreen	vingt-deux
23	tlaata oo 'oshreen	vingt-trois
30	tlateen	trente
31	wa*h*ed oo tlateen	trente et un
32	tenayen oo tlateen	trente-deux
33	tlaata oo tlateen	trente-trois
40	arb'een	quarante
50	khamseen	cinquante
60	setteen	soixante
70	seb'een	soixante-dix
80	tmaaneen	quatre-vingts
90	tes'een	quatre-vingt-dix
100	meya	cent
101	meya oo wa*h*ed	cent un
200	meyateyn	deux cents
500	khamsemeya	cinq cents
800	temnemya	huit cents
1,000	alf	mille
10,000	'ashralaf	dix mille
100,000	meyat alf	cent mille
1,000,000	melyoon	un million

English	Darija (pronunciation)	French
one half	noss	un demi
one third	tooloot	un tiers
one fourth	reba'e / raab'a	un quart

Time

English	Darija (pronunciation)	French
What time is it?	sh-*h*aal fe sa'a?	Quelle heure est-il?
It's one o'clock.	hadi lwe*h*da	Il est une heure.
It's three in the afternoon.	hadi tlata dial le'shiya	Il est trois heures de l'après-midi.
It's three in the morning.	hadi tlata dial sbaa*h*	Il est trois heures du matin.
six-thirty	setta oo nọss	six heures et demi
quarter to eleven	*h*edash la roob'e	onze heures moins quart
quarter past five	khamsa oo rba'e	cinq heures et quart
minute	dqeeqa	minute
hour	sa'a	heure
late	me'aTal	tard
early	bekri	tôt
today	lyoom	aujourd'hui
tomorrow	ghadda	demain
yesterday	l-baara*h*	hier
morning	sbaa*h*	matin
afternoon	le'shiya	après-midi
night	leel	soir
day before yesterday	wel baara*h*	avant-hier
day after tomorrow	ba'ad ghadda	après-demain
in an hour	men daba wa*h*ed sa'a	dans une heure
day	yoom	jour
week	simana	semaine
month	sh-har	mois
after	ba'ad	après
before	q-bel	avant
holiday	'oTla	vacances
long weekend	weekend Tweel	long weekend

Days

English	Darija (pronunciation)	French
Monday	letneen	lundi
Tuesday	tlaata	mardi
Wednesday	larbaa'e	mercredi
Thursday	lekhmees	jeudi
Friday	joom'aa	vendredi
Saturday	sebt	samedi
Sunday	l-*h*add	dimanche

Months

Morocco follows both the Western (or Gregorian) calendar and the Muslim lunar calendar. The first is the one most used. The second is used mainly for religious holidays. Moroccans will generally use the name of the months in French, and in a few instances in classical Arabic, but don't be surprised if some refer to months by numbers ("Sh-har wa*h*ed" or Month 1 for January, "Sh-har jooj" or Month 2 for February, and so on). Be prepared to practice your numbers here, too.

English	Darija (pronunciation)	French
January	yenayer	janvier
February	febrayer	février
March	mars	mars
April	abril	avril
May	may	mai
June	yoonyoo	juin
July	yoolyooz	juillet
August	ghosht	août
September	september	septembre
October	october	octobre
November	nuvember	novembre
December	disamber	décembre

Questions

English	Darija (pronunciation)	French
who	shkoon	qui
what	shenoo	quoi
when	fooqaash	quand
where	feen	où
why	'alaash	pourquoi
how	kifaash	comment

Adjectives and Adverbs

English	Darija (pronunciation)	French
cool; awesome	bikhir / waa'er	cool; génial
clean	n-qi (m.) / nqiya (f.)	propre
dirty	moossakh (m.) / moskha (f.)	sale
broken	m-harres (m.) / m-harsa (f.)	cassé (m.) / cassée (f.)
included	daakhel	inclus
not included	madakhelsh	non inclus
big	kbeer (m.) / kbeera (f.)	grand (m.) / grande (f.)
small	Segheer (m.) / Segheera (f.)	petit (m.) / petite (f.)
medium	mwesseT (m.) / mwesTa (f.)	moyen (m.) / moyenne (f.)
wide, large	waasa'e (m.) / waase'a (f.)	large
narrow	deeyaq (m.) / deeyqa (f.)	étroit (m.) / étroite (f.)
long, tall	Tweel (m.) / Tweela (f.)	long (m.) / longue (f.), grand (m.) / grande (f.)
short	qeseer (m.) / qeseera (f.)	court (m.) / courte (f.)
good	mezyaan	bien
bad	mashi mezyaan	mauvais
sick	mreeD (m.) / mreeDa (f.)	malade
beautiful	zween (m.) / zweena (f.)	beau (m.) / belle (f.)
ugly	khaayeb (m.) / khayba (f.)	moche
full	'aamar	plein
empty	khaawee	vide
a lot/plenty, many, too much	bezzaf	beaucoup, plusieurs, trop
a little, few	shwiyya	un peu, peu
expensive	ghaali (m.) / ghaalya (f.)	cher (m.) / chère (f.)
cheap	rekheeS (m.) / rekheeSa (f.)	pas cher (m.) / chère (f.)
less	qall	moins
more	ktar	plus
not (+ adjective)	mashi (+ …)	pas (+ …)

God-Invoking Expressions

English	Darija (pronunciation)
In the name of God	bismillah (used when you're about to start an action, such as eating, drinking, driving, or pouring tea)
May God save you from (that) evil	allah ya'afoo 'aleek
Thanks be to God/Praise be to God	al*h*amdulillah

English	Darija (pronunciation)
May God help you	allah ye'awen (can be used to mean "goodbye," especially to service providers or people going to work)
If God wills / God willing	inshaa allah
God's blessings be upon you	tbarkellah 'aleek (used to compliment someone for effort or accomplishment)
May God bless you	allah ybaarek feek / baraka allaho feek (used in response to "tbarkellah 'aleek"; can be used to mean "thank you")
May God make it easy for you	allah ysahal / allah yejeeb tisseer (to a beggar if you don't have anything to give them)
May God have mercy on your parents	allah yer*h*am waldeek (used to thank someone or to ask them for help)
Please; May God protect you	allah ykhalleek
Glorious is God	soob*h*aan allah (used to express wonder at something beautiful, such as a landscape or any of God's creations)
May God help with recovery	allah yeshaafi
God forgives	allah ysame*h* (in response to an apology)
Condolences / May God greaten the good deeds	allah ye'aDem l-ajar
To your health	beSa*h*a (to someone who has just taken a bath, had a haircut, bought something new, or had a nice time somewhere)
May God give you health	allah ye'teek Sa*h*a (in response to "beSa*h*a")
Oh my god!	ya rabbee (one can also use wayli (m.) / awilee (f.) as an interjection to mean the same thing)
Forbidden (by God)	*h*araam
Allowed (by God)	*h*alaal

TAMAZIGHT

The language of the Amazigh is complex, heavily regionalized, and can be different from village to village. Knowing a few words in Tamazight is particularly helpful in the rural areas in the mountains and desert. Some of the more common phrases have been adopted from Darija.

English	Tamazight
Hello	la bas dereek (to a man) / la bas dareem (to a woman)
How are you?	iz tna ghrog (to a man)? / iz tna gh-rum (to a woman)?
I am good.	tnaa tia lman
Please	lyrham waladeen
Thank you.	barakaaloufeek
Do you speak English?	iz teewilt lingliziya?

English	Tamazight
What is your name?	msm minum?
My name is ...	... ishm (m.) / ... ishmini (f.)
I like (that).	tehbouh
Yes	eh / ayaa
No	la
How much (is that)?	sh-*h*aal ooya
That's too much!	ighrla bezzaf
OK (agreement)	magheeden (literally "why not?")
hello	azoul
What is your name?	matgit sism?
My name is ________	ism inu ________
What is this?	maynna?
Can you help me?	is imkn ayyi ta3wnt?
Delicious!	izel
How much (is this)?	mnashk atteskr?
good-bye	akki3awn rabbi

Suggested Reading

TRAVELOGUES

Bowles, Paul. *Without Stopping.* 1972. The only autobiography Paul Bowles, the famous Tangier-based American expat, ever wrote, with a few insights into his life, writing, and works and some glimpses of the Tangier gone by.

Choukri, Mohamed. *Tennessee Williams in Tangier.* 1979. Tennessee Williams spent quite some time in Tangier, befriending some of the locals, including Moroccan writer Mohamed Choukri. This book contains Choukri's memories of meeting the famous playwright.

Harris, Walter Burton. *Morocco That Was.* 1921. Another one of the more famous expats to settle in Tangier during the protectorate era, the British-born Walter Burton Harris spent these years in his villa outside of town. He was once captured by the pirate Raisuni, hobnobbed with the Moroccan sultans, and was often involved in political intrigues. This is his often fantastical account of Morocco in the early 20th century.

Shah, Tahir. *The Caliph's House.* 2006. Itinerate traveler, Tahir Shah, purchases the crumbling ruin of a seaside mansion in the middle of a Casablanca city slum. Part laugh aloud comedy, part tear-jerking drama, Shah pens a tale of his family's first year, learning the local customs and fighting through renovations of their new family house that would make any homeowner cringe.

Wharton, Edith. *In Morocco.* 1920. The first known travel guide to Morocco, penned by the aristocratic Wharton and with some fascinating insights into local culture, though perhaps dulled by a sense of French superiority and lack of depth of understanding and peppered with a fine dose of Orientalism. A required read for any traveler to Morocco.

FICTION

Ben Jelloun, Tahar. *This Blinding Absence of Light.* 2001. Based on a true story, this damning and controversial account of a prisoner's suffering in Hassan II's infamous Tazamamart prison during the "Years of Lead" is perhaps Ben Jalloun's best-known work.

Bowles, Paul. *The Spider's House.* 1955. This story follows two Americans and one young Moroccan boy through the complex medina of Fez and into the nearby Middle Atlas mountains. The Fez riots just before the Independence of 1956 in the background of this story serve to add tension and give rise to Bowles's apolitical vision of Morocco.

Burroughs, William. *Naked Lunch.* 1959. This is a story about mugwumps. It's also Burroughs's most famous work, begun in Tangier while it was an international zone. Burroughs worked with Brion Gysin, Allen Ginsberg, and Jack Kerouac on his cut-up technique while also working through a severe drug addiction. It gives some wonderfully kaleidoscopic visions of Tangier during the time, as seen through the snappy, irreverent prose of one of the Beat Generation's greatest masters.

Choukri, Mohamed. *For Bread Alone.* 1973. A largely true-life account written by Choukri, who, with the help of Paul Bowles, was able to get this moving account of a young boy working through the poorest slums of Morocco with all of its drug abuse and prostitution. Perhaps the greatest Moroccan novel of the 20th century. Though *For Bread Alone* was published in 1973, it was banned in Morocco on grounds of perverse sexuality and frank descriptions of drug use. It wasn't until 2000 that the novel was allowed into the country.

Hardy, Myronn. *Kingdom.* 2015. In this collection of poems, long-time Moroccan expat Myronn Hardy explores the social fabric twined throughout his adopted home. Evoking the Gnawa hymns of the desert and rhythmic chants of the Sufi, this is a studious, quietly sought reflection of a world, often intimate, always interesting.

Lalami, Laila. *Hope and Other Dangerous Pursuits.* 2005. Originally from Casablanca, this Moroccan writer chooses to write in English. This collection of stories follows the plights of several young Moroccans who are grappling with a Morocco at the turn of the century that they want to abandon in the hopes of finding a better life in Europe. Lalami's latest, *A Moor's Account*, though set in North America, often touches on traditional life in Morocco and is a captivating read.

Taïa, Abdellah. *An Arab Melancholia.* 2012. The story follows much of Taïa's adolescence growing up homosexual in the highly patriarchal environs of his hometown of Salé, Morocco. Taïa is the only openly gay Moroccan writer producing work today. His books are highly controversial, sparking debate and derision throughout the country. He has emigrated to France.

Vida, Vendala. *The Diver's Clothes Lie Empty.* 2015. A woman boards a plane from Miami to Casablanca and her life is forever altered, her identity shed, and a country discovered in this pensive, wry, edgy yarn that is part mystery, part thriller, and part travelogue, firmly set in today's Morocco.

GENERAL NONFICTION

Clarke, Suzanna. *A House in Fez*. 2007. This real-life story follows Australian photojournalist Suzanna Clarke and her husband, Sandy, as they arrive in Fez for the first time, fall in love with the medieval city, and decide to purchase a *riad* and make Fez their home, with all the never-ending bureaucracy and cultural adaptation that entails.

Hopkins, John. *The Tangier Diaries*. 1998. A cult classic. In his diaries, Hopkins sketches the Tangier of the "Interzone" and much of the rest of Morocco as it was in the 1960s and 1970s, with plenty of appearances by those well known in Morocco, including William Burroughs, Paul and Jane Bowles, Tennessee Williams, Jean Genet, Yves Saint Laurent, and countless others.

Mackintosh-Smith, Tim. *Travels with a Tangerine*. 2001. A writer attempts to follow the path of Tangier's über-explorer, Ibn Battuta, over the course of this compassionate, erudite read. It begins in Tangier before following the footsteps of Battuta to Mecca, India, and China.

Maxwell, Gavin. *The Lords of the Atlas*. 2004. A classic story of the rise and fall of a powerful family. Set in Marrakesh and the High Atlas Mountains, Maxwell follows the wealthy, often ruthless, House of Glaoui at the end of the 19th century. The family's meteoric rise saw 50 years of rule and influence followed by a spectacular collapse worthy of one of Shakespeare's finest dramas.

Mernissi, Fatima. *Beyond the Veil*. 1975. Morocco's foremost feminist writes about the need for feminism in her discussion of Moroccan male-female dynamics. Though *Beyond the Veil* was originally published in the 1970s, her discussion is still very much valid today, as this dynamic has remained largely unchanged.

Milton, Giles. *White Gold*. 2005. In the summer of 1716, Barbary pirates take over a ship at sea, enslaving 52 crew members, including Thomas Pellow, an 11-year-old boy from Cornwall. In this tense, harrowing narrative, Milton weaves the story of Pellow's 20-year slavery and eventual escape against the oft-forgotten, but all-too-real truth of white slavery in Africa.

The Holy Quran. Combined with the *Sunnah*, the teachings of the Prophet Mohammed, this forms the basis of Islam and is considered the direct word of God. Required reading for travelers looking for a full cultural experience in Morocco. The best English translation with commentary is the recent *The Study Quran*, edited by Seyyed Hossein Nasr (HarperOne, 2015). By far one of the best resources for anglophones looking to learn more about Islam.

Shoemake, Josh. *Tangier*. 2013. Dubbed "A Literary Guide for Travelers," this fascinating work takes you into the individual neighborhoods of Tangier for a glimpse at its long literary history, stretching back to Ibn Battuta and forward to Mohamed Choukri while paying plenty of tribute to many expats and travelers, such as Mark Twain and George Orwell, that put Tangier on the literary map.

Žvan-Elliott, Katja. *Modernizing Patriarchy*. 2015. A compelling work examining the wide gap between governmental regulation and legal reforms meant to support the further advancement of women's rights and the reality of women struggling in a country that is still largely patriarchal.

Suggested Films

DRAMA

Casablanca (Michael Curtiz, 1942). The classic American romance, starring Humphrey Bogart and Ingrid Bergman, that likely gives today's Casablanca its cultural caché. From this classic, we get a real-live Rick's Café, a tribute to the film's finest gin joint, as well as the nostalgic tune, "As Time Goes By."

Hideous Kinky (Gillies McKinnon, 1998). Starring Kate Winslet and based on the 1992 semi-autobiographical novel by Esther Freud by the same name, the story follows a young English mother's quest to live outside the gears and boxes she finds too stifling for her and her children in her home city of London.

Horses of God (Nabil Ayouch, 2012). This intense film follows the boys of Sidi Moumen, a poor neighborhood in Casablanca, and highlights the rise of Islamic terrorism. A must watch for those looking for something outside of the regular Hollywood delights.

Marrakesh Express (Gabriele Salvatores, 1989). This film is based on the only autobiography Paul Bowles, the famous Tangier-based American expat, ever wrote. It gives a few insights into his life, writing, and works and some glimpses of the Tangier gone by.

Morocco (Josef von Sternberg, 1930). A classic romance that follows a cabaret singer and Legionnaire who fall in love during the Rif War but struggle with womanizing and infidelity. Scandalous at the time of its release in 1930, though tame by today's standard.

Much Loved (Nabil Ayouch, 2015). Morocco's most controversial filmmaker struck hard with this glimpse into the country's seedy nightlife. This film was banned in Morocco for its brash portrayal of prostitution and homosexuality in and around Marrakesh. A must-watch for those interested in contemporary Morocco.

The Sheltering Sky (Bernardo Bertolucci, 1990). While Paul Bowles's novel, *The Sheltering Sky*, followed three American travelers from Oran in Algeria, Bertolucci's classic adaptation relocated the beginning of the movie to Tangier and features a cameo of Bowles in a storied Tangier café.

The Source (Les Sources des Femmes) (Radu Mihailanu, 2011). Nominated for a Palme d'Or at the Cannes International Festival, this intimate, often humorous, look at life in a small village in Morocco follows one courageous group of women, led by Leila, who go on a sex strike to oppose the conditions they live in.

DOCUMENTARY

475 (Nadir Bouhmouch, 2013). This short, complex documentary examines the controversial Article 475 of the Moroccan Penal Code, which made legal precedent for a rape victim to be forcibly married to her rapist.

My Makhzen and Me (Nadir Bouhmouch, 2012). Another documentary by San Diego-based Bouhmouch that portrays the pro-democracy struggles of the young February 20 movement.

Leo Africanus: A Man Between Worlds (Jeremy Jeffs, 2011). This BBC-produced documentary tracks the life of Leo Africanus, born Hasan al-Wazzan in Grenada. Leo Africanus relocated to Fez after the fall of Grenada to Spanish forces and spent his life traveling Africa and the Middle East before settling in Rome and converting to Christianity.

Internet Resources and Apps

ACCOMMODATIONS

www.riadsmorocco.com
Hotels & Ryads of Morocco is the dedicated booking search engine for Moroccan *riads*. The site's curator, Pierre Yves, works one-on-one with *riad* owners around the country.

www.hipmarrakech.com
Another good resources to find a trendy *riad*, particularly in Marrakesh.

DINING, CULTURE, AND EVENTS

www.bestrestaurantsmaroc.com
Updated reviews, hours, and menus for Morocco's high-end dining. If you're looking for a nice place for date night with a French flair, this is a good place to start. However, options outside of the main cities are sparse.

www.moroccofestivals.co.uk
Dedicated U.K.-run website with updated information for all of Morocco's numerous festivals. Check this before your departure to see if your visit will happily coincide with a festival.

http://riadzany.blogspot.com
The View from Fez has some up-to-date information for events around the country, as well as insights into the culture and people of Fez. Edited by Susanne Clarke, author of *A House in Fez*, an Australian photojournalist now living with her family in Fez.

www.journeybeyondtravel.com/blog
Voted the #1 English-language travel blog by Blogger for Morocco in 2019, this blog has been edited and curated by yours truly since 2017. I strive to provide in-depth cultural insight. The lengthier articles on the site are usually coupled with some good photography, making for fun reading, while the blog is easily searchable for culture, events, locations, and everything else Morocco-related.

https://marocmama.com
A busy mother of three and Marrakeshia-transplant, Amanda Moutakki, writes often about the vibrant environs of Marrakesh as well as expat life. She is a foodie at heart and has an entire section of her website dedicated to food, so foodies, tune in!

EMBASSIES AND VISAS

www.canadainternational.gc.ca/morocco-maroc
The Canadian Embassy in Morocco has information available in English and French with a series of updated notices. The embassy covers **Australians** and Mauritanians, as well.

www.mfat.govt.nz/spain
The New Zealand embassy in Madrid, Spain, is accredited for helping their citizens in Morocco. Look here for the latest travel and safety information.

www.gov.uk/government/world/organisations/british-embassy-rabat
British citizens can find consular information here, along with updated safety information and information for British nationals living in Morocco.

http://morocco.usembassy.gov
You can register your travel plans with the U.S. embassy in case of emergencies and find updated safety, visa, and other important information. For most matters, including lost or stolen passports, you will want to contact the consulate in Casablanca.

LANGUAGE COURSES

www.alif-fes.com
The Arabic Language Institute of Fez offers intensive language courses is Modern Standard Arabic as well as Moroccan Arabic (Darija).

www.qalamcenter.com
Qalam Center for Arabic Studies is located in Rabat. This immersion-based center offers courses in both Modern Standard and Moroccan Arabic.

NEWS AND MEDIA

http://lematin.ma
Le Matin is the leading French-language newspaper in Morocco, with a circulation of around 60,000.

www.moroccoworldnews.com
Morocco World News has English-language news sources focused on Morocco that are growing in popularity.

www.tingismagazine.com
For Anglophones, this online magazine is worth reading for a more in-depth look at some major issues affecting Morocco.

NONPROFITS

www.corpsafrica.org
Initiated by former Peace Corps volunteers, Corps Africa helps Africans volunteer in their own country.

www.moroccoexchange.org
Alternative exchange programs focus on possible exchanges with American and European students.

www.morocco-foundation.org
A group of Moroccan professionals dedicated to fighting poverty and illiteracy throughout the country.

www.peacecorps.gov
Morocco is one of the most active countries in the Peace Corps. Volunteers are found throughout the rural areas helping with projects to develop the region.

http://whc.unesco.org/en/statesparties/ma
History and other information regarding the UNESCO World Heritage Sites found around Morocco.

ROCK-CLIMBING

climbmorocco.com
Regional information on climbing around Morocco, including the Rif, Todra Gorge, and Tafraoute.

www.moroccorock.com
Updated trad climbing information focusing on the Anti-Atlas.

TRANSPORTATION

www.ctm.ma
Generally the most reliable bus company operating in Morocco. Find hours, prices, and schedules.

www.oncf.ma
The website of Morocco's only train company. Find schedules and times, though you will have to purchase tickets at the train station. ONCF is linked with the Supratours bus company. Times for Supratours buses are found here as well.

TRAVEL COMPANIES

www.journeybeyondtravel.com
An eco-friendly tour company dedicated to sustainable economies founded by a former Peace Corps volunteer and a longtime Moroccan transplant. They specialize in small, English-speaking groups and families. The best all-around tour company in Morocco for those looking for a customized experience.

www.amazing-morocco.com
This tour company focuses on desert tours. Guides are English-speaking, reliable, and friendly. Perhaps the best tour outfit in the desert and highly recommended.

www.toubkal-peaks.com
If you're looking to climb Mount Toubkal or just explore the mountainous regions of Morocco, this is by far your best bet. Guides

can pick you up directly in Marrakesh and have hikes for all ability levels. The guides here all speak good English, are certified, and know the mountains and trails extremely well.

TRAVEL INFORMATION

www.madeinmedina.com

An online travel resource with updated information focusing on city life, events, and activities in Morocco's major cities.

www.morocco.com

An online travel resource dedicated to all things Moroccan, with some general information about attractions, beaches, and national parks.

ESSENTIAL TRAVEL APPS

You likely already have the following apps on your phone: maps with GPS, flashlight, music, podcasts, movies, e-reader, and weather. Make sure these apps are running before you board the plane. They can be indispensable. You'll be thankful when you land in Morocco. To add to your app collection, make sure you add these other apps that will help in your journey from the Blue City of Chefchaouen to the Red City of Marrakesh.

Careem

Uber was quick-lived in Morocco. Careem, a Dubai-based alternative, has filled the void. You can try Careem to hail a taxi if you're planning on staying out in Casablanca, Rabat, or Tangier if you're not having any luck otherwise. It's handy to have in a pinch.

Google Translate

Though many people around Morocco do speak some English, most do not. With Moroccan Arabic (Darija) and French being two of the most common languages spoken, this app is almost a necessity for anyone. Quick tip: You won't find "Moroccan Arabic" or "Darija" under the list of possibilities, but if you're with a Moroccan speaking Arabic, you'll likely have the best luck with the "Maltese" language setting for anything in Latin script.

maps.me

Never has a map app made as much sense. These are apps you don't need to be connected to the Internet to use. Download before you leave home or leave your hotel. Though not perfect, they make navigating the confusing medinas so much easier and can be extremely helpful while road-tripping.

Rome2Rio

If you're using public transportation to get around, this app is a necessity. It will help you find the best routes to get to some of the real out-of-the-way places around Morocco.

Trail Wallet

If you're anything like me, you could use some help tracking expenses. I'm awful at this. I'm less awful since I've been using the Trail Wallet app. Easy to understand and customizable, this will help you with your travel accounting and make sure you don't break the bank while you're traveling the country.

TripIt

So much is done right with this app. Once you receive your confirmation emails for your flight, hotel, restaurant, or even car rental, just forward this on to the TripIt app and it will put together an easy-to-understand itinerary for you, helping you keep track of your vacation so you can spend more time relaxing and less time stressing about schedule.

Index

A

B

C

D

E

F

G

J

K

L

M

R

S

T

UV

WZ

List of Maps

Front Map

Discover Morocco

Casablanca

Rabat

Tangier and the Mediterranean Coast

Fez and the Middle Atlas

Marrakesh

The High Atlas

Ouarzazate and the Southern Oases

Acknowledgments

First off, thank you, dear reader, for supporting travel writing! A book like this doesn't come together without a lot of help. I've been lucky in my friends and family from Morocco all the way back to the US. Whether they've helped me explore the country, understand the culture, values, and more, put this guide together, and/or encouraged and supported away, I have a lot of people deserving of much more thanks than I can give them on this page. That said, I'll do my best.

In the last decade I've been traveling around Morocco, I've made a lot of friends. They're in all corners of the country and they are genuine, kind, and willing to aid me in my quest to uncover the best addresses and most adventurous outings in their neighborhood. Thanks to each and every one you for helping me around the country: Naim Abdelaziz, Kamal Abdelfadil, Lahsen Alkouch, Hamid Bennani, Hamid Bidbid, Abdelghani Bouimzgane, Youssef el-Khorib, Driss el-Khoukhi, Ilias el-Mejdoub, Rabie el-Mesnani, Tara Knies-Fraiture, Fatima Habte, Ilias Lkhanjal, Brahim Jarrou, Hamid Jarrou, Omar Jellah, Leila Lebbar, Rachid Mchehori, Redouaine Naji, Amanda Ponzio-Mouttaki, Naim Souhel, Mohamed Tabalquit, and Abdelkarim Tata.

A giant thanks for your kindness, great food, shopping tips, and wonderful restaurant suggestions to the teams at Auberge le Festival in the Todra Gorge, Bivouac Chergui in the Sahara, Casa Perleta in Chefchaouen, Chez Pierre in the Dades Gorge, Dar Chams in Tangier, Dar Shâan in Rabat, Domaine Malika in the High Atlas, Douar Samra in the High Atlas, Hotel Point du Jour in Casablanca, Kammy Hostel in Marrakesh, La Rose du Desert in Erfoud, Le Petit Riad in Ouarzazate, Riad Boussa in Marrakesh, Riad Chbanate in Essaouira, Riad Chergui in Marrakesh, Riad Janoub in Tiznit, Riad Laaroussa in Fez, Ryad Salama in Fez, Riad Zyo in Rabat, and Scorpion House in Moulay Idriss. And a big thank you to my friends at Al Akhawayn University for clueing me into some local hot spots.

A shout-out to Megan, Hannah, Lucie, and Albert, my awesome team at Moon (Hachette) for spending tremendous amounts of their time getting this guidebook to come alive. This book wouldn't be what it is without you.

A giant *shokran bezzaf* to my family in Tangier for all of their patience with my Arabic, French, and Spanish, not to mention the authentic cultural insights that just wouldn't be possible otherwise: Souad Abbad, Nabiha Abbad, Mohktar Abbad, Lina Alouche, Celina Nana, and Mohcine Regragui. And another big thank you to my family and friends spread across the US, Europe, and the rest of the world for their unwavering support, especially Jill and Bob Stone; Dev, Nate, and Nicholas Prouty; Sylvain, Laura, and Miles Gasser; Mike, Zhueng and Mina Miello; Thomas Hollowell; Gregory Hubbs; Fazia Farrook; and Tahir Shah (who convinced me to quit the 9-5). You all make travel special.

Amina Lahbabi, my incredible Tangerina wife, took many of the photos that appear in these pages, has (patiently) traveled the length and breadth of the country with me, and lent her translator's expertise to this phrasebook. For the second edition, Amina and I have been blessed to travel with our son, Zephyr. He unwittingly opened the door to another Morocco I had never before seen. These two have shown me another depth of what it means to travel.

Photo Credits

Title page photo: Lucas Peters

All interior photos © Lucas Peters, except: page 6 © (bottom) Anibal Trejo | Dreamstime.com; page 7 © (bottom left) Amina Lahbabi; page 9 © (bottom left) Amina Lahbabi; pages 14-15 © (bottom) Simon Hack | Dreamstime.com; page 18 © (bottom) Amina Lahbabi; page 20 © Simon Hack | Dreamstime.com; page 22 © (right) Amina Lahbabi; page 25 © (bottom) Luis2007 | Dreamstime.com; page 29 © (left) Ed Francissen | Dreamstime.com; (right) Marcin Jucha | Dreamstime.com; page 34: © Danny Walden; page 36 © (top left) Amina Lahbabi; page 63 © (top and bottom) Amina Lahbabi; page 75 © (bottom) Amina Lahbabi; page 78 © (left middle) Amina Lahbabi; page 83 © Amina Lahbabi; page 92 © (top and bottom) Amina Lahbabi; page 102 © (top left and right) Amina Lahbabi; page 116 © Amina Lahbabi; page 128 © (bottom right) Amina Lahbabi; page 133 © (top right and bottom) Amina Lahbabi; page 152 © (left middle and bottom) Amina Lahbabi; page 156 © (top and bottom) Amina Lahbabi; page 168 © (top left) Amina Lahbabi; page 170 © Amina Lahbabi; page 174 © Petr Švec | Dreamstime.com; page 184 © (top) Hoang Bao Nguyen | Dreamstime.com; (bottom) Amina Lahbabi; page 189 © (left middle) Amina Lahbabi; page 219 © (all) Amina Lahbabi; page 232 © (top and middle right) Amina Lahbabi; page 243 © (top left) Laura Facchini | Dreamstime.com; page 253 © Amina Lahbabi; page 255 © (top and bottom) Amina Lahbabi; page 279 © (left middle) Amina Lahbabi; page 286 © Amina Lahbabi; page 296 © (top left) Amina Lahbabi; page 304 © (top left) Amina Lahbabi; (top right) Checco | Dreamstime.com; page 318 © (bottom) Amina Lahbabi; page 321 © (top) Amina Lahbabi; (right middle) Marc Johnson | Dreamstime.com; (bottom) Amina Lahbabi; page 324 © (top right) Typhoonski | Dreamstime.com; page 329 © Amina Lahbabi; page 331 © (top right and bottom left) Amina Lahbabi; page 372 © Danny Walden; page 389 © (top left) Amina Lahbabi; page 402 © (top and bottom) Amina Lahbabi; page 405 © Amina Lahbabi; page 408 (bottom) Amina Lahbabi; page 414 © Amina Lahbabi; page 438 © Krajinar | Dreamstime.com

GO BIG AND GO BEYOND!

These savvy city guides include strategies to help you see the top sights and find adventure beyond the tourist crowds.

OR TAKE THINGS ONE STEP AT A TIME

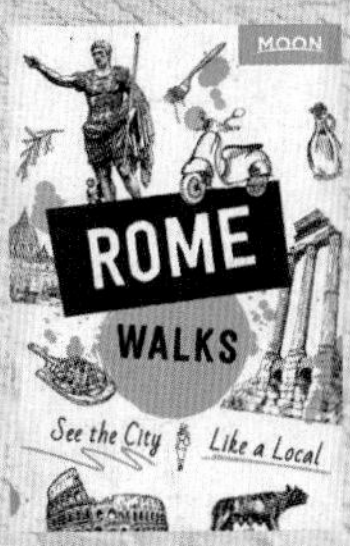

MAP SYMBOLS

Expressway	City/Town	Information Center	Park
Primary Road	State Capital	Parking Area	Golf Course
Secondary Road	National Capital	Church	Unique Feature
Unpaved Road	Highlight	Winery/Vineyard	Waterfall
Trail	Point of Interest	Trailhead	Camping
Ferry	Accommodation	Train Station	Mountain
Railroad	Restaurant/Bar	Airport	Ski Area
Pedestrian Walkway	Other Location	Airfield	Glacier
Stairs			

CONVERSION TABLES

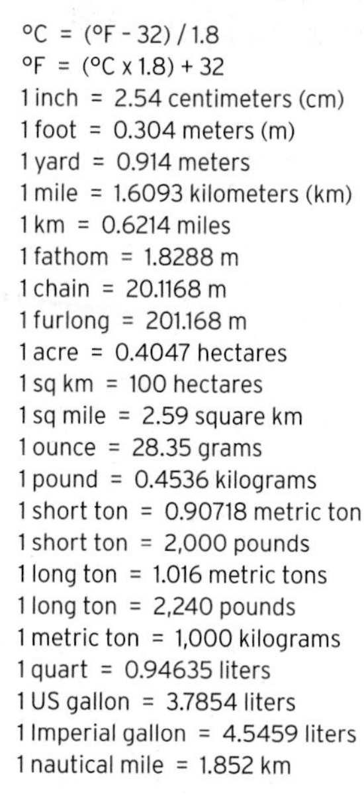

°C = (°F - 32) / 1.8
°F = (°C x 1.8) + 32
1 inch = 2.54 centimeters (cm)
1 foot = 0.304 meters (m)
1 yard = 0.914 meters
1 mile = 1.6093 kilometers (km)
1 km = 0.6214 miles
1 fathom = 1.8288 m
1 chain = 20.1168 m
1 furlong = 201.168 m
1 acre = 0.4047 hectares
1 sq km = 100 hectares
1 sq mile = 2.59 square km
1 ounce = 28.35 grams
1 pound = 0.4536 kilograms
1 short ton = 0.90718 metric ton
1 short ton = 2,000 pounds
1 long ton = 1.016 metric tons
1 long ton = 2,240 pounds
1 metric ton = 1,000 kilograms
1 quart = 0.94635 liters
1 US gallon = 3.7854 liters
1 Imperial gallon = 4.5459 liters
1 nautical mile = 1.852 km

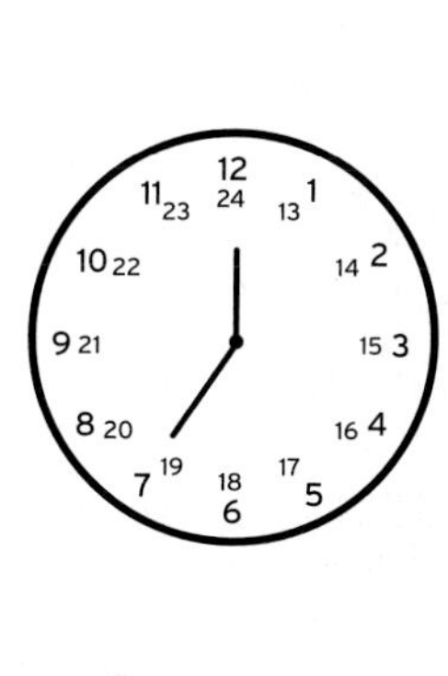

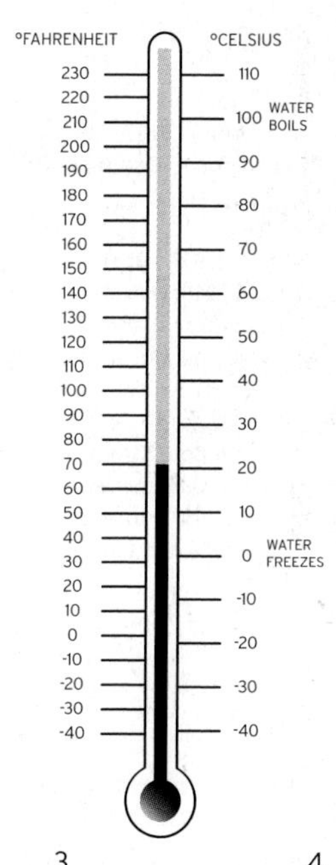

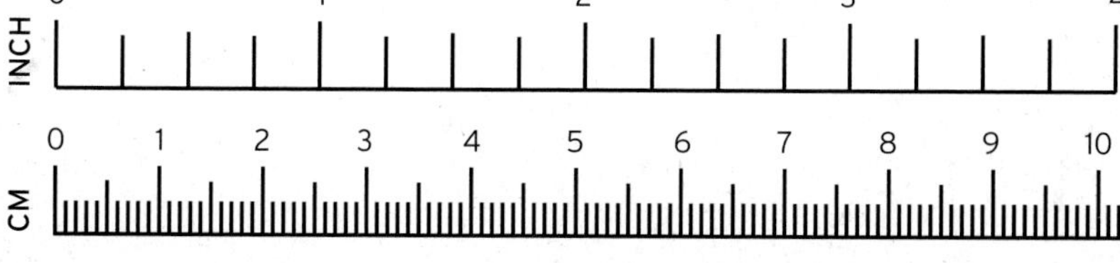

MOON MOROCCO
Avalon Travel
Hachette Book Group
1700 Fourth Street
Berkeley, CA 94710, USA
www.moon.com

Editor: Megan Anderluh
Copy Editor: Jessica Gould
Graphics and Production Coordinator: Lucie Ericksen
Cover Design: Faceout Studios, Charles Brock
Interior Design: Domini Dragoone
Moon Logo: Tim McGrath
Map Editor: Albert Angulo
Cartographers: John Culp, Brian Shotwell, and Albert Angulo
Proofreader: Lina Carmona
Indexer: François Trahan

ISBN-13: 978-1-64049-133-5

Printing History
1st Edition — 2017
2nd Edition — December 2019
5 4 3 2 1

Front cover photo: Ornate exterior of Hassan II Mosque in Casablanca © danm/GettyImages
Back cover photo: a street in Chefchaouen © Lucas Peters

Printed in China by RR Donnelley